KV-638-333

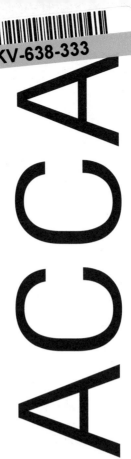

Paper 2.5

FINANCIAL REPORTING

For exams in December 2006 and June 2007

Study Text

In this June 2006 new edition

- A new **user-friendly format** for easy navigation

- **Exam-centred topic coverage**, directly linked to ACCA's syllabus and study guide

- **Exam focus points** showing you what the examiner will want you to do

- Regular **fast forward** summaries emphasising the key points in each chapter

- **Questions** and **quick quizzes** to test your understanding

- **Exam question bank** containing exam standard questions with answers

- **A full index**

BPP's **i-Learn** and **i-Pass** products also support this paper.

FOR EXAMS IN DECEMBER 2006 AND JUNE 2007

First edition 2001
Sixth edition July 2006

ISBN 0 7517 2668 0 (Previous edition 0 7517 2319 3)

British Library Cataloguing-in-Publication Data
A catalogue record for this book
is available from the British Library

Published by

BPP Professional Education
Aldine House, Aldine Place
London W12 8AW

www.bpp.com

Printed in Great Britain by Page Bros
Mile Cross Lane
Norwich
NR6 6SA

All our rights reserved. No part of this publication may
be reproduced, stored in a retrieval system or
transmitted, in any form or by any means, electronic,
mechanical, photocopying, recording or otherwise,
without the prior written permission of BPP
Professional Education.

We are grateful to the Association of Chartered
Certified Accountants for permission to reproduce past
examination questions. The suggested solutions in the
exam answer bank have been prepared by BPP
Professional Education.

©
BPP Professional Education
2006

Contents

Introduction

The introduction pages contain lots of valuable advice and information. They include tips on studying for and passing the exam, also the content of the syllabus and what has been examined.

The BPP Effective Study Package – How the BPP Study Text can help you pass – Help yourself study for your ACCA exams – Syllabus and Study Guide – The exam paper – Oxford Brookes BSc (Hons) in Applied Accounting – ACAC Professional Development requirements

Review form and free prize draw

Computer-based learning products from BPP

If you want to reinforce your studies by **interactive** learning, try BPP's **i-Learn** product, covering major syllabus areas in an interactive format. For **self-testing**, try **i-Pass,** which offers a large number of **objective test questions**, particularly useful where objective test questions form part of the exam.

Learn Online

Learn Online uses BPP's wealth of teaching experience to produce a fully **interactive** e-learning resource **delivered via the Internet**. The site offers comprehensive **tutor support** and features areas such as **study, practice**, **email service**, **revision** and **useful resources**.

Visit our website www.bpp.com/acca/learnonline to sample aspects of Learn Online free of charge.

Learning to Learn Accountancy

BPP's ground-breaking **Learning to Learn Accountancy** book is designed to be used both at the outset of your ACCA studies and throughout the process of learning accountancy. It challenges you to consider how you study and gives you helpful hints about how to approach the various types of paper which you will encounter. It can help you **focus your studies on the subject and exam**, enabling you to **acquire knowledge, practise and revise efficiently and effectively**.

The BPP Effective Study Package

Recommended period of use	The BPP Effective Study Package
From the outset and throughout	**Learning to Learn Accountancy** Read this invaluable book as you begin your studies and refer to it as you work through the various elements of the BPP Effective Study Package. It will help you to acquire knowledge, practise and revise, efficiently and effectively.
Three to twelve months before the exam	**Study Text and i-Learn** Use the Study Text to acquire knowledge, understanding, skills and the ability to apply techniques. Use BPP's **i-Learn** product to reinforce your learning.
Throughout	**Learn Online** Study, practise, revise and take advantage of other useful resources with BPP's fully interactive e-learning site with comprehensive tutor support.
Throughout	**i-Pass** **i-Pass**, our computer-based testing package, provides objective test questions in a variety of formats and is ideal for self-assessment.
One to six months before the exam	**Practice & Revision Kit** Try the numerous examination-format questions, for which there are realistic suggested solutions prepared by BPP's own authors. Then attempt the two mock exams.
From three months before the exam until the last minute	**Passcards** Work through these short, memorable notes which are focused on what is most likely to come up in the exam you will be sitting.
One to six months before the exam	**Success CDs** The CDs cover the vital elements of your syllabus in less than 90 minutes per subject. They also contain exam hints to help you fine tune your strategy.

How the BPP Study Text can help you pass

> **It provides you with the knowledge and understanding, skills and application techniques that you need to be successful in your exams**

This Study Text has been targeted at the **Financial Reporting** syllabus.

- It is **comprehensive**. It covers the syllabus content. No more, no less.

- It is written at the **right level**. Each chapter is written with ACCA's syllabus and study guide in mind.

- It is aimed at the **exam**. We have taken account of recent exams, guidance the examiner has given and the assessment methodology.

> **It allows you to study in the way that best suits your learning style and the time you have available, by following your personal Study Plan (see page (viii))**

You may be studying at home on your own or you may be attending a full-time course. You may like to read every word, or you may prefer to skim-read and practise questions the rest of the time. However you study, you will find the BPP Study Text meets your needs in designing and following your personal Study Plan.

> **It ties in with the other components of the BPP Effective Study Package to ensure you have the best possible chance of passing the exam (see page (v))**

Help yourself study for your ACCA exams

Exams for professional bodies such as ACCA are very different from those you have taken at college or university. You will be under **greater time pressure before** the exam – as you may be combining your study with work. Here are some hints and tips.

The right approach

1 **Develop the right attitude**

Believe in yourself	Yes, there is a lot to learn. But thousands have succeeded before and you can too.
Remember why you're doing it	You are studying for a good reason: to advance your career.

2 **Focus on the exam**

Read through the Syllabus and Study Guide	These tell you what you are expected to know and are supplemented by **Exam focus points** in the text.
Study the Exam paper section	Past papers are likely to be good guides to what you should expect in the exam.

3 **The right method**

See the whole picture	Keeping in mind how all the detail you need to know fits into the whole picture will help you understand it better. • The **Introduction** of each chapter puts the material in context. • The **Syllabus content, Study guide** and **Exam focus points** show you what you need to **grasp**.
Use your own words	To absorb the information (and to practise your written communication skills), you need to **put it into your own words**. • **Take notes.** • Answer the **questions** in each chapter. • Draw **mindmaps**. We have an example for the whole syllabus. • Try **'teaching' a subject** to a colleague or friend.
Give yourself cues to jog your memory	The BPP Study Text uses **bold** to **highlight key points**. • Try **colour coding** with a highlighter pen. • Write **key points** on cards.

4 **The right recap**

Review, review, review	Regularly reviewing a topic in summary form can **fix it in your memory**. The BPP Study Text helps you review in many ways. • **Chapter roundups** summarise the 'Fast forward' key points in each chapter. Use them to recap each study session. • The **Quick quiz** actively tests your grasp of the essentials. • Go through the **Examples** in each chapter a second or third time.

Developing your personal Study Plan

BPP's **Learning to Learn Accountancy** book emphasises the need to use a study plan. Planning and sticking to the plan are key elements of learning successfully.
There are five steps you should work through.

Step 1   **How do you learn?**

First you need to be aware of your style of learning. BPP's **Learning to Learn Accountancy** book commits a chapter to this **self-discovery**. What types of intelligence do you display when learning? You might be advised to brush up on certain study skills before launching into this Study Text.

BPP's **Learning to Learn Accountancy** book helps you to identify what intelligences you show more strongly and then details how you can tailor your study process to your preferences. It also includes handy hints on how to develop intelligences you exhibit less strongly, but which might be needed as you study accountancy.

Step 2   **What do you prefer to do first?**

If you prefer to get to grips with a theory before seeing how it is applied, we suggest you concentrate first on the explanations we give in each chapter before looking at the examples and case studies. If you prefer to see first how things work in practice, skim through the detail in each chapter, and concentrate on the examples and case studies, before supplementing your understanding by reading the detail.

Step 3   **How much time do you have?**

Work out the time you have available per week, given the following.

- The standard you have set yourself
- The time you need to set aside later for work on the Practice & Revision Kit and Passcards
- The other exam(s) you are sitting
- Practical matters such as work, travel, exercise, sleep and social life

Note your time available in box A.   A   [   ]   **Hours**

Step 4   **Allocate your time**

- Take the time you have available per week for this Study Text shown in box A, multiply it by the number of weeks available and insert the result in box B.   B   [   ]

- Divide the figure in box B by the number of chapters in this text and insert the result in box C.   C   [   ]

Remember that this is only a rough guide. Some of the chapters in this book are longer and more complicated than others, and you will find some subjects easier to understand than others.

Step 5   Implement

Set about studying each chapter in the time shown in box C, following the key study steps in the order suggested by your particular learning style.

This is your personal **Study Plan**. You should try to combine it with the study sequence outlined below. You may want to modify the sequence to adapt it to your **personal style**.

> BPP's **Learning to Learn Accountancy** gives further guidance on developing a study plan, and deciding where and when to study.

Tackling your studies

The best way to approach this Study Text is to tackle the chapters in order. Taking into account your individual learning style, you could follow this sequence for each chapter.

Key study steps	Activity
Step 1 **Topic list**	This topic list helps you navigate each chapter; each numbered topic is a numbered section in the chapter.
Step 2 **Introduction**	This sets your objectives for study by giving you the big picture in terms of the context of the chapter. The content is referenced to the Study Guide, and Exam guidance shows how the topic is likely to be examined. The Introduction tells you **why** the topics covered in the chapter need to be studied.
Step 3 **Knowledge brought forward boxes**	These highlight information and techniques that it is assumed you have 'brought forward' with you from your earlier studies. Remember that you may be tested on these areas in the exam. If you are unsure of these areas, you should consider revising your more detailed study material from earlier papers.
Step 4 **Fast forward**	Fast forward boxes give you a quick summary of the content of each of the main chapter sections. They are listed together in the roundup at the end of each chapter to help you review each chapter quickly.
Step 5 **Explanations**	Proceed methodically through each chapter, particularly focussing on areas highlighted as significant in the chapter introduction, or areas that are frequently examined.
Step 6 **Key terms and Exam focus points**	• Key terms can often earn you **easy marks** if you state them clearly and correctly in an exam answer. They are highlighted in the index at the back of this text. • Exam focus points state how the topic has been or may be examined, difficulties that can occur in questions about the topic, and examiner feedback on common weaknesses in answers.
Step 7 **Note taking**	Take brief notes, if you wish. Don't copy out too much. Remember that being able to record something yourself is a sign of being able to understand it. Your notes can be in whatever format you find most helpful; lists, diagrams, mindmaps.
Step 8 **Examples**	Work through the examples very carefully as they illustrate key knowledge and techniques.
Step 9 **Case studies**	Study each one, and try to add flesh to them from your own experience. They are designed to show how the topics you are studying come alive in the real world.
Step 10 **Questions**	Attempt each one, as they will illustrate how well you've understood what you've read.

Key study steps	Activity
Step 11 **Answers**	Check yours against ours, and make sure you understand any discrepancies.
Step 12 **Chapter roundup**	Review it carefully, to make sure you have grasped the significance of all the important points in the chapter.
Step 13 **Quick quiz**	Use the Quick quiz to check how much you have remembered of the topics covered and to practise questions in a variety of formats.
Step 14 **Question practice**	Attempt the Question(s) suggested at the very end of the chapter. You can find these in the Exam Question Bank at the end of the Study Text, along with the answers so you can see how you did. If you have bought i-Pass, use this too.

Short of time: Skim study technique?

You may find you simply do not have the time available to follow all the key study steps for each chapter, however you adapt them for your particular learning style. If this is the case, follow the **skim study** technique below.

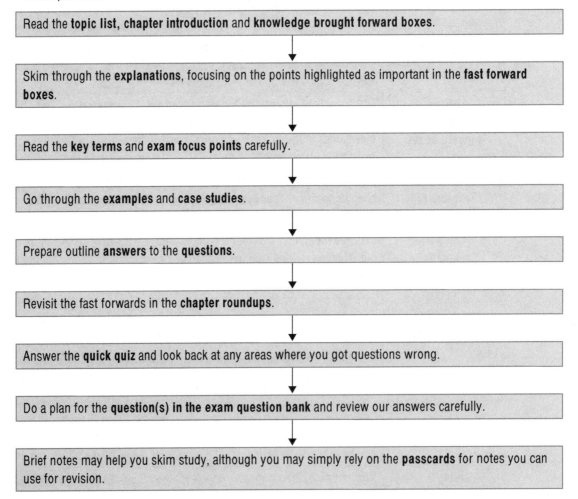

Read the **topic list, chapter introduction** and **knowledge brought forward boxes**.

Skim through the **explanations**, focusing on the points highlighted as important in the **fast forward boxes**.

Read the **key terms** and **exam focus points** carefully.

Go through the **examples** and **case studies**.

Prepare outline **answers** to the **questions**.

Revisit the fast forwards in the **chapter roundups**.

Answer the **quick quiz** and look back at any areas where you got questions wrong.

Do a plan for the **question(s) in the exam question bank** and review our answers carefully.

Brief notes may help you skim study, although you may simply rely on the **passcards** for notes you can use for revision.

BPP
PROFESSIONAL EDUCATION

Moving on...

When you are ready to start revising, you should still refer back to this Study Text.

- As a source of **reference** (you should find the index particularly helpful for this)

- As a way to **review** (the Fast forwards, Exam focus points, Chapter roundups and Quick quizzes help you here)

Remember to keep careful hold of this Study Text – you will find it invaluable in your work.

> More advice on Study Skills can be found in BPP's **Learning to Learn Accountancy** book.

Paper 2.5

Financial Reporting (GBR)

AIM

To build on the basic techniques in Paper 1.1 Preparing Financial Statements and to develop knowledge and understanding of more advanced financial accounting concepts and principles. Candidates will be required to apply this understanding by preparing and interpreting financial reports in a practical context.

OBJECTIVES

On completion of this paper candidates should be able to:

- appraise and apply specified accounting concepts and theories to practical work place situations
- appraise and apply the regulatory framework of financial reporting
- prepare financial statements for different entities to comply with the Companies Acts and specified Accounting Standards and other related pronouncements
- prepare group financial statements (excluding group cash flow statements) to include a single subsidiary. An associate or joint venture may also be included
- analyse, interpret and report on financial statements (including cash flow statements) and related information to a variety of user groups
- discuss and apply the requirements of specified Accounting Standards.
- demonstrate the skills expected in Part 2.

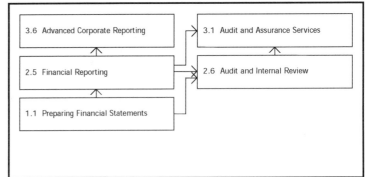

POSITION OF THE PAPER IN THE OVERALL SYLLABUS

Paper 2.5 builds on the techniques developed at Paper 1.1 Preparing Financial Statements and tests the conceptual and technical financial accounting knowledge that candidates will require in order to progress to the higher level analytical, judgmental and communication skills of Paper 3.6 Advanced Corporate Reporting.

Paper 2.5 also provides essential financial accounting knowledge and principles that need to be fully understood by auditors, thus it forms some of the prerequisite knowledge of Paper 2.6 Audit and Internal Review, and the option Paper 3.1 Audit and Assurance services.

Prerequisite knowledge for Paper 2.5 is largely the basic knowledge and skills demonstrated at Paper 1.1, but many accounting standards require the use of

discounting techniques which candidates will have acquired at Paper 2.4 Financial Management and Control.

SYLLABUS CONTENT

1 **Accounting principles, concepts and theory**
   (a) The ASB's Statement of Principles for Financial Reporting.
   (b) Agency theory.
   (c) Price level changes, capital maintenance.

2 **Regulatory framework**
   (a) Structure of the UK regulatory framework
       (i) EC directives
       (ii) Companies Acts.
   (b) Standard setting process: the Financial Reporting Council (FRC) and its subsidiary bodies; the role of the International Accounting Standards Board (IASB).

Financial Reporting (GBR)   (Continued)

3 Preparation and presentation of financial statements for limited liability companies and other entities
(a) Accounting for share capital and reserves
    (i) issue and redemption of shares
    (ii) distributable profits.
(b) Tangible and intangible fixed assets.
(c) Net current assets.
(d) Earnings per share.
(e) Tax in company accounts including
    (i) current tax
    (ii) deferred tax.
(f) SSAPs, FRSs, UITF abstracts and IFRSs as specified in the examinable documents.

4 Preparation of consolidated financial statements
(a) Definition of subsidiary companies.
(b) Exclusions from consolidations.
(c) Preparation of consolidated profit and loss accounts and balance sheets including:
    (i) elimination of intra-group transactions
    (ii) fair value adjustments.
(d) Associates and joint ventures.

5 Analysis and interpretation of financial statements and related information
(a) Analysis of corporate information.
(b) Preparation of reports on financial performance for various user groups.
(c) Preparation and analysis of cash flow statements of a single company.
(d) Related party transactions.

(e) Segmental information.

EXCLUDED TOPICS
The following topics are specifically excluded from the syllabus:
- partnership and branch financial statements
- preparing group financial statements involving more than one subsidiary
- piecemeal acquisitions, disposal of subsidiaries and group reconstructions
- foreign currency translation/ consolidations, hedging, hyperinflationary economics
- financial statements of banks and similar financial institutions
- group cash flows
- schemes of reorganisation/reconstruction
- company/share valuation
- derivative transactions
- accounting for pension costs
- share based payments
- the ASB's Financial Reporting Exposure Drafts and Discussion Drafts / Papers.

KEY AREAS OF THE SYLLABUS
The key topic areas are as follows:

Accounting principles and concepts, accounting theory
- Statement of Principles.
- Revenue recognition.
- Substance over form.

Preparation of financial statements of limited companies
- Form and content of published financial statements.
- Accounting and disclosure requirements of the Companies Acts and Accounting Standards.

Preparation of consolidated financial statements
- Definitions of subsidiaries: exclusions from consolidation.
- Simple groups.

Analysis and interpretation of financial statements
- Preparation of reports for various user groups
- Preparation and analysis of cash flow statements.

Other topic areas
Note these may be examined as part of a question within the above key areas or as a substantial part of a separate optional question:
- hire purchase and leasing
- long-term contracts
- earnings per share
- impairment of fixed assets, provisions
- discontinued operations

Financial Reporting (GBR)   (Continued)

- goodwill and other intangibles.

APPROACH TO EXAMINING THE SYLLABUS

The examination is a three hour paper in two sections. It will contain both computational and discursive elements. Some questions will adopt a scenario/case study approach.

The Section A compulsory question will be the preparation of group financial statements and/or extracts thereof, and may include a small related discussion element. Computations will be designed to test an understanding of principles. At least one of the optional questions in Section B will be a conceptual/discursive question that may include illustrative numerical calculations.

An individual question may often involve elements that relate to different areas of the syllabus. For example a published financial statements question could include elements relating to several accounting standards. In scenario questions candidates may be expected to comment on management's chosen accounting treatment and determine a more appropriate one, based on circumstances described in the question.

Questions on topic areas that are also included in Paper 1.1 will be examined at an appropriately greater depth in Paper 2.5. Some Accounting Standards are very detailed and complex.

At Paper 2.5 candidates need to be aware of the principles and key elements of these Standards. Candidates will also be expected to have an appreciation of the need for an accounting standard and why it has been introduced.

	Number of Marks
Section A: One compulsory question	25
Section B: Choice of 3 from 4 questions (25 marks each)	75
	100

ADDITIONAL INFORMATION

Candidates need to be aware that questions involving knowledge of new examinable regulations will not be set until at least six months after the last day of the month in which the regulation was issued.

The Study Guide provides more detailed guidance on the syllabus. Examinable documents are listed in the 'Exam Notes' section of *student accountant*

Financial Reporting (GBR)   (Continued)

STUDY SESSIONS

1 Review of basic concepts and the Statement of Principles for Financial Reporting
(a) Discuss what is meant by a conceptual framework and GAAP
(b) Describe the objectives of financial statements and the qualitative characteristics of financial information
(c) Define the elements of financial statements
(d) Apply the above definitions to practical situations
(e) Revision of Paper 1.1 – prepare the final accounts of a company from a trial balance

2 Accounting concepts and accounting theory
(a) Outline the concept of 'comprehensive income'
(b) Explain the principle of fair value
(c) Discuss and apply accounting policies
(d) Describe the deficiencies of historic cost accounts (HCA) during periods of rising prices and explain in principle alternatives to HCA.

3 Revenue recognition
(a) Outline the principles of the timing of revenue recognition
(b) Explain the role of the concept of substance over form in relation to recognising sales revenue
(c) Explain and define realised profits

(d) Discuss the various points in the production and sales cycle where it may, depending on circumstances, be appropriate to recognise gains and losses – give examples of this
(e) Describe the ASB's 'balance sheet approach' to revenue recognition within its Statement of Principles and compare this to requirements of relevant accounting standards.

4 The structure of the UK regulatory framework
(a) Describe the influence of EC directives
(b) Explain the role of the Companies Acts
(c) Outline the Standard setting process and the role of the:
  (i) Financial Reporting Council (FRC)
  (ii) Accounting Standards Board (ASB)
  (iii) Urgent Issues Task Force (UITF)
  (iv) Financial Reporting Review Panel (FRRP)
(d) Explain the relationship between UK and International Accounting Standards (IASs)/International Financial Reporting Standards (IFRSs).

5 Preparation of financial statements for limited companies
(a) State the requirements of the Companies Act regarding the form and content of the prescribed

formats
(b) Prepare the financial statements of limited companies in accordance with the prescribed formats and relevant accounting standards
(c) Describe the main issues involved when a company adopts International Financial Reporting Standards (IFRSs) for the first time
(d) Apply the requirements of the IASB to the preparation of financial statements of a first time adopter of International Financial Reporting Standards

6 Reporting financial performance I
(a) Explain the need for an accounting standard in this area
(b) Discuss the importance of identifying and reporting the results of discontinued operations; define discontinued operations
(c) Distinguish between extraordinary and exceptional items, including their accounting treatment and required disclosures

7 Reporting financial performance II
(a) Explain the contents and purpose of the statement of total recognised gains and losses, linking it to the Statement of Principles and the concept of comprehensive income
(b) Describe and prepare, a:
  (i) note of historical cost profits and losses
  (ii) reconciliation of movements in

Financial Reporting (GBR)   (Continued)

shareholders' funds

(iii) statement of movements in reserves

(c) Define prior period adjustments and account for the correction of fundamental errors and changes in accounting policies.

(d) Prepare a profit and loss account in accordance with the requirements of the relevant Financial Reporting Standard.

8 Share capital and reserves

(a) Explain the need for an accounting standard on Financial Instruments

(b) Distinguish between debt and share capital

(c) Apply the requirements of relevant accounting standards to the issue and finance costs of:

(i) equity and preference shares

(ii) debt instruments with no conversion rights, and

(iii) convertible debt

(d) Explain and apply the general requirements to purchase or redemption of shares

(e) Apply the requirements that allow private companies to redeem shares out of capital

(f) Discuss the advantages of companies being able to redeem shares

(g) Define and discuss the Companies Acts rules relating to profits available for distribution

9 Fixed assets – tangible

(a) Define the initial cost of a fixed asset (including a self-constructed asset) and apply this to various examples of expenditure distinguishing between capital and revenue items

(b) Describe, and be able to identify, subsequent expenditure that may be capitalised

(c) State and appraise the effects of accounting standards on the revaluation of fixed assets

(d) Account for gains and losses on the disposal of revalued assets

(e) Calculate depreciation on:

(i) revalued assets, and

(ii) assets that have two or more major components

(f) Apply the provisions of accounting standards on Government Grants

(g) Discuss why the treatment of investment properties should differ from other properties

(h) Apply the requirements of accounting standard on Accounting for Investment Properties.

10 Hire purchase and leasing

(a) Distinguish between a hire purchase contract and a lease

(b) Describe and apply the method of determining a lease type (i.e. an operating or finance lease)

(c) Explain the effect on the financial statements of a finance lease being incorrectly treated as an operating lease

(d) Account for operating leases in financial statements

(e) Account for finance leases in the financial statements of lessors and lessees

(f) Outline the principles of the accounting standard on leasing and its main disclosure requirements
Note: the net cash investment method will not be examined.

11 Fixed assets – goodwill and intangible assets

(a) Discuss the nature and possible accounting treatments of both internally generated and purchased goodwill

(b) Distinguish between goodwill and other intangible assets

(c) Describe the criteria for the initial recognition and measurement of intangible assets

(d) Describe the subsequent accounting treatment, including amortisation and the principle of impairment testing in relation to purchased goodwill

(e) Describe the circumstances in which negative goodwill arises, and its subsequent accounting treatment and disclosure

(f) Describe and apply the requirements of accounting standards on Research and Development.

12 Fixed assets – impairment of fixed assets and goodwill

Financial Reporting (GBR)   (Continued)

(a) Define the recoverable amount of an asset; define impairment losses

(b) Give examples of, and be able to identify circumstances that may indicate that an impairment of fixed assets has occurred

(c) Describe what is meant by an income generating unit

(d) State the basis on which impairment losses should be allocated, and allocate a given impairment loss to the assets of an income generating unit.

13 Liabilities – provisions, contingent liabilities and contingent assets

(a) Explain why an accounting standard on provisions is necessary – give examples of previous abuses in this area

(b) Define provisions, legal and constructive obligations, past events and the transfer of economic benefits

(c) State when provisions may and may not be made, and how they should be accounted for

(d) Explain how provisions should be measured

(e) Define contingent assets and liabilities – give examples and describe their accounting treatment

(f) Be able to identify and account for:
(i) warranties/guarantees
(ii) onerous contracts
(iii) environmental and similar provisions

(g) Discuss the validity of making provisions for future repairs or

refurbishments.

14 Stock and long-term contracts

(a) Review the principles of stock valuation covered in Paper 1.1

(b) Define a long-term contract and describe why recognising profit before completion is generally considered to be desirable and the circumstances where it may not be; discuss if this may be profit smoothing

(c) Describe the ways in which attributable profit may be measured

(d) Calculate and disclose the amounts to be shown in the financial statements for long-term contracts.

15 Earnings per share

(a) Explain the importance of comparability in relation to the calculation of earnings per share (eps) and its importance as a stock market indicator

(b) Explain why the trend of eps may be a more accurate indicator of performance than a company's profit trend

(c) Define earnings and the basic number of shares

(d) Calculate the eps in accordance with relevant accounting standards in the following circumstances:
(i) basic eps
(ii) where there has been a bonus issue of shares during the year, and
(iii) where there has been a rights issue of shares during the year

(e) Explain the relevance to existing shareholders of the diluted eps and describe the circumstances that will give rise to a future dilution of the eps

(f) Calculate the diluted eps in the following circumstances:
(i) where convertible debt or preference shares are in issue; and
(ii) where share options and warrants exist.

16 Taxation in financial statements

(a) Account for current taxation in accordance with relevant accounting standards

(b) Record entries relating to corporation tax in the accounting records

(c) Apply requirements of accounting standard on VAT

(d) Explain the effect of timing differences on accounting and taxable profits

(e) Outline the principles of accounting for deferred tax

(f) Outline the requirements of accounting standards on Deferred tax

(g) Calculate and record deferred tax amounts in the financial statements.

17 Accounting for the substance of transactions

(a) Explain the importance of recording the substance rather than the legal form of transactions – give examples of previous abuses in this area

(b) Describe the features which may indicate that the substance of

Financial Reporting (GBR)   (Continued)

transactions may differ from their legal form

(c) Explain and apply the principles in accounting standards for the recognition and derecognition of assets and liabilities

(d) Be able to recognise the substance of transactions in general, and specifically account for the following types of transaction:
(i) stock sold on sale or return/consignment stock
(ii) sale and repurchase/leaseback agreements
(iii) factoring of debtors.

18 & 19 Group accounting – introduction

(a) Describe the concept of a group and the objective and usefulness of consolidated financial statements

(b) Explain the different methods which could be used to prepare group accounts

(c) Explain and apply the definition of subsidiary companies in the Companies Acts and accounting standards

(d) Describe the circumstances and reasoning for subsidiaries to be excluded from consolidated financial statements

(e) Prepare a consolidated balance sheet for a simple group dealing with pre and post acquisition profits, minority interests and consolidated goodwill

(f) Explain the need for using coterminous year ends and uniform accounting polices when preparing consolidated financial statements

(g) Describe how the above is achieved in practice

(h) Prepare a consolidated profit and loss account for a simple group, including an example where an acquisition occurs during the year and there is a minority interest.

20 Group accounting – intra group adjustments

(a) Explain why intra-group transactions should be eliminated on consolidation

(b) Explain the nature of a dividend paid out of pre-acquisition profits

(c) Account for the effects (in the profit and loss account and balance sheet) of intra-group trading and other transactions including:
(i) unrealised profits in stock and fixed assets
(ii) intra-group loans and interest and other intra-group charges, and
(iii) intra-group dividends including those paid out of pre-acquisition profits.

21 Group accounting – fair value adjustments

(a) Explain why it is necessary for both the consideration paid for a subsidiary and the subsidiary's identifiable assets and liabilities to be accounted for at

their fair values when preparing consolidated financial statements

(b) Prepare consolidated financial statements dealing with fair value adjustments (including their effect on consolidated goodwill) in respect of:
(i) depreciating and non-depreciating fixed assets
(ii) stock
(iii) monetary liabilities (basic discounting techniques may be required)
(iv) assets and liabilities (including contingencies) not included in the subsidiary's own balance sheet.

22 & 23 Group accounting – associates and joint ventures

(a) Define associates and joint ventures, including an arrangement that is not an entity

(b) Distinguish between equity accounting and proportional consolidation

(c) Describe the equity and gross equity methods

(d) Prepare consolidated financial statements to include a single subsidiary and an associate or a joint venture.

24 Analysis and interpretation of financial statements

(a) Calculate useful financial ratios for a single company or for group financial statements

Financial Reporting (GBR)   (Continued)

(b) Analyse and interpret ratios to give an assessment of a company's performance in comparison with:
  (i) a company's previous period's financial statements
  (ii) another similar company for the same period
  (iii) industry average ratios
(c) Discuss the effect that changes in accounting policies or the use of different accounting polices between companies can have on the ability to interpret performance
(d) Discuss how the interpretation of current value information would differ from that of historical cost information
(e) Discuss the limitations in the use of ratio analysis for assessing corporate performance, outlining other information that may be of relevance.

Note: the content of reports should draw upon knowledge acquired in other sessions.
These sessions concentrate on the preparation of reports and report writing skills.

25 & 26 Cash flow statements
(a) Prepare a cash flow statement, including relevant notes, for an individual company in accordance with relevant accounting standards
  Note: questions may specify the use of the direct or the indirect method

(b) Appraise the usefulness of, and interpret the information in, a cash flow statement.

27 Related parties
(a) Define and apply the definition of related parties in accordance with relevant accounting standards
(b) Describe the potential to mislead users when related party transactions are included in a company's financial statements
(c) Adjust financial statements (for comparative purposes) for the effects of non-commercial related party transactions
(d) Describe the disclosure requirements for related party transactions.

28 Segmental reporting
(a) Discuss the usefulness and problems associated with the provision of segmental information
(b) Define a reportable segment and the information that is to be reported
(c) Prepare segmental reports in accordance with relevant accounting standards
(d) Assess the performance of a company based on the information contained in its segmental report.

The exam paper

The examination is a three hour paper in two sections. It will contain a mix of computational and discursive elements. Some questions will adopt a scenario/case study approach.

The Section A compulsory question will be the preparation of group financial statements, and may include a small related discussion element. Computations will be designed to test an understanding of principles. At least one of the optional questions in Section B will be conceptual/discursive question that may include a simple illustrative numerical element.

An individual question may often involve elements that relate to different areas of the syllabus. For example a published financial statements question could include elements relating to several accounting standards. In scenario questions candidates may be expected to comment on management's chosen accounting treatment and determine a more appropriate one, based on circumstances described in the question.

Questions on topic areas that are also included in Paper 1.1 will be examined at an appropriately greater depth in Paper 2.5. Some Accounting Standards are very detailed and complex, particularly recent ones. At Paper 2.5 candidates need to be aware of the principles and key elements of these Standards. Candidates will also be expected to have an appreciation of the background need for an accounting standard and why it has been introduced.

		Number of Marks
Section A:	One compulsory question	25
Section B:	Choice of 3 from 4 questions (25 marks each)	75
		100

Additional information

Candidates need to be aware that questions involving knowledge of new examinable regulations will not be set until at least six months after the last day of the month in which the regulation was issued.

The Study Guide provides more detailed guidance on the syllabus. Examinable documents are listed in the 'Exam Notes' section of the Students' Newsletter.

Analysis of past papers

The analysis below shows the topics which have been examined in all sittings of the current syllabus so far and in the Pilot Paper.

December 2005

Section A

1   Consolidated balance sheet for group having one subsidiary and associate.

Section B

2   Single company profit and loss account and balance sheet including commission income, fixed asset disposal, capitalised development expenditure and EPS.

3   Discussion and scenarios based on FRS 11.

4   Cash flow statement and comment on change in company's financial position.

5   Scenario question covering depreciation and related parties.

Examiners Comments

The best answered questions were Q1, Q2 and Q4. A number of candidates only answered 3 questions and a small number failed to do the compulsory Q1. Quite a number of candidates only attempted the numerical, and not the written, parts of the questions. This shows a lack of analytical, interpretive and communication skills.

June 2005

Section A

1   Consolidated balance sheet extracts with deferred consideration, development expenditure and inter company trading. Explain why consolidated financial statements are useful to users.

Section B

2   Redraft profit and loss account and balance sheet and prepare statement of movement on reserves for private limited company, including revaluation of fixed assets, rights issue and deferred tax adjustment.

3   Discussion question on IFRS 1. Preparation of IFRS 1 balance sheet.

4   Cash flow statement. Discuss extent to which cash flow statement may be more useful and reliable than profit and loss account.

5   Scenarios concerning private company accounts: provision for decommissioning, material losses due to fraud, sale and repurchase agreement.

Examiners comments

Questions 2 and 4 were popular and well answered. Question 1 was quite straightforward. Some candidates failed to go into enough depth in Questions 3 and 5. Marks were lost for poor exam technique, such as not cross-referencing the workings to the answer and not keeping the workings for a question in one place. If an answer is wrong and the marker cannot find the workings, no marks can be given.

December 2004

Section A

1   Consolidated profit and loss account with associate, acquisition by share exchange and fair value adjustment. Show movement on consolidated profit and loss reserve

Section B

2   Profit and loss account and balance sheet in accordance with Companies Acts and accounting standards, including construction contracts, leasing and deferred development expenditure

3   Discussion of UK regulatory framework and standard setting process

4   Cash flow statement using indirect method and financial performance report using ratios

5   Balance sheet extracts to show share issue and repurchase transactions and movements on fixed assets, including revaluation and impairment

Examiners comments

The overall pass rate for this sitting showed some improvement, but there was evidence that candidates had not spent an equal amount of time on each question and that some had not studied the breadth of the syllabus. Questions 3 and 5 were unpopular and poorly answered. A number of candidates rely on the computational part of the paper to gain their marks. This is unwise, as paper 2.5 often contains substantial written elements.

June 2004

Section A

1   Consolidated balance sheet including associate and deferred consideration. Discussion of equity accounting

Section B

2   Redraft single company balance sheet to incorporate adjustments for: leased assets; depreciation; fall in value of an investment property; damaged stock; provision for machinery overhaul; deferred tax; and loan costs in accordance with FRS 4

3   Discussion of FRS 10, including goodwill. Five intangible asset scenarios. Determine correct accounting treatment for each

4   Cash flow statement

5   Long-term contracts and segmental reporting

December 2003

Section A

1   Consolidated balance sheet with contingent consideration

Section B

2   Profit and loss account and STRGL with discontinued operation, sale and leaseback
3   FRS 12; explain need for standard on provisions and deal with two scenarios
4   Ratio analysis, discussion of interfirm comparisons, and report analysing financial performance
5   Deferred tax, leasing, events after the balance sheet date

Examiners comments

Questions 1, 2 and 4 were the best answered questions. Q3 and 5 were not answered well, probably because they were not considered 'banker' topics, so few candidates had studied them in any depth. There is no substitute for substantially covering all the syllabus. There were a number of failures due to poor examination technique – not showing workings, doing unnecessary workings and even producing pro–forma answers to Questions 1 and 2 without entering any figures in them.

June 2003

Section A

1   Consolidated financial statements; discussion of unrealised profit

Section B

2   Preparation of financial statements; STRGL; sale and repurchase; revaluation of investments
3   Revenue recognition; Statement of Principles; substance over form; government grants
4   Cash flow statement with ratio analysis; operating performance and financial position
5   Defects of historical cost; CCP, CCA; EPS; diluted EPS; dividend cover

December 2002

Section A

1   Consolidated accounts using acquisition accounting; consolidated P+L account and shareholders' funds using merger accounting; FRS 6 criteria for using merger accounting

Section B

2   Financial statements presentation: P+L account, balance sheet, STRGL

3   FRS 5; creative accounting; consignment stock; sale and repurchase arrangements

4   Cash flow statement preparation; comment on financial position of the company

5   Discontinued operations; diluted EPS and explanation. Discussion of tax charge shown in P+L account

June 2002

Section A

1   Consolidated balance sheet; Associated company status

Section B

2   Preparation of financial statements; EPS calculations
3   Impairment of fixed assets and goodwill; FRS7; R&D expenditure
4   Related party transactions; Interpretation of financial statements
5   Long term contracts; Property transactions

December 2001

Section A

1   Consolidated balance sheet

Section B

2   Preparation of financial statements
3   FRS 15; cost; revaluation
4   Cash flow statement
5   Intangible assets; investment property; stocks

Pilot paper

Section A

1   Preparation of consolidated balance sheet and profit and loss account. Discussion of treatment of investment.

Section B

2   Preparation of balance sheet and profit and loss. Discussion on fixed assets
3   Revenue recognition
4   Interpretation of financial statements
5   Loan stock, impairment losses, closure of a division and long term contract

Oxford Brookes BSc (Hons) in Applied Accounting

The standard required of candidates completing Part 2 is that required in the final year of a UK degree. Students completing Parts 1 and 2 will have satisfied the examination requirement for an honours degree in Applied Accounting, awarded by Oxford Brookes University.

To achieve the degree, you must also submit two pieces of work based on a **Research and Analysis Project.**

- A 5,000 word **Report** on your chosen topic, which demonstrates that you have acquired the necessary research, analytical and IT skills.

- A 1,500 word **Key Skills Statement**, indicating how you have developed your interpersonal and communication skills.

BPP was selected by the ACCA and Oxford Brookes University to produce the official text *Success in your Research and Analysis Project* to support students in this task. The book pays particular attention to key skills not covered in the professional examinations.

BPP also offers courses and mentoring services.

For further information, please see BPP's website: www.bpp.com/bsc

ACCA professional development requirements

Soon, you will possess a professional qualification. You know its value by the effort you have put in. To uphold the prestige of the qualification, ACCA, with the other professional bodies that form the International Federation of Accountants (IFAC), requires its members to undertake continuous professional development (CPD). This requirement applies to all members, not just those with a practising certificate. Happily, BPP Professional Education is here to support you in your professional development with materials, courses and qualifications.

> For further information, please see ACCA's website: www.accaglobal.com

Professional development with BPP

You do not have to do exams for professional development (PD) – but you need relevant technical updating and you may also benefit from other work-related training. BPP can provide you with both. Visit our professional development website, www.bpp.com/pd for details of our PD courses in accounting, law, general business skills and other important areas. Offering defined hours of structured CPD, and delivered by top professionals throughout the year and in many locations, our courses are designed to fit around your busy work schedule. Our unique PD passport will give you access to these PD services at an attractive discount.

> For further information, please see BPP's website: www.bpp.com/pd

Master of Business Administration (MBA)

This is a joint venture between ACCA and Oxford Brookes University, a leading UK university. The MBA, accredited by AMBA (the Association of MBAs), lasts 21 months for ACCA members, and is taught by distance learning with online seminars delivered to a global student base over the Internet. BPP provides the user-friendly materials. As an ACCA member, you will receive credits towards this MBA and you can begin your studies when you have completed your ACCA professional exams. Flexibility, global reach and value for money underpin a high quality learning experience.

The qualification features an introductory module (*Foundations of Management*). Other modules include *Global Business Strategy*, *Managing Self Development*, and *Organisational Change and Transformation*.

Research Methods are also taught, as they underpin the **research dissertation**.

> For further information, please see the Oxford Institutes's website: www.oxfordinstitute.org and BPP's website: www.bpp.com/mba

Diploma in International Financial Reporting

The ACCA's Diploma in International Financial Reporting is designed for those whose country-specific accounting knowledge needs to be supplemented by knowledge of international accounting standards. BPP offers books and courses in this useful qualification – it also earns you valuable CPD points.

> For further information, please see ACCA's website: www.accaglobal.com and BPP's website: www.bpp.com/dipifr

Tax and financial services

If you are interested in tax, BPP offers courses for the ATT (tax technician) and CTA (Chartered Tax Adviser, formerly ATII) qualifications. You can also buy our user-friendly CTA texts to keep up-to-date with tax practice.

> For further information, please see BPP's website: www.bpp.com/att and www.bpp.com/cta

If your role involves selling financial services products, such as pensions, or offering investment advice, BPP provides learning materials and training for relevant qualifications. BPP also offers training for specialist financial markets qualifications (eg CFA®) and insolvency.

> For further information, please see BPP's website: www.bpp.com/financialadvisers

Other business qualifications

BPP supports many business disciplines, such as market research, marketing, human resources management and law. We are the official provider of distance learning programmes for the Market Research Society. We train for the Chartered Institute of Personnel and Development qualification, with a number of other supporting qualifications in training and personnel management. BPP's law school is an industry leader.

> Visit www.bpp.com for further details of all that we can offer you. BPP's personalised online information service, My BPP, will help you keep track of the details you submit to BPP.

Part A
The regulatory framework

BPP
PROFESSIONAL EDUCATION

Review of basic accounting concepts

Topic list	Syllabus reference
1 A conceptual framework of accounting	1 (a)
2 Generally accepted accounting practice (GAAP)	2 (a)
3 Objectives of financial statements	1 (a)
4 Qualitative characteristics of financial statements	1 (a)
5 Elements of financial statements	1 (a)
6 Recognition in financial statements	1 (a)
7 Measurement in financial statements	1 (a)
8 Revision: basic accounts	-

Introduction

The syllabus for Paper 2.5 is very large and varied. You should be OK if you work through the book steadily and systematically We have provided several diagrams and graphics to provide a visual element to your learning.

Good time management is vital. Try to draw up a timetable and ensure you allow yourself enough time. You must not skimp on any area of the syllabus, tempting though it is when faced with the volume of material. So at the outset – good luck and loads of hard work!

This chapter sets out the underlying concepts that go to the heart of modern financial reporting and helps to equip you with the basic tools you will need for future studies. Take this opportunity to master the key terms you will need for your exams, especially the definitions of assets and liabilities.

Study guide

- Discuss what is meant by a conceptual framework and GAAP
- Describe the objectives of financial statements and the qualitative characteristics of financial information
- Define the elements of financial statements
- Apply the above definitions to practical situations
- Revision of Paper 1.1 – prepare the final accounts of a company from a trial balance

Exam guide

You are unlikely to get a full question on the material in this chapter but it is important that you read through and understand the content of this chapter. It provides you with many of the vital building blocks you will need in the exams.

1 A conceptual framework of accounting

FAST FORWARD

You must be able to define a **conceptual framework** and discuss the conceptual framework in the UK. The key aspects are:

- Definition of assets and liabilities
- Recognition and derecognition process
- Concept of materiality

Prior to the formation of the Accounting Standards Board (ASB) in 1990, accounting standards were developed in an *ad hoc* manner in response to **specific problems** or issues as they arose. This approach, commonly referred to as 'fire fighting', entailed a variety of **weaknesses**.

(a) Accounting standards were **developed piecemeal** at different times and were **not necessarily consistent with one another**

(b) Some of them were **not** up to date with **modern developments** and business practices.

   (i) Many had their **origins in manufacturing** companies with an emphasis on accounting for stock and fixed assets

   (ii) Overall, they were **not effective** in addressing **complex financial reporting issues**, such as those arising from intangibles and complex contractual arrangements

(c) Some were out of line with international developments in financial reporting.

Key term

> A **conceptual framework** is 'a constitution, a coherent system of interrelated objectives and fundamentals that can lead to consistent standards and that prescribes the nature, function and limits of financial accounting and financial statements.'

The ASB therefore developed and issued a *Statement of Principles for financial reporting*, in December 1999.

The ASB *Statement of Principles* comprises several key objectives.

(a) Specification of principles that should underpin the preparation and presentation of **general purpose financial statements**

(b) Clarification of the **conceptual foundations** of proposed accounting standards

(c)   **Reduction** of the need to **debate** fundamental issues each time a standard is developed or revised

(d)   **Assisting auditors** in arriving at their **opinion** on whether a set of financial statements conforms with accounting standards

(e)   Helping **users** to **understand** the **function** of information contained in financial statements

The ASB *Statement of Principles* is covered in detail in Chapter 21.

Remember, however, the ASB *SOP* is only one of the factors taken into account when setting standards. The ASB considers a **range** of **other factors** when setting financial reporting standards.

(a)   Legal requirements
(b)   Cost/benefit issues
(c)   Industry-specific issues
(d)   Desirability of evolutionary change
(e)   Practical implementation issues

Here are some examples of how concepts covered by the ASB *SOP* have been included in various financial reporting standards.

Financial reporting standard	*Statement of Principles* concept
FRS 2 Accounting for subsidiary undertakings	Reporting entity concept
FRS 26 Financial instruments: Recognition and measurement	
FRS 5 Reporting the substance of transactions	Definition of assets and
FRS 7 Fair values in acquisition accounting	liabilities
FRS 12 Provisions, contingent liabilities and contingent assets	
FRS 11 Impairment of fixed assets and goodwill	Recoverable amount notion

2 Generally Accepted Accounting Practice (GAAP)

FAST FORWARD

GAAP is taken to be all the rules, from whatever source, which govern accounting. This varies from country to country and changes over time as new regulations are issued and others are withdrawn or superseded.

This term has emerged in recent years and it **signifies all the rules**, from whatever source, **which govern accounting**. In the UK this is seen primarily as a combination of various sources.

- **Company law** (mainly CA 1985)
- Financial reporting **standards**
- **Stock exchange requirements**

Although those sources are the basis for UK GAAP, the concept also includes the effects of non-mandatory sources such as:

(a)   **International** financial reporting **standards**
(b)   **Statutory requirements in other countries**, particularly the USA.

In the UK, **GAAP** does **not have** any **statutory or regulatory authority** or definition (unlike other countries, such as the USA). The term is mentioned rarely in legislation, and only then in fairly limited terms.

GAAP is in fact a **dynamic concept**: it **changes constantly as circumstances alter through new legislation, standards *and* practice.** This idea that GAAP is constantly changing is recognised by the ASB in its *Statement of Aims* where it states that it expects to issue new standards and amend old ones in response to:

'Evolving business practices, new economic developments and deficiencies identified in current practice.'

The emphasis has shifted from 'principles' to 'practice' in UK GAAP.

The problem of what is '**generally accepted**' is **not easy to settle**, because new practices will obviously not be generally adopted yet. The criteria for a practice being 'generally accepted' will depend on factors such as whether the practice is addressed by UK financial reporting **standards** or **legislation**, their international equivalents, and whether other companies have **adopted the practice**. Most importantly perhaps, the question should be whether the practice is consistent with the **needs of users** and the **objectives of financial reporting** and whether it is consistent with the **'true and fair' concept**.

From January 2005 UK listed companies will be preparing their group accounts under IFRS. This is the first stage in the transition from UK GAAP to IFRS.

3 Objectives of financial statements

FAST FORWARD   The main objective of financial statements is to provide information that is useful to users.

The objectives of financial statements might be depicted diagrammatically.

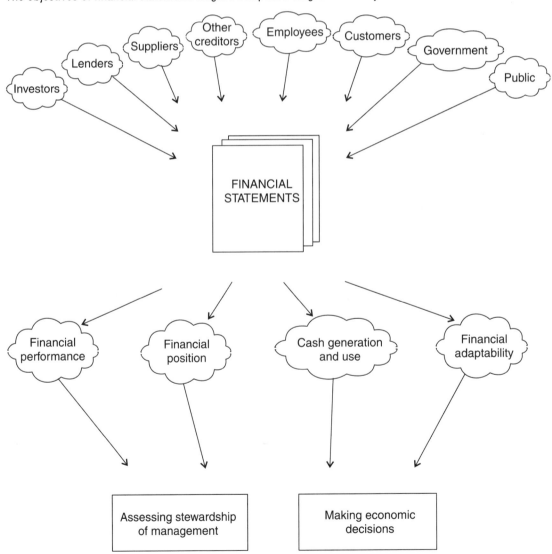

BPP
PROFESSIONAL EDUCATION

4 Qualitative characteristics of financial statements

FAST FORWARD

The qualitative characteristics of useful financial information are **relevance**, **reliability**, **comparability** and **understandability**. **Materiality** exerts a **quality threshold**.

Key term

The ASB *Statement of Principles* states that in deciding which information to include in financial statements, when to include it and how to present it, the **aim** is to ensure that **financial statements yield information that is useful**.

The qualitative characteristics that make information useful may be depicted by the following diagram.

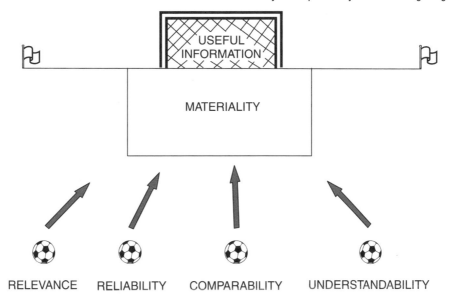

RELEVANCE   RELIABILITY   COMPARABILITY   UNDERSTANDABILITY

4.1 Materiality

For information to be useful it must also be material. The **materiality test** asks whether the **information** involved is of **such significance** as to **require** its **inclusion** in the financial statements. It exerts a **quality threshold** on financial information.

Key term

An item of information is **material** to the financial statements if its **misstatement** or **omission** might reasonably be expected to **influence** the **economic decisions** of users of those financial statements, including their assessments of **management's stewardship**.

Immaterial information can result in **clutter** that **impairs** the **understandability** of the other information provided.

The principal factors to be taken into account are set out below. It will usually be a **combination of these factors**, rather than any one in particular, that will **determine materiality**.

(a)   The item's **size** is judged in the **context** both of the **financial statements** as a **whole** and of the **other information available** to users that would affect their evaluation of the financial statements. This includes, for example, considering how the item affects the evaluation of **trends** and **similar considerations**.

(b)   Consideration is given to the **item's nature** in relation to:

(i)   the **transactions** or other **events giving rise** to it

(ii) the **legality, sensitivity, normality** and **potential consequences** of the event or transaction

(iii) the identity of the **parties involved**

(iv) The particular **headings** and **disclosures** that are affected

If there are **two or more similar items**, the materiality of the items in **aggregate as well as** of the items **individually** needs to be considered. In practice, accountants often keep separate sheets of adjustments that have not been processed to the financial statements. This should be reviewed and evaluated to ensure that the combined effect of supposedly immaterial items do not, when considered together, represent a material misstatement.

4.2 Relevance, reliability, comparability and understanding

These characteristics may be summarised as per the following table.

Characteristic	Qualities
Relevance	
• Ability to influence economic decisions • Provided in time to influence decisions	• **Predictive value.** To evaluate/assess past, present or future events • **Confirmatory value.** Helps to confirm past evaluations/ assessments • **Both** of the above should be maximised
Reliability	
• Entails information that is a complete and faithful representation	• **Faithful representation.** Reflecting the substance of transactions • **Neutral.** Free from bias, not overstating or understating • **Complete.** Free from material omissions or errors • **Prudent.** Exercising due caution where uncertainty exists
Comparability	
• Similarities and differences can be discerned and evaluated	• Enables identification of **trends** in financial position and performance **over time** for an entity • Helps compare **financial performance** between entities • Achieved through **consistency** and **disclosure**

Characteristic	Qualities
Understandability	
• The significance of the information can be perceived	Depends on various factors. • How transactions are **characterised, aggregated** and **classified** • Way in which information is **presented** • Capability of user – assumed **reasonably knowledgeable** and diligent

5 Elements of financial statements

Key terms

Assets are rights or other access to **future economic benefits** controlled by an entity as a result of **past transactions** or events.

Liabilities are **obligations** of an entity to **transfer economic benefits** as a result of **past transactions** or events.

Ownership interest is the residual amount found by **deducting** all of the entity's **liabilities** from all of the entity's **assets**.

Gains are **increases** in **ownership interest**, other than those relating to contributions from owners.

Losses are **decreases** in **ownership interest**, other than those relating to distributions to owners.

Contributions from owners are increases in ownership interest resulting from **investments** made by owners in their **capacity as owners**.

Distributions to owners are **decreases** in ownership interest resulting from **transfers** made to owners in their **capacity as owners**.

Any item that does not fall within one of the definitions of elements should not be included in financial statements.

6 Recognition in financial statements

FAST FORWARD

Recognition involves deciding whether, and at what point, assets and liabilities should be included in the financial statements. There must be **sufficient evidence** of the existence of an asset or liability and it must be capable of **reliable measurement**.

Exam focus point

Recognition is a key element of Paper 2.5 and appears in many guises in the exam. It would be wise to ensure you revise this sub-section until you have it well mastered.

6.1 Recognition

The **process** of **recognising assets** and **liabilities** can be depicted by the following diagram.

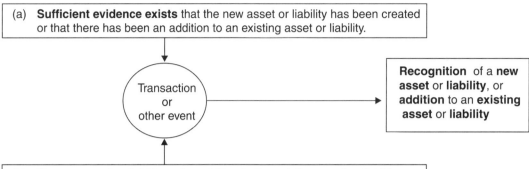

(a) **Sufficient evidence exists** that the new asset or liability has been created or that there has been an addition to an existing asset or liability.

Transaction or other event

Recognition of a **new asset** or **liability**, or **addition** to an **existing asset** or **liability**

(b) The new asset or liability or the addition to the existing asset or liability can be **measured** at a **monetary amount** with **sufficient reliability**.

In a transaction involving the **provision** of **services** or **goods** for a **net gain**, the **recognition** criteria described above will be met on the occurrence of the **critical event** in the **operating cycle** involved. (The critical event approach will be covered in detail later.)

6.2 Derecognition

An asset or liability will be wholly or partly **derecognised** if:

(a) **Sufficient evidence** exists that a **transaction** or other **past event** has **eliminated** a **previously recognised asset or liability**.

(b) Although the item continues to be an asset or a liability the **criteria** for recognition are **no longer met**.

The objective of financial statements is achieved to a large extent through the recognition of elements in the primary financial statements – in other words, the depiction of elements both in **words** and by **monetary amounts**, and the inclusion of those amounts in the primary financial statement totals. Recognition is a process that has the **following stages**.

Initial recognition. An item is depicted in the primary financial statements for the first time.

Subsequent remeasurement. Involves changing the amount at which an already recognised asset or liability is stated in the primary financial statements.

Derecognition. An item that was until then recognised ceases to be recognised.

In practice, entities operate in an uncertain environment and this **uncertainty** may sometimes make it necessary to delay the recognition process. The uncertainty is twofold.

- **Element uncertainty** – does the item exist and meet the definition of the elements of financial statements?

- **Measurement uncertainty** – at what monetary amount should the item be recognised?

Even though matching is not used by the *SOP* to drive the recognition process, it still plays a role in the approach in allocating the cost of assets across reporting periods and in telling preparers where they may find assets and liabilities.

Question Elements

Consider the following situations. In each case, do we have an asset or liability within the definitions of the elements of financial statements? Give reasons for your answer.

(a) Amanda Ltd has purchased a patent for £20,000. The patent gives the company sole use of a particular manufacturing process which will save £3,000 a year for the next five years.

(b) Barry Ltd paid Les Lilley £10,000 to set up a car repair shop, on condition that priority treatment is given to cars from the company's fleet.

(c) Cars U Like Ltd provides a warranty with every car sold.

(d) Donna Ltd has signed a contract with a human resources consultant. The terms of the contract are that the consultant is to stay for six months and be paid £3,000 per month.

(e) Emma Ltd owns a building which for many years it had let out to students. The building has been declared unsafe by the local council. Not only is it unfit for human habitation, but on more than one occasion slates have fallen off the roof, nearly killing passers-by. To rectify all the damage would cost £300,000; to eliminate the danger to the public would cost £200,000. The building could then be sold for £100,000.

Answer

(a) This is an asset, albeit an intangible one. There is a past event, control and future economic benefit (through cost savings).

(b) This cannot be classified as an asset. Barry Ltd has no control over the car repair shop and it is difficult to argue that there are 'future economic benefits'.

(c) This is a liability; the business has taken on an obligation. It would be recognised when the warranty is issued rather than when a claim is made.

(d) As a firm financial commitment, this has all the appearance of a liability. However, as the consultant has not done any work yet, there has been no past event which could give rise to a liability. Similarly, because there has been no past event there is no asset.

(e) The situation is not clear cut. It could be argued that there is a liability, depending on the whether the potential danger to the public arising from the building creates a legal obligation to do the repairs. If there is such a liability, it might be possible to set off the sale proceeds of £100,000 against the cost of essential repairs of £200,000, giving a net obligation to transfer economic benefits of £100,000.

The building is clearly not an asset, because although there is control and there has been a past event, there is no expected access to economic benefit.

7 Measurement in financial statements

A monetary carrying amount needs to be assigned so an asset or liability can be recognised. There are two measuring bases that can be used.

- Historical cost
- Current value

Initially, when an **asset** is **purchased** or a **liability incurred**, the asset/liability is recorded at the **transaction** cost, that is **historical cost**, which at that time is **equal** to **current value.**

An asset/liability may subsequently be 'remeasured'. In a historical cost system, this can involve writing down an asset to its **recoverable amount**. For a liability, the corresponding treatment would be amendment of the monetary amount to the amount ultimately expected to be paid.

Such re-measurements will, however, only be recognised if:

(a)   There is **sufficient evidence** that the monetary amount of the asset/liability has changed

(b)   The new amount can be **measured** with **sufficient reliability**

The *Statement of Principles* does not specify a single obligatory measurement basis. The basis selected will be the one that **best meets** the **objectives** of the financial statements and the demands of the **qualitative characteristics** of financial information.

8 Revision: basic accounts

Question	Financial statements

The accountant of Hola plc has begun preparing final accounts but the work is not yet complete. At this stage the items included in the trial balance are as follows.

	£'000
Land	100
Buildings	120
Plant and machinery	170
Depreciation provision	120
Share capital	100
Profit and loss balance brought forward	200
Debtors	200
Creditors	110
Stock	190
Operating profit	80
Debentures (16%)	180
Allowance for debtors	3
Bank balance (asset)	12
Suspense	1

Notes (i) to (vii) below are to be taken in to account.

(i)   The debtors control account figure, which is used in the trial balance, does not agree with the total of the debtors ledger. A contra of £5,000 has been entered correctly in the individual ledger accounts but has been entered on the wrong side of both control accounts.

A batch total of sales of £12,345 had been entered in the double entry system as £13,345, although the individual ledger accounts entries for these sales were correct. The balance of £4,000 on sales returns account has inadvertently been omitted from the trial balance though correctly entered in the ledger records.

(ii)   A standing order of receipt from a regular customer for £2,000, and bank charges of £1,000, have been completely omitted from the records.

(iii)   A debtor for £1,000 is to be written off. The debtor's allowance balance is to be adjusted to 1% of debtors.

(iv)   The opening stock figure had been overstated by £1,000 and the closing stock figure had been understated by £2,000.

(v)   Any remaining balance on suspense account should be treated as purchases if a debit balance and as sales if a credit balance.

(vi)   The debentures were issued three months before the year end. No entries have been made as regards interest.

Required

(a)   Prepare journal entries to cover items in notes (i) to (v) above. You are not to open any new accounts and may use only those accounts included in the trial balance as given.

(b)   Prepare final accounts for internal use in good order within the limits of the available information. For presentation purposes all the items arising from notes (i) to (vii) above should be regarded as material.

Answer

(a)   JOURNAL ENTRIES FOR ADJUSTMENTS

		Debit £	Credit £
(i)	Creditors	10,000	
	Debtors		10,000
	Operating profit	1,000	
	Debtors		1,000
	Operating profit	4,000	
	Suspense		4,000
(ii)	Bank	2,000	
	Debtors		2,000
	Operating profit	1,000	
	Bank		1,000
(iii)	Operating profit	1,000	
	Debtors		1,000
	Debtors allowance (W1)	1,140	
	Operating profit		1,140
(iv)	Stocks	2,000	
	Operating profit		2,000
	Profit and loss brought forward	1,000	
	Operating profit		1,000
(v)	Suspense	3,000	
	Operating profit		3,000

(b)   HOLA PLC
      BALANCE SHEET

	£	£	£
Fixed assets			
Land and buildings		220,000	
Fixtures and fittings		170,000	
		390,000	
Provision for depreciation		(120,000)	
			270,000
Current assets			
Stock (190 + 2)	192,000		
Debtors (W1)	186,000		
Less allowance	(1,860)		
		184,140	
Bank (12 + 2 – 1)		13,000	
		389,140	
Current liabilities			
Creditors (110 – 10)		100,000	
Debenture interest payable		7,200	
		117,200	
Net current assets			281,940
Debentures			(180,000)
Net assets			371,940
Represented by			
Share capital			100,000
Profit and loss account			271,940
			371,940

HOLA PLC
PROFIT AND LOSS ACCOUNT

	£
Operating profit (W2)	80,140
Debenture interest (£180,000 × 16% × 3/12)	(7,200)
Profit for the period	72,940

Workings

1		£
	Debtors per opening trial balance	200,000
	Contra	(10,000)
	Miscasting	(1,000)
	Standing order	(2,000)
	Written off	(1,000)
		186,000

	£
Allowance b/f	3,000
Allowance required	1,860
Journal	1,140

BPP PROFESSIONAL EDUCATION

2 *Operating profit*

	£
Per question	80,000
Wrong batch total	(1,000)
Returns	(4,000)
Bank charges	(1,000)
Irrecoverable debt	(1,000)
Debtor's allowance	1,140
Stock (2,000 + 1,000)	3,000
Suspense (sales)	3,000
	80,140

3 *Profit and loss account*

	£
Balance brought forward (200,000 – 1,000)	199,000
Profit for the period	72,940
Balance carried forward	271,940

Chapter Roundup

- You must be able to define a **conceptual framework** and discuss the conceptual framework in the UK.

- You must know the key aspects of a conceptual framework.

    - Definition of assets and liabilities
    - Recognition and derecognition process
    - Concept of materiality

- GAAP is taken to be all the rules, from whatever source, which govern accounting. This varies from country to country and changes over time as new regulations are issued and others are withdrawn or superseded.

- The main objective of financial statements is to provide information that is useful to users.

- The qualitative characteristics of useful financial information are **relevance**, **reliability**, **comparability** and **understandability**. **Materiality** exerts a **quality threshold**.

- **Recognition** involves deciding whether, and at what point, assets and liabilities should be included in the financial statements. There must be **sufficient evidence** of the existence of an asset or liability and it must be capable of **reliable measurement**.

Quick Quiz

1   *Fill in the five missing words below.*

A conceptual framework is a constitution, a .... system of .... objectives and .... that can lead to .... standards and that prescribes the nature, function and .... of financial accounting and financial statements.

2   *Tick the appropriate box to indicate your response.*

To meet user needs, financial statements should yield information that is:

(a)   Interesting   ☐

(b)   Correct   ☐

(c)   Useful   ☐

(d)   Objective   ☐

3   For financial information to be relevant what two values should it possess?

4   The application of *prudence* requires that

(a)   Where alternative accounting treatments are available, the most cautious or conservative should be selected   ☐

(b)   Unrealised gains should never be recognised in financial statements   ☐

(c)   Where profits are volatile from year to year, provisions may be used to smooth out reported earnings   ☐

(d)   Where uncertainty exists, caution must be exercised in preparing accounting estimates   ☐

5   The financial accounting recognition process involves two types of uncertainty. State what these are:

(a)   .... uncertainty

(b)   .... uncertainty

6   Explain the concept of neutrality.

7   For financial information to be comparable, consistency is mandatory. Tick the appropriate box below to indicate your response.

True   ☐

False   ☐

8   Fill in the five missing words below.

An item of information is material to the financial statements if its .... or .... might reasonably be expected to .... the economic .... of users of those financial statements, including their assessments of management's ....

9   Explain what the ASB means by the expression 'asset'. Use no more than 25 words in your answer.

10   What two conditions must be satisfied before an asset or liability may be recognised?

BPP PROFESSIONAL EDUCATION

Answers to Quick Quiz

1   A conceptual framework is a constitution, a **coherent** system of **interrelated** objectives and **fundamentals** that can lead to **consistent** standards and that prescribes the nature, function and **limits** of financial accounting and financial statements.

2   C. To meet user needs, financial statements should yield information that is **useful**.

3   For financial information to be relevant it should have

      A   Predictive value
      B   Confirmatory value

4   D. The application of *prudence* requires that **where uncertainty exists, caution must be exercised in preparing accounting estimates**.

5   The financial accounting recognition process involves two types of uncertainty.

      (a)   **Element** uncertainty
      (b)   **Measurement** uncertainty

6   Neutral means free from **deliberate** or **systematic bias**. Financial information should not be selected or presented in such a way as to influence the making of an **economic decision** so as to achieve a **predetermined results** or **outcome**.

7   False. Comparability generally implies consistency throughout the reporting entity within each accounting period and from one period to the next. However, consistency is not an end in itself nor should it be allowed to become an impediment to the introduction of improved accounting practices. Consistency can also be useful in enhancing comparability between entities, although it should not be confused with a need for absolute uniformity.

8   An item of information is material to the financial statements if its **misstatement** or **omission** might reasonably be expected to **influence** the economic **decisions** of users of those financial statements, including their assessments of management's **stewardship**.

9   Assets are rights or other access to future economic benefits by an entity as a result of past transactions or events.

10   (a)   Sufficient evidence exists that a transaction or other past event has eliminated a previously recognised asset or liability.

      (b)   Although the item continues to be an asset or a liability the criteria for recognition are no longer met.

Now try the question below from the Exam Question Bank

Number	Level	Marks	Time
Q1	Introductory	n/a	45 mins

The regulatory framework

Topic list	Syllabus reference
1 The regulatory system	2 (a)
2 Role of company law	2 (a) (ii)
3 Influence of EC Directives	2 (a) (i)
4 Overall regulatory framework	2 (a)
5 The Urgent Issues Task Force (UITF)	2 (a)
6 International Accounting Standards	2 (b)
7 IFRS 1 First time adoption of IFRSs	2 (a)
8 Big GAAP/little GAAP	2 (a)
9 Operating and Financial Review	2 (a)

Introduction

In this chapter, the current financial reporting environment is examined, including the process leading to the creation of Financial Reporting Standards (FRSs). The role and structure of the major bodies involved in the financial reporting regime are discussed, particularly the Accounting Standards Board (ASB).

The work of the ASB in securing convergence with international standards is also covered.

Study guide

- Explain the role of the Companies Acts
- Describe the influence of EC directives
- Outline the Standard setting process and the role of the:

    - Financial Reporting Council
    - Accounting Standards Board
    - Urgent Issues Task Force
    - Financial Reporting Review Panel

- Explain the relationship between UK and International Accounting Standards (IASs)/International Financial Reporting Standards (IFRSs).

- Describe the main issues involved when a company adopts International Financial Reporting Standards (IFRSs) for the first time.

- Apply the requirements of the IASB to the preparation of financial statements of a first time adopter of International Financial Reporting Standards.

Exam guide

Both this chapter and Chapter 3 are extremely important. Make sure that you understand and learn their contents before going on to look at individual items and standards in the following chapters

1 The regulatory system

FAST FORWARD

The UK regulatory system derives from:

- Company law
- Stock exchange requirements
- Accounting standards and financial reporting standards
- International accounting and financial reporting standards

1.1 Unincorporated businesses

In the UK these can usually prepare their **financial statements** in **any form** they choose (subject to the constraints of specific legislation, such as the Financial Services Act 1986 for investment businesses, for example).

1.2 Companies

All **companies** must **comply** with the provisions of the Companies Act 1985 in preparing their financial statements and also with the provisions of *Statements of Standard Accounting Practice* (**SSAPs**) and *Financial Reporting Standards* (**FRSs**).

In its *Foreword to Accounting Standards* the Accounting Standards Board states that **accounting standards are applicable to all financial statements whose purpose is to give a true and fair view**. This necessarily includes the financial statements of every company incorporated in the UK. Obviously if the financial statements of an unincorporated undertaking needs to show a true and fair view, they should also satisfy the requirements of the accounting standards.

The **regulatory framework** over **company accounts** is based on **several sources**.

(a)   **Company law**.

(b)   **Accounting** or **financial reporting standards** and other related pronouncements.

(c)   **International accounting standards** (and the influence of other national standard setting bodies).

(d)   The requirements of the **Stock Exchange**.

2 Role of company law

The Companies Act 1985 (CA 1985) consolidated the bulk of previous company legislation which is relevant to your syllabus. This was substantially amended by the Companies Act 1989 (CA 1989), and all references in this text are to CA 1985 as amended by CA 1989.

The CA 1985 has various key impacts on financial reporting requirements.

(a)   Every UK registered company is required to prepare a balance sheet and profit and loss account for each financial year which gives a true and fair view.

(b)   The financial statements must comply with Schedule 4 to CA 1985 as regards format and additional information provided by way of note.

(c)   Where a company is a parent company, group accounts are also required.

(d)   Accounting standards are accorded legal definition as 'statements of standard accounting practice by such body or bodies as may be prescribed by regulators', ie the Accounting Standards Board.

2.1 Company law review

Currently the DTI is carrying out a comprehensive review of UK company law, following the initial consultation paper *Modern company law for a competitive economy* published in 1998.

The review project has now reached the *Government white paper* stage. The topics covered by the white paper, *Modernising Company Law,* issued on 16 July 2002, include the following matters.

- Small and private companies
- Corporate governance
- Capital maintenance
- Groups of companies
- Reconstructions and mergers

2.2 The Stock Exchange

In the UK there are two different markets on which it is possible for a company to have its securities quoted:

(a)   The Stock Exchange
(b)   The Alternative Investment Market (AIM)

Shares quoted on the main market, the Stock Exchange, are said to be 'listed' or to have obtained a 'listing'. In order to receive a listing for its securities, a company must conform with Stock Exchange regulations contained in the Listing Rules or Yellow Book issued by the Council of The Stock Exchange. The company commits itself to certain procedures and standards, including matters concerning the disclosure of accounting information, which are more extensive than the disclosure requirements of the

Companies Acts. **The requirements of the AIM are less stringent** than the main Stock Exchange. **It is aimed at new, higher risk or smaller companies.**

Many requirements of the Yellow Book do not have the backing of law, but the ultimate sanction which can be imposed on a listed company which fails to abide by them is the withdrawal of its securities from the Stock Exchange List: the company's shares would no longer be traded on the market.

3 Influence of EC directives

Exam focus points

> Although your syllabus does not require you to be an expert on EU procedure, you should be aware that the form and content of company accounts can be influenced by international developments.
>
> Also remember the role of the EU in driving the implementation of *International financial reporting standards*.

Since the United Kingdom became a member of the European Union (EU) it has been obliged to comply with legal requirements decided on by the EU. It does this by enacting UK laws to implement EU directives. For example, the CA 1989 was enacted in part to implement the provisions of the seventh and eighth EU directives, which deal with consolidated accounts and auditors.

Remember EU directives are only mandatory when enacted into legislation by Parliament. Other EU directives only hold advisory status.

EU directives have influenced the UK financial reporting regime in various key areas.

(a) Implementation of prescribed formats and detailed disclosure requirements for financial statements.

(b) Definition of a subsidiary and permission of various exemptions from Companies Act requirements.

(c) Introduction of various exemptions from Companies Act requirements in respect of small and medium sized companies.

4 Overall regulatory framework

The Financial Reporting Council (FRC) with its subsidiaries, the Accounting Standards Board (ASB) and Financial Reporting Review Panel (FRRP) together make up an organisation whose purpose is to promote and secure good financial reporting. Although the FRC is the parent of the ASB and the FRRP, they are independent of the FRC, and of each another, in the performance of their functions.

The ASB has various committees including:

(a) Urgent Issues Task Force (UITF)
(b) Committee on Accounting for Smaller Entities (CASE)

The structure can be depicted in the following diagram.

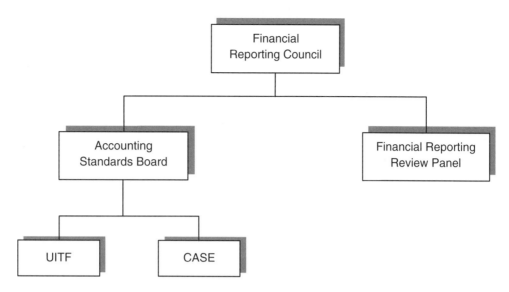

The FRC, ASB and FRRP enjoy strong governmental support but are not government controlled. **They are a part of the private sector process of self-regulation.**

4.1 Financial Reporting Council

The remit of the FRC is to provide support to the ASB and FRRP and to encourage good financial reporting generally. In meeting its remit, the FRC carries out various functions.

(a)   From time to time, making **representations to Government** on the current working of legislation and any desirable developments.

(b)   Providing **guidance** to the **ASB** on **work programmes** and on **broad policy issues**.

(c)   Verifying new arrangements are constructed with **efficiency** and **cost effectiveness**, as well as being adequately funded.

Each year the FRC publishes:

- An annual review describing the activities during the year of the ASB and the FRRP
- Report and financial statements, as required by the Companies Act
- Press releases
- Other relevant information

Projects in which the FRC was involved in 2002 include:

(a)   Participation in a group set up by the government, post-Enron, to co-ordinate the work of UK regulations in the audit and accounting sectors.

(b)   Submitting a report to the Treasury Select Committee, which, in the wake of Enron is enquiring into the financial regulation of public limited companies.

(c)   Advising the *Department of Trade and Industry* on ways in which the *Company Law Revisions* might be implemented.

In 2003, the FRC was involved in preparing a revised text for the *Higgs model code of corporate governance*. Derek Higgs, the deputy chairman of a listed company was asked by the government to conduct an independent review into the role and effectiveness of non-executive directors. The Higgs Report was issued in February 2003 and the FRC is taking feedback before providing a revised model text.

There are currently discussions on the restructuring of the FRC; please keep up-to-date with developments on the FRC web site www.frc.org.uk

4.2 The Accounting Standards Board

4.2.1 Role

The role of the ASB, as recognised by the Companies Act, is to **issue accounting standards**. It took over this role from its predecessor, the Accounting Standards Committee (ASC) in 1990.

Unlike the ASC, the ASB can **issue accounting standards** on its **own authority**, without the approval of any other body.

ASB accounting standards are developed having regard to the ASB's *Statement of Principles*.

4.2.2 Membership

The ASB has a **maximum membership** of ten (plus three observers) which may be depicted as follows.

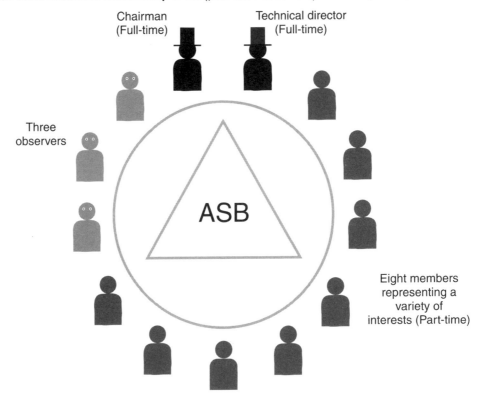

4.2.3 Voting criteria

Any decision to **adopt, revise** or **withdraw** an accounting standard usually requires the **vote** of **seven** members, (**six** when there are fewer than ten members).

4.2.4 Objectives of the ASB

The objectives of the ASB as set out in its *Statement of aims* are to **establish** and **improve standards of financial accounting and reporting**, for the **benefit** of:

- **Users**
- **Preparers**
- **Auditors**

The ASB states that it intends to achieve its objectives by:

(a) **Developing principles** to guide it in establishing standards and to provide a **framework** within which others can **exercise judgement** in **resolving accounting issues**.

(b) **Issuing new accounting standards**, or amending existing ones, in **response** to evolving **business practices**, new **economic developments** and deficiencies being identified in **current practice**.

(c) **Addressing urgent issues promptly**.

Accounting standards developed by the ASB are contained in *Financial Reporting Standards* (FRSs). The ASB has adopted the *Statements of Standards Accounting Practice* (SSAPs) issued by the ASC, so that they also fall within the **legal definition** of accounting standards. Some of the SSAPs have been superseded by FRSs, others remain in force.

Key term

> The *Foreword to Accounting Standards* explains the authority, scope and application of accounting standards.
>
> (a) It will normally be necessary to **comply** with the **standards** to show a **true and fair view**.
>
> (b) In applying the standards, the **user** should be **guided** by their **spirit** and **reasoning**.
>
> (c) **In rare cases** it may be necessary to **depart** from a standard to show a fair view.
>
> (d) **Departures** should be dealt with **objectively** according to the 'economic and commercial characteristics' of the circumstances'; the departure and its financial effect should be **disclosed**.
>
> (e) The **Review Panel** and the **DTI** have powers and procedures to **investigate departures** and to require a **restatement** through the **court**.
>
> (f) Accounting standards **need not** be **applied** to **immaterial items**.

4.2.5 Activities of ASB

The ASB collaborates with accounting standard-setters from other countries and the International Accounting Standards Board (IASB) in order to ensure that its standards are developed with due regard to international developments.

The ASB publicises its activities through press releases and its quarterly newsletter *Inside Track* which provides a broad, non-technical report on the ASB's activities. The ASB also runs a website at www.asb.org.uk.

4.3 ASB standard setting process

The ASB standard setting process can be best viewed in the diagram set out below, which is based on information shown in the ASB's own website.

STEP 1

Identify topic based on own research or input from outside

STEP 2

Set up management structure and identify project resources and expertise

STEP 3

Publish a *Discussion Paper.* The objective here is to canvas the views of the interested public on the possible approaches

STEP 4

Analyse and publish feedback received

STEP 5

Publish *Financial reporting exposure draft* (FRED) for further public comment. Sometimes comments on alternative approaches might be invited

STEP 6

Conduct any necessary further research or field-test possible procedures

STEP 7

Analyse and consider further feedback received from interested parties

STEP 8

Issue final pronouncement in the form of a *Financial Reporting Standard* (FRS) or other publication, which specifies the date on which it becomes effective

Exam focus point

The December 2005 exam had a 25-mark discussion question on the ASB and the standard setting process.

4.4 Accounting standards

Some accounting principles (such as valuation of assets) **are embodied in legislation, while others** (for example cash flow statements) **are regulated by accounting standards**.

Key term

An **accounting standard** is a rule or set of rules which prescribes the method (or methods) by which accounts should be prepared and presented. These 'working regulations' are issued by a national or international body of the accountancy profession.

Accounting standards interact with company law in several ways.

(a)   **'Realised' profits** and **losses** are determined by reference to **generally accepted accounting practice**, ie SSAPs and FRSs: s 262 (3).

(b)   The **accounts must state** whether the provisions of **accounting standards** have been **followed** or give reasons for, and disclosures of any **material departures**: para 36A, Sch 4.

4.4.1 Authority of accounting standards

As discussed above, accounting standards are intended to **apply** to all **financial accounts** which were 'intended to **give a true and fair view** of the financial position and profit and loss'. This includes overseas companies included in UK group accounts. A standard can, however, specify (ie restrict) the 'scope' of its application. For example, FRS 14 on earnings per share applies only to the audited accounts of **publicly traded** companies (companies whose shares are listed on the Stock Exchange).

The **Stock Exchange** requires **listed companies** to **comply** with **accounting standards**. Failure to comply will also usually lead to the auditors qualifying their report, which the company will want to avoid.

Although there are some areas where the contents of accounting standards overlap with provisions of company law, standards are detailed working regulations within the framework of government legislation, and **they cover areas in which the law is silent**. In addition, standards are not intended to override exemptions from disclosure which are allowed to special cases of companies by law.

The Companies Act 1985 states that a departure from its provisions is permissible if that provision is inconsistent with the true and fair view. This may lead to situations in which an accounting standard recommends departure from the legal rules. For example, SSAP 19 *Accounting for investment properties* sanctions such a departure by stating that investment properties need not be depreciated. Other areas of possible conflict between accounting standards and statute will be covered in later chapters.

Members of the Consultative Committee of Accounting Bodies (CCAB), of which the ACCA is a member, are expected to observe accounting standards in their roles either as preparers or auditors of financial information.

4.5 Current accounting standards

The standards in the list are extant at the date of writing. The SSAPs which were in force at the date the ASB was formed have been adopted by the Board. They are gradually being superseded by the new Financial Reporting Standards.

On 7 December 2004, the ASB issued five new accounting standards based on IASs, as part of its strategy for convergence with IFRS.

- FRS 22 (IAS 33) *Earnings per share*
- FRS 23 (IAS 21) *The effect of changes in foreign exchange rates*
- FRS 24 (IAS 29) *Reporting in hyperinflationary economies*
- FRS 25 (IAS 32) *Financial instruments: disclosure and presentation*
- FRS 26 (IAS 39) *Financial instruments: measurement*

FRSs 22, 25 and 26 are part of your syllabus and are covered in this text.

These were followed by FRS 27 *Life Assurance* (not part of your syllabus) and FRS 28 *Corresponding Amounts*, which is explained in Chapter 3.

UK accounting standards

Title		Issue date
	Foreword to accounting standards	Jun 93
FRS 1	Cash flow statements (revised Oct 96)	Sep 91
FRS 2	Accounting for subsidiary undertakings	Jul 92
FRS 3	Reporting financial performance	Oct 92
FRS 4	Capital instruments	Dec 93*
FRS 5	Reporting the substance of transactions	Apr 94
FRS 6	Acquisitions and mergers	Sep 94
FRS 7	Fair values in acquisition accounting	Sep 94
FRS 8	Related party disclosures	Oct 95
FRS 9	Associates and joint ventures	Nov 97
FRS 10	Goodwill and intangible assets	Dec 97
FRS 11	Impairment of fixed assets and goodwill	Jul 98
FRS 12	Provisions, contingent liabilities and contingent assets	Sep 98
FRS 13	Derivatives and other financial instruments: disclosures	Sep 98*
FRS 15	Tangible fixed assets	Feb 99
FRS 16	Current tax	Dec 99
FRS 17	Retirement benefits	Nov 00*
FRS 18	Accounting policies	Dec 00
FRS 19	Deferred tax	Dec 00
FRS 20	Share-based payment	Apr 04*
FRS 21	Events after the balance sheet date	May 04
FRS 22	Earnings per share	Dec 04*
FRS 23	The effect of changes in foreign exchange rates	Dec 04*
FRS 24	Reporting in hyperinflationary economies	Dec 04
FRS 25	Financial instruments: presentation	Dec 04
FRS 26	Financial instruments: recognition and measurement	Dec 04
FRS 27	Life assurance	Dec 04*
FRS 28	Corresponding amounts	Oct 05
FRS 29	Financial instruments: disclosures	Dec 05
FRSSE	Financial Reporting Standard for Smaller Entities	Dec 99
SSAP 4	Accounting for government grants	Jul 90
SSAP 5	Accounting for value added tax	Apr 74
SSAP 9	Stocks and long-term contracts	Sep 88
SSAP 13	Accounting for research and development	Jan 89
SSAP 19	Accounting for investment properties	Nov 81
SSAP 21	Accounting for leases and hire purchase contracts	Aug 84
SSAP 25	Segmental reporting	Jun 90
RS1	Operating and financial review	May 05

Exam focus point

Standards marked * are not examinable in Paper 2.5. In the case of newer accounting standards, you may be asked to discuss why such a standard was needed and how the standard was developed. You *must* therefore follow current developments in the field to be able to understand the impact of standards – it is not sufficient to learn their content.

Question   ASB actions

In between now and your examination, make sure you set aside time *every* week or month to read the *Students' Newsletter* and either the *Financial Times, The Economist* or any other equivalent publication. Look for news about the actions of the Accounting Standards Board and the other bodies we have discussed in this chapter and read about the accounts of individual companies as they are discussed in the press. It is a good idea to keep in touch on a regular basis, eg once every few weeks, with the ASB website.

4.6 Financial Reporting Review Panel

The role of the Review Panel is to **examine departures** from the accounting requirements of the Companies Act 1985, including applicable accounting standards, and if necessary to **seek** an **order** from the **court** to **remedy** them.

By agreement with the Department of Trade and Industry the normal ambit of the Panel is **public** and **large private companies**, the Department dealing with all other cases.

The Panel is concerned with an examination of **material departures** from accounting standards with a view to considering whether the accounts in question nevertheless meet the statutory requirement to give a **true and fair view**. While such a departure does not necessarily mean that a company's accounts fail the true and fair test. It will raise that question. Remember that the Companies Act 1985 requires large companies to **disclose** in their accounts any such **departures** together with the **reasons** for them, thus enabling them to be readily identified and considered.

The Panel does **not scrutinise on a routine basis all companies accounts** falling within its ambit. Instead it **acts on matters drawn to its attention, either directly or indirectly.** (*Note.* Under the new structure being discussed, the FRRP may become more proactive in searching itself, for cases that might have a market impact.)

The Panel normally aims to discharge its tasks by **seeking voluntary agreement** with the directors of a company on any **necessary revisions** to the accounts in question. But if that **approach fails** and the Panel believes that revisions to the accounts are necessary, it will seek:

(a) A **declaration from the court** that the **annual accounts** of the company concerned do **not comply** with the requirements of the Companies Act 1985

(b) An order requiring the directors of the company to **prepare revised accounts**. If the court grants such an order it may also require the directors to meet the **costs** of the proceedings and of revising the accounts.

STEP 1. Voluntary agreement to revise   **STEP 2.** Court order to revise

Where accounts are revised at the instance of the Panel, either voluntarily or by order of the court, but the company's **auditor** had **not qualified his audit report** on the **defective accounts** the Panel will draw this fact to the **attention** of the **auditor's professional body**.

5 The Urgent Issues Task Force (UITF)

The main role of the UITF is to **assist the ASB** in areas where an accounting standard or Companies Act provision exists, but where **unsatisfactory** or **conflicting interpretations** have developed or seem likely to develop.

Its **consensus pronouncements** are issued as UITF Abstracts, which the ASB expects be regarded as **accepted practice** in the area in question, and part of the collection of practices forming the **basis** for what determines a **true and fair view**.

A UITF Abstract may be taken into **consideration** by the **FRRP** in deciding whether a company's financial statements **call for review**.

The UITF abstracts tend to become effective within approximately one month of publication date. The UITF has so far issued twenty two abstracts. Abstracts 1, 2, 3, 7, 8 and 14 have all been superseded by new FRSs and Financial Reporting Exposure Drafts (FREDs). **Only Abstracts 4, 5 and 15 are included in the ACCA's list of examinable documents**. These are discussed briefly here and they are mentioned in the relevant parts of this text when necessary.

5.1 Abstract 4 Presentation of long-term debtors in current assets

Where the figure of debtors due after more than one year is material in the context of the total net current assets then it should be **disclosed on the face of the balance sheet**, rather than just by way of a note (as has been the practice in the past where long-term debtors were included in current assets). The figure would be material in relation to net current assets if its non-disclosure on the balance sheet would cause readers to misinterpret the accounts. You should bear this in mind when considering the Companies Acts formats, given in Chapter 3.

5.2 Abstract 5 Transfers from current assets to fixed assets

This abstract requires transfers from current assets to fixed assets to be made **at the lower of cost and net realisable value**. This prevents the practice of transfers being made at a value higher than NRV. This avoids charging the profit and loss account with any diminution in value of what are, in effect, unsold trading assets. Once transferred to fixed assets, the CA 1985 alternative accounting rules could be used to take the debit reflecting the diminution in value to a revaluation reserve. This abstract follows the statement of Principles and was triggered by a Review Panel Judgement on Trafalgar House's 1991 accounts. In that incidence, commercial properties were transferred out of current assets into tangible fixed assets, thereby avoiding a £102 million hit to pre-tax profits in the original accounts. Fixed assets are dealt with in Chapter 4.

5.3 Abstract 15 Disclosure of substantial acquisitions

This clarifies the threshold for **disclosure of substantial acquisitions** under the Stock Exchange Listing Rules.

The UITF is currently considering another topic, marking current asset investments to market.

5.4 Abstract 40 Revenue recognition and service contracts

Abstract 40 applies the provisions of Application Note G to FRS 5 to all contracts for services. It requires that unbilled revenue relating to service contracts should be accrued as per SSAP 9 where a point has been reached at which an invoice could be raised. This is explained further in Chapter 13, para 1.6.

5.5 Foreword to UITF Abstracts

This foreword was issued in February 1994. It is closely associated with the *Foreword to accounting standards* in its scope and application and users are asked to 'be guided by the spirit and reasoning' behind the abstracts.

Most importantly, the document sets out the following criteria for compliance with the UITF abstracts.

'The Councils of the CCAB bodies expect their members who assume responsibilities in respect of financial statements to **observe UITF Abstracts until they are replaced by accounting standards or otherwise withdrawn** by the ASB.'

The scope of and compliance with the abstracts are similar to those associated with accounting standards (accounts which show a true and fair view, non-compliance must be justified and disclosed etc).

5.6 The effectiveness of the UITF

There is no doubt that the prompt action of the UITF has **closed many loopholes** as soon as they have become apparent. Some of the abstracts have been triggered by the accounts of individual companies, whereas others reflect concern which has arisen over a period of time. Another aspect of the success of the UITF is the **relative speed** with which the abstracts have been included in new standards, or exposure drafts. In other words, the topics were obviously important enough, not only for the attention of the UITF, but also for the ASB.

In combination with the Review Panel, the UITF can halt abuses in financial reporting as soon as they occur. This will also act as a preventative measure, causing many companies and their auditors to hesitate before breaking (or even bending) the rules.

6 International Accounting Standards

FAST FORWARD

International Accounting Standards (IASs) and International Financial Reporting Standards (IFRSs) are ultimately intended to be **global** standards. There is currently a process of **convergence** taking place between UK and International standards.

International Accounting Standards (IASs) were originally produced by the **International Accounting Standards Committee** (IASC), now the **International Accounting Standards Board** (IASB). The IASB **develops accounting standards through an international process that involves the world-wide accountancy profession, the preparers and users of financial statements, and national standard setting bodies.**

The objectives of the IASB are to:

(a)   **Develop**, in the public interest, a **single set** of high quality, understandable and **enforceable global accounting standards** that require high quality, transparent and comparable information in financial statements and other financial reporting to help participants in the various **capital markets** of the world and other users of the **information** to make **economic decisions**

(b)   **Promote** the use and **rigorous application** of those standards

(c)   Work actively with national standard-setters to bring about **convergence** of national accounting standards and International Financial Reporting Standards (IFRSs) to **high quality solutions**

A substantial number of **multinational companies** now prepare financial statements in accordance with IASs. IASs are also endorsed by many countries as their own standards, whether unchanged or with minor amendments.

A great many **stock exchanges** now **accept IASs** for **cross-border listing purposes** (ie when a company in one country wishes to list its shares on another country's stock exchange), but Canada, Japan and the United States are exceptions.

In May 2000, the Presidents Committee of the International Organisation of Securities Commissions (IOSCO) recommended the IOSCO members permit **incoming multi-national issuers** to use the **IASC core standards** to prepare their financial statements for **cross-border offerings and listings**. The core standards include all IASs except for IAS 15, IAS 26 and the recently issued IASs 40 and 41.

On 25 May 2000, the US Securities and Exchange Commission recommended that IASs should now be accepted for use in **cross-border listings** in the United States, without reconciliation to results under US GAAP.

As the use of IASs grew, the role of the IASC expanded and as a result, the member bodies approved the restructuring of the IASC. As a result, on 1 April 2001, the new IASB assumed the IASC's standard-setting responsibilities. Current standards issued by the IASB are known as *International Financial Reporting Standards* (IFRSs). Existing IASs and SICs were adopted by the IASB.

6.1 The use and application of IASs

IASs have helped to both **improve** and **harmonise** financial reporting around the world. The standards are used:

- As national requirements, often after a national process
- As the basis for all or some national requirements
- As an international benchmark for those countries which develop their own requirements
- By regulatory authorities for domestic and foreign companies
- By companies themselves

6.2 Effects of IASs on UK regulation

Before the ASB came into existence, the effect of IASs and other IASC publications on UK standard setting was limited and haphazard. Many SSAPs and IASs were in agreement, but some were not, and some covered completely different topics.

In its FRSs, usually in an appendix, the ASB identifies where the UK standards are in agreement with or are different from IASs or IAS exposure drafts. The ASB sees itself as closely aligned with the IASC, now the IASB. However, it seems that the ASB will only follow the relevant IAS if it fits in with the desired UK practice. The IASB is revising and improving its current IASs and one of the reasons is the elimination or reduction of alternative accounting treatments.

6.3 Harmonisation in Europe

In June 2000, the European Commission proposed that all **publicly listed companies** should be required to implement IASs and IFRs for their **consolidated financial statements** with **accounting periods beginning on 1 January 2005**.

The objective of the European Commission is to build a fully integrated, **globally competitive capital market**. A key element of this is the establishment of a level playing field for EU financial reporting, supported by an effective enforcement regime.

Harmonised financial reporting standards are intended to provide a variety of benefits.

(a)   A platform for **wider investment choice**
(b)   A more efficient capital market
(c)   Lower cost of capital
(d)   Enhanced business development

In March 2002, the European Parliament voted to endorse the use of international standards for publicly limited companies in the EU in respect of their group accounts.

In August 2002, the UK Department of Trade and Industry (DTI) set into motion processes to **extend** the **use** of international financial reporting standards in the UK **beyond publicly listed companies**. The EU would also like to implement IFRSs for all companies.

Exam focus point

> Roger Adams, the ACCA Executive Director – Technical, has published a superb article entitled *Preparing for 2005* in the UK *Times* newspaper.
>
> Have a look at it on the ACCA website.

6.4 The ASB's convergence policy

The following statement is taken from the Convergence Handbook.

> 'The ASB is working with the IASB and other national standard setters in order to seek improvements in IFRS and convergence of national and international standards. The ASB is one of several national standard setters that have a formal liaison relationship with the IASB. This relationship involves regular meetings and other consultations as well as several joint standard setting projects, including the ASB's joint project with the IASB on reporting financial performance.
>
> The ASB intends to **align UK accounting standards** with IFRS whenever practicable. It proposes to do this, in the main, by a **phased replacement** of existing UK standards **with new UK standards based on the equivalent IFRS**.'

Exam focus point

> Consider the likelihood of small general discursive question on how the work of the ASB, IASB, EU etc link into the process of globalisation.

7 IFRS 1 First time adoption of International Financial Reporting Standards

FAST FORWARD

> IFRS 1 sets out the precise way in which an entity should implement a change from local accounting standards to IASs and IFRSs.

IFRS 1 sets out the precise way in which companies should implement a **change from local accounting standards (their previous GAAP) to IASs and IFRSs**.

Exam focus point

> Although this is an IFRS, it is more relevant to the UK stream, as it deals with questions of transition. Accordingly, it is examinable.

One of the main reasons for issuing a new standard is that listed companies in the EU will be required to prepare their consolidated financial statements in accordance with IFRSs from 2005 onwards. Many companies in the EU (for example, in the UK) will be making the transition to IFRS over the next few months.

The standard is intended to ensure that an entity's **first IFRS financial statements** contain **high quality information** that is transparent for users and comparable over all periods presented; provides a suitable starting point for accounting under IFRSs; and can be generated at a cost that does not exceed the benefits to users.

Key terms

> **Date of transition to IFRSs.** The beginning of the earliest period for which an entity presents full comparative information under IFRSs in its first IFRS financial statements.
>
> **Deemed cost** An amount used as a surrogate for cost or depreciated cost at a given date.
>
> **Fair value** The amount for which an asset could be exchanged, or a liability settled, between knowledgeable, willing parties in an arm's length transaction.
>
> **First IFRS financial statements** The first annual financial statements in which an entity adopts International Financial Reporting Standards (IFRSs), by an explicit and unreserved statement of compliance with IFRSs.
>
> **Opening IFRS balance sheet** An entity's balance sheet (published or unpublished) at the date of transition to IFRSs.
>
> **Previous GAAP** The basis of accounting that a first time adopter used immediately before adopting IFRSs.
>
> **Reporting date** The end of the latest period covered by financial statements or by an interim financial report. *(IFRS 1)*

IFRS 1 **only applies** where an entity prepares IFRS financial statements **for the first time**. Changes in accounting policies made by an entity that already applies IFRSs should be dealt with by applying either IAS 8 or specific transitional requirements in other standards.

7.1 Making the transition to IFRS

An entity should:

(a)   Select accounting policies that comply with IFRSs **at the reporting date** for the entity's first IFRS financial statements.

(b)   Prepare an **opening IFRS balance sheet** at the **date of transition to IFRSs.** This is the starting point for subsequent accounting under IFRSs. The date of transition to IFRSs is the beginning of the earliest comparative period presented in an entity's first IFRS financial statements.

(c) **Disclose the effect** of the change in the financial statements.

7.2 Example: Reporting date and opening IFRS balance sheet

An EU listed company has a 31 December year-end and will be required to comply with IFRSs from 1 January 2005.

Required

What is the date of transition to IFRSs?

Solution

The company's first IFRS financial statements will be for the **year ended 31 December 2005**.

IFRS 1 requires that at least one year's comparative figures are presented in the first IFRS financial statements. The comparative figures will be for the year ended 31 December 2004.

Therefore the date of transition to IFRSs is **1 January 2004** and the company prepares an opening IFRS balance sheet at this date.

7.3 Preparing the opening IFRS balance sheet

IFRS 1 states that in its opening IFRS balance sheet an entity must:

(a) **Recognise all assets and liabilities** whose recognition is required by IFRSs

(b) Not recognise items as assets or liabilities if IFRSs do not permit such recognition

(c) **Reclassify items** that it recognised under previous GAAP as one type of asset, liability or component of equity, but are a different type of asset liability or component of equity under IFRSs

(d) **Apply IFRS in measuring** all recognised assets and liabilities

This involves restating the balance sheet prepared at the same date under the entity's previous GAAP so that it complies with IASs and IFRSs in force **at the first reporting date**. In our example above, the company prepares its opening IFRS balance sheet at **1 January 2004**, following accounting policies that comply with IFRSs in force at **31 December 2005**.

The accounting policies that an entity uses in its opening IFRS balance sheet may differ from those it used for the same date using its previous GAAP. The resulting adjustments are recognised directly **in retained earnings** (in equity) **at the date of transition**. (This is because the adjustments arise from events and transactions before the date of transition to IFRS.)

7.4 Exemptions from other IFRSs

A business may elect to use **any or all** of a range of exemptions. These enable an entity not to apply certain requirements of specific accounting standards retrospectively in drawing up its opening IFRS balance sheet. Their purpose is to ensure that the cost of producing IFRS financial statements does not exceed the benefits to users.

7.4.1 Business combinations

IFRS 3 need not be applied retrospectively to business combinations that occurred before the date of the opening IFRS balance sheet. This has the following consequences.

(a)   **All acquired assets and liabilities are recognised** other than:

    (i)   Some financial assets and financial liabilities derecognised under the previous GAAP (derivatives and special purpose entities must be recognised);

    (ii)   Assets (including goodwill) and liabilities that were not recognised under previous GAAP and would not qualify for recognition under IFRSs.

Any resulting change is recognised by **adjusting retained earnings** (ie equity) unless the change results from the recognition of an intangible asset that was previously subsumed within goodwill.

(b)   **Items which do not qualify for recognition** as an asset or liability under IFRSs must be excluded from the opening IFRS balance sheet. For example, intangible assets that do not qualify for separate recognition under IAS 38 must be reclassified as part of goodwill.

(c)   The carrying amount of **goodwill** in the opening IFRS balance sheet is the same as its carrying amount **under previous GAAP**. However, goodwill must be tested for impairment at the transition date, to comply with the treatment of goodwill under international standards.

7.4.2 Property, plant and equipment

An entity may measure an item of property, plant and equipment at its **fair value at the transition** date and then use the fair value as its **deemed** cost at that date.

An entity may use a **previous GAAP revaluation**, or a valuation for the purpose of a privatisation or initial public offering, as the deemed cost at the transition date, so long as the revaluation was **broadly comparable** to fair value or depreciated replacement cost at the date of the valuation.

These exemptions are also available for:

(a)   Investment properties measured under the cost model in IAS 40 *Investment property*

(b)   Intangible assets that meet the recognition criteria and the criteria for revaluation in IAS 38 *Intangible assets*

7.4.3 Compound financial instruments

IAS 32 requires compound financial instruments to be split at inception into separate liability and equity components. If the liability component is no longer outstanding at the date of the translation to IFRSs, the split is not required.

7.4.4 Designation of previously recognised financial instruments

When financial instruments are first recognised, they may be designated as financial assets or financial liabilities 'at fair value through profit or loss' or as 'available for sale' under IAS 39. An entity may make such a designation at the date of transition to IFRSs.

 Question   Adoption of IFRS

Russell Co will adopt International Financial Reporting Standards (IFRSs) for the first time in its financial statements for the year ended 31 December 20X4.

In its previous financial statements for 31 December 20X2 and 20X3, which were prepared under local GAAP, the company made a number of routine accounting estimates, including accrued expenses. It also recognised a general provision for liabilities, calculated at a fixed percentage of its retained profits for the year. This is required under its local GAAP.

Subsequently, some of the accruals were found to be overestimates and some were found to be underestimates.

Required

Discuss how the matters above should be dealt with in the IFRS financial statements of Russell Co for the year ended 31 December 20X4.

Answer

Provided that the routine accounting estimates have been made in a manner consistent with IFRSs no adjustments are made in the first IFRS financial statements. The only exception to this is if the company has subsequently discovered that these estimates were in error. Although there were some overestimates and some underestimates, this is probably not the case here.

The general provision is a different matter. This provision would definitely not have met the criteria for recognition under IAS 37 and therefore it will not be recognised in the opening IFRS balance sheet (1 January 20X3) or at subsequent year-ends.

7.5 Presentation and disclosure

An entity's first IFRS financial statements must include **at least one year of comparative information.**

An entity must also **explain the effect** of the transition from previous GAAP to IFRSs on its financial position, financial performance and cash flows by providing **reconciliations**:

(a) Of **equity** reported under previous GAAP to equity under IFRSs at the **date of transition and at the balance sheet date**

(b) Of the **profit or loss** reported under previous GAAP to profit or loss reported under IFRSs for the period

The reconciliations must give sufficient detail to enable users to understand the material adjustments to the balance sheet and income statement.

If an entity presented a cash flow statement under its previous GAAP, it should also explain the material **adjustments to the cash flow statement**.

If an entity recognised or reversed any **impairment losses** for the first time in preparing its opening IFRS balance sheet, it must provide the disclosures that IAS 36 *Impairment of assets* would have required if the entity had recognised those impairment losses or reversals in the period beginning with the date of transition to IFRSs.

If an entity corrects **errors made under previous GAAP**, the reconciliations must distinguish the correction of errors from changes in accounting policies.

Where **fair value has been used as deemed cost** for a non-current asset in the opening IFRS balance sheet as deemed cost for a non-current asset, the financial statements must disclose the aggregate of fair values and the aggregate adjustments to the carrying amounts reported under previous GAAP for each line in the opening IFRS balance sheet.

7.6 Managing the change to International Standards

The implementation of the above technical aspects is likely to entail careful management in most companies. Here are some of the **change management considerations** that should be addressed.

(a)   **Accurate assessment of the task involved**. Underestimation or wishful thinking may hamper the effectiveness of the conversion and may ultimately prove inefficient.

(b)   **Proper planning**. This should take place at the overall project level, but a **detailed** task **analysis** could be drawn up to **control work performed**.

(c)   **Human resource management**. The project must be properly structured and staffed.

(d)   **Training**. Where there are **skills gaps**, remedial training should be provided.

(e)   **Monitoring and accountability**. A relaxed 'it will be alright on the night' attitude could spell danger. Implementation **progress** should be **monitored** and **regular meetings** set up so that participants can **personally account for what they are doing** as well as **flag up any problems** as early as possible. **Project drift should be avoided**.

(f)   **Achieving milestones**. Successful completion of key steps and tasks should be appropriately acknowledged, ie what managers call 'celebrating success', so as to **sustain motivation and performance**.

(g)   **Physical resourcing**. The need for IT **equipment** and **office space** should be properly assessed.

(h)   **Process review**. Care should be taken not to perceive the change as a one-off quick fix. Any charge in **future systems** and processes should be assessed and properly implemented.

(i)   **Follow-up procedures**. As with general good management practice, the **follow up procedures** should be planned in to **make sure that the changes stick** and that any further changes are identified and addressed.

Exam focus point

> Where you get a narrative or discursive question in the exam you must:
>
> (a)   Ensure you focus on the examiner's requirements
>
> (b)   Write sufficient for the marker to be able to award you the marks for the question
>
> (c)   Avoid long sentences where several valid points are subsumed into one point and probably lost
>
> (d)   Set your answer out in easily identifiable points to help the marker award you as many marks as possible

8 Big GAAP/little GAAP

Most UK companies are small and it is felt that **accounting standards**, being designed for large companies, are less relevant to smaller companies.

Most UK companies are **small companies**. They are generally owned and managed by one person or a family. The owners have invested their own money in the business and there are **no outside shareholders to protect**.

Large companies, by contrast, particularly public limited companies may have shareholders who have invested their money, possibly through a pension fund, with no knowledge whatever of the company. These **shareholders need protection and the regulations for such companies need to be more stringent**.

Key term

> It could therefore be argued that company accounts should be of two types: 'simple' ones for small companies with fewer regulations and disclosure requirements and 'complicated' ones for larger companies with extensive and detailed requirements. This is the **'big GAAP/little GAAP'** divide.

In 1994 a working party of the Consultative Committee of Accountancy Bodies was set up to consider whether small companies should be exempt from most of or all accounting standards. In November 1994 the working party concluded that:

> 'the current form of financial reporting may not best serve the needs of some users. Indeed it could be argued that the application of the full range of present requirements may make some information less understandable, or even result in a distorted presentation, compared with figures that users understand.'

The working party proposed that companies meeting the Companies Act definition of **small** (turnover of less than £5.6m, balance sheet total of £2.8m and an average of 50 employees) would be **exempt from all standards, except for certain core ones**, after taking into account the fact that the accounting regime specified by the Companies Act lays down most of the fundamental principles necessary to produce accounts which show a true and fair. The proposed 'core' standards were as follows.

SSAP 4 *Accounting for government grants*

SSAP 9 *Stocks and long-term contracts*

SSAP 13 *Accounting for research and development*

SSAP 17 *Accounting for post balance sheet events* (now replaced by FRS 21 *Events after the balance sheet date*)

SSAP 18 *Accounting for contingencies* (now replaced by FRS 12 *Provisions, contingent liabilities and contingent assets*).

Initially the proposals met with a **frosty reception** by the profession, with the ACCA, for example, warning that they were 'too radical' and would lead to a 'serious decline in the quality of financial reporting'. It was suggested that small company accounts might not show a true and fair view if they do not follow the majority of standards.

However, in July 1995 it was reported in *Accountancy* that the proposals were beginning to find favour. Moreover, the Department of Trade and Industry published a consultation paper *Accounting Simplifications* which addressed the legal aspects of small company accounts.

8.1 FRS for smaller entities

FAST FORWARD

The FRSSE contains in a simplified form the requirements from existing accounting standards that are relevant to the majority of smaller entities.

In December 1995, the debate was significantly accelerated. The working party published its discussion paper *Designed to fit – a reporting standard for smaller entities*. Then in December 1996 the ASB published an Exposure Draft of the *Financial Reporting Standard for Smaller Entities* and this was published in final form in December 1997. It brings together in one brief document all the accounting guidance which UK small businesses will require to draw up their financial statements.

The **FRSSE retains all of the basic principles of accounting standards while discarding the detailed explanatory notes**. This slims down the volume of accounting standards dramatically. For example, FRS 4 *Capital instruments* and FRS 5 *Reporting the substance of transactions* have been reduced to just a couple of paragraphs. The original standards are very substantial. Disclosure requirements are greatly reduced.

The FRSSE is applicable to all companies that satisfy the definition of a small company in companies legislation and is available to other entities that would meet that definition if they were companies. A company that chooses to comply with the FRSSE is exempt from all other accounting standards and UITF Abstracts.

The FRSSE contains in a simplified form the requirements from existing accounting standards that are relevant to the majority of smaller entities.

In order to keep the FRSSE as user-friendly as possible some of the requirements in accounting standards relating to more complex transactions, eg the treatment of convertible debt in FRS 4 *Capital instruments*, have not been included in the FRSSE, as they do not affect most smaller entities. Where guidance is needed on a matter not contained in the FRSSE, regard should be paid to existing practice as set out in the relevant accounting standards.

8.1.1 Measurement

The measurement bases in the FRSSE are the same as, or a simplification of, those in existing accounting standards. For example, under the FRSSE a lessee that is a small company could account for the finance charges on a finance lease on a straight-line basis over the life of the lease, rather than, as in SSAP 21, using a constant periodic rate of return.

8.1.2 Detailed requirements

The main headings of the FRSSE are listed below with explanatory notes, where appropriate, indicating changes from the original standards or other points of significance. (The FRSSE will not be discussed in detail as many of the standards on which it is based are covered elsewhere in this Study Text.)

(a) **Scope**. The FRSSE is capable of application to smaller **entities** and not just smaller companies. It applies to the companies entitled to the exemptions available in ss 246 and 247 CA 1985 for small companies and which state that they have taken advantage of such exemptions. The FRSSE is also applicable to small groups (as defined by companies legislation) even though there is no statutory requirement for them to prepare consolidated accounts.

(b) **General**. The financial statements should state that they have been prepared in accordance with the FRSSE.

(c) **Profit and loss account**. The requirement of FRS 3 *Reporting financial performance* to **analyse the profit and loss account** into continuing, discontinued and acquired operations has been **lifted**.

(d) **Statement of total recognised gains and losses**. This statement has been **retained**. However, where the only recognised gains and losses are those included in the profit and loss account, no separate statement to that effect is required. This cuts out a large amount of disclosure which, for small companies, was felt to be superfluous. There is no need to show historical cost profits and losses or a reconciliation of movements in shareholders' funds.

(e) **Foreign currency translation**

(f) **Taxation**

(g) **Goodwill**

(h) **Investment properties**

(i) **Depreciation**

(j) **Government grants**

(k) **Research and development**

(l) **Short and long-term contracts**

(m) **Leases**. SSAP 21 *Accounting for leases and hire purchase contracts* is modified such that, for finance leases, charges can normally be spread on a **straight-line basis** and assets and liabilities can normally be recorded at their fair value, rather than the value of the minimum lease payments.

(n)   **Pensions**. There is **no requirement to disclose** the accounting policy for pension scheme contributions, or funding policy, or circumstances where the actuary is an employee or officer of the company.

(o)   **Capital instruments**. FRS 4 *Capital instruments* has been **simplified** such that arrangement fees can be charged directly to the profit and loss account rather than spread over the term of the debt where they are not considered significant in amount.

(p)   **Contingencies**

(q)   **Related parties.** The disclosure requirements for related party transactions in the FRSSE represent a useful dispensation for smaller entities compared with those in FRS 8 *Related party disclosures*. Under FRS 8, related party transactions that are material to the related party, where that related party is an individual, are required to be disclosed in the accounts of the reporting entity even if the transaction is not material to the entity. This is not so for smaller entities adopting the FRSSE, as they need disclose only those related party transactions that are material in relation to the reporting entity.

(r)   **Definitions**

8.1.3 Cash flow statement

Since small entities are already exempt from the requirements of FRS 1 *Cash flow statements* the FRSSE does not include a requirement for a cash flow statement. The ASB nevertheless believes that a cash flow statement is an important aid to the understanding of an entity's financial position and performance and the FRSSE therefore includes a 'voluntary disclosures' section, recommending that smaller entities present a simplified cash flow statement using the indirect method (ie starting with operating profit and reconciling it to the total cash generated (or utilised) in the period).

8.1.4 Small groups

Small groups are not required by law to prepare consolidated accounts, and therefore in practice not many do so, at least on a statutory basis. The Working Party and the Board, however, agreed with respondents that it would be unfair to those small groups that voluntarily prepare group accounts, if they were not able to take advantage of the provisions in the FRSSE. To import all the necessary requirements from accounting standards and UITF Abstracts into the FRSSE to deal with consolidated accounts would have added substantially to its length and complexity, even though it would have been of interest to only a small percentage of entities. Accordingly, the Working Party and the Board preferred to extend the FRSSE in certain areas and then require small groups adopting the FRSSE to follow those accounting standards and UITF Abstracts that deal with consolidated financial statements. This approach was supported by the majority of respondents to the Exposure Draft commenting on the matter.

The FRSSE has been described by Barry Johnson (*Certified Accountant,* February 1996) as 'a commendable summary of UK GAAP .... succinct and to the point'. The need for and advantages of such a standard have been indicated above.

Adverse feedback on the *FRSSE*

(a)   The FRSSE is **unlikely to make it easier or cheaper** to prepare financial statements.

(b)   The case in favour of relaxing **measurement** GAAP for smaller companies has not yet been made convincingly. The only exemptions are from disclosure, rather than from measurement. Some argue that this could be achieved more easily by simply stating in the individual FRSs and SSAPs what disclosure requirements apply to all companies and what applies only to large ones.

(c)   It is questionable whether accounts prepared under the FRSSE would give a **true and fair view** under company law. The true and fair view requirement applies to all companies, whatever their size.

(d)   The present document is **not a 'stand-alone' document**. Users would still need to refer to 'mainstream' standards if they are to prepare financial statements which show a true and fair view.

However, some commentators back the concept of a financial reporting standard for smaller entities; they feel that the FRSSE provides a satisfactory and workable solution to the problems of smaller entities caused by the increasing complexity of accounting standards.

8.2 January 2005 'one stop shop' FRSSE

FAST FORWARD

The updated FRSSE also contains the company law requirements applicable to smaller entities.

The ASB published in April 2005 an updated Financial Reporting Standard for Smaller Entities (FRSSE) which is effective for accounting periods beginning on or after 1 January 2005. The standard was developed from the 'one stop shop' proposals set out in the March 2004 Discussion Paper and the recent Exposure Draft.

8.2.1 Company law incorporated

For the convenience of small companies using the FRSSE, this version **reflects the accounting requirements of applicable company law**. These are clearly distinguished from the requirements of accounting standards by the use of small capitals throughout the text.

Recent amendments to the Companies Act introduced a requirement, in reporting transactions, to have regard to their substance in accordance with generally accepted accounting principles or practice. One effect of this is that some preference shares will be shown as liabilities. The FRSSE has been amended to reflect this change.

8.2.2 Updated for new accounting standards

The FRSSE has also been updated to reflect where appropriate the accounting standards and UITF Abstracts issued, or amended, between the last update and October 2004:

(a)   The basic principles of **FRS 5 Application Note G** *Revenue recognition* are incorporated into a new section. Guidance on bill and hold arrangements, sales with rights of return and presentation of turnover as principal or as agent is included in an appendix.

(b)   The section on post balance sheet events has been updated to reflect the language used in **FRS 21** *Events after the balance sheet date*.

(c)   The change to the effective date of the **transitional arrangements** for accounting for defined benefit **pension schemes** is incorporated.

The FRSSE continues to be available for smaller entities to **prepare consolidated accounts**. The relevant legal requirements for small companies on the **form and content of group accounts** are summarised together with references to the relevant accounting standards.

The ASB intends to consult in a future update on the incorporation of the requirements of FRS 20 *Share-based payment* which requires and entity to recognise chare-based payment transactions (including those with employees or other parties) and the associated assets, liabilities and expenses.

8.3 Changes to small company limits

In January 2004, the thresholds for small companies, ie those eligible to use the FRSSE increased to:

(a) Turnover not more than £5.6m
(b) Balance sheet total not more than £2.8m
(c) Number of employees unchanged from the limit of 50

9 Operating and Financial Review

FAST FORWARD

The **Operating and Financial Review** should be of considerable benefit to less sophisticated users. It is not a statutory requirement but is the subject of a Reporting Statement, setting out best practice.

In January 2006, the Accounting Standards Board (ASB) issued a Reporting Statement *Operating and Financial Review.*

9.1 Overview

The ASB originally issued the Statement Operating and Financial Review in 1993. The process of developing the Statement was started in May 2004, when the UK government announced its proposals for a **statutory operating and financial review** and indicated that it intended to specify the ASB as the body to make reporting standards for the OFR.

In May 2005 Reporting Standard 1 was issued. However, in November 2005 the government announced its intention to remove the statutory requirement on quoted companies to publish an OFR. As a consequence, RS 1 was withdrawn and 'converted' into a Statement of Best Practice. The Reporting Statement recommends that directors prepare an OFR addressed to members, setting out their analysis of the business, with a forward looking orientation. It sets out principles regarded as best practice, namely that the review should both complement and supplement the financial statements, be comprehensive and understandable, balanced and neutral and comparable over time.

Amongst other key areas of business operations, the OFR sets out a framework for directors to consider and report on the **main risks** facing their company and the **measures** that are taken to **control and manage those risks**.

The Statement leaves it to directors to consider how best to structure their review, in the light of the particular circumstances of the entity. Similarly, it does not specify any specific **key performance indicators** (KPIs) that entities should disclose, nor how many, on the grounds that this is a matter for directors to decide.

The Statement is accompanied by **implementation guidance**, which the ASB believes will be useful to directors in considering what to include in their OFR. The guidance sets out some illustrations and suggestions of specific content and related KPIs that might be included in an OFR.

From a risk perspective the implementation guidance looks at ways of reporting on customer and stakeholder risks; environmental risks; employee risks and social responsibility risks.

9.2 Objective

The objective of this Reporting Statement is to specify best practice for an Operating and Financial Review, which should be a balanced and comprehensive analysis, consistent with the size and complexity of the business, of:

(a) The **development and performance** of the business of the entity during the financial year

(b) The **position** of the entity at the end of the year

(c) The **main trends and factors underlying the development, performance and position** of the business of the entity during the financial year

(d) The main trends and factors which are likely to affect the entity's **future development**, performance and position, prepared so as to assist members to assess the strategies adopted by the entity and the potential for those strategies to succeed

9.3 Scope

The Reporting Statement has been written with quoted companies in mind but is also applicable to any other entities that purport to prepare on OFR.

9.4 Principles

The standard sets out the following principles.

(a) The OFR should set out the analysis of the business **through the eyes of the directors**.

(b) The OFR should focus on matters that are of **interest to members**. Other users will be interested in the information, but members' needs must be paramount.

(c) The OFR should have a **forward-looking orientation**, identifying those trends and factors relevant to the members' assessment of the current and future performance of the business and the progress towards the achievement of long-term business objectives. (The directors may warn readers to treat predictive information with caution.)

(d) The OFR should to **complement as well as supplement the financial statements** in order to enhance the overall corporate disclosure.

(e) The OFR should be **comprehensive and understandable**. For example, it must consider whether omitting information might influence users of financial statements.

(f) It should be **balanced and neutral** dealing evenhandedly with good and bad aspects.

(g) It should be **comparable over time**.

9.5 Disclosure framework

The key elements of the disclosure framework are set out below.

(a) The **nature, objectives and strategies** of the business. This includes a description of the business and the external environment in which it operates, the objectives to generate and preserve value over the longer term, the directors' strategies for achieving the objectives of the business and the inclusion of other performance indicators and evidence.

(b) The **development and performance of the business**, both in the period under review and in the future. This will focus on the business segments that are relevant to an understanding of the development and performance as a whole.

(c) The **resources, risks and uncertainties and relationships** that may affect the entity's long-term value. It will analyse the main trends and factors likely to impact future prospects, and describe the resources available, the principle risks and uncertainties faced by the entity and significant relationships with stakeholders.

(d) **Position of the business** including a description of the capital structure, treasury policies and objectives and liquidity of the entity (particularly cash flow), both in the period under review and the future.

9.5.1 Information required for disclosures

To the extent necessary to meet the requirements set out above, the OFR should include information about:

(a) Environmental matters (including the impact of the business of the entity on the environment)

(b) The entity's employees

(c) Social and community issues

(d) Persons with whom the entity has contractual or other arrangements which are essential to the business of the entity

(e) Receipts from, and returns to, members of the entity in respect of shares held by them

(f) All other matters the directors consider to be relevant

For items (a) to (c) the OFR must include the policies of the entity in relation to those matters and the extent to which they have been successively implemented.

9.6 Key performance indicators

An entity should provide information that enables investors to understand each KPI disclosed in the OFR.

For each KPI disclosed in the OFR:

(a) The **definition and its calculation method** must be explained.

(b) Its **purpose** must be explained.

(c) The **source of underlying data** must be disclosed and, where relevant, **assumptions** explained.

(d) **Quantification or commentary** on future targets must be provided.

(e) Where information from the financial statements has been **adjusted** for inclusion in the OFR, that fact must be highlighted and a **reconciliation** provided.

(f) Where available, **corresponding amounts** for the financial year immediately preceding the current year must be disclosed.

(g) **Any changes to KPIs** must be disclosed and the calculation method used compared to previous periods, including significant changes in the underlying accounting policies adopted in the financial statements, must be identified and explained.

Chapter Roundup

- The UK regulatory system derives from:

  - Company law
  - Stock exchange requirements
  - Accounting standards and financial reporting standards
  - International accounting and financial reporting standards

- International Accounting Standards (IASs) and International Financial Reporting Standards (IFRSs) are ultimately intended to be **global** standards. There is currently a process of **convergence** taking place between UK and international standards.

- IFRS 1 sets out the precise way in which an entity should implement a change from local accounting standards to IASs and IFRSs.

- Most UK companies are small and it is felt that **accounting standards**, being designed for large companies, are less relevant to smaller companies.

- The FRSSE contains in a simplified form the requirements from existing accounting standards that are relevant to the majority of smaller entities.

- The updated FRSSE also contains the company law requirements applicable to smaller entities.

- The **Operating and Financial Review** should be of considerable benefit to less sophisticated users. It is not a statutory requirement, but is the subject of a Reporting Statement, setting out best practice.

BPP)))
PROFESSIONAL EDUCATION

Quick Quiz

1   The Financial Reporting Council (FRC) draws its strength from the fact that it reports to the Department of Trade and Industry (DTI). *True or false?*

2   *Fill in the six missing words at the end of the following sentence.*

Accounting standards apply to all companies, and other kinds of entities that prepare accounts that are intended to

....

....

3   Because the FRC is the parent undertaking of the ASB, FRSs produced by the ASB must be sanctioned by the FRC. *True or false?*

4   *Fill in the two missing words below.*

In applying financial reporting standards, users should be guided by their .... and

....

5   Explain when it is permissible to depart from the requirements of a financial reporting standard.

6   The Review Panel has a monitoring unit that reviews the published financial statements of listed companies to identify any material departures from accounting standards. *True or false?*

7   How are international standards required to be implemented by companies in the European Union?

8   Describe the process by which the FRRP enforces the revision to financial statements that it requires.

9   Under FRSSE, small companies need not comply with FRS 3's requirement to analyse the profit and loss account into continuing, discontinuing and acquired operations. *True or false?*

10   UITF Abstracts should not be taken into consideration by the FRRP in deciding whether a company's financial statements call for review. *True or false?*

11   Describe the steps the ASB takes in developing and issuing financial statements.

Answers to Quick Quiz

1   False. The FRC enjoys strong government support but is **not government controlled**. It is part of the private sector process of self-regulation.

2   Accounting standards apply to all companies, and other kinds of entities that prepare accounts that are intended to **provide a true and fair view**.

3   False. The ASB can issue accounting standards on its own authority. It does not need to obtain the approval of any other body.

4   In applying financial reporting standards, users should be guided by their **spirit** and **reasoning**.

5   It is permissible to depart from the requirements of a financial reporting standard where this is necessary to ensure the true and fair view is maintained.

6   False. The FRRP in effect has a 'watching brief'. It reacts to matters brought to its attention.

7   All EU publicly-listed companies are required to implement IASs and IFRSs for their consolidated financial statements with accounting periods beginning on 1 January 2005.

8   The FRRP will initially try to get the company to voluntarily agree to make the necessary revisions to their accounts. Failing that the FRRP will seek a court order.

9   True – see 8.1.2 for full details.

10   False. UITF *Abstracts* **should be** taken into consideration by the FRRP in deciding whether a company's financial statements call for review.

11   **ASB standards setting process**

   The following is a summary drawn from the ASB website.

   (a)   **Identify topic** based on ASB research or input from outside.

   (b)   Set up **project management structure** and identify project resources and expertise.

   (c)   Publish a *Discussion Paper.* The objective here is to canvass the **views** of the **interested public** on possible approaches.

   (d)   Analyse and publish **feedback** received.

   (e)   Publish *Financial reporting exposure draft* (FRED); sometimes comments on alternative approaches might be invited.

   (f)   Analyse and consider **further feedback** received from interested parties.

   (g)   Issue **final pronouncement** in the form of a *Financial Reporting Standard* (FRS) or other publication, which specifies the date on which it becomes effective.

Now try the question below from the Exam Question Bank

Number	Level	Marks	Time
Q2	Full exam	20	36 mins

Part B
Preparing the financial statements of limited liability companies

PROFESSIONAL EDUCATION

Presentation of published financial statements

Topic list	Syllabus reference
1 SSAP 2 Disclosure of accounting policies	3 (f)
2 FRS 18 Accounting policies	3 (f)
3 True and fair view	3 (f)
4 Published accounts	2 (a)
5 The format of accounts	2 (a)
6 Notes to the accounts	2 (b)
7 Directors' report	2 (a)
8 Auditors' report and chairman's report	2 (a)

Introduction

This chapter is as important as Chapter 2 and it may look rather daunting. It lays out the Companies Act formats for the balance sheet and profit and loss account as well as the disclosures required in the notes to the accounts. These are fundamental to the study of financial accounting.

Before we look at the Companies Act, we will refresh your memory of the accounting standard which lays out some of the basic premises upon which accounts are based, FRS 18 *Accounting Policies*.

This chapter is predominantly concerned with Companies Act requirements, but you should refer back to this chapter when you get to Chapter 12 because of the way FRS 3 has affected the format of published accounts and the notes required.

We will mention the Companies Act requirements for each of the individual items mentioned in the rest of the chapters in this part of the Study Text. You should refer back to this chapter frequently to remind yourself of the position of each item in the accounts.

Study guide

- Describe the influence of EC directives
- Explain the role of the Companies Acts
- State the requirement of the Companies Act regarding the form and content of the prescribed formats
- Prepare the financial statements of limited companies in accordance with the prescribed formats and relevant accounting standards

Exam guide

FRS 18 is an important standard. Make sure you understand how to use it, as well as the subtle ways it differs from the withdrawn SSAP 2. Practise the format of the accounts until you can quickly lay out a proforma in the exam.

1 SSAP 2 Disclosure of accounting policies

FAST FORWARD

SSAP 2 specified four fundamental accounting concepts – going concern, accruals, consistency and prudence. It was withdrawn in 2000 and replaced by FRS 18.

You may be familiar with SSAP 2 *Disclosure of accounting policies* from your earlier studies. This was withdrawn in 2000 and replaced by FRS 18. A brief summary of SSAP 2 is nevertheless provided here as a point of reference for when SSAP 2 still comes up in discussions.

Knowledge brought forward from earlier studies

SSAP 2 Disclosure of accounting policies

SSAP 2 defines three important terms.

- **Fundamental accounting concepts** are the broad basic assumptions which underlie the periodic financial accounts of business entities.

- **Accounting bases** are the methods developed for applying fundamental accounting concepts to financial transactions and items, for the purpose of financial accounts; and in particular:

  - For determining the accounting periods in which revenue and costs should be recognised in the P & L a/c.

  - For determining the amounts at which material items should be stated in the B/S.

- **Accounting policies:** a business entity's accounting policies are simply the accounting bases which they have chosen to follow in a situation where there is a choice of accounting bases: eg depreciation of fixed assets.

Fundamental concepts

SSAP deals with the four fundamental concepts.

- The **'going concern' concept:** the entity will continue in operational existence for the foreseeable future.

- The **'accruals' concept:** revenue and costs are accrued (that is, recognised as they are earned or incurred, not as money is received or paid).

- The **'consistency' concept:** there is consistency of accounting treatment of like items within each accounting period and from one period to the next.

- The **concept of 'prudence':** revenue and profits are not anticipated, but are recognised by inclusion in the P&L a/c only when realised in the form either of cash or of assets, the ultimate cash realisation of which can be assessed with reasonable certainty.

There is always a presumption that these concepts have been observed. If this is not the case, the facts should be explained.

The CA 1985 and SSAP 2 share the following requirements.

(a) **Accounting policies should be applied consistently** from one financial year to the next.

(b) If accounts are prepared on the basis of assumptions which differ in material respects from any of the generally accepted fundamental accounting concepts (principles) the details, **reasons for and the effect of, the departure from the fundamental concepts must be given in a note to the accounts**.

(c) The **accounting policies** adopted by a company in determining the (material) amounts to be included in the balance sheet and in determining the profit or loss for the year **must be stated by a note to the accounts**.

Exam focus point

For examination purposes, it is useful to give the accounting policy note as the first note to the accounts, making sure that the explanations are clear, fair and as brief as possible.

2 FRS 18 Accounting policies

FAST FORWARD

FRS 18 emphasises **accruals** and **going concern** as **bedrocks** of accounting. Prudence and consistency are simply 'desirable features'.

Exam focus points

Some aspects of FRS 18 may look like the old SSAP 2 but you need to understand the differences, so that when you use the terminology in your answers it reflects the new flavours of FRS 18 rather than serving up the old SSAP 2 terminology and interpretation we have become accustomed to in the past. FRS 18 is an important standard as it impacts extensively on financial reporting work.

The *Student Accountant* of 17 October 2001 included an excellent article on FRS 18 written by Mr Paul Robins. The section below draws on his perspective.

FRS 18 *Accounting policies* replaced SSAP 2 *Disclosure of accounting policies.* It builds on the concepts outlined in SSAP 2 (issued almost 30 years ago) and attempts to align them with the ASB *Statement of Principles.* FRS 18 can be said to provide a '**bridge**' between the ideas and concepts envisaged by the *Statement of Principles* and enshrined in SSAP 2 for a long time in the past.

The objective of FRS 18 is to ensure that for all **material items**:

(a) An entity adopts the accounting policies **most appropriate** to its particular circumstances for the purpose of giving a **true and fair view**

(b)   The accounting policies adopted are **reviewed regularly** to ensure that they remain appropriate, and are changed when a new policy becomes more appropriate, and are changed when a new policy becomes more appropriate to the entity's particular circumstances

(c)   **Sufficient information** is disclosed in the financial statements to enable users to **understand** the accounting policies adopted and how they have been implemented.

2.1 Desirable features

The most obvious change is the relegation of two fundamental accounting concepts

- **Prudence**
- **Consistency**

These concepts are now **desirable features** of financial statements. This mirrors their **role** within the *Statement of Principles.*

2.2 Pervasive concepts

The bedrocks of accounting are

- **Accruals** basis of accounting
- **Going concern** assumption

FRS 18 places great **importance** upon these concepts. Although these are on the face of it, similar to the previously matching and going concern concepts, there are subtle but important differences.

2.3 Accruals

Within FRS 18, the accruals concept goes to the heart of the definition of assets and liabilities, and plays an important role in the way these items are recognised.

Basic requirement

> The accruals basis of accounting requires the **non-cash impact** of transactions to be reflected in the financial statements for the **period in which they occur**, and not, for example, in the period any cash involved is received or paid.

From the above, it can be seen that FRS 18 adopts a slightly different approach to SSAP 2 on the accruals concept. Together with the definitions of assets and liabilities set out in FRS 5, *Reporting the Substance of Transactions*, FRS 18 in effect provides a discipline within which the old SSAP 2 matching process can operate.

Key terms

> - **Asset**: right to **future economic benefits** controlled by an entity as result of past events.
> - **Liability**: entity's **obligation** to **transfer economic benefits** as result of past events.

FRS 18, like CA 1985, does not refer to matching.

2.4 Example

How would you assess whether expenditure such as unexpired advertising or unused stationery should be carried forward to the next year?

Solution

Under the old SSAP 2 regime, the decision on whether to carry expenditure forward into next year would involve the matching concept and whether there is a reasonable expectation of future revenue.

Under the new FRS 18 regime, the **decision to carry forward** depends on whether the item being considered meets the **definition of an asset**.

FRS 18 effectively updates SSAP 2 within the ambit of the **Statement of Principles** and FRS 5.

The article written by Mr Paul Robins, in the *Student Accountant* of October 2001 suggests that the concept of accruals is also closely related to the concept of **realisation**. CA 1985 only allows realised profits to be recognised in the **profit and loss account**. However, CA 1985 does not adequately define the expression 'realised'. Neither does FRS 18 define 'realised'. What FRS 18 does do is to link realisation with the **creation of new assets and liabilities** and hence with the **concept of accruals**.

2.5 Going concern

2.5.1 Criteria

FRS 18 requires financial statements to be prepared on a going concern basis, except where:

(a)   An entity is being liquidated and has ceased trading

(b)   The directors have no realistic alternative but to cease trading or liquidate the business.

In these circumstances, the **directors have an option** to prepare its financial statements on a **basis other than that of a going concern**. Remember, where the criteria are met, the **decision is discretionary** rather than mandatory, to prepare the financial statements on a non-going concern basis.

The going concern hypothesis assumes that the entity will **continue** in **operational existence** for the **foreseeable future**. The justification for this is that financial statements prepared on a **break up basis** do **not provide** users with much **useful information**, such as on financial adaptability and cash generation ability.

2.5.2 Directors responsibilities

The directors have an obligation to **assess** whether there are **significant doubts** about an entity's ability to continue as a **going concern**, when preparing financial statements.

FRS 18 suggests that directors should review the following factors:

- History of company's profitability
- Access to financial resources
- Debt repayment schedules

Such considerations also govern the **length of time** for which the going concern assessment should be made.

2.5.3 Disclosures

The following information should be disclosed in the financial statements in relation to the going concern assessment required by FRS 18.

(a)   Any material uncertainties, of which the directors are aware in making their assessment, related to events or conditions that may cast significant doubt upon the entity's ability to continue as a going concern.

(b)   Where the foreseeable future considered by the directors has been limited to a period of less than one year from the date of approval of the financial statements, that fact.

(c)   When the financial statements are not prepared on a going concern basis, that fact, together with the basis on which the financial statements are prepared and the reason why the entity is not regarded as a going concern.

2.5.4 Statement of Principles

As you will have gathered from the above, FRS 18 is designed to sit alongside the *Statement of Principles* framework. This helps explain the downplaying of the previously important prudence and consistency concepts.

FRS 18 can be said to provide a **'bridge'** between the ideas and concepts envisaged by the *Statement of Principles* and the concepts enshrined in SSAP 2 for a long time.

The preparers of financial statements must now consider the following **objectives** and constraints in **assessing** the appropriateness of **accounting policies:**

- Relevance
- Reliability
- Comparability
- Understandability

2.5.5 Relevance

Information is **relevant** if it possess **certain qualities**.

(a)   Ability to **influence economic decisions** of users

(b)   Is sufficiently **timely** to influence the decision

(c)   Has **predictive** or **confirmatory** value, or both.

Eg the FRS 3 requirement for separate analyses of the results of discontinued operations can be said to improve the predictive value of a set of financial statements.

2.5.6 Reliability

Financial information is reliable if:

(a)   It can be depended upon by users to **represent faithfully** what it either purports to represent or could reasonably be expected to represent, and therefore reflects the **substance of the transactions** and other events that have taken place

(b)   It is **free** from deliberate or systematic **bias** (ie it is **neutral**)

(c)   It is **free** from **material error**

(d)   It is **complete** within the bounds of **materiality**

(e)   Under conditions of **uncertainty**, it has been **prudently prepared**

2.5.7 Prudence

In terms of FRS 18, **prudence** relates to the **uncertainty** that may be associated with the **recognition** and **measurement** of **assets** and **liabilities.**

FRS 18 suggest different levels of confirmatory evidence regarding the recognition of assets and liabilities, where uncertainty exists. In such circumstances, the existence of an **asset or gain** requires **stronger confirmatory evidence** than that required to acknowledge the existence of a liability or loss.

FRS 18 emphasises that prudence may only be called upon to justify setting up a provision if uncertainty exists. **Prudence** should **not** be **invoked** to **justify setting up hidden reserves, excessive provisions** or **understating assets**. Prudence should not be seen as a tool for smoothing profits in financial statements.

FRS 18 emphasises that **if financial statements are not neutral they cannot be reliable**. Neutrality means that the information is **free from deliberate** or **systematic bias**. Financial information cannot be neutral if it has been selected or presented in such a way so as to influence the making of a decision so as to achieve a predetermined result or outcome.

Tension often exists between neutrality and prudence. This should be reconciled by finding a balance that ensures that the deliberate and systematic understatement of assets and gains, and overstatement of liabilities and losses, does not occur.

Several recent FRSs, especially FRS 12, have adopted a more **'even-handed'** approach to the challenge of **measuring** and **recognising** income, expenses, assets and liabilities in financial statements.

2.5.8 Comparability

FRS 18 suggest that this is achieved through:

    (a)   Consistency
    (b)   Disclosure

Hence, consistency, no longer a fundamental accounting concept it its own right, is subsumed under the objective of comparability. Under the old SSAP 2 regime, **consistency implied** a *status quo* approach to financial reporting.

In practice, **comparability** will often be achieved through **consistency**. However, there may be circumstances where a change in the method of presenting financial information increases the usefulness of the financial report for users.

2.5.9 Understandability

FRS 18 stipulates that information provided by financial statements should be capable of being understood by users who have

    (a)   A **reasonable knowledge** of business and economic activities.
    (b)   A willingness and **reasonable diligence** to study the information provided.

There can be tensions between the different objectives set out above. In particular, sometimes the accounting policy that is most relevant to a particular entity's circumstances is not the most reliable, and vice versa. In such circumstances, the most appropriate accounting policy will usually be that which is the **most relevant of those that are reliable**.

Generally, FRS 18 encourages an approach that leads to the most appropriate policies for the company. Note also that FRS 18 does not use the word "conflict" but prefers a process of resolving "tensions" between different objectives.

The relationship between pervasive concepts, desirable features and accounting policy objectives may be summarised briefly in the following diagram.

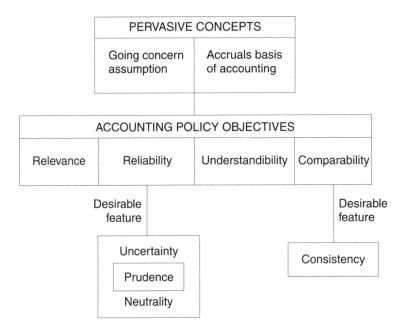

2.6 Accounting policies

FRS 18 prescribes the **regular consideration of the entity's accounting policies**. The **best** accounting policy should be adopted at all times. This is the major reason for downplaying consistency (and to a lesser extent prudence). An entity **cannot retain** an **accounting policy** merely **because** it was **used last** year **or** because it **gives a prudent view**.

However, the entity should consider how a **change** in accounting policy may affect **comparability**. Essentially a **balance** must be struck between selecting the **most appropriate policies** and presenting **coherent and useful** financial statements. The **overriding guidance** is that the financial statements should give a **true and fair view** of the entity's business. Chopping and changing accounting policies year on year is likely to jeopardise the true and fair view but so too is retaining accounting policies which do not present the most useful information to the users of the accounts.

FRS 18 suggests that the need to balance the cost of providing information should be balanced with the likely benefit of such information to the users of the entity's financial statements. However, FRS 18 also cautions against the use of cost and benefit considerations to justify the adoption of an accounting policy that is inconsistent with the requirements of accounting standards, UITF Abstracts and CA 1985.

Exam focus point

The June 2003 exam required candidates to assess whether a given scenario represented a change of accounting policy.

2.6.1 Disclosure

FRS 18 requires the disclosure of

- A **description of each accounting policy** which is material to the entity's financial statements
- A description of any significant estimation technique
- **Changes** to accounting policies
- The effects of any material change to an estimation technique

2.6.2 Estimation techniques

An estimation technique is material **only where a large range** of monetary values may be arrived at. The entity should **vary** the **assumptions** it uses, to **assess** how **sensitive** monetary values are under that **technique**. In most cases the range of values will be relatively narrow (consider the useful life of motor vehicles for example).

2.6.3 Changes to accounting policies

The disclosure of new accounting policies also requires

- An explanation of the **reason for change**

- The **effects of a prior period adjustment** on the previous years results (in accordance with FRS 3)

- The **effects of the change in policy** on the previous year's results

If it is **not possible** to disclose the last two points then the **reason** for this should be disclosed instead.

Exam focus point

> You need to be confident about the application of FRS 18. Make sure that you can **identify** a change in accounting policy and the **reason** that it is a change in accounting policy as opposed to a change in estimation technique. You will have to **discuss** the decision you have reached **and justify** your conclusions.

The most complex aspect to FRS 18 is the **application of the terms and definitions** within the standard. SSAP 2 defined accounting policies and accounting bases. There was some confusion as to what an accounting base was. FRS 18 has dispensed with the term accounting base. However, the term which seems to replace it**, estimation technique**, may prove difficult to apply in practice.

It is essential that you **understand the following definitions** so you can apply them in an examination situation.

Key term

> **Accounting policies.** The principles, conventions, rules and practices applied by an entity that prescribe how transactions and other events are to be reflected in its financial statements.

Accounting policies are **not** estimation techniques.

An accounting policy includes the

- Recognition
- Presentation
- Measurement basis

… of assets, liabilities, gains, losses and changes to shareholders funds.

Key term

> **Estimation technique.** The methods used by an entity to establish the estimated monetary amounts associated with the measurement bases selected for assets, liabilities, gains, losses and changes to shareholder's funds.

Estimation techniques are used to **implement the measurement basis** of an accounting policy. The accounting policy specifies the measurement basis and the estimation technique is used when there is an uncertainty over this amount.

The method of **depreciation is an estimation technique**. The accounting policy is to spread the cost of the asset over its useful economic life. **Depreciation** is the **measurement basis**. The **estimation technique** would be, say, **straight line** depreciation as opposed to **reducing balance**.

A change of estimation technique should **not** be accounted for as a prior period adjustment unless the following apply.

- It is the correction of a fundamental error
- The Companies Act, an accounting standard or a UITF Abstract **requires the change to be accounted** for as a prior period adjustment.

2.7 Application of FRS 18

FRS 18 gives a number of examples of its application in an appendix to the standard. When a change is required to an accounting policy then **three criteria** must be **considered** to ensure that the change is affecting the accounting policy and not an estimation technique.

1 Recognition
2 Presentation
3 Measurement basis

If **any one of the criteria apply** then a change has been made to the accounting policy. If they do **not** apply then a change to an estimation technique has taken place.

You should note that where an **accounting standard gives a choice** of treatments (i.e. SSAP 9 states that stock can be recognised on a FIFO or weighted average cost basis) then adopting the alternative treatment is a **change of accounting policy.** Also note that FRS 15 states that a **change in depreciation method is not** a change in accounting policy.

	Example	Recognition	Change to Presentation	Change to Measurement basis?	Change of Accounting Policy
1	Changing from capitalisation of finance costs associated with the construction of fixed assets to charging them through the profit and loss	Yes	Yes	No	Yes
2	A reassessment of an entity's cost centres means that all three will have production overheads allocated to them instead of just two	No	No	No	No
3	Overheads are reclassified from distribution to cost of sales	No	Yes	No	Yes
4	Change from straight-line depreciation to machine hours	No	No	No	No
5	Reallocate depreciation from administration to cost of sales	No	Yes	No	Yes
6	A provision is revised upwards and the estimates of future cash flows are now discounted in accordance with FRS 12. They were not discounted previously as the amounts involved were not material	No	No	No	No
7	Deferred tax is now reported on a discounted basis. It was previously undiscounted	No	No	Yes	Yes

	Example	Recognition	Change to Presentation	Change to Measurement basis?	Change of Accounting Policy
8	A foreign subsidiary's profit and loss account is now to be translated at the closing rate. It was previously translated at the average rate	No	No	Yes	Yes
9	Fungible stocks are to be measured on the weighted average cost basis instead of the previously used FIFO basis	No	No	Yes	Yes

2.8 Fungible assets

Key term

> **Fungible assets** are similar assets which are grouped together as there is no reason to view them separately in economic terms. Shares and items of stock are examples of fungible assets.

The last example (example 9) is based on a **change to fungible assets**. The standard states that when fungible assets are considered in **aggregate** a change from weighted average cost to FIFO (or vice versa), is a change to the **measurement base**. The standard also recommends that fungible assets should **always be considered in aggregate** in order to enhance **comparability** of financial statements.

Question   Accounting policies 1

The board of Sarah plc decide to change the depreciation method they use on their plant and machinery from 30% reducing balance to 20% straight line to better reflect the way the assets are used within the business. Is this a change of accounting policy ?

Answer

No. This is a change to the **estimation technique**. The same measurement basis is used. The historic cost is allocated over the asset's estimated useful life.

Question   Accounting policies 2

The board of Sarah plc also decide to change their stock valuation. They replace their FIFO valuation method for an AVCO method to better reflect the way that stock is used within the business. Is this a change in accounting policy?

Answer

Yes. This is a change to the **measurement basis**. The paragraphs on fungible assets discuss this further.

Question   Accounting policies 3

The board of Sarah plc decide in the following year that the development costs the business incurs should not be capitalised and presented on the balance sheet. Instead they agree that all development expenditure should be expensed in the profit and loss account. Is this an accounting policy change?

Answer

Yes. The choice to capitalise or not is given in SSAP 13. The criteria affected by this decision are **recognition and presentation.**

 Question   Accounting policies 4

Sarah plc's board are also considering reallocating the depreciation charges made on its large fleet of company cars to administration expenses, they were previously shown in cost of sales. Is this an accounting policy change?

Answer

Yes. Sarah plc would be changing the way they **presented** the depreciation figure.

Exam focus point

In the current financial reporting climate, companies may be tempted to utilise a change of accounting policy or estimation technique to give more favourable reported results. Be prepared for a question in the area perhaps linked to accounting ratios and the interpretation of financial statements.

2.9 Summary

FRS 18 requires an entity to conduct a review on an annual basis in order to ensure that it is using the most appropriate accounting policies.

- The three criteria
- Recognition
- Presentation
- Measurement basis

Are considered in order to establish whether there has been a change of accounting policy or merely a change of measurement basis. The objectives of

- Reliability
- Relevance
- Comparability
- Understandability

The above must be fulfilled by the accounting policies adopted. This requirement helps prevent entities from changing accounting policies too often.

FRS 18 introduces subtle changes into the meaning of accruals and going concern. Whereas matching was driven by the need to ensure completeness in the profit and loss account, the accruals basis approaches recognition from the need to ensure the validity of assets and liabilities.

Prudence and consistency have a lesser role in the accounting policy framework. There may be tension between prudence and neutrality. Prudence should not be used as an excuse for setting up excessive provisions or understating assets. The use of prudence must be linked to uncertainty.

FRS 18 provides a bridge between the standards setting process and the *Statement of Principles*.

3 True and fair view

FAST FORWARD

The overriding requirement for financial statements is that they should present a 'true and fair view'. This concept has not been formally defined.

3.1 Interpretation of true and fair

Section 226 of CA 1985 states that:

> 'the balance sheet shall give a true and fair view of the state of affairs of the company as at the end of the financial year, and the profit and loss account shall give a true and fair view of the profit or loss of the company for the financial year.'

The balance sheet and profit and loss account should also comply with the requirements of the Fourth Schedule (s 226(3) CA 1985).

Key term

> **'True and fair view'** has no set definition. Broadly speaking it means 'reasonably accurate and not misleading'.

The term 'true and fair view' is **not defined** in the **Companies Acts**, nor in **SSAPs** or **FRSs**, which also claim to be authoritative statements on what is a true and fair view. Moreover, the **courts** have **never tried to define it**.

In view of the ASB's policy of **reviewing** and, if necessary, **altering** or **replacing existing accounting standards**, a question **arises** as to whether the concept defined by '**true and fair view**' is constant or is **evolving** over a period of years.

The ASC has sought Counsel's opinion on this question. Very briefly, Counsel's opinion included the following key points:

- **Accuracy** and **completeness** are two key ingredients that contribute to a true and fair view.

- There might **not** be **consensus** amongst reasonable businessman and accountants as to the degree of accuracy and completeness required.

- The concept of **true and fair is dynamic**.

- **Judges** will look for **guidance** to the **ordinary practices** of **professional accountants**.

A later opinion obtained by the ASB, confirms the above views. This opinion also provides further clues on how to interpret the expression true and fair. The opinion suggests that the courts are **unlikely** to **look for synonyms** for the words **'true'** and **'fair'**. **Instead**, the courts will take an approach of trying to **apply** the **concepts implied** by the expression **'true and fair'**.

The **Statement of Principles** echoes the above, but carefully avoids providing a formal definition of **true and fair**.

- The true and fair view is a **dynamic concept** and evolves in **response** to changes in **accounting** and **business practice**.

- **Relevance** and **reliability** and **prime indicators** of the **quality** of **financial information**.

3.2 True and fair override

Important!

S 226 (5) CA 1985 makes an important statement about the need to give a true and fair view. It states that if, in **special circumstances**, compliance with any of the Act's provisions would be inconsistent with the requirement to give a true and fair view, then the directors should depart from that provision to the extent necessary to give a true and fair view. This is the **true and fair override.**

If a balance sheet or profit and loss account drawn up in compliance with these other requirements of the Act would not provide enough information to give a true and fair view, then any **necessary additional information** must **also** be **given**.

The overriding priority to give a true and fair view **has in the past been treated as an important 'loophole' in the law,** and has been a cause of some argument or debate within the accounting profession. For example, the CA 1985 permits only realised profits to be recognised in the profit and loss account, whereas SSAP 9 requires unrealised profits on long-term contracts to be credited to profit and loss. Such a policy can only be justified by **invoking** the **overriding requirement** to show a true and fair view.

If companies do depart from the other requirements of the Act in order to give a true and fair view, they **must explain the particulars of and reasons for the departure**, **and its effects on the accounts**, in a note to the accounts. As already stated, the **Fourth Schedule** also requires a statement in a **note to the accounts** that the accounts have been prepared in accordance with **applicable accounting standards** and **particulars of any material departure from** those **standards and the reasons** (s 36A Sch 4).

3.3 True and fair override disclosures

As we saw above, where the directors depart from provisions of CA 1985 to the extent necessary to give a true and fair view, the Act required that 'particulars of any such departure, the reasons for it and its effect shall be given in a note to the accounts'. **FRS 18 *Accounting Policies*** seeks to clarify the meaning of that sentence. Any **material departure** from the Companies Act, an accounting standard or a UITF abstract should lead to the following information being disclosed.

(a) **A statement that there has been a departure** from the requirements of companies legislation, an accounting standard or a UITF abstract, and that the departure is **necessary to give a true and fair view.**

(b) **A description of the treatment normally required** and also a description of the **treatment actually used.**

(c) An explanation of why the **prescribed treatment would not give a true and fair view**.

(d) **Its effect**: a description of how the position shown in the accounts is different as a result of the departure, with quantification if possible, or an explanation of the circumstances.

The disclosures required should either be **included in or cross referenced** to the note required about **compliance with accounting standards**, **particulars** of any material departure from those standards and the **reasons** for it (Paragraph 36A Sch 4).

If the departure occurs in **subsequent accounting periods**, the above disclosures should be made in **subsequent financial statements including** the **corresponding amounts** for previous years. If the departure only affects the corresponding amounts then the disclosure should relate to the corresponding amounts.

4 Published accounts

FAST FORWARD

Statutory accounts are part of the price to be paid for the benefits of limited liability. **Limited companies must produce such accounts annually and they must appoint an independent person to audit and report on them.**

Once prepared, **a copy** of the accounts **must be sent to the Registrar of Companies**, who maintains a separate file for every company. The Registrar's files may be inspected for a nominal fee by any member of the public. This is why the statutory accounts are often referred to as *published accounts*.

It is the responsibility of the company's directors to produce accounts which show a true and fair view of the company's results for the period and its financial position at the end of the period (see Section 3 of this chapter). The board evidence their approval of the accounts by the signature of one director on the balance sheet. Once this has been done, and the auditors have completed their report, the accounts are laid before the members of the company in general meeting. When the members have adopted the accounts they are sent to the Registrar for filing.

The requirement that the accounts show a true and fair view is paramount; although statute lays down numerous rules on the information to be included in the published accounts and the format of its presentation, any such rule **may be overridden** if compliance with it would prevent the accounts from showing a true and fair view.

4.1 Documents included in the accounts

The documents which **must be included by law** in the accounts laid before a general meeting of the members are:

(a)   A **profit and loss account** (or an income and expenditure account in the case of a non-trading company).

(b)   A **balance sheet** as at the date to which the profit and loss account is made up.

(c)   A **directors' report**.

(d)   An **auditors' report** addressed to the members (not to the directors) of the company.

In addition, FRS 1 requires a cash flow statement to be given. This statement is discussed in Chapter 10. FRS 3 has also introduced the Statement of Total Recognised Gains and Losses, covered in Chapter 9. Here we will look at the profit and loss account and balance sheet.

4.2 The accounting reference period

The Companies Act 1985 contains the following rules about the length of a company's accounting period and the frequency with which it may be altered (ss 223 to 225).

(a)   **Accounts must be prepared for an accounting reference period** (ARP), known as the 'financial year' of the company (whether it is a calendar year or not).

(b)   **The profit and loss account should cover the ARP or a period ending not more than seven days before or after the accounting reference date**. Subsequent accounts should cover the period beginning on the day following the last day covered by the previous profit and loss account, and ending as specified above.

(c)   **The balance sheet should give a true and fair view** of the state of affairs of the company as at the end of the financial year.

(d)   **A company can decide its accounting reference period by giving notice to the Registrar of the date on which the accounting period will end each year.** This date will be the accounting reference date. S 225 makes provisions for the alteration of the accounting reference date.

4.3 The laying and delivery of accounts

Exam focus point

You should know Paragraphs 4.1 and 4.2 from your earlier studies, so the material is unlikely to come up in the exam.

S 241 CA 1985 specifies that the directors shall lay before the company in general meeting and also deliver to the Registrar, in respect of each accounting reference period, a copy of every document comprising the accounts for that period. However, the CA 1989 has amended the CA 1985 to allow the members of private companies to elect unanimously to dispense with general meetings. This does *not*, however, exempt the company from providing accounts to members.

Unlimited companies (with some exceptions) are exempt from the duty to deliver copies of their accounts to the Registrar.

The **period allowed for laying and delivering accounts** varies, and (s 244):

(a)   For **private companies**, it is **ten months** after the end of the accounting reference period.

(b)   For **other (public etc) companies**, it is **seven** months.

4.4 Accounting records

S 221 requires that every company's **accounting records must:**

(a)   Be sufficient to show and explain the company's transactions.

(b)   Disclose with reasonable accuracy at any time the financial position of the company at that time.

(c)   Enable the directors to ensure that any profit and loss account or balance sheet gives a true and fair view of the company's financial position.

S 221 also specifies that accounting records **should contain**:

(a)   Day-to-day entries for money received and paid, with an explanation of why the receipts and payments occurred (ie the nature of the transactions).

(b)   A record of the company's assets and liabilities.

(c)   Where the company deals in goods:

(i)   Statements of stocks held at the financial year end.

(ii)   Statements of stocktakings on which the figures in (c)(i) are based.

(iii)   With the exception of goods sold on retail, statements of all goods bought and sold identifying for each item the suppliers or customers.

S 222 specifies that the **accounting records are to be kept at the registered office** of the company or at such other place as the directors think fit, and they **should be open to inspection at all times by officers of the company.**

Also in s 222 is a **requirement for companies to preserve their accounting records:**

(a)   **Private** companies, for **3 years.**

(b)   **Other** companies, for **6 years.**

4.5 The classification of companies

A company is considered to be private unless it is registered as a public company. A major advantage for a public company is that it can raise new funds from the general public by issuing shares or loan stock; s 81 CA 1985 prohibits a private company from offering shares or debentures to the public.

4.6 Related party transactions

It is generally agreed that separate disclosure of transactions between a company and related parties may be needed if the user of the accounts is to be able to gain a full understanding of the results for the accounting period.

Two parties are considered to be related when:

    (a)   One party is able to exercise control or significant influence over the other party.

    (b)   Both parties are subject to common control or significant influence from the same source.

For example, companies within the same group will be related parties, or a company and its directors will be related parties.

This is governed by FRS 8, which is explained more fully in Chapter 22.

5 The format of accounts

FAST FORWARD

> The CA85 sets out balance sheet and profit and loss account proformas for **published accounts**. Learn the main headings so that you can write them out quickly in the exam.

Exam focus point

> If you are in a hurry or revising, skip or skim the explanations in Paragraph 5.1 and go straight to the proformas in Paragraphs 5.2 and 6.

5.1 The form and content of the balance sheet

The Companies Act 1985 sets out **two formats** for the balance sheet, one **horizontal and** the other **vertical. Once a company has chosen a format it must adhere to it for subsequent financial years** unless, in the opinion of the directors, there are special reasons for a change. Details of any change and the reason for it must be disclosed by note to the accounts.

Each item on the balance sheet format is referenced by letters and roman and Arabic numbers. These reference labels do not have to be shown in a company's published accounts but are given in the Act for the guidance of companies and are relevant in identifying the:

    (a)   Extent to which information may be combined or disclosed by note (rather than on the face of the accounts).

    (b)   Headings and sub-headings which may be adapted or re-arranged to suit the special nature of the company.

    (c)   Items which do not need to be disclosed in modified accounts for small and medium-sized companies.

The following points should be borne in mind.

    (a)   Any item preceded by letters or roman numbers **must** be shown on the face of the balance sheet, unless it has a nil value for both the current and the previous year.

    (b)   Items preceded by arabic numbers **may** be amalgamated:

(i)   If their individual amounts are not material.

(ii) If amalgamation facilitates the assessment of the company's state of affairs (but then the individual items must be disclosed by note).

(c)   Items preceded by arabic numbers **may** be:

(i)   Adapted (eg title altered)

(ii) Re-arranged (in position)

In any case where the special nature of the company's business requires such an alteration.

(d)   Any item required to be shown **may** be shown in greater detail than required by the prescribed format.

(e)   A company's balance sheet (or profit and loss account) **may** include an item not otherwise covered by any of the items listed, except that the following must not be treated as assets in any company's balance sheet:

(i)   Preliminary expenses.

(ii) Expenses of and commission on any issue of shares or debentures.

(iii) Costs of research.

Schedule 4 includes the following notes about the balance sheet format.

(a)   **Concessions, patents, licences, trademarks**, etc (Item B I 2) may only be shown if:

(i)   They were acquired at a purchase cost, and do not consist of goodwill

(ii) Or they are assets created by the company itself.

(b)   **Goodwill** (Item B I 3) should be included only to the extent that it is purchased goodwill.

(c)   **Own shares** (Item B III 7). CA 1985 allows a company to purchase or acquire its own shares.

(d)   **Debtors** (Items C II 1 – 6). Any amounts not falling due until after more than one year should be disclosed separately.

(e)   **Debenture loans** (Items E1 and H1). Convertible loans should be shown separately from other debenture loans.

(f)   **Payments received (in advance) on account** (Items E3 and H3). These should be shown unless they are accounted for as deductions from the value of stocks (as in the case of progress payments for work in progress on long-term contracts).

5.2 The form and content of the profit and loss account

The Companies Act 1985 sets out two **horizontal and** two **vertical formats** for the profit and loss account. The rules applying to the balance sheet formats described above also apply to the profit and loss account.

The two different formats are distinguished by the way in which expenditure is analysed. Format 1 analyses costs by type of operation or function, whereas Format 2 analyses costs by items of expense.

The following points should be borne in mind.

(a)   Every profit and loss account **must show the company's profit or loss on ordinary activities before taxation**, no matter what format is used nor how much it might be amended to suit the circumstances of a particular case.

(b)   Every profit and loss account must also show, as additional items:

(i)   Amounts to be **transferred to reserves**, or amounts to be withdrawn from reserves.

(c)   Amounts representing income may not be set off against items representing expenditure (just as assets and liabilities may not be 'netted off' in the balance sheet).

Below are proforma balance sheets and profit and loss accounts.

PROFORMA BALANCE SHEET (VERTICAL FORMAT)

			£	£	£
A	CALLED UP SHARE CAPITAL NOT PAID*				X
B	**FIXED ASSETS**				
	I	Intangible assets			
		1 Development costs	X		
		2 Concessions, patents, licences, trade marks and similar rights and assets	X		
		3 Goodwill	X		
		4 Payments on account	X̲		
				X	
	II	Tangible assets			
		1 Land and buildings	X		
		2 Plant and machinery	X		
		3 Fixtures, fittings, tools and equipment	X		
		4 Payments on account and assets in course of construction	X̲		
				X	
	III	Investments			
		1 Shares in group undertakings †	X		
		2 Loans to group undertakings †	X		
		3 Participating interest †	X		
		4 Loans to undertakings in which the company has a participating interest †	X		
		5 Other investments other than loans	X		
		6 Other loans	X		
		7 Own shares	X̲		
				X̲	
					X̲
C	**CURRENT ASSETS**				
	I	Stocks			
		1 Raw materials	X		
		2 Work in progress	X		
		3 Finished goods and goods for resale	X		
		4 Payments on account	X̲		
				X	

II   Debtors

    1   Trade debtors   X
    2   Amounts owed by group undertakings †   X
    3   Amounts owed by undertakings in which
          the company has a participating interest †   X
    4   Other debtors   X
    5   Called up share capital not paid*   X
    6   Prepayments and accrued income**   X̲

    X

III   Investments

    1   Shares in group undertakings †   X
    2   Own shares   X
    3   Other investments   X̲

IV   Cash at bank and in hand   X̲

    X

D   PREPAYMENTS AND ACCRUED INCOME**   X

E   CREDITORS: AMOUNTS FALLING DUE WITHIN ONE YEAR

    1   Debenture loans   X
    2   Bank loans and overdrafts   X
    3   Payments received on account   X
    4   Trade creditors   X
    5   Bills of exchange payable   X
    6   Amounts owed to group undertakings †   X
    7   Amounts owed to undertakings in which
          the company has a participating interest †   X
    8   Other creditors including taxation and social security   X
    9   Accruals and deferred income ***   X̲

    (X)

F   NET CURRENT ASSETS (LIABILITIES)   X̲

G   TOTAL ASSETS LESS CURRENT LIABILITIES   X

H   CREDITORS: AMOUNTS FALLING DUE AFTER MORE THAN ONE YEAR

    1   Debenture loans   X
    2   Bank loans and overdrafts   X
    3   Payments received on account   X
    4   Trade creditors   X
    5   Bills of exchange payable   X
    6   Amounts owed to group undertakings †   X
    7   Amounts owed to undertakings in which the
          company has a participating interest †   X
    8   Other creditors including taxation and social security   X
    9   Accruals and deferred income***   X̲

    (X)

PROFORMA BALANCE SHEET (VERTICAL FORMAT)

			£	£	£
I	PROVISIONS FOR LIABILITIES				
	1	Pensions and similar obligations †	X		
	2	Taxation, including deferred taxation	X		
	3	Other provisions	X̲		
				(X)	
J	ACCRUALS AND DEFERRED INCOME ***			(X̲)	
					(X̲)
					X̲
K	CAPITAL AND RESERVES				
	I	Called up share capital			X
	II	Share premium account			X
	III	Revaluation reserve			X
	IV	Other reserves			
		1 Capital redemption reserve			X
		2 Reserve for own shares			X
		3 Reserves provided for by the articles of association			X
		4 Other reserves			X̲
					X
	V	Profit and loss account			X̲
					X̲

(*), (**), (***). These items may be shown in either of the positions indicated.

Both vertical formats of the profit and loss account are reproduced below.

PROFORMA PROFIT AND LOSS ACCOUNT: FORMAT 1

		£	£
1	Turnover		X
2	Cost of sales *		(X)
3	Gross profit or loss *		X
4	Distribution costs *	(X)	
5	Administrative expenses *	(X)	
	(X)		
	X		
6	Other operating income		X
	X		
7	Income from shares in group undertakings †	X	
8	Income from shares in undertakings in which the company		
	has a participating interest †	X	
9	Income from other fixed asset investments	X	
10	Other interest receivable and similar income	X	
	X		
	X		
11	Amounts written off investments	(X)	
12	Interest payable and similar charges	(X)	
			(X)
	Profit or loss on ordinary activities before taxation		X
13	Tax on profit or loss on ordinary activities		(X)
14	Profit or loss on ordinary activities after taxation		X
15	Extraordinary income	X	
16	Extraordinary charges	(X)	
17	Extraordinary profit or loss	X	
18	Tax on extraordinary profit or loss	(X)	
			X
			X
19	Other taxes not shown under the above items		(X)
20	Profit or loss for the financial year		X

* These figures will all include depreciation.

PROFORMA PROFIT AND LOSS ACCOUNT: FORMAT 2

			£		£		£
1	Turnover						X
2	Change in stocks of finished goods and work in progress				(X)	or	X
3	Own work capitalised						X
4	Other operating income						X
							X
5	(a) Raw materials and consumables		(X)				
	(b) Other external charges		(X)				
					(X)		
6	Staff costs:						
	(a) wages and salaries		(X)				
	(b) social security costs		(X)				
	(c) other pension costs		(X)				
					(X)		
					(X)		
7	(a) Depreciation and other amounts written off tangible and intangible fixed assets **		(X)				
	(b) Exceptional amounts written off current assets		(X)				
					(X)		
8	Other operating charges				(X)		
							(X)
9	Income from shares in group undertakings †				X		
10	Income from shares in undertakings in which the company has a participating interest †				X		
11	Income from other fixed asset investments				X		
12	Other interest receivable and similar income				X		
							X
							X
13	Amounts written off investments				(X)		
14	Interest payable and similar charges				(X)		
							(X)
	Profit or loss on ordinary activities before taxation						X
15	Tax on profit or loss on ordinary activities						(X)
16	Profit or loss on ordinary activities after taxation						X
17	Extraordinary income				X		
18	Extraordinary charges				(X)		
19	Extraordinary profit or loss				X		
20	Tax on extraordinary profit or loss				(X)		
							X
							X
21	Other taxes not shown under the above items						(X)
22	Profit or loss for the financial year						X

** This figure will be disclosed by way of a note in Format 1.

Note that because the captions have Arabic number references, they do not have to be shown on the face of the profit and loss account but may instead be shown in the notes.

5.3 FRS 28 Corresponding amounts

Corresponding amounts for the previous financial year **must be shown for items in the primary financial statements and the notes. Where** a corresponding amount for the previous year is **not properly comparable** with an amount disclosed for the current year, **the previous year's amount should be adjusted** and the basis for adjustment disclosed in a note to the financial statements.

5.4 Some items in more detail

In the balance sheet, item A and item CII5 are 'called up share capital not paid'. This item is more relevant to other countries in the EU than to Britain (remember that the Fourth Directive applies to all EU countries). However, if at the balance sheet date a company has called up some share capital and not all the called up amounts have been paid, these will be a short-term debt (see Chapter 12 on the issue of shares). This would probably be shown (if material) as item CII5. Item A should not be expected in the accounts of British companies.

Item BIII7 in the balance sheet, investments in 'own shares', refers to shares which have been bought back by the company, but which have not yet been cancelled.

'**Turnover**' is defined by the 1985 Act as '**the amounts derived from the provision of goods and services, falling within the company's ordinary activities, after deduction of:**

(a) **Trade discounts.**
(b) **Value added tax.**
(c) **Any other taxes based on the amounts so derived'.**

'**Cost of sales**' (format 1) is **not defined**, nor are 'distribution costs', nor are 'administrative expenses'. The division of costs between these three categories is based on accepted practice.

Format 1, unlike Format 2, does not itemise depreciation and wages costs, but:

(a) Provisions for depreciation charged in the year
(b) Wages and salaries, social security costs and other pension costs

Must be disclosed separately in notes to the accounts.

The Act extends the requirements of FRS 3 about extraordinary profits or losses (see later chapters). The extraordinary profit or loss must be shown as the gross amount, with taxation on it separately disclosed. **Extraordinary items are now extremely rare**.

The profit and loss account must show profit or loss for the financial year. Statutory Instrument 2947 now brings UK practice into line with International, in that dividends paid are no longer shown on the face of the profit and loss account. They will be shown in the reconciliation of movements in shareholders' funds. Proposed dividends are no longer accounted for.

In itemising staff costs, wages and salaries consist of gross amounts (net pay plus deductions) and social security costs comprise employer's National Insurance contributions.

6 Notes to the accounts

Part III of the Fourth Schedule deals with notes to the balance sheet and profit and loss account. These are sub-divided into:

(a) Disclosure of accounting policies.
(b) Notes to the balance sheet.
(c) Notes to the profit and loss account.

A note to the accounts must disclose the accounting policies adopted by the company (including the policy used to account for depreciation or the fall in value of assets). This gives statutory backing to the disclosure requirement in FRS 18. Companies must also now state that all relevant accounting standards have been complied with and if not, what the departures are and the reasons for the departure.

The following example shows a *pro forma* profit and loss account and balance sheet with the required notes covering your syllabus. These notes are expanded in the subsequent chapters on different accounting standards and disclosures.

STANDARD PLC
PROFIT AND LOSS ACCOUNT FOR THE YEAR ENDED
31 DECEMBER 20X5

	Notes	£'000	£'000
Turnover	2		X
Cost of sales			X
Gross profit			X
Distribution costs			X
Administrative expenses			X
Operating profit	3		X
Income from fixed asset investments			X
			X
Interest payable and similar charges	6		X
Profit before taxation			X
Taxation	7		X
Profit for the period			X

STANDARD PLC
BALANCE SHEET AS AT 31 DECEMBER 20X5

	Notes	£'000	£'000
Fixed assets			
Intangible assets	9		X
Tangible assets	10		X
Fixed asset investments	11		X
			X
Current assets			
Stocks	12	X	
Debtors	13	X	
Cash at bank and in hand		X	
		X	
Creditors: amounts falling due within one year	14	X	
Net current assets			X
Total assets less current liabilities			X
Creditors: amounts falling due after more than one year	16		X
Accruals and deferred income	17		X
			X
Capital and reserves			
Called up share capital	18		X
Share premium account	19		X
Revaluation reserve	19		X
General reserve	19		X
Profit and loss account	19		X
			X

Approved by the board on .... Director

The notes on pages XX to XX form part of these accounts.

NOTES TO THE ACCOUNTS

1 **Accounting policies**

(a) These accounts have been prepared under the historical cost convention of accounting and in accordance with applicable accounting standards.

(b) Depreciation has been provided on a straight line basis in order to write off the cost of depreciable fixed assets over their estimated useful lives. The rates used are:

Buildings	X%
Plant and machinery	X%
Fixtures and fittings	X%

(c) Stocks have been valued at the lower of cost and net realisable value.

(d) Development expenditure relating to specific projects intended for commercial exploitation is carried forward and amortised over the period expected to benefit commencing with the period in which related sales are first made. Expenditure on pure and applied research is written off as incurred.

Notes

(a) Accounting policies are those followed by the company and used in arriving at the figures shown in the profit and loss accounts and balance sheet.

(b) CA 1985 requires policies in respect of depreciation and foreign currency translation to be included. Others are required by accounting standards insofar as they apply to the company.

2 **Turnover**

Turnover represents amounts derived from the provision of goods and services falling within the company's ordinary activities, after deduction of trade discounts, value added tax and any other tax based on the amounts so derived.

	Turnover £'000	Profit before tax £'000
Principal activities		
Electrical components	X	X
Domestic appliances	X	X
	X	X
Geographical analysis		
UK	X	
America	X	
Europe	X	
	X	

Notes

(a) Directors are to decide on classification and then apply them consistently.

(b) Geographical analysis must be by destination of sale.

(c) If the directors believe this disclosure to be seriously prejudicial to the business the information need not be disclosed.

(d) The profit after tax figures are only required by SSAP 25 (see Chapter 14) for larger companies.

3 Operating profit

Operating profit is stated after charging:

	£'000
Depreciation	X
Amortisation	X
Hire of plant and machinery (SSAP 21: see Chapter 6)	X
Auditors' remuneration	X
Exceptional items	X
Directors' emoluments (see note 4)	X
Staff costs (see note 5)	X
Research and development	X

Notes

Separate totals are required to be disclosed for:

(a)   Audit fees and expenses
(b)   Fees paid to auditors for non-audit work

This disclosure is not required for small or medium-sized companies.

Question   **Auditors' remuneration**

Alvis Ltd receives an invoice in respect of the current year from its auditors made up as follows.

	£
Audit of accounts	10,000
Taxation computation and advice	1,500
Travelling expenses: audit	1,100
Consultancy fees charged by another firm of accountants	1,600
	14,200

What figure should be disclosed as auditors' remuneration in the notes to the profit and loss account?

Answer

	£
Audit of accounts	10,000
Expenses	1,100
Taxation computation and advice	1,500
	12,600

The consultancy fees are not received by the auditors.

4 Directors' emoluments

New requirements for the disclosure of directors' remuneration were introduced by *The Company Accounts (Disclosure of Directors' Emoluments) Regulations 1997* (SI 1997/570). A distinction is made between listed/AIM companies and unlisted companies.

	£'000
Directors	
Aggregate emoluments	X
Gains made on exercise of share options (listed/AIM company only)	X
Amounts receivable (unlisted company: excludes shares) under long-term incentive schemes	X
Company pension contributions	X
Compensation for loss of office	X
Sums paid to third parties for directors' services	X
	X
Highest paid director	
Aggregate emoluments, gains on share options exercised and benefits under long-term incentive schemes (listed/AIM company only)	X
Company pension contributions	X
Accrued pension	X
	X

Notes

(a)   All companies must disclose aggregate emoluments paid to/receivable by a director in respect of 'qualifying services'.

(b)   Unlisted companies do not need to disclose:

    (i)   The amount of gains made when directors exercise options, only the number of directors who exercised options.

    (ii)   The net value of any assets that comprise shares, which would otherwise be disclosed in respect of assets received under long-term incentive schemes, but only the number of directors in respect of whose qualifying service shares were receivable under long-term incentive schemes.

(c)   For listed companies, the disclosure requirements for share options do not refer to qualifying services, so gains made on the exercise of shares before appointment must therefore be included.

(d)   Information about the highest paid director only needs to be given if the aggregate of emoluments, gains on exercise of share options, and amounts receivable by the directors under long-term incentive schemes is > £200,000. For unlisted companies, state whether the highest paid direct or exercised any share options and/or received any shares in respect of qualifying services under a long-term incentive scheme.

(e)   The details relating to pensions are beyond the scope of your syllabus.

(f)   **Definitions**

    (i)   **Emoluments**. Salary, fees, bonuses, expense allowances, money value of other benefits, except share options granted, pension amounts and amounts paid under a long-term incentive scheme. Includes 'golden hellos'.

    (ii)   **Qualifying services**. Services as a director of a company and services in connection with the management of the company's affairs.

    (iii)   **Listed company**. A company whose securities have been admitted to the Official List of the Stock Exchange (or AIM).

    (iv)   **Long-term incentive schemes.** Any agreement or arrangement under which money or other assets become receivable by a director and where one or more of the qualifying candidates relating to service cannot be fulfilled in a single financial year.

Bonuses relating to an individual year, termination payments and retirement benefits are excluded.

5 **Employee information**

(a) The **average number of persons** employed during the year was:

By product	
Electrical components	X
Domestic appliances	X
	X
By activity	
Production	X
Selling	X
Administration	X
	X

(b) **Employment costs**

	£'000
Aggregate wages and salaries	X
Social security costs	X
Other pension costs	X
	X

Notes

(a) Classification to be decided by the directors and applied consistently year on year. Must state whether executive directors are included or excluded.

(b) Social security costs are employer's NI.

(c) Other pension costs are contributions by the company to a pension scheme.

(d) **Definitions**

(i) **Staff costs**. Costs incurred in respect of persons employed under contract of service. They include part time employees under contract.

(ii) **Average number**

(1) Ascertain number employed under contracts each week.
(2) Aggregate these numbers.
(3) Divide by the number of months in the period.

Include those persons working wholly or mainly overseas.

 Question   **Employee information**

During a 12 month accounting period, the administration department of Tariq Ltd had the following employees.

(a) 12 worked overseas, of whom 1 returned to work in the UK and 2 resigned after 6 months.

(b) 30 UK employees (including 1 executive director).

(c) 20 part-timers who only worked over the three months' summer season and of whom only 8 were employed under a service contract.

Determine the average number of employees (assuming executive directors are included) to be disclosed for the administration department.

Note. The employee information note may include or exclude executive directors and the company must state which option they have chosen.

Answer

Average number

	No
Overseas $(12 - (2 \times \frac{1}{2}))$	11
UK employees	30
Contract part-timers (8 for 3 months, which averages out at 2 per year)	2
	43

6 Interest payable and similar charges

	£'000
Interest payable on:	
Bank overdrafts and loans	X
Other loans	X
Lease and HP finance charges allocated for the year	X
	X

Note

Similar charges might include arrangement fees for loans.

7 Taxation

	£'000
UK corporation tax (at x% on taxable profit for the year)	X
Transfer to/from deferred taxation	X
Under/over provision in prior years	X
Unrelieved overseas taxation	X
	X

Note

The rate of tax must be disclosed (FRS 16: see Chapter 8).

8 Dividends

These are no longer shown on the face of the profit and loss account.

9 Intangible fixed assets

	Development expenditure £'000
Cost	
At 1 January 20X5	X
Expenditure	X
At 31 December 20X5	X
Amortisation	
At 1 January 20X5	X
Charge for year	X
At 31 December 20X5	X
Net book value at 31 December 20X5	X
Net book value 31 December 20X4	X

Note

The above disclosure should be given for each intangible asset.

BPP PROFESSIONAL EDUCATION

10 Tangible fixed assets

| | Freehold land and Buildings £'000 | Leasehold land and Buildings | | Plant and machinery £'000 | Fixtures and fittings £'000 | Total £'000 |
		Long leases £'000	Short leases £'000			
Cost (or valuation)						
At 1 Jan 20X5	X	X	X	X	X	X
Additions	X	-	X	-	X	X
Revaluation	X	-	-	-	-	X
Disposals	(X)	-	-	(X)	(X)	(X)
At 31 Dec 20X5	X	X	X	X	X	X
Depreciation						
At 1 Jan 20X5	X	X	X	X	X	X
Charge for year	X	X	X	X	X	X
Revaluation	(X)	-	-	-	-	(X)
Disposals	(X)	-	-	(X)	(X)	(X)
At 31 Dec 20X5	X	X	X	X	X	X
Net book value						
At 31 Dec 20X5	X	X	X	X	X	X
At 31 Dec 20X4	X	X	X	X	X	X

Notes

(a) Long leases are $\geq$ 50 years unexpired at balance sheet date.

(b) Classification by asset type represents arabic numbers from formats.

(c) Motor vehicles (unless material) are usually included within plant and machinery.

(d) Revaluations in the year. state for each asset revalued:

   (i) Method of valuation

   (ii) Date of valuation

   (iii) The historical cost equivalent of the above information as if the asset had not been revalued

11 Fixed asset investments

	£'000
Shares at cost	
At 1 January 20X5	X
Additions	X
Disposals	(X)
At 31 December 20X5	X

The market value (in aggregate) of the listed investments is £X.

Note

An AIM investment is *not* a listed investment. All stock exchanges of repute allowed. Aggregate market value (ie profits less losses) to be disclosed if material.

12   Stocks

	£'000
Raw materials and consumables	X
Work in progress	X
Finished goods	X
	X

The replacement cost of stock is £X higher than its book value.

13   Debtors

	£'000
Trade debtors	X
Other debtors	X
Prepayments and accrued income	X
	X

14   Creditors: amounts falling due within one year

	£'000
Debenture loans: 8% stock 20X9	X
Bank loans and overdrafts	X
Trade creditors	X
Other creditors including taxation and social security (see note 15)	X
Accruals and deferred income	X
	X

The bank loans and overdraft are secured by a floating charge over the company's assets.

Notes

(a)   Give details of security given for all secured creditors.

(b)   Include the current portion of instalment creditors here.

15   Other creditors including taxation and social security

	£'000
UK corporation tax	X
Social security	X
	X

Notes

(a)   Liabilities for taxation and social security must be shown separately from other creditors.

(b)   Dividend liabilities to be disclosed separately.

16   Creditors: amounts falling due after more than one year

	£'000
8½% unsecured loan stock 20Y9	X

Notes

(a)   Very long-term creditors:

   (i)   Disclose the aggregate amount of debentures and other loans:

      (1)   Payable after more than five years

      (2)   Payable by instalments, any of which fall due after more than five years

   (ii)   For (1) and (2) disclose the terms of repayment and rates of interest.

(b)   Debentures during the year, disclose:

   (i)   Class issued

        (ii)   For each class

             (1)   Amount issued
             (2)   Consideration received

(c)   As per FRS 25, redeemable preference shares will now appear under long-term creditors.

17   Accruals and deferred income

	£'000
Government grants received	X
Credited to profit and loss account	(X)
	X

Note

Alternative presentation if not included as part of creditors, which saves dividing the accruals or deferred income amount between within and greater than one year.

18   Called up share capital

	£1 ordinary shares £'000	10% preference Shares (non-redeemable) £'000
Authorised		
Number	X	X
Value	X	X
Allotted		
Number	X	X
Value	X	X

Notes

(a)   Disclose number and nominal value for each class, both authorised and allotted.

(b)   *Shares issued during the year*, disclose:

        (i)   Classes allotted
        (ii)   For each class

             (1)   Number and aggregate nominal value allotted
             (2)   Consideration received

(c)   Only non-redeemable preference shares are now included under equity

19   Reserves

Reserve movements are no longer shown on the face of the profit and loss account. They will be shown in the reconciliation of movements in shareholders funds.

	Share premium £'000	Revaluation £'000	General £'000	Profit and loss £'000
At 1 January 20X5	X	X	X	X
Retained profit for the year				X
Revaluation		X		
Transfers			X	X
At 31 December 2095	X	X	X	X

20   Contingent liabilities

Note: governed by FRS 12 (see Chapter 11).

21   Events after the balance sheet date

Note: governed by FRS 21 (see Chapter 11).

22   **Capital commitments**

	£'000
Amounts contracted but not provided for	X

Note

This figure is not included in the balance sheet as it is simply a note of future obligations to warn users of likely future capital expenditure.

Question
Formats

The best way to learn the format and content of published accounts and notes is to practice questions. However, you must start somewhere, so try to learn the above formats, then close this text and write out on a piece of paper:

(a)   A standard layout for a balance sheet and profit and loss account

(b)   A list of notes to these accounts which are generally required

6.1 Filing exemptions for small and medium-sized companies

Small and medium-sized entities (SMEs) are allowed certain 'filing exemptions': **the accounts they lodge with the Registrar of companies, and which are available for public inspection, need not contain all the information which must be published by large companies.**

This concession allows small and medium-sized companies to reduce the amount of information about themselves available to, say, trading rivals. It **does *not* relieve them of their obligation to prepare full statutory accounts, because all companies,** regardless of their size, **must prepare full accounts for approval by the shareholders.**

Small and medium-sized companies must therefore balance the expense of preparing two different sets of accounts against the advantage of publishing as little information about themselves as possible. Many such companies may decide that the risk of assisting their competitors is preferable to the expense of preparing accounts twice over, and will therefore not take advantage of the filing exemptions.

A company qualifies as a **small or medium sized** company in a particular financial year **if**, for that year, **two or more** of the following **conditions are satisfied**.

	Small	Medium
(a) **Turnover** (must be adjusted proportionately in the case of an accounting period greater than or less than 12 months)	≤ £5.6m	≤ £22.8m
(b) **Balance sheet total** (total assets before deduction of any liabilities; A-D in the statutory balance sheet format)	≤ £2.8m	≤ £11.4m
(c) **Average number of employees**	≤ 50	≤ 250

Public companies can never be entitled to the filing exemptions whatever their size; nor can banking and insurance companies; nor can companies which are authorised persons under the Financial Services Act 1986; nor can members of groups containing any of these exceptions.

The form and content of the abbreviated accounts are contained in separate schedules of the Act: Schedule 8A for small companies and Schedule 245A for medium-sized companies. **Small companies may file an abbreviated balance sheet** showing only the items which, in the statutory format, are denoted by a letter or Roman number. They are **not required to file either a profit and loss account or a directors' report. No details need be filed of the emoluments of directors. Only limited notes to the accounts are required.**

The only exemptions allowed to medium-sized companies are in the profit and loss account. Turnover need not be analysed between a company's different classes of businesses, or its different geographical markets. The profit and loss account may begin with the figure of gross profit (or loss) by amalgamation of items 1, 2, 3 and 6 in Format 1, or of items 1 to 5 in Format 2.

If a small or medium-sized company files 'abbreviated accounts' a statement by the directors must appear above the director's signature on the balance sheet. The statement must be that the financial statements have been prepared in accordance with the special provisions of Part VII of the Act relating to small or (as the case may be) medium-sized companies.

Abbreviated accounts **must be accompanied by a special report** of the company's auditors stating that, in their opinion, the directors are entitled to deliver abbreviated accounts and those accounts are properly prepared. The text of the auditors' report on the full statutory accounts must be included as a part of this special report. A true and fair view is still required, however; if the shorter-form financial statements fail to give a true and fair view because of the use of exemptions, or for any other reason, the auditors should qualify their audit report in the normal way.

The requirements of the Companies Acts regarding SMEs are now incorporated into the 'one stop shop' FRSSE (Chapter 2).

6.2 Summary financial statements

CA 1989 amended CA 1985 so that **listed companies need not send all their members their full financial statements but can instead send them summary financial statements** (SFSs). All members who want to receive full financial statements are still entitled to them, however.

An SFS must:

(a) State that it is only a summary of information in the company's annual accounts and the directors' report.

(b) Contain a statement by the company's auditors of their opinion as to whether the summary financial statement is consistent with those accounts and that report and complies with the relevant statutory requirements.

(c) State whether the auditors' report on the annual accounts was unqualified or qualified, and if it was qualified set out the report in full together with any further material needed to understand the qualification.

SFSs must be derived from the company's annual accounts and the directors' report and the form and content are specified by regulations made by the Secretary of State.

The key figures from the full statements must be included along with the review of the business and future developments shown in the directors' report. Comparative figures must be shown.

7 Directors' report

FAST FORWARD

The directors' report provides additional information regarding the directors and their holdings in the company, details of share capital transactions and other significant matters of interest to shareholders and others.

Attached to every balance sheet there must be a directors' report (s 234 CA 1985). (The Companies Act 1985 allows small companies exemption from delivering a copy of the directors' report to the Registrar of companies.) CA 1985 states specifically what information must be included in the directors' report (as well as what must be shown in the accounts themselves or in notes to the accounts as we saw above).

The directors' report is **largely a narrative report**, but certain figures must be included in it. **The purpose of the report is to give the users of accounts a more complete picture of the state of affairs of the company**. Narrative descriptions should help to 'put flesh on' the skeleton of details provided by the figures of the accounts themselves. However, in practice the directors' report is often a rather dry and uninformative document, perhaps because it must be verified by the company's external auditors, whereas the chairman's report need not be.

The directors' report is **expected to contain a fair review of the development of the business of the company during that year and of its position at the end of it.** No guidance is given on the form of the review, nor the amount of detail it should go into.

S 234 CA 1985 also requires the report to **show the** amount, if any, **recommended** for **dividend**.

Other disclosure requirements are as follows.

(a)   The **principal activities** of the company in the course of the financial year, and any significant changes in those activities during the year.

(b)   Where significant, an estimate should be provided of the **difference between the book value of land held as fixed assets and its realistic market value.**

(c)   **Disabled persons.** Information about the **company's policy** for:

(i)   Giving fair consideration to applications for jobs from disabled persons.

(ii)   Continuing to employ (and train) people who have become disabled whilst employed by the company.

(iii)   Training, career development and promotion of disabled employees.

(Companies with fewer than 250 employees are exempt from (c).)

(d)   The names of persons who were **directors** at any time during the financial year.

(e)   For those persons who were directors at the year end, the **interests of each** (or of their spouse or infant children) in shares or debentures of the company:

(i)   At the beginning of the year, or at the date of appointment as director, if this occurred during the year.

(ii)   At the end of the year.

If a director has no such interests at either date, this fact must be disclosed. (The information in (e) may be shown as a note to the accounts instead of in the directors' report.)

(f)   **Political and charitable contributions made**, if these together exceeded more than £200 in the year, giving:

(i)   Separate totals for political contributions and charitable contributions.

(ii)   The amount of each separate political contribution exceeding £200, and the name of the recipient.

(g)   Particulars of any **important events** affecting the company or any of its subsidiaries which have occurred since the end of the financial year (significant 'post-balance sheet events').

(h)   An indication of likely **future developments** in the business of the company and of its subsidiaries.

(i)   An indication of the activities (if any) of the company and its subsidiaries in the field of **research and development**.

(j)   Particulars of **purchases** (if any) of **its own shares** by the company during the year, including reasons for the purchase.

(k)   Particulars of **other acquisitions of its own shares** during the year (perhaps because shares were forfeited or surrendered, or because its shares were acquired by the company's nominee or with its financial assistance).

Note that the 1985 Act requires details of important events after the balance sheet date to be explained in the directors' report. The requirements of FRS 21 (see Chapter 11), which should be considered in conjunction with the 1985 Act, are either for the accounts themselves to be altered, or for the amount of the adjustment to results to be disclosed in a note to the accounts.

A further requirement relating to the directors' report is contained in the Employment Act 1982. The requirement relates to any company **employing on average more than 250 people each week**. The **directors** of such a company **must state in their report what action** has been **taken** during the financial year **to introduce, maintain or develop arrangements aimed at:**

(a)   **Employee information**, providing employees systematically with information on matters of concern to them.

(b)   **Employee consultation**, consulting employees or their representatives on a regular basis so that the views of employees can be taken into account in making decisions which are likely to affect their interest.

(c)   **Employee involvement**, encouraging the involvement of employees in the company's performance through an employees' share scheme or by some other means.

(d)   **Company performance**, achieving common **awareness** on the part of all employees of the financial and economic factors affecting the performance of the company.

It should be noted that **these provisions do not mean that any such action must be taken, only that if it is taken it must be disclosed** in the directors' report. Moreover, wide discretion is granted to the directors in deciding what needs to be disclosed, since no definition is given ot such terms as 'matters of concern to them' or 'decisions which are likely to affect their interests'.

7.1 Creditor payment policy

A recent amendment to CA 1985 requires companies to disclose details of the company's policy on the payment of creditors. This **disclosure requirement applies if:**

(a)   **The company was at any time during the year a public company**.

(b)   **The company did not qualify as a small or medium-sized company under s 247 and was at any time within the year a member of a group of which the parent company was a public company.**

The **directors' report needs to state**, with respect to the financial year immediately following that covered by the report:

(a)   Whether in respect of some or all of its suppliers (ie those classified as 'trade creditors') it is the company's policy to follow **any code or standard on payment practice**, and if so, the name of the code or standard, and the place where information about, and copies of, the code or standard can be obtained;

(b)   whether in respect of some or all of its suppliers, it is the company's **policy to:**

(i)   **Settle the terms of payment** with those suppliers when agreeing the terms of each transaction.

(ii)   Ensure that those suppliers are **made aware** of the terms of payment.

(iii)   **Abide** by the terms of payment.

(c)   **Where** the company's policy is **not as mentioned** in either of the two paragraphs **above**, in respect of some or all of its suppliers, **what its policy is** with respect to the payment of those suppliers.

If the company's policy is different from different suppliers or classes of suppliers, the directors' must identify the suppliers or classes of suppliers to which the different policies apply.

7.2 Operating and Financial Review

The Operating and Financial Review (OFR) has been in existence for some time as a voluntary report to shareholders. In May 2005 the ASB issued Reporting Standard 1 (RS1) *Operating and Financial Review*, which made the OFR mandatory for al listed companies. In November 2005 the Chancellor of Exchequer removed the statutory requirement for the OFR. The ASB then issued it as a **Statement** of Best **Practice**. So it is once again a **voluntary** report.

Directors are required in the OFR to provide a balanced and comprehensive analysis of:

- The business's development and performance during the financial year.

- The company's (or group's) position at the end of the year.

- The main trends and factors underlying the company's position and performance and likely to affect it in the future. These may include environment, employee and social and community issues.

The statement recommends that the directors report specifically on:

- The nature, objectives and strategy of the business.
- Current and future development and performance.
- The financial position of the entity
- The cash inflows and outflows during the year and the entity's ability to generate cash
- The entity's current and prospective liquidity.

The OFR should include *key performance indicators* ('KPIs) relevant to the business. Examples would be return on capital employed (ROCE), market position and market share.

More detail on the OFR is in Chapter 2 Section 9.

8 Auditors' report and chairman's report

8.1 The auditors' report

The annual accounts of a limited company must be audited by persons independent of the company. In practice, this means that the members of the company appoint a firm of Chartered Accountants or Chartered Certified Accountants to investigate the accounts prepared by the company **and report as to whether or not they show a true and fair** view of the company's results for the year and its financial position at the end of the year. **The audit report is governed by auditing regulations**.

When the auditors have completed their work they must prepare a report explaining the work that they have done and the opinion they have formed. In simple cases they will be able to report that they have carried out their work in accordance with auditing standards and that, in their opinion, the accounts show a true and fair view and are properly prepared in accordance with the Companies Act 1985. This is described as an **unqualified audit report**.

Sometimes the auditors may disagree with the directors on a point concerned with the accounts. If they are unable to persuade the directors to change the accounts, and if the item at issue is material, it is the auditors' duty to prepare a **qualified report**, setting out the matter(s) on which they disagree with the directors.

The financial statements to which the auditors refer in their report comprise the:

   (a)   **Profit and loss account.**
   (b)   **Balance sheet.**
   (c)   **Notes to the accounts.**
   (d)   **Cash flow statement.**

In addition they **must consider whether the information given in the directors' report is consistent with the audited accounts**. If they believes it is not consistent then they must state that fact in their report. Note that the cash flow statement is not mentioned outright.

The auditors' report is included as a part of the company's published accounts. It is **addressed to the members** of the company (not to the directors).

8.2 The chairman's report

Most large companies include a **chairman's report** in their published financial statements. This is **purely voluntary** as there is no statutory requirement to do so.

The chairman's report is not governed by any regulations and is often unduly optimistic. Many listed companies now include an Operating and Financial Review (OFR) in the annual report. This has been introduced to encourage more meaningful analysis.

Question	Company accounts

In between now and your examination obtain as many sets of company accounts or annual reports as you can. (You may like to use the Financial Times Free Annual Report Service for this purpose – look for the advert on the share price pages of the FT for information.) Read through the whole of each report and compare the format of the accounts and the disclosure of the notes with the contents of this chapter, and with the rest of this Study Text

Exam focus point

Accounts preparation questions will, of course, cover a wide range of issues.

The accounts preparation question in the June 2002 exam included *inter alia:*

   (a)   Finance leases v operating leases
   (b)   Treatment of convertible loan notes
   (c)   Deferred taxation
   (d)   Bonus issue using the revaluation reserve
   (e)   Basic and diluted EPS

The June 2003 accounts preparation question included *inter alia:*

   (a)   Net realisable value of stocks
   (b)   Revaluation of fixed assets
   (c)   Revaluation of investments to market price
   (d)   Substance over form
   (e)   Treatment of discovery of a major fraud
   (f)   Deferred taxation
   (g)   Preparation of STRGL

Chapter Roundup

- SSAP 2 specified four fundamental accounting concepts – going concern, accruals, consistency and prudence. It was withdrawn in 2000 and replaced by FRS 18.

- FRS 18 emphasises **accruals** and **going concern** as **bedrocks** of accounting. Prudence and consistency are simply 'desirable features'.

- The overriding requirement for financial statements is that they should present a 'true and fair view'. This concept has not been formally defined.

- Statutory accounts are part of the price to be paid for the benefits of limited liability. **Limited companies must produce such accounts annually and they must appoint an independent person to audit and report on them.**

- The CA85 sets out balance sheet and profit and loss account proformas for **published accounts**. Learn the main headings so that you can write them out quickly in the exam.

- The directors' report provides additional information regarding the directors and their holdings in the company, details of share capital transactions and other significant matters of interest to shareholders and others.

BPP
PROFESSIONAL EDUCATION

Quick quiz

1   The two bedrocks of accounting are:

    A   Accruals, prudence
    B   Prudence, consistency
    C   Consistency, accruals
    D   Going concern, accruals

2   An estimation technique is the method used to establish the estimated monetary amounts associated with the selected measurement bases.

    True   ☐

    False   ☐

3   What does CA 1985 say about a 'true and fair view'?

4   What points are made by the legal opinions sought regarding a 'true and fair view'?

5   The period allowed for layout and delivery of accounts.

    •   Private companies .... months

    •   Public companies .... months

6   Turnover is defined by the Companies Act as the amounts derived from the provision of goods and services falling within the company's ordinary activities after deduction of which of the following.

    A   Carriage inwards
    B   Trade discounts
    C   VAT
    D   Carriage out
    E   Other sales taxes
    F   Stock losses

7

	Small company	Medium company
Turnover	....	....
Total assets	....	....
Average number of employees	....	....

8   List eight disclosures required in the directors' report.

9   Companies must disclose their creditor payment policy in the financial statements.

    True   ☐

    False   ☐

10   The chairman's report is a statutory requirement.

    True   ☐

    False   ☐

11   Explain the accruals basis of accounting in no more than fifty words.

Answers to Quick Quiz

1   Going concern and accruals

2   True

3   CA 1985 does not define a 'true and fair view' (see para 3.1)

4   Accuracy and completeness are required. It is a dynamic concept. Judges will have regard to the practices of professional accountants, but acknowledge there may be no consensus among them.

5   Ten, seven

6   B, C and E

7
	Small company	Medium company
Turnover	≤£5.6m	≤£22.8m
Total assets	≤£2.8m	≤£11.4m
Average number of employees	≤50	≤250
		(5.7)

8   See paragraph 7.

9   False, Only if they are a public company or they fail to meet the requirements for small or medium companies.

10   False.

11   The accruals basis of accounting requires the **non-cash impact** of transactions to be reflected in the financial statements for the **period in which they occur** and not, for example, in the period any cash involved is received or paid.

Now try the question below from the Exam Question Bank

Number	Level	Marks	Time
Q3	Full exam	25	45 mins

Distributable profits and capital transactions

4

Topic list	Syllabus reference
1 Revenue recognition	1 (a)
2 Distributable profits	3 (a)
3 Redemption of shares	3 (a)

Introduction

The topics in this chapter are relevant to all types of accounting transactions, providing a theoretical framework for the topics already covered and for accounting in general.

This chapter also leads on to the legal aspects of financial reporting in the next two chapters. A great deal of the legislation governing distributions and capital transactions is concerned with protection of creditors; the aim is to prevent companies favouring shareholders over creditors.

Study guide

- Outline the principles of the timing of revenue recognition.

- Explain the role of the concept of substance over form in relation to recognising sales revenue.

- Explain and define realised profits.

- Discuss the various points in the production and sales cycle where it may, depending on circumstances, be appropriate to recognise gains and losses - give examples of this.

- Describe the ASB's 'balance sheet approach' to revenue recognition within its Statement of Principles and compare this to requirements of relevant accounting standards.

- Explain and apply the general requirements to purchase or redemption of shares.

- Discuss the advantages of companies being able to redeem shares.

- Define and discuss the Companies Acts rules relating to profits available for distribution.

Exam guide

Revenue recognition is a particularly important area. It is fairly straightforward especially if you take time to relate the concepts to real life situations as you work through the material

1 Revenue recognition

FAST FORWARD

Revenue recognition is straightforward in most business transactions, but some situations are more complicated. It is necessary to determine the **substance of each transaction, rather than the legal form**.

Generally revenue is recognised when the entity has transferred to the buyer the **significant risks and rewards of ownership** and when the revenue can be **measured reliably**.

Exam focus point

The ACCA syllabus places emphasis upon revenue recognition and a full 25-mark question appeared in the pilot paper. This is a key area, approach it in a systematic and methodical manner and you should master how and when to recognise revenue.

The June 2003 exam required candidates to explain the implications that the ASB's *Statement of Principles* and the application of substance over form have on the recognition of income. Candidates were also required to provide examples of how this may conflict with traditional practice and some accounting standards.

1.1 ASB balance sheet driven approach

FAST FORWARD

You should learn the conditions for revenue recognition for all transactions. You should also bear in mind the ASB's **balance sheet driven** approach to revenue recognition.

Accruals accounting is based on the requirement that the **non-cash impact** of transactions are recognised in the **period of occurrence** rather than in the period any cash is received or paid. It is crucially important under this convention that we can establish the **point** at which **revenue may be recognised** and **related costs** treated as an **asset**, being representative of a **right** to **future economic benefits**. For example, the costs of producing an item of finished goods should be carried as an asset in the balance sheet until such time as it is sold; they should then be derecognised as an asset and written off as a charge to the trading account. The treatment which should be applied cannot be decided upon until it is clear at what moment the sale of the item takes place; when one form of **right to economic benefits** is **replaced** by **another form** of **right to economic benefits**, ie **stock replaced by a debtor**.

The decision has a direct impact on profit since under the prudence concept, where there is **uncertainty** regarding the **right to receive economic** benefits, **appropriate caution** must be **exercised in recognising revenue** and **profit** from a sale.

Exam focus point

> Given the current USA controversies over the reporting of earnings by public companies there, consider how you might respond to a proposition by a director to accelerate revenue recognition.

1.2 Point of sale

Revenue is generally recognised as earned at the point of sale, because at that point four criteria will generally have been met.

(a)   The product or service has been **provided** to the buyer.

(b)   The buyer has **recognised** his **liability** to **pay** for the goods or services provided. The converse of this is that the seller has **recognised** that **ownership** of **goods** has **passed** from himself to the buyer.

(c)   The buyer has indicated his **willingness** to **hand over cash** or other assets in **settlement** of his liability.

(d)   The **monetary value** of the goods or services has been **established**.

At **earlier points** in the **business cycle** there will not in general be firm evidence that the above criteria will be met. **Until work** on a product is **complete**, there is a **risk** that some flaw in the manufacturing process will necessitate its **writing off**; even when the product is complete there is no guarantee that it will find a buyer, ie there is **uncertainty** whether the **stock** will **yield future economic benefits**, and the stock might need to be derecognised from the balance sheet.

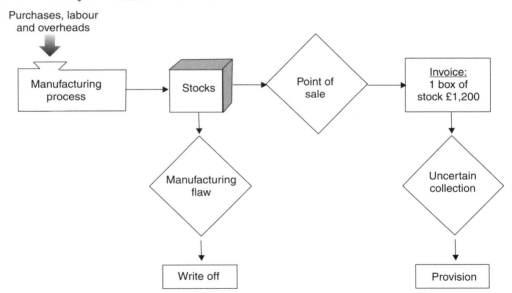

At **later points** in the **business cycle**, for example when cash is received for the sale, the recognition of revenue may occur in a period later than that in which the related costs were charged. Revenue recognition would then depend on **fortuitous circumstances**, such as the **cash flow** of a company's **debtors**, and might **fluctuate** misleadingly from one period to another. Again if collection of payment from any debtors is uncertain, they may need to be derecognised from the balance sheet.

1.3 Times other than point of sale

However, **occasionally revenue is recognised at other times** than at the completion of a sale.

(a)   **Recognition of profit on long-term contract work in progress**. Under SSAP 9 *Stocks and long-term contracts*, credit is taken in the profit and loss account for 'that part of the total profit currently estimated to arise over the duration of the contract which fairly reflects the profit attributable to that part of the work performed at the accounting date'.

   (i)   Owing to the length of time taken to complete such contracts, to defer taking profit into account until completion may result in the profit and loss account reflecting not so much a fair view of the activity of the company during the year but rather the results relating to contracts which have been completed by the year end.

   (ii)   Revenue in this case is recognised when production on, say, a section of the total contract is complete, even though no sale can be made until the whole is complete.

(b)   **Sale on hire purchase.** Title to goods provided on hire purchase terms does not pass until the last payment is made, at which point the sale is complete.

   (i)   To defer the recognition of revenue until that point, however, would be to distort the nature of the revenue earned.

   (ii)   The profits of an HP retailer in effect represent the interest charged on finance provided and such interest arises over the course of the HP agreement rather than at its completion. Revenue in this case is recognised when each instalment of cash is received.

The determination of whether revenue should be recognised is based partly on the accruals concept, but also on the often conflicting accounting concept of prudence. Under the prudence concept revenue and profits are not anticipated and anticipated losses are provided for as soon as they are foreseen (preventing costs being deferred if there is doubt as to their recoverability).

The question of revenue recognition is obviously closely associated with the definition of realised profits, and this is discussed in the next section.

In general terms, under the historical cost system, the following general practice has developed.

(a)   Revenue from the sale of goods is recognised on the date of delivery to the customer.

(b)   Revenue from services is recognised when the services have been performed and are billable.

(c)   Revenue derived from letting others use the resources of the businesses (for example royalty income, rent and interest) is recognised either as the resources are used or on a time basis.

(d)   Revenue from the sale of assets (other than products of the business) is recognised at the date of the sale.

1.4 Problem areas

The problem with revenue recognition is that there are some areas where accounting standards have not (yet) been issued which deal with all types of transaction. We will not go into too much detail here about these situations, but you should be aware of them, and a list is given below (the list is not comprehensive).

(a)   **Receipt of initial fees**, at the beginning of a service, may not have been 'earned' and it is often difficult to determine what they represent.

(b) **Franchise fees** can be incurred in complex franchise agreements and no standard form of agreement has allowed an accepted accounting practice to develop. Each agreement must be dealt with on its own merits.

(c) **Advance royalty or licence receipts** would normally be dealt with as deferred income and released to the profit and loss account when earned under the agreement. In some businesses, however, such advances consist of a number of different components which require different accounting treatments, for example in the record industry.

(d) **Loan arrangement fees** could be recognised in the year the loan is arranged or spread over the life of the loan.

(e) **Credit card fees** charged by credit card companies on their cardholders might be recognised on receipt or spread over the period that the fee allows the cardholder to use the card.

1.5 Revenue

Revenue recognition should be when it is probable that **future economic benefits** will flow to the enterprise and when these benefits can be **measured reliably**.

Income includes both revenues and gains. Revenue is income arising in the ordinary course of an enterprise's activities and it may be called different names, such as sales, fees, interest, dividends or royalties.

Interest, royalties and dividends are included as income because they arise from the use of an enterprise's assets by other parties.

Key terms

> **Interest** is the charge for the use of cash or cash equivalents or amounts due to the enterprise.
>
> **Royalties** are charges for the use of non-current assets of the enterprise, eg patents, computer software and trademarks.
>
> **Dividends** are distributions of profit to holders of equity investments, in proportion with their holdings, of each relevant class of capital.

1.6 Definitions

Key terms

> **Revenue** is the gross inflow of economic benefits during the period arising in the course of the ordinary activities of an entity when those inflows result in increases in equity, other than increases relating to contributions from equity participants.
>
> **Fair value** is the amount for which an asset could be exchanged, or a liability settled, between knowledgeable, willing parties in an arm's length transaction.

Revenue **does not include** sales taxes, value added taxes or goods and service taxes which are only collected for third parties, because these do not represent an economic benefit flowing to the entity. The same is true for revenues collected by an agent on behalf of a principal. Revenue for the agent is only the commission receive for acting as agent.

1.7 UITF Abstract 40

In November 2003 revenue recognition by professional firms (mainly law and accountancy firms) was further regulated by application note G to FRS 5 *Reporting the Substance of Transactions*.

Under the application note, **unbilled fee income**, which would previously have been classified as WIP in the financial statements and valued at cost in accordance with SSAP 9, should now be classified as **accrued income** and valued at expected recovery value, where the point has been reached at which the firm is contractually allowed to raise a fee note.

This has the effect of accelerating the revenue recognised by the firm and accelerating its taxation charge. It will not ultimately increase the amount of tax payable, but it will require it to be paid in an earlier period, so this is a cash management issue for professional firms.

The real impact will be felt by **retiring partners**. It makes a difference to a retiring partner whether unbilled income in his final year is classified as WIP or as accrued income. If it is accounted for as accrued income, he will receive a share of the profit. If it is accounted for as WIP, it will be income the following year, and he will not receive a share of the profit.

In March 2005 UITF Abstract 40 *Revenue recognition and service contracts* was issued. This applied the provisions of Application Note G to *all* contracts for services.

Where there are distinguishable phases of a single contract it may be appropriate to account for the contract as two or more separate transactions, provided the value of each phase can be reliably estimated.

Contracts for services should not be accounted for as long-term contracts unless they involve the provision of a single service, or a number of services that constitute a single project.

A contract for services should be accounted for as a long-term contract where contract activity falls into different accounting periods and the effect of this is material. Revenue accrued should reflect the value of the work performed as the contract progresses.

Where the substance of a contract is that a right to consideration does not arise until the occurrence of a critical event, revenue is not recognised until that event occurs.

1.8 Measurement of revenue

When a transaction takes place, the amount of revenue is usually decided by the **agreement of the buyer and seller**. The revenue is actually measured, however, as the **fair value of the consideration received**, which will take account of any trade discounts and volume rebates.

1.9 Identification of the transaction

Normally, each transaction can be looked at **as a whole**. Sometimes, however, transactions are more complicated, and it is necessary to break a transaction down into its **component parts**. For example, a sale may include the transfer of goods and the provision of future servicing, the revenue for which should be deferred over the period the service is performed.

At the other end of the scale, **seemingly separate transactions must be considered together** if apart they lose their commercial meaning. An example would be to sell an asset with an agreement to buy it back at a later date. The second transaction cancels the first and so both must be considered together.

1.10 Sale of goods

Revenue from the sale of goods should only be recognised when *all* these conditions are satisfied.

(a) The enterprise has transferred the **significant risks and rewards** of ownership of the goods to the buyer

(b) The enterprise has **no continuing managerial involvement** to the degree usually associated with ownership, and no longer has effective control over the goods sold

(c) The amount of revenue can be **measured reliably**

(d)   It is probable that the **economic benefits** associated with the transaction will flow to the enterprise

(e)   The **costs incurred** in respect of the transaction can be measured reliably

The transfer of risks and rewards can only be decided by examining each transaction. Mainly, the transfer occurs at the same time as either the **transfer of legal title**, or the **passing of possession** to the buyer - this is what happens when you buy something in a shop.

If **significant risks and rewards remain with the seller**, then the transaction is *not* a sale and revenue cannot be recognised, for example if the receipt of the revenue from a particular sale depends on the buyer receiving revenue from his own sale of the goods.

It is possible for the seller to retain only an **'insignificant' risk of ownership** and for the sale and revenue to be recognised. The main example here is where the seller retains title only to ensure collection of what is owed on the goods. This is a common commercial situation, and when it arises the revenue should be recognised on the date of sale.

The probability of the enterprise receiving the revenue arising from a transaction must be assessed. It may only become probable that the economic benefits will be received when an uncertainty is removed, for example government permission for funds to be received from another country. Only when the uncertainty is removed should the revenue be recognised. This is in contrast with the situation where revenue has already been recognised but where the **collectability of the cash** is brought into doubt. Where recovery has ceased to be probable, the amount should be recognised as an expense, *not* an adjustment of the revenue previously recognised. These points also refer to services and interest, royalties and dividends below.

The traditional approach is that **matching** should take place, ie the revenue and expenses relating to the same transaction should be recognised at the same time. It is usually easy to estimate expenses at the date of sale (eg warranty costs, shipment costs, etc). Where they cannot be estimated reliably, then revenue cannot be recognised; any consideration which has already been received is treated as a liability.

1.11 Rendering of services

When the outcome of a transaction involving the rendering of services can be estimated reliably, the associated revenue should be recognised by reference to the **stage of completion of the transaction** at the balance sheet date. The outcome of a transaction can be estimated reliably when *all* these conditions are satisfied.

(a)   The amount of revenue can be **measured reliably**

(b)   It is probable that the **economic benefits** associated with the transaction will flow to the enterprise

(c)   The **stage of completion** of the transaction at the balance sheet date can be measured reliably

(d)   The **costs incurred** for the transaction and the costs to complete the transaction can be measured reliably

The parties to the transaction will normally have to agree the following before an entity can make reliable estimates.

(a)   Each party's **enforceable rights** regarding the service to be provided and received by the parties

(b)   The **consideration** to be exchanged

(c)   The **manner and terms of settlement**

There are various methods of determining the stage of completion of a transaction, but for practical purposes, when services are performed by an indeterminate number of acts over a period of time, revenue should be recognised on a **straight line basis** over the period, unless there is evidence for the use of a more appropriate method. If one act is of more significance than the others, then the significant act should be carried out *before* revenue is recognised.

In uncertain situations, when the outcome of the transaction involving the rendering of services cannot be estimated reliably, then it may be appropriate to adopt a **no loss/no gain approach**. Revenue is recognised only to the extent of the expenses recognised that are recoverable.

This is particularly likely during the **early stages of a transaction**, but it is still probable that the entity will recover the costs incurred. So the revenue recognised in such a period will be equal to the expenses incurred, with no profit.

Obviously, if the costs are not likely to be reimbursed, then they must be recognised as an expense immediately. **When the uncertainties cease to exist**, revenue should be recognised as laid out in above.

1.12 Interest, royalties and dividends

When others use the entity's assets yielding interest, royalties and dividends, the revenue should be recognised on the bases set out below when:

(a) It is probable that the **economic benefits** associated with the transaction will flow to the entity

(b) The amount of the revenue can be **measured reliably**

The revenue is recognised on the following bases.

(a) **Interest** is recognised on a time proportion basis that takes into account the effective yield on the asset

(b) **Royalties** are recognised on an accruals basis in accordance with the substance of the relevant agreement

(c) **Dividends** are recognised when the shareholder's right to receive payment is established

It is unlikely that you would be asked about anything as complex as this in the exam, but you should be aware of the basics. The **effective yield** on an asset mentioned above is the rate of interest required to discount the stream of future cash receipts expected over the life of the asset to equate to the initial carrying amount of the asset.

Royalties are usually recognised on the same basis that they accrue **under the relevant agreement**. Sometimes the true substance of the agreement may require some other systematic and rational method of recognition.

Once again, the points made above about **probability and collectability** on sale of goods also apply here.

Exam focus point

> Because of the recent financial reporting scandals, revenue recognition is very topical and you should be prepared for a question on it.

 Question — Revenue recognition

Given that prudence is the main consideration, discuss under what circumstances, if any, revenue might be recognised at the following stages of a sale.

(a) Goods are acquired by the business which it confidently expects to resell very quickly.
(b) A customer places a firm order for goods.

(c)   Goods are delivered to the customer.

(d)   The customer is invoiced for goods.

(e)   The customer pays for the goods.

(f)   The customer's cheque in payment for the goods has been cleared by the bank.

Answer

(a)   A sale must never be recognised before the goods have even been ordered by a customer. There is no certainty about the value of the sale, nor when it will take place, even if it is virtually certain that goods will be sold.

(b)   A sale must never be recognised when the customer places an order. Even though the order will be for a specific quantity of goods at a specific price, it is not yet certain that the sale transaction will go through. The customer may cancel the order, the supplier might be unable to deliver the goods as ordered or it may be decided that the customer is not a good credit risk.

(c)   A sale will be recognised when delivery of the goods is made only when:

(i)   The sale is for cash, and so the cash is received at the same time

(ii)   Or the sale is on credit and the customer accepts delivery (eg by signing a delivery note)

(d)   The critical event for a credit sale is usually the despatch of an invoice to the customer. There is then a legally enforceable debt, payable on specified terms, for a completed sale transaction.

(e)   The critical event for a cash sale is when delivery takes place and when cash is received; both take place at the same time.

It would be too cautious or 'prudent' to await cash payment for a credit sale transaction before recognising the sale, unless the customer is a high credit risk and there is a serious doubt about his ability or intention to pay.

(f)   It would again be over-cautious to wait for clearance of the customer's cheques before recognising sales revenue. Such a precaution would only be justified in cases where there is a very high risk of the bank refusing to honour the cheque.

2 Distributable profits

FAST FORWARD

You should be able to calculate **maximum distributions available to private and public companies** and to discuss the meaning of **distributable** and **realisable** profits.

Exam focus point

This is an important section which you must look at. The June 2002 paper required candidates to deal with a bonus issue using a revaluation reserve.

A **distribution** is defined by s 263(2) CA 1985 as every description of distribution of a company's assets to members (shareholders) of the company, whether in cash or otherwise, with the exceptions of:

(a)   An issue of bonus shares.

(b)   The redemption or purchase of the company's own shares out of capital (including the proceeds of a new issue) or out of unrealised profits.

(c)   The reduction of share capital by:

(i)   Reducing the liability on shares in respect of share capital not fully paid up

    (ii)   Paying off paid-up share capital

(d)   A distribution of assets to shareholders in a winding up of the company.

Important!

> Companies must not make a distribution except out of profits available for the purpose. These available profits are:

(a)   Its **accumulated realised profits**, insofar as these have not already been used for an earlier distribution or for 'capitalisation'.

(b)   **Minus its accumulated realised losses**, insofar as these have not already been written off in a reduction or reconstruction scheme.

Capital profits and revenue profits (if realised) are taken together and capital losses and revenue losses (if realised) are similarly grouped together. *Unrealised profits* cannot be distributed (for example profit on the revaluation of fixed assets); nor must a company apply unrealised profits to pay up debentures or any unpaid amounts on issued shares.

Capitalisation of realised profits is the use of profits:

(a)   To issue bonus shares
(b)   As a transfer to the capital redemption reserve

As a point of detail, s 275(2) allows that any **excess depreciation on a revalued fixed asset above the amount of depreciation that would have been charged on its historical cost can be treated as a realised profit for the purpose of distributions.** This is to avoid penalising companies that make an unrealised profit on the revaluation of an asset, and must then charge depreciation on the revalued amount. For example, suppose that a company buys an asset at a cost of £20,000. It has a life of 4 years and a nil residual value. If it is immediately revalued to £30,000, an unrealised profit of £10,000 would be credited to the revaluation reserve. Annual depreciation must be based on the revalued amount, in this case, ¼ of £30,000 or £7,500. This exceeds depreciation which would have been charged on the asset's cost (£5,000 pa) by £2,500 per annum. This £2,500 can be treated as a distributable profit under s 275(2).

Section 264 imposes **further restrictions on the distributions of public companies**.

Important!

> A public company cannot make a distribution if at the time:
>
> (a)   The amount of its net assets is less than the combined total of its called-up share capital plus its undistributable reserves.
>
> (b)   The distribution will reduce the amount of its net assets to below the combined total of its called-up share capital plus its undistributable reserves.

'Undistributable reserves' are:

(a)   The share premium account.

(b)   The capital redemption reserve.

(c)   Any accumulated surplus of unrealised profits over unrealised losses.

(d)   Any other reserve which cannot be distributed, whether by statute, or the company's memorandum or articles of association.

The key feature of s 264 is that all **accumulated distributable profits, both realised and unrealised, must exceed the accumulated realised and unrealised losses of the company before any distribution can be made**. The difference between the profits and losses is the maximum possible distribution.

In contrast with s 263, s 264 **includes consideration of unrealised profits and losses**, so that if unrealised losses exceed unrealised profits, the amount of distributions which can be made will be reduced by the amount of the 'deficit'.

2.1 Example: Private company v public company distributions

Jelli Ltd is a private company and Kustard plc is a public limited company. Both companies have a financial year ending on 31 December. On 31 December 20X5, the balance sheets of the companies, by a remarkable coincidence, were identical, as follows.

	Jelli Ltd		Kustard plc	
	£'000	£'000	£'000	£'000
Net assets		365		365
Share capital		300		300
Share premium account		60		60
Unrealised losses on asset revaluations		(25)		(25)
Realised profits	50		50	
Realised losses	(20)		(20)	
		30		30
		365		365

What is the maximum distribution that each company can make?

Solution

(a) S 263 restricts the distributable profits of Jelli Ltd to £30,000.

(b) S 264 further restricts the distributable profits of Kustard plc to £30,000 – £25,000 = £5,000 (or alternatively, £365,000 – £300,000 – £60,000 = £5,000. This is the surplus of net assets over share capital plus undistributable reserves, which in this example are represented by the share premium account).

2.2 Realised and distributable profits

Legislation does not define realised profits very clearly. As a **'rule of thumb'**, according to the Consultative Committee of Accounting Bodies, **profits in the profit and loss account are realised, while unrealised profits are credited directly to reserves**.

FRS 18 *Accounting policies* provides a framework for recognising realised profits. If FRS 18, is followed, profit and loss account profits will be realisable.

2.2.1 Exceptions

In the case of **sale of revalued fixed assets**, the **unrealised profit on revaluation previously credited to the revaluation reserve** does not pass through the profit and loss account. It is nevertheless to be **regarded as distributable**.

Where an asset has been revalued, the **increase in depreciation charge** can be treated as a realised profit.

Development expenditure is a realised loss in the year in which it is incurred, except when the costs are capitalised within SSAP 13 guidelines, in which case the costs are amortised as realised losses over a number of years.

Provisions are generally treated as realised losses.

2.3 The relevant accounts

S 270 defines the 'relevant accounts' which should be used to determine the distributable profits. These are the most recent audited annual accounts of the company, prepared in compliance with the Companies Acts. If the accounts are qualified by the auditors, the auditors must state in their report whether they consider that the proposed distribution would contravene the Act.

Companies may also base a distribution on interim accounts, which need not be audited. However, in the case of a public company, such interim accounts must be properly prepared and comply with:

    (a)   s 228(2) (accounts to give a true and fair view)

    (b)   s 238 (directors to sign the company's balance sheet)

    A copy of the interim accounts should be delivered to the Registrar.

2.4 Investment and insurance companies

S 265 makes a **special provision for investment companies which are public companies.** Investment companies may make a distribution out of realised revenue profits (insofar as they have not already been utilised or capitalised) less its realised and unrealised revenue losses (insofar as these have not already been written off in a capital reduction or reconstruction) provided that its assets equal at least one and a half times the aggregate amount of its liabilities.

S 268 refers to insurance companies which have long-term business. Any surplus of assets over liabilities on long-term business which has been properly transferred to the company's profit and loss account should be regarded as a *realised* profit. (This section makes a specific point of clarification, and is therefore relatively minor in importance.)

2.5 The duties of directors

S 309 CA 1985 states that the directors of a company must have regard to the interests of the company's employees in general, as well as to the interests of shareholders. This is a duty which is owed by directors to the company alone.

Question
Available profits

Explain the implications of the following items to profits available for distribution in a public company:

    (a)   Research and development activities

    (b)   Net deficit on revaluation reserve arising from an overall deficit on the revaluation of fixed assets

    (c)   Excess depreciation

    (d)   Goodwill

Answer

    (a)   S 263 of the Companies Act 1985 provides that, for the purposes of calculating realised profits, development expenditure carried forward in the balance sheet should be treated as a realised loss. This means that development expenditure may not be regarded as part of net assets.

           If, however, there are special circumstances which, in the opinion of the directors, justify the treatment of development expenditure as an asset and not as a loss, then this requirement need not apply. It is generally considered that, if the development expenditure qualifies for treatment as an asset under the provisions of SSAP 13, then it may be treated as an asset and not a loss for the purposes of calculating distributable profits.

(b)   A revaluation reserve is a non-distributable reserve because it reflects unrealised profits and losses. A public company cannot make a distribution which reduces its net assets to below the total of called-up share capital and non-distributable reserves. Consequently, any reduction in a revaluation reserve (or an increase in a debit balance) reduces the profits available for distribution.

(c)   Excess depreciation is the depreciation on revalued assets in excess of cost. Since excess depreciation is regarded as the realisation (through use) of part of the corresponding revaluation reserve, it is added back to profits available for distribution.

(d)   Under FRS10, goodwill must be capitalised and amortised. The annual amount written off is considered a realised loss and reduces distributable profits.

3 Redemption of shares

FAST FORWARD

You must be able to carry out **simple calculations** showing the amounts to be transferred to the **capital redemption reserve** on purchase or redemption of own shares and how the amount of any **premium** on redemption would be treated.

Any limited company is permitted without restriction to cancel unissued shares and in that way to reduce its authorised share capital. That change does not alter its financial position.

Three factors need to be in place to give effect to a reduction of a company's issued share capital.

ARTICLES OF ASSOCIATION	+	SPECIAL RESOLUTION	+	COURT ORDER
These must contain the necessary authority.		A special resolution must be passed.		Must be confirmed by the court per s 135.

Articles usually contain the necessary power. If not, the company in general meeting would first pass a special resolution to alter the articles appropriately and then proceed, as the second item on the agenda of the meeting, to pass a special resolution to reduce the capital.

There are **three basic methods of reducing share capital** specified in s 35(2).

(a)   **Extinguish or reduce liability on partly paid shares**. A company may have issued £1 (nominal) shares 75p paid up. The outstanding liability of 25p per share may be eliminated altogether by reducing each share to 75p (nominal) fully paid or some intermediate figure, eg 80p (nominal) 75p paid. Nothing is returned to the shareholders but the company gives up a claim against them for money which it could call up whenever needed.

(b)   **Cancel paid up share capital which has been lost or which is no longer represented by available assets.** Suppose that the issued shares are £1 (nominal) fully paid but the net assets now represent a value of only 50p per share. The difference is probably matched by a debit balance on profit and loss account (or provision for fall in value of assets). The company could reduce the nominal value of its £1 shares to 50p (or some intermediate figure) and apply the amount to write off the debit balance or provision wholly or in part. It would then be able to resume payment of dividends out of future profits without being obliged to make good past losses. The resources of the company are not reduced by this procedure of part cancellation of nominal value of shares but it avoids having to rebuild lost capital by retaining profits.

(c)   **Pay off part of the paid up share capital out of surplus assets.** The company might repay to shareholders, say, 30p in cash per £1 share by reducing the nominal value of the share to 70p. This reduces the assets of the company by 30p per share.

3.1 Role of court in reduction of capital

Exam focus point

> These paragraphs are included for completeness, but they are unlikely to be examined.
>
> The December 2004 exam asked for balance sheet extracts showing share issue and repurchase transactions.

When application is made to the court for approval of the reduction, its first concern is the effect of the reduction on the company's ability to pay its debts: s 136. If the reduction is by method (a) or (c) the court must, and where method (b) is used the court may, require that creditors shall be invited by advertisement to state their objections (if any) to the reduction to the court unless the court decides to dispense with this procedure.

In modern practice the company usually persuades the court to dispense with advertising for creditors' objections (which can be commercially damaging to the company if its purpose is misunderstood since it may suggest to creditors that the company is insolvent). Two possible methods are:

(a)   Paying off all creditors before application is made to the court; or, if that is not practicable.

(b)   Producing to the court a guarantee, perhaps from the company's bank, that its existing debts will be paid in full.

The statutory procedure itself, if it is followed, provides that if a creditor does object his claim shall be met by providing security for his debt or such part of it (if it is in dispute) as the court may decide.

The court also considers whether, if there is more than one class of share, the reduction is fair in its **effect on different classes of shareholder**. If, for example, the company has both ordinary and preference shares, the holders of the preference shares may be entitled in a winding up to repayment of their capital in priority to any repayment to ordinary shareholders. If that is the position then:

(a)   Under method (c) the preference shares must be repaid in full under a reduction of capital before any reduction of ordinary shares is made. For example, the reduction might provide for repayment of £1 per £1 share to the holders of preference shares and then, say, 10p per £1 share (thereby reduced to 90p) for ordinary shareholders.

(b)   When method (b) is used (where the reduction reflects a loss which would in winding up diminish the surplus available to ordinary shareholders), the reduction would be made by cancellation of part of the nominal value of the ordinary shares without altering the value of the preference shares, so as to preserve the priority rights of preference shares to whatever assets are available in a winding up.

If the court is satisfied that the reduction does not prejudice creditors and is fair in its effect on shareholders, it approves the reduction by making an order to that effect. The court has power to require the company to add the words 'and reduced' to its name at the end or to publish the reasons for or information about the reduction: s 137. But neither condition is ever imposed in modern practice.

A copy of the court order and of a minute, approved by the court, to show the altered share capital is delivered to the registrar who issues a certificate of registration. The reduction then takes effect and, if method (c) is used, the payment to shareholders may then be made: s 138.

3.2 Share premium account

Whenever a company obtains for its shares a consideration in excess of their nominal value, it must transfer the excess to a share premium account. The general rule is that the **share premium account is subject to the same restriction as share capital. However, a bonus issue can be made using the share premium account** (reducing share premium in order to increase issued share capital).

Following the decision in *Shearer v Bercain 1980,* there is an exemption from the general rules on setting up a share premium account, in certain circumstances where new shares are issued as consideration for the acquisition of shares in another company (see Chapter 18).

The **other permitted uses of share premium** are to pay:

(a)   Capital expenses such as preliminary expenses of forming the company.
(b)   Discount on the issue of shares or debentures.
(c)   Premium (if any) paid on redemption of debentures: s 130(2).

Private companies (but not public companies) may also use a share premium account in purchasing or redeeming their own shares out of capital.

3.3 Practical reasons for purchase or redemption

Companies may wish to repurchase or redeem their issued shares for a variety of reasons.

(a)   The company may have **surplus funds** for which it **cannot identify** sufficient **attractive business opportunities**.

(b)   A reduction in the number of issued shares helps to **improve earnings per share** (EPS) and **return on capital employed** (ROCE).

(c)   Dividend payments may be reduced, allowing the **cash** to be **used** for **other purposes.**

- Funding operating activities
- Capital expenditure
- Repayment of debt

(d)   The remaining shareholders' holdings will increase. Hence, and if the overall total dividends might not increase, some **shareholders** could receive **more cash individually**.

(e)   Problem or **dissident shareholders** in private companies can be **paid off** and leave the company without spreading the membership of the company beyond the existing shareholders.

(f)   It provides a potential **exit route** for **venture capitalists** who intend to be involved in the business for a limited period.

(g)   It provides an **escape route** for **entrepreneurs** who have taken their companies to market to take them **back into private ownership**, eg Virgin, Amstrad and Harvey Nichols.

3.4 Purchase or redemption by a company of its own shares

There is a **general prohibition** (s 143) against any voluntary acquisition by a company of its own shares, but that prohibition is subject to **exceptions**.

A company may:

(a)   Purchase its own shares in compliance with an **order of the court**.
(b)   Issue **redeemable shares** and then redeem them.
(c)   Purchase its own shares under certain **specified procedures**.
(d)   **Forfeit** or accept the surrender of its shares.

These restrictions relate to the **purchase** of shares: there is no objection to accepting a gift.

The **conditions for the issue and redemption of redeemable shares** are set out in ss 159 to 161.

(a)   The articles must give authority for the issue of redeemable shares. Articles do usually provide for it, but if they do not, the articles must be altered before the shares are issued: s 159.

(b)   Redeemable shares may only be issued if at the time of issue the company also has issued shares which are not redeemable: a company's capital may not consist entirely of redeemable shares: s 159.

(c)   Redeemable shares may only be redeemed if they are fully paid: s 159.

(d)   The terms of redemption must provide for payment on redemption: s 159.

(e)   The shares may be redeemed out of distributable profits, or the proceeds of a new issue of shares, or capital (if it is a private company) in accordance with the relevant rules: s 160.

(f)   Any premium payable on redemption must be provided out of distributable profits subject to an exception described below: s 160.

The 1948 Act provided regulations which prevented companies from redeeming shares except by transferring a sum equal to the nominal value of shares redeemed from distributable profit reserves to a non-distributable 'capital redemption reserve'. This reduction in distributable reserves is an example of the **capitalisation of profits, where previously distributable profits become undistributable.**

The purpose of these regulations was to prevent companies from reducing their share capital investment so as to put creditors of the company at risk.

Note. Following FRS 26, **redeemable preference shares** are no longer classified as equity, they are classified as **financial liabilities**.

3.5 Example: Capitalisation of profits

Suppose, for example, that Muffin Ltd decided to repurchase and cancel £100,000 of its ordinary share capital. A balance sheet of the company is currently as follows.

	£	£
Assets		
Cash	100,000	
Other assets	300,000	
		400,000
Liabilities		
Trade creditors		120,000
Net assets		280,000
Capital and reserves		
Ordinary shares		130,000
Profit and loss account		150,000
		280,000

Now if Muffin Ltd were able to repurchase the shares without making any transfer from the profit and loss account to a capital redemption reserve, the effect of the share redemption on the balance sheet would be as follows.

	£
Net assets	
Non-cash assets	300,000
Less trade creditors	120,000
	180,000

Capital and reserves	
Ordinary shares	30,000
Profit and loss account	150,000
	180,000

In this example, the company would still be able to pay dividends out of profits of up to £150,000. If it did, the creditors of the company would be highly vulnerable, financing £120,000 out of a total of £150,000 assets of the company.

The regulations in the 1948 Act were intended to prevent such extreme situations arising. On repurchase of the shares, Muffin Ltd would have been required to transfer £100,000 from its profit and loss account to a non-distributable reserve, called a capital redemption reserve. The effect of the redemption of shares on the balance sheet would have been:

	£	£
Net assets		
Non-cash assets		300,000
Less trade creditors		120,000
		180,000
Capital and reserves		
Ordinary shares		30,000
Reserves		
Distributable (profit and loss account)	50,000	
Non-distributable (capital redemption reserve)	100,000	
		150,000
		180,000

The maximum distributable profits are now £50,000. If Muffin Ltd paid all these as a dividend, there would still be £250,000 of assets left in the company, just over half of which would be financed by non-distributable equity capital.

When a company redeems some shares, or purchases some of its own shares, they **should be redeemed**:

(a)   **Out of distributable profits**

(b)   **Out of the proceeds of a new issue of shares**

and if there is any premium on redemption, **the premium must be paid out of distributable profits**, except that if the shares were issued at a premium, then any premium payable on their redemption may be paid out of the proceeds of a new share issue made for the purpose, up to an amount equal to the lesser of:

(a)   The aggregate premiums received on issue of the shares

(b)   The balance on the share premium account (including premium on issue of the new shares)

3.6 Example: Repurchase of shares

A numerical example might help to clarify this point. Suppose that Just Desserts Ltd intends to repurchase 10,000 shares of £1 each at a premium of 5 pence per share. The redemption must be financed out of:

(i)   Distributable profits (10,000 × £1.05 = £10,500).

(ii)   The proceeds of a new share issue (say, by issuing 10,000 new £1 shares at par). The premium of £500 must be paid out of distributable profits.

(iii)   Combination of a new share issue and distributable profits.

(iv)   Out of the proceeds of a new share issue where the shares to be repurchased were issued at a premium. For example, if the shares had been issued at a premium of 3p per share, then (assuming that the balance on the share premium account after the new share issue was at least £300) £300 of the premium on redemption could be debited to the share premium account and only £200 need be debited to distributable profits.

(a)   Where a company purchases its own shares wholly out of distributable profits, it must transfer to the capital redemption reserve an amount equal to the nominal value of the shares repurchased (s 170 (1)).

In example (a) above the accounting entries would be:

		£	£
DEBIT	Share capital account	10,000	
	Profit and loss account (premium on redemption)	500	
CREDIT	Cash		10,500
DEBIT	Profit and loss account	10,000	
CREDIT	Capital redemption reserve		10,000

(b)   Where a company redeems shares or purchases its shares wholly or partly out of the proceeds of a new share issue, it must transfer to the capital redemption reserve an amount by which the nominal value of the shares redeemed exceeds the *aggregate* proceeds from the new issue (ie nominal value of new shares issued plus share premium) (s 170 (2)).

(i)   In example (b) the accounting entries would be:

		£	£
DEBIT	Share capital account (redeemed shares)	10,000	
	Profit and loss account (premium)	500	
CREDIT	Cash (redemption of shares)		10,500
DEBIT	Cash (from new issue)	10,000	
CREDIT	Share capital account		10,000

No credit to the capital redemption reserve is necessary because there is no decrease in the creditors' buffer.

(ii)   If the redemption in the same example were made by issuing 5,000 new £1 shares at par, and paying £5,500 out of distributable profits:

		£	£
DEBIT	Share capital account (redeemed shares)	10,000	
	Profit and loss account (premium)	500	
CREDIT	Cash (redemption of shares)		10,500
DEBIT	Cash (from new issue)	5,000	
CREDIT	Share capital account		5,000
DEBIT	Profit and loss account	5,000	
CREDIT	Capital redemption reserve		5,000

(iii)   In the example (d) above (assuming a new issue of 10,000 £1 shares at a premium of 8p per share) the accounting entries would be:

		£	£
DEBIT	Cash (from new issue)	10,800	
CREDIT	Share capital account		10,000
	Share premium account		800
DEBIT	Share capital account (redeemed shares)	10,000	
	Share premium account	300	
	Profit and loss account	200	
CREDIT	Cash (redemption of shares)		10,500

BPP PROFESSIONAL EDUCATION

No capital redemption reserve is required, as in (i) above. The redemption is financed entirely by a new issue of shares.

Note

We are dealing here with the situation where a company repurchases and cancels its shares. Where shares are repurchased and held as 'treasury shares' they are dealt with as explained in Chapter 12 paragraph 2.7.

3.7 Commercial reasons for altering capital structure

These include the following.

- Greater security of finance.
- Better image for third parties.
- A 'neater' balance sheet.
- Borrowing repaid sooner.
- Cost of borrowing reduced.

Question	Share repurchase

Set out below is the summarised balance sheet of Krumpet plc at 30 June 20X5.

	Krumpet plc £'000
Capital and reserves	
Called up share capital £1 ordinary shares	300
Share premium account	60
Profit and loss account	160
	520
Net assets	520

On 1 July 20X5 Krumpet plc and Skone Ltd each purchased 50,000 of their its ordinary shares at £1.50 each.

The shares were originally issued at a premium of 20p. The redemption was partly financed by the issue at par of 5,000 new shares of £1 each.

Required

Prepare the summarised balance sheet of Krumpet plc at 1 July 20X5 immediately after the above transactions have been effected.

Answer

Workings for Krumpet

	£	£
Cost of redemption (50,000 × £1.50)		75,000
Premium on redemption (50,000 × 50p)		25,000
No premium arises on the new issue.		
Distributable profits		
Profit and loss account before redemption		160,000
Premium on redemption (must come out of distributable		
profits, not premium on new issue)		(25,000)
		135,000
Remainder of redemption costs	50,000	
Proceeds of new issue 5,000 × £1	(5,000)	
Remainder out of distributable profits		(45,000)
Balance on profit and loss account		90,000
Transfer to capital redemption reserve		
Nominal value of shares redeemed		50,000
Proceeds of new issue		(5,000)
Balance on CRR		45,000

BALANCE SHEET OF KRUMPET PLC AS AT 1 JULY 20X5

	£'000
Capital and reserves	
Ordinary shares	255
Share premium	60
Capital redemption reserve	45
	360
Profit and loss account	90
	450
Net assets	450

Chapter Roundup

- **Revenue recognition** is straightforward in most business transactions, but some situations are more complicated. It is necessary to determine the **substance of each transaction, rather than the legal form**.

- Generally revenue is recognised when the entity has transferred to the buyer the **significant risks and rewards of ownership** and when the revenue can be **measured reliably**.

- You should learn the conditions for revenue recognition for all transactions. You should also bear in mind the ASB's **balance sheet driven** approach to revenue recognition.

- You should be able to calculate **maximum distributions available to private and public companies** and to discuss the meaning of **distributable** and **realisable** profits.

- You must be able to carry out **simple calculations** showing the amounts to be transferred to the **capital redemption reserve** on purchase or redemption of own shares and how the amount of any **premium** on redemption would be treated.

Quick Quiz

1   Generally, revenue is recognised at the ……………… …….. ……………… .

2   When will revenue be recognised at other times than on the completion of a sale?

3   What are the general procedures for recognising revenue under the historical cost system?

4   Define 'revenue'.

5   Profits statutorily available for distribution are accumulated realised profits less accumulated realised losses.

    True ☐

    False ☐

6   What additional restriction is placed on the distributions of public companies?

7   'Relevant accounts' for the purposes of determining distributable profits are the most ……………………………… …………………………… of the company.

8   The rules which require the setting up of a capital redemption reserve were put in place to protect which group?

    A   Shareholders
    B   The bank
    C   Creditors
    D   Employees

9   When a company repurchases shares, out of what sources of funds can the shares be repurchased?

Answers to Quick Quiz

1   At the point of sale

2   Long term contracts and hire purchase

3   The general procedures are as follows:

    Sale of goods – revenue recognised at date of delivery
    Services – revenue recognised when services have been performed
    Rent, interest, royalties – recognised as resources used, or on time basis
    Sale of assets – date of sale

4   The gross inflow of economic benefits during the period resulting in an increase in equity, other than contributions from equity holders.

5   True

6   A public company cannot make a distribution if at the time:

    (a)   The amount of its net assets is less than the combined total of its called-up share capital plus its undistributable reserves.

    (b)   The distribution will reduce the amount of its net assets to below the combined total of its called-up share capital plus is undistributable reserves.

7   Most recent audited accounts

8   C   Creditors

9   Distributable profits or proceeds of a new issue

Now try the questions below from the Exam Question Bank

Number	Level	Marks	Time
Q13	Full exam	20	36 mins
Q14	Full exam	25	45 mins

BPP PROFESSIONAL EDUCATION

Fixed assets: Tangible assets

Topic list	Syllabus reference
1 Statutory provisions relating to all fixed assets	3 (b)
2 FRS 15 *Tangible fixed assets*	3 (b)
3 Revaluation	3 (b)
4 SSAP 19 *Accounting for investment properties*	3 (b)
5 SSAP 4 *Accounting for government grants*	3 (b)

Introduction

In Section 1, before we look at individual accounting standards, we will review the **Companies Act disclosure requirements** relating to fixed assets. Refer back to Chapter 3 to put these requirements into context. Remember that these provisions apply to *all* fixed assets.

You should already have examined the principles of **depreciation** in your earlier studies. If you are in any doubt about the possible methods of depreciation, refer back to your Paper 1.1 study material.

The other two standards covered in this chapter are on **investment properties** and **government grants**. These are quite straightforward. Develop a sound knowledge of their main provisions and make sure that you can do the relevant exercises.

Study guide

- Define the initial cost of a fixed asset (including a self-constructed asset) and apply this to various examples of expenditures distinguishing between capital and revenue items.

- Describe, and be able to identify, subsequent expenditures that may be capitalised.

- State and appraise the effects of accounting standards on the revaluation of fixed assets.

- Account for gains and losses on the disposal of revalued assets.

- Calculate depreciation on:

  - revalued assets, and
  - assets that have two or more major components.

- Apply the provisions of accounting standards on government grants.

- Discuss why the treatment of investment properties should differ from other properties.

- Apply the requirements of accounting standards on accounting for investment properties.

Exam guide

This is a key area and quite straightforward. Tangible fixed assets may come up as part of a question or subject matter from two or more sections of this chapter may be tested in a full question.

1 Statutory provisions relating to all fixed assets

FAST FORWARD

A number of accounting regulations on the valuation and disclosure of fixed assets are contained in the **Companies Act 1985**.

The standard balance sheet format of CA 1985 divides fixed assets into three categories:

    (a)   **Intangible assets** (BI in the CA 1985 format).
    (b)   **Tangible assets** (BII).
    (c)   **Investments** (BIII).

In this chapter we will deal with the general rules of the CA 1985 relating to *all* fixed assets. These may be considered under two headings.

    (a)   **Valuation:** the amounts at which fixed assets should be stated in the balance sheet.
    (b)   **Disclosure:** the information that should be disclosed in the accounts regarding:

        - Valuation of fixed assets
        - Movements on fixed asset accounts during the year.

1.1 Valuation of fixed assets

1.1.1 Cost

The two key ways of acquiring a tangible fixed asset are either by purchase or by self-production.

Purchased asset: Its cost is simply the purchase price plus any expenses incidental to its acquisition.

Asset produced by a company for its own use: This should be included at 'production cost' which *must* include:

- **Cost of raw materials**
- **Consumables** used
- Other **attributable direct costs** (such as labour)

Production cost **may** additionally **include:**

- **A reasonable proportion of indirect costs**
- **Interest** on any capital borrowed to **finance production** of the asset.

The amount of capitalised interest must however be disclosed in a note to the accounts.

1.1.2 Depreciation

The **'cost'** of any fixed asset having a limited economic life, whether purchase price or production cost, **must be reduced by provisions for depreciation** calculated to write off the cost, less any residual value, **systematically over the period of the asset's useful life**. This very general requirement is supplemented by the more detailed provisions of FRS 15 *Tangible fixed assets* which is dealt with in the next section.

Any provision for **impairment** should be disclosed on the **face of the profit and loss account or by way of note**. Where a provision becomes **no longer necessary**, because the conditions giving rise to it have altered, it should be **written back**, and again **disclosure** should be made.

1.2 Fixed assets valuation: alternative accounting rules

Although the Companies Act 1985 maintains **historical cost** principles as the **normal basis** for the preparation of accounts, **alternative bases** allowing for **revaluations** and **current cost accounting are permitted provided that**:

(a)   The **items affected** and the **basis of valuation** are **disclosed** in a note to the accounts;

(b)   The **historical cost** in the current and previous years is **separately disclosed** in the balance sheet or in a note to the accounts. Alternatively, the difference between the revalued amount and historical cost may be disclosed.

Key term

> Using the **alternative accounting rules**, the appropriate value of any fixed asset (ie its **current cost or market value**), rather than its purchase price or production cost, **may be included in the balance sheet**.

Here is a diagram to help clarify the options available under CA 1985, schedule 4.

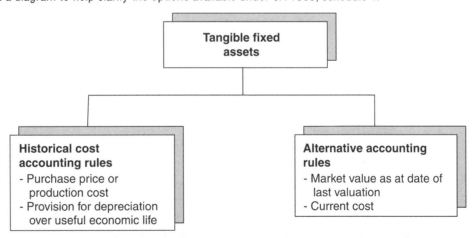

Where appropriate, depreciation may be provided on the basis of the new valuation(s), such depreciation being referred to in the Companies Act 1985 as the **'adjusted amount'** of depreciation. For profit and loss account purposes, **FRS 15** (see below) specifically states that depreciation must be charged on the **revalued amount** and that the *whole* charge must be taken to the **profit and loss account**.

1.3 Revaluation reserve

Key term

> Where the value of any fixed asset is determined by using the **alternative accounting rules**, the amount of **profit or loss arising** must be credited or (as the case may be) debited to a separate reserve, the **revaluation reserve**. (Revised asset value – Net book value prior to valuation = Transfer to revaluation reserve)

1.3.1 Uses of revaluation reserve

The Companies Act 1985 states that an amount may be transferred from the revaluation reserve to the profit and loss account ie debit revaluation reserve and credit profit and loss reserve, if the amount:

- was previously charged to profit and loss account
- represents realised profit
- relates to taxation on a profit or loss taken to the revaluation reserve, or
- is no longer necessary for the valuation method used.

The revaluation reserve may also be used for a **bonus issue** of shares. No other debits to revaluation reserve are allowed.

The revaluation reserve must be **reduced** to the extent that the amounts standing to the credit of the reserves are, in the opinion of directors of the company **no longer necessary** for the purposes of the accounting policies adopted by the company.

The amount of a revaluation reserve must be shown under a **separate sub-heading** in **position KIII** on the **balance sheet**. However, the reserve need not necessarily be called a 'revaluation reserve'.

Question
Revaluation

Studivation Ltd revalued a freehold building on 31 March 20X5 to £300,000. The original purchase cost 10 years ago was £180,000. Studivation Ltd depreciates freehold buildings over 40 years.

Show the accounting entries for the revaluation and the depreciation charge for the year ended 31 March 20X6.

Answer

		£	£
(a)	*Revaluation*		
	DEBIT Fixed asset cost (£300,000 – £180,000)	120,000	
	DEBIT Accumulated depreciation (£180,000 ÷ 40 × 10)	45,000	
	CREDIT Revaluation reserve		165,000
(b)	*Depreciation charge*		
	DEBIT Depreciation (£300,000 ÷ 30)	10,000	
	CREDIT Accumulated depreciation		10,000

1.4 Fixed assets: companies act disclosures

Notes to the accounts must show, for **each class** of **fixed assets**, an analysis of the **movements** on both **costs** and **depreciation provisions**. Refer back to the note on fixed assets in Chapter 3.

Where any **fixed assets** of a company (other than listed investments) are included in the accounts at an alternative accounting valuation, the **following information** must also be given:

(a) The **years** (so far as they are known to the directors) in which the assets were **severally valued** and the **several values**.

(b) In the case of assets that have been **valued** during the **financial period**, the **names** of the **persons** who valued them or particulars of their **qualifications** for doing so and (whichever is stated) the **bases of valuation** used by them.

A **note to the accounts** must **classify land and buildings** under the headings of:

(a) **Freehold property**.
(b) **Leasehold property**, distinguishing between:

   (i) **Long leaseholds**, in which the **unexpired term** of the lease at the balance sheet date is **not less than 50 years**.

   (ii) **Short leaseholds** which are all leaseholds other than long leaseholds.

2 FRS 15 Tangible fixed assets

FAST FORWARD

In the case of **tangible fixed assets**, Companies Act requirements are supplemented by the provisions of FRS 15 *Tangible fixed assets*.

Key term

Tangible fixed assets have physical substance and are held for:

- use in the production or supply of goods or services
- rental to others
- administration purposes

on a **continuing basis** in the **reporting entity's activities**.

They are held to **earn revenue** by their **use**, **not** from their **resale**.

2.1 Objective

FRS 15 deals with accounting for the initial measurement, valuation and depreciation of tangible fixed assets. It also sets out the information that should be disclosed to enable readers to understand the impact of the accounting policies adopted in relation to these issues.

2.2 Initial measurement

Exam focus point

Initial measurement and capitalisation of subsequent expenditure were tested in the December 2001 paper.

A tangible fixed asset should **initially be measured at cost**.

Key term

Cost is purchase price plus any costs directly attributable to bringing the asset into working condition for its intended use.

2.3 Directly attributable costs

Directly attributable costs include:

- **Direct labour** costs of using **own employees**
- **Acquisition costs**, eg stamp duty, import duties
- Cost of **site preparation** and clearance
- Initial **delivery and handling** costs
- **Installation** costs
- **Professional fees** eg legal and architect's fees
- The estimated cost of **dismantling and removing** the asset and restoring the site, to the extent that it is recognised as a provision under FRS 12 *Provisions, contingent liabilities and contingent assets* (discussed in Chapter 11). The fact that the prospect of such decommissioning costs emerges only some time after the original capitalisation of the asset (eg because of legislative changes) does not preclude their capitalisation.

Administration and other general overhead costs and employee costs not related to the specific tangible fixed asset are not directly attributable costs.

In general terms, directly attributable costs can be regarded as incremental costs that would have been avoided only if the tangible fixed asset had not been constructed as required.

2.3.1 Abnormal costs

Costs such as those arising from design error, wasted materials, industrial disputes, idle capacity or production delays are considered to be **abnormal** and **not directly attributable** to bringing the asset into **working condition** and its **intended use**. This approach is consistent with SSAP 9. They should therefore should **not be capitalised** as part of the cost of the asset.

2.3.2 Time frame for capitalisation

Capitalisation of **directly attributable costs** should **cease** when substantially all the activities that are necessary to get the tangible fixed asset ready for use are complete, even if the asset has not actually been brought into use. A tangible fixed asset is considered to be ready for use when its **physical construction is complete**.

2.3.3 Start-up or commissioning period

The costs associated with a **start-up** or **commissioning period** should be **included** in the cost of the tangible fixed asset **only where** the **asset is available for use** but **incapable** of operating at **normal levels without** such a **start-up** or **commissioning period**.

The costs of an **essential commissioning period** are included as part of the **cost of bringing the asset up to its normal operating potential**, and **therefore** as **part** of its **cost**.

However, there is no justification for regarding costs relating to other start-up periods, where the asset is available for use but not yet operating at normal levels.

Question	Start-up period 1

Halliday Inn has been is being built and opens for business in January 20X9. Demand is expected to build up slowly and high levels of room occupancy are only likely to be achieved over a period of several months.

Should any of the costs incurred in the run up to optimal occupancy of hotel be capitalised.

Answer	

No. The hotel is able to operate at normal levels immediately on opening without necessarily having to go through a start up period in a slack season.

Question	Start-up period 2

Duncan Donatz Ltd has constructed a high speed machine for making holes of different shapes in doughnuts.

The machine is to be commissioned in two stages:

(a)   *Test run phase.* This phase is designed to ensure that the shapes are punched properly and the process operates smoothly and efficiently. During this run in phase, output will be restricted to test runs.

(b)   *Demand building phase.* During this phase output is expected to be low because the company is trying to achieve product acceptance of a different innovative type of doughnut. However, the machine is capable of operating at a normal level of output.

How should the costs relating to these two start up phases be treated?

Answer	

Phase 1.   The relevant costs should be capitalised together with the cost of machine because the machine is **not capable** of operating at normal levels without such a start up or commissioning period.

Phase 2.   Costs associated with this period should be written off to profit and loss account. The machine is now capable of operating at normal levels and the low volumes are due to market factors.

From the above, it is important to be aware of the **practical distinction** between **two phases**:

(a)   **Essential start-up** and **commissioning** phase, without which the asset is **incapable** of operating at normal levels.

(b)   **Demand building phase** when output is built up to **full utilisation**.

2.3.4 Suspension of a revenue activity during construction

Operating losses that occur because a revenue activity has been suspended during the construction of a tangible fixed asset are not directly attributable costs. For example, if a restaurant closes for rebuilding, the revenue losses and other costs arising from the suspension of trading are not part of the cost of the new restaurant. Such losses are considered to be **too indirect** and **not linked sufficiently closely** with the **future economic benefits** to be obtained from the new asset.

Question   Suspension of trading

Café Edmondo Ltd has to close its restaurant for rebuilding.

Should the revenue losses and other costs arising from the suspension of trading be capitalised?

Answer

No. These losses are too indirect and not linked sufficiently closely with the economic benefits to be derived from the rebuilt restaurant.

Remember that the FRS 15 approach differs from the SSAP 9 approach to initial recognition. FRS 15 works on an **incremental cost approach,** whereas **SSAP 9** is based on **total absorption costing basis** and therefore does not prohibit recognition of general overheads.

2.3.5 Finance costs

Finance costs directly attributable to the construction of a fixed asset **may be capitalised** if it is **company policy** to do so. However, this **policy must be applied consistently**.

All finance costs that are **directly attributable** to the construction of a tangible fixed asset should be **capitalised** as part of the **cost of the asset**.

Key term

> **Directly attributable finance costs** are those that would have been **avoided** if there had been **no expenditure on the asset**.

If finance costs are capitalised, capitalisation should start when:

- Finance **costs** are being **incurred**
- Expenditure on the **asset** is being **incurred**
- **Activities** necessary to get the **asset ready** for use are **in progress**

Capitalisation of finance costs should cease when the asset is ready for use.

Sometimes construction of an asset may be completed in parts and each part is capable of being used while construction continues on other parts. An example of such an asset is a retail park consisting of several units. In such cases capitalisation of borrowing costs relating to a part should cease when substantially all the activities that are necessary to get that part ready for use are completed.

Sometimes **active development** on a tangible fixed asset might be **interrupted** for extended periods. During such periods, **capitalisation** of finance costs should be **suspended**.

The following disclosures are required in respect of capitalisation of borrowing costs.

(a)   The accounting policy adopted

(b)   The amount of borrowing costs capitalised during the period

(c)   The amount of borrowing costs recognised in the profit and loss account during the period

(d)   The capitalisation (interest) rate used to determine the amount of capitalised borrowing costs

2.3.6 Recoverable amount

The **amount recognised** when a tangible fixed asset is acquired or constructed should **not exceed its recoverable amount**. If it does, it should be written down accordingly to its recoverable amount.

Recoverable amount is defined as being the higher of

(a)   Net realisable value (NRV)

(b)   Value in use (VU)

It is not necessary to review tangible fixed assets for **impairment** when they are acquired or constructed. They need to be **reviewed for impairment** only if there is some **indication** that impairment has occurred. Such indications are specified in the current FRS 11 *Impairment of fixed assets and goodwill*. We will look at impairment in more detail later.

2.4 Subsequent expenditure

After a tangible fixed asset has been brought into use, in practice, there is likely to be **further money spent**.

(a)   **Revenue expenditure** which should be **written off** to the profit and loss account.

(b)   **Capital expenditure** which should be debited to **tangible fixed assets**.

2.4.1 Expenditure to be written off to profit and loss account

General rule

Subsequent expenditure to ensure that a tangible fixed asset maintains its previously assessed standard of performance should be written off to profit and loss account as it is incurred.

Question   Subsequent expenditure

Yummy Foods Ltd has to regularly service and overhaul its labelling machines to ensure that the labels are properly aligned and the tins roll off the production line efficiently, in accordance with the company's production targets.

How should these cost be treated?

Answer

Such expenditure ensures that the machinery sustains its originally assessed standard of performance. Without such expenditure, the useful economic life or residual value is likely to be reduced and in consequence the depreciation charge would increase.

Hence the expenditure is effectively 'repairs and maintenance' to be expensed in the profit and loss account.

2.4.2 Expenditure to be capitalised

FRS 15 specifies three scenarios where subsequent expenditure should be capitalised.

(a)   It **enhances** the **economic benefits** over and **above previously assessed standards of performance**.

(b)   A **component** of an asset that has been treated **separately** for **depreciation purposes** (because it has a substantially different useful economic life from the rest of the asset) has been **restored** or **replaced**.

(c)   The expenditure related to a **major inspection** or **overhaul** that **restores economic benefits** that have been consumed and reflected in the depreciation charge.

2.4.3 Enhancement of economic benefits

FRS 15 offers two ways of **enhancing** the **economic benefits** that a tangible fixed asset might deliver:

    (a)   Mod**ifying the asset** to increase its capacity.

           Eg a hotel reduces its non-productive communal areas to give it more bedrooms.

    (b)   **Upgrading the asset** to achieve a substantial **improvement** in the **quality** of the product or service provided to customers.

           Eg a hotel re-upholsters its fabric furniture with leather to improve the quality of service provided to its guests.

2.4.4 Replacement of separately depreciated component

In these circumstances, the component is disposed of and replaced by a new asset.

Question	Separate component 1

Safeair Ltd treats its aircraft engines separately for depreciation purposes. The engine on one of its aircraft caught fire on take off and has had to be replaced.

How should the cost of the replacement engine be treated?

Answer

The new engine should be capitalised as a fixed asset addition with the destroyed engine taken to disposal account and expensed via the profit and loss account.

General rule

> **Each component** is depreciated over its **individual** useful life, so that the depreciation profile over the whole asset **more accurately reflects** the **actual** consumption of the asset's economic benefits.

2.4.5 Major overhauls and inspections

In addition to routine repairs and maintenance, some assets also require substantial expenditure every few years on major overhauls or inspections. Some examples found in practice are aircraft airworthiness inspections, ocean liner refits, theme park ride overhauls, refurbishment of kiln linings and replacing roofs of buildings.

Question	Overhauls

Safeair Ltd is required by law to overhaul its aircraft once every three years. Unless the overhauls are done, the aircraft cannot be flown.

How should the costs of the overhauls be treated?

Answer

The cost of the overhaul is capitalised when incurred because it restores the economic benefits flowing from the tangible fixed assets. The carrying amount representing the cost of benefits consumed is removed from the balance sheet.

The need to undertake an overhaul or inspection is acknowledged in the accounts by depreciating an amount of the asset that is equivalent to the inspection or overhaul costs over the period until the next inspection or overhaul. Hence, a **new asset** is **treated**, **in effect**, as being made up of **two elements**.

(a)   **The core asset**. This is depreciated over its expected useful economic life.

(b)   **The built-in overhaul cost**. This is depreciated over the period until the first actual overhaul takes place.

Exam focus point

The June 2004 exam had part of a question dealing with a provision for machinery overhaul.

2.4.6 Decision to identify several economic lives

The **decision** whether to **identify separate components** or **future expenditures** on **overhauls** or **inspections** for **depreciation** over a **shorter useful economic life** than the rest of the tangible fixed asset is likely to **reflect various factors**.

(a)   Whether the **useful economic lives** of the components are, or the period until the next inspection or overhaul is, **substantially different** from the useful economic life of the remainder of the asset

(b)   The **degree of irregularity** in the **level of expenditures** required to restate the component or asset in different accounting periods

(c)   Their **materiality** in the context of the financial statements.

The decision may be not to account for each tangible fixed asset as several different asset components or to depreciate part of the asset over a different timescale from the rest of the asset. In these circumstances, the cost of replacing, restoring, overhauling or inspecting the asset or components of the asset is not capitalised, but instead is recognised in the profit and loss account as incurred.

2.5 Depreciation

Exam focus point

The pilot paper required a discussion on the subject of a policy of depreciation of fixed assets. You need to have a good working knowledge of FRS 15.

The important point to note is that depreciation is the allocation of cost (or revalued amount), less estimated residual value, over expected useful life. It is not intended as a process of valuing assets.

Depreciation is consistent with the FRS 18 accruals basis of accounting. The cost is spread over the periods to which the cost relates, rather than being charged to the period in which the payment is made. This is in keeping with what the ASB *Statement of principles* refers to as 'time matching'.

2.5.1 Purpose of depreciation

As noted earlier, the Companies Act 1985 requires that all fixed assets having a limited economic life should be depreciated. **FRS 15** provides a useful discussion of the **purpose of depreciation** and supplements the statutory requirements in important ways.

Key term

> **Depreciation** is defined in FRS 15 as the measure of the cost or revalued amount of the **economic benefits** of the tangible fixed asset that have been **consumed during the period**.
>
> Consumption includes:
>
> - wearing out
> - using up
> - other reduction in the useful economic life
>
> of a tangible fixed asset, whether arising from:
>
> - use
> - effluxion (passage) of time
> - obsolescence through either:
>   - changes in technology
>   - reduction in demand for the goods and services produced by the asset.

This definition includes

- **amortisation** of **assets** with a **pre-determined life**, such as a **leasehold**
- **depletion** of **wasting assets** such as **mines**.

2.5.2 General requirements

FRS 15 specifies the following general rules regarding depreciation.

(a)   The depreciable amount of a tangible fixed asset should be allocated on a **systematic basis** over its **useful economic life**

(b)   The depreciation method used should **reflect** as fairly as possible the **pattern** in which the asset's **economic benefits** are **consumed** by the company

(c)   The depreciation charge for each period should be recognised as an **expense** in the profit and loss account unless it is permitted to be included in the carrying amount of another asset.

The general requirements of FRS 15 entail three key issues.

- Selecting a method which reflects the pattern of consumption
- Estimating the useful economic life and residual value
- Dealing with the impact of subsequent expenditure on depreciation

2.6 Methods of depreciation

A **variety of methods** can be used to allocate the depreciable amount of a tangible fixed asset. No specific method is stipulated.

FRS 15 mentions two common methods of depreciation.

(a)   **Straight-line**. This method assumes that equal amounts of economic benefit are consumed in each year of the asset's life. Therefore the asset is written off in **equal instalments** over its **estimated useful economic life**.

(b)   **Reducing balance**. Here the **depreciation rate** is applied to the **opening net book value**. This method charges more depreciation in the early years of an asset's life than in later years.

The closest FRS 15 gets to making a recommendation is to suggest that where the pattern of consumption of an asset's economic benefits is uncertain, straight-line method of depreciation is usually adopted. In practice this is the most widely used method.

2.7 Factors affecting depreciation

FRS 15 outlines the factors to be considered in determining the useful economic life, residual value and depreciation method of an asset.

(a) The **expected usage** of the asset by the entity, assessed by reference to the asset's **expected capacity** or **physical output**

(b) The **expected physical deterioration** of the asset through use or **effluxion of time**; this will depend upon the **repair and maintenance programme** of the entity both when the asset is in **use** and when it is **idle**

(c) Economic or technological obsolescence, for example arising from changes or improvements in production, or a change in the market demand for the product or service output of that asset

(d) Legal or similar limits on the use of the asset, such as the expiry dates of related leases

2.8 Review of useful economic life

General rule

> The **useful economic life** of a tangible fixed asset should be **reviewed** at the **end of each reporting period** and revised if expectations are significantly different from previous estimates.

If **useful economic life** is **revised**, the **carrying amount** (ie book value) of the tangible fixed asset at the date of revision is **depreciated** over the **revised remaining useful economic life** from that point onwards.

Remember that the useful economic life of a tangible fixed asset is an **accounting estimate**, not an accounting policy. In such cases, the standard accounting practice is **not to restate previous years' figures** when estimates are revised.

The approach is to depreciate the carrying amount of the tangible fixed asset over the remaining useful economic life, beginning in the period in which the change is made.

However, if future results could be materially distorted, the adjustment to accumulated deprecation should be recognised in the accounts in accordance with FRS 3 (normally as an exceptional item).

Exam focus point

> The June 2002 paper asked candidates to respond to a reduction in UEL of fixed assets.

2.9 Revision of residual value

General rule

> Where residual value is material, it should be reviewed at the end of each period to take account of **expected technological changes**, but still based on prices prevailing at the date of acquisition (or revaluation).

A change in estimated residual value is **accounted for prospectively** over the asset's remaining useful economic life, except where the asset is impaired. If an impairment occurs, the asset should be written down immediately. (Impairment will be covered in more detail later in this text.)

When an asset is revalued, the residual value should also be reassessed, based on prices at the date of revaluation.

2.10 Revision of method of depreciation

General rule

> A change in depreciation method is permissible only on the grounds that the new method will give a **fairer presentation** of the results and of the financial position.

The depreciation method is an **accounting estimate**. Therefore, a change of method is not a change of accounting policy.

The carrying amount (ie book value) of the asset is depreciated on the new method over the remaining useful economic life, beginning in the period in which the change is made.

2.11 Two or more components of a fixed asset

General rule

> Where the tangible fixed asset comprises two or more major components with substantially different useful economic lives, each component should be accounted for separately for depreciation purposes and depreciated over its useful economic life.

Examples include:

- Land and buildings
- The structure of a building and items within the structure, such as general fittings

Freehold land usually has an indefinite life, unless subject to depletion (eg a quarry). Buildings have a limited life and are therefore depreciated.

Question   Separate component 2

What about the trading potential associated with a property valued as an operational entity, such as a hotel, pub or club? Should this be treated as a separate component?

Answer

No. The value and life of any trading potential is inherently inseparable from that of the property.

In effect, the asset is treated as though it were several different assets for depreciation purposes. FRS 15 also requires component depreciation if subsequent expenditure on replacing a component is to be capitalised.

2.12 Impact of subsequent expenditure

In calculating the useful economic life of an asset it is assumed that **subsequent expenditure** will be undertaken to **maintain** the **originally assessed standard of performance** of the asset (for example the cost of servicing or overhauling plant and equipment). Without such expenditure the depreciation expense would be increased because the useful life and/or residual value of the asset would be reduced. This type of expenditure is **recognised as an expense when incurred**.

In addition, subsequent expenditure may be undertaken that results in a **restoration** or **replacement** of a component of the asset that has been depreciated or an **enhancement** of **economic benefits** of the asset in excess of the originally assessed standard of performance. This type of expenditure may result in an extension of the **useful economic life of the asset** and represents **capital expenditure**.

Important!

Subsequent expenditure does not obviate the need to charge depreciation.

2.13 Non-depreciation

General rule

For tangible fixed assets other than non-depreciable land, the **only grounds** for not charging depreciation are that the depreciation charge and accumulated depreciation are **immaterial**.

The depreciation charge and accumulated depreciation are immaterial if they would **not reasonably influence** the **decisions** of a **user** of the accounts.

An entity must be able to justify that the uncharged depreciation is not material in **aggregate** as well as for **each tangible fixed asset**. Depreciation may be immaterial because of **very long useful economic lives** or **high residual values** (or both). A high residual value will reflect the remaining economic value of the asset at the end of its useful economic life to the entity. These conditions may occur when **all the following are met**:

(a) The entity has a policy and practice of **regular maintenance and repair** (charges for which are recognised in the profit and loss account) such that the asset is kept to its previously assessed **standard of performance**

(b) The asset is **unlikely** to **suffer** from economic or technological **obsolescence** (eg due to potential changes in demand in the market following changes in fashion)

(c) Where estimated residual values are material:

(i) The entity has a policy and practice of disposing of similar assets well before and end of their economic lives

(ii) The **disposal proceeds** of similar assets (after excluding the effect of price changes since the date of acquisition or last revaluation) have **not** been **materially less than** their **carrying amounts**.

The above rules come into play in relation to what are known as **'trophy assets'**.

- **Top quality** buildings in desirable areas
- **Antique** fixtures and fittings
- **Historic** buildings

This approach was also advocated by the hotel, catering and public house industry on the grounds that their assets were regularly maintained and refurbished and therefore their useful economic life were not restricted.

However, where entities have avoided changing depreciation on the grounds of immateriality, they will nevertheless be required to perform impairment reviews under FRS 11. In practice, the **impairment review route** may prove **costly** and **counter-productive**, when the profit and loss account has nevertheless and **inevitably to suffer a hit** resulting from an impairment loss.

2.14 Impairment requirements

The application of impairment reviews in relation specifically to trophy assets has been touched as above. **Generally** tangible fixed assets other than non depreciable land, should be **reviewed for impairment** at the **end of the reporting** period where:

- **No depreciation** is charged on the **grounds** that it would be **immaterial**.
- The **estimated remaining useful economic life exceeds 50 years**.

The review should be in accordance with FRS 11 *Impairment of fixed assets and goodwill,* which will be discussed in more detail in the **next chapter**

2.15 Depreciation on revalued assets

Many companies **carry fixed assets** in their balance sheets at **revalued amounts**, particularly in the case of freehold buildings. When this is done, the **depreciation charge** should be calculated **on the basis of the revalued amount** (not the original cost).

As discussed above where the **residual value is material**, it should be **reviewed** at the **end of each reporting period** to take account of reasonably **expected technological changes**. A **change** in the **estimated residual value** should be **accounted for prospectively** over the asset's remaining useful economic life, **except** to the **extent** that the asset has been **impaired** at the **balance sheet date**.

2.16 Renewals accounting

Key term

> Where **renewals accounting** is adopted, the level of annual expenditure required to maintain the operating capacity of the infrastructure asset is treated as the depreciation charged for the period and is deducted from the carrying amount of the asset (as part of accumulated depreciation). Actual expenditure is capitalised (as part of the cost of the asset) as incurred.

Definable major assets or components within an infrastructure system or network with determinable finite lives should be treated separately and depreciated over their useful economic lives. For the remaining tangible fixed assets within the system or network, renewals accounting may be used if:

- (a) The infrastructure asset is a system that as a whole is intended to be maintained at a specified level of service by the continuing replacement and refurbishment of its components.
- (b) The level of annual expenditure required to maintain the operating capacity or service capability of the infrastructure asset is calculated from an asset management plan certified by a qualified, independent person.
- (c) The system or network is in a mature or steady state.

2.17 Disclosure requirements of FRS 15

The following information should be disclosed separately in the financial statements for each class of tangible fixed assets.

- (a) The depreciation methods used
- (b) The useful economic lives or the depreciation rates used
- (c) Total depreciation charged for the period
- (d) Where material, the financial effect of a change during the period in either the estimate of useful economic lives or the estimate of residual values
- (e) The cost or revalued amount at the beginning of the financial period and at the balance sheet date
- (f) The cumulative amount of provisions for depreciation or impairment at the beginning of the financial period and at the balance sheet date
- (g) A reconciliation of the movements, separately disclosing additions, disposals, revaluations, transfers, depreciation, impairment losses, and reversals of past impairment losses written back in the financial period

(h)   The net carrying amount at the beginning of the financial period and at the balance sheet date

2.18 Adverse feedback on FRS 15

FRS 15 has been largely welcomed, particularly the rules on revaluations (see below). However, some commentators have found problematic the treatment of subsequent expenditure where there is a major overhaul. As mentioned previously, the treatment has been described as 'contrived'.

3 Revaluation

FAST FORWARD

FRS 15 lays down detailed requirements concerning the revaluation of fixed assets. Directors can no longer choose to revalue certain assets and not others.

Exam focus point

The June 2002 paper required candidates to deal with the revaluation of land and buildings.

The December 2002 accounts preparation question involved dealing with a revaluation of leasehold land and buildings.

The revaluation of fixed assets was examined again in June 2003.

The December 2004 paper asked for balance sheet extracts dealing with revaluation and impairment of fixed assets.

3.1 Policy basis

Before FRS 15, companies could pick and choose which of their assets they wished to revalue and when. This allowed companies to massage their balance sheet figures through the inclusion of meaningless **out of date valuations**, thereby **hindering comparability** between companies from year to year. FRS 15 puts a stop to this '**cherry picking**'.

Basic requirements

An entity may adopt a policy of **revaluing tangible fixed assets**. Where this policy is adopted **it must be applied consistently** to all assets of the same class.

Where an asset is revalued its carrying amount should be its **current value** as at the balance sheet date, current value being the **lower of replacement cost and recoverable amount**. The recoverable amount, in turn, is the **higher** of **net realisable value** and **value in use.**

A **class of fixed assets** is 'a category of tangible fixed assets having a similar nature, function or use in the business of an entity'. (FRS 15)

Key terms

Replacement cost. The cost at which an **identical asset** could be **purchased** or **constructed**.

Depreciated replacement cost. Replacement cost with appropriate **deduction** for **age, condition and obsolescence**.

Recoverable amount. The higher of net realisable value and value in use.

Net realisable value. The **amount** at which an **asset could be disposed of**, less any **direct selling costs.**

Value in use. The **present value** of **future cash flows** obtainable as result of an asset's **continued use**, **including** those resulting from **ultimate disposal**.

Key terms

> **Open market value**. The **best price** that could be obtained between a **willing seller** and a **knowledgeable buyer**, assuming **normal market conditions**.
>
> **Existing use value**. As for **open market value**, except that value is based on the **assumption** that the property can be used for the **foreseeable future** only for its **existing use**.

The above basic requirements can be summarised by the following diagram.

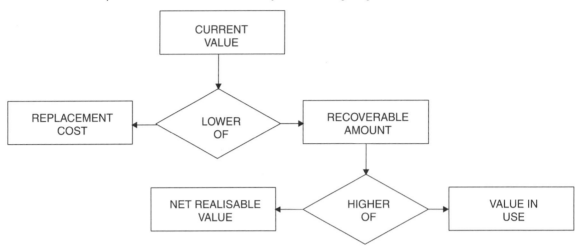

Remember the decision to adopt a policy of revaluation of tangible fixed assets is discretionary. Do not confuse this with other scenarios where the carrying value of a fixed asset should be adjusted:

(a)   **FRS 15 rule** that:

"if the amount recognised when a tangible fixed asset is acquired or constructed exceeds its recoverable amount, it should be written down to its recoverable amount."

(b)   FRS 11 response to indications of impairment that requires:

"A review for impairment of a fixed asset (or goodwill) should be carried out if events or circumstances indicate that the carrying amount of the fixed asset (or goodwill) may not be recoverable."

You may find the following diagram helpful in clarifying the scenarios where, in addition to annual depreciation, the carrying value of a tangible fixed asset needs to be adjusted.

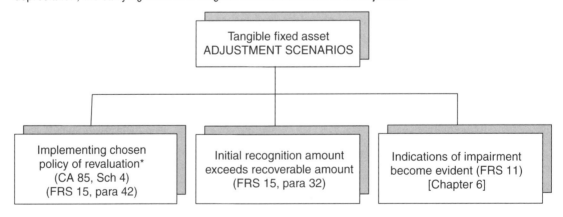

* We shall see later that in certain circumstances, a loss arising on revaluation is effectively tantamount to an impairment loss. However, you must remember that this arises from the revaluation policy route rather than the indications of impairment route.

3.2 Frequency of valuation

3.2.1 General rule

The valuation of properties should be carried out on the basis of a 5 year cycle.

(a) A **full valuation** every **5 years**

(b) An **interim valuation** in **year 3 of the five-year cycle**.

(c) An **interim valuation also in years 1, 2 and 4** of the five-year cycle should also be done where it is likely that there has been a **material change in value**.

3.2.2 Non-specialised properties

For portfolios of non-specialised properties, eg factories, warehouses, shops and offices, there is another alternative. A **full valuation** may be performed on a **rolling basis** designed to cover all the properties over a **five-year cycle**. An **interim valuation** on the **remaining four-fifths** of the portfolio should be done where it is likely that there has been a **material change** in value.

This approach is appropriate only where the property portfolio held by the entity under either of **two specified scenarios**.

(a) The portfolio consists of a number of **broadly similar properties** whose characteristics are such that their values are likely to be affected by the **same market factors**.

(b) The portfolio can be divided on a **continuing basis** into **five groups of a broadly similar spread**.

3.2.3 Valuers

FRS 15 specifies who may carry out a **full valuation**.

(a) A qualified external valuer (eg a surveyor, who is independent of the company), or
(b) A qualified internal valuer, but subject to review by a qualified external valuer.

An **interim valuation** may be done by an internal or external, qualified valuer.

3.2.4 Other tangible fixed assets

For certain types of assets (other than properties) eg company cars, there may be an **active second hand market** for the asset or **appropriate indices** may exist, so that the directors can establish the asset's value with **reasonable reliability** and therefore avoid the need to use the services of a qualified valuer.

For an index to be appropriate:

(a) It must be appropriate to the class of asset, its location and conditions.
(b) It must take into account the impact of technological change.
(c) It must have a proven track record of regular publication.
(d) It is expected to be available in the foreseeable future.

Such valuations must be performed **every five years**, and also in the **intervening years** where there has been a **material change in value**.

3.3 Valuation basis

The following valuation bases should be used for properties that are not impaired.

TYPE	BASIS
Specialised properties	• These should be valued on the basis of **depreciated replacement cost**. • Specialised properties are those which, due to their **specialised** nature, there is **no general market** in their existing use or condition, except as part of a sale of the business in occupation. Eg oil refineries, hospitals, chemical works, power stations, schools, colleges and universities where there is no competing market demand from other organisations using these types of property in the locality. • The objectives of using depreciated replacement cost is to make a realistic estimate of the current cost of constructing an asset that has the same service potential as the existing asset.
Non-specialised properties	• These should be valued on the basis of **existing use value** (EUV), plus notional directly attributable acquisition costs where material.
Properties surplus to an entity's requirements	• These should be valued on the basis of open market value (OMV) less expected direct selling costs where these are material. They may be specialised or non-specialised properties. • The **assumption** supporting the specified accounting treatment is that they **will be sold**.

Where there is an indication of impairment, an impairment review should be carried out in accordance with FRS 11. The asset should be recorded at the lower of revalued amount (as above) and recoverable amount.

Tangible fixed assets other than properties should be valued using market value or, if not obtainable, depreciated replacement cost.

3.4 Reporting gains and losses on revaluations

3.4.1 General points

A revaluation gain or loss arises when there is a difference between the valuation of a tangible fixed asset when compared to its carrying amount.

Revaluation gains and losses are dealt with through either:

- Profit and loss account; or
- Statement of total recognised gains and losses

This will depend on the underlying scenarios, which are explored below.

3.5 Tangible fixed asset revalued upwards

Gain	Treatment of gain
Asset not previously revalued	• Gain credited to revaluation reserve. • Reported in STRGL.
Asset previously revalued upwards	• Gain credited to revaluation reserve. • Reported in STRGL.

Gain	Treatment of gain
Asset subjected to previous revaluation loss	• Portion of gain that in effect reverses the prior revaluation losses should be credited to profit and loss account, ie restores the asset to its depreciated historical cost. • Any gain in excess of the above should be credited to revaluation reserve and reported via STRGL.

The above points are covered in the example 3.24, below.

3.6 Tangible fixed asset revalued downwards

Loss	Treatment of loss
Loss clearly due to consumption of economic benefits eg physical damage or deterioration in quality of goods or services provided by the asset.	All of the loss must be debited to profit and loss account. It does not matter that the asset involved might have been previously revalued upwards. (FRS 15 suggests that this is really an impairment loss)
Losses owing to other causes than the above. Asset previously revalued upwards.	These losses should be recognised in the following order. (a) In STRGL until the carrying amount reaches depreciated historical cost. (b) In the profit and loss account.
Losses owing to other causes than top item above. Asset not previously revalued upwards.	These losses should be recognised in the profit and loss account.

3.7 Depreciation on revalued assets

Basic requirements

Where an asset has been revalued, the depreciation charge is based on the revaluation amount, less residual value, from the date of revaluation.

The asset's residual value should also be re-estimated on revaluation, based on values prevailing at that date.

This approach entails two different and conflicting issues.

(a) The profit and loss account bears the cost of the economic benefits consumed, as measured by the enhanced depreciation charge based on the revalued figure for the tangible fixed asset.

(b) Distributable profits should not be prejudiced by the additional depreciation caused by the revaluation.

The remedy to this problem is to make an annual transfer from revaluation reserve to profit and loss account covering the amount for the addition depreciation caused by the revaluation. This is permitted by Companies Act 1985 and also represents best practice. This is illustrated in the example below.

3.8 Example: impact of revaluation on depreciation

Kevin Ltd acquires a buffing machine costing £100,000 on 1 July 20X4, which it depreciates at 10% straight line. The company policy is to charge a full year's depreciation in the year of acquisition but none in the year of disposal.

When the directors came to prepare the accounts for the year ended 31 December 20X7, the directors decided to obtain a full professional valuation, to be incorporated into the financial statements.

Yasmin, Nicole and Associates, Chartered Surveyors, valued the asset at £108,000.

It is now 31 December 20X9. Show the entries in the relevant accounts in the book of Kevin Ltd.

Solution

PLANT AND EQUIPMENT

		£			£
1.7.X4	Cost of buffing machine	100,000	31.12.X7	Balance c/d	108,000
31.12.X7	Revaluation reserve (W3)	8,000			
		108,000			108,000
1.1.X8	Balance b/d	108,000			

PROVISION FOR DEPRECIATION

		£			£
1.7.X7	Revaluation reserve (W3)	40,000	31.12.X4	Charge for year (W1)	10,000
			31.12.X5	Charge for year (W1)	10,000
			31.12.X6	Charge for year (W1)	10,000
			31.12.X7	Charge for year (W1)	10,000
		40,000			40,000
			31.12.X8	Charge for year (W2)	18,000
			31.12.X9	Charge for year (W2)	18,000

DEPRECIATION CHARGE

		£			£
31.12.X4	Provision (W1)	10,000	31.12.X4	Tfr to P+L a/c	10,000
31.12.X5	Provision (W1)	10,000	31.12.X5	Tfr to P+L a/c	10,000
31.12.X6	Provision (W1)	10,000	31.12.X6	Tfr to P+L a/c	10,000
31.12.X7	Provision (W1)	10,000	31.12.X7	Tfr to P+L a/c	10,000
31.12.X8	Provision (W2)	18,000	31.12.X8	Tfr to P+L a/c	18,000
31.12.X9	Provision (W2)	18,000	31.12.X9	Tfr to P+L a/c	18,000

REVALUATION RESERVE

		£			£
31.12.X8	Add'l depn to P+L a/c	8,000	31.12.X7	Adj. On buffing machine (W3)	48,000
31.12.X9	Add'l depn to P+L a/c	8,000			

Note: These adjustments go directly to P+L reserve, avoiding the current year's P+L account.	*Note:* This adjustment will be done via STRGL.

PROFIT AND LOSS RESERVE (depreciation adjustments only)

			£
	31.12.X8	Depn adj	8,000
	31.12.X9	Depn adj	8,000

BPP
PROFESSIONAL EDUCATION

Workings

1   £100,000 ÷ 10 years = £10,000 per annum.

2   £108,000 ÷ 6 years = 18,000 per annum.

3   *Revaluation of buffing machine*

	£
Cost	100,000
Accumulated depreciation to 31.12.X7	(40,000)
Net book value at 31.12.X7	60,000
Revaluation increase	48,000
Valuation as at 31.12.X7	108,000

Note that the concept of 'split depreciation' is not acceptable ie. the charge for the year may not be split between a portion based on historical cost and a portion based on the revaluation increase with these being debited to profit and loss account and revaluation reserve, respectively.

3.9 Example: Revaluation movements

The following details relate to Moggy Ltd which has a December year end.

• *Year ended 31 December 20X0:*	Acquired a building for £100 million Depreciation; 5% straight line
• *31 December 20X5:*	A professional valuation was obtained in the amount of £42 million.
• *31 December 20X8:*	Due to improved economic circumstances, the value of the building increased to £132 million.
• *31 December 20Y1:*	An interim valuation of £30 million.

Identify the adjustments required and indicate what statements would be affected.

Solution

20X0 to 20X5

- Annual depreciation charge £5m (£100m × 5%)
- Recognised via the profit and loss account.

31 December 20X5

	£m
Cost	100
Accumulated depreciation (£5m × 6 years)	(30)
Net book value	70
Revalued amount 20X5	42
Revaluation loss charged to profit and loss account	28

20X6 to 20X8

- Annual depreciation of £42m ÷ 14 = £3m
- Processed through the profit and loss account.

31 December 20X8

	£m
Previous revalued amount	42
Accumulated depreciation (£3m × 3 years)	(9)
Carrying value before 20X8 valuation	33
New valuation 20X8	132
Revaluation gain 20X8	99

The portion of the gain that in effect reverses the prior revaluation loss should be credited to profit and loss account, ie restores the asset to depreciated historical cost.

	£m
Historical cost	100
Less depreciation (£5m × 9 years)	(45)
Depreciated historical cost 30.12.X8	55

Hence:

	£m
Depreciated historical cost 30.12.X8	55
Carrying value before 20X8 revaluation	(33)
Portion of gain credited to profit and loss	22
Remainder of gain credited to revaluation reserve via STRGL	77
Revaluation gain 20X8, as above	99

Reconciliation of movements in reserves:

	£m
Depreciation – £5m × 6 years	30
– £3m × 3 years	9
Depreciation 20X0 to 20X8	39
Revaluation loss 31.12.X5	28
Revaluation gain 31.12.X8	(22)
Total debits to profit and loss account 20X0 to 20X8	45
Credit to revaluation reserve 31.21.X8	(77)
Net movement 20X0 to 20X8	(32)

Being:

	£m
Historical cost 20X0	100
Valuation 20X8	(132)
Net amount written up	(32)

20X9 to 20Y1

- Annual depreciation of £12m (£132m ÷ 11 years)
- Debited to profit and loss account.

And

- Annual transfer from revaluation reserve to profit and loss account of £7m. (£77m ÷ 11 years).
- Debit revaluation reserve, credit profit and loss account.

31 December 20Y1

	£m
Previous revalued amount	132
Accumulated depreciation (£12m × 3 years)	(36)
Carrying value before 20Y1 valuation	96
New valuation 20Y1	(30)
Revaluation loss 20Y1	66

The loss should be recognised in the following order:

(a)   In the STRGL until the carrying amount reaches depreciated historical cost.
(b)   In the profit and loss account.

Historical cost	100
Less Depreciation (£5m × 12 years)	(60)
Depreciated historical cost	40

Hence:

	£m
Carrying value before 20Y1 revaluation	96
Depreciated historical cost	(40)
Revaluation loss charged to STRGL	56
Revaluation loss taken to profit and loss account (balancing figure)	10
Revaluation loss 20Y1, as above	66

Proof

REVALUATION RESERVE

		£			£
31.12.X9	Release to P+L a/c	7	31.12.X8	Revaluation gain	77
31.12.Y0	Release to P+L a/c	7			
31.12.Y1	Release to P+L a/c	7			
31.12.Y1	Adj. revaluation 20Y1	56			
		77			77

3.10 Gains and losses on disposal

Basic requirements

Gains or losses on disposal of revalued tangible fixed assets should be accounted for in the profit and loss account of the period in which the disposal occurs.

The profit or loss is calculated as the difference between the

- net sale proceeds
- carrying amount, whether accounted for or
    - the historical cost accounting rules
    - alternative accounting rules

3.11 Credit balance on revaluation reserve

Where this relates to an asset which has been sold, this now becomes realised. It should therefore be transferred to profit and loss account.

Question

Disposal

Refer back to the Moggy Ltd example above in 3.9.

How would you account for the disposal if the building had been sold on 1 January 20Y1 for £35 million?

Answer

	£m
Valuation at 31.12.X8	132
Accumulated depreciation (£12m × 2*years)	24
Carrying value at 31.12.Y0	108
Proceeds of sale disposal 1.1.Y1	(35)
Loss on disposal	73

* No charge in year of disposal

- This loss should be processed to disposals account in the usual way.

- In addition, the balance on the revaluation reserve is now realised and can be taken to profit and loss account.

Adjustments

		DEBIT £m	CREDIT £m
DEBIT	Bank – proceeds of sale	35	
DEBIT	Accumulated depreciation	24	
DEBIT	Loss on disposal of fixed assets	73	
CREDIT	Fixed assets		132

Standard journal entry for disposal

DEBIT	Revaluation reserve (W1)	63	
CREDIT	Profit and loss reserve		63

Transfer of gain, now realised, to profit and loss reserves.

Working

REVALUATION RESERVE

		£m		£m
31.12.X9	Release to P+L a/c	7	31.12.X8 Revaluation gain	77
31.12.Y0	Release to P+L a/c	7		
31.12.Y1	Realised gain transferred to P+L a/c	63		
		77		77

Proof:

	£m
Profit realised per revaluation reserve	63
Loss on carrying value	(73)
Net loss	(10)

Being:

	£m
Historical cost	100
Less depreciation (£5m × 11 years)	(55)
Depreciation historical cost 1.1.Y1	45
Proceeds of disposal 1.1.Y1	(35)
Net loss, as above	10

Exam focus point

Where you get a numerical question, make sure you provide clear workings. Otherwise, in the words of the Paper 2.5 examiner:

> 'If an answer is wrong, it is unlikely that any marks can be awarded, as the marker will not be able to determine how the answer was arrived at.'

4 SSAP 19 Accounting for investment properties

 **FAST FORWARD**

SSAP 19 conflicts with the statutory requirement to depreciate all fixed assets with a finite useful economic life, by stating that **investment properties** need not ordinarily be depreciated.

The introduction of SSAP 12, with its requirement that all fixed assets including freehold buildings (though excluding freehold land) should be depreciated, caused a stir amongst property investment companies who feared that their reported profits would be severely reduced. The lobby was sufficiently strong to result in the publication of a separate standard for such properties.

4.1 Definition of investment properties

SSAP 19 defines an investment property as follows.

Key term

'.... An **investment property** is an interest in land and/or buildings:

(a)   In respect of which **construction** work and **development** have been **completed**

(b)   Which is held for its **investment potential**, any **rental income** being **negotiated** at **arm's length**.

'....The following are **exceptions** from the definition:

(a)   A property which is **owned** and **occupied** by a company for its **own purposes** is not an investment property.

(b)   A property **let to** and **occupied** by **another group company** is not an investment property for the purposes of its own accounts or the group accounts.'

Question   Investment properties

Lucy Limited and its subsidiaries are engaged in manufacturing of sweets and confectionery in Luton. It owns three properties which are held in a different ways.

(a)   **Broadacres** is its factory and office building.

(b)   **Kandikorna** is a retail premises let to Darren Limited a subsidiary which deals directly with the public.

(c)   **High Standards** is an office block which is let to a firm of accountants on an arms length rental basis.

Identify which properties are investment properties.

Answer

(a)   Broadacres is **not** an **investment property** because it is owned and **occupied** by Lucy Limited for its **own purposes**.

(b)   Kandikorna is **not** an **investment property** because it is let and **occupied** by **another group company**.

(c)   High Standards is an **investment property** because it **meets the criteria** for being classified as an investment property.

4.2 Justification for special approach to investment properties

Investment properties, as defined, are **not held** to be **consumed within** the **operations** of an enterprise, but instead for their **investment potential**.

The sale of an investment property is also unlikely to materially impact on the manufacturing trading operations of an enterprise.

What is of **prime importance** to users of accounts, regarding investment properties, is their **current value** and any **charges in their current value**, rather than a systematic calculation of annual depreciation.

4.3 Accounting treatment

Exam focus
point

> The December 2002 accounts preparation question involved a revaluation on investment property.

Per **SSAP 19**, investment properties should not be depreciated. Instead they should be **revalued annually** at their **open market value** and the aggregate **surplus** or **deficit** arising transferred to **investment revaluation reserve** (IRR) via the STRGL.

There may be circumstances where the **deficit** relating to an **individual investment property** is expected to be **permanent**. In such case, the deficit should be charged in the **profit and loss account** for the period.

Sometimes an investment property is held on a **lease** with a relatively **short unexpired term**, ie 20 years or less. Here the **carrying value** of lease must be **depreciated** over its **useful economic life** in accordance with the approach set out in **FRS 15**, the charge going to profit and loss account. The objective is to avoid the situation whereby the rentals received for such short leases are credited to profit and loss accounts whilst on the other hand any annual movements arising from revaluations are processed to investment revaluation reserve via STRGL. Under these requirements, both debit (depreciation) and credit (rental income) would be processed to the profit and loss account.

SSAP 19 specifies various criteria for determining open market value.

(a) The valuation **need not** be made by **qualified** or **independent valuers**.

(b) However, **disclosure** is required regarding:

  * The **names** and **qualifications** of the valuers
  * The **basis** of valuation used
  * **Whether** the person making the valuation is an **employee** or **officer** of the company.

(c) Sometimes investment properties represent a **substantial proportion** of the **total assets** of a **major enterprise** (eg a listed company). In these instances, their **valuation** would normally be carried out:

  (i) **Annually** by a **qualified person** having **recent experience** of valuing **similar properties**

  (ii) At least every **five years** by an **external valuer**.

Question		Revaluation reserve

Kikaround Limited acquired two investment properties in Manchester on 31 December 20X6.

	Keegan Towers £'000	Ferguson Towers £'000	Total £'000
Cost 31.12.X6	100	100	200
Valuation			
31.12.X7	70	140	210
31.12.X8	85	145	230
31.12.X9	120	70	190

The deficits on Keegan Towers arising on 31 December 20X7 and 20X8 are expected to be temporary whereas the deficit on Ferguson Towers arising on 31 December 20X9 is expected to be permanent.

Show the investment revaluation reserve for the years ended 31 December 20X7, 20X8 and 20X9.

Answer

INVESTMENT REVALUATION RESERVE

			£'000				£'000
31.12.X7	Keegan Towers		30	31.12.X7	Ferguson Towers		40
31.12.X7	Balance	c/d	10				
			40				40
31.12.X8	Balance	c/d	30	1.1.X8	Balance b/d		10
				31.12.X8	Keegan Towers		15
				31.12.X8	Ferguson Towers		5
			30				30
31.12.X9	Ferguson Towers*		75	1.1.X9	Balance b/d		30
31.12.X9	Balance	c/d	20	31.12.X9	Keegan Towers		35
				31.12.X9	Transfer to P+L a/c (Ferguson)		30
			95				95

* This could have been debited directly to profit and loss account with a transfer of £45,000 credits from IRR, to give effect to the £30,000 permanent deficit in respect of Ferguson Towers.

The carrying value of investment properties and investment revaluation reserve should be disclosed prominently in the accounts.

Investment properties can be owned by **ordinary trading companies as well as property investment companies**. If the assets of a company consist wholly or mainly of investment properties, this fact should also be disclosed.

Further points to note about SSAP 19 are as follows.

(a)   SSAP 19 acknowledges that exemption from depreciation for investment property is **contrary** to the depreciation rules in the **Companies Act 1985**. This departure is considered permissible because the Act states that compliance with the rules is a subordinate requirement to the **'overriding purpose of giving a true and fair view'**.

Where the true and fair override is invoked the notes to the accounts must disclose particulars of that departure, the reasons for it, and its effect. (See Chapter 3.)

(b)   SSAP 19 **does not apply to immaterial items**.

4.4 Disposals

SSAP 19 does not deal with the problem of accounting for the disposal of investment properties. However, FRS 3 *Reporting financial performance* **states the following** in relation to the disposal of any revalued fixed assets.

(a)   The **profit or loss** on **disposal** of an **asset** should be accounted for as the **difference** between the **sale proceeds** and the **net carrying amount**.

(b)   Any **revaluation surplus** remaining is now **realised**, so FRS 3 requires this to be transferred to the **profit and loss reserve**.

4.5 Diminution in value: Amendment to SSAP 19

Previously, under SSAP 19, any deficit on the IRR had to be taken to the profit and loss account. In other words, where the value of one or more investment property fell so far that the total IRR was insufficient to cover the deficit, then the excess was taken to the profit and loss account. SSAP 19 has now been amended as follows.

(a)   **Any diminution in value which is considered permanent should be charged to the profit and loss account.**

(b)   **Where diminution is temporary, a temporary IRR deficit is allowed.**

Question

Investment properties

Compare the accounting treatment of land and buildings as laid down by FRS 15 with the accounting treatment of investment properties as laid down by SSAP 19 and explain why a building owned for its investment potential should be accounted for differently from one which is occupied by its owners.

Answer

FRS 15 requires that all fixed assets should be depreciated, including freehold buildings. The only exception to this is freehold land which need only be depreciated if it is subject to depletion, for example, quarries or mines.

Where a property is revalued, depreciation should be charged so as to write off the new valuation over the estimated remaining useful life of the building.

SSAP 19, by contrast, recognises that there is a **conceptual difference** between *investment properties* and other fixed assets. Such properties are not depreciated and are carried in the balance sheet at open market value, re-assessed every year. An external valuation should be made at least once every five years.

Changes in the value of an investment property should not be taken to the profit and loss account. In other words, a company **cannot claim profit** on the **unrealised gains on revaluation** of such properties. The revaluation should be disclosed as a movement on an 'investment revaluation reserve'. Should this reserve show a **debit balance** (a loss) the **full amount** of the balance should be removed by charging it to the **profit and loss account**, unless the loss in value is considered to be temporary.

SSAP 19 acknowledges that there is a difference between investment properties and other fixed assets, including non-investment properties. Investment properties are held 'not for consumption in the business operations but as investments, the disposal of which would not materially affect any manufacturing or trading operations of the enterprise'.

It follows from this that the item of prime importance is the current value of the investment properties and changes in their current value rather than a calculation of systematic annual depreciation should be reported.

4.6 Issues relating to SSAP 19

SSAP 19 may in due course be amended to fit in with FRS 15 from which it is excluded. There are criticisms of the standard, mainly because it does give a clear definition of 'market value'. The Royal Institution of Chartered Surveyors defines *market value as the best price at which the sale of an interest in property might reasonably be expected to have been completed unconditionally for cash consideration on the date of valuation, assuming a 'willing seller'*. There is no mention of a 'willing buyer'.

This definition involves various difficulties.

(a)   **A market transaction** cannot take place without **both a seller and a buyer**.

(b)   The concept of 'willing seller' (but not a willing buyer) is largely theoretical in **depressed market conditions** where no willing seller really exists, only **unwilling** and even **forced sellers**.

(c)   This 'willing seller' concept inevitably leads to an **over-emphasis** on **comparable evidence**, forcing the valuer to **look backwards rather than forwards**.

(d)   Following on from (c), such an approach cannot cope with **specialised assets**, such as large regional shopping centres, for which **no ready market** exits.

The **deficiencies** in the **current definition** of open market value do **not** become **apparent in normal market conditions** where there is a liquid market in actively traded properties. However, at the **extremes of the cycle**, the current **definition** is quite **inadequate**, producing **over-valuation** in times of **boom** and **under-valuation** in times of **slump**, exacerbating market cycles in an extremely damaging way.

5 SSAP 4 Accounting for government grants

FAST FORWARD

Government grants can be **revenue-based** or **capital-based**. **Revenue grants** are credited to revenue in line with the revenue costs which they are intended to cover. **Capital grants** are credited to revenue over the useful life of the fixed asset for which they have been granted.

Key term

> **Government grants** are assistance provided by government to an enterprise.
>
> (a)   In the form of **cash** or **transfers** of **other assets**.
>
> (b)   In **return** for compliance with **certain conditions** relating to the operating activities of the enterprise.
>
> *Note*: (Items such as free consultancy services are not grants)

In practice, the range of grants available is quite wide and may change regularly, reflecting changes in policy introduced by various governments. You therefore need to understand the general principles included in SSAP4 and be able to apply them to any scenario you encounter in your exams.

Note that for these purposes, government includes local, national or international government, agencies and similar bodies.

Basic requirements

> (a)   Government grants should be recognised in the profit and loss account so as to match them with the expenditure towards which they are intended to contribute.
>
> (b)   Government grants should not be recognised in the profit and loss account until the conditions for this receipt have been compiled with and there is reasonable assurance that the grant will be received.

5.1 Revenue-based grants

These are given to **cover** some of the costs of various categories of **revenue expenditure**.

No particular problems arise in respect of revenue grants as they can be **credited** to **revenue** in the **same period** in which the **revenue expenditure** to which they **relate** is charged.

5.2 Capital-based grants

These are given to **cover** a **proportion** of the **costs of certain** items of **capital expenditure** (for example buildings, plant and machinery), and may be **treated** in a **number of ways**.

(a)   **Credit** the **full amount** of the capital grant to **profit and loss account**.

(b)   **Credit** the **full amount** of the capital grant to a **non distributable reserve**.

In (a) there is an immediate impact on earnings and in (b) there is no impact on earnings. In both cases the concept of matching costs and revenues is not applied. The grant, like the depreciation cost of fixed assets, should apply to the full life of the assets and so should be spread over that period of time.

SSAP 4 states that grants relating to fixed assets should be credited to revenue over the expected useful life of the assets and this can be done in one of two ways:

(a)   **By reducing the acquisition cost of the fixed asset** by the amount of the grant, and providing depreciation on the reduced amount.

(b)   By **treating** the amount of the grant **as a deferred credit and transferring a portion of it to revenue** annually.

5.3 Example: accounting for government grants

Needham Limited receives a government grant towards the cost of a new grinder.

- Cost £100,000.

- Grant = 20%

- Expected life = four years

- Residual value = Nil.

- Expected profits of the company, before accounting for depreciation on the new machine or the grant = £50,000 per annum over expected life of the grinder.

The two alternative approaches outlined in SSAP 4 would give different accounts presentations.

Solution

(a)   *Reducing the cost of the asset approach*

	Year 1 £	Year 2 £	Year 3 £	Year 4 £	Total £
Profits					
Profit before depreciation	50,000	50,000	50,000	50,000	200,000
Depreciation*	(20,000)	(20,000)	(20,000)	(20,000)	(80,000)
Profit	30,000	30,000	30,000	30,000	120,000

*The depreciation charge on a straight line basis, for each year, is ¼ of £[100,000 − 20,000 (20%)] = £20,000.

Balance sheet at year end (extract)

	£	£	£	£
Fixed asset at cost	80,000	80,000	80,000	80,000
Accumulated depreciation	(20,000)	(40,000)	(60,000)	(80,000)
Net book value	60,000	40,000	20,000	−

(b)   *Treating the grant as a deferred credit approach*

	Year 1 £	Year 2 £	Year 3 £	Year 4 £	Total £
Profits					
Profit before grant & dep'n	50,000	50,000	50,000	50,000	200,000
Depreciation	(25,000)	(25,000)	(25,000)	(25,000)	(100,000)
Grant	5,000	5,000	5,000	5,000	20,000
Profit	30,000	30,000	30,000	30,000	120,000

Balance sheet at year end (extract)

	Year 1	Year 2	Year 3	Year 4
Fixed asset at cost	100,000	100,000	100,000	100,000
Accumulated depreciation	(25,000)	(50,000)	(75,000)	(100,000)
Net book value	75,000	50,000	25,000	–
Deferred income				
Government grant				
deferred credit	15,000	10,000	5,000	–

Exam focus point

> The June 2003 exam asked candidates to consider whether the sliding scale repayment profile for a scenario given in the paper should be used in determining the deferred credit for a grant.

5.4 Assessment of alternative approaches

The annual profits under both methods are the same, and both methods apply the matching concept in arriving at the profit figure. Reducing the cost of the asset is simpler since, by reducing the depreciation charge, the amount of the grant is automatically credited to revenue over the life of the asset.

The **deferred credit method has the advantage of recording fixed assets at their actual cost, which allows for comparability and is independent of government policy**.

However, the netting off **method** may be in **conflict with the Companies Act 1985** in that the asset would no longer be carried at its purchase price or production cost.

Legal opinion confirms the unacceptability of the netting off approach and hence the credit method is preferable.

Where the second method is used then **the amount of the deferred credit, if material, should be shown separately in the balance sheet**. SSAP 4 states that it should not be shown as part of the shareholders' funds and it is suggested that the amount should appear under the heading of '**Accruals and deferred income**' in the balance sheet.

The SSAP requires the **disclosure of the accounting policy** adopted for government grants **and** also requires disclosure of:

(a)   The impact of government grants on the **company's profits** in the period **and/or** on its **financial position** generally.

(b)   Any **potential liability** to repay grants.

(c)   The nature of **government aid other than grants** which has materially affected profits in the period and an estimate of the impact, where possible.

A grant may be awarded to assist the financing of a project as a whole, where both capital and revenue expenditure are combined. In such cases the accounting treatment should be to match the grant with the relative proportions of revenue and capital expenditure incurred in the total project cost. For example, if two thirds of a project's costs are capital in nature and one third is revenue in nature, then any grant awarded against the whole project cost should be treated as one-third revenue-based and two thirds capital-based.

Exam focus point

> The June 2003 exam asked candidates to discuss whether a given company's policy for the treatment of government grants accords with the ASB *Statement of principles*.

Question
Government grant

Kaytal plc is to receive a relocation grant of 30% of total expenses incurred. In 20X8 the company incurred the following costs associated with the relocation.

	£'000
Capital cost of factory	2,000
Training costs	200
Removal/relocation costs	300
	2,500

Required

Show the treatment of the government grant for 20X8.

Answer

	£'000
Grant received = 30% × 2,500 =	750
Capital expenditure	2,000
Revenue expenditure	500
	2,500

$$\text{Revenue grant} = \frac{500}{2,500} \times 750 = \qquad 150$$

$$\text{Capital grant} = \frac{2,000}{2,500} \times 750 = \qquad 600$$

	750

	£'000	£'000
DEBIT Cash	750	
CREDIT P&L account		150
CREDIT Deferred income		600

Section summary

The following accounting treatments apply.

(a)   *Revenue-based grants*

      DEBIT   Cash

      CREDIT   P & L account

      In the period in which the revenue expenditure to which the grant relates is charged.

BPP
PROFESSIONAL EDUCATION

(b)   *Capital-based grants*

DEBIT   Cash
CREDIT   Accruals and deferred income

When the grant is received.

DEBIT   Accruals and deferred income
CREDIT   P & L account

Over the useful life of the related fixed asset.

Disclosure will be as follows.

(a)   *Balance sheet: deferred income note*

	£
Balance at 1.1.20X0	X
Grants received during year	X
Transferred to profit and loss account	(X)
Balance at 31.12.20X0	X

(b)   *Profit and loss account:* credit under 'other operating income'.

Exam focus point | A full question on tangible fixed assets might combine two or even all three of the standards covered here.

Chapter Roundup

- A number of accounting regulations on the valuation and disclosure of fixed assets are contained in the **Companies Act 1985**.

- In the case of **tangible fixed assets**, Companies Act requirements are supplemented by the provisions of FRS 15 *Tangible fixed assets.*

- FRS 15 lays down detailed requirements concerning the revaluation of fixed assets. Directors can no longer choose to revalue certain assets and not others.

- **SSAP 19** conflicts with the statutory requirement to depreciate all fixed assets with a finite useful economic life, by stating that **investment properties** need not ordinarily be depreciated.

- Government grants can be **revenue-based** or **capital-based**. **Revenue grants** are credited to revenue in line with the revenue costs which they are intended to cover. **Capital grants** are credited to revenue over the useful life of the fixed asset for which they have been granted.

Quick Quiz

1   Which of the following elements can be included in the production cost of a fixed asset?

   A   Labour
   B   Raw materials
   C   Electricity and fuel used
   D   Interest on loan taken out to finance production of the asset

2   Define depreciation.

3   When the method of depreciation is changed this constitutes a change of accounting policy and an adjustment should be made to the depreciation charged in previous year.

   True   ☐
   False ☐

4   When are investment properties (as defined by SSAP 19) subject to depreciation?

5   In which two ways can fixed asset grants be credited to revenue?

Answers to Quick Quiz

1   All of them. (see Paras 2.2 – 2.3.5.)

2   See Paragraph 2.5.1 for the FRS 15 definition.

3   False. This is a change of **accounting estimate**.

4   When the property is subject to a lease which has 20 years or less to run.

5   By reducing the cost of the asset, and therefore the depreciation, or by treating the grant as a **deferred credit** (see 5.2)

Now try the question below from the Exam Question Bank

Number	Level	Marks	Time
Q4	Full exam	25	45 mins

BPP
PROFESSIONAL EDUCATION

Fixed assets:
Intangible assets

Topic list	Syllabus reference
1 Intangible assets: Companies Act 1985 requirements	3 (b)
2 SSAP 13 *Accounting for research and development*	3 (b)
3 Goodwill: Introduction	3 (b)
4 FRS 10 *Goodwill and intangible assets*	3 (b)
5 FRS 11 *Impairment of fixed assets and goodwill*	3 (b)

Introduction

We will look at intangible assets in this chapter, the main categories of which are R & D costs and goodwill.

Accounting for research and development according to SSAP 13 is relatively straightforward, and has been covered in your Paper 1.1 studies.

The study material on goodwill is closely connected with the later chapters on group accounts. When you reach these chapters you should refer back to the coverage here on goodwill.

Study guide

- Discuss the nature and possible accounting treatments of both internally generated and purchased goodwill.

- Distinguish between goodwill and other intangible assets.

- Describe the criteria for the initial recognition and measurement of intangible assets.

- Describe the subsequent accounting treatment, including amortisation and the principle of impairment tests in relation to purchased goodwill.

- Describe the circumstances in which negative goodwill arises, and its subsequent accounting treatment and disclosure.

- Describe and apply the requirements of accounting standards on research and development.

- Define the recoverable amount of an asset; define impairment losses.

- Give examples of, and be able to identify, circumstances that may indicate that an impairment of fixed assets has occurred.

- Describe what is meant by an income generating unit.

- State the basis on which impairment losses should be allocated.

- Allocate a given impairment loss to the assets of an income generating unit.

Exam guide

Goodwill is certain to feature in the group accounting questions in the exam. You need to be able to account for goodwill but also understand the reasons for its accounting treatment; FRS 11 could come up as the second part of a question.

1 Intangible assets: Companies Act 1985 requirements

FAST FORWARD

The Companies Act 1985 sets out the **statutory accounting requirements** relating to **intangible fixed assets** and **investments**. These requirements are supplemented in the case of **development costs** by SSAP 13, in the case of **goodwill** by FRS 10 and in the case of **impairment** by FRS 11.

The **statutory balance sheet** format lists the following intangible fixed assets (item BI in the format).

(a)   **Development costs**
(b)   **Concessions, patents, licences, trade marks** and similar rights and assets
(c)   **Goodwill**
(d)   **Payments on account**

1.1 Patents and trade marks

Concessions, patents, licences, trade marks etc should only be **treated**, and **disclosed**, as **assets** if they were **either**:

(a)   **Acquired** for **valuable consideration**
(b)   **Created** by the **company itself.**

1.2 Development costs

Development costs, **may only be treated as an asset** in the balance sheet (rather than being written off immediately) **in 'special circumstances'**. The Act does not define these circumstances and this is a case where a SSAP goes further than statute. **SSAP 13** (see below) lays down **strict criteria** for determining when such expenditure may be **treated** as an **asset**. The **Act merely states** that, if it is **so treated**, the **following disclosures** must be made by **way of note**:

    (a)   The **period** over which the amount of the **costs originally capitalised** is **being** or is to be **written off**

    (b)   The **reasons** for **capitalising** the **development costs**

1.3 Goodwill

The Act implicitly makes a **distinction between inherent goodwill and purchased goodwill.** The distinction will be explained when we review FRS 10 *Goodwill and intangible assets.* For now, please remember that **the Act does not permit inherent goodwill to be included as an asset** in the balance sheet. The **difficulties** of **valuing inherent goodwill** are in any case **so great** that very few companies have ever carried it in their balance sheets. **However**, several **listed companies** have **capitalised brands** which were **developed in-house**.

Purchased goodwill may be treated as an asset in the balance sheet. If it is so treated (rather than being written off immediately):

    (a)   It must be **written off systematically** over a **period chosen by the directors**

    (b)   The period chosen must **not exceed** the **useful economic life** of the goodwill

    (c)   **Disclosure** should be made of the **period chosen** and of the **reasons** for choosing that period.

This statutory requirement to amortise any goodwill capitalised does not extend to goodwill arising on consolidation. Even so, **companies** have to **amortise consolidation** goodwill to comply with the **stricter requirements of FRS 10**. You should note that FRS 10 is stricter than CA 1985 in the case of goodwill on acquisition, as we will see below.

2 SSAP 13 Accounting for research and development

FAST FORWARD

SSAP 13 is a standard which has been around for some time and is generally accepted and well understood. It distinguishes between research expenditure and development expenditure and lays down strict criteria for the capitalisation of development expenditure.

In many companies, especially those which produce food, or 'scientific' products such as medicines, or 'high technology' products, the expenditure on research and development (R & D) is considerable. **When R & D is a large item of cost, its accounting treatment may have a significant influence on the profits of a business and its balance sheet valuation.**

Exam focus point

SSAP 13 might feature in a small way as part of a consolidation question, it is very unlikely to form a major question.

The application of SSAP 13 *Accounting for research and development* was tested in the June 2002 paper.

Knowledge brought forward from earlier studies

SSAP 13 Accounting for research and development

Definitions

- **Pure/basic research** is experimental/theoretical work with no commercial end in view and no practical application.

- **Applied research** is original investigation directed towards a specific practical aim/objective.

- **Development** is the use of scientific/technical knowledge in order to produce new/substantially improved **materials**, **devices**, **processes** etc.

Accounting treatment

- **Pure and applied research** should be **written off** as incurred.

- **Development expenditure** should be **written off** in year of expenditure, *except* in certain circumstances when it *may* be **deferred to future periods**.

S	Separately defined project
E	Expenditure separately identifiable
C	Commercially viable
T	Technically feasible
O	Overall profit expected
R	Resources exist to complete the project

- Show deferred development costs as an **intangible asset amortised** from the beginning of commercial production, **systematically** by reference to sales, etc.

- Deferred costs should be **reviewed annually**; where the above criteria no longer apply, write off the cost immediately.

- Development expenditure previously written off **can be reinstated** if the **uncertainties** which led to it being written off **no longer apply**.

- **R & D fixed assets** should be **capitalised** and **written off** over their estimated **economic lives**.

- Deferral of costs should be **applied consistently** to all projects.

- SSAP 13 does not apply to:

  - Fixed assets used for R&D (except amortisation)
  - The cost of locating mineral deposits in extractive industries
  - Expenditure where there is a firm contract for reimbursement

Disclosure

- R & D activities should be disclosed in the **directors' report**.

- **Private companies** outside groups which include a plc are **exempt** from disclosing R & D expenditures (except amortisation) if they would meet the **criteria** for a **medium-sized company** × 10.

- *Disclose:*

  - **Movements** on deferred development expenditure
  - **R & D charged** to the P & L a/c analysed between **current year expenditure** and **amortisation**
  - An accounting **policy** note

The importance of R & D disclosures was emphasised in another **survey** of what **users really needed** in financial statements.

(a) UK institutional investors said the **top requirement** was **future prospects and plans** (84%). R & D is seen to form a crucial quantitative element of prospects and plans.

(b) When specifically asked about R & D, 64% of UK investors said the data was very, or extremely, important to them.

Unfortunately, the top companies analysed failed dismally to provide the information required. There is a wide variety of treatment and information given on R & D and improvements are required in the reporting of R & D.

Question

Research and development

In connection with SSAP 13 *Accounting for research and development*:

(a) Define 'applied research' and 'development'.

(b) Explain why it is considered necessary to distinguish between applied research and development expenditure and how this distinction affects the accounting treatment.

(c) State whether the following items are included within the SSAP 13 definition of research and development, and give your reasons:

    (i)   Market research
    (ii)   Testing of pre-production prototypes
    (iii)   Operational research
    (iv)   Testing in search of process alternatives

Answer

(a) ***Applied research*** expenditure is expenditure on **original investigations** which are carried out in order to gain **new scientific or technical knowledge**, but which also have a specific practical aim or objective. An example might be research into a disease with the intention of finding a cure or a vaccine.

Development expenditure is expenditure on the application of existing scientific or technical knowledge in order to produce **new or substantially improved materials, devices, products, processes, systems or services** prior to the commencement of **commercial production**. The costs of developing a prototype would be development expenditure.

(b) SSAP 13 considers that:

'pure and **applied research** can be regarded as part of a **continuing operation** required to maintain a company's business and its competitive position. In general, **no one particular period** rather than any other will be expected to **benefit** and **therefore** it is appropriate that these **costs** should be **written off** as they are **incurred**.'

This has the affect that applied research costs must be written off as incurred but **development expenditure can be deferred** (that is, capitalised as an intangible asset) and **amortised** over the life of the product, service, process or system developed. This treatment is only permissible if the project meets **certain criteria** designed to ensure that deferral is prudent.

(c) (i) **Market research** is **not normally** considered to be **research and development** activity. It is **specifically excluded in the SSAP**. This is presumably because it does not depart from routine activity and it does not contain an appreciable element of innovation.

(ii) **Testing of prototypes** is included in SSAP 13's list of activities normally to be considered as **research and development**. A prototype must be constructed and tested before full-scale production can be risked and so it is an **essential stage** in the **development process**.

(iii) '**Operational research not tied** to a **specific research** and development activity' is an activity which SSAP 13 considers should **not normally** be **included in research and development**. 'Operational research' is presumably used here to denote the **branch of applied mathematics** which includes techniques such as linear programming and network analysis. The implication is that routine use of such techniques (to improve production efficiency, for example) does **not fall within the ambit of SSAP 13**, in spite of the use of the word 'research'.

(iv) 'Testing in search for, or evaluation of, product, service or process alternatives' is considered to be research and development work by SSAP 13. It would fall within the definition of applied research.

Question
Development expenditure

R.U. Welle Pharmaceuticals plc incurs the following expenditure in years 20X4-20X8.

	Research £'000	Development £'000
20X4	40	65
20X5	45	70
20X6	49	–
20X7	41	–
20X8	43	–

You are told that R.U. Welle Pharmaceuticals plc capitalises development expenditure when appropriate. The item developed in 20X4 and 20X5 goes on sale on 1 January 20X6 and it will be three years from then until any competitor is expected to have a similar product on the market.

Required

Show the profit and loss account and balance sheet extracts for all five years.

Answer

PROFIT AND LOSS ACCOUNT (EXTRACTS)

	20X4 £'000	20X5 £'000	20X6 £'000	20X7 £'000	20X8 £'000
Research expenditure	40	45	49	41	43
Amortisation of development costs	–	–	45	45	45

BALANCE SHEET (EXTRACT)

	20X4 £'000	20X5 £'000	20X6 £'000	20X7 £'000	20X8 £'000
Intangible fixed assets					
Development costs	65	135	135	135	135
Amortisation	–	–	(45)	(90)	(135)
Net book value	65	135	90	45	–

3 Goodwill: Introduction

3.1 Nature of goodwill

FAST FORWARD By definition, goodwill is an asset which **cannot be realised separately** from the **business as a whole**.

Key term

> **Goodwill** is the difference between:
>
> (a)   the aggregate fair value of the net assets of a business
> (b)   the value of the business as a whole.

There are many factors which may explain why goodwill arises. Examples are:

- skilled management team
- good labour relations
- strategic location
- good customer relations

These factors are **intangible** and it is **difficult** to place a **money value** on them. Until **recently**, it was **not usual** to show **goodwill** as an **asset** in the balance sheet. Any **amount** at which it was valued was **considered** to be **arbitrary** and **subject to fluctuations**.

3.2 Potential factors giving rise to goodwill

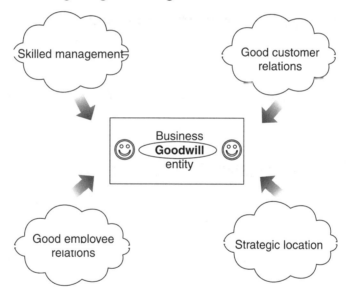

3.3 Inherent goodwill and purchased goodwill

Exam focus point

> FRS 10 *Goodwill and intangible assets* is an attractive area for examiners.

Some form of goodwill is likely to exist in every business. However, the **only circumstances** when **goodwill** is **valued** and may be **disclosed** as an **asset** in the balance sheet is when one **business acquires another as a going concern**. This is because there is then a **positive indication** available of the **value of goodwill acquired**. This is known as **purchased goodwill**.

Goodwill which is presumed to exist, but which has not been evidenced in a purchases transaction, is called non purchased or inherent goodwill.

3.4 Possible accounting treatments for inherent goodwill

There are two possible approaches to accounting for inherent goodwill.

    (a)   Ignore inherent goodwill and make no entries in the accounting records.

    (b)   Estimate the value of inherent goodwill and include this in the records and accounts of the business.

However, remember that FRS 10 stipulates that **inherent goodwill** should **not be recognised** in the financial statements. Its **value cannot** be **measured** with sufficient **reliability** because of the **subjectivity** involved. **It should therefore be ignored.**

3.5 Possible accounting treatments for purchased goodwill

A **wide variety of accounting treatments** are possible regarding **purchased goodwill**.

    (a)   Capitalise goodwill as an **asset** but **amortise** it over its **estimated useful life.**

    (b)   Capitalise **goodwill** as an **asset** but **write down** the value if **impairment becomes evident.**

    (c)   **Write off the entire amount** immediately against:

        (i)   Income
        (ii)   Reserves

    (d)   Show goodwill as a **continuing** and **separately identifiable deduction from shareholders' funds** (the '**dangling debit**' method).

3.6 The case for amortisation approach

    (a)   Goodwill is an asset which at the **date of acquisition** has a **definite value to the business**.

    (b)   This asset is a measure of the extent to which the **earnings** of the **purchased business** will **exceed** those which could be **expected** from the **use of its identifiable assets**. Consequently, it should be **amortised** so as to **match costs against income** (the accruals concept). This is one of the views adopted by FRS 10 *Goodwill and intangible assets*.

3.7 The case for immediate write-off approach

    (a)   (i)   Writing off purchased goodwill immediately would be **consistent with the treatment of inherent goodwill.**

        (ii)   Alternatively, the purchased goodwill becomes **indistinguishable from the total goodwill** of the group and should therefore be written off.

        (iii)   Goodwill might be treated as an asset, but too much **uncertainty exists** over its **value** and **economic life**, therefore **prudence** dictates that it should be written off.

    (b)   (i)   Goodwill is **not an asset** as such and therefore to show it as an asset would be misleading.

        (ii)   Both **inherent** and **purchased** goodwill would be **excluded** (**consistency**, as in (c) above).

        (iii)   **Analysts** may treat goodwill **as they like if it is not amortised.**

Basic requirements

    (a)   Purchased goodwill should be capitalised and classified as an asset on the balance sheet.
    (b)   It should be amortised on a systematic basis over its useful economic life.

3.8 Negative goodwill

Negative goodwill arises when the price paid for a business is less than the fair value of the separable net assets acquired, for example, if the vendor **needed cash quickly** and was forced to sell at a **bargain price**.

4 FRS 10 Goodwill and intangible assets

FAST FORWARD

FRS 10 states that **purchased, positive goodwill** and purchased intangible assets or internally-developed intangible assets which have a **readily ascertainable market value** should be capitalised and amortised over their **useful economic life**.

4.1 Overview

FRS 10 *Goodwill and intangible assets* was published in December 1997. The requirements of the FRS **apply to all intangible assets except those specifically addressed by another accounting standard**, eg SSAP 13. Oil and gas exploration and development costs are also exempt.

FRS 10 applies to **all financial statements except** those entities applying the Financial Reporting Standard for Smaller Entities **(FRSSE)** which do not prepare consolidated accounts.

Although FRS 10 is framed around the purchase of a subsidiary undertaking, it also applies to the acquisition of unincorporated entities.

4.2 Objective of FRS 10

The objectives stated by FRS 10 are to ensure that:

(a) **Capitalised goodwill** and **intangible assets** are charged in the **P&L account** as far as possible in the **periods** in which they are **depleted.**

(b) **Sufficient information** is **disclosed** in the financial statements to enable users to **determine** the **impact of goodwill** and **intangible assets** on the **financial position** and **performance** of the **reporting entity.**

4.3 Definitions

FRS 10 introduces a variety of new definitions, some of which relate to terms used above.

Key terms

- **Class of intangible assets**: a group of intangible assets that have **similar nature** or **function** in the business of the entity.

- **Identifiable assets and liabilities**: the assets and liabilities of an entity that are capable of being **disposed** of or **settled separately**, without disposing of a business of the entity.

- **Purchased goodwill**: the **difference** between:
    - the fair value of the consideration paid for an acquired entity
    - the aggregate of the fair values of that entity's identifiable assets and liabilities.

- **Residual value**: the **net realisable value** of an asset at the **end of its useful economic life**. Residual values are based on prices at the date of acquisition (or revaluation) of the asset and **do not take account** of **expected future price changes**.

- **Useful economic life:** the useful economic life of an **intangible asset** is the **period** over which the entity expects to **derive economic benefit** from that asset.

    The useful economic life of **purchased goodwill** is the period over which the **value** of the **underlying business** is expected to **exceed** the values of its **identifiable net assets**.   *(FRS 10)*

4.4 Ascertaining goodwill

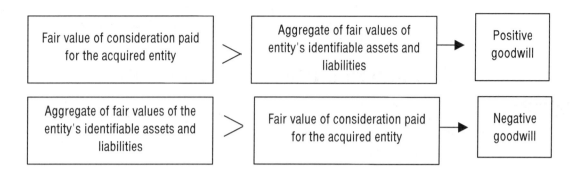

4.5 Example

AJ Limited acquires 80% of VJ Limited at 31 December 20X8.

AJ Limited originally made an initial offer of £75,000 which was rejected. A subsequent offer of £95,000 was however accepted. The total value of VJ Limited is £100,000. Identify the goodwill arising under these two scenarios.

Solution

	Scenario 1 £	Scenario 2 £
Fair value of consideration	75,000	95,000
Fair value of VJ Limited's net assets – 80% of £100,000	(80,000)	80,000
Negative goodwill	5,000	
Positive goodwill		15,000

FRS 10 also includes definitions of the following terms, which are also defined in FRS 11.

- Impairment
- Intangible assets
- Net realisable value
- Readily ascertainable market value
- Recoverable amount
- Value in use

Purchased goodwill is also defined by FRS 11, but the definition given here is fuller.

4.6 Initial recognition and measurement

4.6.1 Goodwill

Positive purchased goodwill should be capitalised and classified as an asset on the balance sheet.

Internally generated goodwill should not be capitalised..

4.6.2 Intangible assets

An intangible asset **purchased separately** from a business should be **capitalised at cost**. Examples of such assets include patents, copyrights and licences.

Where an **intangible** asset is **acquired as part of the acquisition of a business** the treatment **depends** on whether its **value** can be **measured reliably** on its initial recognition.

(a)   If its value **can be measured reliably**, it should initially be **recorded at its fair value**. (The fair value should **not create** or **increase** any **negative goodwill** arising on the acquisition **unless** the asset has a **readily ascertainable market value**.)

(b)   If the value of the asset cannot be measured reliably, the intangible asset must be subsumed within the amount of the purchase price attributed to goodwill.

4.6.3 Internally developed intangibles

FRS 10 states that companies may **capitalise non-purchased** ('internally-developed') **intangibles** but **only if they have a** 'readily ascertainable market value'. This is an important definition that **requires that:**

(a)   The asset belongs to **a group of homogenous assets** (ie they are all of the same kind), that are **equivalent** in **all material respects**.

(b)   There is an **active market** for that **group of assets**, evidenced by **frequent transactions**.

Examples given by FRS 10 of intangibles that may meet these conditions include certain **operating licences**, **franchises** and **quotas**.

FRS 10 also suggests **certain intangibles** that are **not equivalent** in all material aspects, are **indeed unique** and so **do not have readily identifiable market values**.

- Brands
- Publishing titles
- Patented drugs
- Engineering design patents

Hence, FRS 10 effectively precludes the recognition of most internally developed intangibles in financial accounts.

Once they have passed the tests for recognition, FRS 10 requires that intangible assets be treated in exactly the way as goodwill.

4.7 Approach to amortisation and impairment

The FRS 10 approach to amortisation reflects the wish to charge the profit and loss account only to the extent that the **carrying value** of the asset is **not supported** by the **current value** of the asset **within the acquired business**.

The approach is based on a **combination** of:

- **Amortising** over a **limited period** on a **systematic basis**
- An **annual impairment review** (see later coverage)

The first task is to **decide whether** or not the **goodwill** or **intangible** has a **limited useful economic life**.

You may find the following diagram helpful in clarifying the approach outlined above.

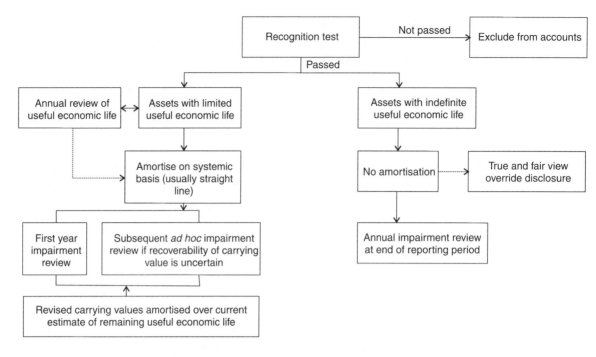

4.8 Assets with a limited useful economic life

4.8.1 Amortisation

FRS 10 states that, where goodwill and intangible assets are regarded as having **limited useful economic lives** they should be **amortised on a systematic basis over those lives**.

FRS 10 gives **little guidance** on how to **predict** an asset's **useful economic life**, which can be very difficult for goodwill and intangibles as it is **impossible** to **see** them **actually wearing out**. It does, however, give **examples** of **relevant considerations**, which include certain **economic** and **legal factors** relating to the asset. An intangible may, for example, be linked to a product with a **specific lifespan**, or there may be time periods attached to **legal rights** (eg patents). It may also be necessary to look at the nature of the business and of the market in which it operates.

There is a **basic assumption** that the **useful economic lives** of **purchased goodwill** and **intangible assets** are limited to periods of **20 years or less**. However, this **presumption** may be **rebutted** and a useful economic life regarded as a longer period or indefinite only if:

(a) The **durability** of the **acquired business** or **intangible asset** can be demonstrated and justifies estimating the **useful economic life** to **exceed 20 years**.

(b) The goodwill or intangible asset is capable of **continued measurement** (so that annual impairment reviews will be feasible).

Question

Goodwill

The circumstances where an indefinite useful economic life longer than 20 years may be legitimately presumed are limited. What factors determine the durability of goodwill?

Answer

FRS 10 mentions the following.

(a)   The **nature** of the business
(b)   The **stability** of the industry in which the acquired business operates

(c)   Typical **lifespans** of the products to which the goodwill attaches

(d)   The extent to which the acquisition **overcomes** market entry **barriers** that will continue to exist

(e)   The expected future **impact** of **competition** on the business

Uncertainty about the **length** of the **useful economic** life is **not a good reason** for choosing one that is **unrealistically short** or for adopting a **20 year** useful economic life **by default**.

In amortising an **intangible asset**, a **residual value** may be assigned to that asset only if such residual value can be **measured reliably**. In practice, the **residual value** of an **intangible asset** is **often insignificant**.

No residual value may be assigned to **goodwill**.

The method of amortisation should be chosen to reflect the **expected pattern of depletion** of the goodwill or intangible asset. A **straight-line method should be chosen unless another method can be demonstrated to be more appropriate**.

Whatever the **useful economic life** chosen, the company should be able to justify it. It **should be reviewed annually and revised if appropriate**.

4.8.2 Impairment review

In addition to the amortisation, the asset should be reviewed for impairment:

(a)   At the end of the first full financial year following the acquisition ('**the first year review**').

(b)   In **other periods** if events or changes in **circumstances** indicate that the **carrying values may not be recoverable**.

If an impairment is identified at the time of the first year review, this impairment is likely to reflect:

(a)   An **overpayment**

(b)   An **event** that occurred **between** the **acquisition** and the **first year review**

(c)   **Depletion** of the acquired goodwill or intangible asset between the acquisition and the first year review that exceeds the amount recognised through amortisation

The requirements of FRS 10 are such that the recognition of an **impairment loss** must be **justified** in the same way as the absence of an impairment loss, is by looking at **expected future cash flows**.

Goodwill and intangible assets that are **amortised** over a period **exceeding 20 years** from the date of acquisition should be **reviewed for impairment at the end of each reporting period**.

Where the **impairment review** indicates a **diminution** in **value**, the goodwill and intangible assets must be **written down accordingly**. The **revised carrying value** should be **amortised** over the current estimate of the **remaining useful economic life**.

4.9 Assets with an indefinite useful economic life

4.9.1 No amortisation

Where goodwill and intangible assets are regarded as having **indefinite useful economic lives**, they **should not be amortised**.

'Indefinite' is not the same as 'infinite', it means merely that no limit can be fixed for it.

Important

> If the option not to amortise is taken, this constitutes a departure from the Companies Act and will need to be justified by invoking the **true and fair override**.

4.9.2 Impairment review

Goodwill and intangible assets that are **not amortised** (because their useful economic life is deemed to be indefinite) should be **reviewed for impairment at the end of each reporting period**.

If an **impairment loss** is **recognised**, the **revised carrying value**, if being amortised, should be **amortised** over the **current estimate** of the **remaining useful economic life**.

If **goodwill** arising on **consolidation** is found to be **impaired**, the carrying amount of the **investment** held in the accounts of the **parent undertaking** should also be **reviewed for impairment**.

The emphasis on impairment reviews is a key feature of FRS 10. The ASB believes that a formal requirement to monitor the value of acquired goodwill and intangible assets using standardised methods and to report any losses in the financial statements will **enhance** the **quality** of the **information** provided to **users of financial statements**.

4.9.3 Reversal of impairment

Normally, once an impairment review has identified a loss, this cannot be restored at a later date. However, **if the loss was caused by an *external* event that later reversed in a way that was not foreseen, the original impairment loss may be restored**. An example of this might be: if a direct competitor came on to the market, leading to an impairment loss, and then the competitor did not survive or produced a different product from the one originally envisaged.

4.9.4 Updating of impairment reviews

After the first period, the reviews need only be updated. If expectations of **future cash flows** and **discount rates** have **not changed significantly**, the updating procedure will be **relatively quick** to **perform**.

If there have been **no adverse changes** in the **key assumptions** and **variables**, or if there was previously substantial leeway between the carrying value and estimated value in use, it **may** even **be possible** to ascertain immediately that an **income generating unit** is **not impaired**.

4.10 Revaluation of goodwill

Goodwill may not be revalued, except in the circumstances described above, ie the **reversal of an impairment**.

If an **intangible asset** has a **readily ascertainable market value**, it may be **revalued** to its **market value**.

Future amortisation should always be made on the revalued amount, just like depreciation for a revalued tangible fixed asset.

Question   Impairment loss

Honeybun Ltd has an income-generating unit with the following details:

(a)   Carrying value of £4,000,000 at 31 December 20X7. This carrying value comprises £1,000,000 relating to goodwill and £3,000,000 relating to net assets.

(b)   The goodwill is not being amortised as its useful life is believed to be indefinite.

(c)   In 20X8, changes in the regulatory framework surrounding its business mean that the income-generating unit has a value in use of £3,200,000. As a result of losses, net assets have decreased to £2,800,000 reducing the total carrying value of the unit to £3,800,000 which has thus suffered an impairment loss of £600,000. This is charged to the profit and loss account. The carrying value of goodwill is reduced to £400,000.

(d)   In 20X9 the company develops a new product with the result that the value in use of the income-generating unit is now £3,400,000. Net tangible assets have remained at £2,800,000.

Can all or any of the impairment loss be reversed?

Answer

No. Despite the value in use of the business unit now being £3,400,000 compared to its carrying value of £3,200,000, it is not possible to reverse £200,000 of the prior year's impairment loss of £600,000 since the reason for the increase in value of the business unit (the launch of the new product) is not the same as the reason for the original impairment loss (the change in the regulatory environment in which the business operates).

4.11 Negative goodwill

4.11.1 How negative goodwill arises

As mentioned earlier, negative goodwill arises when the fair value of the net assets acquired is more than the fair value of the consideration. In other words, the investor has got a bargain.

4.11.2 Subsequent accounting treatment

FRS 10 states that to ensure that any negative goodwill is justified:

(a)   **The investee's assets should be checked for impairment**

(b)   **The liabilities checked for understatement**.

        If indeed any negative goodwill remains after these tests, it needs to be disclosed consistently with positive goodwill.

Rather than being shown on the bottom half of the balance sheet as a capital reserve - as was required by SSAP 22 - **it is now disclosed in the intangible fixed assets category, directly under positive goodwill, ie as a 'negative asset'.** A sub-total of the net amount of positive and negative goodwill should be shown on the face of the balance sheet.

This presentation may seem a little odd. However, the ASB argues that negative goodwill does not meet the definition of a liability under the *Statement of Principles* and that this treatment is consistent with that of positive goodwill.

4.12 Transfers to profit and loss account

Negative goodwill should be **recognised in the profit and loss account in the periods when the non-monetary assets acquired are depreciated or sold.**

There are two important points to note.

(a)   It would be strange for the investor to pay less than its fair value for the monetary items acquired. The value of cash, for example, is pretty universal. Therefore, it is more **likely that the negative goodwill represents a shortfall in the value of the non-monetary items**.

(b) The **benefit** of the 'bargain' of getting these non-monetary items at less than fair value **will only be realised when the non-monetary items themselves are realised**.

[ie it is the non-monetary assets (fixed assets, stock etc) that have been bought on the cheap, effectively at a discount (negative goodwill). Therefore, carry the discount (negative goodwill) in the balance sheet until the relevant assets are sold, or depreciated. Then transfer the relevant chunk of discount (negative goodwill) from the balance sheet to the profit and loss account.]

Hence, any negative goodwill should be credited to the **profit and loss account** only when the **non-monetary assets themselves** are realised, and this is when they are either **depreciated or sold**.

FRS 10 also requires any **remaining goodwill** in **excess** of fair values of the non-monetary assets acquired should be recognised in the **profit and loss account** in the **periods expected to be benefited**.

Question   Negative goodwill

Kewcumber plc acquired its investment in Marrow Ltd during the year ended 31 December 20X8. The goodwill on acquisition was calculated as follows.

	£'000	£'000
Cost of investment		400
Fair value of net assets acquired (remaining useful life - 7 years)		
Fixed assets	700	
Stock	100	
Non-monetary assets	800	
Net monetary assets	200	
		(1,000)
Negative goodwill		(600)

Required

Calculate the amount relating to negative goodwill as reflected in the profit and loss account and balance sheet for the year ended 31 December 20X8.

Answer

Amortisation in the profit and loss account for 20X8

Non-monetary assets recognised through the profit and loss account for the year ended 31 December 20X8:

	£'000
Stock (all sold)	100
Depreciation (£700,000 ÷ 7)	100
Non-monetary assets recognised this year	200
Total non-monetary assets at acquisition	800
∴ Proportion recognised this year	¼

Hence:

	£'000
Negative goodwill arising on acquisition	600
Proportion released to profit and loss account for year to 31.12.X8 (¼)	(150)
Balance at 31.12.X8, shown on balance sheet as deduction from positive goodwill	450

The balance of £450,000 will be carried forward and released into the profit and loss account over the next 6 years at £75,000 per annum, ie in the periods expected to be benefited. (Note: it is assumed that the stock at acquisition was all realised in the year to 31.12.X8.)

4.13 Disclosures

FRS 10 requires various disclosures relating to the following.

- Recognition and measurement
- Amortisation of positive goodwill and intangible assets
- Revaluation
- Negative goodwill
- Impairment (see next section).

The **disclosure requirements are the same as for any other fixed asset**, including the table showing a reconciliation of movements during the year, for every category of intangible assets (including goodwill), details of revaluations, accounting policies and details of amortisation charged.

Significant **additional disclosure** requirements include requirements to explain:

- The **bases of valuation** of intangible assets
- The **grounds for believing a useful economic life to exceed 20 years** or to be indefinite
- The **treatment adopted of negative goodwill**

4.14 Issues relating to FRS 10

FRS 10 has involved **significant changes to the accounts of many companies.** Over 95% of companies in the UK had traditionally adopted the 'immediate write off' treatment permitted under now withdrawn SSAP 22.

The firm Ernst & Young raised issues over the thinking behind the standard.

(a) **FRS 10 still allows a choice of accounting treatments.** Companies can follow a regime that permits the goodwill to be carried as a **permanent asset**. This may allow some **spurious assets** to remain indefinitely in the balance sheet, potentially providing ammunition for challenging of the profession in any likely future wave of accounting scandal.

(b) **The impairment review,** if it is to be based on FRS 11, applies '**labyrinthine methodologies** to very soft numbers'. In other words, it **is subjective**, not least in determining **how** the **business** is to be **segmented. Forecasting cashflows** is also **problematic**.

(c) **The importance of negative goodwill has been underestimated.** It is more likely to arise now that FRS 7 bans reorganisation provisions, thus raising the value of the net assets acquired.

(d) **The treatment of negative goodwill is 'strange'.** It is a '**dangling credit**' in the balance sheet and the profit and loss account treatment simply mirrors that required for depreciation without regard to the fact that this is a **credit** to the profit and loss account.

Section summary

(a) **Purchased goodwill** and **intangible assets** will both be **capitalised** as assets in the balance sheet. The option for goodwill of immediate write off to reserves, by-passing the profit and loss account, will no longer be available as it was under SSAP 22.

(b) Where goodwill and intangible assets have **limited lives** they will be **amortised** to the profit and loss account over their **expected lives**.

(c) Amortisation will not be required for assets that can be justified as having **indefinite lives**. They need to be **written down only if their values drop below those in the balance sheet**.

(d)   There is a **general presumption** that the **lives** of goodwill and intangible assets will be **no more than 20 years**. **A longer or indefinite life** may be assigned only if the **durability** of the asset can be demonstrated and if it is **possible to remeasure** its value **each year** to **identify any reduction**.

(e)   **Impairment reviews** must be **performed annually** where **lives** of **more than 20 years** are chosen. For **lives of less than 20 years**, they are required only in the **year after acquisition**, and in **other years** if there is some **indication** that the asset's **value might have fallen below its recorded value**.

Exam focus point

> The June 2004 exam had a 25-mark question on FRS 10, including intangible asset scenarios.

5 FRS 11 Impairment of fixed assets and goodwill

FAST FORWARD

> FRS 11 deals with impairment losses relating to **tangible fixed assets, intangible fixed assets** and **goodwill**. Where the **recoverable amount** of an asset falls below the amount at which it is carried in the financial statements, an **impairment loss** has occurred.

Exam focus point

> Impairment is a very examinable area as it ties in well with both FRS 15 and FRS 10. It is likely to be part of a 25-mark question as it was in the pilot paper.

It is accepted practice that a **fixed asset** should **not be carried in the financial statements at more than its recoverable amount**, ie the higher of the amount for which it could be sold and the amount recoverable from its future use. FRS 11 has been produced to address impairment of fixed assets and goodwill but first we will review the Companies Act requirements.

5.1 Companies Act 1985 requirements

Under CA 85 the treatment of diminutions in value is as follows.

(a)   **Assets held at cost**

     (i)   **Temporary diminutions** are **not recognised**.

     (ii)   **Permanent diminutions** are **recognised** and **charged to the profit and loss account**.

(b)   **Assets held at valuation**

     (i)   **Temporary diminutions** are **recognised** and **debited to reserves**.

     (ii)   **Permanent diminutions** are **recognised** and charged to the **asset's previous surplus in reserves** and **then to the profit and loss account** for the year.

Further points to note are as follows.

(a)   Where the increase in value relates to the **reversal of a permanent diminution** in value previously charged to the profit and loss account, the increase will be posted to the profit and loss account for the year.

(b)   Any changes in value taken **directly to reserves** must be disclosed in the STRGL.

5.2 FRS 11 Impairment of fixed assets and goodwill

5.2.1 Overview

While statute provides some guidance, it provides none on how the **recoverable amount** should be **measured** and **when impairment losses** should be **recognised**. In consequence, **practice** might be **inconsistent** and perhaps some impairments may **not** be **recognised** on a **timely basis**.

The need for a standard on impairment was increased by the requirement in FRS 10 *Goodwill and intangible assets* (see Section 4) that, where goodwill and intangible assets have a useful life in excess of twenty years or one that is indefinite, the recoverable amount of the goodwill and intangible assets should be reviewed every year.

5.2.2 Objective

The objective of FRS 11 is to ensure that:

    (a)   Fixed assets and goodwill are **recorded** in the financial statements at **no more than** their **recoverable amount**.

    (b)   Any resulting impairment loss is measured and recognised on a consistent basis.

    (c)   **Sufficient information** is **disclosed** in the financial statements to enable users to **understand** the **impact** of the **impairment** on the **financial position** and **performance** of the reporting entity.

5.2.3 Scope

FRS 11 **excludes:**

    (a)   Non-purchased goodwill.

    (b)   Fixed assets which are governed by the ASB's standard on *Derivatives and financial instruments* (FRS 13 see Chapter 12).

    (c)   Investment properties as defined in SSAP 19.

    (d)   Shares held by an ESOP.

    (e)   Cost capitalised pending determination under the Oil Industry Accounting Committee's SORP.

        FRS 11 applies to subsidiary undertakings, associates and joint ventures.

Basic requirement

> A **review for impairment** of a fixed asset or goodwill should be carried out if **events** or **changes** in **circumstances** indicate that the **carrying amount** of the fixed asset or goodwill **may not be recoverable**.

Key term

> **Impairment**: a **reduction** in the **recoverable amount** of a fixed asset or goodwill **below** its **carrying amount**.
> (FRS 11)

Exam focus point

> In June 2002, candidates were required to:
>
> (a)   define an impairment loss and explain why companies should carry out a review for impairment of fixed assets and goodwill.
>
> (b)   describe the circumstances that might indicate that a company's assets may have become impaired.

Impairment occurs due to *either.*

(a)   Something happening to the **fixed asset** itself.

(b)   Something occurring in the **environment** within which the asset operates.

5.3 Indicators of impairment

FRS 11 provides **indicators of impairment** to help determine when an **impairment review** is **required**. Examples of such **events** and **changes** in **circumstances** include the following.

(a)   There is a **current period operating loss** or **net cash outflow** from **operating activities**, combined with *either.*

    (i)   **Past operating losses** or **net cash outflows** from operating activities

    (ii)   An expectation of **continuing operating losses** or **net cash outflows** from operating activities.

(b)   A **fixed asset's market value has declined significantly** during the period.

(c)   Evidence is available of **obsolescence or physical damage** to the fixed asset.

(d)   There is a **significant adverse change** in any of the following.

    (i)   Either the **business or the market** in which the fixed asset or goodwill is involved, such as the entrance of a **major competitor**.

    (ii)   The **statutory or other regulatory environment** in which the business operates.

    (iii) Any **indicator of value** (eg multiples of turnover) used to measure the fair value of a fixed asset on acquisition.

(e)   A **commitment** by management to undertake a **significant reorganisation**.

(f)   A major loss of **key employees**.

(g)   **Market interest rates** or other market rates of return have **increased significantly**, and these increases are likely to **affect materially** the fixed asset's **recoverable amount**.

This diagram may help you to visualise the FRS 11 indicators of impairment.

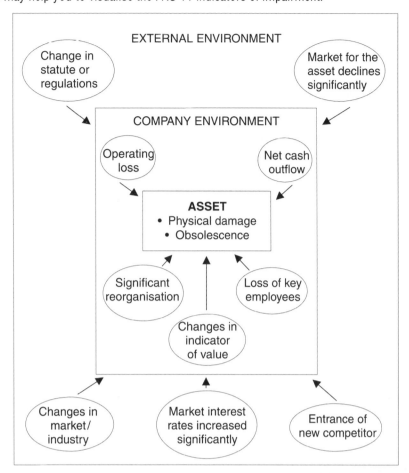

Where any of the above (or similar) **triggers** occur, then an impairment review should be carried out. In the case of **tangible fixed assets**, if there is **no cause** to suspect **any impairment**, then **no impairment review** is necessary. **Intangible assets** and **goodwill may**, however, **still require review**.

Key terms

> **Intangible assets**: **non-financial** fixed assets that do **not have physical substance** but are **identifiable** and **controlled** by the entity through **custody** or **legal rights**.
>
> **Purchased goodwill**: the **difference** between the **cost** of an acquired entity **and** the aggregate of the **fair values** of that entity's identifiable assets and liabilities.
>
> **Tangible fixed assets**: assets that have **physical substance** and are held for **use** in the **production** or **supply of goods or services**, for **rental** to others, or for **administrative purposes** on a **continuing basis** in the reporting entity's activities.
> *(FRS 11)*

5.4 Impairment review

Basic requirements

> FRS 11 specifies the process for conducting an impairment review.
>
> • The impairment review will consist of a **comparison** of the **carrying amount** of the fixed asset or goodwill with its **recoverable amount** (the higher of net realisable value, if known, and value in use).
>
> • To the extent that the **carrying amount exceeds** the **recoverable amount**, the fixed asset or goodwill is **impaired** and should be **written down**.

Key terms

- The impairment loss should be recognised in the profit and loss account unless it arises on a previously revalued fixed asset.

- **Recoverable amount**: the **higher of net realisable value** and **value in use**.

- **Net realisable value**: the **amount** at which an asset **could be disposed** of, **less** any **direct selling costs**.

- **Value in use**: the **present value** of the **future cash flows** obtainable as a result of an asset's continued use, including those resulting from its **ultimate disposal**.

The issues can be summarised by the following diagram.

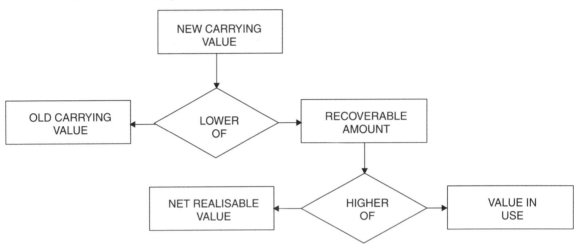

 Question Impairment loss

Determine the impairment loss relating to one of Viegeets Limited's fixed assets for the following four scenarios.

	Scenario 1 £'000	Scenario 2 £'000	Scenario 3 £'000	Scenario 4 £'000
• Carrying amount	750	750	900	900
• Net realisable value *	800	600	800	600
• Value in use **	600	800	600	800

Answer

• Recoverable amount	* 800	** 800	* 800	** 800
• Carrying amount	750	750	900	900
• Impairment	Nil	Nil	100	100

Note the following **rules** here.

(a) If either NRV *or* value in use is higher than the carrying amount, there is no impairment.

(b) If a reliable estimate of NRV cannot be made, the recoverable amount is its value in use.

(c) If NRV is less than the carrying amount, then value in use must be found to see if it is higher still. If it is higher, recoverable amount is based on value in use, not NRV.

Basic
requirements

- When an **impairment loss** on a fixed asset or goodwill is recognised, the **remaining useful economic life** should be **reviewed** and **revised if necessary**.

- The **revised carrying amount** should be **depreciated** over the **revised estimate of the useful economic life**.

5.5 Calculation of net realisable value

The net realisable value of an asset that is **traded on an active market** will be based on **market value**. Disposal costs should include **only** the **essential selling costs** of the fixed asset and *not* **any costs** of reducing or **reorganising** the **business**.

5.6 Calculation of value in use

The process for computing value in use has **two basic** steps.

(a) **Develop projections** of future cash flows.
(b) **Discount** projected cash flows to **determine present value**.

In practice, value in use is **not always easy** to estimate.

(a) The **value in use** of a fixed asset should be estimated **individually** where **reasonably practicable**.

(b) Where it is not reasonably practicable to develop **projected cash flows** arising from an individual fixed asset, value in use should be calculated at the **level of income-generating units**.

(c) The **carrying amount of each income-generating unit** containing the fixed asset or goodwill under review should be compared with the **higher of the value in use and the net realisable value** (if it can be measured reliably) of the unit.

Exam focus point

The June 2002 paper required candidates to deal with the impact of a significant increase in interest rates on the value in use computation of some earthmoving equipment.

5.7 Income generating units

Key term

An **income generating unit** is defined as a group of assets, liabilities and associated goodwill that generates income that is largely independent of the reporting entity's other income streams. The assets and liabilities include those already involved in generating the income and an appropriate portion of those used to generate more than one income stream.

Because it is necessary to **identify only material impairments**, in some cases it may be acceptable to consider a **group of income generating units together** rather than on an individual basis.

In some cases a detailed calculation of value in use will not be necessary. A **simple estimate** may be **sufficient** to **demonstrate** that either **value in use is higher than carrying value**, in which case there is no impairment, or value in use is lower than net realisable value, in which case impairment is measured by reference to net realisable value.

5.8 Identification of income generating units

Basic requirements

FRS 11 specifies that income generating units should be identified by **dividing** the **total income** of the **entity** into as many largely **independent income streams** as is **reasonably practicable**. Each of the entity's identifiable assets and liabilities should be attributed to, or apportioned between, one or more income generating unit(s). However, the following are **excluded**.

- Deferred tax balances
- Interest bearing debt
- Dividends payable
- Other financing items

In general terms, the income streams identified are likely to **follow** the way in which **management** monitors and makes **decisions** about **continuing** or **closing** the **different lines of business** of the entity. **Unique intangible assets**, such as **brands** and **mastheads**, are generally seen to **generate income independently** of each other and are usually **monitored separately**. Hence they can often be used to identify income-generating units. **Other income streams** may be identified by **reference to major products or services**.

5.9 Example: identification of income generating units

Saferail Limited runs a rail network comprising stations fed by a number of routes. Decisions about continuing or closing the routes are not based on the returns generated by the routes in isolation but on the contribution made to the returns generated by the stations.

Solution

An income-generating unit comprises a station plus the routes associated with it because the cash inflows generated by the station's activities are not independent of the routes.

Question   Income generating unit

Identify the income generating unit in the following cases.

(a)   Supasheds Limited, manufactures garden sheds at a number of different sites. Not all the sites are used to full capacity and the manufacturer can choose how much to make at each site. However, there is not enough surplus capacity to enable any one site to be closed. The cash inflows generated by any one site therefore depend on the allocation of production across all sites.

(b)   Dian Xin Limited has a large number of restaurants across the country. The cash inflows of each restaurants can be individually monitored and sensible allocations of costs to each restaurants can be made.

Answer

(a)   The income-generating unit comprises all the sites at which the sheds can be made.

(b)   Each restaurant is an income-generating unit by itself. However, any impairment of individual restaurants is unlikely to be material. A material impairment is likely to occur only when a number of restaurants are affected together by the same economic factors. It may therefore be acceptable to consider groupings of restaurants affected by the same economic factors rather than each individual restaurants.

To perform impairment reviews as accurately as possible:

(a) The **groups of assets and liabilities** that are considered together should be **as small as is reasonably practicable**, but

(b) The **income stream** underlying the **future cash flows** of one group should be **largely independent** of other income streams of the entity and should be **capable** of being **monitored separately**.

Income-generating units are therefore identified by dividing the total income of the business into as many largely independent income streams as is reasonably practicable in the light of the information available to management.

5.10 Central assets

In practice, businesses may have assets and liabilities that are not directly involved in the production and distribution of individual products therefore not attributed directly to one unit. **Central assets**, such as group or regional **head offices** and **working capital** may have to be **apportioned across** the **units** as on a **logical** and **systematic basis**. In such cases, the **sum of the carrying amounts of the units must equal the carrying amount of the net assets (excluding tax and financing items) of the entity as a whole**.

There may be circumstances where it is not **possible** to **apportion certain central assets** meaningfully **across the income generating units** to which they contribute. Such assets **may be excluded from** the **individual income generating units**.

(a) An **additional impairment review** should be performed on the **excluded central assets**.

(b) The **income generating units** to which the **central assets contribute** should be combined and their **combined carrying amount** (including that of the central assets) should be **compared** with their **combined value in use**.

5.11 Working capital

If there is any working capital in the balance sheet that will generate cash flows equal to its carrying amount, the carrying amount of the working capital may be excluded from the income-generating units and the cash flows arising from its realisation/settlement excluded from the value in use calculation.

5.12 Capitalised goodwill

This **should be attributed to income generating** units or groups of similar units, in the same way as are the assets and liabilities of the entity.

5.13 Cash flows

5.13.1 Basis of cash flows

The **expected future cash flows** of the income generating unit, including any allocation of central overheads but excluding cash flows relating to financing and tax, should be:

(a) Based on **reasonable** and **supportable assumptions**.

(b) **Consistent** with the most up-to-date **budgets** and **plans** that have been **formally approved by management**.

(c) Assume a **steady** or **declining growth** rate for the **period beyond** that covered by formal budgets and plans.

Only in **exceptional circumstances** should:

(a) The **period** before the steady or declining growth rate is assumed **extend** to **more than five years**.

(b) The **steady or declining growth rate exceed** the **long-term average growth rate** for the country or **countries** in which the business operates.

5.13.2 Projections of future cash flows

Future cash flows must be estimated for income generating units in their **current condition, ie exclude**:

(a) **Benefits** expected to arise from a **future reorganisation** for which provision has not been made.

(b) **Future capital expenditure** that will improve or **enhance** the income generating units **more than the originally assessed standard of performance**.

5.13.3 Subsequent monitoring of cash flows

For the **five years** following each impairment review where the recoverable amount has been based on value in use, **actual cash flows should be compared with forecast cash flows**.

There may be instances where **actual cash flows** are **significantly less** than forecast. This may **suggest** that the **income** generating **unit might** have required recognition of an **impairment** in **previous periods**. In such cases, the original **impairment calculations should be re-performed** using the actual cash flows. Any **impairment** identified should be **recognised** in the **current period** unless the impairment has reversed.

5.14 Discount rate

The **present value** of the income-generating unit under review should be calculated by **discounting** the expected future cash flows of the unit.

(a) The discount rate used should be an **estimate** of the **rate** that the **market would expect** on an **equally risky investment**.

(b) It should **exclude** the **effects** of **any risk** for which the **cash flows** have **been adjusted** and should be calculated on a **pre-tax basis**.

5.15 Allocation of impairment loss

Exam focus point

The June 2002 paper required candidates to allocate the impairment loss relating to an income generating unit.

Allocation of any impairment loss calculated (ie where carrying amount exceeds value in use) should be allocated:

(a) First, to any **goodwill** in the unit.
(b) Thereafter to any **capitalised intangible asset** in the unit.
(c) Finally, to the **tangible assets** in the unit (pro-rata or other method).

The rationale behind the above allocation is to write down the assets with the most subjective valuations first.

No intangible asset with a **readily ascertainable market value** should be written down to **below NRV**. Similarly, **no tangible asset** with a reliably measured net realisable value should be written down **below its NRV**.

Question   Loss allocation

Nutrinitious Foods Limited has suffered an impairment loss of £90,000 on one of its income generating units because low market entry barriers has enabled competitors to develop and successfully market rival products.

The carrying value of net assets in the income generating unit, before adjusting for the impairment loss are as follows:

	£'000
Goodwill	50
Patent (with no market value)	10
Land and buildings	120
Plant and machinery	60
	240

Demonstrate how the impairment loss of £90,000 should be allocated.

Answer

	£'000
Remember the batting order is:	
• Goodwill	50
• Capitalised intangible fixed assets	10
• Tangible fixed assets, on a pro-rata basis	30
	90

Hence:

	Pre-impairment £'000	Impairment loss £'000	Post-impairment £'000
Goodwill	50	(50)	–
Patent	10	(10)	–
Land and buildings $(30 \times \frac{120}{180})$	120	(20)	100
Plant and machinery $(30 \times \frac{60}{180})$	60	(10)	50
	240	(90)	150

5.16 Reversal of past impairments

Tangible fixed assets and investments are treated differently from goodwill and intangible assets.

5.16.1 Tangible fixed assets and investments

There may be circumstances where, in subsequent periods after an impairment loss has been recognised, the **recoverable amount** of a tangible fixed asset or investment (in subsidiaries, associates and joint ventures) **increases because of an improvement in economic conditions.**

In such instances, the resulting **reversal** of the impairment loss should be **recognised in the current period**. However, recognition is *only* **to the extent that it increases the carrying amount of the fixed asset up to the amount that it would have been had the original impairment not occurred.**

The reversal of the impairment loss should be recognised in the **profit and loss account unless** it arises on a **previously revalued fixed asset.**

BPP PROFESSIONAL EDUCATION

The recognition of an increase in the recoverable amount of a tangible fixed asset above the amount that its carrying amount would have been had the original impairment not occurred is a revaluation, not a reversal of an impairment.

The circumstances we are looking at are those given above (Paragraph 5.9) which would **originally** have **triggered** an **impairment review**. Also, **increases** in value arising as a result of the **passage of time** or through the passing of cash outflows are **not circumstances** that would **give rise** to the **reversal of an impairment loss**.

5.16.2 Goodwill and intangible assets

The reversal of an impairment loss on intangible assets and goodwill should be **recognised in the current period if, and only if**:

(a)   An **external event caused** the **recognition** of the impairment loss in **previous periods**, and **subsequent external events** clearly and demonstrably **reverse** the effects of that event in a way that was **not foreseen in** the **original impairment calculations**.

(b)   The impairment loss related to an intangible asset with a **readily ascertainable market value** and the **net realisable value based on that market value** has increased **to above the intangible asset's impaired carrying amount**.

The reversal of the impairment loss should be **recognised to the extent that it increases the carrying amount of the goodwill or intangible asset up to the amount that it would have been had the original impairment not occurred**.

The recognition of an increase in the recoverable amount of an intangible asset above the amount that its carrying amount would have been had the original impairment not occurred is a revaluation.

Key term

> **Readily ascertainable market value**, in relation to an intangible asset, is the value that is established by reference to a market where:
>
> (a)   The asset belongs to a homogeneous population of assets that are equivalent in all material respects.
>
> (b)   An active market, evidenced by frequent transactions, exists for that population of assets. *(FRS 11)*

Question

Exeler 8 Limited has an income-generating unit comprising a factory, plant and equipment etc and associated purchased goodwill which has become impaired because the product has been overtaken by a technologically more advanced model produced by a competitor. The recoverable amount of the income-generating unit has fallen to £50m, resulting in an impairment loss of £100m, allocated as follows.

	Carrying amounts before impairment £m	Carrying amounts after impairment £m
Goodwill	45	–
Patent (with no market value)	15	–
Tangible fixed assets	90	50
Total	150	50

After three years, Exeler 8 Limited makes a technological breakthrough of its own, and the recoverable amount of the income-generating unit increases to £100m. The carrying amount of the tangible fixed assets had the impairment not occurred would have been £70m.

Required

Calculate the reversal of the impairment loss.

Answer

The reversal of the impairment loss is recognised to the extent that it increases the carrying amount of the tangible fixed assets to what it would have been had the impairment not taken place, ie a reversal of the impairment loss of £20m is recognised and the tangible fixed assets written back to £70m.

Reversal of the impairment is not recognised in relation to the goodwill and patent because the effect of the external event that caused the original impairment has not reversed - the original product is still overtaken by a more advanced model.

5.17 Impairment losses on revalued fixed assets

The general rule is that impairment losses on **revalued fixed assets** should be recognised in the **statement of total recognised gains and losses** until the carrying value of the asset falls **below depreciated historical** cost.

However, there may be specific circumstances where the impairment is clearly caused by a **consumption of economic benefits** eg damage, in which case the loss is recognised in the **profit and loss account**. ie such impairments are regarded as additional depreciation rather than as a decline in value.

Impairments **below depreciated historical** cost are recognised in the **profit and loss account**.

Question   Revalued asset: impairment loss

Rollakoastas Limited has a fixed asset with the following details:

		£
•	Carrying value at 1 January 20X8 based on its revalued amount	£50,000
•	Depreciated historical cost at 1 January 20X8	£36,000
•	Impairment loss owing to entry of a new competitor	£20,000

Explain how this impairment loss should be accounted for in the financial statements for the year ended 31 December 20X8.

Answer

		£
•	Recognised in statement of total gains and losses	14,000
•	Recognised in profit and loss account	6,000

Workings

	£
Carrying value at 1.1.X8	50,000
Write off to STRGL	(14,000)
Depreciated historical cost	36,000
Write off to profit and loss account	(6,000)
Revised carrying value at 31.12.X8	30,000

5.18 Presentation and disclosure

Impairment losses recognised in the profit and loss account should be included within **operating profit** under the **appropriate statutory heading**, and disclosed as an exceptional item if appropriate. Impairment losses recognised in the STRGL should be **disclosed separately** on the face of that statement.

In **the notes** to the financial statements in **accounting periods after the impairment**, the impairment loss should be treated as follows.

(a)   For assets held on a **historical cost basis**, the impairment loss should be included **within cumulative depreciation**: the cost of the asset should not be reduced.

(b)   For **revalued assets held at a market value** (eg existing use value or open market value), the impairment loss should be included **within the revalued carrying amount**.

(c)   For **revalued assets held at depreciated replacement** cost, an impairment loss **charged to the profit and loss account** should be included **within cumulative depreciation**: the carrying amount of the asset should not be reduced; an **impairment loss charged to the STRGL** should be **deducted from the carrying amount** of the asset.

If the impairment loss is measured by reference to **value in use** of a fixed asset or income-generating unit, the **discount rate applied to the cash flows should be disclosed**. If a risk-free discount rate is used, some indication of the risk adjustments made to the cash flows should be given.

Where an impairment loss recognised in a previous period is **reversed** in the current period, the financial statements should **disclose the reason for the reversal**, including any changes in the assumptions upon which the calculation of recoverable amount is based.

Where an impairment loss would have been recognised in a previous period had the forecasts of future cash flows been more accurate but the impairment has reversed and the reversal of the loss is permitted to be recognised, the impairment now identified and its subsequent reversal should be disclosed.

Where, in the measurement of value in use, the period before a steady or declining long-term growth rate has been assumed extends to more than five years, the financial statements should **disclose the length of the longer period** and the circumstances justifying it.

Where, in the measurement of value in use, the long-term growth rate used has exceeded the long-term average growth rate for the country or countries in which the business operates, the financial statements should **disclose the growth rate assumed** and the circumstances justifying it.

5.19 Section summary

The main aspects of FRS 11 to remember are:

- **Indications** of impairment
- Identification of **income-generating** unit
- How an **impairment review** is carried out
- **Restoration of past losses** (tangibles vs intangibles)
- Impairment and restoration of **revalued fixed assets**

Chapter Roundup

- The Companies Act 1985 sets out the **statutory accounting requirements** relating to **intangible fixed assets** and **investments**. These requirements are supplemented in the case of **development costs** by SSAP 13, in the case of **goodwill** by FRS 10 and in the case of **impairment** by FRS 11.

- SSAP 13 is a standard which has been around for some time and is generally accepted and well understood. It distinguishes between research expenditure and development expenditure and lays down strict criteria for the capitalisation of development expenditure.

- By definition, goodwill is an asset which **cannot be realised separately** from the **business as a whole**.

- FRS 10 states that **purchased, positive goodwill** and purchased intangible assets or internally-developed intangible assets which have a **readily ascertainable market value** should be capitalised and amortised over their **useful economic life**.

- FRS 11 deals with impairment losses relating to **tangible fixed assets, intangible fixed assets** and **goodwill**. Where the **recoverable amount** of an asset falls below the amount at which it is carried in the financial statements, an **impairment loss** has occurred.

Quick Quiz

1   Patents can only be treated as assets in a company's accounts if they are:

- .... for valuable consideration

- .... by the company itself

2   What are the criteria which must be met before development expenditure can be deferred?

- S..................... • C..................... • O.....................

- E..................... • T..................... • R.....................

3   Development expenditure written off may be reinstated if the uncertainties which led to the write-off no longer apply.

True   ☐

False ☐

4   How should negative goodwill be accounted for under FRS10?

5   FRS 11 excludes purchased goodwill.

True   ☐

False ☐

6   How is impairment on a revalued fixed asset which has been caused by consumption of economic benefit accounted for?

Answers to Quick Quiz

1   Acquired, created

2   **S**eparately defined project. **E**xpenses identifiable. **C**ommercially viable, **T**echnically feasible, **O**verall profitability, **R**esources to complete it

3   True

4   It should be disclosed in the intangible fixed assets category

5   False. It excludes non-purchased goodwill

6   It is disclosed in the profit and loss account

Now try the questions below from the Exam Question Bank

Number	Level	Marks	Time
Q5	Full exam	30	54 mins

BPP
PROFESSIONAL EDUCATION

7

Stocks and work in progress

Topic list	Syllabus reference
1 Stocks and short-term work in progress	3 (f)
2 Long-term contract work in progress	3 (f)

Introduction

You have encountered stocks and stock valuation in your earlier studies. Stock valuation has a direct impact on a company's gross profit and it is usually a material item in any company's accounts. This is therefore an important subject area. If you have any doubts about accounting for stocks and methods of stock valuation you would be advised to go back to your Paper 1.1 study material and revise this topic.

Section 1 of this chapter goes over some of this ground again, concentrating on the effect of SSAP 9. Section 2 goes on to discuss a new area, long-term contract work in progress.

Study guide

- Review the principles of stock valuation covered in Paper 1.1.

- Define a long-term contract and describe why recognising profit before completion is generally considered to be desirable and the circumstances where it may not be; discuss if this may be profit smoothing.

- Describe the ways in which attributable profit may be measured.

- Calculate and disclose the amounts to be shown in the financial statements for long-term contracts.

Exam guide

You should find long-term contracts fairly logical as long as you work through the examples and exercise carefully.

1 Stocks and short-term work in progress

FAST FORWARD

Stocks comprise:

Raw materials and consumables
Work in progress
Finished goods and goods for resale
Payments on account (of purchases)

They must be revalued at **lower of cost and net realisable value**.

FIFO and **weighted average** are the accepted means of valuation under SSAP 9.

Exam focus point

The June 2003 paper included a small part question on net realisable value of slow moving goods.

In most businesses the value put on stock is an important factor in the determination of profit. Stock valuation is, however, a highly subjective exercise and consequently there is a wide variety of different methods used in practice.

The Companies Act 1985 regulations and SSAP 9 *Stocks and long-term contracts* requirements were developed to achieve greater uniformity in the valuation methods used and in the disclosure in financial statements prepared under the historical cost convention.

SSAP 9 defines stocks and work in progress as:

(a)   Goods or other assets purchased for resale.
(b)   Consumable stores.
(c)   Raw materials and components purchased for incorporation into products for sale.
(d)   Products and services in intermediate stages of completion.
(e)   Long-term contract balances.
(f)   Finished goods.

In published accounts, the Companies Act 1985 requires that these stock categories should be grouped and disclosed under the following headings:

(a)   Raw materials and consumables ((c) and (b) above).

(b)   Work in progress ((d) and (e) above).

(c)   Finished goods and goods for resale ((f) and (a) above).

(d)   Payments on account (presumably intended to cover the case of a company which has paid for stock items but not yet received them into stock).

A distinction is also made in SSAP 9 between:

(a)   Stocks and work in progress other than long-term contract work in progress.

(b)   Long-term contract work in progress.

We will look at long-term contracts later in the chapter. Stocks and short-term work in progress are revised briefly here.

Knowledge brought forward from earlier studies

SSAP 9 Stock and long-term contracts (Stock and short-term WIP)

Under the matching concept costs must be allocated between the cost of goods sold (matched against current revenues) and closing stock (matched against future revenues).

•   Stock should be valued at the **lower of cost and net realisable value** (NRV).

•   **Costs** should include those incurred in the **normal course of business** in bringing a product or service to its **present location and condition**.

•   Costs include direct costs (labour, materials), production overheads and other attributable overheads. Exclude all 'abnormal' overheads, eg exceptional spoilage.

•   CA 1985 also allows the inclusion of interest payable on capital borrowed to finance the production of the asset (allowed by SSAP 9 under 'other attributable overheads').

•   **NRV is the actual or estimated selling price less further costs to be incurred in marketing, selling and distribution.**

•   The method used in allocating costs to stock should produce the fairest approximation to the expenditure incurred.

•   Methods include (per CA 1985): average cost, base stock, current cost, FIFO, LIFO, replacement cost, standard cost, unit cost; however, base stock and LIFO are not allowed under SSAP 9.

•   The principal situation where NRV will be less than cost will be where:

    –   There have been increases in the costs or falls in selling price
    –   Physical deterioration of stock has occurred
    –   Products have become obsolescent
    –   The company has decided to make and sell a product at a loss
    –   There are errors in production or purchasing

The following question is a very simple reminder of how FIFO operates.

Question   FIFO

Digby Pillay, a retailer commenced business on 1 January 20X5, with a capital of £500. He decided to specialise in a single product line and by the end of June 20X5, his purchases and sales of this product were as follows.

	Purchases		Sales	
	Units	Unit price	Units	Unit price
		£		£
January	30	5.00	20	7.00
February	–	–	5	7.20
April	40	6.00	25	8.00
May	25	6.50	30	8.50
June	20	7.00	20	9.00
	115		100	

Required

(a)   Ascertain Digby Pillay's gross profit for the period using FIFO.

(b)   Assuming that all purchases and sales are made for cash and that there are no other transactions for the period, draw up a balance sheet as at 30 June 20X5.

Answer

(a)

	£	£
Sales		811.00
Purchases	692.50	
Less closing stock (15 @ £7.00)	105.00	
		587.50
		223.50

(b)   BALANCE SHEET AS AT 30 JUNE 20X5

	£
Original capital	500.00
Profit	223.50
	723.50
Stock	105.00
Cash	618.50
	723.50

2 Long-term contract work in progress

2.1 Introduction

> The most controversial aspect of SSAP 9 is its approach to the valuation of work in progress for incomplete long-term contracts.

Key term

> A **long-term contract** is defined as: 'a contract entered into for the design, manufacture or construction of a **single substantial asset** or the provision of a service (or of a combination of assets or services which together constitute a **single project**) where the time taken substantially to complete the contract is such that the **contract activity** falls into **different accounting periods**.'

Usually long-term contracts will **exceed one year** in duration, although a **sufficiently material contract** whose activity **straddles a balance sheet date** should still be accounted for as a **long-term contract even if it will last in total less than a year**. This is to ensure that the accounts for **both accounting periods** involved will still give a **true and fair view** of the activities of the company.

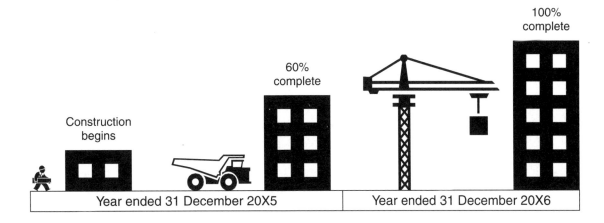

The existence of a proper **contract** is **important**, because it provides a basis of **reasonable certainty** whereby it is nevertheless **prudent** to **allow recognition** of **profits before completion of work.**

2.2 The underlying problem

Turnover and profit should be recognised throughout the duration of the contract. Any foreseeable loss should be recognised immediately.

It is the following requirement which causes the greatest controversy around SSAP 9.

'Separate consideration needs to be given to long-term contracts. Owing to the **length of time** taken to complete such contracts, to defer recording turnover and taking profit into account until completion may result in the profit and loss account reflecting not so much a **fair view** of the results of the **activity** of the company **during the year** but rather the results relating to contracts that have been completed in the year. It is therefore appropriate to take **credit** for **ascertainable turnover** and **profit** while contracts are **in progress** ....'

Some companies might prefer to value work in progress on long-term contracts at cost, and to **defer taking any profit** on the contract into the profit and loss account **until the contract had been completed.** This policy may be considered **prudent**, but there may be an **underlying management motive** to **defer profits** and **tax liabilities.**

2.3 Example: Long-term contracts

Jianzhu Construction Ltd started a contract on 1 January 20X5, with an estimated completion date of 31 December 20X6. In the first year, to 31 December 20X5:

(a)   Costs incurred amounted to £900,000.

(b)   Sixty per cent of the work on the contract was completed.

(c)   The final contract price is £2,000,000.

(d)   Certificates of work completed have been issued, to the value of £1,200,000. (*Note*. It is usual, in a long-term contract, for a qualified person such as an architect or engineer to inspect the work completed, and if it is satisfactory, to issue certificates. This will then be the notification to the customer that progress payments are now due to the contractor. Progress payments are commonly the amount of valuation on the work certificates issued, minus a precautionary retention of 10%.).

(e)   It is estimated with reasonable certainty that further costs to completion in 20X6 will be £600,000.

What is the contract profit in 20X5, and what entries would be made for the contract at 31 December 20X5 if:

(a)   Profits are deferred until the completion of the contract?

(b)   A proportion of the estimated turnover and profit is credited to the profit and loss account in 20X5?

Solution

(a)   *Profits deferred until completion of contract*

	£
• Turnover and profits recognised on the contract in 20X5	Nil
• Value of work in progress at 31 December 20X5	900,000

SSAP 9 takes the view that this policy is unreasonable, because in 20X6, the total profit of £500,000 [2,000,000 – (900,000 + 600,000)] would be recorded. Since the contract revenues are earned throughout 20X5 and 20X6, a profit of nil in 20X5 and £500,000 in 20X6 would be contrary to the accruals basis of accounting.

(b)   It is fairer to recognise turnover and profit throughout the duration of the contract.

As at 31 December 20X5 turnover of £1,200,000 should be matched with cost of sales of £900,000 [(900,000 + 600,000) × 60%] in the profit and loss account, leaving an attributable profit for 20X5 of £300,000.

The only balance sheet entry as at 31 December 20X5 is a debtor of £1,200,000 recognising that the company is owed this amount for work done to date. No balance remains for stock, the whole £900,000 having been recognised in cost of sales.

2.4 Definitions

SSAP 9 gives some other important definitions, as well as that of long-term contracts themselves given above.

Key terms

'**Attributable profit**. That part of the **total profit** currently estimated to arise over the **duration** of the **contract**, after allowing for **estimated remedial** and **maintenance costs** and increases in costs so far as **not recoverable** under the terms of the contract, that fairly reflects the profit attributable to that part of the **work performed** at the accounting date. (There can be no attributable profit until the **profitable outcome** of the contract can be assessed with **reasonable certainty**.)

Foreseeable losses. Losses which are currently estimated to arise over the **duration** of the **contract** (after allowing for **estimated remedial** and **maintenance costs** and increases in costs so far as **not recoverable** under the terms of the contract). This estimate is required irrespective of:

(a)   Whether or not work has yet **commenced** on such contracts

(b)   The **proportion** of work **carried out** at the accounting date

(c)   The amount of **profits expected** to arise on other contracts

Payments on account. All amounts **received** and **receivable** at the accounting date in respect of contracts in progress.'

2.5 Approach for calculating turnover and profit to be taken

The SSAP 9 guidelines for calculating the turnover and profit to be taken on incomplete long-term contracts follow directly from the definitions given above.

(a)   **Turnover and profit**

(i)   Must reflect the **proportion** of **work carried** out at the **accounting date**.

(ii)   Must take into account any **known inequalities of profitability** in the **various stages** of a contract.

  (iii) Must be ascertained in a **manner appropriate** to the **industry** in which the **company operates**.

 (b) **Situations where the outcome of a contract cannot be assessed with reasonable certainty**.

  (i) Generally no profit should be taken up in the profit and loss, especially where the contract is in its early stages.

  (ii) If no loss is expected, it may be appropriate to include in turnover, a proportion of the total contract value using a zero estimate of profit.

 (c) **Situations where there is an expected loss on a contract as a whole**

  Provision must be made for the whole of the loss as soon as it is foreseen, ie, none of the loss should be deferred.

  This has the effect of reducing the value of WIP to its net realisable value. For example, if a contract is 75% complete, and:

  (i) Costs incurred to date are £300,000
  (ii) Further costs to completion are expected to be £100,000
  (iii) The contract price is £360,000

In addition to a **suitable proportion of costs incurred**, then the **full expected loss** of **£40,000** should be **charged against profit** in the current period.

This approach must be applied consistently between different contracts over time.

2.6 Treatment of other costs

The **estimated future costs** must take into account **estimated costs of rectification and guarantee work** and any possible increases in wages, prices of raw materials etc, so far as these are **not recoverable** from the **customer** under the terms of the contract.

Interest payable for finance etc must be **excluded** from **costs unless specifically attributable** to the **contract**.

2.7 Estimating attributable profit

FAST FORWARD

There are generally two alternative formulae for determining the estimated attributable profit for the year.

- Work certified basis
- Costs incurred basis

 (a) $\text{Attributable profit} = \dfrac{\text{Work certified to date}}{\text{Total contract price}} \times \text{Estimated total profit}$

 (b) $\text{Attributable profit} = \dfrac{\text{Cost of work completed to date}}{\text{Total costs}} \times \text{Estimated total profit}$

Care should be exercised in adopting a costs incurred basis eg if there is high initial outlay or perhaps the expensive items only go in towards the end of the contract. The examiner may therefore provide a tailored formula for the specific exam question which you will need to interpret and apply on the day.

2.8 An extra prudent approach

Some companies feel that it is more prudent to take credit for profit only in respect of the cash which has been received from the customer. Hence, the figure for attributable profit obtained above, is subjected to a further fraction.

'Extra prudent' attributable profit = $\dfrac{\text{Cash received}}{\text{Work certified to date}}$ × Attributable profit as above.

With a little bit of basic maths, the above can be expressed as:

'Extra prudent' attributable profit = $\dfrac{\text{Cash received}}{\text{Total contract price}}$ × Estimated total profit

Exam focus point

The extra prudent approach might well not be required by the examiner. It is shown here to demonstrate what some companies use in practice. Read the question carefully to understand the examiner's requirements.

2.9 Available guidance

SSAP 9 does not provide any guidance on how to work out cost of sales, but focuses instead on the approach to determining attributable profit.

The amount of turnover and profit on a long-term contract to be recognised in an accounting period is found using a cumulative approach ie deduct figure total at end of last year from total at end of this year to get figure for the current year.

	£
Cumulative turnover/attributable profit	X
Less any turnover/attributable profit taken into account in previous years	X
Turnover/profit to be recognised in current period	X

Estimates of total profit may change from one year to another. Therefore, attributable profits have to be **recalculated** at the end of **each period**. Remember that at an **early stage** in the contract, in order to show a **true and fair view** of activity in the period, an **appropriate proportion of turnover** should be recorded in the profit and loss account but, on grounds of **prudence**, **no profit** should be recorded until the overall result of the contract is more certain.

2.10 Using a step-by-step approach

Long-term contract WIP can be calculated as:

Costs to date	X
Less Costs transferred to cost of sales	(X)
Less Foreseeable losses	(X)
Less Payments on account in excess of turnover	(X)
WIP	X

In valuing long-term WIP and implementing the other disclosures required under SSAP 9, you may find a step-by-step approach to be helpful. The following suggested process should assist you to tackle the problem in an ordered way.

STEP 1

Calculate the expected total profit or loss on the contract.

	£
Contract value	X
Less: Costs incurred to date	(X)
Expected further costs to complete	(X)
Expected total profit/(loss)	X/(X)

(a) If the contract is expected to make a profit, recognise attributable profit, if outcome is reasonably certain.

(b) If a loss is foreseen (that is, if the costs to date plus estimated costs to completion exceed the contract value) then it must be charged against profits.

(c) If a loss has already been charged in previous years, then only the difference between the loss as previously and currently estimated need be charged (or credited).

STEP 2

Using the percentage certified/completed to date (or other formula given in the question), calculate turnover attributable to the contract for the period.

	£
Total contract value × percentage certified (or formula given in the question)	X
Less Turnover recognised in previous period	(X)
Turnover attributable to current period	X

STEP 3

Calculate the cost of sales attributable to the contract for the period.

	£
Total contract costs × percentage certified (or formula given in question)	X
Less Any costs charged in previous periods	(X)
	X
Add Foreseeable losses in full (not previously charged)	X
Cost of sales attributable to current period	X

STEP 4

Review the balance on work in progress

(a) A debit balance for WIP will remain on the balance sheet
(b) A credit balance on WIP should be shown under provision for liabilities and charges.

STEP 5

Calculate cumulative turnover on the contract (the total turnover recorded in respect of the contract in the profit and loss accounts of all accounting periods since the inception of the contract). Compare this with total progress payments to date.

(a) If turnover exceeds payments on account (from customers), an 'amount recoverable on contracts' is established and separately disclosed within debtors.

(b) If payments on account (from customers) exceed cumulative turnover then the excess is:

  (i) First deducted from any remaining balance on work in progress
  (ii) Any balance is disclosed within creditors

These steps must be done for each contract individually. Only when the amounts under each heading, in respect of contract, have been determined, should they be added together for presentation in the accounts.

2.11 Double entry

The accounting double entry for a long-term contract is as follows.

(a) *During the year*

     (i)   DEBIT   Contract costs account (WIP)
              CREDIT   Bank/creditors
              Being costs incurred on contract

     (ii)   DEBIT   Trade debtors
               CREDIT   Progress payments account
              Being progress payments invoiced to customers

     (iii)   DEBIT   Bank
               CREDIT   Trade debtors
              Being cash received from customers

(b) *At year end*

     (i)   DEBIT   Progress payments account
               CREDIT   Turnover (P&L)
              Being turnover recognised in respect of certified work

     (ii)   DEBIT   Cost of sales (P&L)
               CREDIT   Contract costs account (WIP)
              Being costs matched against turnover

     (iii)   DEBIT   Provisions on long-term contracts (P&L)
               CREDIT   Provision for future losses (B/S)
              Being a provision for future losses

2.12 Summary of accounting treatment

The following is a handy summary of the accounting treatment for long-term contracts.

2.12.1 Profit and loss account

(a) **Turnover and costs**

     (i)   Turnover and associated costs should be recorded in the profit and loss account 'as contract activity progresses'.

     (ii)   Include an 'appropriate proportion of total contract value as turnover' in the profit and loss account.

     (iii)   The costs incurred in reaching that stage of completion are matched with this turnover, resulting in the reporting of results which can be attributed to the proportion of work completed.

     (iv)   Turnover is the 'value of work carried out to date'.

(b) **Attributable profit**

     (i)   It must reflect the proportion of work carried out.

(ii)   It should take into account any known inequalities in profitability in the various stages of a contract.

Balance sheet

(a)   Stocks

	£
Costs to date	X
Less Transfer to profit and loss account	(X)
	X
Less Foreseeable losses	(X)
	X
Less Payments on account in excess of turnover	(X)
Work in progress	X

(b)   **Debtors**

	£
Amounts recoverable on contracts	X
Progress payments receivable (trade debtors)	X

(c)   **Creditors**. Where payments on account exceed both cumulative turnover and net WIP the excess should be included in creditors under 'payments on account'.

(d)   **Provisions**. To the extent foreseeable future losses exceed WIP, the losses should be provided.

Question   Long-term contract

The main business of Fenix Projex Ltd is construction contracts for civil engineering projects such as dams and bridges. At the end of September 20X3 there are two uncompleted contracts on the books, for a bridge over River X and a dam on River Y, details of which are as follows.

CONTRACT	River X	River Y
Date commenced	1.9.X3	1.4.X1
Expected completed date	23.12.X3	23.12.X3
	£	£
Final contract price	70,000	290,000
Costs to 30.9.X3	21,000	210,450
Value of work certified to 30.9.X3	20,000	230,000
Progress payments invoiced to 30.9.X3	20,000	210,000
Cash received to 30.9.X3	18,000	194,000
Estimated costs to completion at 30.9.X3	41,000	20,600

Required

Prepare calculations showing the amounts to be included in the balance sheet at 30 September 20X3 in respect of the above contracts.

Answer

- *River X* is a short-term contract and although it straddles the year end, is not particularly large. It should therefore be included in the balance sheet as work in progress at cost less amounts received and receivable £(21,000 – 20,000) ie £1,000.

- *River Y* is a long-term contract and will be accounted for using long-term contract accounting.

Estimated final profit

	£
Contract value	290,000
Less: Costs incurred to date	(210,450)
Estimated future costs	(20,600)
Expected total profit	58,950

Attributable profit

$$\text{Estimated final profit} \quad \times \quad \frac{\text{Work certified}}{\text{Total contract value}} \quad \times \quad \frac{\text{Cash received}^*}{\text{Work certified}}$$

$$£58,950 \quad \times \quad \frac{230,000}{290,000} \quad \times \quad \frac{194,000}{230,000}$$

Attributable profit   £39,435

* In this instance, the company has adopted the extra prudent approach and applied the cash received fraction. Remember, however, this might not be asked for in your exam.

Profit and loss account (extract)

	£
Turnover	230,000
Cost of sales (W2)	(190,565)
	43,191

Balance sheet (extract)

	£
Stock: long term contracts (W1)	19,885
Debtors:	
Amounts recoverable on contracts (W1)	20,000
Progress payments invoiced less cash received (W1)	16,000

Workings

1

CONTRACT Y (WIP)

	£		£
Bank/creditors	210,450	Tfr to cost of sales	190,565
		Balance c/d	19,885
	210,450		210,450
Balance b/d	23,641		

TRADE DEBTORS

	£		£
Invoices; progress payments	210,000	Cash received	194,000
		Balance c/d	16,000
	210,000		210,000
Balance b/d	16,000		

PROGRESS PAYMENTS – CONTRACT Y (Amount recoverable on contracts)

	£		£
Work certified	230,000	Invoices; progress payments	210,000
		Balance c/d	20,000
	230,000		230,000
Balance c/d	20,000		

TURNOVER

	£		£
		Work certified	230,000

COST OF SALES

	£		£
Tfr from WIP	190,565		

2

	£
Work certified	230,000
Cost of sales (balancing figure)	(190,565)
Attributable profit	39,435

2.13 Profitable and loss-making contracts

Students sometimes find accounting for long-term contracts quite confusing, particularly where contracts are loss-making. We can look at the differences between profitable and loss-making contracts in more depth.

2.13.1 Profitable contracts

PROFIT AND LOSS ACCOUNT (EXTRACT)

	£
Turnover	X
Cost of sales	(X)
Attributable profit	X

BALANCE SHEET (EXTRACT)

	£
Current assets	
Stock: Long-term contracts	
Costs to date	X
Less P&L a/c cost of sales	(X)
Less Excess payments on accounts	(X)
	X
Debtors: amounts recoverable on contracts	
Turnover, work certified	X
Less Progress payments invoiced	(X)
	X
Debtors: trade debtors	
Progress payments invoiced less cash received	X
Current liabilities	
Payments on account (when payments received in excess of turnover which cannot be offset against stock balance)	X

2.13.2 Loss-making contracts

PROFIT AND LOSS ACCOUNT (EXTRACT)

	£
Turnover	X
Cost of sales	(X)
	(X)
Provision for loss (balancing figure to give)	(X)
Total foreseeable loss	(X)

BALANCE SHEET (EXTRACT)

	£
Current assets	
Stock: long-term contracts	
Costs incurred	X
Less Cost of sales	(X)
Less Provision for loss	(X)
Less Negative debtors balance	(X)
Positive/nil balance	X
Debtors: amounts recoverable on contracts	
Turnover; work certified	X
Less Progress payments invoiced	(X)
Positive/nil balance	X
Debtors: trade debtors	
Progress payments invoiced less cash received	X
Current liabilities	
Payments on account	
Negative debtor balance not relieved against stock	X
Provision for liabilities and charges	
Provision for loss not offset against stock balance	X

Exam focus point

> A question is more likely to be set on long-term contracts than on stock or short term WIP, simply because stock and short term WIP were covered in depth for Paper 1.1. The pilot paper covered long-term contracts for 9 marks of a 25-mark question.
>
> The June 2002 paper tested candidates' ability to prepare figures in respect of long-term contracts.
>
> The June 2004 and December 2004 papers both had question parts on long-term contracts.

The following comprehensive question should make things clearer.

Question   Contracts

Znowhyatt plc has two contracts in progress, the details of which are as follows.

	Happy (profitable) £'000	Grumpy (loss-making) £'000
Total contract price	300	300
Costs incurred to date	90	150
Estimated costs to completion	110	225
Progress payments invoiced and received	116	116

Required

Show extracts from the profit and loss account and the balance sheet for each contract, assuming they are both:

(a)   40% complete; and
(b)   36% complete.

Answer

(a)   *Happy contract*

    (i)   *40% complete*

	£'000
Profit and loss account	
Turnover (40% × 300)	120
Cost of sales (40% × 200)	(80)
Gross profit	40
Balance sheet	
Debtors (120 – 116)	4
WIP (90 – 80)	10

    (ii)   *36% complete*

	£'000
Profit and loss account	
Turnover (36% × 300)	108
Cost of sales (36% × 200)	(72)
Gross profit	36
Balance sheet	
Debtors (108 – 116 = –8)	–
WIP (90 – 72 – 8*) =	10

    * Set off excess payments on account against WIP.

(b)   *Grumpy contract*

    (i)   *40% complete*

       Working

	£'000	£'000
Total contract price		300
Less: costs to date	150	
estimated costs to completion	225	
		375
Foreseeable loss		(75)

	£'000
Profit and loss account	
Turnover (40% × 300)	120
Cost of sales (40% × 375)	(150)
	(30)
Provision for future losses (bal fig)	(45)
Gross loss	(75)

	£'000
Balance sheet	
Debtors (120 – 116)	4
WIP (150 – 150)	–
Provision for future losses	(45)

(ii)   *36% complete*

	£'000
Profit and loss account	
Turnover (36% × 300)	108
Cost of sales (36% × 375)	(135)
	(27)
Provision for future losses (balancing figure)	(48)
Gross loss	(75)
Balance sheet	
Debtors (108 − 116 = −8)	–
WIP (150 − 135 − 48* = −33)	–
Creditors: payments on account	8
Provisions: provisions for future losses	33

* Set off provision for losses before excess payments on account.

2.14 Scope for profit smoothing

At the beginning of this section on long term contract accounting, the problems associated with taking profits only on completion of a long term contract were identified.

However, the reference provided by **SSAP 9**, whereby **turnover** and **prudently calculated attributable profit** are **recognised** as the **contract progresses**, might create a **different** set of **financial reporting issues**, particularly in terms of the **scope for profit smoothing**.

(a)   The scope for adopting **various formulae** or methods for calculating attributable profit can provide opportunities for profit smoothing. There is **no prescribed formula** provided in **SSAP 9**.

(b)   Given the adoption of a particular formula for determining attributable profit, a company could '**manage**' the **underlying transactions** to provide the desired year by year profit profile over the duration of a long-term contract.

    (i)   **Cost incurred basis**. Actual expenditure could be incurred in a manner that gives the desired level of profit to be taken for a particular year. Eg. putting in an expensive piece of equipment to accelerate profit recognition.

    (ii)   **Work certified basis**. Here, scope for influencing the level of attributable profits recognised, depends on the arrangements for raising certificates.

    (iii)   **Other basis**. There may be other industry or company specific methods that give a particular outcome. The formula may be a basis that ensures a smooth profile of attributable profit but this does not necessarily accord with the underlying commercial reality. The method should be scrutinised to see whether it will produce figures that meet the true and fair criteria.

(c)   The process of determining attributable profits includes potentially subjective estimates eg. costs to complete the contract.

(d)   SSAP 9 specifies that **profit** on a contract should be recognised only when the **outcome can be foreseen** with **reasonable certainty**. SSAP 9 does not provide any guidance on how this assessment can be quantified. Professional judgement has therefore to be used and commonly used rules of thumb can vary between 25% to 30% of contract completion.

PROFESSIONAL EDUCATION

2.15 Example

Kikabout Konstruction Ltd is building a new £4,000,000 millennium football stadium for a newly promoted club Shepherds Bush Authorials. The contract commenced on 1 June 20X4 and is planned to be completed by 31 July 20X6 in time for the new 20X6/X7 season.

- Costs incurred by Kikabout Konstruction Ltd on the contract to year end 30 December 20X4 amounted to £1,040,000.

- During the year, Kikabout Konstruction issued two invoices for progress payments:

Progress payment 1 £600,000

Progress payment 2 £520,000

- Work certified by architects for the year amounts to £1,240,000.
- The estimated costs to completion on 31 July 20X6 are £1,960,000.

Show how the above transactions should be accounted for by Kikabout Konstruction Ltd in the year ended 31 December 20X6.

Solution

Calculation of contract profitability

		£
Contract value		4,000,000
Costs incurred to date	1,040,000	
Expected further costs to complete	1,960,000	3,000,000
Expected total profit		1,000,000

Percentage completed

$$\frac{\text{Work certified}}{\text{Contract value}} = \frac{£1,240,000}{£4,000,000} = 31\%$$

Percentage cash received on work certified

$$\text{Percentage completed} \times \frac{\text{Cash received}}{\text{Work certified}} = 31\% \times \frac{£1,120,000}{£1,240,000} = 28\%$$

Note: The above can be short-cut by using the alternative formula:

$$\frac{\text{Cash received}}{\text{Contract value}} = \frac{£1,120,000}{£4,000,000} = 28\%$$

	Estimated total £	Collected 28% £	Recognised previous period £	Recognised this period £
Turnover	4,000,000	1,120,000	–	1,120,000
Cost of sales (balancing figure)	3,000,000	840,000	–	840,000
Gross profit	1,000,000	280,000	–	280,000

WIP – Shepherd's Bush Authorials Millennium Stadium

	£		£
Bank/Creditors	1,040,000	Cost of sales	840,000
		Balance c/d	200,000
	1,040,000		1,040,000
Balance b/d	200,000		

Progress payments (Amounts recoverable on contracts)

	£			£
Work certified	1,240,000	Invoice 1		600,000
		Invoice 2		520,000
		Balance	c/d	120,000
	1,240,000			1,240,000
Balance b/d	120,000			

Turnover

	£		£
		Work certified	1,240,000

Cost of sales

	£		£
Tfr from WIP	840,000		

The WIP account shows costs incurred of £1,040,000 less costs of £840,000 transferred to profit and loss account, via cost of sales. The WIP balance should be disclosed as "long-term contract balances" and disclosed separately under the heading stocks.

The progress payments account provides a record of the extent to which work certified by the architects has been invoiced to the customer. The debit of £1,240,000 is the work certified, with credits of £600,000 and £520,000, in respect of invoices sent to the customer.

The debit balance on the progress payment account reflects unbilled work. The debit balance should be disclosed separately as "Amounts recoverable on contracts" under debtors.

BPP
PROFESSIONAL EDUCATION

Chapter Roundup

- **Stocks** comprise:

  Raw materials and consumables
  Work in progress
  Finished goods and goods for resale
  Payments on account (of purchases)

  They must be revalued at **lower of cost and net realisable value**.

  FIFO and **weighted average** are the accepted means of valuation under SSAP 9.

- The most controversial aspect of SSAP 9 is its approach to the valuation of work in progress for incomplete long-term contracts.

- Turnover and profit should be recognised throughout the duration of the contract. Any foreseeable loss should be recognised immediately.

- There are generally two alternative formulae for determining the estimated attributable profit for the year.

  - Work certified basis
  - Costs incurred basis

- Long-term contract WIP can be calculated as:

Costs to date	X
Less Costs transferred to cost of sales	(X)
Less Foreseeable losses	(X)
Less Payments on account in excess of turnover	(X)
WIP	X

Quick Quiz

1   Net realisable value = Selling price **less** .... **less** ....

2   Which stock costing methods are permissible under SSAP 9?

    A   FIFO, LIFO, average cost, unit cost
    B   Unit cost, job cost, batch cost, LIFO
    C   Process costing, unit cost LIFO, average cost
    D   Job costing, average cost, FIFO, unit cost.

3   Any expected loss on a long-term contract must be recognised, in full, in the year it was identified.

    True   ☐

    False   ☐

4   List the five steps to be taken when valuing long-term contracts.

5   Which items in the profit and loss and balance sheet are potentially affected by long term contracts?

Answers to Quick Quiz

1   Net realisable value = selling price **less** costs to completion **less** costs to market, sell and distribute. (see Para 1)

2   D, LIFO is not an acceptable costing method

3   True.

4   1   Calculate the expected profit or loss
     2   Calculate turnover for the period
     3   Calculate cost of sales
     4   Review balance on WIP
     5   Compare cumulative turnover with payments on account (2.10)

5   Profit and loss: turnover and cost of sales. Balance sheet: stocks, debtors, creditors and provisions

Now try the question below from the Exam Question Bank

Number	Level	Marks	Time
Q8	Full exam	30	54 mins

Financial instruments

Topic list	Syllabus reference
1 Financial instruments	3(a)
2 Presentation of financial instruments	3(a)
3 Disclosure of financial instruments	3(a)
4 Recognition of financial instruments	3(a)
5 Measurement of financial instruments	3(a)

Introduction

Financial instruments sounds like a daunting subject, and indeed this is a complex and controversial area. The numbers involved in financial instruments are often huge, but don't let this put you off. In this chapter we aim to simplify the topic as much as possible and to focus on the important issues.

The debate over **measurement and recognition** of financial instruments is very closely connected to the **off balance sheet finance debate**. Before the issue of FRS 25 and FRS 26 many financial instruments were not recognised or disclosed in financial statements at all.

The issues of disclosure and presentation are addressed in **FRS 25 and 29**. Recognition and measurement issues are dealt with in **FRS 26**. There has been plenty in the financial and accountancy press on this project – keep your eyes open for further press comment.

Study guide

- Explain the need for an accounting standard on financial instruments

- Distinguished between debt and share capital

- Apply the requirements of relevant accounting standards to the issue and finance costs of:

  (i) equity and preference shares

  (ii) debt instruments with no conversion rights

  (iii) convertible debt

Exam guide

This is a highly controversial topic and therefore, likely to be examined, probably in Section B.

Exam focus point

> You will not be expected to deal with transactions.

1 Financial instruments

FAST FORWARD

> Financial instruments can be very complex, particularly **derivative instruments**, although **primary instruments** are more straightforward.

If you read the financial press you will probably be aware of **rapid international expansion** in the use of financial instruments. These vary from straightforward, traditional instruments, eg bonds, through to various forms of so-called 'derivative instruments'

We can perhaps summarise the reasons why a project on financial instruments was considered necessary as follows.

(a) The **significant growth of financial instruments** over recent years has outstripped the development of guidance for their accounting.

(b) The topic is of **international concern**, other national standard-setters are involved as well as the IASB.

(c) There have been recent **high-profile disasters** involving derivatives (eg Barings) which, while not caused by accounting failures, have raised questions about accounting and disclosure practices.

There are three standards on financial instruments, all issued as part of the ASB's convergence programme, and all of which implement IAS.

(a) FRS 25 *Financial instruments: presentation*, which deals with:

  (i)   The classification of financial instruments between liabilities and equity
  (ii)   Presentation of certain compound instruments

(b) FRS 29 *Financial instruments: disclosures,* which revised, simplified and incorporated disclosure requirements previously in FRS 25.

(c) FRS 26 *Financial Instruments: recognition and measurement*, which deals with:

  (i)   Recognition and derecognition
  (ii)   The measurement of financial instruments
  (iii) Hedge accounting

Note: The recognition and derecognition rules were introduced in April 2006 by an amendment.

1.1 Definitions

FAST FORWARD

The important definitions to learn are:

- **Financial asset**
- **Financial liability**
- **Equity instrument**

The most important definitions are common to all three standards.

Key terms

Financial instrument. Any contract that gives rise to both a financial asset of one entity and a financial liability or equity instrument of another entity.

Financial asset. Any asset that is:

(a)   Cash

(b)   An equity instrument of another entity

(c)   A contractual right to receive cash or another financial asset from another entity; or to exchange financial instruments with another entity under conditions that are potentially favourable to the entity, or

(d)   A contract that will or may be settled in the entity's own equity instruments and is:

    (i)   A non-derivative for which the entity is or may be obliged to receive a variable number of the entity's own equity instruments; or

    (ii)   A derivative that will or may be settled other than by the exchange of a fixed amount of cash or another financial asset for a fixed number of the entity's own equity instruments.

Financial liability. Any liability that is:

(a)   A contractual obligation:

    (i)   To deliver cash or another financial asset to another entity, or

    (ii)   To exchange financial instruments with another entity under conditions that are potentially unfavourable; or

Key terms

(b)   a contract that will or may be settled in the entity's own equity instruments and is:

  (i)   A non-derivative for which the entity is or may be obliged to deliver a variable number of the entity's own equity instruments; or

  (ii)   A derivative that will or may be settled other than by the exchange of a fixed amount of cash or another financial asset for a fixed number of the entity's own equity instruments.

Equity instrument. Any contract that evidences a residual interest in the assets of an entity after deducting all of its liabilities.

Fair value is the amount for which an asset could be exchanged, or a liability settled, between knowledgeable, willing parties in an arm's length transaction

Derivative. A financial instrument or other contract with all three of the following characteristics:

(a)   Its value changes in response to the change in a specified interest rate, financial instrument price, commodity price, foreign exchange rate, index of prices or rates, credit rating or credit index, or other variable (sometimes called the 'underlying');

(b)   It requires no initial net investment or an initial net investment that is smaller than would be required for other types of contracts that would be expected to have a similar response to changes in market factors; and

(c)   It is settled at a future date.   *(FRS 25, FRS 26 and FRS 29)*

Exam focus point

These are very important – particularly the first three – so learn them.

1.1.1 More detail

We should clarify some points arising from these definitions. Firstly, one or two terms above should be themselves defined.

(a)   A '**contract**' need not be in writing, but it must comprise an agreement that has 'clear economic consequences' and which the parties to it cannot avoid, usually because the agreement is enforceable in law.

(b)   An '**entity**' here could be an individual, partnership, incorporated body or government agency.

The definitions of **financial assets and financial liabilities** may seem rather circular, referring as they do to the terms financial asset and financial instrument. The point is that there may be a chain of contractual rights and obligations, but it will lead ultimately to the receipt or payment of cash *or* the acquisition or issue of an equity instrument.

Examples of **financial assets** include:

(a)   Trade debtors
(b)   Options
(c)   Shares (when used as an investment)

Examples of **financial liabilities** include:

(a)   Trade creditors
(b)   Debenture loans payable
(c)   Redeemable preference (non-equity) shares
(d)   Forward contracts standing at a loss

As we have already noted, financial instruments include both of the following.

(a) **Primary instruments**: eg receivables, payables and equity securities

(b) **Derivative instruments**: eg financial options, futures and forwards, interest rate swaps and currency swaps, **whether recognised or unrecognised**

FRS 25 makes it clear that the following items are *not* financial instruments.

- **Physical assets**, eg stocks, property, plant and equipment, leased assets and intangible assets (patents, trademarks etc)

- **Prepaid expenses**, deferred revenue and most warranty obligations

- Liabilities or assets that are **not contractual** in nature

- Contractual rights/obligations that **do not involve transfer of a financial asset**, eg commodity futures contracts, operating leases

Question | Financial instruments

Can you give the reasons why the first two items listed above do not qualify as financial instruments?

Answer

Refer to the definitions of financial assets and liabilities given above.

(a) **Physical assets**: control of these creates an opportunity to generate an inflow of cash or other assets, but it does not give rise to a present right to receive cash or other financial assets.

(b) **Prepaid expenses, etc**: the future economic benefit is the receipt of goods/services rather than the right to receive cash or other financial assets.

(c) **Deferred revenue, warranty obligations**: the probable outflow of economic benefits is the delivery of goods/services rather than cash or another financial asset.

Contingent rights and obligations meet the definition of financial assets and financial liabilities respectively, even though many do not qualify for recognition in financial statements. This is because the contractual rights or obligations exist because of a past transaction or event (eg assumption of a guarantee).

1.2 Derivatives

A **derivative** is a financial instrument that **derives** its value from the price or rate of an underlying item. Common **examples** of derivatives include:

(a) **Forward contracts**: agreements to buy or sell an asset at a fixed price at a fixed future date

(b) **Futures contracts**: similar to forward contracts except that contracts are standardised and traded on an exchange

(c) **Options**: rights (but not obligations) for the option holder to exercise at a pre-determined price; the option writer loses out if the option is exercised

(d) **Swaps**: agreements to swap one set of cash flows for another (normally interest rate or currency swaps).

The nature of derivatives often gives rise to **particular problems**. The **value** of a derivative (and the amount at which it is eventually settled) depends on **movements** in an underlying item (such as an exchange rate). This means that settlement of a derivative can lead to a very different result from the one originally envisaged. A company which has derivatives is exposed to **uncertainty and risk** (potential for gain or loss) and this can have a very material effect on its financial performance, financial position and cash flows.

Yet because a derivative contract normally has **little or no initial cost**, under traditional accounting it **may not be recognised** in the financial statements at all. Alternatively it may be recognised at an amount which bears no relation to its current value. This is clearly **misleading** and leaves users of the financial statements unaware of the **level of risk** that the company faces. The IASs on which FRS 25 and 26 are based were developed in order to correct this situation.

1.3 Section summary

- Three accounting standards are relevant:

    - FRS 25 *Financial instruments: presentation*
    - FRS 26 *Financial instruments: measurement*
    - FRS 29 *Financial instruments: disclosures*

- The definitions of **financial asset, financial liability** and **equity instrument** are fundamental to FRS 25, FRS 26 and FRS 29.

- Financial instruments include:

    - **Primary** instruments
    - **Derivative** instruments

2 Presentation of financial instruments

The objective of FRS 25 is:

'to enhance financial statement users' understanding of the significance of on-balance-sheet and off-balance-sheet financial instruments to an entity's financial position, performance and cash flows.'

2.1 Scope

FRS 25 should be applied in the presentation and disclosure of **all types of financial instruments**, whether recognised or unrecognised.

Certain items are **excluded**.

- Interests in subsidiaries (FRS 2, FRS 5)

- Interests in associates (FRS 9)

- Interests in joint ventures (FRS 9)

- Pensions and other post-retirement benefits (FRS 17)

- Insurance contracts

- Contracts for contingent consideration in a business combination

- Contracts that require a payment based on climatic, geographic or other physical variables

- Financial instruments, contracts and obligations under share-based payment transactions (FRS 20)

2.2 Liabilities and equity

FAST FORWARD Financial instruments must be classified as **liabilities** or **equity** according to their **substance**.

The main thrust of FRS 25 here is that financial instruments should be presented according to their **substance**, **not merely their legal form**. In particular, entities which issue financial instruments should classify them (or their component parts) as **either financial liabilities, or equity**.

The classification of a financial instrument as a liability or as equity depends on the following.

- The **substance of the contractual arrangement** on initial recognition
- The definitions of a financial liability and an equity instrument

FAST FORWARD The critical feature of a financial liability is the **contractual obligation to deliver cash** or another financial instrument.

How should a **financial liability be distinguished from an equity instrument**? The critical feature of a **liability** is an **obligation** to transfer economic benefit. Therefore a financial instrument is a financial liability if there is a **contractual obligation** on the issuer either to deliver cash or another financial asset to the holder or to exchange another financial instrument with the holder under potentially unfavourable conditions to the issuer.

The financial liability exists **regardless of the way in which the contractual obligation will be settled**. The issuer's ability to satisfy an obligation may be restricted, eg by lack of access to foreign currency, but this is irrelevant as it does not remove the issuer's obligation or the holder's right under the instrument.

Where the above critical feature is *not* met, then the financial instrument is an **equity instrument**. FRS 25 explains that although the holder of an equity instrument may be entitled to a *pro rata* share of any distributions out of equity, the issuer does *not* have a contractual obligation to make such a distribution.

Although substance and legal form are often **consistent with each other**, this is not always the case. In particular, a financial instrument may have the legal form of equity, but in substance it is in fact a liability. Other instruments may combine features of both equity instruments and financial liabilities.

For example, many entities issue **preference shares** which must be **redeemed** by the issuer for a fixed (or determinable) amount at a fixed (or determinable) future date. Alternatively, the holder may have the right to require the issuer to redeem the shares at or after a certain date for a fixed amount. In such cases, the issuer has an **obligation**. Therefore the instrument is a **financial liability** and should be classified as such.

The classification of the financial instrument is made when it is **first recognised** and this classification will continue until the financial instrument is removed from the entity's balance sheet.

2.3 Contingent settlement provisions

An entity may issue a financial instrument where the way in which it is settled depends on:

(a) The occurrence or non-occurrence of uncertain future events, or
(b) The outcome of uncertain circumstances,

that are beyond the control of both the holder and the issuer of the instrument. For example, an entity might have to deliver cash instead of issuing equity shares. In this situation it is not immediately clear whether the entity has an equity instrument or a financial liability.

Such financial instruments should be classified as **financial liabilities** unless the possibility of settlement is remote.

2.4 Settlement options

When a derivative financial instrument gives one party a **choice** over how it is settled (eg, the issuer can choose whether to settle in cash or by issuing shares) the instrument is a **financial asset** or a **financial liability** unless **all the alternative choices** would result in it being an equity instrument.

2.5 Compound financial instruments

FAST FORWARD

> **Compound instruments** are split into **equity** and **liability** components and presented in the balance sheet accordingly.

Some financial instruments contain both a liability and an equity element. In such cases, FRS 25 requires the component parts of the instrument to be **classified separately**, according to the substance of the contractual arrangement and the definitions of a financial liability and an equity instrument.

One of the most common types of compound instrument is **convertible debt**. This creates a primary financial liability of the issuer and grants an option to the holder of the instrument to convert it into an equity instrument (usually ordinary shares) of the issuer. This is the economic equivalent of the issue of conventional debt plus a warrant to acquire shares in the future.

Although in theory there are several possible ways of calculating the split, FRS 25 requires the following method:

(a) Calculate the value for the liability component.

(b) Deduct this from the instrument as a whole to leave a residual value for the equity component.

The reasoning behind this approach is that an entity's equity is its residual interest in its assets amount after deducting all its liabilities.

The **sum of the carrying amounts** assigned to liability and equity will always be equal to the carrying amount that would be ascribed to the instrument **as a whole**.

2.6 Example: Valuation of compound instruments

Rathbone Co issues 2,000 convertible bonds at the start of 20X2. The bonds have a three year term, and are issued at par with a face value of £1,000 per bond, giving total proceeds of £2,000,000. Interest is payable annually in arrears at a nominal annual interest rate of 6%. Each bond is convertible at any time up to maturity into 250 common shares.

When the bonds are issued, the prevailing market interest rate for similar debt without conversion options is 9%. At the issue date, the market price of one common share is £3. The dividends expected over the three year term of the bonds amount to 14p per share at the end of each year. The risk-free annual interest rate for a three year term is 5%.

Required

What is the value of the equity component in the bond?

Solution

The liability component is valued first, and the difference between the proceeds of the bond issue and the fair value of the liability is assigned to the equity component. The present value of the liability component is calculated using a discount rate of 9%, the market interest rate for similar bonds having no conversion rights, as shown.

	£
Present value of the principal: £2,000,000 payable at the end of three years (£2m ×0.772)*	1,544,00
Present value of the interest: £120,000 payable annually in arrears for three years (£120,000 ×2.531)*	303,720
Total liability component	1,847,720
Equity component (balancing figure)	152,280
Proceeds of the bond issue	2,000,000

* These figures can be obtained from discount and annuity tables.

The split between the liability and equity components remains the same throughout the term of the instrument, even if there are changes in the **likelihood of the option being exercised.** This is because it is not always possible to predict how a holder will behave. The issuer continues to have an obligation to make future payments until conversion, maturity of the instrument or some other relevant transaction takes place.

2.7 Treasury shares

Treasury shares are an example of an equity instrument.

An entity can choose to reaquire its own shares and, rather than cancelling them, hold them in treasury. These are then classified as 'treasury shares' and can be issued for cash or issued as part of an employee share scheme, at some point in the future.

Treasury shares are shown on the balance sheet as a deduction from equity. For instance, a company has 500,000 £1 shares in issue and £200,000 in share premium. It requires 100,000 shares for £1.40. The shares reaquired are classified as treasury shares and presented as follows:

	£'000
Share capital – £1 shares	500
Share premium	200
	700
Treasury shares	(140)
	560

2.8 Interest, dividends, losses and gains

As well as looking at balance sheet presentation, FRS 25 considers how financial instruments affect the profit and loss account (and movements in equity). The treatment varies according to whether interest, dividends, losses or gains relate to a financial liability or an equity instrument.

(a)   Interest, dividends, losses and gains relating to a financial instrument (or component part) classified as a **financial liability** should be recognised as **income or expense** in profit or loss.

(b)   Distributions to holders of a financial instrument classified as an **equity instrument** should be **debited directly to equity** by the issuer.

(c)   **Transaction costs** of an equity transaction shall be accounted for as a **deduction from equity** (unless they are directly attributable to the acquisition of a business, in which case they are accounted for under FRS 2).

2.9 Offsetting a financial asset and a financial liability

A financial asset and financial liability should **only** be **offset**, with the net amount reported in the balance sheet, when an entity:

    (a)   has a **legally enforceable right of set off**, *and*

    (b)   intends to settle on a **net basis**, or to realise the asset and settle the liability simultaneously, ie at the same moment.

This will reflect the expected **future cash flows** of the entity in these specific circumstances. In all other cases, financial assets and financial liabilities are presented separately.

2.10 Current liabilities

A **long-term financial liability** due to be **settled within twelve months** of the balance sheet date should be classified as a **current liability**, even if an agreement to refinance, or to reschedule payments, on a long-term basis is completed after the balance sheet date and before the financial statements are authorised for issue.

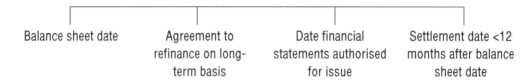

| Balance sheet date | Agreement to refinance on long-term basis | Date financial statements authorised for issue | Settlement date <12 months after balance sheet date |

A **long-term financial liability** that is payable on **demand** because the entity **breached** a **condition** of its loan agreement should be classified as **current** at the balance sheet date even if the **lender** has agreed **after the balance sheet date**, and **before** the financial statements are **authorised for issue**, **not** to **demand payment** as a consequence of the breach.

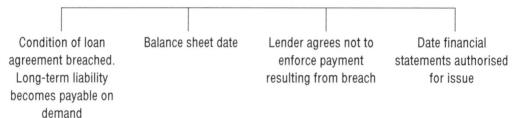

| Condition of loan agreement breached. Long-term liability becomes payable on demand | Balance sheet date | Lender agrees not to enforce payment resulting from breach | Date financial statements authorised for issue |

However, if the **lender** has **agreed** by the **balance sheet date** to provide a **period of grace** ending **at least twelve months after the balance sheet date** within which the entity can rectify the breach and during that time the lender cannot demand immediate repayment, the liability is classified as **non-current.**

2.11 Section summary

- Financial instruments must be classified as **liabilities** or **equity**
- The **substance** of the financial instrument is more important than its **legal form**
- The **critical feature of a financial liability** is the contractual obligation to deliver cash or another financial instrument
- **Compound instruments** are split into equity and liability parts and presented accordingly
- **Interest, dividends, losses and gains** are treated according to whether they relate to a financial asset or a financial liability
- Rules apply stating whether liabilities should be classified as **current or non current**

3 Disclosure of financial instruments

FAST FORWARD

FRS 29 specifies the **disclosures** required for financial instruments. The standard requires qualitative and quantitative disclosures about exposure to risks arising from financial instruments and specifies minimum disclosures about credit risk, liquidity risk and market risk.

The IASB and ASB maintain that users of financial instruments need information about an entity's exposures to risks and how those risks are managed, as this information can **influence a user's assessment of the financial position and financial performance of an entity** or of the amount, timing and uncertainty of its **future cash flows.**

There have been new techniques and approaches to measuring risk management, which highlighted the need for guidance.

Accordingly, FRS 29 *Financial instruments: disclosures* was issued in December 2005. This embodies IFRS 7 of the same name, amended for UK entities.

3.1 General requirements

The extent of disclosure required depends on the extent of the entity's use of financial instruments and of its exposure to risk. It **adds to the requirements previously in FRS 25** by requiring:

- Enhanced balance sheet and income statement disclosures

- Disclosures about an allowance account when one is used to reduce the carrying amount of impaired financial instruments.

The standard requires **qualitative and quantitative disclosures about exposure to risks** arising from financial instruments, and specifies minimum disclosures about **credit risk**, **liquidity risk** and **market risk**.

3.2 Objective

The objective of the standard is to require entities to provide disclosures in their financial statements that enable users to evaluate:

(a)   The significance of financial instruments for the entity's financial position and performance

(b)   The nature and extent of risks arising from financial instruments to which the entity is exposed during the period and at the reporting date, and how the entity manages those risks.

The principles in FRS 29 complement the principles for recognising, measuring and presenting financial assets and financial liabilities in FRS 25 *Financial instruments: presentation* and FRS 26 *Financial instruments: recognition and measurement.*

3.3 Classes of financial instruments and levels of disclosure

The entity must group financial instruments into classes **appropriate to the nature of the information disclosed**. An entity must decide in the light of its circumstances how much detail it provides. Sufficient information must be provided to permit reconciliation to the line items presented in the balance sheet.

3.3.1 Balance sheet

The following must be disclosed.

(a)   **Carrying amount** of financial assets and liabilities by FRS 26 category

(b)   **Reason for any reclassification** between fair value and amortised cost (and vice versa)

(c)   **Details** of the assets and exposure to risk where the entity has made a **transfer** such that part or all of the financial assets do not qualify for derecognition.

(d)   The **carrying amount** of financial assets the entity has **pledged as collateral** for liabilities or contingent liabilities and the associated terms and conditions.

(e)   When financial assets are impaired by credit losses and the entity records the impairment in a separate account (eg an **allowance account** used to record individual impairments or a similar account used to record a collective impairment of assets) rather than directly reducing the carrying amount of the asset, it must disclose a **reconciliation** of changes in that account during the period for each class of financial assets.

(f)   The **existence of multiple embedded derivatives**, where compound instruments contain these.

(g)   **Defaults and breaches**

3.3.2 Income statement and equity

The entity must disclose the following **items of income, expense, gains or losses**, either on the face of the financial statements or in the notes.

(a)   Net gains/losses by FRS 26 category (broken down as appropriate: eg interest, fair value changes, dividend income)

(b)   Interest income/expense

(c)   Impairments losses by class of financial asset

3.3.3 Other disclosures

Entities must disclose in the summary of **significant accounting policies** the measurement basis used in preparing the financial statements and the other accounting policies that are relevant to an understanding of the financial statements.

Disclosures must be made relating to **fair value**:

(a)   **By class** in a way that allows comparison to balance sheet value. (Financial assets and liabilities may only be offset to the extent that their carrying amounts are offset in the balance sheet.)

(b)   The **methods and assumptions** used, for example by reference to an active market, and any change in these assumptions. If the market for a financial instrument is not active, a valuation technique, as per FRS 26, must be used. There could be a difference between the fair value at initial recognition and the amount that would be determined using the valuation technique. The accounting policy for recognising that difference in profit or loss, the aggregate difference yet to be recognised in profit or loss at the beginning and end of the period and a reconciliation of the changes in the balance of this difference, should be disclosed.

3.4 Nature and extent of risks arising from financial instruments

In undertaking transactions in financial instruments, an entity may assume or transfer to another party one or more of **different types of financial risk** as defined below. The disclosures required by the standard show the extent to which an entity is exposed to these different types of risk, relating to both recognised and unrecognised financial instruments.

The examiner has stated that you will not be examined on the financial risks of financial instruments.

4 Recognition of financial instruments

FRS 26 *Financial instruments: recognition and measurement* establishes principles for recognising and measuring financial assets and financial liabilities.

4.1 Amendment

FAST FORWARD

> The Amendment to FRS 26 brings in the recognition and de-recognition rules of IAS 39.

In April 2006, the ASB issued *Amendment to FRS 26 (IAS 39) Financial instruments: measurement, recognition and derecognition.* This implements the recognition and derecognition rules in IAS 39. For items falling within the definition of financial instruments, recognition and derecognition are no longer governed by FRS 5.

In this section, FRS 26 will be known by its new name *Financial instruments: recognition and measurement.*

4.2 Initial recognition

Financial instruments should be recognised in the balance sheet when the entity becomes a party to the **contractual provisions of the instrument**.

Point to note

An important consequence of this is that all derivatives should be on the balance sheet.

Notice that this is **different** from the recognition criteria in the IASB *Framework,* the ASB *Statement of Principles* and in most other standards. Items are normally recognised when there is a probable inflow or outflow of resources and the item has a cost or value that can be measured reliably.

4.3 Example: Initial recognition

An entity has entered into two separate contracts.

(a)   A firm commitment (an order) to buy a specific quantity of iron
(b)   A forward contract to buy a specific quantity of iron at a specified price on a specified date.

Contract (a) is a **normal trading contract**. The entity does not recognise a liability for the iron until the goods have actually been delivered. (Note that this contract is not a financial instrument because it involves a physical asset, rather than a financial asset.)

Contract (b) is a **financial instrument**. Under FRS 26 the entity recognises a financial liability (an obligation to deliver cash) on the **commitment date**, rather than waiting for the closing date on which the exchange takes place.

Note that planned future transactions, no matter how likely, are not assets and liabilities of an entity – the entity has not yet become a party to the contract.

4.4 Derecognition

Derecognition is the removal of a previously recognised financial instrument from an entity's balance sheet.

An entity should derecognise a **financial asset** when:

(a)   The **contractual rights** to the cash flows from the financial asset **expire**, or

(b)   The entity **transfers substantially all the risks and rewards of ownership** of the financial asset to another party.

Question	Risks and rewards

Can you think of an example of sales of financial assets in which:

(a)   An entity has transferred substantially all the risks and rewards of ownership?

(b)   An entity has retained substantially all the risks and rewards of ownership?

Answer

FRS 26 includes the following examples:

(a)   (i)   An unconditional sale of a financial asset

(ii)   A sale of a financial asset together with an option to repurchase the financial asset at its fair value at the time of repurchase

(b)   (i)   A sale and repurchase transaction where the repurchase price is a fixed price or the sale price plus a lender's return

(ii)   A sale of a financial asset together with a total return swap that transfers the market risk exposure back to the entity

Exam focus point

The principle here is that of **substance over form**.

An entity should derecognise a **financial liability** when it is **extinguished** – ie, when the obligation specified in the contract is discharged or cancelled or expires.

It is possible for only **part** of a financial asset or liability to be derecognised. This is allowed if the part comprises:

(a)   Only specifically identified cash flows; or

(b)   Only a fully proportionate (pro rata) share of the total cash flows.

For example, if an entity holds a bond it has the right to two separate sets of cash inflows: those relating to the principal and those relating to the interest. It could sell the right to receive the interest to another party while retaining the right to receive the principal.

On derecognition, the amount to be included in net profit or loss for the period is calculated as follows:

Formula to learn

	£	£
Carrying amount of asset/liability (or the portion of asset/liability) transferred		X
Less: Proceeds received/paid	X	
Any cumulative gain or loss reported in equity	X	
		(X)
Difference to net profit/loss		X

Where only part of a financial asset is derecognised, the carrying amount of the asset should be allocated between the part retained and the part transferred based on their relative fair values on the date of transfer. A gain or loss should be recognised based on the proceeds for the portion transferred.

4.5 Section summary

- **All financial assets** and **liabilities** should be **recognised on the balance sheet**, including derivatives.

- Financial assets should be derecognised when the **rights to the cash flows** from the asset **expire** or where **substantially all the risks and rewards of ownership are transferred** to another party.

- Financial liabilities should be derecognised when they are **extinguished**.

5 Measurement of financial instruments

FRS 26 *Financial instruments: recognition and measurement* was published in 2004, and amended in 2006 to include the IAS 39 rules on recognition and derecognition. It applies to listed entities or entities whose financial statements are prepared in accordance with the fair value accounting rules of CA 85. Entities applying the FRSSE are exempt.

5.1 Initial measurement

Financial instruments are initially measured at the **fair value** of the consideration given or received (ie, **cost**) **plus** (in most cases) **transaction costs** that are **directly attributable** to the acquisition or issue of the financial instrument.

The **exception** to this rule is where a financial instrument is designated as **at fair value through profit or loss** (this term is explained below). In this case, **transaction costs** are **not** added to fair value at initial recognition.

The fair value of the consideration is normally the transaction price or market prices. If market prices are not reliable, the fair value may be **estimated** using a valuation technique (for example, by discounting cash flows).

5.2 Subsequent measurement

For the purposes of measuring a financial asset held subsequent to initial recognition, FRS 26 classifies financial assets into four categories defined here.

Key terms

A financial asset or liability at fair value through profit or loss meets either of the following conditions:

(a)   It is classified as held for trading. A financial instrument is classified as held for trading if it is:

    (i)   Acquired or incurred principally for the purpose of selling or repurchasing it in the near term

    (ii)   Part of a portfolio of identified financial instruments that are managed together and for which there is evidence of a recent actual pattern of short-term profit-taking or

    (iii)   A derivative (unless it is a designated and effective hedging instrument)

(b)   Upon initial recognition it is designated by the entity as at fair value through profit or loss. Any financial instrument may be so designated when it is initially recognised except for investments in equity instruments that do not have a quoted market price in an active market and whose fair value cannot be reliably measured.

Held-to-maturity investments are non-derivative financial assets with fixed or determinable payments and fixed maturity that an entity has the positive intent and ability to hold to maturity other than:

(a)   Those that the entity upon initial recognition designates as at fair value through profit or loss

(b)   Those that the entity designates as available for sale and

(c)   Those that meet the definition of loans and receivables.

Key terms

Loans and receivables are non-derivative financial assets with fixed or determinable payments that are not quoted in an active market, other than:

(a) Those that the entity intends to sell immediately or in the near term, which should be classified as held for trading and those that the entity upon initial recognition designates as at fair value through profit or loss

(b) Those that the entity upon initial recognition designates as available-for-sale or

(c) Those for which the holder may not recover substantially all of the initial investment, other than because of credit deterioration, which shall be classified as available for sale

An interest acquired in a pool of assets that are not loans or receivables (for example, an interest in a mutual fund or a similar fund) is not a loan or a receivable.

Available-for-sale financial assets are those financial assets that are not:

(a) Loans and receivables originated by the entity,
(b) Held-to-maturity investments, or
(c) Financial assets at fair value through profit or loss. *(FRS 26)*

FAST FORWARD

Subsequently they should be **re-measured to fair value** except for

(a) Loans and receivables not held for trading
(b) Other **held-to-maturity investments**
(c) **Financial assets** whose value **cannot be reliably measured**

After initial recognition, all financial assets should be **remeasured to fair value**, without any deduction for transaction costs that may be incurred on sale of other disposal, except for:

(a) **Loans and receivables**

(b) **Held to maturity investments**

(c) Investments in **equity instruments** that do not have a quoted market price in an active market and whose **fair value cannot be reliably measured** and derivatives that are linked to and must be settled by delivery of such unquoted equity instruments

Loans and receivables and **held to maturity investments** should be measured at **amortised cost using the effective interest method**.

Key term

Amortised cost of a financial asset or financial liability is the amount at which the financial asset or liability is measured at initial recognition minus principal repayments, plus or minus the cumulative amortisation of any difference between that initial amount and the maturity amount, and minus any write-down (directly or through the use of an allowance account) for impairment or uncollectability.

The **effective interest method** is a method of calculating the amortised cost of a financial instrument and of allocating the interest income or interest expense over the relevant period.

The **effective interest rate** is the rate that exactly discounts estimated future cash payments or receipts through the expected life of the financial instrument. *(FRS 26)*

5.3 Example: Amortised cost

On 1 January 20X1 Abacus Co purchases a debt instrument for its fair value of £1,000. The debt instrument is due to mature on 31 December 20X5. The instrument has a principal amount of £1,250 and the instrument carries fixed interest at 4.72% that is paid annually. The effective interest rate is 10%.

How should Abacus Co account for the debt instrument over its five year term?

Solution

Abacus Co will receive interest of £59 (1,250 × 4.72%) each year and £1,250 when the instrument matures.

Abacus must allocate the discount of £250 and the interest receivable over the five year term at a constant rate on the carrying amount of the debt. To do this, it must apply the effective interest rate of 10%.

The following table shows the allocation over the years:

Year	Amortised cost at beginning of year	Profit and loss account: Interest income for year (@10%)	Interest received during year (cash inflow)	Amortised cost at end of year
	£	£	£	£
20X1	1,000	100	(59)	1,041
20X2	1,041	104	(59)	1,086
20X3	1,086	109	(59)	1,136
20X4	1,136	113	(59)	1,190
20X5	1,190	119	(1,250+59)	–

Each year the carrying amount of the financial asset is increased by the interest income for the year and reduced by the interest actually received during the year.

Investments whose **fair value cannot be reliably measured** should be measured at **cost**.

5.4 Classification

On initial recognition, certain financial instruments must be designated at fair value through profit and loss.

In contrast, it is quite difficult for an entity **not** to remeasure financial instruments to fair value.

For a financial instrument to be held to maturity it must meet several extremely narrow criteria. The entity must have a **positive intent** and a **demonstrated ability** to hold the investment to maturity. These conditions are not met if:

(a)   The entity intends to hold the financial asset for an undefined period

(b)   The entity stands ready to sell the financial asset in response to changes in interest rates or risks, liquidity needs and similar factors (unless these situations could not possibly have been reasonably anticipated)

(c)   The issuer has the right to settle the financial asset at an amount significantly below its amortised cost (because this right will almost certainly be exercised)

(d)   It does not have the financial resources available to continue to finance the investment until maturity

(e)   It is subject to an existing legal or other constraint that could frustrate its intention to hold the financial asset to maturity

In addition, an **equity** instrument is **unlikely** to meet the criteria for classification as held to maturity.

There is a **penalty** for selling or reclassifying a 'held-to-maturity' investment other than in certain very tightly defined circumstances. If this has occurred during the **current** financial year or during the **two preceding** financial years **no** financial asset can be classified as held-to-maturity.

If an entity can no longer hold an investment to maturity, it is no longer appropriate to use amortised cost and the asset must be re-measured to fair value. **All** remaining held-to-maturity investments must also be re-measured to fair value and classified as available-for-sale (see above).

5.5 Subsequent measurement of financial liabilities

After initial recognition, all financial liabilities should be measured at **amortised cost**, with the exception of financial liabilities at fair value through profit or loss (including most derivatives). These should be measured at **fair value**, but where the fair value **is not capable of reliable measurement**, they should be measured at **cost**.

| Question | Deep discount bond |

Galaxy Co issues a bond for £503,778 on 1 January 20X2. No interest is payable on the bond, but it will be redeemed on 31 December 20X4 for £600,000. The bond has **not** been designated as at fair value through profit or loss.

Required

Calculate the charge to the profit and loss account of Galaxy Co for the year ended 31 December 20X2 and the balance outstanding at 31 December 20X2.

Answer

The bond is a 'deep discount' bond and is a financial liability of Galaxy Co. It is measured at amortised cost. Although there is no interest as such, the difference between the initial cost of the bond and the price at which it will be redeemed is a finance cost. This must be allocated over the term of the bond at a constant rate on the carrying amount.

To calculate amortised cost we need to calculate the effective interest rate of the bond:

$$\frac{600,000}{503,778} = 1.191 \text{ over three years.}$$

To calculate **an annual rate**, we have to take the cube root, $(1.191)^{1/3}$, so the annual interest rate is 6%.

From tables, the interest rate is 6%.

The charge to the profit and loss account is £30,226 (503,778 × 6%)

The balance outstanding at 31 December 20X2 is £534,004 (503,778 + 30,226)

5.6 Gains and losses

Instruments at **fair value through profit or loss**: gains and losses are recognised **in profit or loss** (ie, in the profit and loss account).

Available for sale financial assets: gains and losses are recognised **in the statement of total recognised gains and losses.** When the asset is derecognised the cumulative gain or loss previously recognised in the STRGL should be recognised in profit and loss.

Financial instruments carried at **amortised cost**: gains and losses are recognised **in profit and loss** as a result of the amortisation process and when the asset is derecognised.

Financial assets and financial assets that are **hedged items**: special rules apply (discussed later in this chapter).

Question

Ellesmere Co entered into the following transactions during the year ended 31 December 20X3:

(1) Entered into a speculative interest rate option costing £10,000 on 1 January 20X3 to borrow £6,000,000 from AB Bank commencing 31 March 20X5 for 6 months at 4%. The value of the option at 31 December 20X3 was £15,250.

(2) Purchased 6% debentures in FG Co on 1 January 20X1 (their issue date) for £150,000 as an investment. Ellesmere Co intends to hold the debentures until their redemption at a premium in 5 year's time. The effective rate of interest of the bond is 8.0%.

(3) Purchased 50,000 shares in ST Co on 1 July 20X3 for £3.50 each as an investment. The share price on 31 December 20X3 was £3.75.

Required

Show the accounting treatment and relevant extracts from the financial statements for the year ended 31 December 20X3.

Answer

BALANCE SHEET EXTRACTS

	£
Financial assets:	
Interest rate option (W1)	15,250
4% debentures in MT Co (W2)	153,000
Shares in EG Co (W3)	187,500

PROFIT AND LOSS ACCOUNT EXTRACTS

	£
Finance income:	
Gain on interest rate option (W1)	5,250
Effective interest on 6% debentures (W2)	12,000

Workings

1   *Interest rate option*

This is a derivative and so it must be treated as at fair value through profit or loss.

Initial measurement (at cost):

DEBIT	Financial asset	£10,000	
CREDIT	Cash		£10,000

At 31.12.20X3 (re-measured to fair value)

DEBIT	Financial asset (£15,250 – £10,000)	£5,250	
CREDIT	Profit and loss account		£5,250

2   *Debentures*

On the basis of the information provided, this can be treated as a held-to-maturity investment.

Initial measurement (at cost):

DEBIT	Financial asset	£150,000	
CREDIT	Cash		£150,000

At 31.12.20X3 (amortised cost):

DEBIT	Financial asset (150,000 × 8%)	£12,000	
CREDIT	Finance income		£12,000
DEBIT	Cash (150,000 × 6%)	£9,000	
CREDIT	Financial asset		£9,000

Amortised cost at 31.12.20X3:

(150,000 + 12,000 – 9,000)	£153,000

3   *Shares*

These are treated as an available for sale financial asset (shares cannot normally be held to maturity and they are clearly not loans or receivables).

Initial measurement (at cost):

DEBIT	Financial asset (50,000 × £3.50)	£175,000	
CREDIT	Cash		£175,000

At 31.12.20X3 (re-measured to fair value)

DEBIT	Financial asset ((50,000 × £3.75) – £175,000))	£12,500	
CREDIT	Statement of total recognised gains and losses		£12,500

5.7 Impairment and uncollectability of financial assets

At each balance sheet date, an entity should assess whether there is any objective evidence that a financial asset or group of assets is impaired.

Question   Impairment

Give examples of indications that a financial asset or group of assets may be impaired.

Answer

FRS 26 lists the following:

(a)   Significant financial difficulty of the issuer

(b)   A breach of contract, such as a default in interest or principal payments

(c)   The lender granting a concession to the borrower that the lender would not otherwise consider, for reasons relating to the borrower's financial difficulty

(d)   It becomes probable that the borrower will enter bankruptcy

(e)   The disappearance of an active market for that financial asset because of financial difficulties

Where there is objective evidence of impairment, the entity should **determine the amount** of any impairment loss.

5.7.1 Financial assets carried at amortised cost

The impairment loss is the **difference** between the asset's **carrying amount** and its **recoverable amount**. The asset's recoverable amount is the present value of estimated future cash flows, discounted at the financial instrument's **original** effective interest rate.

The amount of the loss should be **recognised in profit or loss.**

If the impairment loss decreases at a later date (and the decrease relates to an event occurring **after** the impairment was recognised) the reversal is recognised in profit or loss. The carrying amount of the asset must not exceed the original amortised cost.

5.7.2 Financial assets carried at cost

Unquoted equity instruments are carried at cost if their fair value cannot be reliably measured. The impairment loss is the difference between the asset's **carrying amount** and the **present value of estimated future cash flows**, discounted at the current market rate of return for a similar financial instrument. Such impairment losses cannot be reversed.

5.7.3 Available for sale financial assets

Available for sale financial assets are carried at fair value and gains and losses are recognised in the statement of total recognised gains and losses. Any impairment loss on an available for sale financial asset should be **removed from statement of total recognised gains and losses** and **recognised in net profit or loss for the period** even though the financial asset has not been derecognised.

The impairment loss is the difference between its **acquisition cost** (net of any principal repayment and amortisation) and **current fair value** (for equity instruments) or recoverable amount (for debt instruments), less any impairment loss on that asset previously recognised in profit or loss.

Impairment losses relating to equity instruments cannot be reversed. Impairment losses relating to debt instruments may be reversed if, in a later period, the fair value of the instrument increases and the increase can be objectively related to an event occurring after the loss was recognised.

5.8 Example: Impairment

Broadfield Co purchased 5% debentures in X Co at 1 January 20X3 (their issue date) for £100,000. The term of the debentures was 5 years and the maturity value is £130,525. The effective rate of interest on the debentures is 10% and the company has classified them as a held-to-maturity financial asset.

At the end of 20X4 X Co went into liquidation. All interest had been paid until that date. On 31 December 20X4 the liquidator of X Co announced that no further interest would be paid and only 80% of the maturity value would be repaid, on the original repayment date.

The market interest rate on similar bonds is 8% on that date.

Required

(a) What value should the debentures have been stated at just before the impairment became apparent?

(b) At what value should the debentures be stated at 31 December 20X4, after the impairment?

(c) How will the impairment be reported in the financial statements for the year ended 31 December 20X4?

Solution

(a) The debentures are classified as a held-to-maturity financial asset and so they would have been stated at amortised cost:

	£
Initial cost	100,000
Interest at 10%	10,000
Cash at 5%	(5,000)
At 31 December 20X3	105,000
Interest at 10%	10,500
Cash at 5%	(5,000)
At 31 December 20X4	110,500

(b) After the impairment, the debentures are stated at their recoverable amount (using the **original** effective interest rate of 10%, which, from tables, gives a discount factor of 0.751):

80% × £130,525 × 0.751 = £78,419

(c) The impairment of £32,081 (£110,500 – £78,419) should be recorded:

debit Profit and loss account	£32,081	
credit Financial asset		£32,081

5.9 Section summary

- On initial recognition, financial instruments are measured at **cost**.

- Subsequent measurement depends on how a financial asset is **classified**.

- Financial assets at **fair value through profit or loss** are measured at **fair value**; gains and losses are recognised in **profit or loss**.

- **Available for sale** assets are measured at **fair value**; gains and losses are taken to **the STRGL**.

- **Loans and receivables** and **held to maturity** investments are measured at **amortised cost**; gains and losses are recognised in **profit or loss**.

- Financial **liabilities** are normally measured at **amortised cost**, unless they have been classified as at fair value through profit and loss.

Chapter Roundup

- Financial instruments can be very complex, particularly **derivative instruments**, although **primary instruments** are more straightforward.

- The important definitions to learn are:
  - **Financial asset**
  - **Financial liability**
  - **Equity instrument**

- Financial instruments must be classified as **liabilities** or **equity** according to their **substance**.

- The critical feature of a financial liability is the **contractual obligation to deliver cash** or another financial instrument. On this basis **redeemable preferences** shares are clarified as a libility, not as equity.

- **Compound instruments** are split into **equity** and **liability** components and presented in the balance sheet accordingly.

- **FRS 29** Specifies the **disclosures** required for financial instruments. The standard requires quantitative and qualitative disclosures about exposure to risks arising from financial instruments.

- **FRS 26** *Financial instruments: measurement* has been amended to include the recognition and derecognition rules of IAS 39.

- **Financial assets** should **initially** be measured at **cost = fair value**.

- Subsequently they should be **re-measured to fair value** except for

  (a)   Loans and receivables not held for trading
  (b)   Other **held-to-maturity investments**
  (c)   **Financial assets** whose value **cannot be reliably measured**

Quick Quiz

1   A **financial liability** involves an obligation to ....

2   How are redeemable preference shares classified?

3   How should financial assets be initially measured?

4   What is the effective interest rate?

Answers to quick quiz

1   A financial liability involves an obligation to deliver cash or another financial asset to another entity, or to exchange financial instruments with another entity under conditions that are potentially unfavourable.

2   As financial liabilities.

3   Financial assets should be initially measured at fair value or cost.

4   The rate that exactly discounts estimated future cash payments or receipts through the expected life of the financial instrument.

Now try the questions below from the Exam Question Bank

Number	Level	Marks	Time
Q12	Full exam	25	45 mins

Accounting for leases

Topic list	Syllabus reference
1 Distinction between hire purchase contract and a lease	3 (f)
2 Types of leases	3 (f)
3 Accounting for operating leases	3 (f)
4 Lessees	3 (f)
5 Lessors	3 (f)

Introduction

Leasing transactions are extremely common so this is an important practical subject. **Lease accounting is regulated by SSAP 21**, which was introduced because of abuses in the use of lease accounting by companies.

These companies effectively 'owned' an asset and 'owed' a debt for its purchase, but showed neither the asset nor the liability on the balance sheet because they were not required to do so. This is called **'off balance sheet finance',** a term which you will meet again later in this Text.

Study guide

- Distinguish between a hire purchase contract and a lease.

- Describe and apply the method of determining a lease type (ie an operating or finance lease).

- Explain the effect on the financial statements of a finance lease being incorrectly treated as an operating lease.

- Account for operating leases in financial statements.

- Account for finance leases in the financial statements of lessor and lessees.
- Outline the principles of SSAP 21 and its main disclosure requirements.

  Note: the net cash investment method will not be examined.

Exam guide

You must learn how to deal with leases. Make sure you can cope with the numbers.

1 Distinction between hire purchase contract and a lease

SSAP 21 provides the following definitions.

Key terms

> A '**hire purchase contract**' is a contract for the hire of an asset which contains a provision giving the hirer an option to acquire legal title to the asset upon the fulfilment of certain conditions stated in the contract.
>
> A **lease** is a contract between a lessor and a lessee for the hire of a specific asset. The lessor retains ownership of the asset but conveys the right to the use of the asset to the lessee for an agreed period of time in return for the payment of specified rentals.
>
> The term 'lease' as used in SSAP 21 also applies to other arrangements in which one party retains ownership of an asset but conveys the right to the use of the asset to another party for an agreed period of time in return for specified payments.

2 Types of leases

FAST FORWARD

> **Finance leases** are like HP contracts. In both cases:
>
> - Assets acquired should be capitalised
> - Interest element of instalments should be charged against profit.

2.1 Definitions

SSAP 21 recognises two types of lease.

Key term

> A **finance lease** transfers substantially all the risks and rewards of ownership to the lessee. Although strictly the leased asset remains the property of the lessor, in substance the lessee may be considered to have acquired the asset and to have financed the acquisition by obtaining a loan from the lessor.

Key term

> An **operating lease** is any lease which is not a finance lease. An operating lease has the character of a rental agreement with the lessor usually being responsible for repairs and maintenance of the asset. Often these are relatively short-term agreements with the same asset being leased, in succession, to different lessees.

A *finance lease* is very similar in substance to a *hire purchase agreement*. (The difference in law is that under a hire purchase agreement the customer eventually, after paying an agreed number of instalments, becomes entitled to exercise an option to purchase the asset. Under a leasing agreement, ownership remains forever with the lessor.)

In this chapter the **user** of an asset will often be referred to simply as the **lessee**, and the **supplier** as the **lessor**. You should bear in mind that identical requirements apply in the case of hirers and vendors respectively under hire purchase agreements.

2.2 Ninety per cent rule

Transfer of risks and ownership can be presumed if at the inception of a lease the present value of the minimum lease payments amounts to substantially all (normally 90% or more) of the fair value of the leased asset.

The present value should be calculated by using the **interest rate implicit in the lease**.

Key terms

> The **minimum lease payments** are the minimum payments over the remaining part of the lease term plus any residual amounts guaranteed by the lessee or by a party related to the lessee.
>
> **Fair value** is the price at which an asset could be exchanged in an arm's length transaction.
>
> The **interest rate implicit in the lease** is the discount rate that, at the inception of a lease, when applied to the amounts which the lessor expects to receive and retain, produces an amount equal to the fair value of the leased asset.
>
> The **lease term** is the period for which the lessee has contracted to lease the asset and any further terms for which the lessee has the option to continue to lease the asset, with or without further payment, which option it is reasonably certain at the inception of the lease that the lessee will exercise.

3 Accounting for operating leases

FAST FORWARD

Operating leases are **rental agreements** and all instalments are charged against profit.

Operating leases do not really pose an accounting problem.

- In the books of the lessee payments are debited to the profit and loss account
- In the books of the lessor, the asset is recorded in fixed assets and receipts from the lessee are credited to profit and loss account

For assets held **under finance leases or hire purchase** the above accounting treatment would not disclose the reality of the situation. From a **lessor's perspective,** if an asset is leased out on a finance lease, the asset will probably never be seen on his premises or used in his business again. It would be inappropriate for a lessor to record such an asset as a fixed asset. In reality, **the asset is a debtor rather than a fixed asset.**

Similarly, from the lessee's point of view, a finance lease may be used to fund the 'acquisition' of a major asset which he will then use in his business perhaps for many years. **The substance of the transaction is** that the lessee has acquired a fixed asset, and this is reflected in the accounting treatment prescribed by SSAP 21, even though in law the lessee never becomes the owner of the asset.

Exam focus point

Questions on leasing could involve a discussion of the reasons for the different accounting treatments of operating and finance leases, from the perspectives of both the lessor and the lessee.

Practical questions could involve preparation of the relevant ledger accounts and/or extracts from the financial statements.

Both the June 2004 and December 2004 papers had question parts on leasing.

4 Lessees

FAST FORWARD

You must learn how to apply actuarial method of **interest allocation**.

4.1 Accounting treatment

In light of the above, **SSAP 21 requires that, when an asset changes hands under a finance lease or HP agreement, lessor and lessee should account for the transaction as though it were a credit sale.** In the lessee's books therefore:

DEBIT   Asset account
CREDIT   Lessor (liability) account

The amount to be recorded in this way is the capital cost or fair value of the asset. This may be taken as the amount which the lessee might expect to pay for it in a cash transaction.

The asset should be depreciated over the shorter of:

    (a)   The lease term
    (b)   Its useful life

4.2 Apportionment of rental payments

When the lessee makes **a rental payment** it **will comprise two elements.**

    (a)   **An interest charge on the finance provided by the lessor.** This proportion of each payment is interest payable and interest receivable in the profit and loss accounts of the lessee and lessor respectively.

    (b)   **A repayment of part of the capital cost of the asset.** In the lessee's books this proportion of each rental payment must be debited to the lessor's account to reduce the outstanding liability. In the lessor's books, it must be credited to the lessee's account to reduce the amount owing (the debit of course is to cash).

The accounting problem is to decide what proportion of each instalment paid by the lessee **represents interest, and what proportion represents a repayment of the capital** advanced by the lessor. There are **three methods** you may encounter:

    (a)   The **level spread method**.
    (b)   The **actuarial method**.
    (c)   The **sum-of-the-digits method**.

Exam focus point

The examiner has said that he will not examine the sum-of-the-digits method. So you will be expected to use the actuarial method.

The level spread method is based on the assumption that finance charges accrue evenly over the term of the lease agreement. For example, if an asset with a fair value of £3,000 is being 'acquired' on a finance lease for five payments of £700 each, the total interest is £(3,500 – 3,000) = £500. This is assumed to accrue evenly and therefore there is £100 interest comprised in each rental payment, the £600 balance of each instalment being the capital repayment.

The level spread method is quite **unscientific and takes no account of the commercial realities of the transaction.** You should use it in the examination only if you are specifically instructed to or if there is insufficient information to use another method.

The actuarial method is the best and most scientific method. It derives from the commonsense assumption that the **interest charged by a lessor company will equal the rate of return desired by the company, multiplied by the amount of capital it has invested.**

    (a)   At the beginning of the lease the capital invested is equal to the fair value of the asset (less any initial deposit paid by the lessee).

    (b)   This amount reduces as each instalment is paid. It follows that the interest accruing is greatest in the early part of the lease term, and gradually reduces as capital is repaid. In this section, we will look at a simple example of the actuarial method.

The sum-of-the-digits method approximates to the actuarial method, splitting the total interest (without reference to a rate of interest) in such a way that the greater proportion falls in the earlier years. The procedure is as follows.

    (a)   **Assign a digit to each instalment.** The digit 1 should be assigned to the final instalment, 2 to the penultimate instalment and so on.

    (b)   **Add the digits.** If there are twelve instalments, then the sum of the digits will be 78. For this reason, the sum of the digits method is sometimes called the *rule of 78.*

    (c)   **Calculate the interest charge included in each instalment.** Do this by multiplying the total interest accruing over the lease term by the fraction:

$$\frac{\text{Digit applicable to the instalment}}{\text{Sum of the digits}}$$

We will now concentrate on the actuarial method.

4.3 Example: Apportionment

On 1 January 20X0 Bacchus Ltd, wine merchants, buys a small bottling and labelling machine from Silenus Limited on hire purchase terms. The cash price of the machine was £7,710 while the HP price was £10,000. The HP agreement required the immediate payment of a £2,000 deposit with the balance being settled in four equal annual instalments commencing on 31 December 20X0. The HP charge of £2,290 represents interest of 15% per annum, calculated on the remaining balance of the liability during each accounting period. Depreciation on the plant is to be provided for at the rate of 20% per annum on a straight line basis assuming a residual value of nil.

You are required to show the breakdown of each instalment between interest and capital, using the actuarial method.

Solution

Interest is calculated as 15% of the outstanding *capital* balance at the beginning of each year. The outstanding capital balance reduces each year by the capital element comprised in each instalment. The outstanding capital balance at 1 January 20X0 is £5,710 (£7,710 fair value less £2,000 deposit).

	Total £	Capital £	Interest £
Capital balance at 1 Jan 20X0		5,710	
1st instalment			
(interest = £5,710 × 15%)	2,000	1,144	856
Capital balance at 1 Jan 20X1		4,566	
2nd instalment			
(interest = £4,566 × 15%)	2,000	1,315	685
Capital balance at 1 Jan 20X2		3,251	
3rd instalment			
(interest = £3,251 × 15%)	2,000	1,512	488
Capital balance at 1 Jan 20X3		1,739	
4th instalment			
(interest = £1,739 × 15%)	2,000	1,739	261
	8,000		2,290
Capital balance at 1 Jan 20X4		-	

Exam focus point

> Where you get a numerical question, make sure you provide clear workings. In the words of the Paper 2.5 examiner, where workings are not shown:
>
> 'If an answer is wrong, it is unlikely that any marks can be awarded, as the marker will not be able to determine how the answer was arrived at.'

4.4 Disclosure requirements for lessees

SSAP 21 requires lessees to disclose the following information.

(a)   The **gross amounts of assets held under finance leases* together with the related accumulated depreciation, analysed by class of asset**. This information may be consolidated with the corresponding information for owned assets, and not shown separately. In that case, the net amount of assets held under finance leases* included in the overall total should also be disclosed.

(b)   The **amounts of obligations related to finance leases* (net of finance charges allocated to future periods).** These should be disclosed separately from other obligations and liabilities and should be analysed between amounts payable in the next year, amounts payable in the second to fifth years inclusive from the balance sheet date and the aggregate amounts payable thereafter.

(c)   The **aggregate finance charges allocated for the period** in respect of finance leases.*

* Including the equivalent information in respect of hire purchase contracts.

These disclosure requirements will be illustrated for Bacchus Ltd (above example). We will assume that Bacchus Ltd makes up its accounts to 31 December and uses the actuarial method to apportion finance charges. The company's accounts for the first year of the HP agreement, the year ended 31 December 20X0, would include the information given below.

BALANCE SHEET AS AT 31 DECEMBER 20X0 (EXTRACTS)

	£	£
Fixed assets		
Tangible assets held under hire purchase agreements		
Plant and machinery at cost	7,710	
Less accumulated depreciation (20% × £7,710)	1,542	
		6,168
Creditors: amounts falling due within one year		
Obligations under hire purchase agreements		1,315
Creditors: amounts falling due after more than one year		
Obligations under hire purchase agreements, falling due		
within two to five years £(1,512 + 1,739)		3,251

(Notice that only the outstanding *capital* element is disclosed under creditors. That is what is meant by the phrase 'net of finance charges allocated to future periods' in Paragraph 2.7(b) above.)

PROFIT AND LOSS ACCOUNT
FOR THE YEAR ENDED 31 DECEMBER 20X0

	£
Interest payable and similar charges	
Hire purchase finance charges	856

As noted above, SSAP 21 requires that **leased assets should be depreciated over the shorter of the lease term and their useful lives; but assets acquired under HP agreements** resembling finance leases **should be depreciated over their useful lives**, because such assets are legally the debtor's property. Bacchus can therefore depreciate the machine over five years, not four years.

For operating leases the disclosure is simpler.

(a) The **total of operating lease rentals** charged as an expense in the profit and loss account should be disclosed, distinguishing between rentals payable for hire of plant and machinery and other rentals.

(b) Disclosure should be made of **payments to which the lessee is committed** under operating leases, analysed between those in which the commitment expires:

    (i)   **Within a year** from the balance sheet date
    (ii)   In the **second to fifth** years inclusive
    (iii)   **Later than five years** from the balance sheet date

Commitments in respect of land and buildings should be shown separately from other commitments.

5 Lessors

FAST FORWARD

> You must also learn the **disclosure requirements of SSAP 21** for both lessors and lessees.

5.1 Accounting treatment

In principle, accounting for a finance lease by a **lessor** is a **mirror image of the entries for the lessee**. The asset is recorded in the lessor's books as follows.

DEBIT   Lessee (debtor) account
CREDIT   Sales

The income derived from the lease is spread over accounting periods so as to give a constant periodic rate of return for the lessor. The complex methods of achieving this are beyond the scope of your syllabus.

5.2 FRS 5: Sale and leaseback transactions

We will discuss FRS 5 *Reporting the substance of transactions* in Chapter 11. Leases were a common form of off balance sheet finance before SSAP 21 was introduced. Ever since then, businesses have attempted to undertake types of arrangement whereby an asset is 'sold' but in fact the use is still retained.

FRS 5 states that where such a transaction is, in effect, a sale and leaseback, no profit should be recognised on entering into the arrangement and no adjustment made to the carrying value of the asset. As stated in the guidance notes to SSAP 21, **this represents the substance of the transactions,** 'namely the raising of finance secured on an asset that continues to be held and is not disposed of'.

5.3 Disclosure requirements for lessors

SSAP 21 requires lessors to disclose their **net investments in (a) finance leases and (b) hire purchase contracts at each balance sheet date.**

The accounts of Silenus Ltd (example above) for the year ended 31 December 20X0 would show the information given below.

BALANCE SHEET AS AT 31 DECEMBER 20X0 (EXTRACTS)

	£
Current assets	
Debtors	
Net investment in finance leases (note)	4,566

NOTES TO THE BALANCE SHEET

Net investment in finance leases	£
Falling due within one year	1,315
Falling due after more than one year	3,251
	4,566

(The Companies Act 1985 requires amounts included as debtors to be separately disclosed if they fall due more than one year after the balance sheet date.)

SSAP 21 also requires **disclosure by lessors** of the:

(a)   **Gross amounts of assets** held for use **in operating leases**, and the related **accumulated depreciation charges**.

(b)   **Policy** adopted for accounting for operating leases and finance leases and, in detail, the policy for accounting for finance lease income.

(c)   **Aggregate rentals receivable** in respect of an accounting period in relation to finance leases and operating leases separately.

(d)   **Cost of assets acquired**, whether by purchase or finance lease, for the purpose of letting under finance leases.

Chapter Roundup

- **Finance leases** are like HP contracts. In both cases:
    - Assets acquired should be capitalised
    - Interest element of instalments should be charged against profit.

- **Operating leases** are **rental agreements** and all instalments are charged against profit.

- You must learn how to apply the actuarial method of **interest allocation**.

- You must also learn the **disclosure requirements of SSAP 21** for both lessors and lessees.

Quick Quiz

1   (a)   ....leases transfer substantially the risks and rewards of ownership.

    (b)   ....leases are usually short-term rental agreements with the lessor being responsible for the repairs and maintenance of the asset.

2   The present value of the minimum lease payments is equal to 89% of the fair value of the leased asset. What type of lease is this likely to be?

3   A business acquires an asset under an HP agreement. What is the double entry?

    DEBIT
    CREDIT

4   List the disclosures required under SSAP 21.

5   A lorry has an expected useful life of six years. It is acquired under a four year finance lease. Over which period should it be depreciated?

6   A company leases a photocopier under an operating lease which expires in June 20X2. Its office is leased under an operating lease due to expire in January 20X3. How should past and future operating leases be disclosed in its 31 December 20X1 accounts?

Answers to Quick Quiz

1   (a)   Finance leases
    (b)   Operating leases

2   Per SSAP 21, an operating lease

3   DEBIT   Asset account
    CREDIT   Lessor account

4   See Paragraph 4.4.

5   The six year term per SSAP 21. See Para 4.4.

6   The total operating lease rentals charged though the profit and loss should be disclosed. The payments committed to should be disclosed, analysing them between those falling due in the next year and the second to fifth years. (Para 4.4)

Now try the question below from the Exam Question Bank

Number	Level	Marks	Time
Q7	Full exam	20	36 mins

BPP
PROFESSIONAL EDUCATION

Accounting for taxation

Topic list	Syllabus reference
1 FRS 16 *Current Tax*	3 (e)
2 SSAP 5 *Accounting for value added tax*	3 (e)
3 FRS 19 *Deferred tax*	3 (e)
4 Taxation in company accounts	3 (e)
5 Disclosure requirements	3 (e)

Introduction

Tax is a straightforward area. There are plenty of exercises here - make sure that you attempt each one yourself without referring to the solution immediately.

Accounting for VAT is particularly easy and you should be relatively familiar with the workings of the tax. Do not overlook the SSAP 5 requirements.

In relation to corporation tax you must be able to calculate the relevant tax figures *and* know how they should be disclosed in the accounts according to FRS 16.

Deferred taxation is probably the most difficult topic in this chapter. Concentrate on trying to understand the logic behind the adjustment and the reasons why the FRS 19 approach has been adopted.

Study guide

- Account for current taxation in accordance with relevant accounting standards.

- Record entries relating to corporation tax in the accounting records.

- Apply requirements of accounting standards on VAT.

- Explain the effect of timing differences on accounting and taxable profits.

- Outline the principles of accounting for deferred tax.

- Outline the requirements of accounting standards on deferred tax.

- Calculate and record deferred tax amounts in the financial statements.

Exam guide

Learn the disclosures, they are bound to come up in an accounts preparation question

1 FRS 16 current tax

> **FAST FORWARD**
>
> The **FRS 16 requirements** relating to company taxation are straightforward but **must be learned**. The best way is to practise on past exam questions.

Companies pay corporation tax, usually nine months after the year end. FRS 16 *Current tax*, which was published in December 1999, specifies how current tax should be reflected in the financial statements. This should be done in a **'consistent and transparent manner'**.

Specifically, the FRS deals with **tax credits** and **withholding tax**. Consider these definitions.

Key terms

- **Current tax**. The amount of tax estimated to be payable or recoverable in respect of the taxable profit or loss for a period, along with adjustments to estimates in respect of previous periods.

- **Withholding tax**. Tax on dividends or other income that is deducted by the payer of the income and paid to the tax authorities wholly on behalf of the recipient.

- **Tax credit**. The tax credit given under UK tax legislation to the recipient of a dividend from a UK company. The credit is given to acknowledge that the income out of which the dividend has been paid has already been charged to tax, rather than because any withholding tax has been deducted at source. The tax credit may discharge or reduce the recipient's liability to tax on the dividend. Non-taxpayers may or may not be able to recover the tax credit.

You can see from these definitions that a tax credit is different from a withholding tax.

- A tax credit **gives credit for** tax paid by a company
- A **withholding tax withholds** the taxable part of the income

Accordingly, the tax credit and the withholding tax are treated differently in the financial statements.

1.1 Treatment in financial statements

Learn this treatment.

Outgoing dividends paid, interest or other amounts payable

- Include withholding tax
- Exclude tax credit

Incoming dividends, interest or other amounts payable

- Include withholding tax
- Exclude tax credit
- Include the effect of withholding tax suffered as part of the tax charge

---

1.2 Example: current tax

Taxus Ltd made a profit of £1,000,000. It received a dividend of £80,000 on which there was a tax credit of £20,000. From an overseas company it received a dividend of £3,000 on which 25% withholding tax had been deducted. The corporation tax charge was £300,000.

Required

Show how this information would be presented in the financial statements in accordance with FRS 16 *Current tax*.

Solution

	£
Operating profit	1,000,000
Income from fixed asset investments	
UK (note 1)	80,000
Foreign (note 2)	4,000
Profit before tax	1,084,000
Taxation (note 3)	301,000
Profit after tax	783,000

Notes

1   Excludes tax credit

2   Includes withholding tax: £3,000 + £1,000 = £4,000. Read the question carefully - 25% had been deducted already

3   Add back withholding tax of £1,000

1.2.1 Other requirements of FRS 16

Current tax should be recognised in the **profit and loss account**. But if it is attributable to a gain or loss that has been recognised in the statement of total recognised gains and losses it should be recognised in that statement.

Current tax should be measured using tax rates and laws that have been enacted or substantially enacted by the balance sheet date.

Generally (apart from the treatment of withholding tax) income and expenses are **not adjusted** to reflect a **notional amount** of tax that would have been paid or received if the transaction had been taxable or allowable on a different basis. Income and expenses are included in pre-tax results on the basis of amounts **actually receivable or payable**.

1.2.2 Income tax withheld

If a company reasonably believes the receipt of payments of annual interest, royalties or annuities is chargeable to corporation tax on the payment, with effect from 1 April 2001, the paying company is not required to withhold income tax on the payment. However, such payments made to individuals, partnerships etc (ie non-companies) are still made under deduction of income tax.

1.2.3 Tax disclosure in the notes

This example, taken from the appendix to FRS 16, illustrates one method of showing by way of a note the tax items required to be disclosed under CA 1985 and the FRS.

	£'000	£'000
UK corporation tax		
Current tax on income for the period	X	
Adjustments in respect of prior periods	X	
	X	
Double taxation relief*	(X)	
		X
Foreign tax		
Current tax on income for the period	X	
Adjustments in respect of prior periods	X	
		X
Tax on profit on ordinary activities		X

*Don't worry about this - it's unlikely to come up in your exam.

2 SSAP 5 Accounting for value added tax

VAT is a tax on the supply of goods and services. The tax authority responsible for collecting VAT is HM Customs & Excise. **Tax is collected at each transfer point in the chain from prime producer to final consumer**. Eventually, the consumer bears the tax in full and any tax paid earlier in the chain can be recovered by the trader who paid it.

2.1 Example: VAT

A manufacturing company, Alyson Ltd, purchases raw materials at a cost of £1,000 plus VAT at 17½%. From the raw materials Alyson Ltd makes finished products which it sells to a retail outlet, Barry Ltd, for £1,600 plus VAT. Barry Ltd sells the products to customers at a total price of £2,000 plus VAT. How much VAT is paid to Customs & Excise at each stage in the chain?

Solution

	Value of goods sold £	VAT at 17½% £
Supplier of raw materials	1,000	175
Value added by Alyson Ltd	600	105
Sale to Barry Ltd	1,600	280
Value added by Barry Ltd	400	70
Sales to 'consumers'	2,000	350

2.2 How is VAT collected?

Although it is the final consumer who eventually bears the full tax of £350, the sum is **collected and paid over to Customs & Excise by the traders who make up the chain.** Each trader must assume that his customer is the final consumer and must collect and pay over VAT at the appropriate rate on the full sales value of the goods sold. He is entitled to reclaim VAT paid on his own purchases (inputs) and so makes a net payment to Customs & Excise equal to the tax on value added by himself.

In the example above, the supplier of raw materials collects from Alyson Ltd VAT of £175, all of which he pays over to Customs & Excise. When Alyson Ltd sells goods to Barry Ltd VAT is charged at the rate of 17½% on £1,600 = £280. Only £105, however, is paid by Alyson Ltd to Customs & Excise because the company is entitled to deduct VAT of £175 suffered on its own purchases. Similarly, Barry Ltd must charge its customers £350 in VAT but need only pay over the net amount of £70 after deducting the £280 VAT suffered on its purchase from Alyson Ltd.

2.3 Registered and non-registered persons

Traders whose sales (outputs) are below a certain minimum need not register for VAT. Such traders neither charge VAT on their outputs nor are entitled to reclaim VAT on their inputs. They are in the same position as a final consumer.

All outputs of registered traders are either taxable or exempt. Traders carrying on exempt activities (such as banks) cannot charge VAT on their outputs and consequently cannot reclaim VAT paid on their inputs.

Taxable outputs are usually (fuel being an exception as it is charged at 5%) chargeable at one of **two rates**:

    (a)   **Zero per cent (zero-rated items)**

    (b)   **17½% (standard-rated items)**

Customs & Excise publish lists of supplies falling into each category. **Persons carrying on taxable activities** (even activities taxable at zero per cent) **are entitled to reclaim VAT paid on their inputs.**

Some traders carry on a **mixture of taxable and exempt activities**. Such traders need to apportion the VAT suffered on inputs and **can only reclaim the proportion relating to taxable outputs.**

2.4 Accounting for VAT

As a general principle the treatment of VAT in the accounts of a trader should reflect his role as a collector of the tax and **VAT should not be included in income or in expenditure whether of a capital or of a revenue nature.**

2.4.1 Irrecoverable VAT

Where the **trader bears the VAT** himself, as in the following cases, this should be reflected in the accounts.

    (a)   **Persons not registered** for VAT will suffer VAT on inputs. This will effectively increase the cost of their consumable materials and their fixed assets and must be so reflected, ie shown **inclusive of VAT.**

    (b)   **Registered persons** who also carry on **exempted** activities will have a residue of VAT which falls directly on them. In this situation the costs to which this residue applies will be inflated by the **irrecoverable VAT.**

    (c)   **Non-deductible inputs will be borne** by all traders (examples are tax on cars bought which are not for resale, entertaining expenses and provision of domestic accommodation for a company's directors).

Exam focus point

> Where VAT is not recoverable it must be regarded as an inherent part of the cost of the items purchased and included in the P&L charge or balance sheet as appropriate.

2.5 Further points

VAT is charged on the price net of any discount and this general principle is carried to the extent that where a cash discount is offered, VAT is charged on the net amount **even where the discount is not taken up.**

Most VAT registered persons are obliged to record VAT when a supply is received or made (effectively when a credit sales invoice is raised or a purchase invoice recorded). This has the effect that **the net VAT liability has on occasion to be paid to Customs & Excise before all output tax has been paid by customers**. If a debt is subsequently written off, the VAT element may not be recovered from Customs & Excise for six months from the date of sale, even if the customer becomes insolvent.

Some small businesses can join the cash accounting scheme whereby VAT is only paid to Customs & Excise after it is received from customers. This delays recovery of input tax but improves cash flow overall, although it may involve extra record keeping. Bad debt relief is automatic under this scheme since if VAT is not paid by the customer it is not due to Customs & Excise.

 Question

VAT

Sunglo Ltd is preparing accounts for the year ended 31 May 20X9. Included in its balance sheet as at 31 May 20X8 was a balance for VAT recoverable of £15,000.

Its summary profit and loss account for the year is as follows.

	£'000
Sales (all standard rated)	500
Purchases (all standard rated)	120
Gross profit	380
Expenses	280
Operating profit	100
Interest receivable	20
Profit before tax	120

	£'000
Note: expenses	
Wages and salaries	200
Entertainment expenditure	10
Other (all standard rated)	70
	280

Payments of £5,000, £15,000 and £20,000 have been made in the year and a repayment of £12,000 was received. What is the balance for VAT in the balance sheet as at 31 May 20X9? Assume a 17.5% standard rate of VAT.

BPP
PROFESSIONAL EDUCATION

Answer

SUNGLO LIMITED: VAT ACCOUNT

	£		£
Balance b/d	15,000	Sales (£500,000 × 17.5%)	87,500
Purchases (£120,000 × 17.5%)	21,000	Bank	12,000
Expenses (£70,000 × 17.5%)	12,250		
Bank	40,000		
Balance c/d	11,250		
	99,500		99,500

2.6 Requirements of SSAP 5

SSAP 5 requires the following accounting rules to be followed.

(a) **Turnover** shown in the profit and loss account should **exclude VAT** on taxable outputs. If gross turnover must be shown then the VAT in that figure must also be shown as a deduction in arriving at the turnover exclusive of VAT.

(b) **Irrecoverable VAT** allocated to fixed assets and other items separately disclosed should be **included in their cost** where material and practical.

(c) The **net amount due to (or from) Customs & Excise** should be **included in the total for creditors** (or **debtors**), and need not be separately disclosed.

Note that the CA 1985 also requires disclosure of the cost of sales figure in the published accounts. This amount should exclude VAT on taxable inputs.

3 FRS 19 Deferred tax

FAST FORWARD

FRS 19 requires full provision for **deferred** tax. It is unlikely that complicated numerical questions will be set in the exam so concentrate on **understanding** deferred tax.

Exam focus point

This topic appears almost in every paper, so do work through the material thoroughly, learn and inwardly digest. The June 2004 paper included a deferred tax adjustment.

You may already be aware from your studies of taxation that accounting profits and taxable profits are not the same. There are several reasons for this but they may conveniently be considered under two headings.

(a) **Permanent differences** arise because certain expenditure, such as entertainment of UK customers, is not allowed as a deduction for tax purposes although it is quite properly deducted in arriving at accounting profit. Similarly, certain income (such as UK dividend income) is not subject to corporation tax, although it forms part of accounting profit.

(b) **Timing differences** arise because certain items are included in the accounts of a period which is different from that in which they are dealt with for taxation purposes.

Deferred taxation is the tax attributable to timing differences.

Key term

Deferred tax. Estimated future tax consequences of transactions and events recognised in the financial statements of the current and previous periods.

Deferred taxation is therefore a means of ironing out the tax inequalities arising from timing differences.

(a) In years when **corporation tax is saved** by timing differences such as accelerated capital allowances, a charge for deferred taxation is made in the P&L account and a provision set up in the balance sheet.

(b) In years when **timing differences reverse**, because the depreciation charge exceeds the capital allowances available, a deferred tax credit is made in the P&L account and the balance sheet provision is reduced.

Deferred tax is the subject of a new standard, FRS 19 *Deferred tax*. Before we look at the detailed requirements of FRS 19, we will explore some of the issues surrounding deferred tax.

You should be clear in your mind that the tax actually payable to the Inland Revenue is the **corporation tax liability**. The credit balance on the deferred taxation account represents an estimate of tax saved because of timing differences but expected ultimately to become payable when those differences reverse.

FRS 19 identifies the main categories in which timing differences can occur.

(a) **Accelerated capital allowances.** Tax deductions for the cost of a fixed asset are accelerated or decelerated, ie received before or after the cost of the fixed asset is recognised in the profit and loss account.

(b) **Pension liabilities** are accrued in the financial statements but are allowed for tax purposes only when paid or contributed at a later date (pensions are not in the paper 2.5 syllabus).

(c) **Interest charges or development costs** are capitalised on the balance sheet but are treated as revenue expenditure and allowed as incurred for tax purposes.

(d) **Intragroup profits in stock**, unrealised at group level, are reversed on consolidation.

(e) **Revaluations.** An asset is revalued in the financial statements but the revaluation gain becomes taxable only if and when the asset is sold.

(f) **Unrelieved tax losses.** A tax loss is not relieved against past or present taxable profits but can be carried forward to reduce future taxable profits.

(g) **Unremitted earnings of subsidiaries.** The unremitted earnings of subsidiary and associated undertakings and joint ventures are recognised in the group results but will be subject to further taxation only if and when remitted to the parent undertaking.

Deferred taxation is therefore an accounting convention which is introduced in order to apply the accruals concept to income reporting where timing differences occur. However, **deferred tax assets** are not included in accounts as a rule, because it would not be prudent, given that the recovery of the tax is uncertain.

3.1 Basis of provision

A comprehensive tax allocation system is one in which deferred taxation is computed for every instance of timing differences: **full provision**. The opposite extreme would be the **nil provision** approach ('**flow through** method'), where only the tax payable in the period would be charged to that period.

3.2 SSAP 15

SSAP 15, the forerunner of FRS 19, rejected both these approaches and prescribe a middle course, called **partial provision**.

'Tax deferred or accelerated by the effect of timing differences should be accounted for to the extent that it is probable that a liability or asset will crystallise. Tax deferred or accelerated by the effect of timing differences should not be accounted for to the extent that it is probable that a liability or asset will not crystallise.'

The **probability** that a liability or asset would crystallise was assessed by the directors on the basis of **reasonable assumptions**. They had to take into account all relevant information available up to the date on which they approved the financial statements, and also their intentions for the future. Ideally, financial projections of future plans had to be made for a number (undefined) of years ahead. The directors' judgement had to be exercised with prudence.

If a company predicted, for example, that capital expenditure would **continue at the same rate** for the foreseeable future, so that capital allowances and depreciation would remain at the same levels, then no originating or reversing differences of any significance to the continuing trend of the tax charge would arise and so no change to the provision for deferred tax needed to be made (unless there were other significant timing differences).

3.3 The three different methods compared

Under the **flow-through method**, the tax liability recognised is the expected legal tax liability for the period (ie no provision is made for deferred tax). The main **advantages** of the method are that it is straightforward to apply and the tax liability recognised is closer to many people's idea of a 'real' liability than that recognised under either full or partial provision.

The main **disadvantages** of flow-through are that it can lead to large fluctuations in the tax charge and that it does not allow tax relief for long-term liabilities to be recognised until those liabilities are settled. The method is not used internationally.

The **full provision method** has the **advantage** that it is consistent with general international practice. It also recognises that each timing difference at the balance sheet date has an effect on future tax payments. If a company claims an accelerated capital allowance on an item of plant, future tax assessments will be bigger than they would have been otherwise. Future transactions may well affect those assessments still further, but that is not relevant in assessing the position at the balance sheet date. The **disadvantage** of full provision is that, under certain types of tax system, it gives rise to large liabilities that may fall due only far in the future. The full provision method is the one prescribed by FRS 19.

The **partial provision method** addresses this disadvantage by providing for deferred tax only to the extent that it is expected to be paid in the foreseeable future. This has an obvious intuitive appeal, but its effect is that deferred tax recognised at the balance sheet date includes the tax effects of future transactions that have not been recognised in the financial statements, and which the reporting company has neither undertaken nor even committed to undertake at that date. It is difficult to reconcile this with the ASB's *Statement of Principles*, which defines assets and liabilities as arising from past events.

Exam focus point

> You need to understand the concept of deferred tax, it is unlikely that you will need to perform detailed calculations.

It is important that you understand the issues properly so consider the example below.

3.4 Example: The three methods compared

Suppose that Pamella plc begins trading on 1 January 20X7. In its first year it makes profits of £5m, the depreciation charge is £1m and the capital allowances on those assets is £1.5m. The rate of corporation tax is 33%.

Solution: Flow through method

The tax liability for the year is 33% £(5.0 + 1.0 – 1.5)m = £1.485m. The potential deferred tax liability of 33% × (£1.5m – £1m) is completely ignored and no judgement is required on the part of the preparer.

Solution: Full provision

The tax liability is £1.485m again, but the debit in the P&L account is increased by the deferred tax liability of 33% × £0.5m = £165,000. The total charge to the P&L account is therefore £1,650,000 which is an effective tax rate of 33% on accounting profits (ie 33% × £5.0m). Again, no judgement is involved in using this method.

Solution: Partial provision

Is a deferred tax provision necessary under partial provision? It is now necessary to look ahead at future capital expenditure plans. Will capital allowances exceed depreciation over the next few years? If *yes*, no provision for deferred tax is required. If *no*, then a reversal is expected, ie there is a year in which depreciation is greater than capital allowances. The deferred tax provision is made on the maximum reversal which will be created, and any not provided is disclosed by note.

If we assume that the review of expected future capital expenditure under the partial method required a deferred tax charge of £82,500 (33% × £250,000), we can then summarise the position.

3.5 Summary

The methods can be compared as follows.

Method	Provision £	Disclosure £
Flow-through	–	–
Full provision	165,000	–
Partial provision	82,500	82,500

3.6 FRS 19 Deferred tax

In December 2000 the ASB published FRS 19. The FRS replaced SSAP 15 and came into effect for accounting periods ending on or after 23 January 2002. It requires entities to provide for tax timing differences on a **full, rather than partial provision basis.**

3.7 Objective

The objective of FRS 19 is to ensure that:

(a)   Future tax consequences of past transactions and events are recognised as liabilities or assets in the financial statements

(b)   The financial statements disclose any other special circumstances that may have an effect on future tax charges.

3.8 Scope

The FRS applies **to all financial statements that are intended to give a true and fair view** of a reporting entity's financial position and profit or loss (or income and expenditure) for a period. The FRS applies to taxes calculated on the basis of taxable profits, including withholding taxes paid on behalf of the reporting entity.

Reporting entities applying the Financial Reporting Standard for Smaller Entities **(FRSSE)** currently applicable are **exempt** from the FRS.

3.9 Recognition of deferred tax assets and liabilities

Remember!

Deferred tax should be recognised in respect of **all timing differences that have originated but not reversed by the balance sheet date**.

Deferred tax should **not be recognised on permanent differences.**

Question	Timing differences

Can you remember some examples of timing differences?

Answer

- Accelerated capital allowances
- Pension liabilities accrued but taxed when paid
- Interest charges and development costs capitalised but allowed for tax purposes when incurred
- Unrealised intra-group stock profits reversed on consolidation
- Revaluation gains
- Tax losses
- Unremitted earnings of subsidiaries, associates and joint ventures recognised in group results.

Key term

Permanent differences. Differences between an entity's taxable profits and its results as stated in the financial statements that arise because certain types of income and expenditure are non-taxable or disallowable, or because certain tax charges or allowances have no corresponding amount in the financial statements.

3.9.1 Allowances for fixed asset expenditure

Deferred tax **should be recognised** when the **allowances** for the cost of a fixed asset are **received before or after the cost of the fixed asset is recognised in the profit and loss account.** However, if and when **all conditions** for retaining the allowances have been met, the **deferred tax should be reversed.**

If an asset is not being depreciated (and has not otherwise been written down to a carrying value less than cost), the timing difference is the amount of capital allowances received.

Most capital allowances are received on a **conditional basis**, ie they are repayable (for example, via a balancing charge) if the assets to which they relate are sold for more than their tax written-down value. However, some, such as industrial buildings allowances, are repayable only if the assets to which they relate are sold within a specified period. Once that period has expired, all conditions for retaining the allowance have been met. At that point, deferred tax that has been recognised (ie on the excess of the allowance over any depreciation) is reversed.

Question	Tax allowances

An industrial building qualifies for an IBA when purchased in 20X1. The building is still held by the company in 20Z6. What happens to the deferred tax?

Answer

All the conditions for retaining tax allowances have been met. This means that the timing differences have become permanent and the deferred tax recognised should be reversed. Before the 25 year period has passed, deferred tax should be provided on the difference between the amount of the industrial building allowance and any depreciation charged on the asset.

3.9.2 Revaluation of fixed assets

Revaluation of a fixed asset does not create an unavoidable tax liability and so does not affect the deferred tax provision. The exception to this is where an agreement has been entered into to dispose of the asset at the revalued amount, and the gains and losses expected to arise on the sale have been recognised at the balance sheet date. In this case, FRS 19 requires deferred tax to be recognised on the timing difference. As the revaluation gain will be shown under reserves in the statement of total recognised gains and losses, the deferred tax on the revaluation gain or loss will also be adjusted directly in the revaluation reserve.

3.9.3 Example:

Z Ltd owns a property which has a carrying value at the beginning of 20X9 of £1,500,000. At the year end, it has entered into a contract to sell the property for £1,800,000. The tax rate is 30%. How will this be shown in the financial statements?

Solution

STATEMENT OF TOTAL RECOGNISED GAINS AND LOSSES

	£'000
Profit for the financial year	X
Unrealised surplus on revaluation of property	(300)
Deferred tax on revaluation surplus	(90)
Total gains and losses relating to year	X

The journal entries will be as follows:

	Dr £'000	Cr £'000
Property	300	
Deferred tax		90
Revaluation reserve		210

Question   **Current and deferred tax**

Jonquil Co buys equipment for £50,000 on 1 January 20X1 and depreciates it on a straight line basis over its expected useful life of five years. For tax purposes, the equipment is depreciated at 25% per annum on a straight line basis. Tax losses may be carried back against taxable profit of the previous five years. In year 20X0, the entity's taxable profit was £25,000. The tax rate is 40%.

Required

Assuming nil profits/losses after depreciation in years 20X1 to 20X5 show the current and deferred tax impact in years 20X1 to 20X5 of the acquisition of the equipment.

Answer

Jonquil Co will recover the carrying amount of the equipment by using it to manufacture goods for resale. Therefore, the entity's current tax computation is as follows.

(1)

	Year				
	20X1	20X2	20X3	20X4	20X5
	£	£	£	£	£
Taxable income*	10,000	10,000	10,000	10,000	10,000
Depreciation for tax purposes	12,500	12,500	12,500	12,500	0
Taxable profit (tax loss)	(2,500)	(2,500)	(2,500)	(2,500)	10,000
Current tax expense (income) at 40%	(1,000)	(1,000)	(1,000)	(1,000)	4,000

* ie nil profit plus $50,000 ÷ 5 depreciation add-back.

The entity recognises a current tax asset at the end of years 20X1 to 20X4 because it recovers the benefit of the tax loss against the taxable profit of year 20X5.

The temporary differences associated with the equipment and the resulting deferred tax asset and liability and deferred tax expense and income are as follows.

(2)

	Year				
	20X1	20X2	20X3	20X4	20X5
	£	£	£	£	£
Depreciation	10,000	20,000	30,000	40,000	50,000
Capital allowances	12,500	25,000	37,500	50,000	50,000
Taxable temporary difference	2,500	5,000	7,500	10,000	0
Opening deferred tax liability @ 40%	0	1,000	2,000	3,000	4,000
Deferred tax expense (income): bal fig	1,000	1,000	1,000	1,000	(4,000)
Closing deferred tax liability @ 40%	1,000	2,000	3,000	4,000	0

The entity recognises the deferred tax liability in years 20X1 to 20X4 because the reversal of the taxable temporary difference will create taxable income in subsequent years. The entity's profit and loss account is as follows.

	Year				
	20X1	20X2	20X3	20X4	20X5
	£	£	£	£	£
Income	10,000	10,000	10,000	10,000	10,000
Depreciation	10,000	10,000	10,000	10,000	10,000
Profit before tax	0	0	0	0	0
Current tax expense (income) as (1) above	(1,000)	(1,000)	(1,000)	(1,000)	4,000
Deferred tax expense (income) as (2) above	1,000	1,000	1,000	1,000	(4,000)
Total tax expense (income)	0	0	0	0	0
Net profit for the period	0	0	0	0	0

3.10 Measurement – discounting

Reporting entities are **permitted but not required** to discount deferred tax assets and liabilities to reflect the time value of money.

The ASB believes that, just as other long-term liabilities such as provisions and debt are discounted, so too in principle should long-term deferred tax balances. The FRS therefore permits discounting and provides guidance on how it should be done. However, the ASB stopped short of making discounting mandatory, acknowledging that there is as yet **no internationally accepted methodology** for discounting deferred tax, and that for some entities **the costs might outweigh the benefits.** Entities are encouraged to select the more appropriate policy, taking account of factors such as materiality and the policies of other entities in their sector.

Question	Discounting

Can you think of a situation where it might be appropriate to discount deferred tax liabilities?

Answer

Where the reversal is fairly slow, for example with industrial buildings allowances.

Discounting should be **applied consistently** to all tax flows on timing differences where the effect is expected to be **material** and where the **tax flows have not already been discounted**.

No account should be taken of **future timing differences** including future tax losses.

The **scheduling of the reversals** should take account of the **remaining tax effect of transactions already reflected in the financial statements**, for example tax losses at the balance sheet date.

The **discount rate** should be the **post tax return** that could be obtained at the balance sheet date on **government bonds** with **similar maturity dates** and in **currencies similar to those of the deferred tax assets or liabilities.** It may be possible to use average rates without introducing material errors.

3.11 Presentation

In the **balance sheet** classify:

- Net deferred tax liabilities as 'provisions for liabilities'
- Net deferred tax assets as debtors, as a separate subhead if material where taxes are levied by the same tax authority or in a group where tax losses of one entity can reduce the taxable profits of another.

Balances are to be **disclosed separately** on the face of the balance sheet **if** so **material** as to distort the financial statements.

In the **profit and loss account** classify as part of **tax on profit or loss on ordinary activities.**

3.12 Problems

FRS 19 has the effect of **increasing the liabilities** reported by entities that at present have **large amounts of unprovided deferred tax** arising from capital allowances in excess of depreciation.

Criticisms that may be made of the FRS 19 approach include the following.

(a) The provisions on **discounting** are somewhat **confusing**.

(b) The standard is **complicated,** and there is **scope for manipulation and inconsistency**, since discounting is optional.

(c) It is **open to question whether deferred tax is a liability** as defined in the *Statement of Principles*. It is not, strictly speaking, a present obligation arising as a result of a past event. However, it is being recognised as such under the FRS.

(d) Arguably the flow-through or **nil provision method is closer to the ASB definition**, but this method, although much simpler, has been rejected to bring the standard closer to the IAS.

3.13 Section summary

- Deferred tax is tax relating to timing differences.
- Full provision must be made for tax timing differences.
- Discounting is allowed but not required.

Exam focus point

Questions on deferred tax for Paper 2.5 should be fairly straightforward. It is likely to be tested as part of a larger question rather than a question in its own right.

4 Taxation in company accounts

FAST FORWARD

The balance sheet liability for tax payable is the tax charge for the year. In the income statement the tax charge for the year is adjusted for transfers to or from deferred tax and for prior year under- or over-provisions.

We have now looked at the 'ingredients' of taxation in company accounts. There are two aspects to be learned:

(a) Taxation on profits in the profit and loss account.
(b) Taxation payments due, shown as a liability in the balance sheet.

4.1 Taxation in the profit and loss account

The tax on profit on ordinary activities is calculated by **aggregating**:

(a) **Corporation tax** on taxable profits
(b) **Transfers to or from deferred taxation**
(c) Any **under provision or overprovision** of corporation tax on profits of previous years

When corporation tax on profits is calculated for the profit and loss account, **the calculation is only an estimate of what the company thinks its tax liability will be. In subsequent dealings with the Inland Revenue, a different corporation tax charge might eventually be agreed.**

The difference between the estimated tax on profits for one year and the actual tax charge finally agreed for the year is made as an adjustment to taxation on profits in the following year, **resulting in the disclosure of either an underprovision or an overprovision of tax.**

Question   Tax payable

In the accounting year to 31 December 20X3, Neil Down Ltd made an operating profit before taxation of £110,000.

Corporation tax on the operating profit has been estimated as £45,000. In the previous year (20X2) corporation tax on 20X2 profits had been estimated as £38,000 but it was subsequently agreed at £40,500 with the Inland Revenue.

A transfer to the deferred taxation account of £16,000 will be made in 20X3.

Required

(a) Calculate the tax on profits for 20X3 for disclosure in the accounts.
(b) Calculate the amount of mainstream corporation tax payable on 30 September 20X4.

Answer

(a)

	£
Corporation tax on profits	45,000
Deferred taxation	16,000
Underprovision of tax in previous year £(40,500 – 38,000)	2,500
Tax on profits for 20X3	63,500

(b)

	£
Tax payable on 20X3 profits	45,000
Mainstream corporation tax liability	45,000

4.2 Taxation in the balance sheet

It should already be apparent from the previous examples that the corporation tax charge in the profit and loss account will not be the same as corporation tax liabilities in the balance sheet.

In the balance sheet, there are several items which we might expect to find.

(a)   **Income tax may be payable** in respect of (say) interest payments paid in the last accounting return period of the year, or accrued.

(b)   If no corporation tax is payable (or very little), then there might be an **income tax recoverable asset** disclosed in current assets (income tax is normally recovered by offset against the tax liability for the year).

(c)   There will usually be a **liability for mainstream corporation tax**, possibly including the amounts due in respect of previous years but not yet paid.

(d)   We may also find a **liability on the deferred taxation account**. Deferred taxation is shown under 'provisions for liabilities' in the balance sheet.

Question

Tax charge

For the year ended 31 July 20X4 Norman Kronkest Ltd made taxable trading profits of £1,200,000 on which corporation tax is payable at 30%.

(a)   A transfer of £20,000 will be made to the deferred taxation account. The balance on this account was £100,000 before making any adjustments for items listed in this paragraph.

(b)   The estimated tax on profits for the year ended 31 July 20X3 was £80,000, but tax has now been agreed with the Inland Revenue at £84,000 and fully paid.

(c)   Mainstream corporation tax on profits for the year to 31 July 20X4 is payable on 1 May 20X5.

(d)   In the year to 31 July 20X4 the company made a capital gain of £60,000 on the sale of some property. This gain is taxable at a rate of 30%.

Required

(a)   Calculate the tax charge for the year to 31 July 20X4.
(b)   Calculate the tax liabilities in the balance sheet of Norman Kronkest as at 31 July 20X4.

Answer

(a)   *Tax charge for the year*

		£
(i)	Tax on trading profits (30% of £1,200,000)	360,000
	Tax on capital gain	18,000
	Deferred taxation	20,000
		398,000
	Underprovision of taxation in previous years £(84,000 – 80,000)	4,000
	Tax charge on ordinary activities	402,000

(ii)   *Note.* The profit and loss account will show the following.

	£
Operating profit (assumed here to be the same as taxable profits)	1,200,000
Profit from sale of asset (exceptional)	60,000
Profit on ordinary activities before taxation	1,260,000
Tax on profit on ordinary activities	402,000
Retained profits for the year	858,000

	£
Deferred taxation	
Balance brought forward	100,000
Transferred from profit and loss account	20,000
Deferred taxation in the balance sheet	120,000

The mainstream corporation tax liability is as follows.

	£
Payable on 1 May 20X5	
Tax on ordinary profits (30% of £1,200,000)	360,000
Tax on capital gain (30% of £60,000)	18,000
Due on 1 May 20X5	378,000

Summary

	£
Creditors: amounts falling due within one year	
Mainstream corporation tax, payable on 1 May 20X5	378,000
Provisions for liabilities	
Deferred taxation	120,000

Note. It may be helpful to show the journal entries for these items.

		£	£
(b) DEBIT	Tax charge (profit and loss account)	402,000	
CREDIT	Corporation tax creditor		*382,000
	Deferred tax		20,000

* This account will show a debit balance of £4,000 until the underprovision is recorded, since payment has already been made: (360,000 + 18,000 + 4,000).

5 Disclosure requirements

> You must also be able to prepare the **notes to the accounts** on tax for publication. This means mastering the disclosure requirements of FRS 16, FRS 19 and the CA 1985.

The CA 1985 requires that the **'tax on profit or loss on ordinary activities' is disclosed on the face of the profit and loss account or in a note to the accounts**. In addition, the **notes** to the profit and loss account **must state:**

(a)   The **basis** on which the charge for UK corporation tax and UK income tax is computed

(b)   The **amounts** of the charge for:

    (i)   UK corporation tax (showing separately the amount, if greater, of UK corporation tax before any double taxation relief)

    (ii)   UK income tax

    (iii)   Non-UK taxation on profits, income and capital gains

(*Note*. The same details must be given, if relevant, in respect of the 'tax on extraordinary profit or loss'.)

5.1 FRS 16

FRS 16 *Current Tax* supplements and extends these provisions requiring that a company's *profit and loss account* should disclose separately (if material):

(a)   The **amount of the UK corporation** tax specifying:

    (i)   **The current charge for corporation tax** on the income of the year (stating the rate used to make the provision).

    (ii)   Adjustments in respect of prior periods.

(b)   The **total foreign taxation** specifying:

    (i)   The current foreign tax charge on the income of the year.
    (ii)   Adjustments in respect of prior periods.

5.2 FRS 19

FRS 19 requires that **deferred** tax relating to the ordinary activities of the enterprise should be **shown separately** as a part of the tax on profit or loss on ordinary activities, either on the face of the profit and loss account, or by note.

Adjustments to deferred tax arising from changes in tax rates and tax allowances should normally be **disclosed separately** as part of the tax charge for the period.

The **deferred liabilities and assets**, should be **disclosed in the balance sheet or notes**. They should be disclosed separately on the face of the balance sheet if the amounts are so material that the absence of disclosure would affect interpretation of the Financial Statements.

5.3 CA 1985

Finally, the **Companies Act 1985 requires certain disclosures in respect of deferred tax.**

(a)   Deferred tax should be shown **in the balance sheet under the heading 'provisions for liabilities and charges'** and in the category of provision for 'taxation, including deferred taxation'. The amount of any provision for taxation other than deferred taxation must be disclosed. The provision for taxation is different from tax liabilities which are shown as creditors in the balance sheet.

(b) **Movements on reserves and provisions** must be disclosed, including provisions for deferred tax:

    (i)   The amount of the provision at the beginning of the year and the end of the year

    (ii)   The amounts transferred to or from the provision during the year

    (iii)   The source/application of any amount so transferred

(c) Information must be disclosed about any **contingent liability** not provided for in the accounts **(such as deferred tax not provided for) and its legal nature**. It is understood that deferred tax not provided for is a contingent liability within the terms of the Act.

(d) The **basis on which the charge for UK tax is computed** has to be stated. Particulars are required of any special circumstances affecting the tax liability for the financial year or succeeding financial years.

Chapter Roundup

- The **FRS 16 requirements** relating to company taxation are straightforward but **must be learned**. The best way is to practise on past exam questions.

- **FRS 19** requires full provision for **deferred** tax. It is unlikely that complicated numerical questions will be set in the exam so concentrate on **understanding** deferred tax.

- The balance sheet liability for tax payable is the tax charge for the year. In the income statement the tax charge for the year is adjusted for transfers to or from deferred tax and for prior year under- or over-provisions.

- You must also be able to prepare the **notes to the accounts** on tax for publication. This means mastering the disclosure requirements of FRS 16, FRS 19 and the CA 1985.

Quick Quiz

1   The due date of payment of corporation tax is:

    A   Twelve months after the company's financial statements have been filed at Companies House

    B   Nine months after the end of the relevant accounting period

    C   Nine months after the company's financial statements have been filed at Companies House

    D   Twelve months after the end of the relevant accounting period

2   What is the SSAP 5 requirement relating to the disclosure of turnover in company accounts?

3   What are the three bases under which deferred tax can be computed?

4   Which method does FRS 19 require to be used?

5   Under FRS 19 deferred tax assets and liabilities may/must be discounted. (*Delete as applicable.*)

6   Tax on profit on ordinary activities is the aggregate of:

    .... + ... + ...

7   List the disclosure requirements set out by the CA 1985, in respect of deferred tax.

Answers to Quick Quiz

1   B (see Para 1)

2   Generally turnover should exclude VAT

3   The nil provision basis, the full provision basis and the partial provision basis

4   Full provision

5   May

6   Corporation tax on taxable profits, transfers to/from deferred tax, under/over provisions from previous years

7   (a)   The deferred tax balance is shown under 'provisions for liabilities'.
     (b)   Movement on the deferred tax provision must be disclosed
     (c)   Any deferred tax not provided for must be disclosed as a contingent liability.
     (d)   Basis on which the charge is computed must be stated, ie full provision basis.

Now try the question below from the Exam Question Bank

Number	Level	Marks	Time
Q9	Full exam	20	36 mins

Liabilities and provisions: reporting and substance of transactions

Topic list	Syllabus reference
1 FRS 21 Events after the balance sheet date	3 (f)
2 FRS 12 Provisions, contingent liabilities and contingent assets	3 (f)
3 Creditors, provisions and reserves	3 (f)
4 Substance over form	3 (f)
5 Off balance sheet finance	3 (f)

Introduction

FRS 21 *Events after the balance sheet date* and FRS 12 *Provisions, contingent liabilities and contingent assets* are very important as they can affect many items in the accounts. Make sure you learn all the relevant definitions and understand the standard accounting treatment.

There are various disclosures relating to creditors, provisions and reserves, and share capital which it is convenient to mention here. The profit and loss disclosures are additional to the FRS 3 disclosures mentioned in the last chapter.

FRS 5 *Reporting the substance of transactions* is a key standard which you need to understand. Make sure you get to grips with why such a standard was put together.

Study guide

- Explain why an accounting standard on provisions is necessary - give examples of previous abuses in this area.

- Define provisions, legal and constructive obligations, past events and the transfer of economic benefits.

- State when provisions may and may not be made, and how they should be accounted for.

- Explain how provisions should be measured.

- Define contingent assets and liabilities - give examples and describe their accounting treatment.

- Be able to identify and account for:

    - warranties/guarantees
    - onerous contracts
    - environmental and similar provisions

- Discuss the validity of making provisions for future repairs or refurbishment.

- Explain the importance of recording the substance rather than the legal form of transactions - give examples of previous abuses in this area.

- Describe the features which may indicate that the substance of transactions may differ from their legal form.

- Explain and apply the principles in accounting standards for the recognition and derecognition of assets and liabilities.

- Be able to recognise the substance of transactions in general, and specifically account for the following types of transactions:

    - stock sold on sale or return/consignment stock.
    - sale and repurchase/leaseback agreements.
    - factoring of debtors.

Exam guide

Substance over form has been highlighted as a key area in the syllabus.

1 FRS 21 Events after the balance sheet date

FAST FORWARD

FRS 21 deals with events after the balance sheet date.

- It distinguishes between adjusting and non-adjusting events and gives examples.

- Where deterioration in operating results and financial position indicates that the going concern concept is no longer appropriate, then the accounts may have to be restated on a break-up basis.

- It stipulates that dividends declared after the balance sheet date are not recognised in the financial statements

FRS 21 *Events after the balance sheet date* is a new standard replacing SSAP 17 *Accounting for post balance sheet events*. The provisions of FRS 21 do not differ greatly from those of SSAP 17

The standard gives the following definitions.

Events after the balance sheet date are those events, favourable and unfavourable, that occur between the balance sheet date and the date when the financial statements are authorised for issue.

Adjusting events after the balance sheet date provide evidence of conditions that existed at the balance sheet date.

Non-adjusting events after the balance sheet date are indicative of conditions that arose after the balance sheet date.

FRS 21 gives the following examples of **adjusting events.**

- The settlement after the balance sheet date of a court case that confirms that the entity had a present obligation at the balance sheet date.

- The receipt of information after the balance sheet date indicating that an asset was impaired at the balance sheet date. This could apply, for instance, to stock valuation or the recoverability of a debtor.

- The determination after the balance sheet date of the cost of assets purchased or the proceeds from assets sold before the balance sheet date.

- The determination after the balance sheet date of the amount of profit sharing or bonus which the entity had a constructive obligation to make at the balance sheet date.

- The discovery of fraud or errors that show that the financial statements are incorrect.

An entity is required to adjust the amounts recognised in its financial statements to reflect adjusting events after the balance sheet date.

1.1 Dividends

This provision was not in SSAP 17. If an entity declares a dividend after the balance sheet date, that dividend is not recognised as a liability at the balance sheet date. It is disclosed by note. In practice, all final dividends are declared after the balance sheet date. A proposed dividend will therefore never appear in the accounts as a current liability.

1.2 Going concern

Deteriorating results after the balance sheet date may indicate a need to reconsider the going concern basis. The financial statements should not be prepared on a going concern basis if management determines after the balance sheet date that it intends to liquidate the entity or cease trading, or that it has no realistic alternative but to do so.

1.3 Material non-adjusting events

For **material** non adjusting events an entity shall **disclose**

(a) The nature of the event
(b) An estimate of its financial effect or a statement that such an estimate cannot be made.

1.4 Examples of material non-adjusting events after the balance sheet date are as follows.

- Acquisition or disposal of a major subsidiary
- Announcing a plan to discontinue an operation
- Major purchases and disposals of assets
- Destruction of a major production plant by fire
- Announcing or commencing a major restructuring

- Major ordinary share or potential ordinary share transactions
- Major changes in asset prices or foreign exchange rates
- Changes in tax rates or laws that significantly affect deferred tax assets
- Entering into significant capital commitments or contingent liabilities
- Commencing major litigation arising solely out of events since the balance sheet date

2 FRS 12 Provisions, contingent liabilities and contingent assets

FAST FORWARD

Under FRS 12, a **provision** should be recognised

– When an entity has a **present obligation**, legal or constructive
– It is probable that a **transfer of economic benefits** will be required to settle it
– A **reliable estimate** can be made of its amount

As we have seen with regard to post balance sheet events, financial statements must include **all the information necessary for an understanding of the company's financial position**.

Provisions, contingent liabilities and contingent assets are 'uncertainties' that must be accounted for consistently if are to achieve this understanding.

2.1 Objective

FRS 12 *Provisions, contingent liabilities and contingent assets* aims to ensure that appropriate **recognition criteria** and **measurement bases** are applied to provisions, contingent liabilities and contingent assets and that **sufficient information** is disclosed in the **notes** to the financial statements to enable users to understand their nature, timing and amount.

2.2 Provisions

You will be familiar with provisions for depreciation and doubtful debts from your earlier studies. The sorts of provisions addressed by FRS 12 are, however, rather different.

Before FRS 12, there was no accounting standard dealing with provisions. Companies wanting to show their results in the most favourable light used to make large **'one off' provisions** in years where a high level of underlying profits was generated. These provisions, often known as **'big bath'** provisions, were then available to shield expenditure in future years when perhaps the underlying profits were not as good.

In other words, **provisions were used for profit smoothing**. Profit smoothing is misleading.

Important

The key aim of FRS 12 is to ensure that provisions are made only where there are valid grounds for them.

FRS 12 views a provision as a **liability**.

Key terms

A **provision** is a **liability** of uncertain timing or amount. A **liability** is an obligation of an entity to transfer economic benefits as a result of past transactions or events.   *(FRS 12)*

The FRS distinguishes provisions from other liabilities such as trade creditors and accruals. This is on the basis that for a provision there is **uncertainty** about the timing or amount of the future expenditure. Whilst uncertainty is clearly present in the case of certain accruals the uncertainty is generally much less than for provisions.

2.3 Recognition

FRS 12 states that a provision should be **recognised** as a liability in the financial statements when:

(a)   An entity has a **present obligation** (legal or constructive) as a result of a past event.

(b)   It is probable that a **transfer of economic benefits** will be required to settle the obligation.

(c)   A **reliable estimate** can be made of the obligation.

2.4 Meaning of obligation

It is fairly clear what a legal obligation is. However, you may not know what a **constructive obligation** is.

Key term

FRS 12 defines a **constructive obligation** as

'An obligation that derives from an entity's actions where:

- By an established pattern of past practice, published policies or a sufficiently specific current statement the entity has indicated to other parties that it will accept certain responsibilities.

- As a result, the entity has created a valid expectation on the part of those other parties that it will discharge those responsibilities.'

Question

Provisions 1

In which of the following circumstances might a provision be recognised?

(a)   On 13 December 20X9 the board of an entity decided to close down a division. The accounting date of the company is 31 December. Before 31 December 20X9 the decision was not communicated to any of those affected and no other steps were taken to implement the decision.

(b)   The board agreed a detailed closure plan on 20 December 20X9 and details were given to customers and employees.

(c)   A company is obliged to incur clean up costs for environmental damage (that has already been caused).

(d)   A company intends to carry out future expenditure to operate in a particular way in the future.

Answer

(a)   No provision would be recognised as the decision has not been communicated.

(b)   A provision would be made in the 20X9 financial statements.

(c)   A provision for such costs is appropriate.

(d)   No present obligation exists and under FRS 12 no provision would be appropriate. This is because the entity could avoid the future expenditure by its future actions, maybe by changing its method of operation.

2.4.1 Probable transfer of economic benefits

For the purpose of the FRS, a transfer of economic benefits is regarded as **'probable'** if the event is **more likely than not** to occur. This appears to indicate a probability of more than 50%. However, the standard makes it clear that where there is a number of similar obligations the probability should be based on considering the population as a whole, rather than one single item.

2.5 Example: Transfer of economic benefits

If a company has entered into a warranty obligation then the probability of transfer of economic benefits may well be extremely small in respect of one specific item. However, when considering the population as a whole the probability of some transfer of economic benefits is quite likely to be much higher. If there is a **greater than 50% probability** of some transfer of economic benefits then a **provision** should be made for the **expected amount**.

2.5.1 Measurement of provisions

Important!

> The amount recognised as a provision should be the best estimate of the expenditure required to settle the present obligation at the balance sheet date.

The estimates will be determined by the **judgement** of the entity's management supplemented by the experience of similar transactions.

Allowance is made for **uncertainty**. Where the provision being measured involves a large population of items, the obligation is estimated by weighting all possible outcomes by their discounted probabilities, ie **expected value**.

Question   Expected value

Patel plc sells goods with a warranty under which customers are covered for the cost of repairs of any manufacturing defect that becomes apparent within the first six months of purchase. The company's past experience and future expectations indicate the following pattern of likely repairs.

% of goods sold	Defects	Cost of repairs £m
75	None	–
20	Minor	1.0
5	Major	4.0

What is the expected cost of repairs?

Answer

The cost is found using 'expected values' (75% × £nil) + (20% × £1.0m) + (5% × £4.0m) = £400,000.

2.5.2 Future events

Future events which are reasonably expected to occur (eg new legislation, changes in technology) may affect the amount required to settle the entity's obligation and should be taken into account.

2.5.3 Expected disposal of assets

Gains from the expected disposal of assets should not be taken into account in measuring a provision.

2.5.4 Reimbursements

Some or all of the expenditure needed to settle a provision may be expected to be recovered form a third party. If so, the **reimbursement should be recognised only when it is virtually certain that reimbursement will be received if the entity settles the obligation**.

(a) The reimbursement should be treated as a separate asset, and the amount recognised should not be greater than the provision itself.

(b) The provision and the amount recognised for reimbursement may be netted off in the profit and loss account.

2.5.5 Changes in provisions

Provisions should be renewed at each balance sheet date and adjusted to reflect the current best estimate. If it is no longer probable that a transfer of economic benefits will be required to settle the obligation, the provision should be reversed.

2.5.6 Use of provisions

A provision should be used only for expenditures for which the provision was originally recognised. Setting expenditures against a provision that was originally recognised for another purpose would conceal the impact of two different events.

2.5.7 Recognising an asset when recognising a provision

Normally the setting up of a provision should be charged immediately to the profit and loss account. But **if the incurring of the present obligation recognised as a provision gives access to future economic benefits an asset should be recognised.**

2.6 Example: Recognising an asset

An obligation for decommissioning costs is incurred by commissioning an oil rig. At the same time, the commissioning gives access to oil reserves over the years of the oil rig's operation. Therefore an asset representing future access to oil reserves is recognised at the same time as the provision for decommissioning costs.

2.6.1 Future operating losses

Provisions should not be recognised for future operating losses. They do not meet the definition of a liability and the general recognition criteria set out in the standard.

2.6.2 Onerous contracts

If an entity has a contract that is onerous, the present obligation under the contract **should be recognised and measured** as a provision. An example might be vacant leasehold property.

Key term

> An **onerous contract** is a contract entered into with another party under which the unavoidable costs of fulfilling the terms of the contract exceed any revenues expected to be received from the goods or services supplied or purchased directly or indirectly under the contract and where the entity would have to compensate the other party if it did not fulfil the terms of the contract.

2.7 Examples of possible provisions

It is easier to see what FRS 12 is driving at if you look at examples of those items which are possible provisions under this standard. Some of these we have already touched on.

(a) **Warranties.** These are argued to be genuine provisions as on past experience it is probable, ie more likely than not, that some claims will emerge. The provision must be estimated, however, on the basis of the class as a whole and not on individual claims. There is a clear legal obligation in this case.

(b)   **Major repairs**. In the past it has been quite popular for companies to provide for expenditure on a major overhaul to be accrued gradually over the intervening years between overhauls. Under FRS 12 this will no longer be possible as FRS 12 would argue that this is a mere intention to carry out repairs, not an obligation. The entity can always sell the asset in the meantime. The only solution is to treat major assets such as aircraft, ships, furnaces etc as a series of smaller assets where each part is depreciated over shorter lives. Thus any major overhaul may be argued to be replacement and therefore capital rather than revenue expenditure.

(c)   **Self insurance**. A number of companies have created a provision for self insurance based on the expected cost of making good fire damage etc instead of paying premiums to an insurance company. Under FRS 12 this provision would no longer be justifiable as the entity has no obligation until a fire or accident occurs. No obligation exists until that time.

(d)   **Environmental contamination**. If the company has an environment policy such that other parties would expect the company to clean up any contamination or if the company has broken current environmental legislation then a provision for environmental damage must be made.

(e)   **Decommissioning or abandonment costs**. When an oil company initially purchases an oilfield it is put under a legal obligation to decommission the site at the end of its life. Prior to FRS 12 most oil companies applied the SORP on *Accounting for abandonment costs* published by the Oil Industry Accounting Committee and they built up the provision gradually over the life of the field so that no one year would be unduly burdened with the cost.

FRS 12, however, insists that a legal obligation exists on the initial expenditure on the field and therefore a liability exists immediately. This would appear to result in a large charge to profit and loss in the first year of operation of the field. However, the FRS takes the view that the cost of purchasing the field in the first place is not only the cost of the field itself but also the costs of putting it right again. Thus all the costs of abandonment may be capitalised.

(f)   **Restructuring**. This is considered in detail below.

2.7.1 Provisions for restructuring

One of the main purposes of FRS 12 was to target abuses of provisions for restructuring. Accordingly, FRS 12 lays down **strict criteria** to determine when such a provision can be made.

Key term

FRS 12 defines a **restructuring** as:

A programme that is planned and is controlled by management and materially changes either:

- The scope of a business undertaken by an entity
- The manner in which that business is conducted

The FRS gives the following **examples** of events that may fall under the definition of restructuring.

- The **sale or termination** of a line of business

- The **closure of business locations** in a country or region or the **relocation** of business activities from one country region to another

- **Changes in management structure**, for example, the elimination of a layer of management

- **Fundamental reorganisations** that have a material effect on the **nature and focus** of the entity's operations

The question is whether or not an entity has an obligation - legal or constructive - at the balance sheet date.

- An entity must have a **detailed formal plan** for the restructuring.
- It must have **raised a valid expectation** in those affected that it will carry out the restructuring by starting to implement that plan or announcing its main features to those affected by it

Important!

> **A mere management decision is not normally sufficient**. Management decisions may sometimes trigger off recognition, but only if earlier events such as negotiations with employee representatives and other interested parties have been concluded subject only to management approval.

Where the restructuring involves the **sale of an operation** then FRS 12 states that no obligation arises until the entity has entered into a **binding sale agreement**. This is because until this has occurred the entity will be able to change its mind and withdraw from the sale even if its intentions have been announced publicly.

2.7.2 Costs to be included within a restructuring provision

The FRS states that a restructuring provision should include only the **direct expenditures** arising from the restructuring, which are those that are both:

- **Necessarily entailed** by the restructuring; and
- Not associated with the **ongoing activities** of the entity.

The following costs should specifically **not** be included within a restructuring provision.

- **Retraining** or relocating continuing staff
- **Marketing**
- **Investment in new systems** and distribution networks

2.7.3 Disclosure

Disclosures for provisions fall into two parts.

(a) Disclosure of details of the **change in carrying value** of a provision from the beginning to the end of the year

(b) Disclosure of the **background** to the making of the provision and the uncertainties affecting its outcome

2.8 Contingent liabilities

FAST FORWARD

> An entity should not recognise a contingent asset or liability, but they should be disclosed.

Now you understand provisions it will be easier to understand contingent assets and liabilities.

Key term

> FRS 12 defines a **contingent liability** as:
>
> - A possible obligation that arises from past events and whose existence will be confirmed only by the occurrence or non-occurrence of one or more uncertain future events not wholly within the entity's control; or
>
> - A present obligation that arises from past events but is not recognised because:
>   - It is not probable that a transfer of economic benefits will be required to settle the obligation
>   - The amount of the obligation cannot be measured with sufficient reliability

As a rule of thumb, probable means more than 50% likely. **If an obligation is probable, it is not a contingent liability** - instead, a **provision is needed**.

2.8.1 Treatment of contingent liabilities

Contingent liabilities **should not be recognised in financial statements** but they **should be disclosed**. The required disclosures are:

- A brief description of the nature of the contingent liability
- An estimate of its financial effect
- An indication of the uncertainties that exist
- The possibility of any reimbursement

2.9 Contingent assets

Key term

> FRS 12 defines a **contingent asset** as:
>
> A possible asset that arises from past events and whose existence will be confirmed by the occurrence of one or more uncertain future events not wholly within the entity's control.

A contingent asset must not be recognised. Only when the realisation of the related economic benefits is **virtually certain** should recognition take place. At that point, **the asset is no longer a contingent asset**!

2.9.1 Disclosure: contingent liabilities

A **brief description** must be provided of all material contingent liabilities unless they are likely to be remote. In addition, provide

- An estimate of their **financial effect**
- Details of **any uncertainties**

Disclosure: contingent assets

Contingent assets must only be disclosed in the notes if they are **probable**. In that case a brief description of the contingent asset should be provided along with an estimate of its likely financial effect.

2.9.2 'Let out'

FRS 12 permits reporting entities to avoid disclosure requirements relating to provisions, contingent liabilities and contingent assets if they would be expected to **seriously prejudice** the position of the entity in dispute with other parties. However, this should only be employed in **extremely rare** cases. Details of the general nature of the provision/contingencies must still be provided, together with an explanation of why it has not been disclosed.

You must practise the questions below to get the hang of FRS 12. But first, study the flow chart, taken from FRS 12, which is a good summary of its requirements.

Exam focus
point

> If you learn this flow chart you should be able to deal with most of the questions you are likely to meet in the exam.

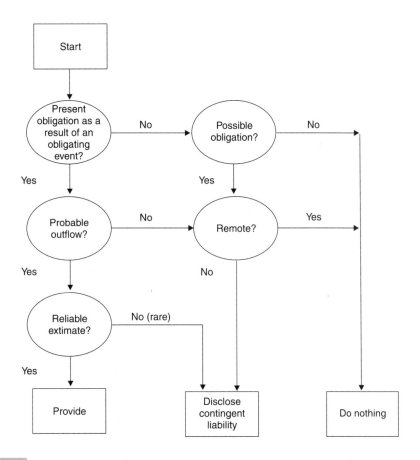

Question

During 20X9 Avocado Ltd gives a guarantee of certain borrowings of Banana Ltd, whose financial condition at that time is sound. During 20Y0, the financial condition of Banana Ltd deteriorates and at 30 June 20Y0 Banana Ltd goes into administration.

What accounting treatment is required:

(a)   At 31 December 20X9?
(b)   At 31 December 20Y0?

Answer

(a)   *At 31 December 20X9*

There is a present obligation as a result of a past obligating event. The obligating event is the giving of the guarantee, which gives rise to a legal obligation. However, at 31 December 20X9 no transfer of economic benefits is probable in settlement of the obligation.

No provision is recognised. The guarantee is disclosed as a contingent liability unless the probability of any transfer is regarded as remote.

(b)   *At 31 December 20Y0*

As above, there is a present obligation as a result of a past obligating event, namely the giving of the guarantee.

At 31 December 20Y0 it is probable that a transfer of economic events will be required to settle the obligation. A provision is therefore recognised for the best estimate of the obligation.

Question

Super Produx Ltd gives warranties at the time of sale to purchasers of its products. Under the terms of the warranty the manufacturer undertakes to make good, by repair or replacement, manufacturing defects that become apparent within a period of three years from the date of the sale. Should a provision be recognised?

Answer

Super Produx Ltd **cannot avoid** the cost of repairing or replacing all items of product that manifest manufacturing defects in respect of which warranties are given before the balance sheet date, and a provision for the cost of this should therefore be made.

Super Produx Ltd is obliged to repair or replace items that fail within the entire warranty period. Therefore, in respect of **this year's sales**, the obligation provided for at the balance sheet date should be the cost of making good items for which defects have been notified but not yet processed, **plus** an estimate of costs in respect of the other items sold for which there is sufficient evidence that manufacturing defects **will** manifest themselves during their remaining periods of warranty cover.

Question

After a wedding in 20X0 ten people died, possibly as a result of food poisoning from products sold by Crippen Ltd. Legal proceedings are started seeking damages from Crippen but it disputes liability. Up to the date of approval of the financial statements for the year to 31 December 20X0, Crippen's lawyers advise that it is probable that it will not be found liable. However, when Crippen prepares the financial statements for the year to 31 December 20X1 its lawyers advise that, owing to developments in the case, it is probable that it will be found liable.

What is the required accounting treatment:

(a)   At 31 December 20X0?

(b)   At 31 December 20X1?

Answer

(a)   *At 31 December 20X0*

On the basis of the evidence available when the financial statements were approved, there is no obligation as a result of past events. No provision is recognised. The matter is disclosed as a contingent liability unless the probability of any transfer is regarded as remote.

(b)   *At 31 December 20X1*

On the basis of the evidence available, there is a present obligation. A transfer of economic benefits in settlement is probable.

A provision is recognised for the best estimate of the amount needed to settle the present obligation.

2.10 Section summary

- The objective of FRS 12 is to ensure that appropriate recognition criteria and measurement bases are applied to provisions and contingencies and that sufficient information is disclosed.

- The FRS seeks to ensure that provisions are only recognised when a measurable obligation exists. It includes detailed rules that can be used to ascertain when an obligation exists and how to measure the obligation.

- The standard attempts to eliminate the 'profit smoothing' which has gone on before it was issued.

Exam focus point

Where you get a narrative or discursive question in the exam you must:

(a) Ensure you focus on the examiner's requirements

(b) Write sufficient for the marker to be able to award you the marks for the question

(c) Avoid long sentences where several valid points are subsumed into one point and probably lost

(d) Set your answer out in easily identifiable points to help the marker award you as many marks as possible

3 Creditors, provisions and reserves

3.1 Creditors

If any liabilities included under creditors have been **secured**, the amounts secured and the nature of the security must be **stated**.

Any amounts included which are **payable** (or repayable) **more than five years** after the balance sheet date must be **specified**, together with the terms of payment or repayment and the rate of any Interest payable.

The amount of any **declared dividend** should be stated. A dividend is only recognised if it was declared before the year end. Details of any arrears of dividends on cumulative preference shares must also be given.

Where **debentures** have been issued during the year, **details of the issue** (including the reasons why it was made) should be given in a note.

3.2 Provisions and reserves

As defined in the CA 1985, **provisions for liabilities and charges** are amounts retained to provide for any liability or loss which is either likely to be incurred or certain to be incurred, but uncertain as to amount or as to the date on which it will crystallise.

Where a reserve or provision is disclosed as a separate item in a company's balance sheet or in a note, any movements on the account during the year should be specified. The amount of any **provisions for taxation other than deferred taxation must be stated and details must be given of any pension commitments.**

The pro-forma balance sheet requires that any **share premium account** (KII) **and any revaluation reserve** (KIII) be **shown separately**. Any other reserves built up by a company should be disclosed under the appropriate headings (or amalgamated if not material) with the profit and loss account balance (KV) being shown separately.

4 Substance over form

FAST FORWARD

Transactions must be accounted for according to their **substance**, **not** just their legal **form**.

There are a number of '**creative accounting**' techniques, the purpose of which is to manipulate figures for a desired result.

Exam focus point

December 2002 candidates were asked to discuss the importance of recording the substance rather than the legal form of transactions and describe what might indicate that the substance of a transaction is different from its legal form.

In the December 2002 exam, candidates were given a scenario and were required to discuss which party bears the risks and rewards and to arrive at a conclusion on how the transactions involved should be treated by each party.

The June 2003 paper required candidates to correctly account for goods legally sold to a merchant bank with an option to reacquire for the original price plus a facilitating fee.

FRS 5 has featured strongly in recent exams, both by way of separate questions but perhaps more importantly candidates must be able to apply it to a variety of scenarios. It is vital to develop a sound grasp of FRS 5 before entering the exam room.

'Substance over form' is a very important concept and it **has been used to determine accounting treatment in financial statements through accounting standards and so prevent off balance sheet transactions**. The following paragraphs give examples of where the principle of substance over form is enforced, particularly in accounting standards.

4.1 SSAP 21 Accounting for leases and hire purchase contracts

In SSAP 21, as we saw in the previous chapter, there is an explicit requirement that if the lessor transfers substantially all the risks and rewards of ownership to the lessee then, even though the legal title has not passed, the item being leased should be shown as an asset in the balance sheet of the lessee and the amount due to the lessor should be shown as a liability.

4.2 FRS 8 Related party disclosures

FRS 8 requires financial statements to disclose fully material transactions undertaken with a related party by the reporting entity, regardless of any price charged.

4.3 SSAP 9 Stocks and long-term contracts

In SSAP 9 there is a requirement to account for attributable profits on long-term contracts under the accruals convention. However, there may be a problem with realisation, since it is arguable whether we should account for profit which, although attributable to the work done, may not have yet been invoiced to the customer. It is argued that the convention of substance over form is applied to justify ignoring the strict legal position.

4.4 FRS 2 Accounting for subsidiary undertakings

This is perhaps the most important area of off balance sheet finance which has been prevented by the application of the substance over form concept.

The use of quasi-subsidiaries was very common in the 1980s. A **quasi-subsidiary** is defined by FRS 5: in effect it **is a vehicle which does not fulfil the definition of a subsidiary, but it operates just like a subsidiary.**

The main off balance sheet transactions involving quasi-subsidiaries were as follows.

(a) **Sale of assets**. The sale of assets to a quasi-subsidiary was carried out to remove the associated borrowings from the balance sheet and so reduce gearing; or perhaps so that the company could credit a profit in such a transaction. The asset could then be rented back to the vendor company under an operating lease (no capitalisation required by the lessee).

(b) **Purchase of companies or assets**. One reason for such a purchase through a quasi-subsidiary is if the acquired entity is expected to make losses in the near future. Post-acquisition losses can be avoided by postponing the date of acquisition to the date the holding company acquires the purchase from the quasi-subsidiary.

(c) **Business activities conducted outside the group**. Such a subsidiary might have been excluded through a quasi-subsidiary or not consolidated on the grounds of 'dissimilar activities'. Exclusion from consolidation might be undertaken because the activities are high risk and have high gearing.

CA 1989 introduced a new definition of a subsidiary based on *control* rather than just ownership rights and this definition (along with other related matters) was incorporated into FRS 2, thus substantially reducing the effectiveness of this method of off-balance sheet finance.

An amendment to FRS 2 by way of statutory instrument 2947 in 2004 removed the need for a parent company to have a 'participating interest' in a subsidiary, ie a 20% shareholding. Instead, the criterion is '… it has the power to exercise, or actually exercises, dominant influence or control over it.' So this moves the definition of a subsidiary away from 'interest' (shareholding) to 'control'. This parallels the situation with a 'quasi-subsidiary' and should have the effect of brining certain types of quasi-subsidiaries into group accounts.

4.5 Creative accounting

Exam focus point

December 2002 candidates were required to explain the meaning of the term 'creative accounting' and to provide examples.

Creative accounting, the **manipulation of figures for a desired result**, takes many forms. Off balance sheet finance is a major type of creative accounting and it probably has the most serious implications. Before we look at some of the other types of creative accounting, we should consider some important points.

Firstly, **it is very rare for a company, its directors or employees to manipulate results for the purpose of fraud. The major consideration is usually the effect the results will have on the share price of the company**. If the share price falls, the company becomes vulnerable to takeover.

Analysts, brokers and economists, whose opinions affect the stock markets, are often perceived as having an outlook which is both short-term and superficial. Consequently, **companies will attempt to produce the results the market expects or wants.** The companies will aim for steady progress in a few key numbers and ratios and they will aim to meet the market's stated expectation.

Another point to consider, particularly when you approach this topic in an examination, is that the **number of methods** available for creative accounting and the determination and imagination of those who wish to perpetrate such acts are **endless**. It has been seen in the past that, wherever an accounting standard or law closes a loophole, another one is found. This has produced a change of approach in regulators and standard setters, towards general principles rather than detailed rules.

Let us now examine some examples of creative accounting, the reaction of the standard setters and possible actions in the future which may halt or change such practices. Remember that this list is not comprehensive and that the frequency and materiality of the use of each method will vary a great deal. Remember also that we have already covered several methods in our examination of off balance sheet finance.

4.5.1 Income recognition and cut-off

Manipulation of cut-off is relatively straightforward. A company may issue invoices before the year end and inflate sales for the year when in fact they have not received firm orders for the goods. Income recognition can be manipulated in a variety of ways.

One example is where a company sells software under contract. The sales contracts will only be realised in full over a period of time, but the company might recognise the full sales value of the contract once it has been secured, even though some payments from clients will fall due over several years. This is clearly imprudent, but the company might justify it by pointing to the irrevocable nature of the contract. But what if a customer should go in to liquidation? No income would be forthcoming from the contract under such circumstances.

4.5.2 Reserves

Reserves are often used to manipulate figures, avoiding any impact on the profit and loss account. This occurs particularly in situations where an accounting standard allows a choice of treatments.

4.5.3 Revaluations

The optional nature of the revaluation of fixed assets leaves such practices open to manipulation. The choice of whether to revalue can have a significant impact on a company's balance sheet. Companies which carried out such revaluations would expect to suffer a much higher depreciation charge as a result. However, many companies charged depreciation in the profit and loss account based on the historical cost only. The rest of the depreciation charge (on the excess of the revalued amount over cost) was transferred to reserves and offset against the revaluation reserve.

Again, this is an abuse of the use of reserves and it was outlawed by the revised SSAP 12 (now superseded by FRS 15). Companies must now charge depreciation on the revalued amount and pass the whole charge through the profit and loss account.

4.5.4 Other creative accounting techniques

The examples given above are some of the major 'abuses' in accounting over recent years. A few more are mentioned here and you should aim to think up as many examples of each as you can. You may also know of other creative accounting techniques which we have not mentioned here.

(a)   **Window dressing**. This is where transactions are passed through the books at the year end to make figures look better, but in fact they have not taken place and are often reversed after the year end. An example is where cheques are written to creditors, entered in the cash book, but not sent out until well after the year end.

(b)   **Change of accounting policies**. This tends to be a last resort because companies which change accounting policies know they will not be able to do so again for some time. The effect in the year of change can be substantial and prime candidates for such treatment are depreciation, stock valuation, changes from current cost to historical cost (practised frequently by privatised public utilities) and foreign currency losses.

(c)   **Manipulation of accruals, prepayments and contingencies**. These figures can often be very subjective, particularly contingencies. In the case of impending legal action, for example, a contingent liability is difficult to estimate, the case may be far off and the solicitors cannot give any indication of likely success, or failure. In such cases companies will often only disclose the possibility of such a liability, even though the eventual costs may be substantial.

Question

Creative accounting

Creative accounting, off balance sheet finance and related matters (in particular how ratio analysis can be used to discover these practices) often come up in articles in, for example, the *Financial Times* and *The Economist*. Find a library, preferably a good technical library, which can provide you with copies of back issues of such newspapers or journals and look for articles on creative accounting. Alternatively you may have access to the Internet and could therefore search the relevant websites.

5 Off balance sheet finance

FAST FORWARD

The subject of **off balance sheet finance** is complex and difficult to understand. In practice, off balance sheet finance schemes are often very sophisticated and they are beyond the range of this syllabus.

Key term

> **Off balance sheet finance** has been described as 'the funding or refinancing of a company's operations in such a way that, under legal requirements and existing accounting conventions, some or all of the finance may not be shown on its balance sheet.'

Off balance sheet transactions' is the term used for transactions which meet the above objective. These transactions may involve the removal of assets from the balance sheet, as well as liabilities, and they are likely to have a significant impact on the profit and loss account.

5.1 The off balance sheet finance problem

The result of the use of increasingly sophisticated off balance sheet finance transactions is a situation where the users of financial statements do not have a proper or clear view of the state of the company's affairs. The disclosures required by company law and current accounting standards do not provide sufficient rules for disclosure of off balance sheet finance transactions and so very little of the true nature of the transaction is exposed.

Whatever the purpose of such transactions, insufficient disclosure creates a problem. This problem has been debated over the years by the accountancy profession and other interested parties and some progress has been made (see the later sections of this chapter).

The incidence of company collapses over the last few years has risen due to the recession and a great many of these have revealed much higher borrowings than originally thought, because part of the borrowing was off balance sheet.

The main argument used for disallowing off balance sheet finance is that the true substance of the transactions should be shown, not merely the legal form, particularly when it is exacerbated by poor disclosure.

5.2 ASB initiatives

Although the ASB wanted to give the old exposure draft on this subject priority in its work programme, there were problems. A general problem was how to ensure that any new standard was consistent with the revised *Statement of Principles*. There was also a specific problem with securitisation because of opposition from the banking industry. All these aspects are discussed below.

Two chapters of the *Statement of Principles* affect the question of off balance sheet finance: *The elements of financial statements* and *The recognition of items in financial statements*.

The definitions are as follows.

Key terms

> (a) **Assets** are defined as 'rights or other access to future economic benefits controlled by an entity as a result of past transactions or events'.
>
> (b) **Liabilities** are defined as 'an entity's obligations to transfer economic benefits as a result of past transactions or events'.

This chapter also lays out the **criteria for recognition** and derecognition of assets and liabilities.

- (a) An item should be recognised in financial statements if:
    - (i) The item meets the definition of an element of financial statements (such as an asset or a liability).
    - (ii) There is enough evidence that the change in assets or liabilities inherent in the item has occurred (including evidence that a future inflow or outflow of benefit will occur).
    - (iii) The item can be measured in monetary terms with sufficient reliability.
- (b) An item should cease to be recognised as an asset or liability if:
    - (i) The item no longer meets the definition of the relevant element of financial statements.
    - (ii) There is no longer enough evidence that the entity has access to future economic benefits or an obligation to transfer economic benefits.

5.3 FRS 5 Reporting the substance of transactions

After many years' work on the subject of off balance sheet finance (some of it detailed above), the ASB has finally published FRS 5 *Reporting the substance of transactions*. It is a daunting document, running to well over 100 pages, although the standard section itself is relatively short.

5.3.1 Scope and exclusions

FRS 5 applies to all entities whose accounts are intended to give a true and fair view, with no exemptions for any particular type or size of companies. However, it excludes a number of transactions from its scope, unless they are part of a larger series of transactions that is within the scope of the standard. These exclusions are:

- (a) **Forward contracts and futures** (such as those for foreign currencies or commodities).
- (b) **Foreign exchange and interest rate swaps**.
- (c) contracts where a net amount will be paid or received based on the movement in a price or an index (sometimes referred to as **'contracts for differences'**).
- (d) **Expenditure commitments** (such as purchase commitments) and orders placed, until the earlier of delivery or payment.
- (e) **Employment contracts**.

5.3.2 Relationship to other standards

The interaction of FRS 5 with other standards and statutory requirements is also an important issue; **whichever rules are the more specific should be applied**. Leasing provides a good example (as we will see in the next chapter): straightforward leases which fall squarely within the terms of SSAP 21 should continue to be accounted for without any need to refer to FRS 5, but where their terms are more complex, or the lease is only one element in a larger series of transactions, then FRS 5 comes into play.

In addition, the standard requires that its general principle of substance over form should apply to the application of other existing rules.

Exam focus point

A full question on FRS 5, covering both knowledge and application could be set.

5.3.3 Application notes

FRS 5 deals with certain specific aspects of off balance sheet finance in detailed **application notes**. The topics covered are:

(a) **Consignment stock**
(b) **Sale and repurchase agreements**
(c) **Factoring of debts**
(d) **Securitised assets**
(e) **Loan transfers**
(f) **Private Finance Initiative and similar contracts**
(g) **Revenue recognition**

The application notes explain how to apply the standard to the particular transactions which they describe, and also contain specific disclosure requirements in relation to those transactions. The application notes are not exhaustive and they do not override the general principles of the standard itself, but they are regarded as authoritative insofar as they assist in interpreting it. The notes are discussed in more detail in the next section.

5.3.4 Basic principles

FRS 5's fundamental principle is that the substance of an entity's transactions should be reflected in its accounts. The key considerations are whether a transaction has given rise to new assets and liabilities, and whether it has changed any existing assets and liabilities. Definitions of assets and liabilities and rules for their recognition and derecognition are discussed below.

Sometimes there will be a series of connected transactions to be evaluated, not just a single transaction. It is necessary to identify and account for the substance of the series of transactions as a whole, rather than addressing each transaction individually.

5.3.5 Definitions of assets and liabilities

According to the standard:

'**Assets** are rights or other access to future economic benefits controlled by an entity as a result of past transactions or events.'

'**Liabilities** are an entity's obligations to transfer economic benefits as a result of past transactions or events.'

The standard goes on to say that identification of who has the risks relating to an asset will generally indicate who has the benefits and hence who has the asset. It also says that if an entity is in certain circumstances unable to avoid an outflow of benefits, this will provide evidence that it has a liability. The various risks and benefits relating to particular assets and liabilities are discussed in the application notes.

5.3.6 Recognition

The next key question is deciding **when** something which satisfies the definition of an asset or liability has to be recognised in the balance. sheet. The standard seeks to answer this by saying that:

'where a transaction results in an item that meets the definition of an asset or liability, that item should be recognised in the balance sheet if:

(a)   There is sufficient evidence of the existence of the item (including, where appropriate, evidence that a future inflow or outflow of benefit will occur), and

(b)   The item can be measured at a monetary amount with sufficient reliability.'

5.3.7 Derecognition

As the name suggests, derecognition is the opposite of recognition. It **concerns the question of when to remove from the balance sheet the assets and liabilities which have previously been recognised**. FRS 5 addresses this issue only in relation to assets, not liabilities, and its rules are designed to determine one of three outcomes, discussed below: complete derecognition, no derecognition, and the in-between case, partial derecognition.

The issue of derecognition is perhaps one of the most common aspects of off balance sheet transactions; has an asset been sold or has it been used to secure borrowings? The concept of partial derecognition is a new addition to FRS 5 and attempts to deal with the in-between situation of where sufficient benefits and risks have been transferred to warrant at least some derecognition of an asset.

5.3.8 Complete derecognition

In the simplest case, where a transaction results in the transfer to another party of all the significant benefits and risks relating to an asset, the entire asset should cease to be recognised. In this context, the word 'significant' is explained further: it should not be judged in relation to all the conceivable benefits and risks that could exist, but only in relation to those that are likely to occur in practice. This means that the importance of the risk retained must be assessed in relation to the magnitude of the total realistic risk which exists.

5.3.9 No derecognition

At the other end of the spectrum, **where a transaction results in no significant change to the benefits or to the risks relating to the asset in question, no sale can be recorded and the entire asset should continue to be recognised.** Retaining *either* the benefits or the risks is sufficient to keep the asset on the balance sheet. This means that the elimination of risk by financing the asset on a non-recourse basis will not remove it from the balance sheet; it would be necessary to dispose of the upside as well in order to justify recording a sale. (A further possible treatment, the special case of a 'linked presentation', is discussed below.)

The standard says that **any transaction that is 'in substance a financing' will not qualify for derecognition**; the item will therefore stay on the balance sheet, and the finance will be introduced as a liability.

5.3.10 Partial derecognition

As can be seen, the above criteria are relatively restrictive. The standard therefore goes on to deal with circumstances where, although not all significant benefits and risks have been transferred, the transaction is more than a mere financing and has transferred enough of the benefits and risks to warrant at least some derecognition of the asset. It addresses three such cases.

(a) **Where an asset has been subdivided**

Where an identifiable part of an asset is separated and sold off, with the remainder being retained, the asset should be split and a partial sale recorded. Examples include the sale of a proportionate part of a loan receivable, where all future receipts are shared equally between the parties, or the stripping of interest payments from the principal of a loan instrument.

(b) **Where an item is sold for less than its full life**

This exception arises where the seller retains a residual value risk by offering to buy the asset back at a predetermined price at a later stage in the asset's life. Such an arrangement is sometimes offered in relation to commercial vehicles, aircraft, and so on. The standard says that in such cases the original asset will have been replaced by a residual interest in the asset together with a liability for its obligation to pay the repurchase price.

(c) **Where an item is transferred for its full life but some risk or benefit is retained**

This may arise, for example, where a company gives a warranty or residual value guarantee in relation to the product being sold. Under the standard, this does not preclude the recording of the sale so long as the exposure under the warranty or guarantee can be assessed and provided for if necessary. Companies may also sometimes retain the possibility of an upward adjustment to the sale price of an asset based on its future performance, for example, when a business is sold subject to an earn-out clause, but again this should not preclude the recognition of the sale.

In all of these cases of partial disposals, the amount of the initial profit or loss may be uncertain. **FRS 5 says that the normal rules of prudence should be applied, but also that the uncertainty should be disclosed if it could have a material effect on the accounts.**

5.3.11 Linked presentation

FAST FORWARD

You need to understand **linked presentation**. This was originally an FRS 5 Application Note and is now part of FRS 26.

This requires **non-recourse finance** to be **shown on the face of the balance sheet as a deduction from the asset to which it relates** (rather than in the liabilities section of the balance sheet), provided certain stringent criteria are met. This is really a question of how, rather than whether, to show the asset and liability in the balance sheet, so it is not the same as derecognition of these items, although there are some similarities in the result.

Linked presentation should be used when an asset is financed in such a way that:

(a) The finance will be repaid only from proceeds generated by the specific item it finances (or by transfer of the item itself) and there is no possibility whatsoever of a claim on the entity being established other than against funds generated by that item (or against the item itself).

(b) There is no provision whereby the entity may either keep the item on repayment of the finance or reacquire it at any time.

There are also several more specific conditions which elaborate on these principles.

5.3.12 Consolidation of other entities

The Companies Act definition of a 'subsidiary undertaking' means that the consolidation of other entities is based largely on *de facto* control. However, FRS 5 takes the view that this is not conclusive in determining which entities are to be included in consolidated accounts. It envisages that there will be occasions where the need to give a true and fair view will require the inclusion of **'quasi subsidiaries'**. FRS 5 defines a quasi subsidiary in these terms.

Key term

> 'A **quasi subsidiary** of a reporting entity is a company, trust, partnership or other vehicle that, though not fulfilling the definition of a subsidiary, is directly or indirectly controlled by the reporting entity and gives rise to benefits for that entity that are in substance no different from those that would arise were the vehicle a subsidiary.'

Statutory instrument 2947 has brought some quasi subsidiaries into the net for consolidation – see 4.4 above.

5.3.13 Disclosure

FRS 5 has a general requirement to **disclose transactions in sufficient detail to enable the reader to understand their commercial effect**, whether or not they have given rise to the recognition of assets and liabilities. This means that where transactions or schemes give rise to assets and liabilities which are *not* recognised in the accounts, disclosure of their nature and effects still has to be considered in order to ensure that the accounts give a true and fair view.

A second general principle is that an **explanation** should be given **where there are any assets or liabilities whose nature is different from that which the reader might expect** of assets or liabilities appearing in the accounts under that description. The standard also calls for specific disclosures in relation to the use of the linked presentation, the inclusion of quasi subsidiaries in the accounts, and the various transactions dealt with in the application notes.

5.4 Common forms of off balance sheet finance

The application notes attached to FRS 5 are intended to clarify and develop the methods of applying the proposed standard to the particular transactions which they describe and to provide guidance on how to interpret it in relation to other similar transactions. These transactions are the more common types.

5.4.1 Consignment stock

Consignment stock is an arrangement where stock is **held by one party** (say a distributor) but is **owned by another party** (for example a manufacturer or a finance company). Consignment stock is common in the motor trade and is similar to goods sold on a 'sale or return' basis.

To identify the correct treatment, it is necessary to identify the point at which the distributor acquired the benefits of the asset (the stock) **rather than the point at which legal title was acquired**. If the manufacturer has the right to require the return of the stock, and if that right is likely to be exercised, then the stock is not an asset of the dealer. If the dealer is rarely required to return the stock, then this part of the transaction will have little commercial effect in practice and should be ignored for accounting purposes. The potential liability would need to be disclosed in the accounts.

5.4.2 Sale and leaseback transactions

These are arrangements under which the company sells an asset to another person on terms that allow the company to repurchase the assets in certain circumstances. **The key question is whether the transaction is a straightforward sale, or whether it is, in effect, a secured loan**. It is necessary to look at the arrangement to determine who has the rights to the economic benefits that the asset generates, and the terms on which the asset is to be repurchased.

If the seller has the right to the benefits of the use of the asset, and the repurchase terms are such that the repurchase is likely to take place, the transaction should be accounted for as a loan.

Exam focus
point

> The June 2002 paper linked sale and leaseback of property to accounting ratios.

5.4.3 FRS 26

The FRS 5 application notes on debt factoring and loan transfers have now been transferred to FRS 26, but are included in this chapter as they deal with substance over form.

5.4.4 Factoring of debts

Where debts are factored, the original creditor sells the debts to the factor. The sales price may be fixed at the outset or may be adjusted later. It is also common for the factor to offer a credit facility that allows the seller to draw upon a proportion of the amounts owed.

In order to determine the correct accounting treatment it is **necessary to consider whether the benefit of the debts has been passed on to the factor, or whether the factor is, in effect, providing a loan on the security of the debtors.** If the seller has to pay interest on the difference between the amounts advanced to him and the amounts that the factor has received, and if the seller bears the risks of non-payment by the debtor, then the indications would be that the transaction is, in effect, a loan. Depending on the circumstances, either a linked presentation or separate presentation may be appropriate.

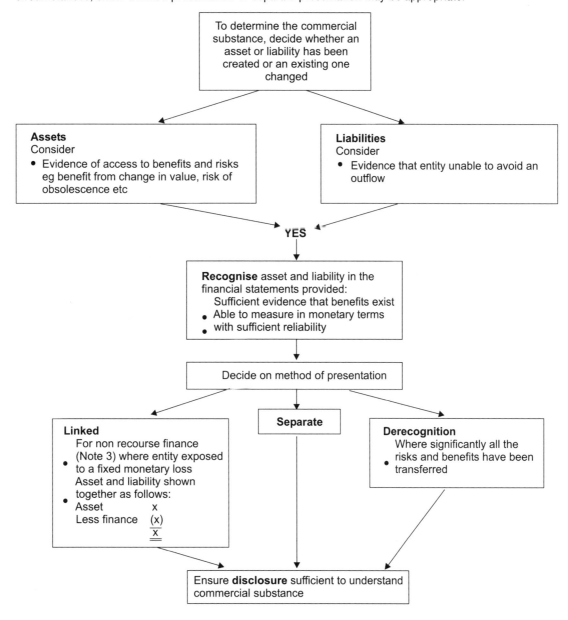

5.4.5 Loan transfers

These are arrangements where a loan is transferred to a transferee from an original lender. This will usually be done by the assignment of rights and obligations by the lender, or the creation of a new agreement between the borrower and the transferee. The **same principles apply to loan transfers as apply to debt factoring**.

5.4.6 Revenue recognition

Application Note G on revenue recognition is now the subject of UITF Abstract 40. See Chapter 4 Para 1.7.

Chapter Roundup

- FRS 21 deals with events after the balance sheet date.

  - It distinguishes between adjusting and non-adjusting events and gives examples.

  - Where deterioration in operating results and financial position indicates that the going concern concept is no longer appropriate, then the accounts may have to be restated on a break-up basis.

  - It stipulates that dividends declared after the balance sheet date are not recognised in the financial statements

- Under FRS 12, a **provision** should be recognised

  - When an entity has a **present obligation**, legal or constructive
  - It is probable that a **transfer of economic benefits** will be required to settle it
  - A **reliable estimate** can be made of its amount

- An entity should not recognise a contingent asset or liability, but they should be disclosed.

- Transactions must be accounted for according to their **substance**, **not** just their legal **form.**

- There are a number of '**creative accounting**' techniques, the purpose of which is to manipulate figures for a desired result.

- The subject of **off balance sheet finance** is complex and difficult to understand. In practice, off balance sheet finance schemes are often very sophisticated and they are beyond the range of this syllabus.

- You need to understand the methods of presentation described in FRS 5, particularly **linked presentation**.

Quick Quiz

1   Define 'events after the balance sheet date'.

2   A property is valued and a permanent diminution in value is identified.

Adjusting event ☐

Non-adjusting event ☐

3   Stocks are lost in a fire.

Adjusting event ☐

Non-adjusting event ☐

4   A provision is a .... of .... timing or amount.

5   A programme is undertaken by management which converts the previously wholly owned chain of restaurants they ran into franchises. Is this restructuring?

6   Define contingent asset and contingent liability.

7   What are the statutory disclosure requirements in respect of reserves?

8   What is meant by 'substance over form'?

9   How are assets and liabilities defined in the *Statement of Principles*?

10   Describe 'linked presentation' as set out in FRS 5.

11   What topics does FRS 5 discuss in the application notes?

Answers to Quick Quiz

1   Those events unfavourable and favourable which occur between the balance sheet date and the date of approval of the financial statements. (see knowledge b/f)

2   Adjusting.

3   Non-adjusting.

4   Liability of uncertain timing or amount.

5   Yes. The manner in which the business is conducted has changed.

6   A contingent asset is a possible asset that arises from past events and whose existence will be confirmed by the occurrence of one or more uncertain future events not wholly within the entity's control.

     A contingent liability is a possible obligation that arises from past events and whose existence will be confirmed by the occurrence of one or more uncertain future events not wholly within the entity's control.

7   Refer to Paragraph 3.2

8   Transactions should be accounted for in accordance with their substance and financial reality, not their legal form (4.1)

9   Assets are defined as 'rights or other access to future economic benefits controlled by an entity as a result of past transactions or events'.

     Liabilities are defined as 'an entity's obligations to transfer economic benefits as a result of past transactions or events'.

10   Refer to Paragraph 5.3.11.

11   Consignment stock, sale and leaseback transactions, factoring of debts, securitised assets and loan transfers, PFI contracts and revenue recognition.

Now try the question below from the Exam Question Bank

Number	Level	Marks	Time
Q11	Introductory	n/a	10 mins

Earnings per share and reporting financial performance

Topic list	Syllabus reference
1 FRS 22 *Earnings per share*	3 (d)
2 FRS 3 *Reporting financial performance*	3 (f)

Introduction

Section 1 of this chapter involves the description of EPS, the mechanics of its calculation and the disclosure required by FRS 22. EPS is an important indicator of a company's performance.

FRS 22 is a relatively new standard and therefore topical.

FRS 3 *Reporting financial performance* introduced radical changes to the format of the profit and loss account and the associated notes to the accounts. Of major importance are the definitions of extraordinary and exceptional items and prior year adjustments. You may be asked to produce a statement of total recognised gains and losses.

Remember that you will appreciate the contents of this chapter far more if you obtain and examine some company reports (those of *public companies* are required in this case).

Study guide

- Explain the importance of comparability in relation to the calculation of earnings per (EPS) share and its importance as a stock market indicator.

- Explain why the trend of EPS may be a more accurate indicator of performance than a company's profit trend.

- Define earnings and the basic number of shares.

- Calculate the EPS in accordance with relevant accounting standards in the following circumstances:

  - basic EPS
  - where there has been a bonus issue of shares during the year, and
  - where there has been a rights issue of shares during the year.

- Explain the relevance to existing shareholders of the diluted EPS, and describe the circumstances that will give rise to a future dilution of the EPS.

- Calculate the diluted EPS in the following circumstances:

  - where convertible debt or preference shares are in issue; and
  - where share options and warrants exist.

- Explain the need for an accounting standard in this area.

- Discuss the importance of identifying and reporting the results of discontinued operations; define discontinued operations.

- Distinguish between extraordinary and exceptional items, including their accounting treatment and required disclosures.

- Explain the contents and purpose of the statement of total recognised gains and losses, linking it to the Statement of Principles and the concept of comprehensive income.

- Describe and prepare a:

  (i)   note of historical cost profits and losses

  (ii)   reconciliation of movements in shareholders' funds

  (iii) statement of movements in reverse

- Define prior period adjustments and account for the correction of fundamental errors and charges in accounting policies..

- Prepare a profit and loss account in accordance with the requirements of the relevant Financial Reporting Standard.

Exam guide

Both of these standards can appear alongside a requirement to interpret financial statements. You not only need to learn the disclosure but also about the information you arrive at.

**Exam focus
point**

> The June 2002 paper required candidates to calculate basic EPS and diluted EPS.
>
> The June 2003 paper required candidates to calculate basic EPS and fully diluted EPS and to advise a prospective investor of the significance of diluted EPS.

1 FRS 22 Earnings per share

FAST FORWARD

FRS 22 has superseded FRS 14. This has brought the UK's treatment of the EPS calculation into line with international standards.

Earnings per share is a measure of the amount of profits earned by a company for each ordinary share. Earnings are profits after tax and preference dividends.

Exam focus point

You studied earnings per share for earlier papers, so we will skim over basic EPS and spend more time looking at diluted EPS, which is much more likely to come up in a Paper 2.5 exam.

FRS 22 *Earnings per share* was published in December 2004 as part of the ASB's convergence programme. It implements IAS 33 of the same name. The objective of FRS 22 is to improve the **comparison** of the performance of different entities in the same period and of the same entity in different accounting periods.

1.1 Definitions

The following definitions are given in FRS 22.

Key terms

- **Ordinary share**: an equity instrument that is subordinate to all other classes of equity instruments.

- **Potential ordinary share:** a financial instrument or other contract that may entitle its holder to ordinary shares.

- **Options, warrants and their equivalents**: financial instruments that give the holder the right to purchase ordinary shares.

- **Contingently issuable ordinary shares** are ordinary shares issuable for little or no cash or other consideration upon the satisfaction of certain conditions in a contingent share agreement.

- **Contingent share agreement:** an agreement to issue shares that is dependent on the satisfaction of specified conditions.

- **Dilution** is a reduction in earnings per share or an increase in loss per share resulting from the assumption that convertible instruments are converted, that options or warrants are exercised, or that ordinary shares are issued upon the satisfaction of certain conditions.

- **Antidilution** is an increase in earnings per share or a reduction in loss per share resulting from the assumption that convertible instruments are converted, that options or warrants are exercised, or that ordinary shares are issued upon the satisfaction of certain conditions. *(FRS 22)*

1.1.1 Ordinary shares

There may be more than one class of ordinary shares, but ordinary shares of the same class will have the same rights to receive dividends. Ordinary shares participate in the net profit for the period **only after other types of shares**, eg preference shares.

1.1.2 Potential ordinary shares

FRS 22 identifies the following examples of financial instrument and other contracts generating potential ordinary shares.

    (a) **Debts** (financial liabilities) **or equity instruments**, including preference shares, that are convertible into ordinary shares

(b)   **Share warrants and options**

(c)   Shares that would be issued upon the satisfaction of **certain conditions** resulting from contractual arrangements, such as the purchase of a business or other assets

1.2 Scope

FRS 22 has the following **scope restrictions**.

(a)   Only companies with (potential) ordinary shares which are **publicly traded** need to present EPS (including companies in the process of being listed).

(b)   EPS need only be presented on the basis of **consolidated results** where the parent's results are shown as well.

(b)   Where companies **choose** to present EPS, even when they have no (potential) ordinary shares which are traded, they must do so according to FRS 22.

(c)   Entities applying the Financial Reporting Standard for Smaller Entities (FRSSE) are exempt.

1.3 Basic EPS

FAST FORWARD

Basic EPS is calculated by dividing the net profit or loss for the period attributable to ordinary shareholders by the weighted average number of ordinary shares outstanding during the period.

You should know how to calculate **basic EPS** and how to deal with related complications (issue of shares for cash, bonus issue, share splits/reverse share splits, rights issues).

Basic EPS should be calculated for **profit or loss attributable to ordinary equity holders** of the parent entity and **profit or loss from continuing operations** attributable to those equity holders (if this is presented).

Basic EPS should be calculated by dividing the **net profit** or loss for the period attributable to ordinary equity holders by the **weighted average number of ordinary shares** outstanding during the period.

$$\frac{\text{Net profit/(loss) attribtable to ordinary shareholders}}{\text{Weighted average number of ordinary shares outstanding during the period}}$$

1.3.1 Earnings

Earnings includes **all items of income and expense** (including tax and minority interests) *less* net profit attributable to **preference shareholders**, including preference dividends.

1.3.2 Per share

The number of ordinary shares used should be the weighted average number of ordinary shares during the period. This figure (for all periods presented) should be **adjusted for events**, other than the conversion of potential ordinary shares, that have changed the number of shares outstanding without a corresponding change in resources.

The **time-weighting factor** is the number of days the shares were outstanding compared with the total number of days in the period. A reasonable approximation is usually adequate.

Shares are usually included in the weighted average number of shares from the **date consideration is receivable** which is usually the date of issue. In other cases consider the specific terms attached to their issue (consider the substance of any contract). The treatment for the issue of ordinary shares in different circumstances is as follows.

Consideration	Start date for inclusion
In exchange for cash	When cash is receivable
On the voluntary reinvestment of dividends on ordinary or preferred shares	The dividend payment date
As a result of the conversion of a debt instrument to ordinary shares	Date interest ceases accruing
In place of interest or principal on other financial instruments	Date interest ceases accruing
In exchange for the settlement of a liability of the entity	The settlement date
As consideration for the acquisition of an asset other than cash	The date on which the acquisition is recognised
For the rendering of services to the entity	As services are rendered

Ordinary shares issued as **purchase consideration** in an acquisition should be included as of the date of acquisition because the acquired entity's results will also be included from that date.

Ordinary shares that will be issued on the **conversion** of a mandatorily convertible instrument are included in the calculation from the **date the contract is entered into**.

If ordinary shares are **partly paid**, they are treated as a fraction of an ordinary share to the extent they are entitled to dividends relative to fully paid ordinary shares.

Contingently issuable shares (including those subject to recall) are included in the computation when all necessary conditions for issue have been satisfied.

1.4 Effect on basic EPS of changes in capital structure

1.4.1 New issues/buy backs

When there has been an issue of new shares or a buy-back of shares, the corresponding figures for EPS for the previous year will be comparable with the current year because, as the weighted average of shares has risen or fallen, there has been a **corresponding increase or decrease in resources**. Money has been received when shares were issued, and money has been paid out to repurchase shares. It is assumed that the sale or purchase has been made at full market price.

There are other events, however, which change the number of shares outstanding, **without a corresponding change in resources**. In these circumstances (four of which are considered by FRS 22) it is necessary to make adjustments so that the current and prior period EPS figures are comparable.

1.4.2 Capitalisation/bonus issue and share split/reverse share split

These two types of event can be considered together as they have a similar effect. In both cases, ordinary shares are issued to existing shareholders for **no additional consideration**. The number of ordinary shares has increased without an increase in resources.

This problem is solved by **adjusting the number of ordinary shares outstanding before the event** for the proportionate change in the number of shares outstanding as if the event had occurred at the beginning of the earliest period reported.

1.4.3 Rights issue

A rights issue of shares is an issue of new shares to existing shareholders **at a price below the current market value**. The offer of new shares is made on the basis of x new shares for every y shares currently held, eg a 1 for 3 rights issue is an offer of 1 new share at the offer price for every 3 shares currently held. This means that there is a bonus element included.

To arrive at figures for EPS when a rights issue is made, we first calculate the **theoretical ex-rights price**. This is a weighted average value per share.

The procedures for calculating the EPS for the current year and a corresponding figure for the previous year are as follows.

(a)   The **EPS for the corresponding previous period** should be multiplied by the following fraction. (*Note.* The market price on the last day of quotation is taken as the fair value immediately prior to exercise of the rights, as required by the standard.)

$$\frac{\text{Theoretical ex-rights price}}{\text{Market price on last day of quotation (with rights)}}$$

(b)   To obtain the **EPS for the current year** you should:

(i)   multiply the number of shares before the rights issue by the fraction of the year before the date of issue and by the following fraction.

$$\frac{\text{Market price on last day of quotation with rights}}{\text{Theoretical ex-rights price}}$$

(ii)   multiply the number of shares after the rights issue by the fraction of the year after the date of issue and add to the figure arrived at in (i).

The total earnings should then be divided by the total number of shares so calculated.

Question   Were you awake?

Give the formula for the 'bonus element' of a rights issue.

Answer

$$\frac{\text{Actual cum-rights price}}{\text{Theoretical ex-rights price}}$$

Question   Basic EPS

Macarone Co has produced the following net profit figures.

	£m
20X6	1.1
20X7	1.5
20X8	1.8

On 1 January 20X7 the number of shares outstanding was 500,000. During 20X7 the company announced a rights issue with the following details.

Rights:	1 new share for each 5 outstanding (100,000 new shares in total)
Exercise price:	£5.00
Last date to exercise rights:	1 March 20X7

The market (fair) value of one share in Marcoli immediately prior to exercise on 1 March 20X7 = £11.00.

Required

Calculate the EPS for 20X6, 20X7 and 20X8.

Answer

Computation of theoretical ex-rights price

This computation uses the total fair value and number of shares.

$$\frac{\text{Fair value of all outstanding shares + total received from exercise of rights}}{\text{No shares outstanding prior to exercise + no shares issued in exercise}}$$

$$= \frac{(£11.00 \times 500,000) + (\$5.00 \times 100,000)}{500,000 + 100,000} = £10.00$$

Computation of EPS

		20X6 £	20X7 £	20X8 £
20X6	EPS as originally reported $\dfrac{£1,100,000}{500,000}$	2.20		
20X6	EPS restated for rights issue = $\dfrac{£1,100,000}{500,000} \times \dfrac{10}{11}$	2.00		
20X7	EPS including effects of rights issue $\dfrac{£1,500,000}{(500,000 \times 2/12 \times 11/10) + (600,000 \times 10/12)}$		2.54	
20X8	EPS = $\dfrac{£1,800,000}{600,000}$			3.00

1.5 Diluted EPS

FAST FORWARD

Diluted EPS is calculated by adjusting the net profit attributable to ordinary shareholders and the weighted average number of shares outstanding for the effects of all dilutive potential ordinary shares.

You must be able to deal with **options** and all other **dilutive potential ordinary shares**.

At the end of an accounting period, a company may have in issue some **securities** which do not (at present) have any 'claim' to a share of equity earnings, but **may give rise to such a claim in the future**.

(a) A **separate class of equity shares** which at present is not entitled to any dividend, but will be entitled after some future date.

(b) **Convertible loan stock** or **convertible preferred shares** which give their holders the right at some future date to exchange their securities for ordinary shares of the company, at a pre-determined conversion rate.

(c) **Options** or **warrants**.

In such circumstances, the future number of shares ranking for dividend might increase, which in turn results in a fall in the EPS. In other words, a **future increase** in the **number of equity shares will cause a dilution or 'watering down' of equity**, and it is possible to calculate a **diluted earnings per share** (ie the EPS that would have been obtained during the financial period if the dilution had already taken place). This will indicate to investors the possible effects of a future dilution.

1.5.1 Earnings

The earnings calculated for basic EPS should be adjusted by the **post-tax** (including deferred tax) effect of the following.

(a)   Any **dividends** on dilutive potential ordinary shares that were deducted to arrive at earnings for basic EPS.

(b)   **Interest recognised** in the period for the dilutive potential ordinary shares.

(c)   Any **other changes in income or expenses** (fees and discount, premium accounted for as yield adjustments) that would result from the conversion of the dilutive potential ordinary shares.

The conversion of some potential ordinary shares may lead to changes in **other income or expenses**. For example, the reduction of interest expense related to potential ordinary shares and the resulting increase in net profit for the period may lead to an increase in the expense relating to a non-discretionary employee profit-sharing plan. When calculating diluted EPS, the net profit or loss for the period is adjusted for any such consequential changes in income or expense.

1.5.2 Per share

The number of ordinary shares is the weighted average number of ordinary shares calculated for basic EPS plus the weighted average number of ordinary shares that would be issued on the conversion of all the **dilutive potential ordinary shares** into ordinary shares.

It should be assumed that dilutive ordinary shares were converted into ordinary shares at the **beginning of the period** or, if later, at the actual date of issue. There are two other points.

(a)   The computation assumes the most **advantageous conversion rate** or exercise rate from the standpoint of the holder of the potential ordinary shares.

(b)   A **subsidiary, joint venture or associate** may issue potential ordinary shares that are convertible into either ordinary shares of the subsidiary, joint venture or associate, or ordinary shares of the reporting entity. If these potential ordinary shares have a dilutive effect on the consolidated basic EPS of the reporting entity, they are included in the calculation of diluted EPS.

1.5.3 Example: diluted EPS

In 20X7 Farrah plc had a basic EPS of 105p based on earnings of £105,000 and 100,000 ordinary £1 shares. It also had in issue £40,000 15% Convertible Loan Stock which is convertible in two years' time at the rate of 4 ordinary shares for every £5 of stock. The rate of tax is 30%. In 20X7 gross profit of £150,000 was recorded.

Required

Calculate the diluted EPS.

Solution

Diluted EPS is calculated as follows.

Step 1   **Number of shares**: the additional equity on conversion of the loan stock will be 40,000 × 4/5 = 32,000 shares

Step 2   **Earnings**: Farrah plc will save interest payments of £6,000 but this increase in profits will be taxed. Hence the earnings figure may be recalculated:

	£
Gross profit £(150,000 + 6,000)	156,000
Taxation (30%)	46,800
Profit after tax	109,200

Step 3   **Calculation**: Diluted EPS = $\dfrac{£109,200}{132,000}$ = 82.7p

Step 4   **Dilution**: the dilution in earnings would be 105p − 82.7p = 22.3p per share.

Question

EPS 1

Ardent Co has 5,000,000 ordinary shares of 25 pence each in issue, and also had in issue in 20X4:

(a)   £1,000,000 of 14% convertible loan stock, convertible in three years' time at the rate of 2 shares per £10 of stock.

(b)   £2,000,000 of 10% convertible loan stock, convertible in one year's time at the rate of 3 shares per £5 of stock.

The total earnings in 20X4 were £1,750,000.

The rate of income tax is 35%.

Required

Calculate the EPS and diluted EPS.

Answer

(a)   EPS = $\dfrac{£1,750,000}{5\,\text{million}}$ = 35 pence

(b)   On dilution, the (maximum) number of shares in issue would be:

	Shares
Current	5,000,000
On conversion of 14% stock	200,000
On conversion of 10% stock	1,200,000
	6,400,000

	£	£
Current earnings		1,750,000
Add interest saved (140,000 + 200,000)	340,000	
Less tax thereon at 35%	119,000	
		221,000
Revised earnings		1,971,000

Fully diluted EPS = $\dfrac{£1,971,000}{6.4\,\text{million}}$ = 30.8 pence

1.5.4 Treatment of options

It should be assumed that options are exercised and that the assumed proceeds would have been received from the issue of shares at **fair value**. Fair value for this purpose is calculated on the basis of the average price of the ordinary shares during the period.

Options and other share purchase arrangements are dilutive when they would result in the issue of ordinary shares for **less than fair value**. The amount of the dilution is fair value less the issue price. In order to calculate diluted EPS, each transaction of this type is treated as consisting of two parts.

(a)   A contract to issue a certain number of ordinary shares at their **average market price** during the period. These shares are fairly priced and are assumed to be neither dilutive nor antidilutive. They are ignored in the computation of diluted earnings per share.

(b)   A contract to issue the remaining ordinary shares for **no consideration**. Such ordinary shares generate no proceeds and have no effect on the net profit attributable to ordinary shares outstanding. Therefore such shares are dilutive and they are added to the number of ordinary shares outstanding in the computation of diluted EPS.

To the extent that **partly paid shares** are not entitled to participate in dividends during the period, they are considered the equivalent of **warrants** or **options**.

Employee share options with fixed or determinable terms (ie, **not performance based**) and outstanding shares are treated as **options** in the calculation of diluted earnings per share. **Performance based** employee share options are treated as **contingently issuable shares** because their issue is contingent upon satisfying specified conditions in addition to the passage of time.

Question
EPS 2

Brand plc has the following results for the year ended 31 December 20X7.

Net profit for year	£1,200,000
Weighted average number of ordinary shares outstanding during year	500,000 shares
Average fair value of one ordinary share during year	£20.00
Weighted average number of shares under option during year	100,000 shares
Exercise price for shares under option during year	£15.00

Required

Calculate both basic and diluted earnings per share.

Answer

	Per share	Earnings £	Shares
Net profit for year		1,200,000	
Weighted average shares outstanding during 20X7			500,000
Basic earnings per share	2.40		
Number of shares under option			100,000
Number of shares that would have been issued			
At fair value: (100,000 × £15.00/£20.00)			(75,000) *
Diluted earnings per share	2.29	1,200,000	525,000

*   The earnings have not been increased as the total number of shares has been increased only by the number of shares (25,000) deemed for the purpose of the computation to have been issued for no consideration.

1.5.5 Interim financial reports

Where an entity issues interim financial reports, EPS is based on the earnings and weighted average number of shares for the 'year-to-date'.

FRS 22 states that dilutive potential ordinary shares must be determined **independently for each period presented**. The number of dilutive potential ordinary shares included in the year-to-date period is not a weighted average of the dilutive potential ordinary shares included in each interim computation.

1.5.6 Contingently issuable shares

Contingently issuable (potential) ordinary shares are treated **as for basic EPS**. If the conditions have not been met, the number of contingently issuable shares included in the computation is based on the number of shares **that would be issuable** if the end of the reporting period was the end of the contingency period. Restatement is not allowed if the conditions are not met when the contingency period expires.

1.5.7 Contracts that may be settled in ordinary shares or cash

Where an entity has issued a contract that may be settled either in ordinary shares or in cash at the **issuer's option**, the entity shall **presume** that the contract will be settled **in ordinary shares**, and the resulting potential ordinary shares should be included in diluted earnings per share if the effect is dilutive.

For contracts that may be settled in ordinary shares or cash at the **holder's option**, the **more dilutive** of cash settlement and share settlement should be used in the calculation.

1.6 Dilutive potential ordinary shares

According to FRS 22, potential ordinary shares should be treated as dilutive when, and only when, their conversion to ordinary shares would **decrease net profit per share** from continuing ordinary operations. How is this determined?

The **net profit from continuing ordinary activities** is 'the control number', used to establish whether potential ordinary shares are dilutive or antidilutive. The net profit from continuing ordinary activities is the net profit from ordinary activities **after deducting** preference dividends and after excluding items relating to discontinued operations. It also excludes the effects of changes in accounting policies and of corrections of prior period errors.

Potential ordinary shares are **antidilutive** when their conversion to ordinary shares would increase earnings per share from continuing ordinary operations or decrease loss per share from continuing ordinary operations. The effects of antidilutive potential ordinary shares are ignored in calculating diluted EPS.

In considering whether potential ordinary shares are dilutive or antidilutive, each issue or series of potential ordinary shares is **considered separately**, *not* in aggregate. The sequence in which potential ordinary shares are considered may affect whether or not they are dilutive. Therefore, in order to maximise the dilution of basic EPS, each issue or series of potential ordinary shares is considered in sequence from the most dilutive to the least dilutive. This may sound very confusing, but the following example may help.

1.6.1 Example: dilutive potential ordinary shares

Carter plc has the following results for the year ended 31 December 20X7.

Earnings: net profit attributable to ordinary shareholders	£10,000,000
Ordinary shares outstanding	2,000,000
Average fair value of one ordinary share during the year	£75.00
Tax rate	40%

Potential ordinary shares are as follows.

(a)   Options: 100,000 with exercise price of £60

(b)   Convertible preference shares: 800,000 shares entitled to a cumulative dividend of £8 per share (each preference share is convertible to two ordinary shares)

(c)   5% Convertible bond: nominal amount £100,000,000, each 1,000 bond is convertible to 20 ordinary shares and there is no amortisation of premium or discount affecting the determination of interest expense.

Required

Calculate the diluted EPS.

Solution

Step 1   Calculate the increase in earnings attributable to ordinary shareholders on conversion of the potential ordinary shares.

	Increase in earnings	Increase in number of ordinary shares	Earnings per Incremental shares
	£		£
Options			
Increase in earnings	Nil		
Incremental shares issued for no			
Consideration 100,000 × £(75 − 60)/£75		20,000	Nil
Convertible preference shares			
Increase in net profit £8 × 800,000	6,400,000		
Incremental shares 2 × 800,000		1,600,000	4.00
5% Convertible bonds			
Increase in net profit			
100,000,000 × 0.05 × £1 − 0.4)	3,000,000		
Incremental shares 100,000 × 20		2,000,000	1.50

Step 2   Now calculate the diluted EPS in order of most dilutive to least dilutive.

	Net profit attributable	Ordinary shares	Per share
	£		£
As reported	10,000,000	2,000,000	5.00
Options		20,000	
	10,000,000	2,020,000	4.95 Dilutive
5% Convertible bonds	3,000,000	2,000,000	
	13,000,000	4,020,000	3.23 Dilutive
Convertible preference shares	6,400,000	1,600,000	
	19,400,000	5,620,000	3.45 Dilutive

Note. Since diluted EPS is increased when taking the convertible preference shares into account (from £3.23 to £3.45), the convertible preference shares are antidilutive and are ignored in the calculation of diluted EPS. Therefore, diluted EPS is £3.23.

Potential ordinary shares are **weighted** for the period they were outstanding. Any that were cancelled or allowed to lapse during the reporting period are included in the computation of diluted EPS only for the portion of the period during which they were outstanding. Potential ordinary shares that have been converted into ordinary shares **during the reporting period** are included in the calculation of diluted EPS from the beginning of the period to the date of conversion. From the date of conversion, the resulting ordinary shares are included in both basic and diluted EPS.

1.6.2 Retrospective adjustment

If the number of ordinary or potential ordinary shares outstanding **increases** as a result of a capitalisation, bonus issue or share split, or decreases as a result of a reverse share split, the calculation of basic and diluted EPS for all periods presented should be **adjusted retrospectively**.

If these changes occur **after the balance sheet date** but before issue of the financial statements, the calculations per share for the financial statements and those of any prior period should be based on the **new number of shares** (and this should be disclosed).

In addition, basic and diluted EPS of all periods presented should be adjusted for the effects of **errors**, and adjustments resulting from **changes** in **accounting policies**, accounted for retrospectively.

An entity **does not restate diluted EPS** of any prior period for changes in the assumptions used or for the conversion of potential ordinary shares into ordinary shares outstanding.

1.7 Presentation

A entity should present on the **face of the income statement** basic and diluted EPS for:

(a)   profit or loss from continuing operations; and
(b)   profit or loss for the period

for each class of ordinary share that has a different right to share in the net profit for the period.

The basic and diluted EPS should be presented with **equal prominence** for all periods presented.

Basic and diluted EPS for any **discontinued operations** must also be presented.

Disclosure must still be made where the EPS figures (basic and/or diluted) are **negative** (ie a loss per share).

1.8 Disclosure

An entity should disclose the following.

(a)   The amounts used as the **numerators** in calculating basic and diluted EPS, and a **reconciliation** of those amounts to the net profit or loss for the period.

(b)   The weighted average number of ordinary shares used as the **denominator** in calculating basic and diluted EPS, and a **reconciliation** of these denominators to each other.

(c)   Instruments that could potentially dilute basic EPS but which were **not included** in the calculation because they were **antidilutive** for the period presented.

An entity should also disclose a description of ordinary share transactions or potential ordinary share transactions, other than capitalisation issues and share splits, which occur **after the balance sheet date** when they are of such importance that non-disclosure would affect the ability of the users of the financial statements to make proper evaluations and decisions (see FRS 21). Examples of such transactions include the following.

(a)   Issue of shares for cash

(b)   Issue of shares when the proceeds are used to repay debt or preferred shares outstanding at the balance sheet date

(c)   Redemption of ordinary shares outstanding

(d)   Conversion or exercise of potential ordinary shares, outstanding at the balance sheet date, into ordinary shares

(e)   Issue of warrants, options or convertible securities

    (f)   Achievement of conditions that would result in the issue of contingently issuable shares

EPS amounts are not adjusted for such transactions occurring after the balance sheet date because such transactions **do not affect the amount of capital used** to produce the net profit or loss for the period.

1.9 Alternative EPS figures

An entity may present **alternative EPS figures if it wishes**. However, FRS 22 lays out certain rules where this takes place.

    (a)   The weighted average number of shares as calculated under FRS 22 **must** be used.

    (b)   A **reconciliation** must be given between the component of profit used in the alternative EPS (if it is not a line item in the income statement) and the line item for profit reported in the income statement.

    (c)   The entity must indicate the basis on which the **numerator** is determined.

    (d)   Basic and diluted EPS must be shown with **equal prominence**.

1.10 Significance of earnings per share

Earnings per share (EPS) is one of the most frequently quoted statistics in financial analysis. Because of the widespread use of the price earnings **(P/E) ratio** as a yardstick for investment decisions, it became increasingly important.

It seems that reported and forecast EPS can, through the P/E ratio, have a **significant effect on a company's share price**. Thus, a share price might fall if it looks as if EPS is going to be low. This is not very rational, as EPS can depend on many, often subjective, assumptions used in preparing a historical statement, namely the income statement. It does not necessarily bear any relation to the value of a company, and of its shares. Nevertheless, the market is sensitive to EPS.

EPS has also served as a means of assessing the **stewardship and management** role performed by company directors and managers. Remuneration packages might be linked to EPS growth, thereby increasing the pressure on management to improve EPS. The danger of this, however, is that management effort may go into distorting results to produce a favourable EPS.

1.11 Section summary

EPS is an important measure for investors.

- **Basic EPS** is straightforward, although it may require adjustments for **changes in capital structure**

- **Diluted EPS** is more complex (and more likely in an exam question). You must be able to deal with:
    - Options
    - Dilutive potential ordinary shares
    - Retrospective adjustment

2 FRS 3 Reporting financial performance

FAST FORWARD

FRS 3 *Reporting financial performance* has introduced radical **changes to the profit and loss** account of large and medium sized companies.

You must know the **FRS 3 definitions** of:

- – **Extraordinary items**
- – **Exceptional items**
- – **Prior year adjustments**
- – **Discontinued operations**
- – **Total recognised gains and losses**

Exam focus point

This is an extremely popular exam topic. All recent papers have had a single company accounts preparation question. Make sure that you familiarise yourself fully with the contents of this standard.

FRS 3 represents an attempt by the ASB to improve the quality of financial information provided to shareholders. In particular it was **an attempt to move away from the high profile of the earnings per share**. The main elements of the FRS are as follows.

(a) New structure of the profit and loss account
(b) Extraordinary items
(c) Statement of total recognised gains and losses
(d) Other new disclosures
(e) Earnings per share

Exam focus point

A key way of developing familiarity with this topic is to look at published financial reports. See FT share page for details of free service.

2.1 Exceptional and extraordinary items

A company may experience events or undertake transactions which are 'out of the ordinary', ie they are not the same as what the company normally does.

FRS 3 lays down the rules for dealing with 'out of the ordinary' items in the P & L account and restricts the way companies can manipulate these figures.

2.1.1 Exceptional items

Key terms

FRS 3 defines **exceptional items** as: 'Material items which derive from events or transactions that fall within the ordinary activities of the reporting entity and which individually or, if of a similar type, in aggregate, need to be disclosed by virtue of their *size or incidence* if the financial statements are to give a true and fair view.'

The definition of **ordinary activities** is important.

'Any activities which are undertaken by a reporting entity as **part of its business** and such related activities in which the reporting entity engages in furtherance of, incidental to, or arising from these activities. Ordinary activities include the effects on the reporting entity of any event in the various environments in which it operates including the political, regulatory, economic and geographical environments irrespective of the frequency or unusual nature of the event.'

There are **two** types of exceptional items and their accounting treatment is as follows.

(a)   Firstly there are **three categories of exceptional items,** so called **super exceptionals,** **which must be shown separately on the face of the profit and loss account** after operating profit and before interest and allocated appropriately to discontinued and continued activities.

  (i)   **Profit or loss on the sale or termination** of an operation

  (ii)   **Costs of a fundamental reorganisation** or restructuring that has a material effect on the nature and focus of the reporting entity's operations

  (iii)   **Profit or loss on disposal of fixed assets**

  For both items (i) and (iii) profit and losses may not be offset within categories.

(b)   **All other items should be allocated to the appropriate statutory format heading** and attributed to **continuing** or **discounted** operations as appropriate. If the item is **sufficiently material** that it is needed to show a **true and fair view** it must be disclosed on the **face** of the **profit and loss account**.

In both (a) and (b) an adequate description must be given in the notes to the accounts to enable its nature to be understood.

FRS 3 does not give examples of the type of transaction which is likely to be treated as exceptional. However, its predecessor on the subject, SSAP 6, gave a useful list of examples of items which if of a sufficient size might normally be treated as exceptional.

(a)   Abnormal charges for bad debts and write-offs of stock and work in progress.
(b)   Abnormal provisions for losses on long-term contracts.
(c)   Settlement of insurance claims.

2.1.2 Extraordinary items

The ASB publicly stated that it does not envisage extraordinary items appearing on a company's profit and loss account after the introduction of FRS 3. Its decline in importance has been achieved by tightening of the definition of an extraordinary item.

Key term

> **Extraordinary items** are defined as material items possessing a high degree of abnormality which arise from events or transactions that fall outside the ordinary activities of the reporting entity and which are not expected to recur.

An example given by the chairman of the ASB was that 'if the Martians landed and destroyed a company's factory, that could be treated as an extraordinary item'. Extraordinary items are therefore very rare!

Extraordinary items should be shown on the face of profit and loss account before dividends and other minority interests (for group accounts). Tax and minority interest in the extraordinary item should be shown separately. A description of the extraordinary items should be given in the notes to the accounts.

2.2 Structure of the profit and loss account

All statutory headings from turnover to operating profit must be subdivided between that arising from continuing operations and that arising from discontinued operations. In addition, turnover and operating profit must be further analysed between that from existing and that from newly acquired operations.

Only figures for turnover and operating profit need be shown on the face of the P & L account; all additional information regarding costs may be relegated to a note.

PROFIT AND LOSS
EXAMPLE 1 (as shown in FRS 3)

	1993 £m	1993 £m	1992 as restated £m
Turnover			
Continuing operations	550		500
Acquisitions	50		
	600		
Discontinued operations	175		190
		775	690
Cost of sales		(620)	(555)
Gross profit		155	135
Net operating expenses		(104)	(83)
Operating profit			
Continuing operations	50		40
Acquisitions	6		
	56		
Discontinued operations	(15)		12
Less 1992 provision	10		
		51	52
Profit on sale of properties in continuing operations		9	6
Provision for loss on operations to be discontinued			(30)
Loss on disposal of discontinued operations	(17)		
Less 1992 provision	20		
		3	
Profit on ordinary activities before interest		63	28
Interest payable		(18)	(15)
Profit on ordinary activities before taxation		45	13
Tax on profit on ordinary activities		(14)	(4)
Profit on ordinary activities after taxation		31	9
Minority interests		(2)	(2)
Profit before extraordinary items		29	7
Extraordinary items - included only to show positioning		-	-
Profit for the financial year		29	7
Earnings per share		39p	10p
Adjustments (to be itemised and an adequate description to be given)		Xp	Xp
Adjusted earnings per share		Yp	Yp

Note. Reason for calculating the adjusted earnings per share to be given.

PROFIT AND LOSS ACCOUNT EXAMPLE 2 (to operating profit line)

	Continuing Operations 1993 £m	Acquisitions 1993 £m	Discontinued of operations 1993 £m	Total 1993 £m	Total 1992 as restated £m
Turnover	550	50	175	775	690
Cost of sales	(415)	(40)	(165)	(620)	(555)
Gross profit	135	10	10	155	135
Net operating expenses	(85)	(4)	(25)	(114)	(83)
Less 1992 provision			10	10	—
Operating profit	50	6	(5)	51	52
Profit on sale of properties	9			9	6
Provision for loss on operations to be discontinued					(30)
Loss on disposal of the discontinued operations			(17)	(17)	
Less 1992 provision			20	20	
Profit on ordinary activities before interest	59	6	(2)	63	28

Thereafter example 2 is the same as example 1.

NOTES TO THE FINANCIAL STATEMENTS

Note required in respect of profit and loss account example 1

	1993 Continuing £m	Discontinued £m	Total £m	1992 (as restated) Continuing £m	Discontinued £m	Total £m
Cost of sales	455	165	620	385	170	555
Net operating expenses						
Distribution costs	56	13	69	46	5	51
Administrative expenses	41	12	53	34	3	37
Other operating income	(8)	0	(8)	(5)	0	(5)
	89	25	114	75	8	83
Less 1992 provision	0	(10)	(10)			
	89	15	104			

The total figures for continuing operations in 1993 include the following amounts relating to acquisitions: cost of sales £40 million and net operating expenses £4 million (namely distribution costs £3 million, administrative expenses £3 million and other operating income £2 million).

Note required in respect of profit and loss account example 2

	1993 Continuing £m	Discontinued £m	Total £m	1992 (as restated) Continuing £m	Discontinued £m	Total £m
Turnover				500	190	690
Cost of sales				385	170	555
Net operating expenses						
Distribution costs	56	13	69	46	5	51
Administrative expenses	41	12	53	34	3	37
Other operating income	(8)	0	(8)	(5)	0	(5)
	89	25	114	75	8	83
Operating profit				40	12	52

The total figure of net operating expenses for continuing operations in 1993 includes £4 million in respect of acquisitions (namely distribution costs £3 million, administrative expenses £3 million and other operating income £2 million).

2.2.1 Discontinued operations

A **discontinued operation** is one which **meets all of the following conditions.**

(a) The sale or termination must have been **completed** before the earlier of 3 months after the year end or the date the financial statements are approved. (Terminations not completed by this date may be disclosed in the notes.)

(b) Former activity must have **ceased permanently**.

(c) The sale or termination has a **material effect** on the nature and focus of the entity's operations and represents a material reduction in its operating facilities resulting either from:

(i) Its withdrawal from a particular market (class of business or geographical); or from
(ii) A material reduction in turnover in its continuing markets.

(d) The assets, liabilities, results of operations and activities are **clearly distinguishable**, physically, operationally and for financial reporting purposes.

2.2.2 Accounting for the discontinuation

(a) **Results**

The results of the discontinued operation up to the date of sale or termination or the balance sheet date should be shown **under each of the relevant profit and loss account headings**.

(b) **Profit/loss on discontinuation**

The profit or loss on discontinuation or costs of discontinuation should be **disclosed separately** as an exceptional item after operating profit and before interest.

(c) **Comparative figures**

Figures for the previous year **must be adjusted for** any **activities** which have become **discontinued in the current year.**

2.3 Acquisitions

Acquisitions include **most holdings acquired by a group, as well as unincorporated businesses purchased**. However, start-ups are not acquisitions.

Question	Profit and loss account

Feelgoode plc's profit and loss account for the year ended 31 December 20X2, with comparatives, is as follows.

	20X2	20X1
	£m	£m
Turnover	200	180
Cost of sales	(60)	(80)
Gross profit	140	100
Distribution costs	(25)	(20)
Administration expenses	(50)	(45)
Operating profit	65	35

During the year the company sold a material business operation with all activities ceasing on 14 February 20X3. The loss on the sale of the operation amounted to £2.2m and this is included under administration expenses.. The results of the operation for 20X1 and 20X2 were as follows.

	20X2 £m	20X1 £m
Turnover	22	26
Profit/(loss)	(7)	(6)

In addition, the company acquired a business which contributed £7m to turnover and an operating profit of £1.5m.

Required

Prepare the profit and loss account and related notes for the year ended 31 December 20X2 complying with the requirements of FRS 3 as far as possible.

Answer

	20X2 £m	20X2 £m	20X1 £m	20X1 £m
Turnover				
Continuing operations				
(200 – 22 – 7)/(180 – 26)		171.0		154
Acquisitions		7.0		–
		178.0		154
Discontinued		22.0		26
		200.0		180
Cost of sales		(60.0)		(80)
Gross profit		140.0		100
Distribution costs		(25.0)		(20)
Administration expenses (50 – 2.2)		(47.8)		(45)
Operating profit				
Continuing operations* (bal)	72.7		41	
Acquisitions	1.5		–	
	74.2		41	
Discontinued	(7.0)		(6)	
		67.2		35
Exceptional item		(2.2)		–
		65.0		35

* ie 65.0 + 2.2 + 7.0 – 1.5 = 72.7; 35 + 6 = 41

Note to the profit and loss account

	20X2	20X2	20X2	20X1 (as restated)	20X1 (as restated)	20X1 (as restated)
	Continuing £m	Discontinued £m	Total £m	Continuing £m	Discontinued £m	Total £m
Cost of sales	X	X	60.0	X	X	80
Net operating expenses						
Distribution costs	X	X	25.0	X	X	20
Administration expenses	X	X	47.8	X	X	45
	X	X	72.8	X	X	65

BPP PROFESSIONAL EDUCATION

2.4 FRS 3 Statements and notes

FRS 3 introduced a new statement and a variety of new notes to expand the information required in published accounts which we saw in Chapter 3.

Exam focus point

The December 2002 and June 2003 exams required preparation of a STRGL.

Please make sure you have this topic well mastered.

2.5 Statement of total recognised gains and losses

FAST FORWARD

You must know the format of the **statement of total recognised gains and losses** and understand its contents.

This is required by FRS 3 to be presented with the same prominence as the P & L account, balance sheet and cash flow statement, ie as a **primary statement**.

The statement will include all gains and losses occurring during the period and so would typically include the following.

	£
Profit for the year (per the profit and loss account)	X
Items taken directly to reserves (not goodwill written off to reserves)	
Surplus on revaluation of fixed assets	X
Surplus/deficit on revaluation of investment properties	X
Total recognised gains and losses for the year	X
Prior period adjustments (see later)	(X)
Total gains and losses recognised since last annual report	X

At a glance, It seems that all this new statement does is to reconcile the opening and closing net assets of a business. This is, however, not so since FRS 3 requires that **transactions with shareholders are to be excluded**, ie:

(a) Dividends paid
(b) Share issues and redemptions

since these transactions do not represent either gains or losses.

In the case of goodwill, which is capitalised and amortised under FRS 10, the amortisation charge will appear indirectly (as part of the results for the year) in the statement.

Where the profit or loss for the year is the only recognised gain or loss, a **statement to that effect should be given** immediately below the profit and loss account.

The profit and loss account and the STRGL taken together report **all** gains and losses other than those arising from transactions with equity holders. This concept of **all** gains and losses is sometimes referred to as **'comprehensive income'** and future developments may lead to a single statement of comprehensive income. This is explained further in Chapter 18.

2.6 Realised and distributable profits

At this point it may be worth pointing out that just because gains and losses are 'recognised' in this statement, they are, **not necessarily 'realised'** (described below, or **'distributable'**, ie as a dividend. Realised and distributable profits are covered in Chapter 13).

2.7 Reconciliation of movements in shareholders' funds

This reconciliation is required by FRS 3 to be included in the notes to the accounts. What the statement aims to do is to **pull together financial performance** of the entity as is reflected in:

(a)   The profit and loss account.

(b)   Other movements in shareholders' funds as determined by the statement of total recognised gains and losses.

(c)   All other changes in shareholders funds not recognised in either of the above such as goodwill immediately written off to reserves.

The typical contents of the reconciliation would be as follows.

	£
Profit for the financial year	X
* Dividends	(X)
	X
Other recognised gains and losses (per statement of total recognised gains and losses)	X
* New share capital	X
Net addition to shareholders' funds	X
Opening shareholders' funds	X
Closing shareholders' funds	X

* Items not appearing in the statement of recognised gains and losses

Question   STRGL

Extracts from Zoe Ltd's profit and loss account for the year ended 31 December 20X1 were as follows.

	£'000
Profit after tax	512
Dividend	(120)
Retained profit	392

During the year the following important events took place.

(a)   Assets were revalued upward by £110,000.

(b)   £300,000 share capital was issued during the year.

(c)   Certain stock items were written down by £45,000.

(d)   Opening shareholders' funds at 1 January 20X1 were £3,100,000.

Show how the events for the year would be shown in the statement of total recognised gains and losses and the reconciliation of movements in shareholders' funds.

Answer

STATEMENT OF TOTAL RECOGNISED GAINS AND LOSSES

	£'000
Profit after tax	512
Asset revaluation	110
	622

RECONCILIATION OF MOVEMENTS IN SHAREHOLDERS' FUNDS

	£'000
Profit after tax	512
Dividend	(120)
	392
Other recognised gains and losses (622 – 512)	110
New share capital	300
Net addition to shareholders' funds	802
Opening shareholders' funds	3,100
Closing shareholders' funds	3,902

2.8 Note of historical cost profits and losses

If a company has adopted any of the alternative accounting rules as regards revaluation of assets then the reported profit figure per the profit and loss account may deviate from the historical cost profit figure. If this deviation is material then the financial statements must include a reconciliation statement after the statement of recognised gains and losses or the profit and loss account. The profit figure to be reconciled is profit before tax; however, the retained profit for the year must also be restated.

Note that **FRS 3 requires the profit or loss on the disposal of a revalued asset to be calculated by reference to the difference between proceeds and the net carrying amount** (revalued figure less depreciation). The profit or loss based on historical cost will appear in the note of historical cost profits.

Question	Note of historical cost profits and losses

Faiza Ltd reported a profit before tax of £162,000 for the year ended 31 December 20X8. During the year the following transactions in fixed assets took place.

(a)   An asset with a book value of £40,000 was revalued to £75,000. The remaining useful life is estimated to be five years.

(b)   An asset (with a five year useful life at the date of revaluation) was revalued by £20,000 (to carrying value £30,000) was sold one year after revaluation for £48,000.

Show the reconciliation of profit to historical cost profit for the year ended 31 December 20X8.

Answer

RECONCILIATION OF PROFIT TO HISTORICAL COST PROFIT
FOR THE YEAR ENDED 31 DECEMBER 20X8

	£'000
Reported profit on ordinary activities before taxation	162
Realisation of property revaluation gains*	20
Difference between historical cost depreciation charge and the actual depreciation charge of the year calculated on the revalued amount (75,000 - 40,000)/5	7
	189

* By interpretation of the question, the asset was revalued last year with £20,000 being credited to revaluation reserve. With the asset being sold this year, this gain becomes realised. It is assumed that there has been no annual transfer from revaluation reserve to profit and loss account.

2.9 Prior period adjustments

When the financial statements of a company are compiled, certain items (eg accruals, provisions) represent best estimates at a point in time. Further evidence received in the following year may suggest that previous estimates were incorrect. In most cases the 'error' will not be significant in size and so as a result the difference should be dealt with in the current year's accounts.

There are **two situations where a prior period adjustment is necessary:**

(a)   **Fundamental errors** - evidence is found to suggest last year's accounts were wrong.

(b)   A **change in accounting policy** (see FRS 18 in Chapter 3).

Exam focus point

> Given the upheaval globally in company reporting, many companies have had to admit to fundamental errors, so do consider the likelihood of being examined on the treatment of errors discovered.

The following accounting treatment should be used.

(a)   Restate prior year profit and loss account and balance sheet.

(b)   Restate opening reserves balance.

(c)   Include the adjustment in the reconciliation of movements in shareholders' funds.

(d)   Include a note at the foot of the statement of total recognised gains and losses of the current period.

Prior period adjustments are therefore defined by FRS 3 as follows.

Key term

> **Prior period adjustments** are: 'Material adjustments applicable to prior periods arising from changes in accounting policy or from the correction of fundamental errors. They do not include normal recurring adjustments or corrections of accounting estimates made in prior periods.'

A **fundamental error** is an error which is **so significant that the truth and fairness of the financial statements is not achieved.**

A **change in accounting policy requires a prior period adjustment based on the accounting concept of consistency**. For users of the financial statements to make meaningful comparisons of a company's results it is important that the current year's and the last year's comparatives are prepared on the same basis. Therefore if for any reason a company changes its accounting policy they must go back and represent last year's accounts on the same basis.

Reasons for a change in accounting policy are discussed in Chapter 3.

A prior period adjustment will be shown in the **statement of movements in reserves**.

The format of the statement is as follows:

	Share premium account	Revaluation reserve	Other reserve	Profit and loss account	Total
Balance at beginning of year	X	X	X	X	X
Prior year adjustment	–	–	–	(X)	(X)
Balance at beginning of year restated	X	X	X	X	X
Premium on issue of shares	X				X
Goodwill impairment				(X)	(X)
Profit (loss) for the year				X	X
Transfer of realised profits		(X)		X	–
Decrease in value of investments	–	(X)	–	–	(X)
At end of year	X	X	X	X	X

Exam focus point

The June 2003 paper required candidates to deal with the discovery of a fraud that had been perpetrated in the previous year.

Question
Deferred development expenditure

Jenny Ltd was established on 1 January 20X0. In the first three years' accounts deferred development expenditure was carried forward as an asset in the balance sheet. During 20X3 the directors decided that for the current and future years, all development expenditure should be written off as it is incurred. This decision has not resulted from any change in the expected outcome of development projects on hand, but rather from a desire to favour the prudence concept. The following information is available.

(a) Movements on the deferred development account.

Year	Deferred development expenditure incurred during year £'000	Transfer from deferred development expenditure account to P & L account £'000
20X0	525	–
20X1	780	215
20X2	995	360

(b) The 20X2 accounts showed the following.

	£'000
Retained reserves b/f	2,955
Retained profit for the year	1,825
Retained profits carried forward	4,780

(c) The retained profit for 20X3 after charging the actual development expenditure for the year was £2,030,000.

Required

Show how the change in accounting policy should be reflected in the statement of movements in reserves in the company's 20X3 accounts.

Ignore taxation.

Answer

If the new accounting policy had been adopted since the company was incorporated, the additional profit and loss account charges for development expenditure would have been:

	£'000
20X0	525
20X1 (780 – 215)	565
	1,090
20X2 (995 – 360)	635
	1,725

This means that the reserves brought forward at 1 January 20X3 would have been £1,725,000 less than the reported figure of £4,780,000; while the reserves brought forward at 1 January 20X2 would have been £1,090,000 less than the reported figure of £2,955,000.

The statement of movement in reserves in Jenny Ltd's 20X3 accounts should, therefore, appear as follows.

STATEMENT OF MOVEMENTS IN RESERVES (EXTRACT)	Total 20X3 £'000	Comparative (previous year) figures 20X2 £'000
Retained profits at the beginning of year		
Previously reported	4,780	2,955
Prior year adjustment (note 1)	1,725	1,090
Restated	3,055	1,865
Retained profits for the year	2,030	1,190 (note 2)
Retained profits at the end of the year	5,085	3,055

Notes

1   The accounts should include a note explaining the reasons for and consequences of the changes in accounting policy. (See above workings for 20X3 and 20X2.)

2   The retained profit shown for 20X2 is after charging the additional development expenditure of £635,000.

2.10 Potential problems with FRS 3

FRS 3 was designed to put an end to various abuses, for example extraordinary items. The latter have now been effectively prohibited.

Other aspects of FRS 3 have remained problematic. Two aspects may be highlighted.

2.10.1 Discontinued operations

Companies may take advantage of the requirement to analyse operations into continuing and discontinued and **use the analysis to hide 'bad news'**. A discontinued operation is likely to be a poor performer so it is in the company's interests to remove it from the rest of the results.

Careful consideration should be made as to whether the FRS 3 criteria for classification of an operation as continuing or discontinued have been met. The following should be singled out for close consideration.

(a)   Have sales and costs relating to the discontinued activity been identified? The directors may wish to include sales in continuing operations if possible and costs in discontinued operation if possible.

(b)   Provisions for profits or (more likely) losses on discontinuance must be considered carefully, as there is scope for manipulation.

2.10.2 Lack of consensus

FRS 3 was the first manifestation of the ASB's **balance sheet approach** to income recognition as outlined in the Board's *Statement of Principles* (discussed in Chapter 19). This was highlighted through the introduction into UK GAAP of an `additional primary statement of financial performance - the statement of total recognised gains and losses - which focuses on changes in wealth as the means of performance measurement, rather than traditional historical cost profit and loss.

Concern has been expressed that the ASB seems to be entrenching into an accounting standard a conceptual approach which has not been the subject of due process, has no general agreement and which is still only at an early stage of development and discussion. In fact, one of the most crucial chapters of the ASB's framework – that dealing with measurement – had not even been issued in draft form by the time FRS 3 was issued.

Chapter Roundup

- FRS 22 has superseded FRS 14. This has brought the UK's treatment of the EPS calculation into line with international standards.

- **Earnings per share** is a measure of the amount of profits earned by a company for each ordinary share. Earnings are profits after tax and preference dividends.

- **Basic EPS** is calculated by dividing the net profit or loss for the period attributable to ordinary shareholders by the weighted average number of ordinary shares outstanding during the period.

  You should know how to calculate **basic EPS** and how to deal with related complications (issue of shares for cash, bonus issue, share splits/reverse share splits, rights issues).

- **Diluted EPS** is calculated by adjusting the net profit attributable to ordinary shareholders and the weighted average number of ordinary shares outstanding during the period for the effects of all dilutive potential ordinary shares.

  You must be able to deal with **options** and all other **dilutive potential ordinary shares**.

- FRS 3 *Reporting financial performance* has introduced radical **changes to the profit and loss** account of large and medium sized companies.

- You must know the **FRS 3 definitions** of:

  - **Extraordinary items**
  - **Exceptional items**
  - **Prior year adjustments**
  - **Discontinued operations**
  - **Total recognised gains and losses**

- You must know the format of the **statement of total recognised gains and losses** and understand its contents.

Quick Quiz

1   Define earnings per share.

2   Following a rights issue, what is the fraction by which the EPS for the corresponding previous period should be multiplied?

3   What is diluted EPS?

4   Which of the following exceptional items must be shown on the face of the profit and loss account per FRS 3?

   A   Loss on disposal of manufacturing equipment

   B   Profit on the sale of a branch

   C   A significant insurance claim settlement

   D   The cost of restructuring the entity so that its focus and the nature of its operations are materially different

   E   A write off of 40% of the year end stock due to unforeseen obsolescence

   F   A provision for a major loss on a long term contract

5   A company's year end is 31 December 20X1. The financial statements are approved on 10 February 20X2. A large foreign operation is sold on the 11th February. Should the operation be treated as a discontinued operation?

6   How should a discontinued activity be accounted for?

7   Draw up a proforma statement of total recognised gains and losses.

8   The movement in the reconciliation of movements in shareholders' funds is:

$$\frac{\text{Profit /loss for the}}{\text{financial year}} + \frac{\text{Other recognised}}{\text{gains/losses}} - \text{Dividends} + \text{New share capital}$$

True   ☐

False   ☐

9   The following accounting treatment should be used to make a prior period adjustment.

   • Restate the prior year .... and ....

   • Restate the .... balance.

   • Include the adjustment in the ....

   • Include a .... at the foot of the statement ....
     ....

Answers to Quick Quiz

1   EPS is profit in pence attributable to each equity share.

2   $\dfrac{\text{Fair value of current shares}}{\text{Theoretical ex - rights value per share}}$

3   Diluted EPS shows users of the accounts how EPS would appear taking into account the effects of all dilutive potential ordinary shares.

4   All of them.

5   No. The sale is after the accounts were approved. Disclosure in a note can be made.

6   The **results** of the discontinued activity should be shown along with profit/loss on discontinuation (exceptional item) and comparatives.

7   Compare yours to that in Paragraph 2.5.

8   True

9   • Restate the prior year **profit and loss account** and **balance sheet**
    • Restate the **opening reserves** balance
    • Include the adjustment in the **reconciliation of movements in shareholders' funds**
    • Include a **note** at the foot of the **statement of total recognised gains and losses of the current period**

Now try the question below from the Exam Question Bank

Number	Level	Marks	Time
Q6	Exam	25	45 mins

Part C
Preparation of consolidated financial statements

13

Introduction to groups

Introduction

In this chapter we will look at the major definitions in consolidation and the relevant statutory requirements and accounting standards. These matters are fundamental to your comprehension of group accounts, so make sure you can understand them and then learn them.

The next two chapters deal with the basic techniques of consolidation, and then we move on to more complex aspects in the following chapters.

In all these chapters, make sure that you work through each example and question properly.

Study guide

- Describe the concept of a group and the objective and usefulness of consolidated financial statements.

- Explain the different methods which could be used to prepare group accounts.

- Explain and apply the definition of subsidiary companies in the Companies Acts and accounting standards.

- Describe the circumstances and reasoning for subsidiaries to be excluded from consolidated financial statements.

- Explain the need for using coterminous year ends and uniform accounting policies when preparing consolidated financial statements.

- Describe how the above is achieved in practice.

Exam guide

Group accounts and consolidation are an extremely important area of your Paper 2.5 syllabus as **you are almost certain to face a large compulsory consolidation question in the examination.**

The key to consolidation questions in the examination is to adopt a logical approach and to practise as many questions as possible beforehand.

1 Definitions

FAST FORWARD

A **group** consists of a **parent undertaking** and one or more **subsidiary undertakings**..

There are many reasons for businesses to operate as groups; for the goodwill associated with the names of the subsidiaries, for tax or legal purposes and so forth. Company law requires that the results of a group should be presented as a whole. Unfortunately, it is not possible simply to add all the results together and this chapter and those following will teach you how to **consolidate** all the results of companies within a group.

In traditional accounting terminology, a group of companies consists of a holding company (or parent company) and one or more subsidiary companies which are controlled by the holding company. The CA 1989 widened this definition. (The Act amended the CA 1985 and references below are to the amended sections.) As a result, FRS 2 *Accounting for subsidiary undertakings* was published in July 1992 by the ASB, incorporating the CA 1989 changes.

Exam focus point

If you are revising, go straight to the summary at the end of this section.

There are **two definitions of a group in company law. One** uses the terms 'holding company' and 'subsidiary' and applies **for general purposes. The other** is wider and applies **only for accounting purposes**. It **uses the terms 'parent undertaking' and 'subsidiary undertaking'**. The purpose of this widening of the group for accounting purposes was to curb the practice of structuring a group in such a way that not all companies or ventures within it had to be consolidated. This is an example of off balance sheet financing and has been used extensively to make consolidated accounts look better than is actually justified (see Chapter 11).

We are only really interested in the accounting definitions of parent and subsidiary undertaking here: they automatically include 'holding companies' and 'subsidiaries' under the general definition.

Exam focus point

The June 2003 paper required candidates to suggest why reliance on the entity financial statements of a subsidiary may mislead a potential purchaser of the company.

1.1 Parent and subsidiary undertakings: definition

FRS 2 states that an undertaking is the **parent undertaking** of another undertaking (**a subsidiary undertaking**) if any of the following apply.

Key term

Parent undertaking

(a)   It holds a **majority of the voting rights** in the undertaking.

(b)   It **is a member of the undertaking and has the right to appoint or remove directors** holding a majority of the voting rights at meetings of the board on all, or substantially all, matters.

(c)   **It has the right to exercise a dominant influence over the undertaking**:

   (i)   By virtue of provisions contained in the undertaking's memorandum or articles.

   (ii)   By virtue of a control contract (in writing, authorised by the memorandum or articles of the controlled undertaking, permitted by law).

(d)   **It is a member of the undertaking and controls alone**, under an agreement with other shareholders or members, **a majority of the voting rights in the undertaking.**

(e)   (i)   It actually exercises a dominant influence over the undertaking; ir
        (ii)   It and the undertaking are managed on a unified basis

(f)   A parent undertaking is **also treated as the parent undertaking of the subsidiary undertakings of its subsidiary undertakings.**

This replaced the previous criterion of owning a majority of equity with one of holding a majority of voting rights. **Also, the board is considered to be controlled if the holding company has the right to appoint directors with a majority of the voting rights on the board** (not just to appoint a simple majority of the directors, regardless of their voting rights).

1.1.1 Dominant influence

Key term

FRS 2 defines **dominant influence** as influence that can be exercised to achieve the operating and financial policies desired by the holder of the influence, notwithstanding the rights or influence of any other party.

The standard then distinguishes between the two different situations involving dominant influence.

(a)   In the context of Paragraph 1.6(c) above, **the right to exercise a dominant influence** means that the holder has **a right to give directions** with respect to the operating and financial policies of another undertaking with which its directors are obliged to comply, whether or not they are for the benefit of that undertaking.

(b)   **The actual exercise of dominant influence** is the exercise of an influence that achieves the result that the operating and financial policies of the undertaking influenced are set in accordance with the wishes of the holder of the influence and for the holder's benefit whether or not those wishes are explicit. The actual exercise of dominant influence is identified by its effect in practice rather than by the way in which it is exercised.

315

There are four other important definitions.

Key terms

(a)   **Control** is the ability of an undertaking to direct the financial and operating policies of another undertaking with a view to gaining economic benefits from its activities.

(b)   An **interest held on a long-term basis** is an interest which is held other than exclusively with a view to subsequent resale.

(c)   An **interest held exclusively with a view to subsequent resale** is either:

    (i)   An interest for which a purchaser has been identified or is being sought, and which is reasonably expected to be disposed of within approximately one year of its date of acquisition.

    (ii)   An interest that was acquired as a result of the enforcement of a security, unless the interest has become part of the continuing activities of the group or the holder acts as if it intends the interest to become so.

(d)   **Managed on a unified basis:** two or more undertakings are managed on a unified basis if the whole of the operations of the undertakings are integrated and they are managed as a single unit. Unified management does not arise solely because one undertaking manages another.

Other definitions from the standard will be introduced where relevant over the next few chapters.

1.2 The requirement to consolidate

FRS 2 requires a parent undertaking to prepare consolidated financial statements for its group unless it uses one of the exemptions available in the standard (see Section 2).

Key term

Consolidation is defined as: 'The process of adjusting and combining financial information from the individual financial statements of a parent undertaking and its subsidiary undertaking to prepare consolidated financial statements that present financial information for the group as a single economic entity.'

1.3 Associated undertakings

Another important definition, which applies only for the purposes of preparing group accounts, is that of an 'associated undertaking'. This is not defined by FRS 2, but as CA 1985 (and FRS 9: see Chapter 19).

Key term

'An "**associated undertaking**" means an undertaking in which an undertaking included in the consolidation has a participating interest and over whose operating and financial policy it exercises a significant influence, and which is not:

(a)   A subsidiary undertaking of the parent company

(b)   A joint venture'. (s 20(1) Sch 4A, CA 1985)

'Where an undertaking holds 20% or more of the voting rights in another undertaking, it shall be presumed to exercise such an influence over it unless the contrary is shown.'

                                                       (s 20(2) Sch 4A, CA 1985)

An undertaking **S is a subsidiary undertaking of H** if:

    (a)   H is a member of S and *either* holds or **controls > 50% of the voting rights** *or* controls the board; *OR*

    (b)   S is a **subsidiary** of P (ie S is a sub-subsidiary); *OR*

(c)   H has the right to exercise a **dominant influence** over S (laid down in the memorandum or articles or a control contract); *OR*

(d)   H **actually** exercises a **dominant influence** over S *or* P and S are managed on a unified basis.

∴ Special treatment: consolidate

An undertaking A is an **associated undertaking** of P if:

(a)   P and/or one or more of its subsidiary undertakings **either** hold more than **20%** of the voting rights **or** can otherwise be demonstrated to exercise a **significant** influence over A's operating and financial policy

(b)   A is not a subsidiary undertaking of P nor is it a joint venture.

∴ **Special treatment: equity accounting**

2 Exclusion of subsidiary undertakings from group accounts

FAST FORWARD

An entity may have one or more subsidiaries which it would **like** to exclude from the consolidation, for instance they may be loss-making. For this reason, FRS 2 sets out the exact circumstances in which a subsidiary may be excluded.

Both the Companies Act (S229) and FRS 2 **specify circumstances** where a **subsidiary** undertaking is **allowed or required** to be **omitted** from **group accounts**.

- Immateriality
- Temporary control
- Severe long-term restrictions
- Disproportionate expense and delay

Where **all the subsidiary undertakings** of parent undertaking fall within **one of these exclusions, no group accounts are required**.

2.1 Immateriality

The Companies Act allows an individual subsidiary to be excluded from consolidation if its inclusion is **not material** for the **purposes** of giving a **true and fair view**.

Where **two or more subsidiaries** are involved, these may be excluded only if they are not material, **taken together**.

FRS 2 states that it does not deal with immaterial items and hence this ground for exclusion is not covered by its requirements.

2.2 Temporary control

The **Companies Act allows exclusion** from consolidation where:

"The **interest** of the parent is **held exclusively** with a view to **subsequent resale**."

FRS 2 reiterates the Companies Act terms relating to this exclusion but **makes it mandatory**. So if the **conditions are met**, the relevant subsidiary undertaking **must be excluded** from consolidation.

FRS 2 however, set **tough test for achieving exclusion** via the **held exclusively for subsequent resale route**.

(a)   A **purchaser** has been **identified** or is being **sought**.

(b)   The interest is **reasonably expected** to be **sold** in approximately **one year of its acquisition**.

A **temporary investment** should be shown under **current assets** in the consolidation balance sheet at the **lower of cost and net realisable value**.

2.3 Severe long term restrictions

The **Companies Act allows** a subsidiary undertaking to be excluded from consolidation where severe long-tem restrictions **consistently hinder the exercise of the rights of the parent company** over the **assets** or **management** of that undertaking.

FRS 2 stiffens this Companies Act permissible exclusion to a **mandatory exclusion**. However, the explanatory notes to FRS 2 suggest that severe long-term restrictions justify excluding a subsidiary undertaking only where the **impact** of those restrictions is to **prevent** the parent undertaking from **controlling** its **subsidiary undertaking**, ie the test is harder to pass but once it is passed, the exclusion is mandatory.

Generally, **restrictions** are **better dealt** with by making **appropriate disclosures** rather than going down the exclusion from consolidation route.

Subsidiary undertakings **excluded** from consolidation **because of severe long-term restrictions** are to be **treated as fixed asset investments**. They should be included at their carrying amount when the restrictions came into force, subject to any write-down for impairment, and no further accruals are to be made for profits or losses of those subsidiary undertakings, unless the parent undertaking still exercises significant influence. In the latter case they are to be treated as associated undertakings.

The following information should be **disclosed** in the group accounts.

(a)   It **net assets**.
(b)   Its **profit or loss** for the period.
(c)   Any amounts included in the **consolidated profit and loss account** in respect of:

- **Dividends received** by the holding company from the subsidiary
- **Writing down the value of the investment**

2.4 Disproportionate expense and delay

The **Companies Act allows** a subsidiary company to be excluded from consolidation where the **information** necessary for the preparation of group accounts cannot be obtained without **disproportionate expense** or **undue delay**.

However, **FRS 2 effectively negates** any **scope to exclude** a subsidiary undertaking from consolidation, by stating:

"**Neither disproportionate expense** nor **undue delay** in obtaining the information necessary for the preparation of consolidated financial statements can **justify excluding** from consolidation subsidiary undertakings that are **individually or collectively material** in the **context** of the **group**."

2.5 General disclosure requirements

In all cases given above, FRS 2 states that the consolidated accounts should show:

(a)   The **reasons** for exclusion.
(b)   The **names** of subsidiaries excluded.
(c)   The **premium or discount on acquisition** not written off.
(d)   **Anything else required** by the Companies Acts.

The Companies Act requires that when **consolidated group accounts** are **not prepared**, or if **any subsidiaries** are **excluded** from the group accounts (for any of the reasons given above), **a note to the accounts should be given:**

    (a)   To explain the **reasons** why the subsidiaries are not dealt with in group accounts

    (b)   To disclose any **auditors' qualifications** in the accounts of the **excluded subsidiaries**

A **note** to the (holding) company's accounts (or the consolidated accounts, if any) should **also state**, for **subsidiaries** which are **not consolidated** in group accounts, the aggregate value of the **total investment** of the **holding company** in the subsidiaries, by way of the **'equity method' of valuation**.

2.6 Section summary

The following table summaries the rules relating to exclusion of a subsidiary.

Reason for exclusion	Companies Act	FRS 2	Classification	Accounting treatment
• Immateriality	Optional	Does not deal with immaterial items	–	–
• Temporary control	Optional	Mandatory	Current asset investment	Lower of cost and NRV
• Severe long-term restrictions	Optional	Mandatory	Fixed asset investment	• Record at carrying amount when restrictions come into force, less any impairment. • Where parent exercises significant influence, treat as associate and apply equity accounting
• Disproportionate expense and delay	Optional	Not allowed	–	–

3 Exemption from the requirement to prepare group accounts

The CA 1989 introduced a completely new provision exempting some groups from preparing consolidated accounts. There are two grounds.

    (a)   **Smaller groups** can claim exemptions on grounds of size (see below).

    (b)   **Parent companies** (*except* for listed companies) **whose immediate parent produces accounts in accordance with IFRS** need not prepare consolidated accounts. The accounts must give the name and country of incorporation of the parent and state the fact of the exemption. In addition, a copy of the audited consolidated accounts of the parent must be filed with the UK company's accounts. Minority shareholders can, however, require that consolidated accounts are prepared.

FRS 2 adds that exemption may be gained if all of the parent's subsidiary undertakings gain exemption under s 229 CA 1985 (see Paragraph 2.1).

The **exemption** from preparing consolidated accounts is **not available to:**

(a)   Public companies.
(b)   Banking and insurance companies.
(c)   Authorised persons under the Financial Services Act 1986.
(d)   Companies belonging to a group containing a member of the above classes of undertaking.

Any two of the following **size criteria** for small and medium-sized groups must be met.

	Small	Medium-sized
Aggregate turnover	≤ £5.6 million net/ £6.72 million gross	≤ £22.8 million net/ £27.36 million gross
Aggregate gross assets	≤ £2.8 million net/ £3.36 million gross	≤ £11.4 million net/ £13.68 million gross
Aggregate number of employees (average monthly)	≤ 50	≤ 250

The aggregates can be calculated either before (gross) or after (net) consolidation adjustments for intra-group sales, unrealised profit on stock and so on (see following chapters). The qualifying conditions **must be met:**

(a)   **In the case of the parent's first financial year, in that year**
(b)   **In the case of any subsequent financial year, in that year and the preceding year**

If the qualifying conditions were met in the preceding year but not in the current year, the exemption can be claimed. If, in the subsequent year, the conditions are met again, the exemption can still be claimed, but if they are not met, then the exemption is lost until the conditions are again met for the second of two successive years.

When the exemption is claimed, but the auditors believe that the company is not entitled to it, then they must state in their report that the company is in their opinion not entitled to the exemption and this report must be attached to the individual accounts of the company (ie no report is required when the company *is* entitled to the exemption).

4 Content of group accounts

FAST FORWARD

Group accounts comprise a consolidated profit and loss account, balance sheet and cash flow statement. Each of these financial statements presents the financial position and results of the group as if they were the financial position and results of a single entity.

The information contained in the individual accounts of a holding company and each of its subsidiaries does not give a picture of the group's activities as those of a single entity. To do this, a separate set of accounts can be prepared from the individual accounts. *Note.* **Remember that a group has no separate (legal) existence, except for accounting purposes.**

There is more than one way of amalgamating the information in the individual accounts into a set of group accounts, but the most common way (and now the legally required way) is to prepare consolidated accounts. **Consolidated accounts are one form of group accounts which combines the information contained in the separate accounts of a holding company and its subsidiaries as if they were the accounts of a single entity.** 'Group accounts' and 'consolidated accounts' are often used synonymously, and now that UK law *requires* group accounts to be consolidated accounts, this tendency will no doubt increase.

In simple terms a set of consolidated accounts is prepared by **adding together** the assets and liabilities of the holding company and each subsidiary. The **whole of the assets and liabilities of each company** are included, **even though some subsidiaries may be only partly owned**. The 'capital and reserves' side of the balance sheet will indicate how much of the net assets are attributable to the group and how much to outside investors in partly owned subsidiaries. These **outside investors** are known as **minority interests**.

The CA 1985 requires that group accounts should be prepared whenever a company:

    (a)   Is a parent company at the end of its financial year

    (b)   Is not itself a wholly owned subsidiary of a company incorporated in Great Britain

Most parent companies present their own individual accounts and their group accounts in a single **package**. The package typically comprises a:

    (a)   **Parent company balance sheet**, which will include 'investments in subsidiary undertakings' as an asset.

    (b)   **Consolidated balance sheet.**

    (c)   **Consolidated profit and loss** account.

    (d)   **Consolidated cash flow statement**.

It is not necessary to publish a parent company profit and loss account (s 230 CA 1985), provided the consolidated profit and loss account contains a note stating the profit or loss for the financial year dealt with in the accounts of the parent company and the fact that the statutory exemption is being relied on.

Exam focus point	If you are in a hurry skim or skip the rest of Section 4.

4.1 Co-terminous accounting periods

S 223 (5) CA 1985 requires that the directors of the holding company **should ensure that the financial year of each of the subsidiaries in the group shall coincide with the financial year of the holding company.** This is to prevent any possible 'window dressing' (although financial years need not coincide if the directors hold the opinion that there are reasons against it).

If the financial year end of a subsidiary does not coincide with the financial year of the holding company, the appropriate results to include in the group accounts for the subsidiary will be those for its year ending before the year end of the holding company; or if this ended more than three months previously, from interim accounts prepared as at the holding company's year end (s 2(2) Sch 4A CA 1985). These two provisions are included in FRS 2.

Additionally, FRS 2 requires that a note to the group accounts should disclose the:

    (a)   Reasons why the directors consider that coinciding dates are not appropriate.

    (b)   Name(s) of the subsidiary(ies) concerned.

    (c)   Accounting date and length of the accounting period of each relevant subsidiary.

4.2 Disclosure of subsidiaries

The CA 1985 requires that a parent company disclose, by note:

    (a)   The name of each subsidiary undertaking.

    (b)   Its country of incorporation (or, if unincorporated, address of principal place of business).

    (c)   The identity and proportion of the nominal value of each class of shares held (distinguishing between direct and indirect holdings).

    (d)   The reason for treating a subsidiary undertaking as such *unless* a majority of the voting rights are held and the proportion is the same as that of shares held.

FRS 2 confirms these provisions and also requires that the nature of each subsidiary's business should be indicated.

(*Note.* A subsidiary company must show, in its own accounts, its ultimate holding company's name and country of incorporation.)

4.3 Further provisions of FRS 2

FRS 2 also requires the following.

(a) **Uniform accounting policies should be applied by all companies in the group,** or if this is not done, appropriate adjustments should be made in the consolidated accounts to achieve uniformity. (If, in exceptional cases, such adjustments are impractical, the different accounting policies used, the effect of the difference on the results and net assets, and the reason for the different treatment should all be disclosed). This is also required by the CA 1985.

(b) **Where there are material additions to the group there should be disclosure of the extent to which the results of the group are affected by profits and losses** of subsidiaries brought in for the first time. This is also now required by the CA 1985.

(c) **Outside or minority interests in the share capital and reserves of companies consolidated should be disclosed separately in the consolidated balance sheet** (also required by the CA 1985). Debit balances should be shown only if there is a binding obligation on minority shareholders to make good any losses. Similarly, the profits and losses of such companies attributable to outside interests should be shown separately in the consolidated profit and loss account after arriving at group profit or loss after tax but before extraordinary items. Minority interests in extraordinary items should be deducted from the relevant amounts.

(d) Changes in membership of a group occur on the date control passes, whether by a transaction or other event. **Changes in the membership of the group during the period should be disclosed.**

(e) When a subsidiary undertaking is acquired the FRS requires its **identifiable assets and liabilities to be brought into the consolidation at their fair values at the date that undertaking becomes a subsidiary** undertaking, even if the acquisition has been made in stages. When a group increases its interest in an undertaking that is already its subsidiary undertaking, the identifiable assets and liabilities of that subsidiary undertaking should be calculated by reference to that fair value. This revaluation is not required if the difference between fair values and carrying amounts of the identifiable assets and liabilities attributable to the increase in stake is not material.

(f) The effect of consolidating the parent and its subsidiary undertakings may be that aggregation obscures useful information about the different undertakings and activities included in the consolidated financial statements. Parent undertakings are encouraged to give **segmental analysis to provide** readers of consolidated financial statements with **useful information on the different risks and rewards, growth and prospects of the different parts of the group.** The specification of such analysis, however, falls outside the scope of the FRS.

4.4 Further provisions of the Companies Act 1985

For each material acquisition in the period, in addition to the above disclosures, a note must state:

(a) The composition and **fair value** of the consideration given.

(b) The name of the undertaking (of the parent undertaking in the case of a newly acquired group).

(c) Whether acquisition or merger accounting has been used.

If **acquisition accounting** was used, a table of the book values and *fair values* as at acquisition of each class of assets and liabilities of the undertaking or group acquired is to be given, including a statement of the amount of any goodwill or negative consolidation difference arising and an explanation of any significant adjustments made.

If **merger accounting** is used, then an explanation is to be given of any significant adjustments made together with a statement of adjustments to consolidated reserves. (Note that merger accounting is no longer in your syllabus.)

For each **material disposal** in the period, the name of the subsidiary must be disclosed, along with the FRS 2 requirements (see Section 2).

Finally, the CA 1985 requirement to disclose cumulative goodwill written off has been amended recently to exclude goodwill written off through the profit and loss account. Consequently, only the **cumulative goodwill that has been written off direct to reserves** in the current year or past years need now be disclosed. Note that negative goodwill does not require disclosure.

5 Group structure

FAST FORWARD

> The first issue to look at is always the **structure** of the group. This shows which companies should be included in the consolidation.

With the difficulties of definition and disclosure dealt with, let us now look at group structures. The simplest are those in which a holding company has only a direct interest in the shares of its subsidiary companies. For example:

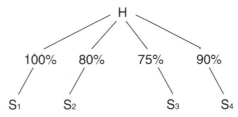

S_1 Ltd is a wholly owned subsidiary of H Ltd. S_2 Ltd, S_3 Ltd and S_4 Ltd are partly owned subsidiaries; a proportion of the shares in these companies is held by outside investors.

Often a holding company will have indirect holdings in its subsidiary companies. This can lead to more complex group structures.

(a)

H Ltd owns 51% of the equity shares in S Ltd, which is therefore its subsidiary. S Ltd in its turn owns 51% of the equity shares in SS Ltd. SS Ltd is therefore a subsidiary of S Ltd and consequently a subsidiary of H Ltd. SS Ltd would describe S Ltd as its **parent** (or holding) company and H Ltd as its **ultimate parent** (or holding) company.

Note that although H Ltd can control the assets and business of SS Ltd by virtue of the chain of control, its interest in the assets of SS Ltd is only 26%. This can be seen by considering a dividend of £100 paid by SS Ltd: as a 51% shareholder, S Ltd would receive £51; H Ltd would have an interest in 51% of this £51 = £26.01.

(b)

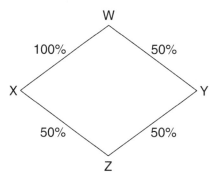

W Ltd owns 100% of the equity of X Ltd and 50% of the equity of Y Ltd. X Ltd and Y Ltd each own 50% of the equity of Z Ltd. Assume that:

(i)   W Ltd does not control the composition of Y Ltd's board; and

(ii)   W Ltd does not hold or control more than 50% of the *voting rights* in Y Ltd; and

(iii)   W Ltd does not have the right to exercise a dominant influence over Y Ltd by virtue of its memorandum, articles or a control contract; and

(iv)   W Ltd and Y Ltd are not managed on a unified basis; and

(v)   W Ltd does not actually exercise a dominant influence over Y Ltd; and

(vi)   none of the above apply to either X Ltd's or Y Ltd's holdings in Z Ltd.

In other words, because W Ltd is not in co-operation with the holder(s) of the other 50% of the shares in Y Ltd, neither Y nor Z can be considered subsidiaries.

In that case:

(i)   X Ltd is a subsidiary of W Ltd;

(ii)   Y Ltd is not a subsidiary of W Ltd;

(iii)   Z Ltd is not a subsidiary of either X Ltd or Y Ltd. Consequently, it is not a subsidiary of W Ltd.

If Z Ltd pays a dividend of £100, X Ltd and Y Ltd will each receive £50. The interest of W Ltd in this dividend is as follows.

	£
Through X Ltd (100% × £50)	50
Through Y Ltd (50% × £50)	25
	75

Although W Ltd has an interest in 75% of Z Ltd's assets, Z Ltd is not a subsidiary of W Ltd.

(c)

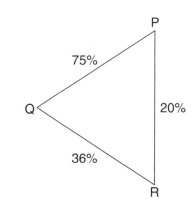

BPP
PROFESSIONAL EDUCATION

Q Ltd is a subsidiary of P Ltd. P Ltd therefore has indirect control over 36% of R Ltd's equity. P Ltd also has direct control over 20% of R Ltd's equity. R Ltd is therefore a subsidiary of P Ltd, although P Ltd's interest in R Ltd's assets is only 20% + (75% $\times$ 36%) = 47%.

Examples (b) and (c) illustrate an important point in company law: in deciding whether a company A holds more than 50% of the equity (or equivalent) of an undertaking B it is necessary to aggregate:

(i)   Shares (or equivalent) in B held directly by A
(ii)   Shares (or equivalent) in B held by undertakings which are subsidiaries of A

Question   Published accounts

During the time until your examination you should obtain as many sets of the published accounts of top quoted companies as possible. Examine the accounting policies in relation to subsidiary and associated companies and consider how these policies are shown in the accounting and consolidation treatment. Consider the effect of any disposals during the year. Also, look at all the disclosures made relating to fair values, goodwill etc and match them to the disclosure requirements outlined in this chapter and in subsequent chapters on FRSs 6 and 7.

Alternatively (or additionally) you should attempt to obtain such information from the financial press.

Chapter Roundup

- A **group** consists of a **parent undertaking** and one or more **subsidiary undertakings**.

- An entity may have one or more subsidiaries which it would **like** to exclude from the consolidation, for instance they may be loss-making. For this reason, FRS 2 sets out the exact circumstances in which a subsidiary may be excluded.

- Group accounts comprise a consolidated profit and loss account, balance sheet and cash flow statement. Each of these financial statements presents the financial position and results of the group as if they were the financial position and results of a single entity.

- The first issue to look at is always the **structure** of the group. This shows which companies should be included in the consolidation.

Quick Quiz

1   *Fill in the blanks* in the statements below, using the words in the box.

Per FRS 2, A is a parent of B if:

(a)   A holds (1) ……………….. in B

(b)   A can appoint or remove (2) ………………..

(c)   A has the right to exercise (3) ……………….. over B

(d)   B is a (4) ……………….. of A

Sub-subsidiary	Dominant influence
Directors holding a majority of the voting rights	A majority of the voting rights

2   If a company holds 20% or more of the shares of another company, it has a participating interest. *True or false*?

3   What is dominant influence?

4   How should a subsidiary excluded on the grounds of temporary control be accounted for in the consolidated balance sheet?

5   What are the size criteria for exemption from preparing group accounts under the CA 1985?

6   It is not necessary for a parent company to publish its profit and loss account.

True   ☐

False   ☐

BPP
PROFESSIONAL EDUCATION

Answers to Quick Quiz

1   (a)   A majority of the voting rights
    (b)   Directors holding a majority of the voting rights
    (c)   Significant influence
    (d)   Sub-subsidiary

2   False. Significant influence is presumed but the presumption may be rebutted.

3   Influence that can be exercised to achieve the operating and financial policies desired by the holder of the influence, notwithstanding the rights or influence of any other party.

4   It should be included under current assets at the lower of cost and NRV.

5   An entity must meet **two** of the size criteria for small and medium-sized groups. See the table in Paragraph 3.

6   True. The parent company's balance sheet must be published but there is an exemption for its profit and loss account.

Now try the question below from the Exam Question Bank

Number	Level	Marks	Time
Q17	Full exam	20	36 mins

BPP
PROFESSIONAL EDUCATION

Consolidated balance sheet

Introduction

This chapter introduces the *basic procedures* required in consolidation and gives a formal step plan for carrying out a balance sheet consolidation. This step procedure should be useful to you as a starting guide for answering any question, but remember that you cannot rely on it to answer the question for you.

The method of consolidation shown here uses schedules for workings (reserves, minority interests etc) rather than the ledger accounts used in some other texts. This is because we believe that ledger accounts lead students to 'learn' the consolidation journals without thinking about what they are doing - always a dangerous practice in consolidation questions.

There are plenty of questions in this chapter - work through *all* of them carefully.

Study guide

- Explain the different methods which could be used to prepare group accounts.

- Prepare a consolidated balance sheet for a simple group dealing with pre and post acquisition profits, minority interests and consolidated goodwill.

- Explain why intra-group transactions should be eliminated on consolidation.

- Account for the effects (in the profit and loss account and balance sheet) of intra-group trading and other transactions including:
    - unrealised profits in stock and fixed assets
    - intra-group loans and interest and other intra-group charges, and
    - intra-group dividends including those paid out of pre-acquisition profits.

Exam guide

Each question must be approached and answered on its own merits. Examiners often put small extra or different problems in because, as they are always reminding students, it is not possible to 'rote-learn' consolidation.

1 Cancellation and part cancellation

1.1 Basic process

FAST FORWARD

The preparation of a consolidated balance sheet, in a very simple form, consists of two procedures.

(a) Take the individual accounts of the holding company and each subsidiary and **cancel out items which appear as an asset in one company and a liability in another.**

(b) **Add together all the uncancelled assets** and liabilities throughout the group.

1.2 Cancellation

Items requiring cancellation may include the following.

(a) The asset **'shares in subsidiary companies'** which appears in the parent company's accounts will be matched with the liability 'share capital' in the subsidiaries' accounts.

(b) There may be **inter-company trading** within the group. For example, S Ltd may sell goods to P Ltd. P Ltd would then be a debtor in the accounts of S Ltd, while S Ltd would be a creditor in the accounts of P Ltd.

1.3 Example: cancellation

Peach Ltd regularly sells goods to its one subsidiary company, Strawberry Ltd. The balance sheets of the two companies on 31 December 20X6 are given below.

PEACH LIMITED
BALANCE SHEET AS AT 31 DECEMBER 20X6

	£	£	£
Fixed assets			
Tangible assets			35,000
40,000 £1 shares in Strawberry Ltd at cost			40,000
			75,000
Current assets			
Stocks		16,000	
Debtors: Strawberry Ltd	2,000		
Other	6,000		
		8,000	
Cash at bank		1,000	
		25,000	
Current liabilities			
Creditors		14,000	
			11,000
			86,000
Capital and reserves			
70,000 £1 ordinary shares			70,000
Reserves			16,000
			86,000

STRAWBERRY LIMITED
BALANCE SHEET AS AT 31 DECEMBER 20X6

	£	£	£
Fixed assets			
Tangible assets			45,000
Current assets			
Stocks		12,000	
Debtors		9,000	
		21,000	
Current liabilities			
Bank overdraft		3,000	
Creditors: Peach Ltd	2,000		
Other	2,000		
		4,000	
		7,000	
			14,000
			59,000
Capital and reserves			
40,000 £1 ordinary shares			40,000
Reserves			19,000
			59,000

Prepare the consolidated balance sheet of Peach Ltd.

Solution

The cancelling items are:

(a)   Peach Ltd's asset 'investment in shares of Strawberry Ltd' (£40,000) cancels with Strawberry Ltd's liability 'share capital' (£40,000);

(b)   Peach Ltd's asset 'debtors: Strawberry Ltd' (£2,000) cancels with Strawberry Ltd's liability 'creditors: Peach Ltd' (£2,000).

The remaining assets and liabilities are added together to produce the following consolidated balance sheet.

PEACH LIMITED
CONSOLIDATED BALANCE SHEET AS AT 31 DECEMBER 20X6

	£	£
Fixed assets		
Tangible assets		80,000
Current assets		
Stocks	28,000	
Debtors	15,000	
Cash at bank	1,000	
	44,000	
Current liabilities		
Bank overdraft	3,000	
Creditors	16,000	
	19,000	
		25,000
		105,000
Capital and reserves		
70,000 £1 ordinary shares		70,000
Reserves		35,000
		105,000

1.3.1 Notes on the example

(a)   Peach Ltd's bank balance is not netted off with Strawberry Ltd's bank overdraft. To offset one against the other would be less informative and would conflict with the statutory principle that assets and liabilities should not be netted off.

(b)   The share capital in the consolidated balance sheet is the share capital of the parent company alone. This must *always* be the case, no matter how complex the consolidation, because the share capital of subsidiary companies must *always* be a wholly cancelling item.

1.4 Part cancellation

An item may appear in the balance sheets of a parent company and its subsidiary, but not at the same amounts.

(a)   **The parent company may have acquired shares in the subsidiary at a price greater or less than their nominal value.** The asset will appear in the parent company's accounts at cost, while the liability will appear in the subsidiary's accounts at nominal value. **This raises the issue of goodwill**, which is dealt with later in this chapter.

(b)   Even if the parent company acquired shares at nominal value, it **may not have acquired all the shares of the subsidiary** (so the subsidiary may be only partly owned). This **raises the issue of minority interests**, which are also dealt with later in this chapter.

PROFESSIONAL EDUCATION

(c)   The inter-company trading balances may be out of step because of **goods or cash in transit**.

(d)   One company may have **issued loan stock of which a proportion only is taken up** by the other company.

The following example illustrates the techniques needed to deal with the second two items. The procedure is to **cancel as far as possible. The remaining uncancelled amounts will appear in the consolidated balance sheet.**

(a)   Uncancelled loan stock will appear as a liability of the group.

(b)   Uncancelled balances on inter-company accounts represent goods or cash in transit, which will appear in the consolidated balance sheet.

Question	Consolidated balance sheet 1

The balance sheets of Parrot Ltd and of its subsidiary Swallow Ltd have been made up to 30 June. Parrot Ltd has owned all the ordinary shares and 40% of the loan stock of Swallow Ltd since its incorporation.

PARROT LIMITED

BALANCE SHEET AS AT 30 JUNE

	£	£
Fixed assets		
Tangible assets		120,000
Investment in Swallow Ltd, at cost		
80,000 ordinary shares of £1 each		80,000
£20,000 of 12% loan stock in Swallow Ltd		20,000
		220,000
Current assets		
Stocks	50,000	
Debtors	40,000	
Current account with Swallow Ltd	18,000	
Cash	4,000	
	112,000	
Creditors: amounts falling due within one year		
Creditors	47,000	
Taxation	15,000	
	62,000	
Net current assets		50,000
		270,000
Creditors: amounts falling due after more than one year		
10% loan stock		75,000
		195,000
Capital and reserves		
Ordinary shares of £1 each, fully paid		100,000
Reserves		95,000
		195,000

SWALLOW LIMITED
BALANCE SHEET AS AT 30 JUNE

	£	£
Tangible fixed assets		100,000
Current assets		
Stocks	60,000	
Debtors	30,000	
Cash	6,000	
	96,000	
Creditors: amounts falling due within one year		
Creditors	16,000	
Taxation	10,000	
Current account with Parrot Ltd	12,000	
	38,000	
		58,000
		158,000
Creditors: amounts falling due after more than one year		
12% Loan stock		50,000
		108,000
Capital and reserves		
80,000 ordinary shares of £1 each, fully paid		80,000
Reserves		28,000
		108,000

The difference on current account arises because of goods in transit. Prepare the consolidated balance sheet of Parrot Ltd.

Answer

PARROT LIMITED
CONSOLIDATED BALANCE SHEET AS AT 30 JUNE

	£	£
Tangible fixed assets		220,000
Current assets		
Stocks	110,000	
Goods in transit	6,000	
Debtors	70,000	
Cash	10,000	
	196,000	
Creditors: amounts falling due within one year		
Creditors	63,000	
Taxation	25,000	
	88,000	
		108,000
		328,000
Creditors: amounts falling due after more than one year		
10% loan stock	75,000	
12% loan stock	30,000	
		105,000
		223,000
Capital and reserves		
Ordinary shares of £1 each, fully paid		100,000
Reserves		123,000
		223,000

BPP
PROFESSIONAL EDUCATION

Note especially how:

(a)   The uncancelled loan stock in Swallow Ltd becomes a liability of the group
(b)   The goods in transit is the difference between the current accounts (£18,000 – £12,000)

2 Minority interests

Where the parent does not own 100% of the shares in the subsidiary, the other shares are held by **minority** shareholders. The proportion of share capital and reserves attributable to this **minority interest** must be shown in the consolidated balance sheet.

Exam focus point

All 2.5 papers will include a group accounts question which is more than likely to involve calculating minority interests.

It was mentioned earlier that the total assets and liabilities of subsidiary companies are included in the consolidated balance sheet, even in the case of subsidiaries which are only partly owned. A proportion of the net assets of such subsidiaries in fact belongs to investors from outside the group (minority interests).

Key term

FRS 2 defines **minority interest** in a subsidiary undertaking as the 'interest in a subsidiary undertaking included in the consolidation that is attributable to the shares held by or on behalf of persons other than the parent undertaking and its subsidiary undertakings'.

In the consolidated balance sheet it is necessary to distinguish this proportion from those assets attributable to the group and financed by shareholders' funds.

The net assets of a company are financed by share capital and reserves. The consolidation procedure for dealing with partly owned subsidiaries is to **calculate the proportion of ordinary shares, preference shares and reserves attributable to minority interests.**

2.1 Example: minority interests

Peppa Ltd has owned 75% of the share capital of Salt Ltd since the date of Salt Ltd's incorporation. Their latest balance sheets are given below.

PEPPA LIMITED – BALANCE SHEET

	£
Fixed assets	
Tangible assets	50,000
30,000 £1 ordinary shares in Salt Ltd at cost	30,000
	80,000
	25,000
Net current assets	105,000
Capital and reserves	
80,000 £1 ordinary shares	80,000
Reserves	25,000
	105,000

SALT LIMITED BALANCE SHEET

	£
Tangible fixed assets	35,000
Net current assets	15,000
	50,000

335

	£
Capital and reserves	
40,000 £1 ordinary shares	40,000
Reserves	10,000
	50,000

Prepare the consolidated balance sheet.

Solution

All of Salt Ltd's net assets are consolidated despite the fact that the company is only 75% owned. The amount of net assets attributable to minority interests is calculated as follows.

	£
Minority share of share capital (25% × £40,000)	10,000
Minority share of reserves (25% × £10,000)	2,500
	12,500

Of Salt Ltd's share capital of £40,000, £10,000 is included in the figure for minority interest, while £30,000 is cancelled with Peppa Ltd's asset 'investment in Salt Limited'.

The consolidated balance sheet can now be prepared.

PEPPA GROUP
CONSOLIDATED BALANCE SHEET

	£
Tangible fixed assets	85,000
Net current assets	40,000
	125,000
Share capital	80,000
Reserves £(25,000 + (75% × 10,000))	32,500
Shareholders' funds	112,500
Minority interest (W)	12,500
	125,000

In this example we have shown minority interest on the 'capital and reserves' side of the balance sheet to illustrate how some of Salt Ltd's net assets are financed by shareholders' funds, while some are financed by outside investors. You may see minority interest as a deduction from the other side of the balance sheet. The second half of the balance sheet will then consist entirely of shareholders' funds. The Companies Act 1985 permits either of the above presentations, but **FRS 4 seems to require the disclosure shown above**.

Exam focus point	In more complicated examples the following technique is recommended for dealing with minority interests.
	Step 1 Cancel common items in the draft balance sheets. If there is a minority interest, the subsidiary company's share capital will be a partly cancelled item. Ascertain the proportion of ordinary shares and the proportion (possibly different) of preference shares held by the minority.
	Step 2 Produce a working for the minority interest. Add in the amounts of preference and ordinary share capital calculated in step 1: this completes the cancellation of the subsidiary's share capital.

BPP
PROFESSIONAL EDUCATION

Exam focus point cont'd

Add also the minority's share of each reserve in the subsidiary company. Reserves belong to equity shareholders; the proportion attributable to minority interests therefore depends on their percentage holding of ordinary shares.

Step 3 Produce a separate working for each reserve (capital, revenue etc) found in the subsidiary company's balance sheet. The initial balances on these accounts will be taken straight from the draft balance sheets of the parent and subsidiary company.2.6

Step 4 The closing balances in these workings can be entered directly onto the consolidated balance sheet.

Question
Consolidated balance sheet 2

Set out below are the draft balance sheets of Plug Ltd and its subsidiary Socket Ltd. You are required to prepare the consolidated balance sheet.

PLUG LIMITED

	£	£
Fixed assets		
Tangible assets		31,000
Investment in Socket Ltd		
12,000 £1 ordinary shares at cost	12,000	
4,000 £1 preference shares at cost	4,000	
£4,000 10% debentures at cost	4,000	
		20,000
		51,000
Net current assets		11,000
		62,000
Capital and reserves		
Ordinary shares of £1 each		40,000
Revenue reserve		22,000
		62,000

SOCKET LIMITED

	£
Tangible fixed assets	34,000
Net current assets	22,000
	56,000
Long-term liability	
10% debentures	10,000
	46,000
Capital and reserves	
Ordinary shares of £1 each	20,000
Preference shares of £1 each	16,000
Capital reserve	6,000
Revenue reserve	4,000
	46,000

Answer

Partly cancelling items are the components of Plug Ltd's investment in Socket Ltd, ie ordinary shares, preference shares and loan stock. Minorities have an interest in 75% (12,000/16,000) of Socket Ltd's preference shares and 40% (8,000/20,000) of Socket Ltd's equity, including reserves.

You should now product workings for minority interests, capital reserve and revenue reserve as follows.

Workings

1 *Minority interests*

		£
Ordinary share capital (40% of 20,000)		8,000
Reserves: capital (40% × 6,000)		2,400
revenue (40% × 4,000)		1,600
		12,000
Preference share capital (75% × 16,000)		12,000
		24,000

2 *Capital reserve*

	Plug Ltd £	Socket Ltd £
Per question		6,000
Group share in Socket Ltd (6,000 × 60%)	3,600	
Group capital reserves	3,600	

3 *Revenue reserve*

	Plug Ltd £	Socket Ltd £
Per question	22,000	4,000
Group share in Socket Ltd (4,000 × 60%)	2,400	
Group revenue reserves	24,400	

The results of the workings are now used to construct the consolidated balance sheet (CBS).

PLUG GROUP
CONSOLIDATED BALANCE SHEET

	£
Tangible fixed assets	65,000
Net current assets	33,000
	98,000
Long-term liability	
10% debentures	6,000
	92,000
Capital and reserves	
Ordinary shares of £1 each	40,000
Capital reserve (W2)	3,600
Revenue reserve (W3)	24,400
Shareholders' funds	68,000
Minority interests (W1)	24,000
	92,000

Notes

(a) Socket Ltd is a subsidiary of Plug Ltd because Plug Ltd owns 60% of its equity capital. It is unimportant how little of the preference share capital is owned by Plug Ltd.

(b) As always, the share capital in the consolidated balance sheet is that of the parent company alone. The share capital in Socket Ltd's balance sheet was partly cancelled against the investment shown in Plug Ltd's balance sheet, while the uncancelled portion was credited to minority interest.

(c) The figure for minority interest comprises the interest of outside investors in the share capital and reserves of the subsidiary. The uncancelled portion of Socket Ltd's loan stock is not shown as part of minority interest but is disclosed separately as a liability of the group.

3 Dividends paid by a subsidiary

FAST FORWARD

When dealing with dividends paid by a subsidiary, make sure that the entry has been made in the accounts of both the **paying** company and the **receiving** company.

When a subsidiary company pays a dividend during the year the accounting treatment is not difficult. Suppose Silva Ltd, a 60% subsidiary of Pink Ltd, pays a dividend of £1,000 on the last day of its accounting period. Its total reserves before paying the dividend stood at £5,000.

    (a)   £400 of the dividend is paid to minority shareholders. The cash leaves the group and will not appear anywhere in the consolidated balance sheet.

    (b)   The parent company receives £600 of the dividend, debiting cash and crediting profit and loss account.

    (c)   The remaining balance of reserves in Silva Ltd's balance sheet (£4,000) will be consolidated in the normal way. The group's share (60% × £4,000 = £2,400) will be included in group reserves in the balance sheet; the minority share (40% × £4,000 = £1,600) is credited to the minority interest account.

Exam focus point

Dividends *proposed* by a subsidiary do not appear in the accounts and will not be examined.

Note. When a subsidiary pays a dividend out of **pre-acquisition profits** the dividend is accounted for differently. This is explained in the next chapter.

4 Goodwill arising on consolidation

FAST FORWARD

When a company acquires shares in another company for an amount which exceeds the value of that proportion of the fair value of its assets, it has paid a 'premium', which is called **goodwill**. This appears as an **intangible fixed asset** in the consolidated balance sheet and is then **amortised** over its useful life.

In the examples we have looked at so far the cost of shares acquired by the parent company has always been equal to the nominal value of those shares. This is seldom the case in practice and we must now consider some more complicated examples. To begin with, **we will examine the entries made by the parent company in its own balance sheet when it acquires shares.**

When a company P Ltd wishes to **purchase shares** in a company S Ltd it must pay the previous owners of those shares. The most obvious form of payment would be in **cash**. Suppose P Ltd purchases all 40,000 £1 shares in S Ltd and pays £60,000 cash to the previous shareholders in consideration. The entries in P Ltd's books would be:

DEBIT	Investment in S Ltd at cost	£60,000	
CREDIT	Bank		£60,000

However, the previous shareholders might be prepared to accept some other form of consideration. For example, they might accept an agreed number of **shares** in P Ltd. P Ltd would then issue new shares in the agreed number and allot them to the former shareholders of S Ltd. This kind of deal might be attractive to P Ltd since it avoids the need for a heavy cash outlay. The former shareholders of S Ltd would retain an indirect interest in that company's profitability via their new holding in its parent company.

Continuing the example, suppose the shareholders of S Ltd agreed to accept one £1 ordinary share in P Ltd for every two £1 ordinary shares in S Ltd. P Ltd would then need to issue and allot 20,000 new £1 shares. How would this transaction be recorded in the books of P Ltd?

The simplest method would be as follows.

DEBIT	Investment in S Ltd	£20,000	
CREDIT	Share capital		£20,000

However, if the 40,000 £1 shares acquired in S Ltd are thought to have a value of £60,000 this would be misleading. The former shareholders of S Ltd have presumably agreed to accept 20,000 shares in P Ltd because they consider each of those shares to have a value of £3. This view of the matter suggests the following method of recording the transaction in P Ltd's books.

DEBIT	Investment in S Ltd	£60,000	
CREDIT	Share capital		£20,000
	Share premium account		£40,000

The second method is the one which the Companies Act 1985 requires should normally be used in preparing consolidated accounts.

The amount which P Ltd records in its books as the cost of its investment in S Ltd may be more or less than the book value of the assets it acquires. Suppose that S Ltd in the previous example has nil reserves, so that its share capital of £40,000 is balanced by net assets with a book value of £40,000. For simplicity, assume that the book value of S Ltd's assets is the same as their market or fair value.

Now when the directors of P Ltd agree to pay £60,000 for a 100% investment in S Ltd they must believe that, in addition to its tangible assets of £40,000, S Ltd must also have intangible assets worth £20,000. This amount of £20,000 paid over and above the value of the tangible assets acquired is called **goodwill arising on consolidation** (sometimes **premium on acquisition**).

Following the normal cancellation procedure the £40,000 share capital in S Ltd's balance sheet could be cancelled against £40,000 of the 'investment in S Limited' in the balance sheet of P Ltd. This would leave a £20,000 debit uncancelled in the parent company's accounts and this £20,000 would appear in the consolidated balance sheet under the caption 'Intangible fixed assets. Goodwill arising on consolidation' (although see below for FRS 10's requirements on this type of goodwill).

4.1 Goodwill and pre-acquisition profits

Up to now we have assumed that S Ltd had nil reserves when its shares were purchased by P Ltd. Assuming instead that S Ltd had earned profits of £8,000 in the period before acquisition, its balance sheet just before the purchase would look as follows.

	£
Net tangible assets	48,000
Share capital	40,000
Reserves	8,000
	48,000

If P Ltd now purchases all the shares in S Ltd it will acquire net tangible assets worth £48,000 at a cost of £60,000. Clearly in this case S Ltd's intangible assets (goodwill) are being valued at £12,000. It should be apparent that **any reserves earned by the subsidiary prior to its acquisition by the parent company must be incorporated in the cancellation process so as to arrive at a figure for goodwill arising on consolidation.** In other words, not only S Ltd's share capital, but also its pre-acquisition reserves, must be cancelled against the asset 'investment in S Ltd' in the accounts of the parent company. The uncancelled balance of £12,000 appears in the consolidated balance sheet.

The consequence of this is that any pre-acquisition reserves of a subsidiary company are not aggregated with the parent company's reserves in the consolidated balance sheet. **The figure of consolidated reserves comprises the reserves of the parent company plus the post-acquisition reserves only of**

subsidiary companies. **The post-acquisition reserves are simply reserves at the consolidation date less reserves at acquisition.**

4.2 Example: goodwill and pre-acquisition profits

Pace Ltd acquired the ordinary shares of Speed Ltd on 31 March when the draft balance sheets of each company were as follows.

PACE LIMITED
BALANCE SHEET AS AT 31 MARCH

	£
Fixed assets	
Investment in 50,000 shares of Speed Ltd at cost	80,000
Net current assets	40,000
	120,000
Capital and reserves	
Ordinary shares	75,000
Revenue reserves	45,000
	120,000

SPEED LIMITED
BALANCE SHEET AS AT 31 MARCH

	£
Net current assets	60,000
Share capital and reserves	
50,000 ordinary shares of £1 each	50,000
Revenue reserves	10,000
	60,00

Prepare the consolidated balance sheet as at 31 March.

Solution

The technique to adopt here is to produce a new working: 'Goodwill'. A proforma working is set out below.

Goodwill

	£	£
Cost of investment		X
Share of net assets acquired as represented by:		
Ordinary share capital	X	
Share premium	X	
Reserves on acquisition	X	
Group share	a%	(X)
		X
b% preference shares		(X)
Goodwill		

Applying this to our example the working will look like this.

	£	£
Cost of investment		80,000
Share of net assets acquired as represented by:		
Ordinary share capital	50,000	
Revenue reserves on acquisition	10,000	
	60,000	
Group share 100%		60,000
Goodwill		20,000

PACE LIMITED
CONSOLIDATED BALANCE SHEET AS AT 31 MARCH

	£
Fixed assets	20,000
Goodwill arising on consolidation	100,000
Net current assets	120,000
Capital and reserves	
Ordinary shares	75,000
Revenue reserves	45,000
	120,000

4.3 FRS 10 Goodwill and intangible assets

Goodwill arising on consolidation is one form of **purchased goodwill**, and is therefore governed by FRS 10. As explained in an earlier chapter FRS 10 requires that purchased goodwill should be capitalised and classified as an asset on the balance sheet. It is then eliminated from the accounts by **amortisation** through the profit and loss account.

A consolidation adjustment will be required each year as follows.

DEBIT	Consolidated P&L account
CREDIT	Provision for amortisation of goodwill

The **unamortised portion** will be included in the consolidated balance sheet under **fixed assets**.

Goodwill arising on consolidation is the difference between the cost of an acquisition and the value of the subsidiary's net assets acquired. This difference can be **negative**: the aggregate of the fair values of the separable net assets acquired may exceed what the holding company paid for them. This 'negative goodwill', also sometimes called 'discount arising on consolidation', is required by FRS 10 to be disclosed in the intangible fixed assets category, directly under positive goodwill, ie as a 'negative asset'

5 Inter-company trading

FAST FORWARD

Where **inter-company trading** has taken place and goods which have been sold at a profit by one group company are still held in stock by another group company, an adjustment must be made to remove the element of **unrealised profit**. The entry will be: **DR Group reserves CR Group stock**. A similar adjustment is made to account for inter-company sales of fixed assets.

We have already come across cases where one company in a group engages in trading with another group company. Any debtor/creditor balances outstanding between the companies are cancelled on consolidation. No further problem arises if all such intra-group transactions are undertaken at cost, without any mark-up for profit.

However, each company in a group is a separate trading entity and may wish to treat other group companies in the same way as any other customer. In this case, a company (say A Ltd) may buy goods at one price and sell them at a higher price to another group company (B Ltd). The accounts of A Ltd will quite properly include the profit earned on sales to B Ltd; and similarly B Ltd's balance sheet will include stocks at their cost to B Ltd at the amount at which they were purchased from A Ltd.

This gives rise to **two problems**.

(a)   Although A Ltd makes a profit as soon as it sells goods to B Ltd, the group does not make a sale or achieve a profit until an outside customer buys the goods from B Ltd.

(b)   Any purchases from A Ltd which remain unsold by B Ltd at the year end will be included in B Ltd's stock. Their balance sheet value will be their cost to B Ltd, which is not the same as their cost to the group.

The objective of consolidated accounts is to present the financial position of several connected companies as that of a single entity, the group. This means that **in a consolidated balance sheet the only profits recognised should be those earned by the group** in providing goods or services to outsiders; and similarly, stock in the consolidated balance sheet should be valued at cost to the group.

Suppose that a parent company P Ltd buys goods for £1,600 and sells them to a wholly owned subsidiary S Ltd for £2,000. The goods are in S Ltd's stock at the year end and appear in S Ltd's balance sheet at £2,000. In this case, P Ltd will record a profit of £400 in its individual accounts, but from the group's point of view the figures are:

Cost	£1,600
External sales	nil
Closing stock at cost	£1,600
Profit/loss	nil

If we add together the figures for retained reserves and stock in the individual balance sheets of P Ltd and S Ltd the resulting figures for consolidated reserves and consolidated stock will each be overstated by £400. A **consolidation adjustment** is therefore necessary as follows.

DEBIT   **Group reserves**
CREDIT   **Group stock (balance sheet)**

with the amount of profit unrealised by the group.

Question   Consolidated balance sheet 3

Pasta Ltd acquired all the shares in Spaghetti Ltd when the reserves of Spaghetti Ltd stood at £10,000. Draft balance sheets for each company are as follows.

	Pasta Ltd		Spaghetti Ltd	
	£	£	£	£
Fixed assets				
Tangible assets		80,000		40,000
Investment in Spaghetti Ltd at cost		46,000		
		126,000		
Current assets	40,000		30,000	
Current liabilities	21,000		18,000	
		19,000		12,000
		145,000		
				52,000
Capital and reserves				
Ordinary shares of £1 each		100,000		30,000
Reserves		45,000		22,000
		145,000		
				52,000

During the year Spaghetti Ltd sold goods to Pasta Ltd for £50,000, the profit to Spaghetti Ltd being 20% of selling price. At the balance sheet date, £15,000 of these goods remained unsold in the stocks of Pasta Ltd. At the same date, Pasta Ltd owed Spaghetti Ltd £12,000 for goods bought and this debt is included in the creditors of Pasta Ltd and the debtors of Spaghetti Ltd.

Note. Goodwill is deemed to have an indefinite useful life and is therefore to remain in the balance sheet.

Required

Prepare a draft consolidated balance sheet for Pasta Ltd.

Answer

1	Goodwill	£	£
	Cost of investment		46,000
	Share of net assets acquired as represented by		
	Share capital	30,000	
	Reserves	10,000	
		40,000	
	Group share (100%)		40,000
	Goodwill		6,000

2	Reserves	Pasta Ltd	Spaghetti Ltd
		£	£
	As per question	45,000	22,000
	Pre acquisition		(10,000)
			12,000
	Pasta share in Spaghetti (100%)	12,000	
	Unrealised profit in stock £5,000 × 20%	(3,000)	
	Group reserves	54,000	

PASTA LIMITED
CONSOLIDATED BALANCE SHEET

	£	£
Intangible fixed assets: goodwill		6,000
Tangible fixed assets		120,000
		126,000
Current assets (W1)	55,000	
Current liabilities (W2)	27,000	
		28,000
		154,000
Capital and reserves		
Ordinary shares of £1 each		100,000
Reserves		54,000
		154,000

Workings

1	*Current assets*	£	£
	In Pasta Ltd's balance sheet		40,000
	In Spaghetti Ltd's balance sheet	30,000	
	Spaghetti Ltd's current account with Pasta Ltd cancelled	(12,000)	
			18,000
			58,000
	Unrealised profit excluded from stock valuation		(3,000)
			55,000

BPP PROFESSIONAL EDUCATION

	£
2 *Current liabilities*	
In Pasta Ltd's balance sheet	21,000
Less Pasta Ltd's current account with Spaghetti Ltd cancelled	12,000
	9,000
In Spaghetti Ltd's balance sheet	18,000
	27,000

5.1 Minority interests in unrealised inter-company profits

A further problem occurs where a subsidiary company which is not wholly owned is involved in inter-company trading within the group. If a subsidiary S Ltd is 75% owned and sells goods to the parent company for £16,000 cost plus £4,000 profit, ie for £20,000 and if these stocks are unsold by P Ltd at the balance sheet date, the 'unrealised' profit of £4,000 earned by S Ltd and charged to P Ltd will be partly owned by the minority interest of S Ltd. As far as the minority interest of S Ltd is concerned, their share (25% of £4,000) amounting to £1,000 of profit on the sale of goods would appear to have been fully realised. It is only the group that has not yet made a profit on the sale.

There are three different possibilities as regards the treatment of these inter-company profits.
Remove:

(a)   **Only** the **group's share** of the profit loading.

(b)   The **whole profit loading**, charging the **minority** with their **proportion**.

(c)   The **whole of the profit** without charging the minority (to **reduce group reserves** by the whole profit loading).

However, FRS 2 does not support the old approach. Instead FRS 2 requires elimination in full.

Basic requirement

> The elimination of profits or losses relating to inter-group transactions should be set against the interests held by the group and the minority interest in **respective proportion** to their **holdings in the undertaking whose individual statements record the eliminated profits or losses.**

The FRS 2 indicates two scenarios regarding unrealised profits in closing stocks.

(a)   **Parent sold the stock to subsidiary.** The **unrealised profits sits in the parent's records** and relates to the **whole group**. Therefore the **entire unrealised profit** is **eliminated** from parent's accounts.

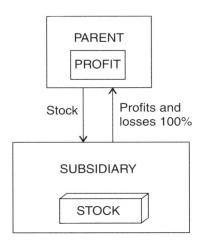

Profit sits in the parent and is attributable to its shareholders. Therefore eliminate 100% of unrealised profit against group profits.

(b)   **Subsidiary sold the stock to the parent**. The **unrealised profit sits in the subsidiary's** records and relates to the subsidiary. Hence, the **minority** will have to **bear** its **share** of the elimination.

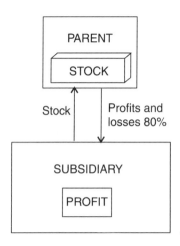

> Minority shares in 20% profits and losses of subsidiary. Therefore minority must suffer its 20% share of the elimination of unrealised profit, with balance 80% borne by the group.

5.2 Example: minority interests and inter-company profits

Pie Ltd has owned 75% of the shares of Sandwich Ltd since the incorporation of that company. Draft balance sheets of each company at 31 December 20X4 were as follows.

	Pie Limited		Sandwich Limited	
Fixed assets	£	£	£	£
Tangible assets		125,000		120,000
Investment: 75,000 shares in Sandwich Ltd				
at cost		75,000		–
		200,000		120,000
Current assets				
Stocks	50,000		48,000	
Trade debtors	20,000		16,000	
	70,000		64,000	
Creditors	40,000		24,000	
		30,000		40,000
		230,000		160,000
Capital and reserves				
Ordinary shares of £1 each fully paid		80,000		100,000
Reserves		150,000		60,000
		230,000		160,000

Prepare the draft consolidated balance sheet of Pie Ltd where during the year:

(a)   Pie Ltd sold goods costing £16,000 to Sandwich at a price of £20,000 and these goods were still unsold at the year end.

(b)   Sandwich Ltd sold the goods to Pie Ltd instead.

Solution

(a)   PIE LTD CONSOLIDATED BALANCE SHEET AS AT 31 DECEMBER 20X4

	£	£
Tangible fixed assets		245,000
Current assets		
Stocks (50,000 + 48,000 – 4,000)	94,000	
Trade debtors	36,000	
	130,000	
Creditors	64,000	
Net current assets		66,000
		311,000
Capital and reserves		
Ordinary shares of £1 each		80,000
Reserves (W3)		191,000
Shareholders' funds		271,000
Minority interest (W2)		40,000
		311,000

Workings

1   The unrealised profit sitting in Pie Ltd's books is £4,000. This relates to the group and should be eliminated in full from the group accounts.

2   *Minority interests in Sandwich*

	£
Share capital	100,000
Reserves	60,000
	160,000
Minority share (25%)	40,000

2   *Goodwill*

	£	£
Cost of investment in Sandwich	75,000	
Net assets of Sandwich at acquisition		
Share capital	100,000	
Pre-acquisition reserves (W3)	60,000	
	100,000	
Group share	75%	75,000
Goodwill arising on acquisition		NIL

3   *Group reserves*

	Pie Ltd £	Sandwich Ltd £
As per accounts	150,000	60,000
Pre-acquisition profit (W2)		–
		60,000
Group share in Sandwich Ltd (60,000 × 75%)	45,000	
Elimination of unrealised profit in stocks		
(20,000 – 16,000) (W1)	(4,000)	
	191,000	

(b)   PIE LIMITED
CONSOLIDATED BALANCE SHEET AS AT 31 DECEMBER 20X4

	£	£
Tangible fixed assets		245,000
Current assets		
Stocks £(50,000 + 48,000 – 4,000)	94,000	
Trade debtors	36,000	
	130,000	
Creditors	64,000	
Net current assets		66,000
		311,000
Capital and reserves		
Ordinary shares of £1 each		80,000
Reserves (W3)		192,000
Shareholders' funds		272,000
Minority interest (W2)		39,000
		311,000

Workings

1   The unrealised profit of £4,000 sits in the books of Sandwich Ltd, a subsidiary. This relates to both the group and also the minority shareholders of Sandwich Ltd. The group as well as the minority must suffer their appropriate share of the elimination of unrealised profit.

2   *Goodwill*

	£	£
Cost of investment in Sandwich	75,000	
Net assets of Sandwich at acquisition		
Share capital	100,000	
Pre-acquisition reserves (W3)	60,000	
	100,000	
Group share	75%	75,000
Goodwill arising on acquisition		NIL

3   *Group reserves*

	Pie Ltd £	Sandwich Ltd £
As per accounts	150,000	60,000
Pre-acquisition profit (W2)		–
Unrealised profit in stocks (20,000 – 16,000) (W1)		(4,000)
		56,000
Group share in Sandwich Ltd (56,000 × 75%)	42,000	
	192,000	

Note: Compare these workings with those for scenario (a).

Exam focus point

Adjustment for unrealised profit in stock is a hardy perennial in Paper 2.5 exams. Make sure you identify which direction the sale is made, the profit involved and how much is left on hand at year end. Most importantly, be careful to identify correctly whether the profit sits in the parent or in a subsidiary.

6 Inter-company sales of fixed assets

As well as engaging in trading activities with each other, **group companies** may on occasion wish to **transfer fixed assets.** In their individual accounts the companies concerned will treat the transfer just like a sale between unconnected parties:

- The **selling company** will record a profit or loss on sale;

- The **purchasing company** will record the asset at the **amount paid** to acquire it
- That amount paid will be used as the basis for calculating **depreciation**

On **consolidation**, the usual **'group entity' principle** applies. The consolidated balance sheet must show **assets** at their **cost to the group**, and any depreciation charged must be based on that cost. Two consolidation adjustments will usually be needed to achieve this.

(a)   An **adjustment** to alter **reserves** and **fixed assets** cost so as to **remove** any element of **unrealised profit or loss**. This is **similar** to the adjustment required in respect of **unrealised profit in stock**.

(b)   An **adjustment** to alter **reserves** and **accumulated depreciation** is made so that **consolidated depreciation** is based on the asset's **cost to the group**.

In practice this can be done simply by one journal entry. The **net** unrealised profit (total profit on the sale less cumulative 'excess' depreciation charges) is eliminated from the carrying amount of the asset and from the profit of the company making the sale.

6.1 Example: parent sells fixed asset to subsidiary

- Potato Ltd owns 60% of Shallot Ltd
- On 1 January 20X8 Potato Ltd sells goods costing £10,000 to Shallot Ltd for £12,500
- Shallot Ltd uses these goods as fixed assets
- Depreciation is 10% straight line.

Identify the necessary consolidation adjustments.

Solution

The **net** unrealised profit is £2,250. (£2,500 unrealised profit less £250 excess depreciation.) This is adjusted as follows:

	Dr £	Cr £
Fixed assets		2,250
Profit and loss account – Potato	2,250	

Note that the value of the fixed asset in the group accounts now becomes:

	£
Sale value	12,500
Net unrealised profit	(2,250)
Depreciation (in Shallot's books)	(1,250)
	9,000

This would have been the carrying value of the asset if it has been transferred at cost (£10,000) and depreciated at 10%.

6.2 Example: subsidiary sells fixed asset to parent

- Parmesan Ltd owns 60% of Stilton Ltd
- On 1 January 20X8, Stilton Ltd sells goods costing £10,000 to Parmesan Ltd for £12,500
- Parmesan Ltd uses these goods as fixed assets
- Depreciation is at 10% straight line

Identify the necessary consolidation adjustments.

Solution

	Dr £	Cr £
Fixed assets		2,250
Profit and loss account – Stilton	2,250	

Note that, as the net unrealised profit has been debited to the profit and loss account of the subsidiary, part of this cost will be borne by the minority.

7 Summary: consolidated balance sheet

Purpose	To show the net assets which P controls and the ownership of those assets.
Net assets	Always 100% P plus 100% S providing P holds a majority of voting rights.
Share capital	P only.
Reason	Simply reporting to the holding company's shareholders in another form.
Reserves	100% P plus group share of post-acquisition retained reserves of S less consolidation adjustments.
Reason	To show the extent to which the group actually owns net assets included in the top half of the balance sheet.
Minority interest	MI share of S's consolidated net assets.
Reason	To show the extent to which other parties own net assets that are under the control of the holding company.

Exam focus point

The June 2002 exam tested the related party implications of a parent company and wholly owned subsidiary undertaking relationship.

The December 2002 group accounts paper involved:

(a) Acquisition of the subsidiary part way through the year
(b) Dealing with fair value adjustments on fixed assets
(c) Consideration involving share for share exchange
(d) Deferred taxation

Chapter Roundup

- The preparation of a consolidated balance sheet, in a very simple form, consists of two procedures.

  - Take the individual accounts of the holding company and each subsidiary and **cancel out items which appear as an asset in one company and a liability in another**.

  - **Add together** all the **uncancelled** assets and liabilities throughout the group.

- Where the parent does not own 100% of the shares in the subsidiary, the other shares are held by **minority** shareholders. The proportion of share capital and reserves attributable to this **minority interest** must be shown in the consolidated balance sheet.

- When dealing with dividends paid by a subsidiary, make sure that the entry ahs been made in the accounts of both the **paying** company and the **receiving** company.

- When a company acquires shares in another company for an amount which exceeds the value of that proportion of the fair value of its assets, it has paid a 'premium', which is called **goodwill**. This appears as an **intangible fixed asset** in the consolidated balance sheet and is then **amortised** over its useful life.

- Where **inter-company trading** has taken place and goods which have been sold at a profit by one group company are still held in stock by another group company, an adjustment must be made to remove the element of **unrealised profit**. The entry will be: **DR Group reserves CR Group stock**. A similar adjustment is made to account for inter-company sales of fixed assets.

Quick Quiz

1   What are the components making up the figure of minority interest in a consolidated balance sheet?

2   The following diagram shows the structure of the Aubergine group.

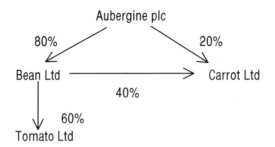

Which are the subsidiaries of Aubergine plc?

A   Bean Ltd
B   Bean Ltd and Tomato Ltd
C   Bean Ltd and Carrot Ltd
D   Bean Ltd, Tomato Ltd and Carrot Ltd

3   Goodwill is always positive. True or false?

4   The following figures relate to Phlox plc and its subsidiary Spirea Ltd for the year ended 31 December 20X9.

	Phlox plc £	Spirea Ltd £
Turnover	600,000	300,000
Cost of sales	(400,000)	(200,000)
Gross profit	200,000	100,000

During the year, Phlox plc sold goods to Spirea Ltd for £20,000 making a profit of £5,000. These goods were all sold by Spirea Ltd before the year end.

What are the amounts for turnover and gross profit in the consolidated profit and loss accounts of Phlox plc for the year ended 31 December 20X9?

BPP
PROFESSIONAL EDUCATION

Answers to Quick Quiz

1   The minority's share of ordinary shares, preference shares and reserves.

2   D   Aubergine has control over Bean's 40% holding in Carrot and has a 20% direct holding. Thus Carrot is a subsidiary.

3   False. Goodwill can be negative if the purchaser has 'got a bargain'.

4
	£
Turnover (600 + 300 – 20)	880
Cost of sales (400 +200 – 20)	580
Gross profit	300

To get you started, the question recommended is rather easier than you could expect in an exam

Number	Level	Marks	Time
Q18	Introductory	n/a	36 mins

Acquisition of subsidiaries

Topic list	Syllabus reference
1 Acquisition of a subsidiary during its accounting period	4 (c)
2 Dividends and pre-acquisition profits	4 (c)
3 FRS 7 *Fair values in acquisition accounting*	4 (c)

Introduction

This chapter deals with the problems associated with the consolidation of a subsidiary acquired during the accounting period (a fairly common occurrence).

Chapter 16 covers the consolidated profit and loss account and Chapter 17 deals with accounting for associated undertakings.

Study guide

- Explain the nature of a dividend paid out of pre-acquisition profits.

- Explain why it is necessary for both the consideration paid for a subsidiary and the subsidiary's identifiable assets and liabilities to be accounted for at their fair values when preparing consolidated financial statements.

- Prepare consolidated financial statements dealing with the fair value adjustments (including their effect on consolidated goodwill) in respect of:

    - depreciating and non-depreciating fixed assets

    - stocks

    - monetary liabilities (basic discounting techniques may be required)

    - assets and liabilities (including contingencies) not included in the subsidiary's own balance sheet.

Exam guide

You will not understand the rest of the chapters on consolidation unless you grasp the principles laid out in this chapter. You should pay particular attention to the determination of pre- and post-acquisition profits and the effect of dividends in Section 2.

1 Acquisition of a subsidiary during its accounting period

FAST FORWARD

When a subsidiary is acquired **during its accounting period**, it will be necessary to distinguish between **pre-acquisition** and **post-acquisition** profits.

In the absence of information to the contrary, the profits earned during the period may be assumed to have **accrued evenly** and should be allocated accordingly.

Exam focus point

The December 2002 and June 2003 papers involved an acquisition of a subsidiary part way through a year. This is a popular requirement favoured by examiners. If necessary, draw a time line to help you picture what happened when.

When a holding company acquires a subsidiary during its accounting period the only accounting entries will be those recording the cost of acquisition in the holding company's books. As we have already seen, at the end of the accounting year it will be necessary to prepare consolidated accounts.

The subsidiary company's accounts to be consolidated will show the subsidiary's profit or loss for the whole year. **For consolidation** purposes, however, it will be necessary to **distinguish between:**

(a) **Profits earned before acquisition**
(b) **Profits earned after acquisition**

In practice, a subsidiary company's profit may not accrue evenly over the year; for example, the subsidiary might be engaged in a trade, such as toy sales, with marked seasonal fluctuations. Nevertheless, statute permits the **assumption** to be made **that profits accrue evenly** whenever it is impracticable to arrive at an accurate split of pre- and post-acquisition profits.

Once the amount of pre-acquisition profit has been established the appropriate consolidation workings (goodwill, reserves) can be produced.

Bear in mind that **in calculating minority interests the distinction between pre- and post-acquisition profits is irrelevant.** The minority shareholders are simply credited with their share of the subsidiary's total reserves at the balance sheet date.

It is worthwhile to summarise what happens on consolidation to the reserves figures extracted from a subsidiary's balance sheet. Suppose the accounts of S Ltd, a 60% subsidiary of P Ltd, show reserves of £20,000 at the balance sheet date, of which £14,000 were earned prior to acquisition. The figure of £20,000 will appear in the consolidated balance sheet as follows.

	£
Minority interests working: their share of total reserves at balance sheet date (40% × £20,000)	8,000
Goodwill working: group share of pre-acquisition profits (60% × £14,000)	8,400
Consolidated reserves working: group share of post-acquisition profits (60% × £6,000)	3,600
	20,000

Question
Consolidated balance sheet

Prawn Ltd acquired 80% of the ordinary shares of Shrimp Ltd on 1 April 20X5. On 31 December 20X4 Shrimp Ltd's accounts showed a share premium account of £4,000 and revenue reserves of £15,000. The balance sheets of the two companies at 31 December 20X5 are set out below. Neither company has paid dividends during the year.

You are required to prepare the consolidated balance sheet of Prawn Ltd at 31 December 20X5.

Note. Goodwill is to be amortised over 25 years. A full year's amortisation is charged in the year of acquisition.

PRAWN LIMITED
BALANCE SHEET AS AT 31 DECEMBER 20X5

	£
Fixed assets	
Tangible assets	32,000
16,000 ordinary shares of 50p each in Shrimp Ltd	50,000
	82,000
Net current assets	65,000
	147,000
Ordinary shares of £1 each	100,000
Share premium account	7,000
Revenue reserves	40,000
	147,000

SHRIMP LIMITED
BALANCE SHEET AS AT 31 DECEMBER 20X5

	£
Tangible fixed assets	30,000
Net current assets	23,000
	53,000
Capital and reserves	
20,000 ordinary shares of 50p each	10,000
Share premium account	4,000
Revenue reserves	39,000
	53,000

Answer

Shrimp Ltd has made a profit of £24,000 (£39,000 – £15,000) for the year. In the absence of any direction to the contrary, this should be assumed to have arisen evenly over the year; £6,000 in the three months to 31 March and £18,000 in the nine months after acquisition. The company's pre-acquisition revenue reserves are therefore as follows.

	£
Balance at 31 December 20X4	15,000
Profit for three months to 31 March 20X5	6,000
Pre-acquisition revenue reserves	21,000

The balance of £4,000 on share premium account is all pre-acquisition.

The consolidation workings can now be drawn up.

1   *Minority interest*

	£
Ordinary share capital (20% × £10,000)	2,000
Revenue reserves (20% × £39,000)	7,800
(pre-acquisition)	
Share premium (20% × £4,000)	800
	10,600

2   *Goodwill*

	£	£
Cost of investment		50,000
Share of net assets acquired		
represented by		
Ordinary share capital	10,000	
Revenue reserves (pre-acquisition) (W3)	21,000	
Share premium	4,000	
	35,000	
Group share (80%)		28,000
Goodwill		22,000
Amortisation (22,000 ÷ 25 (W3)		880
Unamortised goodwill		21,200

3   *Revenue reserves*

	Prawn Ltd	*Shrimp Ltd*
	£	£
As per question	40,000	39,000
Pre-acquisition reserves (W2)		21,000
		18,000

Group share in Shrimp Ltd post-acquisition reserves (18,000 × 80%)		14,400
Amortisation of goodwill in Shrimp Ltd (W2)		(880)
Group revenue reserves		53,520

4   *Share premium account*

	£
Prawn Ltd	7,000

PRAWN LIMITED
CONSOLIDATED BALANCE SHEET AS AT 31 DECEMBER 20X5

	£
Intangible fixed assets: goodwill	21,120
Tangible fixed assets	62,000
Net current assets	88,000
	171,120
Capital and reserves	
Ordinary shares of £1 each	100,000
Reserves	
Share premium account	7,000
Revenue reserves	53,520
Shareholders' funds	160,520
Minority interest	10,600
	171,120

Exam focus point

The examiner has commented in the past that candidates have often made the mistake of showing the share premium of the subsidiary together with the parent company share premium. This must always be set off against the cost of investment or allocated accordingly to minority interest.

1.1 Example: pre-acquisition losses of a subsidiary

As an illustration of the entries arising when a subsidiary has pre-acquisition *losses*, suppose P Ltd acquired all 50,000 £1 ordinary shares in S Ltd for £20,000 on 1 January 20X1 when there was a debit balance of £35,000 on S Ltd's revenue reserves. In the years 20X1 to 20X4 S Ltd makes profits of £40,000 in total, leaving a credit balance of £5,000 on revenue reserves at 31 December 20X4. P Ltd's reserves at the same date are £70,000. Any goodwill is deemed to have an indefinite useful life and should be held in the balance sheet.

The consolidation workings would appear as follows.

1   *Goodwill*

	£	£
Cost of investment		20,000
Share of net assets acquired as represented by		
Ordinary share capital	50,000	
Pre-acquisition revenue reserves (W2)	(35,000)	
	15,000	
Group share (100%)		15,000
Goodwill		5,000

2   *Revenue reserve*

	P Ltd £	S Ltd £
As per question	70,000	5,000
Pre-acquisition debit balance 1.1.X1 (W1)		35,000
		40,000
Group share in S Ltd (40,000 × 100%)	40,000	
Group reserves	110,000	

2 Dividends and pre-acquisition profits

FAST FORWARD

Dividends paid by a subsidiary to its parent company may only be **credited to the parent's profit and loss account** to the extent that they are paid from **post-acquisition profits**.

Dividends received by the holding company **from pre-acquisition profits** should be credited to 'investment in subsidiary' account and treated as **reducing the cost of the shares** acquired.

A further problem in consolidation occurs when a subsidiary pays out a dividend soon after acquisition. The holding company, as a member of the subsidiary, is entitled to its share of the dividends paid but it is necessary to decide whether or not these dividends come out of the pre-acquisition profits of the subsidiary.

If the dividends come from post-acquisition profits there is no problem. **The holding company simply credits the relevant amount to its own profit and loss account**, as with any other dividend income. The double entry is **quite different**, however, **if the dividend is paid from pre-acquisition profits**, being as follows.

DEBIT	**Cash**
CREDIT	**Investment in subsidiary**

The holding company's balance sheet would then disclose the investment as 'Investment in subsidiary at cost less amounts written down'.

It is **very important that you are clear about the reason for this**. Consider the following balance sheets of S_1 Ltd and S_2 Ltd as at 31 March 20X4.

	S_1 Ltd £	S_2 Ltd £
Current assets	30,000	30,000
Current liabilities	10,000	10,000
Ordinary shareholders' funds	20,000	20,000

Both companies have goodwill, not reflected in the books, valued at £5,000 and are identical in every respect, except that the current liabilities of S_1 Ltd are trade creditors while the current liabilities of S_2 Ltd are a proposed ordinary dividend.

P_1 Ltd, a prospective purchaser of S_1 Ltd, is willing to pay £25,000 for 100% of S_1, including goodwill. P_2 Ltd, a prospective purchaser of S_2 Ltd, will clearly be willing to pay £35,000 for the acquisition of that company in the knowledge that £10,000 of the cost will immediately be 'refunded' by way of dividend.

Assume that the two purchases are completed on 31 March 20X4 and on 1 April 20X4 S_1 Ltd and S_2 Ltd pay off their current liabilities as appropriate. P_1 and P_2 will then own identical investments, each consisting of £20,000 of current assets plus £5,000 of goodwill, and it is clearly appropriate that the investment figures in their own balance sheets should be identical. This will be the case if P_2 Ltd sets off the £10,000 dividend receivable against the £35,000 cost of the acquisition, disclosing the investment in S_2 at a net cost of £25,000.

The point to grasp is that P$_2$ Ltd cannot credit the dividend to profit because no profit has been made. The correct way of looking at it is to say that P$_2$ Ltd was willing to pay 'over the odds' for its investment in the presumption that a part of its cost would immediately be repaid. When the dividend is paid, this presumption must be pursued to its conclusion by treating the dividend as a reduction of the cost of the investment.

Note.

Proposed dividends are no longer accounted for as current liabilities or shown on the face of the profit and loss account, so the scenario above is not realistic. What would happen in practice is that the notes to the accounts would detail the proposed dividend.

However, the S$_1$, S$_2$ example does illustrate the rationale behind treating a dividend paid out of pre-acquisition profits as a reduction in the cost of the investment.

This accounting treatment used to be a legal requirement but is not *required* by the CA 1985 (or any current SSAP or FRS). However, it **must be considered best practice.**

2.1 Example: dividends and pre-acquisition profits

Planet Ltd acquired 8,000 of the 10,000 £1 ordinary shares of Star Ltd on 1 January 20X5 for £25,000. Star Ltd's balance sheet at 31 December 20X4 showed retained reserves of £12,000. The balance sheets of the two companies at 31 December 20X5 are given below. During 20X5 Star Ltd paid a dividend of £4,000.

PLANET LIMITED
BALANCE SHEET AS AT 31 DECEMBER 20X5

	£
Fixed assets	
Tangible assets	35,000
Investment in Star Ltd at cost less	
amounts written down	21,800
	56,800
Net current assets	27,000
	83,800
Capital and reserves	
Ordinary shares of £1 each	50,000
Retained reserves	33,800
	83,800

STAR LIMITED
BALANCE SHEET AS AT 31 DECEMBER 20X5

	£
Tangible fixed assets	14,500
Net current assets	12,500
	27,000
Capital and reserves	
Ordinary shares of £1 each	10,000
Retained reserves	17,000
	27,000

Required

Prepare the consolidated balance sheet of Planet Ltd at 31 December 20X5.

Note. Goodwill is deemed to have a useful life of 10 years and is therefore to be amortised over that period.

Solution

During the year Star Ltd has paid £4,000 dividend. This will be paid out of profits earned in 20X4. Planet Ltd's share (80% × £4,000 = £3,200) has been correctly credited by that company to its 'investment in Star Ltd' account. That account appears in the books of Planet Ltd as follows.

INVESTMENT IN STAR LIMITED

	£		£
Bank: purchase of 8,000		Bank: dividend received from	
£1 ordinary shares	25,000	pre-acquisition profits	3,200
		Balance c/f	21,800
	25,000		25,000

If Planet Ltd had incorrectly credited the pre-acquisition dividend to its own profit and loss account, it would have been necessary to make the following adjustments in Planet Ltd's accounts before proceeding to the consolidation.

DEBIT	Retained reserves	£3,200
CREDIT	Investment in Star Ltd	£3,200

This procedure is sometimes necessary in examination questions.

The consolidation workings can be drawn up as follows.

1   *Minority interest*

	£
Share capital (20% × £10,000)	2,000
Reserves (20% × £17,000)	3,400
	5,400

2   *Goodwill*

	£	£
Cost of investment		25,000
Share of pre-acquisition dividend (80% × £4,000)		(3,200)
		21,800
Share of net assets acquired as represented by		
Ordinary share capital	10,000	
Pre-acquisition reserves	12,000	
	22,000	
Group share (80%)		(17,600)
Goodwill		4,200
Amortisation (4,200 ÷ 10)		(420)
Unamortised goodwill		3,780

3   *Reserves*

	Planet Ltd £	Star Ltd £
As per question	33,800	17,000
Pre-acquisition reserves		(12,000)
		5,000
Group share in Star Ltd (5,000 × 80%)	4,000	
Goodwill amortisation (W2)	(420)	
Group reserves	37,380	

BPP
PROFESSIONAL EDUCATION

PLANET LIMITED
CONSOLIDATED BALANCE SHEET AS AT 31 DECEMBER 20X5

	£
Intangible fixed assets	3,780
Tangible fixed assets	49,500
Net current assets	39,500
	92,780
Capital and reserves	
Ordinary shares of £1 each	50,000
Retained reserves	37,380
Shareholders' funds	87,380
Minority interest	5,400
	92,780

The example above included an ordinary dividend paid from pre-acquisition profits. The treatment would be exactly the same if a **preference dividend** had been paid from pre-acquisition profits. Any share of such a preference dividend received by the holding company would be credited not to profit and loss account, but to the investment in subsidiary account.

2.2 Is the dividend paid from pre-acquisition profits?

We need next to consider how it is decided whether a dividend is paid from pre-acquisition profits. In the example above there was no difficulty: Planet Ltd acquired shares in Star Ltd on the first day of an accounting period and the dividend was in respect of the previous accounting period. Clearly, the dividend was paid from profits earned in the period before acquisition.

The position is less straightforward if shares are acquired during the subsidiary's accounting period. In this case, the dividend will have to be time-apportioned over the year.

3 FRS 7 Fair values in acquisition accounting

FAST FORWARD

Goodwill arising on consolidation is the difference between the purchase consideration and the **fair value** of net assets acquired. **Goodwill** should be calculated **after revaluing** the subsidiary company's assets. If the subsidiary does not incorporate the revaluation in its own accounts, it should be done as a **consolidation adjustment**. The accounting requirements and disclosures of the **fair value exercise** are covered by **FRS 7**.

FRS 10 *Goodwill and intangible assets* **defines goodwill as the difference between the purchase consideration paid by the acquiring company and the aggregate of the 'fair values' of the identifiable assets and liabilities acquired.** The balance sheet of a subsidiary company at the date it is acquired may not be a guide to the fair value of its net assets. For example, the market value of a freehold building may have risen greatly since it was acquired, but it may appear in the balance sheet at historical cost less accumulated depreciation.

Exam focus point

The group accounts question invariably includes a part dealing with fair value adjustments.

The December 2004 group accounts question included a fair value adjustment.

3.1 Fair value adjustment calculations

Until now we have calculated goodwill as the difference between the cost of the investment and the **book value** of net assets acquired by the group. If this calculation is to comply with the definition in FRS 10 we **must ensure that the book value of the subsidiary's net assets is the same as their fair value.**

There are **two possible ways** of achieving this.

(a)   **The subsidiary company might incorporate any necessary revaluations in its own books of account.** In this case, we can proceed directly to the consolidation, taking asset values and reserves figures straight from the subsidiary company's balance sheet.

(b)   **The revaluations may be made as a consolidation adjustment without being incorporated in the subsidiary company's books.** In this case, we must make the necessary adjustments to the subsidiary's balance sheet as a working. Only then can we proceed to the consolidation.

Note. Remember that when depreciating assets are revalued there may be a corresponding alteration in the amount of depreciation charged and accumulated.

3.2 Example: fair value adjustments

Panache Ltd acquired 75% of the ordinary shares of Style Ltd on 1 September 20X5. At that date the fair value of Style Ltd's fixed assets was £23,000 greater than their net book value, and the balance of retained profits was £21,000. The balance sheets of both companies at 31 August 20X6 are given below. Style Ltd has not incorporated any revaluation in its books of account.

PANACHE LIMITED
BALANCE SHEET AS AT 31 AUGUST 20X6

	£
Fixed assets	
Tangible assets	63,000
Investment in Style Ltd at cost	51,000
	114,000
Net current assets	62,000
	176,000
Capital and reserves	
Ordinary shares of £1 each	80,000
Retained profits	96,000
	176,000

STYLE LIMITED
BALANCE SHEET AS AT 31 AUGUST 20X6

	£
Tangible fixed assets	28,000
Net current assets	33,000
	61,000
Capital and reserves	
Ordinary shares of £1 each	20,000
Retained profits	41,000
	61,000

If Style Ltd had revalued its fixed assets at 1 September 20X5, an addition of £3,000 would have been made to the depreciation charged in the profit and loss account for 20X5/X6.

Required

Prepare Panache Ltd's consolidated balance sheet as at 31 August 20X6.

Note. Goodwill is deemed to have a useful life of 5 years and is to be amortised over that period.

Solution

Style Ltd has not incorporated the revaluation in its draft balance sheet. Before beginning the consolidation workings we must therefore adjust the company's balance of profits at the date of acquisition and at the balance sheet date.

In the consolidated balance sheet, Style Ltd's fixed assets will appear at their revalued amount: £(28,000 + 23,000 − 3,000) = £48,000. The consolidation workings can now be drawn up.

1   *Minority interest*

	£
Share capital (25% × £20,000)	5,000
Revenue reserves (25% × £41,000)	10,250
Fair value adjustment less depreciation (25% × (23,000 − 3,000))	5,000
	20,250

2   *Goodwill*

	£	£
Cost of investment		51,000
Share of net assets acquired as represented by		
Ordinary share capital	20,000	
Revenue reserves (pre-acquisition) (W3)	21,000	
Fair value adjustment (W4)	23,000	
	64,000	
Group share (75%)		48,000
Goodwill		3,000
Amortisation (3,000 ÷ 5) (W3)		(600)
Unamortised goodwill		2,400

3   *Revenue reserves*

	Panache Ltd £	Style Ltd £
As per question	96,000	41,000
Pre-acquisition reserves (W2)		(21,000)
Depreciation on FV adjustment (W4)		(3,000)
		17,000
Group share in Style Ltd (17,000 × 75%)	12,750	
Goodwill amortisation (W2)	(600)	
Group revenue reserves	108,150	

4   *Fixed assets*

	£	£
Panache per accounts		63,000
Style		
Per accounts	28,000	
FV adjustment (W2)	23,000	
Depreciation adjustment (W3)	(3,000)	
		48,000
		111,000

PANACHE LIMITED CONSOLIDATED BALANCE SHEET AS AT 31 AUGUST 20X6

	£
Intangible fixed assets: goodwill (W2)	2,400
Tangible fixed assets £(63,000 + 48,000) (W4)	111,000
Net current assets	95,000
	208,400
Capital and reserves	
Ordinary shares of £1 each	80,000
Retained profits (W3)	108,150
Shareholders' funds	188,150
Minority interest (W1)	20,250
	208,400

Question
Fair value

An asset is recorded in Shark Ltd's books at its historical cost of £4,000. On 1 January 20X1 Porpoise Ltd bought 80% of Shark Ltd's equity. Its directors attributed a fair value of £3,000 to the asset as at that date. It had been depreciated for two years out of an expected life of four years on the straight line basis. There was no expected residual value. On 30 June 20X1 the asset was sold for £2,600. What is the profit or loss on disposal of this asset to be recorded in Shark Ltd's accounts and in Porpoise Ltd's consolidated accounts for the year ended 31 December 20X1?

Answer

Shark Ltd: NBV at disposal (at historical cost) = £4,000 × 1½/4 = £1,500

∴ Profit on disposal = £1,100 (depreciation charge for the year = £500)

Porpoise Ltd: NBV at disposal (at fair value) = £3,000 × 1½/2 = £2,250

∴ Profit on disposal for consolidation = £350 (depreciation for the year = £750). The minority would be credited with 20% of both items as part of the one line entry in the profit and loss account.

3.3 FRS 7 Fair values in acquisition accounting

FRS 7 and FRS 6 *Acquisitions and mergers* were published together in September 1994 in order to reform both acquisition and merger accounting practices.

Key term

The basic principles stated by FRS 7 are that:

(a)   **All identifiable assets and liabilities** should be **recognised** which are in existence **at the date of acquisition**.

(b)   Such recognised assets and liabilities should be **measured at fair values** which reflect the conditions existing at the date of acquisition.

Fair values should not reflect either the acquirer's intentions or events subsequent to the acquisition.

In addition any **changes** to the acquired assets and liabilities, and the resulting gains and losses, that arise **after control** of the acquired entity has passed to the acquirer should be reported as part of the **post-acquisition profits** of the group.

FRS 7 also sets out specific rules on how fair values should be determined for the main categories of asset and liability. The underlying principle remains that **fair values should reflect the price at which an asset or liability could be exchanged in an arm's length transaction.** For long-term monetary assets and liabilities, fair values may be derived by discounting.

The standard also describes how the value attributed to the consideration given for the acquisition should be determined, and the acquisition expenses that may be included as part of the cost.

3.4 Definitions

The following definitions are given by FRS 7. They are self explanatory except for the highlighted terms.

(a)   Acquisition
(b)   Business combination
(c)   Date of acquisition
(d)   **Fair value**

(e)   Identifiable assets and liabilities
(f)   **Recoverable amount**
(g)   **Value in use**

(a)   In particular note the definition of **fair value**: 'The amount at which an asset or liability could be exchanged in an arm's length transaction between informed and willing parties, other than in a forced or liquidation sale.'

(b)   **Recoverable amount** is the greater of the net realisable value of an asset and, when appropriate, the amount recoverable from its further use.

(c)   **Value in use** is the present value of the future cash flows obtainable as a result of an asset's continued use, including those resulting from the ultimate disposal of the asset.

3.5 Scope

FRS 7 applies to all financial statements that are intended to give a true and fair view. Although the FRS is framed in terms of the acquisition of a subsidiary undertaking by a parent company that prepares consolidated financial statements, it **also applies where an individual company entity acquires a business other than a subsidiary undertaking**. This last point means that companies cannot avoid the provisions of FRS 7 when taking over an unincorporated entity or joint venture vehicle.

3.6 Determining the fair values of identifiable assets and liabilities acquired

Most importantly, the FRS lists those **items which do not affect fair values** at the date of acquisition, and **which are therefore to be treated as post-acquisition items**:

(a)   Changes resulting from the **acquirer's intentions or future actions.**

(b)   **Impairments** or other changes, resulting from events subsequent to the acquisition.

(c)   **Provisions or accruals for future operating losses** or for reorganisation and integration costs expected to be incurred as a result of the acquisition, whether they relate to the acquired entity or to the acquirer.

3.6.1 Assessing fair value of major categories

In general terms, fair values should be determined in accordance with the acquirer's accounting policies for similar assets and liabilities. The standard does, however, go on to describe how the major categories of assets and liabilities should be assessed for fair values.

(a)   **Tangible assets: fair value based on:**

    (i)   **Market value**, if similar assets are sold on the open market.
    (ii) **Depreciated replacement cost**, reflecting normal business practice.

    However, **fair value ≤ replacement cost**.

(b)   **Intangible assets**, where recognised: **fair value should be based on replacement costs**, which will normally be estimated market value.

(c)   **Stocks and work in progress**

    (i)   For stocks which are replaced by purchasing in a **ready market** (commodities, dealing stock etc), the fair value is **market value**.

    (ii) For other stocks, with **no ready market** (most manufacturing stocks), fair value is represented by the **current cost** to the acquired company of reproducing the stocks.

(d)   **Quoted investments:** value at **market price**, adjusted where necessary for unusual price fluctuations or the size of the holding.

(e)   **Monetary assets and liabilities:** fair values should take into account the **amounts expected to be received or paid** and their timing. Reference should be made to market prices (where available) or to the current price if acquiring similar assets or entering into similar obligations, or to the discounted present value.

(f)   **Contingencies: reasonable estimates** of the expected outcome may be used.

(g)   **Pensions and other post-retirement benefits:** the **fair value of a deficiency, a surplus** (to the extent it is expected to be realised) or accrued obligation should be **recognised** as an asset/liability of the acquiring group. Any changes on acquisition should be treated as post-acquisition items.

(h)   **Deferred tax** recognised in a fair value exercise should be measured in accordance with the requirements of FRS 19 (see Chapter 8). Thus deferred tax would not be recognised on an adjustment to recognise a non-monetary asset acquired with the business at its fair value on acquisition.

3.7 Business sold or held with a view to subsequent resale

The fair value exercise for such an entity, 'sold as a single unit, within approximately one year of acquisition', should be carried out on the basis of a **single asset investment**.

'Its fair value should be based on the **net proceeds of the sale, adjusted for the fair value of any assets or liabilities transferred** into or out of the business, unless such adjusted net proceeds are demonstrably different from the fair value at the date of acquisition as a result of a post-acquisition event.'

Any relevant part of the business can be treated in this way if it is separately identifiable, ie it does not have to be a separate subsidiary undertaking.

Where the first financial statements after the date of acquisition come for approval, but the business has not been sold, the above treatment can still be applied if:

(a)   A purchaser has been identified or is being sought.
(b)   The disposal is expected to occur within one year of the date of acquisition.

The interest (or its assets) should be shown in current assets. On determination of the sales price, the original estimate of fair value should be adjusted to reflect the actual sales proceeds.

3.8 Investigation period and goodwill adjustments

FRS 7 states that:

'**The recognition and measurement of assets and liabilities acquired should be completed, if possible, by the date on which the first post-acquisition financial statements of the acquirer are approved by the directors.**'

Where this has not been possible, provisional valuations should be made, amended if necessary in the next financial statements with a corresponding adjustment to goodwill. Such adjustments should be incorporated into the financial statements in the full year following acquisition. After that, any adjustments (except for the correction of fundamental errors by prior year adjustment) should be recognised as profits or losses as they are identified.

3.9 Determining the fair value of purchase consideration

The cost of acquisition is the amount of cash paid and the fair value of other purchase consideration given by the acquirer, together with the expenses of the acquisition. Where a subsidiary undertaking is acquired in stages, the cost of acquisition is the total of the costs of the interests acquired, determined as at the date of each transaction.

The main likely components of purchase consideration are as follows.

    (a)   *Ordinary shares*

        (i)   **Quoted shares** should be valued at **market price** on the date of acquisition.

        (ii)   Where there is **no suitable market**, estimate the value using:

            (1)   The value of **similar quoted securities**
            (2)   The **present value of the future cash** flows of the instrument used
            (3)   Any **cash alternative** which was offered

    (b)   **Other securities:** the value should be based on similar principles to those given in (a).

    (c)   **Cash or monetary amounts:** value at the **amount paid or payable**.

    (d)   **Non-monetary assets:** value at **market price**, estimated realisable value, independent valuation or based on other available evidence.

    (e)   **Deferred consideration: discount** the amounts calculated on the above principles (in (a) to (d)). An appropriate discount rate is that which the acquirer could obtain for a similar borrowing.

    (f)   **Contingent consideration:** use the **probable** amount. When the actual amount is known, it should be recorded in the financial statements and goodwill adjusted accordingly.

Acquisition cost (the fees and expenses mentioned above) should be **included in the cost of the investment**. Internal costs and the costs of issuing capital instruments should *not* be capitalised, according to the provisions of FRS 4, ie they must be written off to the profit and loss account.

Exam focus point

> The June 2002 paper tested the application of FRS 7 *Fair values in acquisition accounting*. Candidates had to deal with a subsequent revision in value of assets and the consequential effects on goodwill amortisation.

3.10 Summary and assessment

The most important effect of FRS 7 is the ban it imposes on making provisions for future trading losses of acquired companies and the costs of any related rationalisation or reorganisation, unless outgoing management had already incurred those liabilities. This is a controversial area, demonstrated by the dissenting view of one member of the ASB.

Some commentators argued that the ASB's approach ignores the commercial reality of the transaction by treating as an expense the costs of reorganisation that the acquirer regards as part of the capital cost of the acquisition; and that within defined limits a provision for planned post-acquisition expenditure should be permitted to be included in the net assets acquired.

Case Study

The Hundred Group of finance directors gave an example. If you buy a house for, say £100,000 that you know needs £50,000 spent on it to bring it into good condition and make it equivalent to a property that sells for £150,000, then you would treat the £50,000 renovation expense as part of the cost of the house and not as part of ordinary outgoings. The group states that FRS 7 goes beyond standards set in other countries, including the US. It also recommends that abuses in this area should be dealt with by tightening existing accounting standards and through 'proper policing' by external auditors (the standard is seen to undermine the professional judgement of the auditor) and 'not by distorting accounting concepts'.

The ASB rejected this view, saying that an intention to incur revenue expenditure subsequent to the acquisition could not properly be regarded as a liability of the acquired business at the date of acquisition.

'Acquisition accounting should reflect the business that is acquired as it stands at the date of acquisition and ought not to take account of the changes that an acquirer might intend to make subsequently. Nor could the ASB accept the proposition that some of the inadequacies of the present system could be met by better disclosure. In the ASB's view deficient accounting cannot be put right by disclosure alone.'

This is still an open area of debate and you should keep track of the arguments in the financial and accountancy press.

Question   Goodwill

Prune plc prepares accounts to 31 December. On 1 September 20X7 Prune plc acquired 6 million £1 shares in Sultana plc at £2.00 per share. The purchase was financed by an additional issue of loan stock at an interest rate of 10%. At that date Sultana plc produced the following interim financial statements.

	£m		£m
Tangible fixed assets (note 1)	16.0	Trade creditors	3.2
Stocks (note 2)	4.0	Taxation	0.6
Debtors	2.9	Bank overdraft	3.9
Cash in hand	1.2	Long-term loans (note 6)	4.0
		Share capital (£1 shares)	8.0
		Profit and loss account	4.4
	24.1		24.1

Notes

1   The following information relates to the tangible fixed assets of Sultana plc at 1 September 20X7.

	£m
Gross replacement cost	28.4
Net replacement cost	16.6
Economic value	18.0
Net realisable value	8.0

The fixed assets of Sultana plc at 1 September 20X7 had a total purchase cost to Sultana plc of £27.0 million. They were all being depreciated at 25% per annum pro rata on that cost. This policy is also appropriate for the consolidated financial statements of Prune plc. No fixed assets of Sultana plc which were included in the interim financial statements drawn up as at 1 September 19X7 were disposed of by Sultana plc prior to 31 December 20X7. No fixed asset was fully depreciated by 31 December 20X7.

2   The stocks of Sultana plc which were shown in the interim financial statements at cost to Sultana plc of £4 million would have cost £4.2 million to replace at 1 September 20X7 and had an estimated net realisable value at that date of £4.8 million. Of the stock of Sultana plc in hand at 1 September 20X7, goods costing Sultana plc £3.0 million were sold for £3.6 million between 1 September 20X7 and 31 December 20X7.

3   The long-term loan of Sultana plc carries a rate of interest of 10% per annum, payable on 31 August annually in arrears. The loan is redeemable at par on 31 August 2001. The interest cost is representative of current market rates. The accrued interest payable by Sultana plc at 31 December 20X7 is included in the trade creditors of Sultana plc at that date.

4   On 1 September 20X7 Prune plc took a decision to rationalise the group so as to integrate Sultana plc. The costs of the rationalisation (which were to be borne by Prune plc) were estimated to total £3.0 million and the process was due to start on 1 March 20X8. No provision for these costs has been made in any of the financial statements given above.

Required

Compute the goodwill on consolidation of Sultana plc that will be included in the consolidated financial statements of the Prune plc group for the year ended 31 December 20X7, explaining your treatment of the items mentioned above. You should refer to the provisions of relevant accounting standards.

Answer

Goodwill on consolidation of Sultana Ltd

	£m	£m
Consideration (£2.00 × 6m)		12.0
Group share of fair value of net assets acquired		
Share capital	8.0	
Pre-acquisition reserves	4.4	
Fair value adjustments		
Tangible fixed assets (16.6 – 16.0)	0.6	
Stocks (4.2 – 4.0)	0.2	
	13.2	
Group share	75%	9.9
Goodwill		2.1

Notes on treatment

(a) It is assumed that the market value (ie fair value) of the loan stock issued to fund the purchase of the shares in Sultana plc is equal to the price of £12.0m. FRS 2 *Accounting for subsidiary undertakings* requires goodwill to be calculated by comparing the fair value of the consideration given with the fair value of the separable net assets of the acquired business or company.

(b) Share capital and pre-acquisition profits represent the book value of the net assets of Sultana plc at the date of acquisition. Adjustments are then required to this book value in order to give the fair value of the net assets at the date of acquisition. For short-term monetary items, fair value is their carrying value on acquisition.

(c) FRS 7 *Fair values in acquisition accounting* states that the fair value of tangible fixed assets should be determined by market value or, if information on a market price is not available (as is the case here), then by reference to depreciated replacement cost, reflecting normal business practice. The net replacement cost (ie £16.6m) represents the gross replacement cost less depreciation based on that amount, and so further adjustment for extra depreciation is unnecessary.

(d) FRS 7 also states that stocks which cannot be replaced by purchasing in a ready market (eg commodities) should be valued at current cost to the acquired company of reproducing the stocks. In this case that amount is £4.2m.

(e)   The fair value of the loan is the present value of the total amount payable, ie on maturity and in interest. If the quoted interest rate was used as a discount factor, this would give the current par value.

(f)   The rationalisation costs must be reported in post-acquisition results under FRS 7 *Fair values in acquisition accounting*, so no adjustment is required in the goodwill calculation.

Exam focus point

Where you get a numerical question, make sure you provide clear workings. In the words of the Paper 2.5 examiner, if no workings are shown:

'If an answer is wrong, it is unlikely that any marks can be awarded, as the marker will not be able to determine how the answer was arrived at.'

BPP))
PROFESSIONAL EDUCATION

Chapter Roundup

- When a subsidiary is acquired **during its accounting period**, it will be necessary to distinguish between **pre-acquisition** and **post-acquisition** profits.

- In the absence of information to the contrary, the profits earned during the period may be assumed to have **accrued evenly** and should be allocated accordingly.

- **Dividends** paid by a subsidiary to its parent company may only be **credited to the parent's profit and loss account** to the extent that they are paid from **post-acquisition profits**.

- **Dividends** received by the holding company **from pre-acquisition profits** should be credited to 'investment in subsidiary' account and treated as **reducing the cost of the shares** acquired.

- **Goodwill arising on consolidation** is the difference between the purchase consideration and the **fair value** of net assets acquired. **Goodwill** should be calculated **after revaluing** the subsidiary company's assets. If the subsidiary does not incorporate the revaluation in its own accounts, it should be done as a **consolidation adjustment**. The accounting requirements and disclosures of the **fair value exercise** are covered by **FRS 7**.

Quick Quiz

1 A holding company can assume that, for a subsidiary acquired during its accounting period, profits accrue evenly during the year. *True or false*?

2 What entries are made in the holding company's accounts to record a dividend received from a subsidiary's pre-acquisition profits? *Fill in the blanks.*

DEBIT
CREDIT

3 How is 'fair value' defined by FRS 7?

4 Which items does FRS 7 state *must* be treated as post-acquisition?

5 How is the cost of an acquisition made up?

6 On 31 March, Plant Ltd purchased 1,800,000 of the 2,000,000 ordinary shares of £1 each in Seed Ltd paying £1.20 per share.

At that date the values of the separable net assets of Seed Ltd were:
Aggregate book value £1,800,000
Aggregate fair value £1,700,000

What is the values of the goodwill on consolidation as at 31 March?

7 On 31 March, Plant Ltd purchased 1,800,000 of the 2,000,000 ordinary shares of £1 each in Seed Ltd paying £1.20 per share.

At that date the value of the separable net assets of Seed Ltd were:
Aggregate book value £1,800,000
Aggregate fair value £1,700,000
What is the value of the minority interest as at 31 March?

Answers to Quick Quiz

1   False in practice, true for the purposes of your exam (unless you are told otherwise).

2   DEBIT   Cash
    CREDIT   Investment in subsidiary

3   The amount at which an asset or liability could be exchanged in an arm's length transaction between informed and willing parties other than in forced liquidation sale.

4   •   Changes resulting from the acquirer's intentions or future actions
    •   Impairments due to subsequent events
    •   Provisions for future losses

5   The amount of cash paid
    The fair value of other purchase consideration given by the acquirer
    The expenses of the acquisition

6
	£'000	
Cost	2,160	
Fair value of separable net assets acquired		
90% × 1,700,000	1,530	
	630	(Section 3)

7   10% × £1,700,000 = £170,000. (Section 3)

Now try the questions below from the Exam Question Bank

Number	Level	Marks	Time
Q19	Full exam	25	45 mins

BPP
PROFESSIONAL EDUCATION

16

The consolidated profit and loss account

Topic list	Syllabus reference
1 The consolidated profit and loss account	4 (c)
2 FRS 6 *Acquisitions and mergers*	4 (e)

Introduction

The consolidated profit and loss account will appear again in Chapter 17 where we consider the treatment of associated companies and joint ventures.

Merger accounting is no longer in your syllabus.

Study guide

- Prepare a consolidated profit and loss account for a simple group, including an example where an acquisition occurs during the year and there is a minority interest.

- Account for the effects (in the profit and loss account and balance sheet) of intra-group trading and other transactions including:
    - unrealised profits in stock and fixed assets
    - intra-group loans and interest and other intra-group charges, and
    - intra-group dividends including those paid out of pre-acquisition profits.

Exam guide

Generally speaking, the preparation of the consolidated profit and loss account is more straightforward than the preparation of the consolidated balance sheet. Complications do arise, however, usually in the form of inter-company transactions and accounting for pre-acquisition profits.

1 The consolidated profit and loss account

FAST FORWARD

The **consolidated profit and loss account** combines the profit and loss accounts of each group company. Adjustments must be made for:
- inter-group trading
- unrealised profit
- minority interest
- inter-group dividends
- elimination of pre-acquisition profits

As always, the source of the consolidated statement is the individual accounts of the separate companies in the group. **It is customary in practice to prepare a working paper** (known as a **consolidation schedule**) **on which the individual profit and loss accounts are set out side by side and totalled to form the basis of the consolidated profit and loss account.**

Exam focus point

In an examination it is very much quicker not to do this. Use workings to show the calculation of complex figures such as the minority interest and show the derivation of others on the face of the profit and loss account, as shown in our examples.

1.1 Consolidated profit and loss account: simple example

Pappadum Ltd acquired 75% of the ordinary shares of Samosa Ltd on that company's incorporation in 20X3. The summarised profit and loss accounts of the two companies for the year ending 31 December 20X6 are set out below.

BPP PROFESSIONAL EDUCATION

	Pappadum Ltd £	Samosa Ltd £
Turnover	75,000	38,000
Cost of sales	30,000	20,000
Gross profit	45,000	18,000
Administrative expenses	14,000	8,000
Profit before taxation	31,000	10,000
Taxation	10,000	2,000
Retained profit for the year	21,000	8,000
Retained profits brought forward	87,000	17,000
Retained profits carried forward	108,000	25,000

Required

Prepare the consolidated profit and loss account.

Solution

PAPPADUM LIMITED
CONSOLIDATED PROFIT AND LOSS ACCOUNT
FOR THE YEAR ENDED 31 DECEMBER 20X6

	£
Turnover (75 + 38)	113,000
Cost of sales (30 + 20)	50,000
Gross profit	63,000
Administrative expenses (14 + 8)	22,000
Profit before taxation	41,000
Taxation (10 + 2)	12,000
Profit after taxation	29,000
Minority interest (25% × £8,000)	2,000
Group retained profit for the year	27,000
Retained profits brought forward	
(group share only: 87 + (17 × 75%))	99,750
Retained profits carried forward	126,750

Notice how the minority interest is dealt with.

(a) **Down to the line 'profit after taxation' the whole of Samosa Ltd's results is included without reference to group share or minority share. A one-line adjustment is then inserted to deduct the minority's share of Samosa Ltd's profit after taxation.**

(b) **The minority's share** (£4,250) **of Samosa Ltd's retained profits brought forward is excluded**. This means that the carried forward figure of £126,750 is the figure which would appear in the balance sheet for group retained reserves.

This last point may be clearer if we revert to our balance sheet technique and construct the working for group reserves.

Group reserves

	Pappadum Ltd £	Samosa Ltd £
As per question	108,000	25,000
Group share in Samosa Ltd (25,000 × 75%)	18,750	
Group reserves	126,750	

The minority share of Samosa Ltd's reserves comprises the minority interest in the £17,000 profits brought forward plus the minority interest (£2,000) in £8,000 retained profits for the year.

377

Notice that a consolidated profit and loss account links up with a consolidated balance sheet exactly as in the case of an individual company's accounts: the figure of retained profits carried forward at the bottom of the profit and loss account appears as the figure for retained profits in the balance sheet.

We will now look at the **complications introduced by inter-company trading and pre-acquisition profits in the subsidiary.**

Exam focus point

Proposed dividends will not be examined in group accounts. Dividends that have been paid will of course be items to cancel out.

1.2 Inter-company trading

Like the consolidated balance sheet, the consolidated profit and loss account should deal with the results of the group as those of a single entity. When one company in a group sells goods to another an identical amount is added to the turnover of the first company and to the cost of sales of the second. Yet as far as the entity's dealings with outsiders are concerned no sale has taken place.

The consolidated figures for turnover and cost of sales should represent sales to, and purchases from, outsiders. An adjustment is therefore necessary to reduce the turnover and cost of sales figures by the value of inter-company sales during the year.

We have also seen in an earlier chapter that any **unrealised profits on inter-company trading should be excluded** from the figure of group profits. This will occur whenever goods sold at a profit within the group remain in the stock of the purchasing company at the year end. The best way to deal with this is to **calculate the unrealised profit** on **unsold stocks at the year end and reduce consolidated gross profit by this amount**. Cost of sales will be the balancing figure.

1.3 Example: inter-company trading

Suppose in our earlier example that Samosa Ltd had recorded sales of £5,000 to Pappadum Ltd during 20X6. Samosa Ltd had purchased these goods from outside suppliers at a cost of £3,000. One half of the goods remained in Pappadum Ltd's stock at 31 December 20X6.

Solution

The consolidated profit and loss account for the year ended 31 December 20X6 would now be as follows.

	Group £
Turnover (75 + 38 – 5)	108,000
Cost of sales (balancing figure)	46,000
Gross profit (45 + 18 – 1*)	62,000
Administrative expenses	(22,000)
Profit before taxation	40,000
Taxation	(12,000)
	28,000
Minority interest (25% × (£8,000 – £1,000*))	1,750
Group retained profit for the year	26,250
Retained profits brought forward	99,750
Retained profits carried forward	126,000

*Provision for unrealised profit: ½ × (£5,000 – £3,000)

A provision will be made for the unrealised profit against the stock figure in the consolidated balance sheet, as explained in chapter 16.

PROFESSIONAL EDUCATION

1.4 Pre-acquisition profits

As explained above, the figure for retained profits at the bottom of the consolidated profit and loss account must be the same as the figure for retained profits in the consolidated balance sheet. We have seen in previous chapters that **retained profits in the consolidated balance sheet comprise:**

(a)   **The whole of the parent company's retained profits,**

(b)   Plus a proportion of the subsidiary company's retained profits. The proportion is **the group's share of post-acquisition retained profits in the subsidiary**. From the total retained profits of the subsidiary we must therefore exclude both the minority's share of total retained profits and the group's share of pre-acquisition retained profits.

A **similar procedure is necessary in the consolidated profit and loss account** if it is to link up with the consolidated balance sheet. Previous examples have shown how the minority share of profits is excluded in the profit and loss account: their share of profits for the year is deducted from profit after tax; while the figure for profits brought forward in the consolidation schedule includes only the group's proportion of the subsidiary's profits.

In the same way, when considering examples which include pre-acquisition profits in a subsidiary, the figure for profits brought forward should include only the group's share of the post-acquisition retained profits. If the subsidiary is acquired *during* the accounting year, it is therefore necessary to apportion its profit for the year between pre-acquisition and post-acquisition elements.

The entire profit and loss account of the subsidiary is split between pre-acquisition and post-acquisition proportions. Only the post-acquisition figures are included in the profit and loss account. **This method is more usual** than the whole-year method and is the one which will be used in this Study Text.

Question	Consolidated profit and loss account 1

Pine Ltd acquired 60% of the equity of Spruce Ltd on 1 April 20X5. The profit and loss accounts and retained earnings of the two companies for the year ended 31 December 20X5 are set out below.

	Pine Ltd £	Spruce Ltd £	Spruce Ltd ($^9/_{12}$) £
Turnover	170,000	80,000	60,000
Cost of sales	65,000	36,000	27,000
Gross profit	105,000	44,000	33,000
Administrative expenses	43,000	12,000	9,000
Profit before tax	62,000	32,000	24,000
Taxation	23,000	8,000	6,000
Profit after tax	39,000	24,000	18,000
Movement on reserves			
Profit for the year	39,000	24,000	
Dividends (paid 31 December)	(12,000)	(6,000)	
Retained profits brought forward	81,000	40,000	
Retained profits carried forward	108,000	58,000	

Pine Ltd has not yet accounted for the dividends received from Spruce Ltd.

Prepare the consolidated profit and loss account.

Answer

The shares in Spruce Ltd were acquired three months into the year. Only the post-acquisition proportion (9/12ths) of Spruce Ltd's P & L account is included in the consolidated profit and loss account. This is shown above for convenience.

PINE LIMITED CONSOLIDATED PROFIT AND LOSS ACCOUNT
FOR THE YEAR ENDED 31 DECEMBER 20X5

	£
Turnover (170 + 60)	230,000
Cost of sales (65 + 27)	92,000
Gross profit	138,000
Administrative expenses (43 + 9)	52,000
Profit before tax	86,000
Taxation (23 + 6)	29,000
Profit after tax	57,000
Minority interest (40% × £18,000)	7,200
Group profit for the year	49,800
Movement on reserves	
Profit for the year	49,800
Dividends (Pine Ltd only)	12,000
Retained profits brought forward*	81,000
Retained profits carried forward	118,800

* All of Spruce Ltd's profits brought forward are pre-acquisition.

1.5 Disclosure requirements

S 230 CA 1985 allows a parent company to dispense with the need to publish its own individual profit and loss account.

(a) Companies taking advantage of this dispensation are obliged to state in their consolidated profit and loss account how much of the group's profit for the financial year is dealt with in the parent company's own profit and loss account.

(b) For internal purposes, of course, it will still be necessary to prepare the parent company's profit and loss account and the profit or loss shown there is the figure to be shown in the note to the group accounts.

(c) This is a point which has been clarified by the CA 1989. In the example above, P Ltd should disclose its own profit after adjustment for its share of the S Ltd dividend (from post-acquisition profits – remember that the pre-acquisition element should be credited to the cost of P's investment in S Ltd).

Where there are **extraordinary items** (now very rare) in the profit and loss account of a group company the **group share only** of such items should be included, after minority interest and the adjustment for inter-company dividends but before dividends payable by the parent company.

If you are required to prepare a consolidated profit and loss account in statutory form, you may need to disclose a figure for **directors' emoluments**. The figure should represent the emoluments of **parent company directors only**, whether those emoluments are paid by the parent company or by subsidiary companies. The emoluments of directors of subsidiary companies should be excluded, unless they are also directors of the parent company.

The movement on reserves statement may be required to show a transfer from the profit and loss account to other reserves. Where this transfer occurs in a subsidiary, only the group's (post-acquisition) share of

PROFESSIONAL EDUCATION

the transfer will be recorded in the movement on reserves statement. Any minority interest or pre-acquisition profits would be excluded.

MOVEMENT ON RESERVES (EXTRACT)

	Total £
Profit and loss account brought forward	X
Add retained profit for the year	X
	X
Less transfer to reserves (all of parent company transfers plus the group share of transfers in a subsidiary)	(X)
Profit and loss account carried forward	X

Section summary

The table below summaries the main points about the consolidated profit and loss account.

Summary: consolidated P & L account

Purpose	To show the results of the group for an accounting period as if it were a single entity.
Turnover to profit after tax	100% P + 100% S (excluding dividend receivable from subsidiary and adjustments for inter-company transactions).
Reason	To show the results of the group which were controlled by the holding company.
Inter-company sales	Strip out inter-company activity from both turnover and cost sales.
Unrealised profit on inter-company sales	(a) Goods sold by P Ltd. Increase cost of sales by unrealised profit. (b) Goods sold by S Ltd. Increase cost of sales by full amount of unrealised profit and decrease minority interest by their share of unrealised profit.
Depreciation	If the value of S Ltd's fixed assets have been subjected to a fair value uplift then any additional depreciation must be charged in the consolidated profit and loss account. The minority interest will need to be adjusted for their share.
Transfer of fixed assets	Any profit on the transfer, less excess depreciation is eliminated from the carrying value of the asset and the profit of the company making the transfer.

Minority interests	S's profit after tax (PAT) X
	 Less: * unrealised profit (X)
	        * profit on disposal of fixed assets (net of (X)
	          additional depreciation)
	                        X
	 MI% X
	
	 * Only applicable if sales of goods and fixed assets made by subsidiary.

Reason	To show the extent to which profits generated through H's control are in fact owned by other parties.

Dividends	P's only.
Reason	S's dividend is due (a) to P; and (b) to MI.
	P has taken in its share by including the results of S in the consolidated P & L a/c. The MI have taken their share by being given a proportion of S's PAT. Remember: PAT = dividends + retained profit.
Retained reserves	As per the balance sheet calculations.

2 FRS 6 Acquisitions and mergers

2.1 Acquisitions and mergers

Merger accounting has been removed from the 2.5 syllabus. This was to be expected, as it is no longer allowed under international standards. FRS 6 is still applicable, but you do not need to study the FRS 6 requirements for merger accounting.

2.2 Acquisitions

In relation to the consideration:

'The composition and fair value of the consideration given by the acquiring company and its subsidiary undertakings should be disclosed. The nature of any deferred or contingent purchase consideration should be stated, including, for contingent consideration, the range of possible outcomes and the principal factors that affect the outcome.'

We have already discussed the disclosure requirements relating to fair values and goodwill in Chapter 11 when we were looking at goodwill. This is a good opportunity for you to go back to that chapter, look at the disclosure requirements, and consider how FRS 6 interacts with FRS 10.

FRS 6 also interacts with FRS 3:

'As required by FRS 3, in the period of acquisition the post-acquisition results of the acquired entity should be shown as a component of continuing operations in the profit and loss account, other than those that are also discontinued in the same period; and where an acquisition has a material impact on a major business segment this should be disclosed and explained.'

You should go back to the section in Chapter 9 on FRS 3 and consider the impact FRS 6 has.

If it is not possible to determine the post-acquisition results to the end of the period of acquisition, an indication of the entity's contribution to turnover and operating results should be given; if not, the reason should be explained.

Also in relation to FRS 3:

'Any exceptional profit or loss in periods following the acquisition that is determined using the fair values recognised on acquisition should be disclosed in accordance with the requirements of FRS 3, and identified as relating to the acquisition.'

The FRS then makes it very clear that any **costs incurred post-acquisition** for **reorganising, restructuring and integrating the acquisition should be shown in the profit and loss account of that period (ie post acquisition).** Such costs are described as those that:

(a)   'Would not have been incurred had the acquisition not taken place.

(b)   Relate to a project identified and controlled by management as part of a reorganisation or integration programme set up at the time of acquisition or as a direct consequence of an immediate post-acquisition review.'

In other words, such costs **cannot be treated as movements on reserves.**

The FRS also lays out disclosure requirements for movements on provisions and accruals made in relation to the acquisition, which should be:

'Disclosed and analysed between the amounts used for the specific purpose for which they were created and the amounts released unused.'

The cash flow impact of the acquisition should be disclosed according to FRS 1 *Cash flow statements* (see Chapter 10).

Finally, for a material acquisition:

'The profit after taxation and minority interests of the acquired entity should be given for:

(a)   The period from the beginning of the acquired entity's financial year to the date of acquisition, giving the date on which this period began.

(b)   Its previous financial year.

2.3 Substantial acquisitions

Extra information should be disclosed for 'substantial acquisitions', which are defined as each business combination accounted for by using acquisition accounting where:

(a)   For listed companies, the combination is a Class I or Super Class I transaction under the Stock Exchange Listing Rules (see below).

(b)   For other entities, either:

(i)   The net assets or operating profits of the acquired entity exceed 15% of those of the acquiring entity.

(ii)   The fair value of the consideration given exceeds 15% of the net assets of the acquiring entity.

and should also be made in other exceptional cases where an acquisition is of such significance that the disclosure is necessary in order to give a true and fair view.

The **extra information** requiring disclosure is a **summarised profit and loss account, and statement of total recognised gains and losses** of the acquired entity from the beginning of the period to the date of acquisition. The **profit after tax and minority interests for the acquired entity's previous financial year** should also be disclosed.

2.4 UITF Abstract 15 *Disclosure of substantial acquisitions*

In relation to Paragraph 3.14 (a) above, in August 1995 the Stock Exchange revised its Listing Rules and they no longer refer to Class 1 transactions.

The Stock Exchange Listing Rules classify transactions by assessing their size relative to that of the company proposing to make the transaction. It does this by ascertaining whether any of a number of ratios (eg the net assets of the target to the net assets of the offeror) exceeds a given percentage. Class 1 transactions used to be those where the percentage exceeded 15%. Super Class 1 are those where the percentage exceeds 25%. FRS 6 uses the 15% criterion for non-listed entities.

The UITF reached a consensus that, in order to retain the ASB's original intentions for FRS 6, the reference to Class 1 transactions should be interpreted as meaning those transactions in which any of the ratios set out in the London Stock Exchange Listing Rules defining Super Class 1 transactions exceeds 15%.

Exam focus point

> FRS 6 and FRS 7 (which was published at the same time) represent a major revision of the principles and practices of merger and acquisition accounting. They are controversial and arguments are likely to be carried on in the financial and accountancy press for some time. You *must* go back to Chapters 15 and 17 to tie in the disclosure and other requirements of FRS 6 to FRS 2 *Accounting for subsidiary undertakings* and FRS 7 *Fair values in acquisition accounting*. **These three standards are interrelated and you should be able to discuss the relationships between them.**

2.5 Example: disclosure of reorganisation costs

In an appendix at the end of the standard, the ASB lays out an illustrative example of the disclosure of reorganisation and integration costs. The explanatory part of the standard suggests that management may wish to include these in the notes to the financial statements. The example given below is optional; the best method will depend on individual circumstances.

COSTS OF REORGANISING AND INTEGRATING ACQUISITIONS

	Acquisition of European business (note (a)) £	Other acquisitions £	Total £
Announced but not charged as at the previous year	–	25	25
Announced in relation to acquisitions during the year	170	–	170
Adjustments to previous year's estimates	–	(5)	(5)
	170	20	190
Charged in the year:			
Operating profit	55	12	67
Elsewhere	65	–	65
	120	12	132
Announced but still to be charged at 31 December 1995	50	8	58

Note (a): Acquisition of European business

	£	£
Cost of acquisition		400
Reorganisation and integration expenditure announced		
Fundamental restructuring		
Withdrawal from existing US business and related redundancies	65	
Other items (to be charged to operating profit)		
Other redundancy costs	75	
Re branding and redesign costs	30	
Announced reorganisation and integration costs as shown in above table		170
Total investment		570

In addition to the £120 million expenditure shown in the above table, reorganisation and integration costs charged during the year include £30 million in respect of write-downs to fixed assets consequent on the closure of XYZ plant.

Chapter Roundup

- The **consolidated profit and loss account** combines the profit and loss accounts of each group company. Adjustments must be made for:

    - inter-group trading
    - unrealised profit
    - minority interest
    - inter-group dividends
    - elimination of pre-acquisition profits

Quick Quiz

1   At what stage in the consolidated profit and loss account does the figure for minority interests appear?

2   What dispensation is granted to a parent company by s 230 CA 1985?

3   Barley Ltd has owned 100% of the issued share capital of Oats Ltd for many years. Barley Ltd sells goods to Oats Ltd at cost plus 20%. The following information is available for the year:

Turnover   – Barley Ltd   £460,000
            – Oats Ltd   £120,000

During the year Barley Ltd sold goods to Oats Ltd for £60,000 of which £18,000 were still held in stock by Oats at the year end.

At what amount should turnover appear in the consolidated profit and loss account?

4   Chicken plc owns 80% of Duck plc. Duck plc sells goods to Chicken plc at cost plus 50%. The total invoiced sales to Chicken plc by Duck plc in the year ended 31 December 20X9 were £900,000 and, of these sales, goods which had been invoiced at £60,000 were held in stock by Chicken plc at 31 December 20X9. What is the reduction in aggregate group gross profit?

5   Pavlova Ltd, which makes up its accounts to 31 December, has an 80% owned subsidiary Sponge Ltd. Sponge Ltd sells goods to Pavlova Ltd at a mark-up on cost of 33.33%. At 31 December 20X8, Pavlova had £12,000 of such goods in stock and at 31 December 20X9 had £15,000 of such goods in stock.

What is a permissible amount by which the consolidated profit attributable to Pavlova Ltd's shareholders should be adjusted in respect of the above?

Ignore taxation

A   £1,000 Debit
B   £800 Credit
C   £750 Credit
D   £600 Debit

Answers to Quick Quiz

1   Down to the line 'profit after taxation', the whole of the subsidiary's results is included. A one line adjustment is then inserted to deduct the minority's share of the subsidiary's PAT.

2   The parent company can choose to not publish its own individual profit and loss account.

3   Turnover: 460 + 120 − 60 = 520.

4   $£60,000 \times \dfrac{50}{150} = £20,000$

5   D $(15,000 - 12,000) \times \dfrac{33.3}{133.3} \times 80\%$

Now try the question below from the Exam Question Bank

Number	Level	Marks	Time
Q20	Full exam	25	45 mins

BPP
PROFESSIONAL EDUCATION

Associates and joint ventures

Introduction

Some investments which do not satisfy the criteria for classification as subsidiaries may nevertheless be much more than trade investments. The most important of these are associates and joint ventures which are the subject of this chapter and of FRS 9 *Associates and joint ventures*.

Study guide

- Define associates and joint ventures, including an arrangement that is not an entity (JANE).

- Distinguish between equity accounting and proportional consolidation.

- Describe the equity and gross equity methods.

- Prepare consolidated financial statements to include a single subsidiary and an associate or a joint venture.

1 Background

In the 1960s it became increasingly common for companies to trade through companies in which a **substantial but not a controlling interest** was held. Traditionally such companies were accounted for in the same way as trade investments. In other words the income from associated companies was only included in the investing company's accounts to the extent of the dividends received and receivable up to its balance sheet date. However, it was felt that this treatment did not reflect the reality of the investment, not least because the investor could in many cases influence the investee's dividend policy. The need thus arose for an **intermediate form of accounting for those investments which lie between full subsidiary and trade investment status**.

1.1 Equity accounting and the Companies Act 1985

The intermediate form of accounting developed for this purpose is known as **equity accounting.** The full, up-to-date (FRS 9) definition of equity accounting will be given later in this chapter. For now, think of it as follows.

Key term

> **Equity accounting** is a modified form of consolidation of the results and assets of the investee where the investor has significant influence but not control. Rather than full, line by line consolidation, it involves incorporating the investor's share of the profit/loss and assets of the investee **in one line** in the investor's profit and loss account and balance sheet.

Equity accounting was first recognised in UK accounting literature in SSAP 1 *Accounting for associated companies* (now superseded by FRS 9). **Parent companies are also required by law to use equity accounting to account for holdings in associated undertakings, defined as follows.**

Key term

> 'An "**associated undertaking**" means an undertaking in which an undertaking included in the consolidation has a participating interest and over whose operating and financial policy it exercises a significant influence, and which is not:
>
> (a)   A subsidiary undertaking of the parent company
> (b)   A joint venture'. (s 20(1) Sch 4A, CA 1985)
>
> 'Where an undertaking holds 20% or more of the voting rights in another undertaking, it shall be presumed to exercise such an influence over it unless the contrary is shown.'   (s 20(2) Sch 4A, CA 1985)

Participating interests which are not in associated undertakings have to be disclosed separately from other investments but do not have to be accounted for by the equity method.

2 FRS 9 Associates and joint ventures

FAST FORWARD

Associates and **joint ventures** are entities in which an investor holds a **substantial but not controlling interest**. They are the subject of an accounting standard: **FRS 9** *Associates and joint ventures.*

FRS 9 *Associates and joint ventures* was issued in November 1997. It sets out the definition and accounting treatments for associates and joint ventures, two types of interests that a reporting entity may have in other entities. The FRS also deals with joint arrangements that are not entities. The definitions and treatments prescribed have been developed to be consistent with the Accounting Standards Board's approach to accounting for subsidiaries (dealt with in FRS 2 *Accounting for subsidiary undertakings*). The requirements are consistent with companies legislation.

2.1 Objective

The objective of FRS 9 is **to reflect the effect on an investor's financial position and performance** of its interest in two special kinds of investments - **associates and joint ventures**. The investor is partly accountable for the activities of these investments because of the closeness of its involvement.

(a) It is closely involved in **associates** as a result of its **participating interest** and **significant influence**.

(b) Its close involvement with **joint ventures** arises as a result of its **long-term interest** and **joint control**.

The FRS **also deals with joint arrangements that do not qualify as associates or joint ventures because they are not entities.**

2.2 Scope

The FRS applies to all financial statements intending to give a true and fair view. It is **not yet required for those smaller entities adopting the Financial Reporting Standard for Smaller Entities** and preparing consolidated financial statements. However, it is envisaged that a future revision to the FRSSE will require such entities to adopt the FRS. The FRS is effective in respect of financial statements of accounting periods ending on or after 23 June 1998.

Exam focus point

- At this stage, read through the summary and example for overview only. Do not expect to understand everything you read.

- At the end of the chapter, when you have worked through the detailed sections on associates and joint ventures, come back to this section to put it in context.

- When you come to revise, look at this section as it contains a clear summary of the requirements of the FRS.

2.3 Summary

The table below, taken from the FRS, describes the **different sorts of interest that a reporting entity may have in other entities or arrangements**. The sections marked with an asterisk (*) are covered by the FRS. The defining relationships described in the table form the basis for the definitions used in the FRS.

Entity/ arrangement	Nature of relationship	Description of the defining relationship - the full definitions are given in the FRS
Subsidiary	Investor controls its investee	Control is the ability of an entity to direct the operating and financial policies of another entity with a view to gaining economic benefits from its activities. To have control an entity must have both: (a) The ability to deploy the economic resources of the investee or to direct it. (b) The ability to ensure that any resulting benefits accrue to itself (with corresponding exposure to losses) and to restrict the access of others to those benefits.
* Joint arrangement that is not an entity	Entities participate in an arrangement to carry on part of their own trades or businesses	A joint arrangement, whether or not subject to joint control, does not constitute an entity unless it carries on a trade or business of its own.
* Joint venture	Investor holds a long-term interest and shares control under a contractual arrangement	The joint venture agreement can override the rights normally conferred by ownership interests with the effect that: • Acting together, the venturers can control the venture and there are procedures for such joint action. • Each venturer has (implicitly or explicitly) a veto over strategic policy decisions. There is usually a procedure for settling disputes between venturers and, possibly, for terminating the joint venture.
* Associate	Investor holds a participating interest and exercises significant influence	The investor has a long-term interest and is actively involved, and influential, in the direction of its investee through its participation in policy decisions covering the aspects of policy relevant to the investor, including decisions on strategic issues such as: (i) The expansion or contraction of the business, participation in other entities or changes in products, markets and activities of its investee. (ii) Determining the balance between dividend and reinvestment.
Simple investment		The investor's interest does not quality the investee as an associate, a joint venture or a subsidiary because the investor has limited influence or its interest is not long-term.

The table below, also taken from the FRS, sets out the **treatments in consolidated financial statements** for the different interests that a reporting entity may have in other entities and for joint arrangements that are not entities - the sections marked with an asterisk (*) are covered by the FRS.

Type of investment	Treatment in consolidated financial statements
Subsidiaries	The investor should consolidate the assets, liabilities, results and cash flows of its subsidiaries.
* Joint arrangements that are not entities	Each party should account for its own share of the assets, liabilities and cash flows in the joint arrangement, measured according to the terms of that arrangement, for example pro rata to their respective interests.

BPP
PROFESSIONAL EDUCATION

Type of investment	Treatment in consolidated financial statements
Joint ventures	The venturer should use the gross equity method showing in addition to the amounts included under the equity method, on the face on the balance sheet, the venturer's share of the gross assets and liabilities of its joint ventures, and, in the profit and loss account, the venturer's share of their turnover distinguished from that of the group. Where the venturer conducts a major part of its business through joint ventures, it may show fuller information provided all amounts are distinguished from those of the group.
Associates	The investor should include its associates in its consolidated financial statements using the equity method. In the investor's consolidated profit and loss account the investor's share of its associates' operating results should be included immediately after group operating results. From the level of profit before tax, the investor's share of the relevant amounts for associates should be included within the amounts for the group. In the consolidated statement of total recognised gains and losses the investor's share of the total recognised gains and losses of its associates should be included, shown separately under each heading, if material. In the balance sheet the investor's share of the net assets of its associates should be included and separately disclosed. The cash flow statement should include the cash flows between the investor and its associates. Goodwill arising on the investor's acquisition of its associates, less any amortisation or write-down, should be included in the carrying amount for the associates but should be disclosed separately. In the profit and loss account the amortisation or write-down of such goodwill should be separately disclosed as part of the investor's share of its associates' results.
Simple investments	The investor includes its interests as investments at either cost or valuation.

2.4 Example: consolidated financial statements

The following example of consolidated financial statements is taken from Appendix IV of FRS 9. Study it for an overview and come back to it when you have finished the chapter.

The format is illustrative only. The amounts shown for 'Associates' and 'joint ventures' are subdivisions of the item for which the statutory prescribed heading is 'Income from interests in associated undertakings'. The subdivisions may be shown in a note rather than on the face of the profit and loss account.

CONSOLIDATED PROFIT AND LOSS ACCOUNT

	£m	£m
Turnover: group and share of joint ventures	320	
Less: share of joint ventures' turnover	(120)	
Group turnover		200
Cost of sales		(120)
Gross profit		80
Administrative expenses		(40)
Group operating profit		40
Share of operating profit in		
Joint ventures	30	
Associates	24	
		54
		94
Interest receivable (group)		6
Interest payable		
Group	(26)	
Joint ventures	(10)	
Associates	(12)	
		(48)
Profit on ordinary activities before tax		52
*Tax on profit on ordinary activities**		(12)
Profit on ordinary activities after tax		40
Minority interests		(6)
Profit on ordinary activities after taxation and minority interest		34
*Tax relates to the following: Parent and subsidiaries		(5)
Joint ventures		(5)
Associates		(2)

CONSOLIDATED BALANCE SHEET

	£m	£m	£m
Fixed assets			
Tangible assets		480	
Investments			
Investments in joint ventures:			
Share of gross assets	130		
Share of gross liabilities	(80)		
		50	
Investments in associates		20	
			550
Current assets			
Stock		15	
Debtors		75	
Cash at bank and in hand		10	
		100	
Creditors (due within one year)		(50)	
Net current assets			50
Total assets less current liabilities			600
Creditors (due after more than one year)			(250)
Provisions for liabilities			(10)
Equity minority interest			(40)
			300

BPP
PROFESSIONAL EDUCATION

	£m
Capital and reserves	
Called up share capital	50
Share premium account	150
Profit and loss account	100
Shareholders' funds (all equity)	300

Notes

In the example, there is no individual associate or joint venture that accounts for more than 25 per cent of any of the following for the investor group (excluding any amount for associates and joint ventures).

- Gross assets
- Gross liabilities
- Turnover
- Operating results (on a three-year average)

Additional disclosures for joint ventures (which in aggregate exceed the 15 per cent threshold)

	£m	£m
Share of assets		
Share of fixed assets	100	
Share of current assets	30	
		130
Share of liabilities		
Liabilities due within one year or less	(10)	
Liabilities due after more than one year	(70)	
		(80)
Share of net assets		50

Additional disclosures for associates (which in aggregate exceed the 15 per cent threshold)

	£m	£m
Share of turnover of associates		90
Share of assets		
Share of fixed assets	4	
Share of current assets	28	
		32
Share of liabilities		
Liabilities due within one year or less	(3)	
Liabilities due after more than one year	(9)	
		(12)
Share of net assets		20

3 Associates

Associates are to be included in the investor's consolidated financial statements using the **equity method**. The investor's share of its associates' results should be included immediately after group operating profit.

Exam focus point

The June 2002 exam required candidates to discuss the matters that should be considered in determining whether an investment in another company constitutes associate status.

The compulsory question in both the June 2004 and December 2004 papers was a consolidation with a subsidiary and an associate.

Associated undertakings **should be included** by an entity **in its consolidated financial statements using the equity method. In the investor's individual statements**, the interest in associates is **shown as a fixed asset investment**, at cost (less any amounts written off) or valuation.

3.1 Definitions

The most important definitions relate to the **identification** of associates.

Key terms

- **Associate**: an entity (other than a subsidiary) in which another entity (the investor) has a participating interest and over whose operating and financial policies the investor exercises a significant influence.

- **Control** the ability of an entity to direct the operating and financial policies of another entity with a view to gaining economic benefits from its activities.

- **Entity**: a body corporate, a partnership or an unincorporated association carrying on a trade or business with or without a view to profit. *(FRS 9)*

3.2 Participating interest

FRS 9 defines 'participating interest' in the same way as FRS 2.

Key term

Participating interest: an interest held in the shares of another entity on a long-term basis for the purpose of securing a contribution to the investor's activities by the exercise of control or influence arising from or related to that interest. *(FRS 9)*

The investor's interest must be **beneficial**, the benefits linked to the exercise of significant influence. An interest convertible to an interest in shares and an option to acquire shares also qualify.

A participating interest is a **continuing relationship**. It confers a right to share in profits.

3.3 Long-term interest

This definition relates to a participating interest.

Key term

Interest held on a long-term basis: an interest that is held other than exclusively with a view to subsequent resale. An interest held exclusively with a view to subsequent resale is:

- An interest for which a purchaser has been identified or is being sought, and which is reasonably expected to be disposed or within approximately one year of its date of acquisition.

- An interest that was acquired as a result of the enforcement of a security, unless the interest has become part of the continuing activities of the group or the holder acts as if it intends the interest to become so. *(FRS 9)*

This definition is extremely important.

Key term

Exercise of significant influence: the exercise of a degree of influence by an investor over the operating and financial policies of its investee that results in the following conditions being fulfilled.

(a)   The investor is actively involved and is influential in the direction of its investee through its participation in policy decisions covering all aspects of policy relevant to the investor, including decisions on strategic issues such as:

    (i)   The expansion or contraction of the business, participation in other entities, changes in products, markets and activities of its investee.

**Key term
cont'd**

(ii)   Determining the balance between dividend and reinvestment.

(b)   Over time, the investee generally implements policies that are consistent with the strategy of the
investor and avoids implementing policies that are contrary to the investor's interests.   *(FRS 9)*

Significant influence is **usually wielded through nomination to the board of directors**, although it may be
achieved in other ways. It presupposes an agreement (formal or informal) between the investor and
investee.

The 20% rule is followed here, so that a holding of 20% or more of the voting rights suggests (but does
not guarantee) that the investor exercises significant influence. At 20% the presumption of the exercise of
significant influence can be rebutted if the criteria above are not fulfilled. The holdings of both parent and
subsidiaries in the entity should be taken into account.

3.4 Accounting for associates

Following FRS 9, a reporting entity that prepares **consolidated financial statements** should include its
associates in those statements using the **equity method in all the primary statements**. In the investor's
individual financial statements, its interests in associates should be treated as **fixed asset investments**
and shown either **at cost less any amounts written off or at valuation**.

The equity method is discussed here in more detail with regard to each of the primary statements.

3.4.1 Consolidated profit and loss account

FRS 9 stipulates the following.

(a)   The investor's **share of its associates' operating results** should be **included immediately
after group operating result** (but after the investor's share of the results of its joint
ventures, if any).

(b)   Any **amortisation** or write-down **of goodwill** arising on acquiring the associates should be
charged at this point **and disclosed.**

(c)   The **investor's share of any exceptional items** included after operating profit (paragraph 20
of FRS 3) or of interest should be **shown separately** from the amounts for the group.

(d)   **At and below the level of profit before tax**, the **investor's share** of the relevant amounts for
associates should be **included within the amounts for the group**, although for items **below
this level**, such as taxation, the **amounts relating to associates should be disclosed.**

(e)   Where it is helpful to give an indication of the size of the business as a whole, a total
combining the investor's share of its associates' turnover with **group turnover may be
shown as a memorandum item** in the profit and loss account **but** the investor's share of its
associates' turnover should be clearly distinguished from group turnover.

(f)   Similarly, the **segmental analysis of turnover and operating profit** (if given) should clearly
distinguish between that of the **group and** that of **associates**.

3.4.2 Consolidated balance sheet

FRS 9 requires the following.

(a)   The investor's **consolidated balance sheet should include as a fixed asset investment the
investor's share of the net assets of its associates** shown as a separate item.

(b)   **Goodwill** arising on the investor's acquisition of its associates, less any amortisation or
write-down, should be **included in the carrying amount for the associates but should be
disclosed separately.**

3.4.3 Consolidated cash flow statement

Cash flow statements are covered in Chapter 10. FRS 9 amends the revised version of FRS 1 to reflect the following.

    (a)   The consolidated cash flow statement should include **dividends received from associates as a separate item** between operating activities and returns on investments and servicing of finance.

    (b)   Any other cash flows between the investor and its associates should be included under the appropriate cash flow heading for the activity giving rise to the cash flow. None of the other cash flows of the associates should be included.

3.4.4 Consolidated statement of total recognised gains and losses

The statement of total recognised gains and losses is discussed in Chapter 9 which deals with FRS 3. FRS 9 requires the **investor's share of the total recognised gains and losses of its associates to be included**. If the amounts included are material they should be shown separately under each heading, either in the statement or in a note that is referred to in the statement.

3.5 Example: associated company in investor's own accounts

Pumpkin Ltd, a company with subsidiaries, acquires 25,000 of the 100,000 £1 ordinary shares in Asparagus Ltd for £60,000 on 1 January 20X0. Asparagus Ltd meets the FRS 9 definitions of an associate. In the year to 31 December 20X0, Asparagus Ltd earns profits after tax of £24,000, from which it declares a dividend of £6,000.

How will Asparagus Ltd's results be accounted for in the individual and consolidated accounts of Pumpkin Ltd for the year ended 31 December 20X0?

Solution

In the individual accounts of Pumpkin Ltd, the investment will be recorded on 1 January 20X0 at cost. Unless there is a permanent diminution in the value of the investment, this amount will remain in the individual balance sheet of Pumpkin Ltd permanently. The only entry in Pumpkin Ltd's individual profit and loss account will be to record dividends received. For the year ended 31 December 20X0, Pumpkin Ltd will:

DEBIT	Cash	£1,500	
CREDIT	Income from shares in associated companies		£1,500

3.6 Consolidated profit and loss account

A consolidation schedule may be used to prepare the consolidated profit and loss account of a group with associates. The treatment of the associate's profits in the following example should be studied carefully.

3.7 Example: associated company in consolidated accounts

The following consolidation schedule relates to the Pisces Ltd group, consisting of the parent company, an 80% owned subsidiary Sagitarius Ltd and an associate Aries Ltd in which the group has a 30% interest.

CONSOLIDATION SCHEDULE

	Group £'000	Pisces Ltd £'000	Sagitarius Ltd £'000	Aries Ltd £'000
Turnover	1,400	600	800	300
Cost of sales	770	370	400	120
Gross profit	630	230	400	180
Distribution costs and administrative expenses (including depreciation, directors' emoluments etc)	290	110	180	80
Group operating profit	340	120	220	100
Share of operating profit in associate	30	–	–	30% 30
	370	120	220	30
Interest receivable (group)	30	30	–	–
	400	150	220	30
Interest payable (group)	(20)	–	(20)	–
Profit on before tax	380	150	200	30
Taxation				
Pisces Ltd	(150)	(60)	(90)	
Associate	(12)	–	–	(12)
Profit after taxation	218	90	110	18
Minority interest	(22)		(22)	
Profit for the period	196	90	88	18

Notes

(a) **Group turnover, group gross profit and costs** such as depreciation etc **exclude** the turnover, gross profit and costs etc of **associates**.

(b) The **group share of the associate's operating profit is credited** to the group profit and loss account (here, 30% of £100,000 = £30,000). If the associated company has been acquired during the year, it would be necessary to deduct the pre-acquisition profits.

(c) **Taxation** consists of:

(i) Taxation **on the parent company and subsidiaries in total.**

(ii) Only the **group's share of the tax charge of the associated company**; Aries Ltd tax would be £40,000, so that the group share is £40,000 × 30% = £12,000.

(d) The **minority interest will only ever apply to subsidiary companies.**

(e) **Inter-company dividends** from subsidiaries and associated companies **should all be recorded**.

(f) **Dividends** paid **relate to the holding company only**.

3.8 Pro-forma consolidated profit and loss account

The following is a **suggested layout** (using the figures given in the illustration above) for a profit and loss account for a company having subsidiaries as well as associates. It follows the FRS 9 example given in Section 2 of this chapter.

	£'000	£'000
Turnover		1,400
Cost of sales		770
Gross profit		630
Distribution costs and administrative expenses		290
Group operating profit		340
Share of operating profit in associate		30
		370
Interest and similar income receivable (group)		30
		400
Interest payable and similar charges (group)		(20)
Profit before tax		380
Taxation		162
Profit after taxation		218
Minority interest (in the current year post tax profits of subsidiary)		(22)
Profit for the financial year attributable to the group		196
(of which £110,000 has been dealt with in the accounts of the holding company)		
Earnings per share		Xp

3.9 Consolidated balance sheet

As explained earlier, the consolidated balance sheet will contain an **asset 'Investment in associates'.** The amount at which this asset is stated will be its original cost plus the group's share of any **profits earned since acquisition** which have not been distributed as dividends.

3.10 Example: consolidated balance sheet

On 1 January 20X6 the net tangible assets of Almond Ltd amount to £220,000, financed by 100,000 £1 ordinary shares and revenue reserves of £120,000. Peanut Ltd, a company with subsidiaries, acquires 30,000 of the shares in Almond Ltd for £75,000. During the year ended 31 December 20X6 Almond Ltd's profit after tax is £30,000, from which dividends of £12,000 are paid.

Show how Peanut Ltd's investment in Almond Ltd would appear in the consolidated balance sheet at 31 December 20X6.

Solution

CONSOLIDATED BALANCE SHEET
AS AT 31 DECEMBER 20X6 (extract)

	£
Fixed assets	
Investment in associate	
Cost	75,000
Group share of post-acquisition retained profits	
(30% × £18,000)	5,400
	80,400

An important point to note is that this figure of £80,400 can be arrived at in a completely different way. It is the sum of:

(a)   The group's share of Almond Ltd's net assets at 31 December 20X6.
(b)   The premium paid over net book value for the shares acquired.

This can be shown as follows.

(a)   Almond Ltd's net assets at 31 December 20X6

	£	£
Net assets at 1 January 20X6	220,000	
Retained profit for year	18,000	
Net assets at 31 December 20X6	238,000	
Group share (30%)		71,400

(b)   Premium on acquisition

	£	£
Net assets acquired by group on 1 Jan 20X6		
(30% × £220,000)	66,000	
Price paid for shares	75,000	
Premium on acquisition		9,000
Investment in associate per balance sheet		80,400

The reason why this is important is because FRS 9 requires the investment in associated companies to be analysed in this way, ie:

(a)   Group share of associate's net assets

(b)   Goodwill arising on acquisition of associate less any amortisation or write down is included in (a) but disclosed separately

Fair values should be attributed to the associate's underlying assets and liabilities. These will provide the basis for subsequent depreciation. Both the consideration paid in the acquisition and the goodwill arising should be calculated in the same way as on the acquisition of a subsidiary. The associate's assets should not include any goodwill earned in the balance sheet of the associate.

The goodwill should be treated in accordance with the provisions of FRS 10 *Goodwill and intangible assets*. The usual treatment would therefore be to capitalise and amortise. (Our example assumes for simplicity that the goodwill has an indefinite life and there is no amortisation.)

Question   Associated company

How should a holding company treat the following items in the financial statements for an associated company, when preparing group accounts:

(a)   Turnover?
(b)   Inter-company profits?
(c)   Goodwill?

Answer

(a)   The holding company should not aggregate the turnover of an associated company with its own turnover.

(b)   Wherever the effect is material, adjustments similar to those adopted for the purpose of presenting consolidated financial statements should be made to exclude from the investing group's consolidated financial statements such items as unrealised profits on stocks transferred to or from associated companies.

(c)   The investing group's balance sheet should disclose 'interest in associated companies'. The amount disclosed under this heading should include both the investing group's share of any goodwill in the associated companies' own financial statements and any premium paid on acquisition of the interests in the associated companies in so far as it has not already been written off or amortised.

Question	Consolidated balance sheet

The balance sheets of J plc and its investee companies, P Ltd and S Ltd, at 31 December 20X5 are shown below.

BALANCE SHEETS AS AT 31 DECEMBER 20X5

	J plc £'000	£'000	P Ltd £'000	£'000	S Ltd £'000	£'000
Tangible fixed assets						
Freehold property	1,950		1,250		500	
Plant and machinery	795		375		285	
		2,745		1,625		785
Investments		1,500		-		-
Current assets						
Stock	575		300		265	
Trade debtors	330		290		370	
Cash	50		120		20	
	955		710		655	
Creditors: due within one year						
Bank overdraft	560		-		-	
Trade creditors	680		350		300	
	1,240		350		300	
Net current (liabilities)/assets		(285)		360		355
Creditors: due after one year						
12% debentures		(500)		(100)		-
		3,460		1,885		1,140
Share capital (£1 ordinary shares)		2,000		1,000		750
Profit and loss account		1,460		885		390
		3,460		1,885		1,140

Additional information

(a)   J plc acquired 600,000 ordinary shares in P Ltd on 1 January 20X0 for £1,000,000 when the reserves of P Ltd were £200,000.

(b)   At the date of acquisition of P Ltd, the fair value of its freehold property was considered to be £400,000 greater than its value in P Ltd's balance sheet. P Ltd had acquired the property in January 20W0 and the buildings element (comprising 50% of the total value) is depreciated on cost over 50 years.

(c)   J plc acquired 225,000 ordinary shares in S Ltd on 1 January 20X4 for £500,000 when the reserves of S Ltd were £150,000.

(d)   P Ltd manufactures a component used by both J plc and S Ltd. Transfers are made by P Ltd at cost plus 25%. J plc held £100,000 stock of these components at 31 December 20X5 and S Ltd held £80,000 at the same date.

(e)   It is the policy of J plc to write off goodwill over a period of five years.

Required

Prepare, in a format suitable for inclusion in the annual report of the J Group, the consolidated balance sheet at 31 December 20X5.

Answer

J GROUP CONSOLIDATED BALANCE SHEET AS AT 31 DECEMBER 20X5

	£'000	£'000
Fixed assets		
Tangible assets		
Freehold property (W2)	3,570.00	
Plant and machinery (795 + 375)	1,170.00	
		4,740.00
Investment in associate (W8)		475.20
		5,215.20
Current assets		
Stock (W3)	855.00	
Debtors (W4)	620.00	
Cash at bank and in hand (50 + 120)	170.00	
	1,645.00	
Creditors: amounts falling due within one year (W5)	1,590.00	
Net current assets		55.00
Total assets less current liabilities		5,270.20
Creditors: amounts falling due after more than one year		
(500 + 100)		600.00
		4,670.20
Capital and reserves		
Called up share capital		2,000.00
Profit and loss account (W9)		1,778.12
Shareholders' funds		3,778.12
Minority interests (W6)		892.08
		4,670.20

Workings

1 *Group structure*

		J		
1.1.X0 (6 years ago)	60%		30%	1.1.X4 (2 years ago)
	P		S	

2 *Freehold property*

	£'000
J plc	1,950
P Ltd	1,250
Fair value adjustment	400
Additional depreciation $(400 \times 50\% \div 40) \times 6$ years (20X0-20X5)	(30)
	3,570

3 *Stock*

	£'000
J plc	575
P Ltd	300
PUP $(100 \times {}^{25}/_{125})$	(20)
	855

4   *Debtors*

	£'000
J plc	330
P Ltd	290
	620

5   *Creditors due < 1 year*

	£'000
J plc: bank overdraft	560
trade creditors	680
P Ltd: trade creditors	350
	1,590

6   *Minority interest*

	£'000
Net assets of P Ltd	1,885.0
Fair value adjustment (W11)	370.0
Less PUP: sales to J plc	(20.0)
sales to S Ltd ($80 \times {}^{25}/_{125} \times 30\%$)	(4.8)
	2,230.2
Minority interest (40%)	892.08

7   *Goodwill*

	£'000	£'000
P Ltd		
Cost of investment		1,000
Share of net assets acquired		
Share capital	1,000	
Reserves	200	
Fair value adjustment	400	
	1,600	
Group share	60%	(960)
Fully amortised		40
S Ltd		
Cost of investment		500
Share of net assets acquired		
Share capital	750	
Reserves	150	
	900	
Group share	30%	(270)
		230
		92

$$\text{Amortisation} = \frac{230}{5} \times 2 =$$

8   *Investment in associate*

	£'000
Share of net assets (30% × 1,140)	342.0
Less PUP	(4.8)
Add unamortised goodwill (230 – 92)	138.0
	475.2

BPP))
PROFESSIONAL EDUCATION

9   *Profit and loss account*

	J	P	S
	£'000	£'000	£'000
Reserves per question	1,460.0	885.0	390.0
Adjustments			
Unrealised profit (W10)		(24.8)	
Fair value adjustments (W11)		(30.0)	
		830.2	390.0
Less pre-acquisition reserves		(200.0)	(150.0)
	1,460.0	630.2	240.0
P: 60% × 630.2	378.1		
S: 30% × 240	72.0		
Less amortisation of goodwill: P	(40.0)		
S	(92.0)		
	1,778.1		

10   *Unrealised profit*

	£'000
On sales to J (parent co) 100 × 25/125	20.0
On sales to S (associate) 80 × 25/125 × 30%	4.8
	24.8

11   *Fair value adjustments*

	Difference at acquisition	Difference now
	£'000	£'000
Property	400	400
Additional depreciation: 200 × 6/40	-	(30)
	400	370

∴ Charge £30,000 to P&L

3.11 Minority interests

FRS 9 does not specifically address the situation where an investment in an associate is held by a subsidiary. However, the FRS does stipulate that in calculating the amounts to be included in the consolidated financial statements the same principles should be applied as are applied in the consolidation of subsidiaries. This implies that the **group accounts should include the 'gross' share of net assets, operating profit, interest payable and receivable (if any) and tax, accounting for the minority interest separately**. For example, we will suppose that P Ltd owns 60% of S Ltd which owns 25% of A Ltd, an associate of P Ltd. The relevant amounts for inclusion in the consolidated financial statements would be as follows.

CONSOLIDATED PROFIT AND LOSS ACCOUNT

Operating profit (P 100% + S 100%)
Share of operating profit of associate (A 25%)
Interest receivable (group) (P 100% + S 100% + A 25%)
Interest payable (P 100% + S 100% + A 25%)
Exceptional items (P 100% + S 100% + A 25%)
Tax (P 100% + S 100% + A 25%)
Minority interest (S 40% + A 10%)
Retained profits (P 100% + S 60% + A 15%)

CONSOLIDATED BALANCE SHEET

Investment in associated company (figures based on 25% holding)

Minority interest ((40% × shareholders' funds of S) + (10% × post-acquisition reserves of A))

Unrealised reserves (15% × post-acquisition reserves of A)

Group profit and loss account ((100% × P) + (60% × post-acquisition of S))

4 Incorporated joint ventures and joint arrangements

FAST FORWARD

Joint ventures are to be included in the venturer's consolidated financial statements by the **gross equity method**. This requires, in addition to the amounts included under the equity method, disclosure of the venturer's share of the turnover, gross assets and gross liabilities of the joint venture.

4.1 Joint ventures

Joint ventures are another form of entity which, while not giving the investor control as with a subsidiary, gives it considerable influence.

There are three important definitions here.

Key terms

> - **Joint venture**: an entity in which the reporting entity holds an interest on a long-term basis and is **jointly controlled** by the reporting entity and one or more other venturers under a contractual arrangement.
>
> - **Joint control**: a reporting entity jointly controls a venture with one or more other entities if none of the entities alone can control that entity but all together can do so and decisions on financial and operating policy essential to the activities, economic performance and financial position of that venture require each venturer's consent.
>
> *(FRS 9)*

Joint control is exercised by the venturers for their mutual benefit, each conducting its part of the contractual arrangement with a view to its own advantage. It is possible within the definition for one venturer to manage the joint venture, provided that the venture's principal operating and financial policies are collectively agreed by the venturers and the venturers have the power to ensure that those policies are followed.

High-level strategic decisions require the consent of each venturer. In effect, each venturer has a veto on such decisions.

Question   Joint control

How is this situation different from that of a minority shareholder in a company?

Answer

A minority shareholder has no veto and is subject to majority rule: *Foss v Harbottle 1843*, except in very limited circumstances.

4.2 Accounting aspects: background

The nature of joint ventures might mean that one line equity accounting is not appropriate. For example, the investor might have a direct interest in certain assets which it has contributed to the venture. Alternatively, it might be considered appropriate to reflect directly in its own financial statements its proportional share of the assets and liabilities of the investee by a form of **proportional consolidation**. This is **a method of accounting where the investor's share of the results, assets and liabilities of its investee is included in its consolidated financial statements on a line-by-line basis.**

The Companies Act contains provisions which permit proportional consolidation for some joint ventures. This is restricted to unincorporated joint ventures and the joint venture should be managed 'jointly with one or more undertakings not included in the consolidation'.

FRED 11 *Associates and joint ventures* proposed identifying two classes of joint ventures: those where the venturers shared in common the benefits and risks, which were to be included by the equity method, and those where each venturer had its own separate interest, which were to be included by proportional consolidation.

4.3 FRS 9 treatment

FRS 9 emphasises the special nature of joint control by identifying joint ventures as a single class of investments wholly separate from associates to be included by a special method of accounting - the gross equity method.

Key term

> **Gross equity method**: a form of equity method under which the investor's share of the aggregate gross assets and liabilities underlying the net amount included for the investment is shown on the face of the balance sheet and, in the profit and loss account, the investor's share of the investee's turnover is noted.
>
> *(FRS 9)*

The gross equity method is like the equity method except with regard to the following.

(a) In the **consolidated profit and loss** account the investor's share of **joint ventures' turnover** is **shown, but not as part of group turnover.** For example:

	£m	£m
Turnover: group and share of joint ventures	560	
Less: share of joint ventures' turnover	130	
Group turnover		430

(b) In the segmental analysis the investor's share of its joint ventures' turnover should also be distinguished from the turnover of the group.

(c) In the **consolidated balance sheet, the investor's share of the gross assets and liabilities** underlying the net equity amount included for joint ventures should be shown in amplification of that amount. For example:

	£m	£m	£m
Fixed assets			
Tangible assets			700
Investments			
Investments in joint ventures:			
Share of gross assets	250		
Share of gross liabilities	(120)		
		130	
Investment in associates		80	
			910

(d) In both the profit and loss account and the balance sheet **any supplemental information given for joint ventures must be shown clearly separate from amounts for the group** and must not be included in the group totals. An exception is made for items below profit before tax in the profit and loss account.

In the investor's individual financial statements, investments in joint ventures should be treated as fixed asset investments and shown at cost, less any amounts written off, or at valuation.

4.4 Further aspects of FRS 9 applying to both joint ventures and associates

4.4.1 Principles of consolidation

As has been mentioned, when calculating the amounts to be included in the investor's consolidated financial statements, whether using the equity method for associates or the gross equity method for joint ventures, the **same principles should be applied as are applied in the consolidation of subsidiaries**. This has the following implications.

(a) **Fair values** are to be attributed to assets and liabilities on acquisition. Goodwill should be treated as per FRS 10. This point was dealt with in connection with associates in Paragraphs 3.27 and 3.28. The same applies to joint ventures.

(b) In arriving at the amounts to be included by the equity method, the **same accounting policies** as those of the investor should be applied.

(c) The financial statements of the investor and the associate or joint venture should be prepared to the **same accounting date** and for the **same accounting period**; associates/joint ventures can prepare three months before if necessary with appropriate adjustments and disclosure.

(d) **Profits or losses resulting from transactions between the investor and its associate/joint venture** may be included in the carrying amount of assets in either party. Where this is the case, the part relating to the **investor's share should be eliminated**. Any impairment of those or similar assets must be taken into account if evidence of it is given by the transactions in question.

4.4.2 Investor is a group

Where the investor is a group, it share of its associate or joint venture is the aggregate of the holdings of the parent and its subsidiaries in that entity. The holdings of any of the group's **other associates or joint ventures should be ignored** for this purpose. Where an associate or joint venture itself has subsidiaries, associates or joint ventures, the results and net assets to be taken into account by the equity method are those reported in that investee's consolidated financial statements (including the investee's share of the results and net assets of its associates and joint ventures), after any adjustment necessary to give effect to the investor's accounting policies.

4.4.3 Options, convertibles and non-equity shares

The investor may hold options, convertibles or non-equity shares in its associate or joint venture. In certain circumstances, the conditions attaching to such holdings are such that the investor should take them into account in reflecting its interest in its investee under the equity or gross equity method. In such cases, the costs of exercising the options or converting the convertibles, or future payments in relation to the non-equity shares, should also be taken into account.

4.4.4 Impairment

In cases where there is impairment in any goodwill attributable to an associate or joint venture the **goodwill should be written down** and the amount written off in the accounting period separately disclosed.

4.4.5 Commencement and cessation of relationship

The following points apply with regard to commencement or cessation of an associate or joint venture relationship.

(a) An investment **becomes an associate on the date on which the investor begins to:**

 (i) Hold a **participating interest**.
 (ii) Exercise **significant influence**.

(b) An investment **ceases to be an associate** on the date **when it ceases to fulfil either of the above.**

(c) An investment **becomes a joint venture on the date on which the investor begins to control it jointly** with other investors, provided it has a long-term interest.

(d) On the date when an investor **ceases to have joint control**, the investment **ceases to be a joint venture.**

(e) The **carrying amount** (percentage of investment retained) should be reviewed and, if necessary, written down to the **recoverable amount**.

4.5 Joint arrangements that are not entities (JANEs)

FAST FORWARD

> Other **joint arrangements,** such as cost-sharing arrangements and one-off construction projects, are to be included in their participants' individual and consolidated financial statements by **each participant including directly** its share of the assets, liabilities and cash flows arising from the arrangements.

Exam focus point

> The December 2002 accounts preparation question involved a JANE under FRS 9.

A reporting entity may operate through a structure that has the appearance of a joint venture but not the reality. It may thus be a separate entity in which the participants hold a long-term interest and exercise joint management, but there may be no common interest because each venturer operates independently of the other venturers within that structure. The framework entity acts merely as an agent for the ventures with each venturer able to identify and control its share of the assets, liabilities and cash flows arising within the entity. **Such arrangements have the form but not the substance of a joint venture.**

The accounting treatment for such joint arrangements required by FRS 9 is that **each venturer should account directly for its share of the assets, liabilities and cash flows held within that structure**. This treatment reflects the substance rather than the form of the arrangement.

4.6 Investors that do not prepare consolidated accounts

A reporting entity may have an associate or joint venture, but **no subsidiaries**. It will thus not prepare group accounts. In such cases it **should present the relevant amounts for associates and joint ventures, as appropriate, by preparing a separate set of financial statements** or by showing the relevant amounts, together with the effects of including them, as additional information to its own financial statements. Investing entities that are exempt from preparing consolidated financial statements, or would be exempt if they had subsidiaries, are exempt from this requirement.

Question

Auden plc is a long established business in office supplies. The nature of its business has expanded and diversified to take account of technological changes which have taken place in recent years. Now in addition to stationery and office furniture, it also supplies photocopiers, fax machines and more recently new computer based technologies. The expansion has occurred organically but also through acquisition of existing companies and joint ventures. Auden plc's investments are as follows.

(a)   **Byron Ltd**. Auden has a 40% interest in the issued share capital of Byron Ltd and representation on the board. Byron Ltd manufactures office furniture and a large proportion of what it produces is sold to Auden. Auden is therefore actively involved in decisions regarding product ranges, designs and pricing to ensure they get the products they want.

(b)   **Chaucer NRG**. Chaucer NRG is a joint venture company which commenced operations on 1 June 19X7. The joint venturers in Chaucer are Auden plc and Dryden Inc, a company also in office automation, specialising in computer products. The purpose of the joint venture was to distribute their products to South America where the demand for office automation is growing rapidly. Auden and Dryden have an equal interest in Chaucer.

(c)   **Elgar Ltd**. Elgar Ltd's principal activities is the supply and fitting of bathroom suites. Its managing director is Mrs Tina Tennyson, wife of Mr Trevor Tennyson, a director of Auden plc. Auden plc has a 25% interest in the share capital of Elgar and the remaining shares are held by various members of the Tennyson family. Mr Tennyson is on the board of Elgar as a non-executive director and this was approved at the last AGM by all the voting members of the Tennyson family. The activities of Elgar and Auden are in totally different markets, the share interest is there for historic reasons and Auden has not exercised its voting rights for several years. During the year Auden plc sold one of the company's executive cars to Elgar Ltd for an agreed open market value of £30,000.

The following are extracts from the financial statements of Byron, Chaucer and Elgar for the year ended 31 March 20X8.

	Byron	Chaucer	Elgar
	£'000	£'000	£'000
Turnover	4,068	17,720	7,640
Operating costs	3,872	16,834	6,980
Operating profit	196	886	660
Interest payable	-	280	30
Profit before tax	196	606	630
Tax	40	152	200
Profit after tax	156	454	430

	Byron	Chaucer	Elgar
	£'000	£'000	£'000
Fixed assets	360	1,720	260
Current assets	2,940	2,130	834
Creditors falling due within one year	(2,214)	(710)	(252)
Creditors falling due after one year	(26)	(1,810)	(400)
	1,060	1,330	442
Cost of investment	600	500	400

Sales of office furniture from Byron to Auden amounted to £160,000 during the year. 10% of the goods remain in the closing stock of Auden. These goods had been sold at a mark up of 25% on cost.

Required

Produce extracts from the consolidated profit and loss account and balance sheet of Auden for the year ended 31 March 20X8 indicating clearly the treatments for Byron, Chaucer and Elgar and where each item would appear.

Answer

AUDEN PLC
EXTRACTS FROM THE CONSOLIDATED PROFIT AND LOSS ACCOUNT
FOR THE YEAR ENDED 31 MARCH 20X8

	£'000	£'000
Turnover	X	
Less share of joint ventures' turnover	(8,860)	
Group turnover		X
Group operating profit		X
Share of operating profit in		
Joint ventures	443	
Associates (W1)	77.2	
Interest payable		
Group	X	
Joint ventures	(140)	
Profit before tax		X
Tax (see below)		X
Profit after tax		X
Tax relates to		
Parent and subsidiary		X
Joint ventures		76
Associates		16

EXTRACTS FROM THE CONSOLIDATED BALANCE SHEET AS AT 31 MARCH 20X8

	£'000	£'000
Fixed assets		
Investments		
Investments in joint ventures		
Share of gross assets	1,925	
Share of gross liabilities	1,260	
		665.0
Investments in associates (W2)		422.8
Other investments		400.0

Workings

1 *Share of associate company profit*

	£'000
Profit of Byron per question	196.0
PUP $(160,000 \times 10\% \times {}^{25}/_{125})$	(3.2)
	192.8
Group share (40%) (rounded)	77.2

2   *Investment in associates*

	£'000
Net assets per question	1,060.0
PUP (W1)	(3.2)
	1,056.8
Group share (40%) (rounded)	422.8

5 Disclosures for associates and joint ventures

The disclosures required by FRS 9 are extensive. Some are required for all associates and joint ventures and other additional disclosures are required if certain thresholds are exceeded. These disclosures are to be made in addition to the amounts required on the face of the financial statements under the equity method or the gross equity method.

Exam focus point

> A detailed question on disclosures is unlikely to come up in your exam, so a summary table is produced below.

FRS 9: Summary of disclosure requirements

All associates and joint ventures	15% threshold*	25% threshold*
• Names of principal associates/joint venture • Proportion of shares held • Accounting date if different • Nature of business • Material differences in accounting policies • Restrictions on distributions • Intercompany balances • Reason for rebutting 20% presumption of participating interest/ significant influence	• Turnover (associates only) • Fixed assets • Current assets • Liabilities due within one year • Liabilities due after one year or more	• Turnover • Profit before tax • Taxation • Profit after tax • Fixed assets • Current assets • Liabilities due within one year • Liabilities due after one year or more

*Threshold refers to investor's aggregate share of gross assets, gross liabilities, turnover or three year average operating result of investee as compared with the corresponding group figure.

BPP
PROFESSIONAL EDUCATION

Chapter Roundup

- **Associates** and **joint ventures** are entities in which an investor holds a **substantial but not controlling interest**. They are the subject of an accounting standard: **FRS 9** *Associates and joint ventures*.

- **Associates** are to be included in the investor's consolidated financial statements using the **equity method**. The investor's share of its associates' results should be included immediately after group operating profit.

- **Joint ventures** are to be included in the venturer's consolidated financial statements by the **gross equity method**. This requires, in addition to the amounts included under the equity method, disclosure of the venturer's share of the turnover, gross assets and gross liabilities of the joint venture.

- Other **joint arrangements**, such as cost-sharing arrangements and one-off construction projects, are to be included in their participants' individual and consolidated financial statements by **each participant including directly** its share of the assets, liabilities and cash flows arising from the arrangements.

Quick Quiz

1 What types of interest does FRS 9 identify?

2 How does FRS 9 define associate?

3 What is meant by 'participating interest'?

4 A group of companies has the following shareholdings.

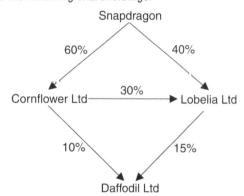

For consolidation purposes what, prima facie, is the relationship of Lobelia Ltd and Daffodil Ltd to Snapdragon plc?

5 What **additional** disclosures are required by FRS 9 when the '25% threshold' is reached (ie not also required when the '15% threshold' is reached). *Circle any that apply.*

   (a) Fixed assets
   (b) Liabilities due within one year
   (c) Profit before tax
   (d) Turnover
   (e) Profit after tax

6 Constable plc owns 40% of Turner plc which it treats as an associated company in accordance with FRS 9. Constable plc also owns 60% of Whistler Ltd. Constable has held both of these shareholdings for more than one year. Turnover of each company for the year ended 30 June 20X0 was as follows.

	£m
Constable	400
Turner	200
Whistler	100

What figure should be shown as turnover in the consolidated profit and loss account of Constable plc?

Answers to Quick Quiz

1   Associates
    Joint ventures
    Joint arrangements that are not entities

2   An entity in which another entity has a participating interest and over whose operating and financial policies the investor exerts a significant influence.

3   An interest held in the shares of another entity on a long-term basis for the purpose of securing a contribution to the investor's activities by the exercise of control or influence.

4   Lobelia Ltd **subsidiary**; Daffodil Ltd **associate**

    Shares held by subsidiary companies count in full. Snapdragon has control of Cornflower's 30% holding in Lobelia. It owns 40% itself, 40 + 30 gives control. Snapdragon therefore controls Lobelia's 15% in Daffodil and Cornflower's 10% in Daffodil (10 + 15 = 25 = associate).

5   (c) and (e)

6   Turnover will be 100% H + 100% S only. Associates are introduced in to the consolidated profit and loss account as a share of their operating profits in the first instance.

	£m
Constable	400
Whistler (subsidiary)	100
	500

Now try the questions below from the Exam Question Bank

Number	Level	Marks	Time
Q21	Examination	20	36 mins

BPP
PROFESSIONAL EDUCATION

Part D
The theoretical framework of accounting

BPP
PROFESSIONAL EDUCATION

Theoretical aspects of accounting

18

Topic list	Syllabus reference
1 Comprehensive income	1(c)
2 Fair value	1(c)
3 Current purchasing power (CPP)	1(c)
4 Current cost accounting (CCA)	1(c)
5 Historical cost accounting	1(c)

Introduction

'Comprehensive income' and 'fair value' are concepts currently under
discussion by standard setters. It is important to understand them as they may
appear as part of a discussion question.

Study guide

- Outline the concept of 'comprehensive income'.

- Explain the principle of fair value.

- Describe the deficiencies of historic cost accounts (HCA) during periods of rising prices and explain in principle alternatives to HCA.

1 Comprehensive income

Exam focus point

This topic can only form part of a discussion question in the exam, but it is useful material for any question on convergence issues and it is a new addition to your syllabus, so the examiner expects you to know about it.

FAST FORWARD

Comprehensive income means **all** transactions for the period, other than those between an entity and its owners. It is not currently reported under either UK or International standards, but it is a likely future development.

The concept of **comprehensive income** has been under discussion in since 2002 and illustrates the fact that, while the convergence process of which we are most aware is that between UK and International standards, a similar process is going on between the IASB and the FASB.

1.1 Comprehensive income and the FASB

In the US, public companies have been required since 1997 to report comprehensive income. 'Comprehensive income' is defined as **all** gains and losses for the period, ie. all changes in equity, other than those arising from transactions with equity holders. So it does not include transactions such as share issues and dividend payments.

The requirement to report comprehensive income in the US was prompted by the fact that certain items were bypassing the Statement of Income and going straight to the statement of changes in stockholders' equity, specifically foreign currency translation gains and losses, adjustments to the minimum pension liability and unrealised gains or losses on available-for-sale investments. In this way, users were not being given important information.

1.2 Comprehensive income and the IASB/ASB

Since 2002 the IASB and the ASB have been running a joint project on **reporting financial performance**. Other than the desire to move into line with the FASB, the project has been motivated by the following considerations:

(a)   The conceptual basis of the distinction between the income statement (profit and loss account) and the statement of changes in equity (STRGL) is felt to be unclear.

(b)   The structure of the income statement/profit and loss account could be more clearly defined, with more helpful categorisation of different items.

(c)   The income statement/profit and loss account and the cash flow statement are closely related but not designed to be read together, so their mutual information content could be improved

The work of this project **may** lead to the formulation of a new accounting standard on the presentation of gains and losses, which would replace FRS 3 in the UK. The focus is on the development of a single statement of **comprehensive income,** which would report all gains and losses for the period, replacing in the UK the profit and loss account and the STRGL.

2 Fair value

FAST FORWARD

The concept of **fair value** has become very important since the issue of IAS 39 and now FRS 26 in the UK. Entities are now permitted to remeasure financial instruments to fair value.

Exam focus point

This topic has been newly-added to the syllabus, so ignore it at your peril! Any question involving FRS 26 will require you to know about fair value and a short discussion of it could be added onto the end of an accounts preparation question which includes a financial instrument.

2.1 Background

The fair value concept is relevant to two major areas of accounting.

Following a joint FASB/IASB project on business combinations it was agreed that fair value should be applied to assets and liabilities acquired in a business combination. In many cases this leads to a 'fair value adjustment'.

The EU **Fair Value Directive** required UK and other member states to permit or require companies to account for some of their financial instruments at **fair value**.

The Directive had the declared objective of enabling companies to use more 'transparent' accounting practices and of bringing those practices into line with IAS 39. The UK response to this was the issue of FRS 26.

2.2 Fair value and FRS 26

Fair value is commonly defined by reference to the **current market value** of a financial instrument. IAS 26 defines **fair value** as "the amount for which an asset could be exchanged or a liability settled, between knowledgeable, willing parties in an arm's length transaction."

FRS 26 permits an entity to designate any financial asset or liability on initial recognition as one to be measured at fair value, with changes to fair value recognised in profit or loss.

Measurement at fair value is, of course, no problem in the case of financial instruments for which market prices are readily available. Where this is not the case, fair value will have to be estimated using either the transaction price or valuation techniques using observable market data. There is some degree of judgement implied here, which could lead to different valuations of similar assets/liabilities from one company to the next.

The recognition of changes to fair value in profit or loss means that what are essentially unrealised gains and losses are reported in the profit and loss account. It will be interesting to see how this one plays out.

3 Current purchasing power (CPP)

FAST FORWARD

CPP accounting is a method of accounting for general (not specific) inflation. It does so by expressing asset values in a stable monetary unit, the £c or £ of current purchasing power.

Exam focus point

The June 2003 exam asked candidates to calculate the depreciation charge for the plant of a company (based on year end values) and its balance sheet carrying values using three bases.

(a)   Historical cost
(b)   Current purchasing power
(c)   Current cost

3.1 Capital maintenance in times of inflation

Profit can be measured as the **difference between how wealthy a company is at the beginning and at the end of an accounting period.**

(a)   This wealth can be expressed in terms of the capital of a company as shown in its opening and closing balance sheets.

(b)   A business which maintains its capital unchanged during an accounting period can be said to have broken even.

(c)   **Once capital has been maintained, anything achieved in excess represents profit.**

For this analysis to be of any use, we must be able to draw up a company's balance sheet at the beginning and at the end of a period, so as to place a value on the opening and closing capital. There are particular difficulties in doing this during a period of rising prices.

In conventional historical cost accounts, assets are stated in the balance sheet at the amount it cost to acquire them (less any amounts written off in respect of depreciation or diminution in value). Capital is simply the difference between assets and liabilities.

Important!

If prices are rising, it is possible for a company to show a profit in its historical cost accounts despite having identical physical assets and owing identical liabilities at the beginning and end of its accounting period.

For example, consider the following opening and closing balance sheets of a company.

	Opening £	Closing £
Stock (100 items at cost)	500	600
Other net assets	1,000	1,000
Capital	1,500	1,600

Assuming that no new capital has been introduced during the year, and no capital has been distributed as dividends, the profit shown in historical cost accounts would be £100, being the excess of closing capital over opening capital. And yet in physical terms the company is no better off: it still has 100 units of stock (which cost £5 each at the beginning of the period, but £6 each at the end) and its other net assets are identical. The 'profit' earned has merely enabled the company to keep pace with inflation.

An alternative to the concept of capital maintenance based on historical costs is to express capital in physical terms. On this basis, no profit would be recognised in the example above because the physical substance of the company is unchanged over the accounting period. In the UK, a system of accounting (called **current cost accounting** or CCA) was introduced in 1980 by SSAP 16 (now withdrawn) and had as its basis a concept of capital maintenance based on 'operating capability'.

Capital is maintained if at the end of the period the company is in a position to achieve the same physical output as it was at the beginning of the period.

You should bear in mind that financial definitions of capital maintenance are not the only ones possible; in theory at least, there is no reason why profit should not be measured as the increase in a company's *physical* capital over an accounting period.

3.2 The unit of measurement

Another way to tackle the problems of capital maintenance in times of rising prices is to look at the unit of measurement in which accounting values are expressed.

It is an axiom of **conventional accounting**, as it has developed over the years, that value should be measured in terms of money. It is also **implicitly assumed that money values are stable**, so that £1 at the start of the financial year has the same value as £1 at the end of that year. **But when prices are rising, this assumption is invalid: £1 at the end of the year has less value (less purchasing power) than it had one year previously.**

This **leads to problems when aggregating amounts which have arisen at different times.** For example, a company's fixed assets may include items bought at different times over a period of many years. They will each have been recorded in £s, but the value of £1 will have varied over the period. In effect the fixed asset figure in a historical cost balance sheet is an aggregate of a number of items expressed in different units. It **could be argued that such a figure is meaningless.**

Faced with this argument, one possibility would be to re-state all accounts items in terms of a stable monetary unit. There would be difficulties in practice, but in theory there is no reason why a stable unit (£ CPP = £s of current purchasing power) should not be devised. In this section we will look at a system of accounting (current purchasing power accounting, or CPP) based on precisely this idea.

3.3 Specific and general price changes

We can identify two different types of price inflation.

When prices are rising, it is likely that the current value of assets will also rise, but not necessarily by the general rate of inflation. For example, if the replacement cost of a machine on 1 January 20X2 was £5,000, and the general rate of inflation in 20X2 was 8%, we would not necessarily expect the replacement cost of the machine at 31 December 20X2 to be £5,000 plus 8% = £5,400. The rate of price increase on the machinery might have been less than 8% or more than 8%. (Conceivably, in spite of general inflation, the replacement cost of the machinery might have gone down.)

(a) There is **specific price inflation**, which **measures price changes over time for a specific asset or group of assets.**

(b) There is **general price inflation**, which **is the average rate of inflation, which reduces the general purchasing power of money.**

To counter the problems of specific price inflation some system of current value accounting may be used (for example, the system of current cost accounting described in the following chapter). The capital maintenance concepts underlying current value systems do not attempt to allow for the maintenance of real value in money terms.

Current purchasing power (CPP) accounting is based on a different concept of capital maintenance.

Key term

> **CPP** measures profits as the increase in the current purchasing power of equity. Profits are therefore stated after allowing for the declining purchasing power of money due to price inflation.

In Britain attempts to introduce CPP accounting have been in a combination with historical cost accounting, and it is on this aspect that this section will concentrate.

When applied to historical cost accounting, **CPP is a system of accounting which makes adjustments to income and capital values to allow for the general rate of price inflation.** An attempt to introduce such a system was made in 1974 with the publication of a Provisional Statement of Standard Accounting Practice, PSSAP 7 *Accounting for changes in the purchasing power of money.* Although it was withdrawn after a year, and was then superseded by SSAP 16, it remains a topic of debate and **some knowledge of CPP accounting is necessary to understand the diversity of views currently held on inflation accounting in general.**

3.4 The principles and procedures of CPP accounting

In CPP accounting, profit is measured after allowing for general price changes. It is a fundamental idea of CPP that capital should be maintained in terms of the same monetary purchasing power, so that:

$$P_{CPP} = D_{CPP} + (E_{t(CPP)} - E_{(t-1)CPP})$$

where P_{CPP} is the CPP accounting profit

            D_{CPP} is distributions to shareholders, re-stated in current purchasing power terms

            E_t the total value of assets attributable to the owners of the business entity at the end of the accounting period, restated in current purchasing power terms

            $E_{(t-1)CPP}$ is the total value of the owners' equity at the beginning of the year re-stated in terms of current purchasing power at the end of the year.

A current purchasing power £ relates to the value of money on the last day of the accounting period.

Profit in CPP accounting is therefore **measured after allowing for maintenance of equity capital.** To the extent that a company is financed by loans, there is no requirement to allow for the maintenance of the purchasing power of the loan creditors' capital. Indeed, as we shall see, the equity of a business can profit from the loss in the purchasing power value of loans.

3.5 Monetary and non-monetary items

FAST FORWARD

> In the CPP balance sheet, **monetary items** are stated at their **face value. Non-monetary items** are stated at their **current purchasing power** as at the balance sheet date.

Key term

> A **monetary item** is an asset or liability whose amount is fixed by contract or statute in terms of £s, regardless of changes in general price levels and the purchasing power of the pound.

The main examples of monetary items are cash, debtors, creditors and loan capital.

Key term

> A **non-monetary item** is an asset or liability whose value is not fixed by contract or statute.

These include land and buildings, plant and machinery and stock.

In CPP accounting, there is an **important difference** between monetary assets and liabilities.

(a) If a company borrows money in a period of inflation, the amount of the debt will remain fixed (by law) so that when the debt is eventually paid, it will be paid in £s of a lower purchasing power.

For example, if a company borrows £2,000 on 1 January 20X5 and repays the loan on 1 January 20X9, the purchasing power of the £2,000 repaid in 20X9 will be much less than the value of £2,000 in 20X5, because of inflation. Since the company by law must repay only £2,000 of principal, it has gained by having the use of the money from the loan for 4 years. (The lender of the £2,000 will try to protect the value of his loan in a period of inflation by charging a higher rate of interest; however, this does not alter the fact that the loan remains fixed at £2,000 in money value.)

(b) If a company holds cash in a period of inflation, its value in terms of current purchasing power will decline. The company will 'lose' by holding the cash instead of converting it into a non-monetary asset. Similarly, if goods are sold on credit, the amount of the debt is fixed by contract; and in a period of inflation, the current purchasing power of the money from the sale, when it is eventually received, will be less than the purchasing power of the debt, when it was first incurred.

In CPP accounting, it is therefore argued that **there are gains from having monetary liabilities and losses from having monetary assets.**

(a) In the case of monetary assets, there is a need to make a provision against profit for the loss in purchasing power, because there will be a need for extra finance when the monetary asset is eventually used for operational activities. For example, if a company has a cash balance of £200, which is just sufficient to buy 100 new items of raw material stock on 1 January 20X5, and if the rate of inflation during 20X5 is 10%, the company would need £220 to buy the same 100 items on 1 January 20X6 (assuming the items increase in value by the general rate of inflation). By holding the £200 as a monetary asset throughout 20X5, the company would need £20 more to buy the same goods and services on 1 January 20X6 that it could have obtained on 1 January 20X5. £20 would be a CPP loss on holding the monetary asset (cash) for a whole year.

(b) In the case of monetary liabilities, the argument in favour of including a 'profit' in CPP accounting is not as strong. By incurring a debt, say, on 1 January 20X5, there will not be any eventual cash input to the business. The 'profit' from the monetary liabilities is a 'paper' profit, and T A Lee has argued against including it in the CPP profit and loss account. PSSAP 7, however, noted that

'It has been argued that the gain on long-term borrowing should not be shown as profit in the CPP accounts because it might not be possible to distribute it without raising additional finance. This argument, however, confuses the measurement of profitability with the measurement of liquidity. Even in the absence of inflation, the whole of a company's profit may not be distributable without raising additional finance, for example, because it has been invested in, or earmarked for investment in, non-liquid assets.'

PSSAP 7 therefore concluded that all gains and losses from having monetary liabilities or assets should be included in the calculation of CPP profit. The concept of monetary gains and losses is an important one, and it was introduced into current cost accounting practice in Britain (see next section).

Question

CPP

Rice and Price set up in business on 1 January 20X5 with no fixed assets, and cash of £5,000. On 1 January they acquired some stocks for the full £5,000 which they sold on 30 June 19X5 for £6,000. On 30

November they obtained a further £2,100 of stock on credit. The index of the general price level gives the following index figures.

Date	Index
1 January 20X5	300
30 June 20X5	330
30 November 20X5	350
31 December 20X5	360

Calculate the CPP profits (or losses) of Rice and Price for the year to 31 December 20X5.

Answer

The approach is to prepare a CPP profit and loss account.

	£c	£c
Sales (6,000 × 360/330)		6,545
Less cost of goods sold (5,000 × 360/300)		6,000
		545
Loss on holding cash for 6 months*	(545)	
Gain by having creditor for 1 month**	60	
		485
CPP profit		60

* (£6,000 × 360/330) – £6,000 = £c 545
**(£2,100 × 360/350) – £2,100 = £c 60

3.6 The advantages and disadvantages of CPP accounting

3.6.1 Advantages

(a)   The **restatement of asset values in terms of a stable money value provides a more meaningful basis of comparison** with other companies. Similarly, provided that previous years' profits are re-valued into CPP terms, it is also possible to compare the current year's results with past performance.

(b)   Profit is measured in 'real' terms and excludes 'inflationary value increments'. This **enables better forecasts of future prospects to be made.**

(c)   CPP **avoids the subjective valuations** of current value accounting, because a single price index is applied to all non-monetary assets.

(d)   CPP **provides a stable monetary unit** with which to value profit and capital; ie £c.

(e)   Since it is based on historical cost accounting, **raw data is easily verified**, and measurements of value can be readily audited.

3.6.2 Disadvantages

(a)   It is **not clear what £c means**. 'Generalised purchasing power' as measured by the Retail Price Index, or indeed any other general price index, has no obvious practical significance.

'Generalised purchasing power has no relevance to any person or entity because no such thing exists in reality, except as a statistician's computation.'   (T A Lee)

(b)   The use of indices **inevitably involves approximations** in the measurements of value.

(c) **The value of assets in a CPP balance sheet has less meaning than a current value balance sheet**. It cannot be supposed that the CPP value of net assets reflects:

    (i)   The general goods and services that could be bought if the assets were released.

    (ii)   The consumption of general goods and services that would have to be forgone to replace those assets.

In this respect, a CPP balance sheet has similar drawbacks to an historical cost balance sheet.

4 Current cost accounting (CCA)

FAST FORWARD

CCA is an alternative to the historical cost convention which attempts to overcome the problems of accounting for **specific price inflation**. Unlike CPP accounting, it does not attempt to cope with general inflation. CCA is based on a physical concept or **capital maintenance**. Profit is recognised after the operating capability of the business has been maintained.

Exam focus point

The June 2003 exam asked candidates to calculate the depreciation charge for the plant of a company (based on year end values) and its balance sheet carrying values using three bases.

(a) Historical cost
(b) Current purchasing power
(c) Current cost

4.1 Value to the business (deprival value)

The **conceptual basis of CCA is that the value of assets consumed or sold, and the value of assets in the balance sheet, should be stated at their value to the business** (also known as 'deprival value').

A system of current cost accounting was introduced into the UK by SSAP 16 *Current cost accounting* in March 1980. This was the culmination of a long process of research into the problems of accounting in times of inflation. One result of this process had been the publication of PSSAP 7 on current purchasing power accounting, described previously. SSAP 16 encountered heavy criticism and was finally withdrawn in April 1988.

In CCA, a physical rather than financial definition of capital is used: capital maintenance is measured by the ability of the business entity to keep up the same level of operating capability.

Key term

The **deprival value** of an asset is the loss which a business entity would suffer if it were deprived of the use of the asset.

Value to the business, or deprival value, can be any of the following values.

(a) **Replacement cost**. In the case of fixed assets, it is assumed that the replacement cost of an asset would be its net replacement cost (NRC), its gross replacement cost minus an appropriate provision for depreciation to reflect the amount of its life already 'used up'.

(b) **Net realisable value** (NRV); what the asset could be sold for, net of any disposal costs.

(c) **Economic value** (EV), or utility; what the existing asset will be worth to the company over the rest of its useful life.

The choice of deprival value from one of the three values listed will depend on circumstances. The decision tree on the next page illustrates the principles involved in the choice, but in simple terms you should remember that in **CCA deprival value is nearly always replacement cost.**

If the asset is worth replacing, its deprival value will always be net replacement cost. If the asset is not worth replacing, it might be disposed of straight away, or else it might be kept in operation until the end of its useful life.

You may therefore come across a statement that deprival value is the **lower of**:

(a)   **Net replacement cost**

(b)   The **higher of net realisable value and economic value**

We have already seen that if an asset is not worth replacing at the end of its life, the deprival value will be NRV or EV. However, there are many assets which will not be replaced either:

(a)   Because the asset is technologically obsolete, and has been (or will be) superseded by more modern equipment.

(b)   Because the business is changing the nature of its operations and will not want to continue in the same line of business once the asset has been used up.

Such assets, even though there are reasons not to replace them, would still be valued (usually) at net replacement cost, because this 'deprival value' still provides an estimate of the operating capability of the company.

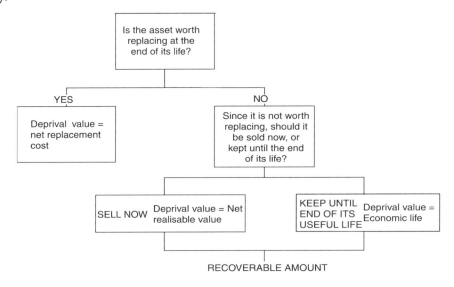

4.2 CCA profits and deprival value

The deprival value of assets is reflected in the CCA profit and loss account by the following means.

(a)   **Depreciation** is **charged** on fixed assets **on the basis of gross replacement cost** of the asset (where NRC is the deprival value).

(b)   Where **NRV or EV** is the deprival value, the **charge against CCA profits will be the loss in value of the asset during the accounting period**; ie from its previous balance sheet value to its current NRV or EV.

(c)   **Goods sold are charged at their replacement cost**. Thus if an item of stock cost £15 to produce, and sells for £20, by which time its replacement cost has risen to £17, the CCA profit would be £3.

BPP
PROFESSIONAL EDUCATION

	£
Sales	20
Less replacement cost of goods sold	17
Current cost profit	3

It is useful to explain the distinction here between CCA and accounting for inflation, and a simple example may help to describe the difference. Suppose that Arthur Smith Ltd buys an asset on 1 January for £10,000. The estimated life of the asset is 5 years, and straight line depreciation is charged. At 31 December the gross replacement cost of the asset is £10,500 (5% higher than on 1 January) but general inflation during the year, as measured by the retail price index, has risen 20%.

(a) To maintain the value of the business against inflation, the asset should be revalued as follows.

	£
Gross (£10,000 × 120%)	12,000
Depreciation charge for the year (@ 20%)	2,400
Net value in the balance sheet	9,600

(b) In CCA, the business maintains its operating capability if we revalue the asset as follows.

	£
Gross replacement cost	10,500
Depreciation charge for the year (note)	2,100
NRC; balance sheet value	8,400

Note	£
Historical cost depreciation	2,000
CCA depreciation adjustment (5%)	100
Total CCA depreciation cost	2,100

CCA preserves the operating capability of the company but does not necessarily preserve it against the declining value in the purchasing power of money (against inflation). As mentioned in the previous chapter, CCA is a system which takes account of specific price inflation (changes in the prices of specific assets or groups of assets) but not of general price inflation.

A strict view of current cost accounting might suggest that a set of CCA accounts should be prepared from the outset on the basis of deprival values. In practice that has not been the procedure adopted in the UK. Instead, current cost accounts have been prepared by starting from historical cost accounts and making appropriate adjustments.

4.3 Current cost adjustments to historical cost profit

FAST FORWARD

The **current cost profit and loss account** is constructed by taking historical cost profit before interest and tax and adjusting as follows:

- Current cost operating adjustments in respect of **cost of sales, monetary working capital** and **depreciation** are made to arrive at **current cost operating profit**.

- A **gearing adjustment** is then necessary to arrive at a figure of current cost profit attributable to shareholders.

In current cost accounting profit is calculated as follows

	£	£
Historical cost profit		X
Less: cost of sales adjustment (COSA)	X	
depreciation adjustment	X	
		(X)
Current cost profit		X

The holding gains, both realised and unrealised, are therefore excluded from current cost profit. The double entry for the debits in the current cost profit and loss account is to credit both COSA and depreciation adjustment to a non-distributable revaluation reserve.

4.3.1 The current cost profit and loss account and balance sheet

The format of the *current cost profit and loss account* would show the following information, although not necessarily in the order given.

	£	£
Historical cost profit (before interest & taxation)		X
Current cost operating adjustments		
Cost of sales adjustment (COSA)	(X)	
Monetary working capital adjustment (loss or gain) (MWCA)	(X) or X	
Depreciation adjustment	(X)	
		(X)
Current cost operating profit (before interest and taxation)		X
Less interest payable and receivable		(X)
Add gearing adjustment		X
Current cost profit attributable to shareholders		X
Less taxation		(X)
Current cost profit after tax		X
Extraordinary items (loss or gain)		(X) or X
Current cost profit or loss for the financial year		X

4.4 Cost of sales adjustment (COSA)

The COSA is **necessary to eliminate realised holding gains on stock**. It **represents the difference between the replacement cost and the historical cost of goods sold.** The exclusion of holding gains from CC profit is a necessary consequence of the need to maintain operating capability. The COSA represent that portion of the HC profit which must be consumed in replacing the stock item sold so that trading can continue. Where practical difficulties arise in estimating replacement cost, a simple indexing system can be used.

4.5 Depreciation adjustment

The depreciation adjustment is **the difference between the depreciation charge on the gross replacement cost of the assets and the historical cost depreciation**. This is (as with the COSA) a realised holding gain which is excluded from the CC profit. Where comparison is made with a different asset for the purposes of calculating replacement cost (because of the obsolescence of the old asset), then allowance must be made for different useful lives and different production capabilities.

4.6 Monetary working capital adjustment (MWCA)

Where a company gives or takes credit for the sale or purchase of goods, the goods are paid for at the end of the credit period at the replacement cost as at the beginning of the credit period. If a company measures profit as the excess of revenue over cost:

(a) **Creditors protect the company** to some extent **from price changes because the company lags behind current prices in its payment.**

(b) **Debtors, in contrast, would be a burden on profits** in a period of rising prices because sales receipts will always relate to previous months' sales at a lower price/cost/profit level.

The MWCA can therefore be either a gain or a loss.

4.7 Gearing adjustment

The gearing adjustment reduces the effect of the current cost adjustments to the extent that the business is financed by external creditors.

For instance, a company's gearing $\left(\dfrac{\text{Net borrowing}}{\text{Equity + net borrowing}} \right)$ is 30%.

It's current cost adjustments are:

	£
MWCA	1,200
COSA	300
Depreciation	100
	1,600
Gearing adjustment (1,600 × 30%)	(480)
Deduction to arrive at current cost profit	1,120

4.8 Summary of double entry: CCA

It may be useful to summarise the double-entry system in CCA, in which the current cost reserve has a central role.

(a) **For fixed assets, there will be an excess of net replacement cost over (historical cost) net book value**. The increase in this excess amount each accounting period will be recorded as:

DEBIT   net assets (assets account and provision for depreciation account) with the increase in the gross replacement cost minus total extra provision for depreciation;

CREDIT   current cost reserve account

(b) The **various adjustments** will be as follows.

DEBIT   current cost profit and loss account
CREDIT   current cost reserve account;

with the amount of the **COSA**, the depreciation adjustment and the MWCA, if this reduces the current cost profit. If the MWCA increases the current cost profit, the entries would be 'credit P & L account' 'debit current cost reserve'.

(c) At the end of an accounting period, there may be some **revaluations of closing stocks**:

DEBIT   stocks
CREDIT   current cost reserve account

with the amount of the revaluation.

On the first day of the next accounting period, this entry is **reversed**; ie

CREDIT   stocks (to reduce them to historical cost)
DEBIT   current cost reserve account.

4.9 The advantages and disadvantages of current cost accounting

4.9.1 Advantages

(a)   By excluding holding gains from profit, CCA **can be used to indicate whether** the **dividends** paid to shareholders (which by UK law can exceed the size of the CCA profit) **will reduce the operating capability** of the business.

(b)   Assets are valued after management has considered the **opportunity cost** of holding them, and the expected benefits from their future use. CCA is therefore **a useful guide for management in deciding whether to hold or sell assets.**

(c)   It is **relevant to the needs of information users** in:

   (i)   Assessing the stability of the business entity.

   (ii)   Assessing the vulnerability of the business (eg to a takeover), or the liquidity of the business.

   (iii) Evaluating the performance of management in maintaining and increasing the business substance.

   (iv)   Judging future prospects.

(d)   It can be **implemented fairly easily** in practice, by making simple adjustments to the historical cost accounting profits. A current cost balance sheet can also be prepared with reasonable simplicity.

4.9.2 Disadvantages

(a)   It is impossible to make valuations of EV or NRV without subjective judgements. The **measurements used are** therefore **not objective.**

(b)   There are **several problems to be overcome in deciding how to provide an estimate of replacement costs for fixed assets.**

   (i)   Depreciation based on replacement costs **does not conform to the traditional accounting view** that depreciation can be viewed as a means of spreading the cost of the asset over its estimated life,

   (ii)   Depreciation based on replacement costs would appear to be a means of providing that sufficient funds are set aside in the business to ensure that the asset can be replaced at the end of its life. But if it is not certain what technological advances might be in the next few years and how the type of assets required might change between the current time and the estimated time of replacement, it is difficult to argue that depreciation based on today's costs is a valid way of providing for the eventual physical replacement of the asset.

   (iii) It is more correct, however, that **depreciation in CCA does not set aside funds for the physical replacement of fixed assets.**

   'CCA aims to maintain no more and no less than the facilities that are available at the accounting date ... despite the fact that the fixed assets which provide those facilities might never be replaced in their existing or currently available form ... In simple language, this means charging depreciation on the basis of the current replacement cost of the assets at the time the facilities are used.'   (Mallinson)

BPP PROFESSIONAL EDUCATION

(iv)   It may be argued that depreciation based on **historical cost is more accurate** than replacement cost depreciation, **because the historical cost is known,** whereas replacement cost is simply an estimate. However, replacement costs are re-assessed each year, so that inaccuracies in the estimates in one year can be rectified in the next year.

(c)   The **mixed value approach** to valuation **means** that some assets will be valued at replacement cost, but others will be valued at net realisable value or economic value. It is arguable that the **total assets** will, therefore, have an **aggregate value** which is **not particularly meaningful** because of this mixture of different concepts.

(d)   It can be argued that **'deprival value' is an unrealistic concept, because the business entity has not been deprived of the use of the asset**. This argument is one which would seem to reject the fundamental approach to 'capital maintenance' on which CCA is based.

5 Historical cost accounting

Exam focus point

The June 2003 paper required candidates to explain the problems that can be encountered when users rely on financial statements prepared under the historical cost convention for their information needs.

5.1 Limitations of historical cost accounting

Historical cost accounting is simple to use and understand but does suffer from several limitations.

(a)   **Fixed asset values are unrealistic**. This is especially so with property and in effect **unrealised holding gains** are not recognised until the year of disposal.

(b)   **Accounting ratios may be unrealistic**. If net assets/capital employed are understated, accounting ratios such as return on capital employed and asset utilisation could be misleading.

(c)   **Inter-company comparisons might be undermined**. For example, Company A may seem to be performing well because it is still coping with old virtually depreciated assets. Company B may be operating with expensive newly acquired assets. Company A's assets may need replacing soon, so there may well be questions about its financial adaptability if it does not have adequate resources.

(d)   **Depreciation charge is inadequate**. Under HCA, only the cost is **spread** over the **economic life** of the asset. Hence the performance statement will report **rosier annual results** than if fixed assets reflected revaluations.

(e)   **Trading performance may be overstated**. Sales revenue may be recognised on up to date selling prices but the cost of sales figure may include stocks brought forward from earlier periods included at out of date values.

For example, an item of stock costing £100 is sold for £150 giving a recorded profit of £50. However, this items is replenished at a cost of £120, suggesting that the make up of the recorded profit is probably:

	£
Holding gain	20
Trading profit	30
	50

Hence, trading profit includes holding gain on stocks.

(f) **Profits (or losses) on holdings of net monetary items are not shown.** For example, £1,000 cash held by a company on 1 January 20X6 could have purchased machine X. However, by 31 December 20X6, the price of the machine was £1,200. HCA does not tell the story of the loss on holding cash.

(g) **Creditworthiness is not enhanced.** If property is used as security to borrow money, current values rather than historical cost are more relevant to potential financiers.

(h) **Comparisons over time are unrealistic.** This effectively reinforces the above. For example, a company's sales are £1 million and £5 million for 1980 and 2005 respectively, which at first sight may seem impressive. However, the impact of inflation should be taken into consideration.

(i) **The time effect of inflation on capital maintenance is not reflected.** As demonstrated above, profits may be distributed to the detriment of the long term viability of the business.

(j) **The company may become a take-over target.** Understated asset values may lead to:

- Higher gearing ratios
- Lower assets per share value

Hence the company may be more susceptible to a take over bid.

5.2 The modified historical cost approach

As discussed in Chapter 4, CA 1985, Sch 4 allows companies to apply both HCA rules and alternative rules subject to certain conditions. FRS 15 also sets out the requirements where a company would like to revalue tangible fixed assets.

The modified HCA approach has several advantages.

(a) The financial statements produced are easy to prepare, easy to read and easy to understand.

(b) The mix and match approach is practical, albeit pragmatic. Revaluation of a class of fixed assets such as property but not plant and equipment is sensible.

(c) In periods of low inflation, cost can be a useful and meaningful figure. Moreover, it is relatively simply to compare cost figures between companies. Any impacts of inflation can be readily identified.

Chapter Roundup

- **Comprehensive income** means **all** transactions for the period, other than those between an entity and its owners. It is not currently reported under either UK or International standards, but it is a likely future development.

- The concept of **fair value** has become very important since the issue of IAS 39 and now FRS 26 in the UK. Entities are now permitted to remeasure financial instruments to fair value.

- **CPP accounting** is a method of accounting for general (not specific) inflation. It does so by expressing asset values in a stable monetary unit, the £c or £ of current purchasing power.

- In the **CPP balance sheet**, **monetary items** are stated at their **face value**. **Non-monetary items** are stated at their **current purchasing power** as at the balance sheet date.

- **CCA** is an alternative to the historical cost convention which attempts to overcome the problems of accounting for **specific price inflation**. Unlike CPP accounting, it does not attempt to cope with general inflation.

- CCA is based on a **physical concept of capital maintenance**. Profit is recognised after the operating capability of the business has been maintained.

- The current cost profit and loss account is constructed by taking **historical cost** profit before interest and taxation as a starting point.

  - Current cost **operating adjustments** in respect of **cost of sales**, **monetary working capital** and **depreciation** are made so as to arrive at **current cost operating profit**.

  - A **gearing adjustment** is then necessary to arrive at a figure of current cost profit attributable to shareholders.

Quick Quiz

1   How would 'comprehensive income' differ from the income currently reported in the profit and loss account?

2   How does FRS 26 define 'fair value'?

3   Stock is a non-monetary item.

    True   ☐

    False   ☐

4   List the advantages and disadvantages of CPP as a method of accounting.

5   *Fill in the three blanks.*

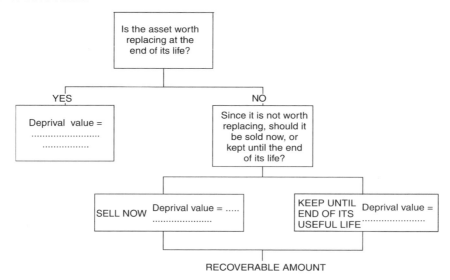

RECOVERABLE AMOUNT

6   List four advantages and four disadvantages of CCA.

Answers to Quick Quiz

1   It would include items such as foreign exchange gains and losses which are currently reported in the STRGL.

2   The amount for which an asset could be exchanged or a liability settled, between knowledgeable, willing parties in an arm's length transaction.

3   True

4   See Paragraph 3.6.

5   Answers (from left to right) net replacement cost, net realisable value and economic value

6   Refer to Paragraph 4.9.

Now try the question below from the Exam Question Bank			
Number	**Level**	**Marks**	**Time**
Q22	Full examination	25	45 mins

BPP
PROFESSIONAL EDUCATION

19

The ASB's Statement of Principles

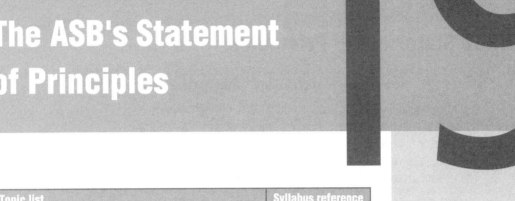

Topic list	Syllabus reference
1 ASB *Statement of Principles*	3(e)

Introduction

By now you should have acquired a thorough grasp of accounting, both for single companies and for groups. You should therefore have little difficulty with this chapter on the ASB's Statement of Principles.

Chapter 1 introduced you to the conceptual framework and in this chapter we will cover in detail the ASB's conceptual framework, the Statement of Principles. The Statement is designed to provide the basis for all new accounting standards. It is therefore very important and also very topical as you will know from your reading of the financial press.

BPP
PROFESSIONAL EDUCATION

Study guide

- Describe the ASB's approach to revenue recognition within its Statement of Principles.

Exam guide

The Statement of Principles is a very pervasive document as it provides a framework for standard setters. You should be able to relate the majority of your written answers to the Statement, especially when discussing the strengths or weaknesses of a standard.

1 ASB Statement of Principles

FAST FORWARD

The *Statement of Principles* is the ASB's conceptual framework. Key points to note are:

- It is not an accounting standard.
- It affects accounting practice by influencing the standard-setting process.
- 'True and fair', FRS 18 and matching are important.
- Current cost accounting is **not** on the agenda.
- The balance sheet and P&L are equally important.

Exam focus point

This topic always comes up in some guise in an exam. You must understand and learn the material covered here. You are most likely to be asked to link it to a particular FRS or given set of circumstances.

The Accounting Standards Board (ASB) published (in November 1995) an exposure draft of its Statement of Principles for Financial Reporting. In March 1999, the text was substantially revised with particular attention being given to the clarity of expression. In December 1999 the Statement was finalised. The ASB issued with the revised draft an introductory booklet and a technical supplement. Together these documents respond to the criticisms raised on the 1995 version by exploding myths, rebutting arguments and making technical changes.

The statement consists of eight chapters.

(1)   The objective of financial statements
(2)   The reporting entity
(3)   The qualitative characteristics of financial information
(4)   The elements of financial statements
(5)   Recognition in financial statements
(6)   Measurement in financial statements
(7)   Presentation of financial information
(8)   Accounting for interests in other entities

1.1 Purpose of the Statement of Principles

The following are the main reasons why the Accounting Standards Board (ASB) developed the Statement of Principles.

(a)   To assist the ASB by providing a basis for reducing the number of alternative accounting treatments permitted by accounting standards and company law

(b)   To provide a framework for the future development of accounting standards

(c)   To assist auditors in forming an opinion as to whether financial statements conform with accounting standards

(d)   To assist users of accounts in interpreting the information contained in them

(e)   To provide guidance in applying accounting standards

(f)   To give guidance on areas which are not yet covered by accounting standards

(g)   To inform interested parties of the approach taken by the ASB in formulating accounting standards

The role of the Statement can thus be summed up as being to provide **consistency, clarity and information**.

1.2 Chapter 1 The objective of financial statements

The main points raised here are as follows.

(a)   'The objective of financial statements is to provide information about the reporting entity's **performance and financial position** that is useful to a wide range of users for assessing the stewardship of management and for making economic decisions.'

(b)   It is acknowledged that while all not all the information needs of users can be met by financial statements, there are needs that are common to all users. Financial statements that meet the needs of providers of risk capital to the enterprise will also meet most of the needs of other users that financial statements can satisfy.

Users of financial statements other than investors include the following.

(i)   Investors
(ii)   Lenders
(iii)   Suppliers and other creditors
(iv)   Employees
(v)   Customers
(vi)   Government and their agencies
(vii)   The public

(c)   The limitations of financial statements are emphasised as well as the strengths.

(d)   Investors are the defining choice of user because they focus on the entity's cash-generation ability or financial adaptability.

(e)   The information required by investors relates to: Financial performance

The exposure draft discusses the importance of each of these elements and why they are disclosed in the financial statements.

1.3 Chapter 2 The reporting entity

This chapter makes the point that it is important that entities that ought to prepare financial statements, in fact do so. The entity must be a cohesive economic unit. It has a determinable boundary and is held to account for all the things it can control. For this purpose, first direct control and secondly direct plus indirect control are taken into account.

Key term

> **Control** means two things:
>
> (a)   The ability to deploy the economic resources involved
> (b)   The ability to benefit (or to suffer) from their deployment
>
> An entity will have control of a second entity if it has the ability to direct that entity's operating and financial policies with a view to gaining economic benefit from its activities.

Control must be distinguished from **management**, where the entity is not exposed to the benefits arising from or risks inherent in the activities of the second entity.

1.4 Chapter 3 Qualitative characteristics of financial information

The ED gives a diagrammatic representation of the discussion, shown below.

(a)   Qualitative characteristics that relate to **content** are **relevance** and **reliability**.

(b)   Qualitative characteristics that relate to **presentation** are **comparability** and **understandability**.

The diagram shown here is reasonably explanatory.

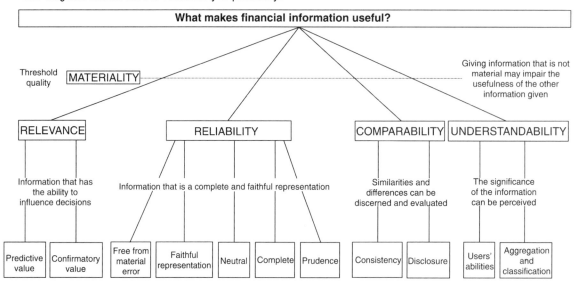

1.5 Chapter 4 Elements of financial statements

The elements of financial statements are listed. They are:

(a)   Assets
(b)   Liabilities
(c)   Ownership interest
(d)   Gains
(e)   Losses
(f)   Contributions from owners
(g)   Distributions to owners

Any item that does not fall within one of the definitions of elements should not be included in financial statements. The definitions are as follows.

(a)   **Assets** are rights or other access to future economic benefits controlled by an entity as a result of past transactions or events.

(b)   **Liabilities** are obligations of an entity to transfer economic benefits as a result of past transactions or events.

(c)   **Ownership interest** is the residual amount found by deducting all of the entity's liabilities from all of the entity's assets.

(d)   **Gains** are increases in ownership interest, other than those relating to contributions from owners.

(e)   **Losses** are decreases in ownership interest, other than those relating to distributions to owners.

(f)   **Contributions from owners** are increases in ownership interest resulting from investments made by owners in their capacity as owners.

(g) **Distributions to owners** are decreases in ownership interest resulting from transfers made to owners in their capacity as owners.

1.6 Chapter 5 Recognition in financial statements

If a transaction or other event has created a new asset or liability or added an existing asset or liability, that effect will be recognised if:

(a) Sufficient evidence exists that the new asset or liability has been created or that there has been an addition to an existing asset or liability.

(b) The new asset or liability or the addition to the existing asset or liability can be measured at a monetary amount with sufficient reliability.

In a transaction involving the provision of services or goods for a net gain, the recognition criteria described above will be met on the occurrence of the critical event in the operating cycle involved.

An asset or liability will be wholly or partly derecognised if:

(a) Sufficient evidence exists that a transaction or other past event has eliminated a previously recognised asset or liability.

(b) Although the item continues to be an asset or a liability the criteria for recognition are no longer met.

The objective of financial statements is achieved to a large extent through the recognition of elements in the primary financial statements – in other words, the depiction of elements both in words and by monetary amounts, and the inclusion of those amounts in the primary financial statement totals. Recognition is a process that has the following stages.

(a) Initial recognition, which is where an item is depicted in the primary financial statements for the first time.

(b) Subsequent remeasurement, which involves changing the amount at which an already recognised asset or liability is stated in the primary financial statements.

(c) Derecognition, which is where an item that was until then recognised ceases to be recognised.

In practice, entities operate in an uncertain environment and this **uncertainty** may sometimes make it necessary to delay the recognition process. The uncertainty is twofold.

- **Element uncertainty** – does the item exist and meet the definition of elements?
- **Measurement uncertainty** – at what monetary amount should the item be recognised?

Even though matching is not used by the Statement to drive the recognition process, it still plays an important role in the approach described in the draft in allocating the cost of assets across reporting periods and in telling preparers where they may find assets and liabilities.

| Question | Assets and liabilities |

Consider the following situations. In each case, do we have an asset or liability within the definitions given by the Statement of Principles? Give reasons for your answer.

(a) Pat Ltd has purchased a patent for £20,000. The patent gives the company sole use of a particular manufacturing process which will save £3,000 a year for the next five years.

(b) Baldwin Ltd paid Don Brennan £10,000 to set up a car repair shop, on condition that priority treatment is given to cars from the company's fleet.

(c) Deals on Wheels Ltd provides a warranty with every car sold.

(d)   Monty Ltd has signed a contract with a human resources consultant. The terms of the contract are that the consultant is to stay for six months and be paid £3,000 per month.

(e)   Rachmann Ltd owns a building which for many years it had let out to students. The building has been declared unsafe by the local council. Not only is it unfit for human habitation, but on more than one occasion slates have fallen off the roof, nearly killing passers-by. To rectify all the damage would cost £300,000; to eliminate the danger to the public would cost £200,000. The building could then be sold for £100,000.

Answer

(a)   This is an asset, albeit an intangible one. There is a past event, control and future economic benefit (through cost savings).

(b)   This cannot be classified as an asset. Baldwin Ltd has no control over the car repair shop and it is difficult to argue that there are 'future economic benefits'.

(c)   This is a liability; the business has taken on an obligation. It would be recognised when the warranty is issued rather than when a claim is made.

(d)   As a firm financial commitment, this has all the appearance of a liability. However, as the consultant has not done any work yet, there has been no past event which could give rise to a liability. Similarly, because there has been no past event there is no asset.

(e)   The situation is not clear cut. It could be argued that there is a liability, depending on the whether the potential danger to the public arising from the building creates a legal obligation to do the repairs. If there is such a liability, it might be possible to set off the sale proceeds of £100,000 against the cost of essential repairs of £200,000, giving a net obligation to transfer economic benefits of £100,000.

The building is clearly not an asset, because although there is control and there has been a past event, there is no expected access to economic benefit.

1.7 Chapter 6 Measurement in financial statements

A monetary carrying amount needs to be assigned so an asset or liability can be recognised. There are two measuring tasks that can be used: **historical cost** or **current value**.

(a)   Initially, when an asset is purchased or a liability incurred, the asset/liability is recorded at the transaction cost, that is historical cost, which at that time is equal to current replacement cost.

(b)   An asset/liability may subsequently be 'remeasured'. In a historical cost system, this can involve writing down an asset to its recoverable amount. For a liability, the corresponding treatment would be amendment of the monetary amount to the amount ultimately expected to be paid.

(c)   Such re-measurements will, however, only be recognised if there is sufficient evidence that the monetary amount of the asset/liability has changed and the new amount can be reliably measured.

1.8 Chapter 7 Presentation of financial information

Aspects of this chapter have also given rise to some controversy. The chapter begins by making the general point that financial statements need to be as simple, straightforward and brief as possible while retaining their relevance and reliability.

1.8.1 Components of financial statements

The primary financial statements are as follows.

Statement	Measure of
Profit and loss account	Financial performance
Statement of total recognised gains and losses	Financial performance
Balance sheet	Financial position
Cash flow statement	Cash inflows and outflows

The notes to the financial statements 'amplify and explore' the primary statements; together they form an 'integrated whole'. Disclosure in the notes does not correct or justify non-disclosure or misrepresentation in the primary financial statements.

'Supplementary information' embraces voluntary disclosures and information which is too subjective for disclosure in the primary financial statement and the notes.

1.9 Chapter 8 Accounting for interests in other entities

Financial statements need to reflect the effect on the reporting entity's financial performance and financial position of its interests in other entities. This involves various measurement, presentation and consolidation issues which are dealt with in this chapter of the Statement.

1.9.1 Different kinds of investments

The **classification** of investments should reflect the way in which they are used to further the business of the investor and their effect on the investor's financial position, performance and financial adaptability. The two key factors here are:

(a)   The **degree of influence** of the investor
(b)   The nature of the **investor's interest** in the results, assets and liabilities of its investee

The different types of investment are summarised in the following table.

Degree of influence	Nature of interest	Resulting categorisation
Control	The investor controls the investee	Subsidiary
Joint control	The investor does not itself control the investee but shares control through some form of arrangement jointly with others	Joint venture
Significant influence	The investor has neither control nor joint control, but exerts a degree of influence over the investee's operating and financial policies that is at the least a significant influence and at the most just short of joint control	Associate
Lesser or no influence	Any influence that the investor has over the investee's operating and financial policies is less than a significant influence	Simple investment

1.9.2 Parent and subsidiary

Parent entities prepare **consolidated financial statements** to provide financial information about the group as a single reporting entity. Consolidation is a process that aggregates the total assets, liabilities and results of the parent and its subsidiaries.

In determining which investments should be consolidated, the principle of control should predominate. However, consolidated financial statements should also reflect the extent of **outside ownership interests** because they are important factors in considering the parent's access and exposure to the results of its subsidiaries.

1.9.3 Associates and joint ventures

There are interests involving significant influence and joint control respectively. The method used should recognise the reporting entity's share of the results and the changes in net assets of the investee and should not misrepresent the extent of its influence. The **equity method** is therefore used.

1.9.4 Business combinations

Two types are recognised.

- **Purchases/acquisitions**. The assets and liabilities of the entity acquired are treated as if the transaction was the purchase of a bundle of assets and liabilities on the open market.

- **Uniting of interests/mergers**. The assets and liabilities of one party to the transaction are treated in the same way as the assets and liabilities of all the other parties; none of the assets or liabilities are treated as being purchased as a bundle of assets and liabilities on the open market.

1.10 Questions and answers

The original November 1995 exposure draft of the Statement of Principles attracted a great deal of criticism, not least from the firm Ernst & Young. In an attempt to address the criticisms raised, the ASB produced a booklet to go with the Statement, called 'Some questions answered'. Below is an outline of the topics covered.

1.10.1 Status and purpose

The points made here are as follows.

(a) The Statement is a description of the fundamental approach that should underpin the financial statements. It is intended to be:

- Comprehensive
- Internally consistent
- Consistent with international approaches

(b) The final version will **not** be an accounting standard.

(c) Its main influence on accounting practice will be through its influence on the standard-setting process. It is only one of the factors that will be taken into account.

1.10.2 Approach

The approach encompasses the following.

(a) There are similarities to existing practice and differences.

(b) The Statement is based on the International Accounting Standard Committee's framework statement and is largely consistent with the framework statements issued in Australia, Canada, New Zealand, the USA and elsewhere. This reflects the view that it will be easier to achieve harmonisation of accounting practice if standard-setters work with a common set of principles.

(c)   The 'true and fair' requirement and the **accounting concepts defined in FRS 18 play a central role** in the revised draft.

(d)   The Statement's development has not been constrained by the requirements of companies legislation because:

- It does not just apply to companies
- Legal frameworks change in response to developments in accounting thought

1.10.3 The use of current costs and values and current cost accounting

These points are made.

(a)   The previous version of the Statement was criticised as heralding a move towards **current cost accounting**. However, the finalised Statement makes it clear that this is **not on the ASB's agenda**.

(b)   The Statement explains that historical cost and current value are **alternative measures**. It also explains that it is envisaged that the approach now adopted by the majority of the larger UK listed companies will continue to be used. This approach involves carrying some categories of balance sheet items at historical cost and others at current value. The Statement then goes on to describe a framework that would guide the choice of an appropriate measurement basis for each balance sheet category.

1.10.4 The focus on assets and liabilities and the role of transactions

Exam focus point

> The ASB balance sheet driven approach should be borne in mind.

These points are made.

(a)   The previous draft placed great emphasis on assets and liabilities and even defined the items that are to be included in the profit and loss account in terms of assets and liabilities. This approach has been retained.

(b)   The approach does not mean that the P&L is unimportant. The primary source of information provided in financial statements is the transactions undertaken by the reporting entity. The primary focus of the accounting process is to allocate these transactions to accounting periods.

(c)   The Statement regards the profit or loss for the period as the difference between the opening and closing balance sheets adjusted for capital constructions and distributions.

1.10.5 Accounting standards based on the Statement

The question was raised as to whether accounting standards published in the future and therefore based on the Statement of Principles will be very different from past accounting standards. The ASB's view is that they won't. Some of the principles have already played very significant roles in accounting standards and have found general acceptance. The standards include:

- FRS 2 Accounting for subsidiary undertakings, which uses the reporting entity concept described in Chapter 2 of the Statement.

- FRS 4 Capital instruments and FRS 5 Reporting the substance of transactions, which use the definitions of assets and liabilities set out in Chapter 4.

- FRS 11 Impairment of fixed assets and goodwill, which uses the recoverable amount notion described in Chapter 6.

Exam focus point

> The *Statement of Principles* is a topical area of the Paper 2.5 syllabus. Keep your eye out for articles on it in the *Student Accountant*.

Question

Purpose

What is the purpose of the ASB's Statement of Principles?

Answer

The following are the main reasons why the ASB developed the Statement of Principles.

(a)   To assist the ASB by providing a basis for reducing the number of alternative accounting treatments permitted by accounting standards and company law

(b)   To provide a framework for the future development of accounting standards

(c)   To assist auditors in forming an opinion as to whether financial statements conform with accounting standards

(d)   To assist users of accounts in interpreting the information contained in them

(e)   To provide guidance in applying accounting standards

(f)   To give guidance on areas which are not yet covered by accounting standards

(g)   To inform interested parties of the approach taken by the ASB in formulating accounting standards

The role of the Statement can thus be summed up as being to provide consistency, clarity and information.

Chapter Roundup

- The *Statement of Principles* is the ASB's conceptual framework. Key points to note are:
    - It is not an accounting standard.
    - It affects accounting practice by influencing the standard-setting process.
    - 'True and fair', FRS 18 and matching are important.
    - Current cost accounting is **not** on the agenda.
    - The balance sheet and P&L are equally important.

Quick Quiz

1   Which of the following are chapters in the Statement of Principles?

    A   Subsidiaries, associates and joint ventures
    B   Profit measurement in financial statements
    C   The objective of financial statements
    D   Accounting for interest in other entities
    E   Recognition in financial statements
    F   Presentation of financial information
    G   Substance of transactions in financial statements
    H   The qualitative characteristics of financial information
    I   The quantitative characteristics of financial information
    J   Measurement in financial statements
    K   The reporting entity
    L   The elements of financial statements.

2   Name **five** of the **six** user groups identified in the Statement of Principles.

3   A **gain** as defined by the Statement of Principles is an increase in the net assets of the entity.

    True   ☐

    False   ☐

4   Financial statements need to be as ...., ... and .... as possible while retaining their .... and ....

5   The Statement favours current cost accounting. *True or false?*

Answers to Quick Quiz

1   C, D, E, F, H, J, K and L.

2   See paragraph 1.2

3   False. A **gain** is an increase in ownership interest, other than one relating to contribution from owners.

4   Simple, straightforward, brief, relevance, reliability.

5   False. The *Statement* favours historical cost accounting, with certain items carried at current value.

Now try the question below from the Exam Question Bank

Number	Level	Marks	Time
Q23	Full examination	20	36 mins

BPP
PROFESSIONAL EDUCATION

Part E

Analysing and interpreting financial and related information

BPP
PROFESSIONAL EDUCATION

Interpretation of financial statements

Topic list	Syllabus reference
1 The broad categories of ratios	5(a),(b)
2 Profitability and return on capital	5(a),(b)
3 Long term solvency and stability	5(a),(b)
4 Short term solvency and liquidity	5(a),(b)
5 Efficiency	5(a),(b)
6 Shareholders' investment ratios	5(a),(h)
7 Accounting policies and the limitations of ratio analysis	5(a),(b)
8 Reports on financial performance	5(a),(b)

Introduction

You may remember some of the basic interpretation of accounts from your earlier studies. This chapter recaps and develops the calculation of ratios and covers more complex accounting relationships. More importantly, perhaps, this chapter looks at how ratios can be analysed, interpreted and how the results should be presented to management.

Wide reading is encouraged in this area. If you want to look at real sets of accounts you could try the Financial Times Free Annual Reports Service - look in the FT at the London Share Service page. In any case, you should read regularly the *Student Accountant* and the *Financial Times at least*.

Study guide

- Calculate useful financial ratios for single company or group financial statements.
- Analyse and interpret ratios to give an assessment of a company's performance in comparison with:
    - a company's previous period's financial statements.
    - another similar company for the same period.
    - industry average ratios.
- Discuss the effect that changes in accounting policies or the use of different accounting policies between companies can have on the ability to interpret performance.
- Discuss how the interpretation of current value information would differ from that of historical cost information.
- Discuss the limitations in the use of ratio analysis for assessing corporate performance, outlining other information that may be of relevance.

Note: the content of reports should draw upon knowledge acquired in other sessions.

These sessions concentrate on the preparation of reports and report writing skills.

Exam guide

You need to master report writing. Ratios are the tools used to interpret financial statements, the most important skill for this area of the syllabus is to develop reasoned arguments which lead to useful and valid conclusions. It is also important to demonstrate real commercial awareness and adopt a holistic perspective in looking at a business.

1 The broad categories of ratios

FAST FORWARD

There are five main categories of ratio:

- Profitability and return
- Long term solvency
- Short term solvency
- Efficiency
- Shareholders' investment ratios

You must select the most appropriate ratios to use.

1.1 Focus on user needs

An underlying purpose of preparing financial statements is to provide **meaningful information** for **potential users** regarding **financial performance**, **financial position** and **financial adaptability**. As identified earlier, they fall into a few key categories.

- Shareholders and potential investors
- Management
- Creditors
- Bankers and other providers of finance.

In general, these users may calculate a range of ratios and performance indicators. However, they are likely to **interpret** them from their **own perspective**, based on their own particular **commercial needs and interests.** In practice, there may well be conflicts of interest between users. For example, **management**

will focus on **profitability** whereas a **bank manager** might be more concerned about **solvency**. **Shareholders** are likely to be interested in how **value** is **generated** and sustained as well as **returns**.

Exam focus point

Ensure you accurately identify who is going to be using the analysis you produce. Your answer must address their specific needs.

At its most basic, ratio analysis involves **comparing one figure against another** to produce a ratio, and then trying to interpret the meaning of the figure produced.

1.2 The broad categories of ratios

Broadly speaking, basic ratios can be grouped into five categories.

- **Profitability and return**
- **Long-term solvency and stability**
- **Short-term solvency and liquidity**
- **Efficiency (turnover ratios)**
- **Shareholders' investment ratios.**

Within each heading there are a number of standard measures or ratios that are traditionally calculated and generally accepted as meaningful indicators. However, **each individual business** must be **considered separately**, and a ratio that is meaningful for a manufacturing company may be completely meaningless for a financial institution. Avoid being **too mechanical when working out ratios.** Always be aware of the importance of **user focus**.

Further **useful insights** might also be gleaned from **companies' financial reports**.

(a) Comments in the **Chairman's report** and **directors' report**.

(b) A review of the **age and nature of the company's assets**.

(c) **Current and future developments** in the company's markets, at home and overseas, recent acquisitions or disposals of a subsidiary by the company.

(d) **Additional statements** and notes such as STRGL, note of historical profits and losses and reconciliation of movements in shareholders funds.

(e) **Exceptional items** in the P&L account.

(f) **Any other noticeable features** of the report and accounts, such as post balance sheet events, contingent liabilities, discontinued activities, qualified auditors' report, the company's taxation position, and so on.

(g) **Notes** dealing with **fixed assets**.

(h) **Notes** dealing with **employee details** and directors' remuneration.

Remember, the nature and scope of the analysis and the amount and quality of information available will depend on the circumstances and the brief provided. A shareholder may only have access to **published information**, whereas a **bank manager** is likely to be in a position to ask to see not only **financial statements**, but also documents such as **business plans**, periodic **management accounts** and **cash flow projections**.

In practice, you may be able to actually speak to management to obtain additional information. However, in an exam situation, you may have to identify what additional information might be useful and **explain tactfully** to the examiner how it might impact on your analysis and interpretation.

Exam focus point

The June 2003 exam asked candidates to write a report analysing the operating performance and financial position for a company.

1.3 Industry specific performance indicators

In practice, businesses may also use a range of **industry and company specific ratios** to help them **manage the business** on a **day to day basis**.

Industry	Performance indicator
Hotels	Room occupancy
Accountants	Chargeable hours utilisation
Farms	Yields per acre
Hospitals	Patient waiting times
Pubs and restaurants	Till overs and unders
Motor manufacturer	Cars produced per worker
Training provider	Exam success rates
Airlines	Daily hours in air per plane

In practice, accounting firm and banks are developing **benchmarking services** for their clients whereby an individual client's **performance indicators** are shown (anonymously) alongside those of other subscribers to the **benchmarking survey**.

1.4 Holistic approach

Accounting ratios are only one part of the accountants diagnostic kit for analysing and interpreting financial statements. Other useful tools or sources of information, if available may comprise:

    (a)   The company's business plan
    (b)   Annual budgets
    (c)   Cash flow projections
    (d)   Management accounts
    (e)   Historic accounts figures (past trends)
    (f)   SWOT analysis
    (g)   Industry benchmark surveys
    (h)   Any other strategy or planning documents
    (i)   On line company and text search services
    (j)   Press releases and comments

The following diagram reinforces the importance of taking a **holistic approach** when reviewing a set of financial statements.

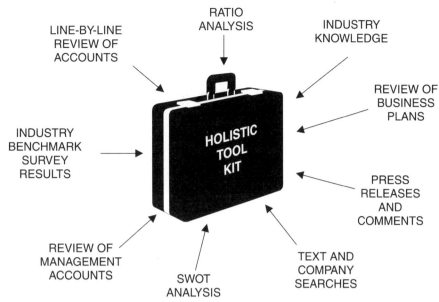

1.5 Basic ratios

The following are the **main accounting ratios** which would **traditionally** be **calculated**. However, in any question that requires you to interpret the financial statements of a company, you should **assess and select** the **most appropriate ratios** to use. Where necessary, you should also **be prepared to apply non-standard industry specific ratios** to support your interpretation.

Accounting ratio **Formula**

Profitability and return

(a) Gross margin

$$\frac{\text{Gross profit}}{\text{Turnover}} \times 100$$

(b) Net margin

$$\frac{\text{Profit on ordinary activities before interest and taxation (PBIT)}}{\text{Turnover}} \times 100$$

(c) Return on capital employed (ROCE)

$$\frac{\text{Profit on ordinary activities before interest and taxation (PBIT)}}{\text{Capital employed}}$$

where capital employed = total assets less current liabilities.

(d) Asset turnover

$$\frac{\text{Turnover}}{\text{Capital employed}}$$

Long term solvency and stability

(a) Debt ratio

$$\frac{\text{Total debt}}{\text{Total assets}}$$

(b) Capital gearing

$$\frac{\text{Prior charge capital}}{\text{Total capital}}$$

(c) Debt/equity ratio

$$\frac{\text{Prior charge capital}}{\text{Ordinary share capital and reserves}}$$

(d) Interest cover

$$\frac{\text{Profit before interest and tax (PBIT)}}{\text{Interest charges}}$$

(e) Cash flow ratio

$$\frac{\text{Net cash inflow}}{\text{Total debts}}$$

BPP PROFESSIONAL EDUCATION

Short term solvency and liquidity

(a)   Current ratio $\dfrac{\text{Current assets}}{\text{Current liabilities}}$

(b)   Quick ratio $\dfrac{\text{Current assets less stocks}}{\text{Current liabilities}}$

(c)   Creditors turnover $\dfrac{\text{Purchases}}{\text{Trade creditors}}$ or $\dfrac{\text{Trade creditors}}{\text{Purchases}} \times 365$

Efficiency

(d)   Stock turnover $\dfrac{\text{Cost of sales}}{\text{Stock}}$ or $\dfrac{\text{Stock}}{\text{Cost of sales}} \times 365$

(e)   Debtors turnover $\dfrac{\text{Credit sales}}{\text{Trade debtors}}$ or $\dfrac{\text{Trade debtors}}{\text{Credit sales}} \times 365$

Shareholders' investment ratios

(a)   Dividend cover $\dfrac{\text{Earnings per share}}{\text{Net dividend per (ordinary) share}}$

(b)   Price earnings (P/E) ratio $\dfrac{\text{Share price}}{\text{Earnings per share}}$

(c)   Dividend yield $\dfrac{\text{Dividend on the share for the year}}{\text{Current market value of the share (ex div)}} \times 100$

1.6 Example: calculating ratios

The balance sheet and profit and loss account figures of Earwigo plc are provided to illustrate the calculation of ratios.

EARWIGO PLC PROFIT AND LOSS ACCOUNT
FOR THE YEAR ENDED 31 DECEMBER 20X8

	Notes	20X8	20X7
		£	£
Turnover	1	3,095,576	1,909,051
Operating profit	1	359,501	244,229
Interest	2	17,371	19,127
Profit on ordinary activities before taxation		342,130	225,102
Taxation		74,200	31,272
Profit on ordinary activities after taxation		267,930	193,830
Earnings per share		12.8p	9.3p

EARWIGO PLC BALANCE SHEET
AS AT 31 DECEMBER 20X8

	Notes	20X8	20X7
Fixed assets			
Tangible fixed assets		802,180	656,071
Current assets			
Stocks and work in progress		64,422	86,550
Debtors	3	1,002,701	853,441
Cash at bank and in hand		1,327	68,363
		1,068,450	1,008,354
Creditors: amounts falling due within one year	4	881,731	912,456
Net current assets		186,719	95,898
Total assets less current liabilities		988,899	751,969
Creditors: amounts falling due after more than one year			
10% first mortgage debenture stock 20Y4/20Y9		(100,000)	(100,000)
Provision for liabilities			
Deferred taxation		(20,000)	(10,000)
		868,899	641,969
Capital and reserves			
Called up share capital	5	210,000	210,000
Share premium account		48,178	48,178
Profit and loss account		610,721	383,791
		868,899	641,969

NOTES TO THE ACCOUNTS

		20X8 £	20X7 £
1	Turnover and profit		
(i)	Turnover	3,095,576	1,909,051
	Cost of sales	2,402,609	1,441,950
	Gross profit	692,967	467,101
	Administration expenses	333,466	222,872
	Operating profit	359,501	244,229
(ii)	Operating profit is stated after charging:		
	Depreciation	151,107	120,147
	Auditors' remuneration	6,500	5,000
	Leasing charges	47,636	46,336
	Directors' emoluments	94,945	66,675
2	Interest		
	Payable on bank overdrafts and other loans	8,115	11,909
	Payable on debenture stock	10,000	10,000
		18,115	21,909
	Receivable on short-term deposits	744	2,782
	Net payable	17,371	19,127
3	Debtors		
	Amounts falling due within one year		
	Trade debtors	884,559	760,252
	Prepayments and accrued income	97,022	45,729
		981,581	805,981
	Amounts falling due after more than one year		
	Trade debtors	21,120	47,460
	Total debtors	1,002,701	853,441

			20X8 £	20X7 £
4	Creditors: amounts falling due within one year			
	Trade creditors		627,018	545,340
	Accruals and deferred income		81,279	280,464
	Corporation tax		108,000	37,200
	Other taxes and social security costs		65,434	49,452
			881,731	912,456
5	Called up share capital			
	Authorised ordinary shares of 10p each		1,000,000	1,000,000
	Issued and fully paid ordinary shares of 10p each		210,000	210,000
6	*Dividends paid:*		41,000	16,800

EARWIGO PLC

Review of year on year movements between 31 December 20X7 and 31 December 20X8

	Increase/(Decrease)
Turnover	62.2%
Operating profit	47.2%
Administration expenses	49.6%
Directors emoluments	42.4%
Net interest payable	(9.1%)
Profit on ordinary activities	52.0%
Taxation	137.3%
Profit on ordinary activities after tax	38.2%
PBIT	45.8%
Dividends	244.1%

Accounting ratios

	20X8	*20X7*
Profitability and return		
Gross margin	$\frac{692,967}{3,095,576} \times 100 = 22.4\%$	$\frac{467,101}{1,909,051} \times 100 = 24.5\%$
Net margin	$\frac{360,245}{3,095,576} \times 100 = 11.6\%$	$\frac{247,011}{1,909,051} \times 100 = 12.9\%$
ROCE	$\frac{360,245}{988,899} \times 100 = 36.4\%$	$\frac{247,011}{751,969} \times 100 = 32.8\%$
Asset turnover	$\frac{3,095,576}{988,899} = 3.1$ times	$\frac{1.909,051}{751,969} = 2.5$ times
Long term stability		
Debt ratio	$\frac{981,731}{1,870,630} \times 100 = 52.5\%$	$\frac{1,012,456}{1,664,425} \times 100 = 60.8\%$
Capital gearing	$\frac{100,000}{988,899} \times 100 = 10.1\%$	$\frac{100,000}{751,969} \times 100 = 13.3\%$
Long term solvency		
Debt/equity ratio	$\frac{100,000}{868,899} \times 100 = 11.5\%$	$\frac{100,000}{641,969} \times 100 = 15.6\%$
Interest cover	$\frac{360,245}{18,115} = 19.9$ times	$\frac{247,011}{21,909} = 11.3$ times
Cash flow ratio	$\frac{510,608}{981,731} \times 100 = 52.0\%$	$\frac{364,376}{1,012,456} \times 100 = 36.0\%$

BPP
PROFESSIONAL EDUCATION

	20X8	20X7

Short term solvency/liquidity

Current ratio $\dfrac{1{,}068{,}450}{881{,}731} \times 100 = 121.2\%$ $\dfrac{1{,}008{,}354}{912{,}456} \times 100 = 110.5\%$

Quick ratio $\dfrac{1{,}004{,}028}{881{,}731} \times 100 = 113.9\%$ $\dfrac{921{,}804}{912{,}456} \times 100 = 101.0\%$

Creditors turnover $\dfrac{627{,}018}{2{,}402{,}609} \times 365 = 95.3 \text{ days}$ $\dfrac{545{,}340}{1{,}441{,}950} \times 365 = 138.0 \text{ days}$

Efficiency

Stock turnover $\dfrac{64{,}422}{2{,}402{,}609} \times 365 = 9.8 \text{ days}$ $\dfrac{86{,}550}{1{,}441{,}950} \times 365 = 21.9 \text{ days}$

Debtors turnover $\dfrac{905{,}679}{3{,}095{,}576} \times 365 = 106.8 \text{ days}$ $\dfrac{807{,}712}{1{,}909{,}051} \times 365 = 154.4 \text{ days}$

Shareholder investment ratios

Dividend cover $\dfrac{267{,}930}{41{,}000} = 6.5 \text{ times}$ $\dfrac{193{,}830}{16{,}800} = 11.5 \text{ times}$

Workings

1 Profit before interest and tax

	20X8 £	20X7 £
Profit on ordinary activities before tax	342,130	225,102
Interest payable	18,115	21,909
PBIT	360,245	247,011

2 Capital employed

Shareholders funds	868,899	641,969
Creditors: amounts falling due after more than one year	100,000	100,000
Long term provision for liabilities and charges	20,000	10,000
	988,899	751,969

3 Total debts

Creditors: amounts falling due within one year	881,731	912,456
Creditors: amounts falling due after more than one year	100,000	100,000
	981,731	1,012,456

4 Total assets

Tangible fixed assets	802,180	656,071
Current assets	1,068,450	1,008,354
	1,870,630	1,664,425

5 Net cash inflow

Operating profit	359,501	244,229
Depreciation	151,107	120,147
Increase in stocks	* –	–
Increase in debtors	* –	–
Increase in creditors	* –	–
	510,608	364,376

* Ignored for this purpose, because figures for 20X7 cannot be calculated as 20X6 accounts are not available.

6 Quick assets

Current assets	1,068,450	1,008,354
Less Stock and works-in-progress	(64,422)	(86,550)
	1,004,028	921,804

2 Profitability and return on capital

FAST FORWARD

The ratios measuring profitability and return on capital are:

- Gross margin on sales
- Return on capital employed
- Net profit %
- Asset turnover ratio

2.1 Gross margin

Earwigo's plc has increased its turnover significantly from 20X7 to 20X8 by 62.2%. Over this period, the gross margin has fallen from 24.5% to 22.4%.

Intuitively, there is a relationship between the level of sales and the gross margin. However, it is important to also consider the potential and **independent causes of fluctuations** in both sales levels and gross margins.

Sales levels	Gross profit margin
• Level of marketing effort and expenditure	• Pricing policy, discounts etc
• Product design and quality	• Sales mix
• Relocation of distribution outlets	• Production efficiency
• Service skills training	• Impact of inflation on costs
• Changes in consumer taste or product usage	• Control of waste and pilferage
• General economic factors	• Sourcing of supplies, discounts etc
• Impact of legislation	• Stock valuation issues (obsolescence, overhead absorption, NRV etc)
• Competition	

Generally, the gross margin is an indicator of trading performance. Remember that **achievable margins** will **differ between industries**. In practice, you are likely to try to obtain additional information, such as **relevant industry benchmarking data**.

2.2 Net margin

Earwigo's net margin has fallen from 12.9% in 20X7 to 11.6% in 20X8. PBIT has increased from 20X7 to 20X8 by 45.8%. This is in line with the increase in operating profit for the year by 47.2%. Other items moving along similar lines are administration expenses and directors remuneration with increases of 49.6% and 42.4%, respectively.

Net margin is **not considered** to be **very meaningful** because of its **susceptibility** to **many factors**. In practice, it is difficult to carry out meaningful comparisons of net margins between companies. For example, one company may have purchased its buildings whereas another company prefer to rent its premises.

Trends in the net margin might provide pointers to the effectiveness of controls over the level of overheads. However, this would seem to be a **blunt tool** because there are **more direct ways** of **financially controlling overheads** for example by monitoring specific overhead accounts.

In practice, net profit is **more usefully compared** to factors such as **number of employees** or **square footage**.

2.3 ROCE

Earwigo's ROCE has improved from 32.8% in 20X7 to 36.4% in 20X8.

To assess the acceptability of these ratios **further information** is necessary.

(a) **Benchmark** against the ROCEs of other companies in the **same industry.**

(b) **Cost of servicing finance**. The level of return should be assessed against the returns available from **alternative investments** and should also reflect the level of **business risk** involved.

(c) **Target ROCE**. A comparison with **budgeted ROCE** may reveal whether management is **achieving expected returns**.

ROCE is probably the **key profitability ratio** in **measuring business performance**. It measures the **return generated** for investors against the **amount invested**. Because of its importance, ROCE is often referred to as the **primary ratio**.

There are certain **factors** which may **obscure** the **assessment** of ROCE.

(a) **Undervalued fixed assets**, such as property, may depress the capital employed figure and show a **rosier ROCE**.

(b) **Capitalised interest**, will increase capital employee and give a **more conservative ROCE**.

(c) **Aging fixed assets** mean lower capital employed and hence higher ROCE. However, this may indicate a variety of potential operational problems.

- Impending obsolescence/impairment
- Inefficiency owing to breakdowns
- Higher maintenance costs
- Probable labour intensive operation
- Competitive inefficiency

Review current carrying values and accumulated depreciation levels for clues of age of fixed assets. Learn to glean meaningful insights about the business from looking at the fixed assets note to the accounts.

(d) **Capitalised development costs**. Like capitalised interest above, will **depress ROCE**. Nevertheless the costs will hit reported profits, but only over a number of years, by way of depreciation or impairment.

(e) **Idle cash balances**. There is a school of thought that advocates these should be removed from capital employed. However, this is likely to give a **misleadingly better** ROCE. The ratio should effectively **measure all aspects of capital employed**.

2.4 Asset turnover

Earwigo plc has improved on its asset utilisation. This went up from 2.5 times in 20X7 to 3.1 times in 20X8.

Again, it is important to asses this ratio against available industry averages. **Manufacturing industries** are likely to be **capital intensive** and therefore have **low asset turnover**. On the other hand, **service industries** tend to be **human resource intensive** and hence likely to have relatively **high asset turnover**.

It might be tempting to think that a high profit margin is good, and a low asset turnover means sluggish trading. In broad terms, this is so. But **there is a trade-off between profit margin and asset turnover, and you cannot look at one without allowing for the other.**

(a)   A high profit margin means a high profit per £1 of sales, but if this also means that sales prices are high, there is a strong possibility that sales turnover will be depressed, and so asset turnover lower.

(b)   A high asset turnover means that the company is generating a lot of sales, but to do this it might have to keep its prices down and so accept a low profit margin per £1 of sales.

Remember that companies may well arrive at the same ROCE via different routes.

	Company A	Company B
Profit margin	20%	5%
Asset turnover	× 1	× 4
ROCE	20%	20%

3 Long term solvency and stability

FAST FORWARD

Long-term solvency and stability is assessed by means of the following ratios:

- Debt ratio
- Gearing ratio
- Debt/equity ratio
- Interest cover
- Cash flow ratio

3.1 Debt ratio

Earwigo's debt ratio has shown an improvement from being 60.8% at the end 20X7 to being 52.5% at the end of 20X8.

There is no absolute guide to the maximum safe debt ratio, but as a **very general guide**, 50% is commonly regarded as a safe limit. In practice, many companies operate successfully with a higher debt ratio than this, but 50% is nonetheless a **helpful benchmark**. In addition, if the debt ratio is over 50% and getting worse, the company's debt position will be worth looking at more carefully.

In Earwigo's case, the debt ratio is quite high, mainly because of the large amount of current liabilities. However, the debt ratio has fallen from 60.8% to 52.5% between 20X7 and 20X8, and so the company appears to be improving its debt position.

3.2 Capital gearing

Earwigo plc's capital gearing ratio has fallen from 13.3% for 20X7 to 10.1% for 20X8.

Gearing **measures** the **relationship** between the **prior charge capital** of a company **and** its **total capital**. It is an indicator of the extent to which a company is reliant on prior charge capital as compared to equity capital.

Preference share capital is normally considered to be **prior charge capital**. Preference dividends must be paid out of profits before ordinary shareholders are entitled to an ordinary dividend. **Debentures** would usually **also** be classified as **prior change capital**.

Total capital is ordinary share capital and reserves plus charge capital plus any long-term liabilities or provisions. In **group accounts** we would also include **minority interests**. Do note that it is easier to identify the same figure for total capital as **total assets less current liabilities**, which you will find given to you in the balance sheet.

The level of gearing maintained by a company is likely to be part of its **corporate** and **financial strategy**. As with the debt ratio, there is **no absolute limit** to what a gearing ratio ought to be. A company with a gearing ratio of more than 50% is said to be high-geared, whereas low gearing means a gearing ratio of less than 50%.

In practice, **many companies** are **highly geared**. However, there are **risks** and **potential problems** associated with **high gearing**.

- **Prior charges** can **consume available profits**, leaving **little earnings for equity shareholders**.

- If **earnings** are **volatile**, this will have a consequential **impact** on the company **share price** (**given** a certain **price/earnings ratio**).

- As the company's **borrowing capacity decreases**, lenders will perceive a **greater risk** and hence the company's **marginal cost** of **borrowing** is **likely to rise**.

- If a **loss situation** prevails, the **financial viability** of the company may become **seriously challenged**.

Here is a little diagram that might help to reinforce your understanding of the implications of different financial structures.

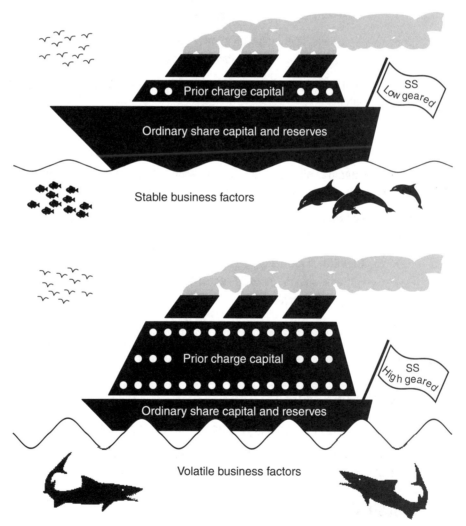

The two above scenarios can be seen within the context of four theoretical scenarios depicted in the two by two matrix below. This provides another tool which you might find useful in looking at a business.

BUSINESS FACTORS

	HIGH	LOW
STABLE	MODERATE RISK	LOW RISK
VOLATILE	HIGH RISK	MODERATE RISK

HIGH   *LOW*

GEARING

- A business operating with a **highly geared financial structure** and **volatile business factors** is likely to face **high business risk**.

- A business operating with a **lowly geared financial structure** and **stable business factors** structure is likely to have **low business risks**.

- **Moderate business risk** would probably be relevant to businesses with combinations of either:

    –   **stable business factors** and **high gearing**.
    –   **volatile business** factors and **low gearing**.

Low geared companies obviously have **more capacity** to **borrow money**. However increases in prior charge capital will in turn compromise the gearing situation!

In practice, the **gearing structure** of a company will be influenced by **company policy** as well **nature of the business**. A highly geared structure is likely to rest on three business factors.

- **Stability** of **profits**
- **Suitable assets** to provide **security**
- **Attitude** of **lenders**

Examples of types of companies likely to satisfy these criteria include property investment companies, hotels and supermarket chains. In general terms, companies in high technology industries are less likely to meet the criteria for sustaining a highly geared structure.

3.3 Debt/equity ratio

Earwigo's debt/equity ratio has improved from 15.6% in 20X7 to 11.5% in 20X8.

This radio provides similar information as the gearing ratio, and here a ratio of 100% or more would indicate high gearing.

3.4 Interest cover

Earwigo's interest cover has improved significantly from 11.3 times in 20X7 to 19.9 times in 20X8.

BPP
PROFESSIONAL EDUCATION

Interest cover is an indicator of whether a company is **earning enough profits before interest and tax to pay its interest costs comfortably**, or whether its interest costs are high in relation to the size of its profits, so that a fall in PBIT would then have a **significant effect on profits available for ordinary shareholders**.

Generally, an interest cover of 2 times or less would be low, and should really exceed 3 times before the company's interest costs are to be considered within acceptable limits.

Remember that although preference share capital is included as prior charge capital for the gearing ratio, **it is usual to exclude preference dividends from 'interest' charges.** We also look at all interest payments, even interest charges on short-term debt, and so interest cover and gearing do not quite look at the same thing. Interest payments should be taken gross from the **notes to the accounts** and not net of interest receipts as shown on the face of the profit and loss account.

Low interest cover suggests:

(a) Shareholders **dividends may be at risk**, because most profits are required to meet interest charges

(b) **Interest charges themselves** could be at **risk** if **profits decline further**.

Earwigo plc has more than sufficient interest cover. In view of the company's low gearing, this is not too surprising and so we finally obtain a picture of Earwigo plc as a company that does not seem to have a debt problem, in spite of its high (although declining) debt ratio.

3.5 Cash flow ratio

Earwigo's cash flow ratio has improved from 35.0% in 20X7 to 52.0% in 20X8.

The cash flow ratio is **the ratio of a company's net cash inflow to its total debts**.

(a) Net cash inflow is the amount of cash which the company has coming into the business from its operations. A suitable figure for net cash inflow can be obtained from the cash flow statement or profit and loss account, with depreciation being added back.

(b) Total debts are short-term and long-term creditors, together with provisions for liabilities and charges. A distinction can be made between debts payable within one year and other debts and provisions.

Obviously, a company needs to be earning enough cash from operations to be able to meet its foreseeable debts and future commitments, and the cash flow ratio, and changes in the cash flow ratio from one year to the next, provide a useful indicator of a company's cash position.

4 Short term solvency/liquidity

Short-term solvency and liquidity is assessed by:

- Current ratio
- Quick ratio (acid test)
- Creditors turnover

4.1 Current ratio

Earwigo's current ratio has improved from 1.1:1 in 20X7 to 1.2:1 in 20X8.

The current ratio is the **perennial 'standard' test of liquidity**. It can be obtained from the balance sheet.

Various books quote a range of acceptable current ratios from 1.0 to 2.0. Obviously 1.0 is a **baseline level** which ensures that the company has sufficient current assets to cover its current liabilities.

Current ratios are likely to **vary between industries** and may even **vary from company to company** within the same industry.

In practice, various factors might influence the level of the current rates.

(a)   **Seasonal factors**. Many companies have year ends after their busy period to minimise stock counting. The timing of the year end may well impact on the level of a company's current ratio.

Example

Santa Specials Limited is a company which specialises in buying and selling a special brand of Xmas Trees made out of genuine high grade Norwegian plastic.

The trees cost £10 each and are sold for £14 each. Details of its current assets and current liabilities per its monthly management accounts are as follows.

The company stocks up with trees in November. In December it sells the trees and in January it pays off the majority of its suppliers.

	31.11.X6 £'000	31.12.X7 £'000	31.1.X8 £'000
Current assets			
Stock	100		
Cash	50	190	91
	150	190	91
Current liabilities			
Trade creditors	100	100	1
Current ratio	1.5:1	1.9:1	91:1

This example illustrates how the **positioning of a company's year end** might **influence** the **level of its current ratio**. You could explore for yourself how the current ratio would change if the company were to pay a dividend in February!

The example also demonstrates the **potential for window dressing** by **processing creditors payments** though the accounting system but **not actually mailing the cheque**!

(b)   **Timing of payment of long term liabilities**. This is an extension of the principle demonstrated in the Santa Specials example above. For example, consider the impact on the current ratio, if in March the company had to pay a long term liability.

The message here is that you need to **develop a good understanding** of the **business** and the **relevant industry** to help you make high quality comments in your examination.

4.2 Quick ratio

Earwigo's quick ratio has improved from 101.0% in 20X7 to 113.9% in 20X8.

Otherwise known as the acid test ratio, this indicator **focuses** on only those **current assets** that are **available** to **pay current liabilities when they fall due**.

Again a quick ratio of 1.0 is desirable but in practice companies might operate effectively at a lower level, depending on the particular business and industry.

Remembering the **holistic kit approach** suggested earlier. In practice, management is likely to use **cash flow forecasts** to enable a **proactive approach** to the **management** of its **liquidity**.

The quick ratio is as susceptible to window dressing as the current ratio, as described above.

4.3 Creditor's payment period

In 20X7, Earwigo took 138.0 days to settle its creditors, but this has accelerated to 95.3 days in 20X8.

This ratio measure the **average number of days taken to pay creditors**. Published financial statements are unlikely to disclose purchases so you may have to resort the using cost of sales in your calculation.

Factors to be considered in setting a supplier payment policy may pull in opposite directions.

(a) Delaying payments to creditors represents a source of interest free finance (However, an obvious question is whether suppliers will build this into their prices!)

(b) Slow payments may give an impression, rightly or wrongly, of liquidity problems. Any potential adverse impacts on the company's credit rating should be considered.

Public companies and members of groups where the parent is a public company, and the company does not qualify as a small or medium sized company under CA 1985, Section 247, must disclose 'creditor days' in respect of amounts due at the year end. This may influence a company's behaviour in relation to how quickly it pays its suppliers.

In addition, public sector bodies such as local authorities are likely to have publicly responsible credit payment targets. Of course, there may be private sector companies that have ethically driven policies for paying their suppliers quickly. It might be worth considering the converse impact on companies that have debtors who like to pay their creditors quickly.

In **certain circumstances**, businesses may be required by their **bankers** to **demonstrate their ability to clear their overdraft** on **specific dates** during the year. This will impact on the creditors payment period as well as the current ratio and quick ratio.

Again, the **creditors payment** period is **susceptible** to being **massaged** by **management**.

5 Efficiency

 The efficiency ratios are:

- Stock turnover
- Debtors turnover

5.1 Stock turnover

Earwigo has significantly refined its stock turnover rate from once every 21.9 days in 20X7 to once every 9.8 days in 20X8.

Stock turnover is an indicator of the **average number** of **days** a business takes to **sell an item of stock**. This can be calculated using the **figures** contained in **published accounts**.

Generally, there is **no universally acceptable level** at which stock should be turned over. A high stock turnover is considered to be better than a low turnover figure. However, in practice several aspects of **stock management policy** have to be balanced in setting a **target stock turnover** for the year.

- Lead times
- Seasonal fluctuations in orders
- Alternative uses of warehouse space
- Bulk buying discounts
- Likelihood of stock perishing or becoming obsolete.
- Minimising of stock holding costs

The **nature of the product traded** will impact on the stock turnover rate. For example, a **fruit and vegetable shop** is likely turnover its stock more frequently than say a **furniture retailer.**

A lengthening stock turnover period from one period to the next could indicate a slowdown in trading or build up in stock levels. **Consideration should be given to both business trading factors as well as stock management issues,** when seeking explanations for movements in stock turnover from one period to the next.

Also remember that:

(a)   Excessively long stock turnover periods tend to increase the **risk of obsolesce**

(b)   The computed turnover rate can be affected by the **timing of orders received or dispatched**, especially where these involve relatively **high values.**

In practice, many companies now use a **'just in time'** approach to stock control. This method seeks to **minimise stock holding costs**. Again, its suitability to a company will depend on the nature of the business included such as **alternative sources** and **level of customer loyalty.**

5.2 Debtor's turnover

Earwigo plc took an average of 118.2 days to collect its debtors in 20X8 as compared to 163.2 days in 20X7.

Debtors turnover is a **rough measure** of the **average length of time for a company's debtors to pay** what they owe the company.

The figure for sales should be taken as the turnover figure in the P & L account. The trade debtors are not the total figure for debtors in the balance sheet, which includes prepayments and non-trade debtors. The trade debtors figure will be itemised in an analysis of the debtors total, in a note to the accounts.

The estimate of debtor days is **only approximate**.

(a)   The balance sheet value of debtors might be abnormally high or low compared with the 'normal' level the company usually has.

(b)   Turnover in the P & L account is exclusive of VAT, but debtors in the balance sheet are inclusive of VAT. We are not strictly comparing like with like. (Some companies show turnover inclusive of VAT as well as turnover exclusive of VAT, and the 'inclusive' figure should therefore be used in these cases.)

Sales are usually made on 'normal credit terms' of payment within 30 days. Debtor days significantly in excess of this might be representative of poor management of funds of a business. However, some companies must allow generous credit terms to win customers. Exporting companies in particular may have to carry large amounts of debtors, and so their average collection period might be well in excess of 30 days.

The **trend of the collection period (debtor days) over time is probably the best guide.** If debtor days are increasing year on year, this is indicative of a poorly managed credit control function (and potentially therefore a poorly managed company).

Stock turnover added to debtors turnover indicates how soon stock is converted into cash.

This is an area where an understanding of the business is important. For example, if you are analysing debtors turnover for a hotel you need to understand and the type of hotel it operates and hence the composition of its sales and debtors mix.

(a)   Accommodation – non corporate guests paying cash for short stays.

(b)   Accommodation – corporate guests staying on credit terms

(c)   Catering – non-corporate guests paying each month

(d)   Catering – corporate guests with debtors accounts

(e)   Conference facilities – corporate usage on debtors accounts.

It may be important to be able to **disaggregate the sale and debtors figures** to enable **meaningful debtors turnover figures** to be calculated. If your calculation can only be done on combined cash and credit sales figures, you should comment accordingly on its limitations and also suggest, in a positive way, what additional information might be useful.

Be careful over **cash oriented businesses** such as supermarket chains where any **debtors turnover** figure you might be able to calculate **is not likely to be very meaningful**.

Again when attempting to explain movements in debtors turnover rates between one year to the next, be aware of both **business trading factors** as well as **credit control factors**.

Business trading factors	Credit control factors
• Trying to attract more custom by allowing easier payment terms • Selling to higher collection risk debtors • Debtors themselves experiencing financial problems eg because of recession • Acquisition/loss of customers with quick settlement policies eg public sector organisations • General change in customer base • Debt factoring	• Efficiency of credit control department • Change in credit terms • Changes in policies on legal action to recover debts • Level of balances already written off.

5.3 The cash cycle

The cash cycle describes the flow of **cash out** of a business and **back into it again** as a result of **normal trading operations**.

Cash goes out to pay for supplies, wages and salaries and other expenses, although payments can be delayed by taking some credit. A business might hold stock for a while and then sell it. Cash will come back into the business from the sales, although customers might delay payment by themselves taking some credit.

The main points about the cash cycle are as follows.

(a)   The timing of cash flows in and out of a business does not coincide with the time when sales and costs of sales occur. **Cash flows out can be postponed by taking credit. Cash flows in can be delayed by having debtors.**

(b)   The **time between making a purchase and making a sale also affects cash flows**. If stocks are held for a long time, the delay between the cash payment for stocks and cash receipts from selling them will also be a long one.

(c)   **Holding stocks and having debtors** can therefore be seen as **two reasons why cash receipts are delayed**. Another way of saying this is that if a company invests in working capital, its cash position will show a corresponding decrease.

(d)   Similarly, **taking credit** from creditors can be seen as a reason why **cash payments are delayed**. The company's liquidity position will worsen when it has to pay the creditors, unless it can get more cash in from sales and debtors in the meantime.

The liquidity ratios and working capital turnover ratios are used to test a company's liquidity, length of cash cycle, and investment in working capital.

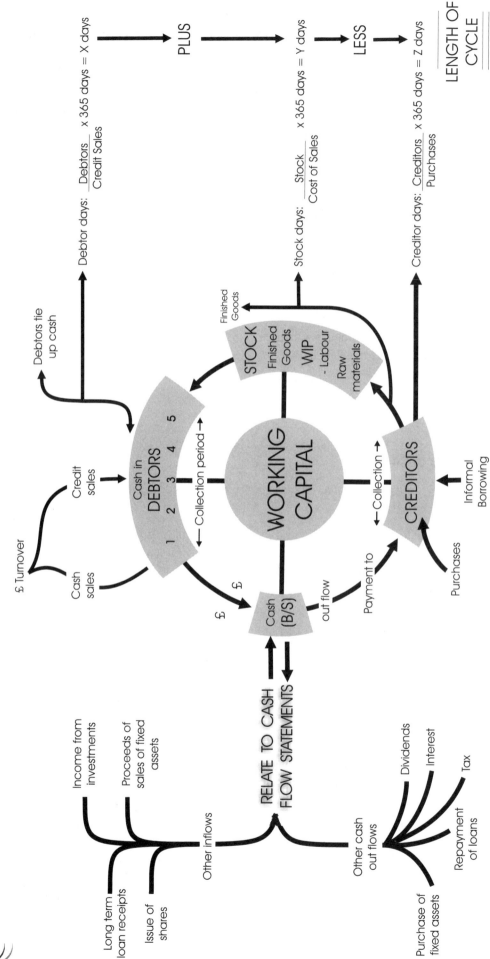

BPP PROFESSIONAL EDUCATION

6 Shareholders' investment ratios

FAST FORWARD

The shareholders' investment ratios are:

- Earnings per share
- Dividend cover
- P/E ratio
- Dividend yield
- Earnings yield

Earnings per share and dividend yield can be calculated from information in a company's published accounts. The other three ratios require the share price.

These are the ratios which **help equity shareholders and other investors to assess the value and quality of an investment in the ordinary shares of a company.** The value of an investment in ordinary shares in a listed company is its **market value**, and so investment ratios must have regard not only to information in the company's published accounts, but also to the current price, and **some of these ratios involve using the share price**.

Earnings per share is a valuable indicator of an ordinary share's performance and is the subject of FRS 14. This was dealt with in Chapter 9.

6.1 Dividend cover

Earwigo's dividend cover has fallen from 11.5 times in 20X7 to 6.5 times in 20X8. This is because the dividend paid has gone up by 244.1% over this period when the net profit after tax has only increased by 38.2%.

Divided cover is an indicator of how secure shareholders can expect to be in terms of their dividend being paid. It measures the number of times the current dividend could have been paid from available current earnings

Exam focus point

The June 2003 exam asked candidates to calculate dividend cover and explain its significance.

6.2 P/E ratio

A high P/E ratio indicates **strong shareholder confidence** in the company and its future, eg in profit growth, and a lower P/E ratio indicates lower confidence.

The P/E ratio of one company can be **compared** with the P/E ratios of:

(a) Other **companies** in the **same business sector**.
(b) Other **companies generally**.

The P/E ratio is a generally used stock market ratio.

6.3 Dividend yield

Dividend yield is **the return a shareholder is currently expecting on the shares of a company.**

Shareholders look for both dividend yield and capital growth. Obviously, dividend yield is therefore an important aspect of a share's performance.

In the year to 30 September 20X8, Wat-u-like plc declared an interim ordinary dividend of 7.4p per share and a final ordinary dividend of 8.6p per share. Assuming an ex div share price of 315 pence, what is the dividend yield?

Answer

The dividend per share is (7.4 + 8.6) = 16 pence

Dividend yield is $\dfrac{16}{315} \times 100$ = 5.1%

6.4 Earnings yield

Earnings yield is **a performance indicator** that is not given the same publicity as EPS, P/E ratio, dividend cover and dividend yield. It is **measured as earnings per share, grossed up, as a percentage of the current share price**. It therefore, indicates what the dividend yield could be if:

(a) The company paid out all its profits as dividend and retained nothing in the business.
(b) There were no extraordinary items in the P & L account.

Some companies retain a bigger proportion of their profits than others, and so the dividend yield between companies can vary for this reason. **Earnings yield overcomes the problem of comparison by assuming that all earnings are paid out as dividends**. *Note*. The earnings yield is equal to the dividend yield multiplied by the dividend cover.

7 Accounting policies and the limitations of ratio analysis

FAST FORWARD

Ratios provide information **through comparison**:

- trends in a company's ratios **from one year to the next**
- in some cases, against an industry norm or standard
- comparison with the ratios of other companies in the same industry

But note that the use of different accounting policies may distort comparisons between companies.

We discussed the disclosure of accounting policies in our examination of FRS 18. The choice of accounting policy and the effect of its implementation are almost as important as its disclosure. This is because the results of a company can be altered significantly by the choice of accounting policy.

7.1 The impact of choice of accounting policies

Where accounting standards allow alternative treatment of items in the accounts, then the accounting policy note should declare which policy has been chosen. It should then be applied consistently.

The problem of comparability arises where companies with similar business adopt different policies. In recent years, financial reporting standard have restricted the selection of accounting treatments. However, there are a few areas where preparers are allowed significant choice.

7.2 Development expenditure

Although the criteria for capitalising development expenditure are very strict, the **choice** of whether to **capitalise and amortise or write off such costs** can have a significant impact on profit.

The **capitalisation** of development costs has **various impacts** on the figures used for analysing accounts.

(a) The capitalised development cost will be **amortised annually** and will **hit earnings**, including EPS, **until fully written off**.

(b) The capitalised development costs are included as part of **capital employed** and hence **ROCE will fall**.

(c) The **gearing ratio** will be **reduced** whilst any of the **capitalised development costs** are still **carried in the balance sheet**.

7.3 Capitalisation of finance costs

FRS 15 allows the capitalisation of finance costs that are **directly attributable** to the **construction** of tangible fixed assets. An entity **need not capitalise** finance costs. However, if an entity adopts a **policy of capitalisation** of finance costs, then it should be **applied consistently** to all tangible fixed assets where finance cost fall to be capitalised.

The impacts of capitalising finance costs in relation to tangible fixed assets on the calculation of accounting ratios is **similar** to those outlined above for **capitalised development costs**.

Remember that capitalisation of interest does not impact on interest cover because an appropriate adjustment must be made to include capitalised interest in the interest cover calculation.

7.4 Leases and the ninety per cent test

Companies might use the 90% test in such a way that ensures that leases are classified as **operating leases** and thereby kept **off the balance sheet**. This would entail **various impacts** on the accounting ratios.

(a) The **profit and loss account** would show a **lease charge instead of finance charges and depreciation**.

(b) The **balance sheet** would **not reflect the asset nor the corresponding liability. Capital employed** and ROCE would remain **roughly the same**.

(c) **Long term debt** will be **less** under an **operating lease scenario** with little impact on equity interests. Hence, the **gearing ratio** is **likely** to **fall significantly**.

7.5 Tangible fixed asset revaluation

Revaluation of fixed affects various figures shown in the accounts.

(a) The total amount of **depreciation written off** through the profit and loss account over the life of the asset **will increase. Reported profits** will therefore be **lower**.

(b) **Distributable profits** are however **not affected. A portion of revaluation reserves** may be **transferred to profit and loss reserves** as they become realised as result of additional depreciation of disposal.

(c) **Shareholder** funds, **capital employed** and **total net assets** will **increase**.

(d) **Debt** will be **unaffected**.

These changes in accounts balances will have consequential impacts on accounting ratios.

- The **gearing ratio** will **decrease**
- **ROCE** will **fall**
- **EPS** will also **fall**.

7.6 Areas of judgment and estimation

The accounting standards specify detailed requirements in many areas of accounting and financial reporting. However, there still remains **significant scope** for the area of **professional judgement** in preparing accounts.

Accounts area	Scope for professional judgement on:
Tangible fixed assets	Depreciation rates and methods
Stocks	Overhead cost inclusion
	Net realisable value estimate
Long-term contracts	Turnover and profit recognition
	Decision to treat as long-term contract
General provisions	Existence of obligation
	Likelihood of transfer of economic benefit
	Measurement of liability

7.7 Limitations of ratio analysis

The consideration of how accounting policies may be used to massage company results leads us to some of the other limitations of ratio analysis. These can be summarised as follows.

- (a)   **Availability of comparable information.**
- (b)   **Use of historical/out of date information.**
- (c)   **Ratios are not definitive – they are only a guide.**
- (d)   **Interpretation needs careful analysis and should not be considered in isolation.**
- (e)   **It is a subjective exercise.**
- (f)   **It can be subject to manipulation and window dressing.**
- (g)   **Ratios are not defined in standard form.**
- (h)   **They are a type of tool in a more holistic approach (see section 1.4)**

Exam focus point

In the exam, always bear these points in mind; you may even be asked to discuss such limitations, but in any case they should have an impact on your analysis of a set of results.

 Question   Ratios

The following are a selection of accounting ratios for a range of UK listed public companies in various industries ie

- Furniture
- Recruitment and business services
- Supermarket
- Cruise liner holidays
- Bakery shops

Review the table provided, then have a go at trying to identify which ratios relate to which industry. Write your response into the space provided at the foot of the table.

Standard ratios	Company A	Company B	Company C	Company D	Company E
Gross margin	8.0%	61.3%	49.6%	24.0%	-
ROCE	17.4%	26.3%	11.6%	10.1%	29.2%
Asset turnover	2.9 times	3.4 times	2.5 times	0.7 times	2.7 times
Current ratio	0.8:1	0.7:1	1.4:1	0.7:1	1.1:1
Stock turnover	20.4 days	15.7 days	102.2 days	12.0 days	N/A
Debtors turnover	1.1 days	0.5 days	15.0 days	5.8 days	56.2 days
Creditors turnover	40.0 days	54.7 days	53.7 days	30.2 days	-
Non-standard ratio					
Staff costs per employee	£17,566	£9,211	£22,279	£9,672	£24,646
Report date	1999	2000	2001	2000	2001
Industry involved					

Answer

Company	Industry
A	Supermarket chain
B	Bakery shop chain
C	Furniture retailer
D	Cruise holiday operator
E	Recruitment and business services

8 Reports on financial performance

FAST FORWARD

Always bear in mind:

(a) However many ratios you calculate, **numbers alone will not answer a question**. You must **interpret** all the available information and support your interpretation with ratio calculations.

(b) Financial ratios must be viewed alongside **commercial and business issues** that may impact on a business. Your report must demonstrate **commercial awareness**.

Exam focus point

The June 2002 exam required candidates to prepare a report for a Chief Executive on the overall financial position of a company, with the aid of suitable accounting ratios. Candidates were also required to include comments on matters that gave cause for concern or required further investigation. These matters included:

(a) A sale and leaseback of property and its impact on the figures
(b) Issue of a loan note and share capital

You may have experience already in writing reports within your organisation. Accountants are called upon to write reports for many different purposes. These range from very formal reports, such as those addressed to the board of directors or the audit committee, to one-off reports of a more informal nature.

8.1 A step-by-step approach

The following chart is provided as an aid memoire to help you tackle accounts analysis questions in exams. You, of course, **may have an equally valid approach**, based on your **own practical experience**.

Identify:

- The purpose of your analysis and interpretation.
- The audience to which your comments are to be addressed.

Review the accounts to develop an overall familiarity with the nature of the company, the industry in which it operates, company size, key account balances, significant changes between years etc.

Do a quick brainstorm of the general business issues behind the accounts; market conditions, policies, consumer behaviour, management skills, competition, stability, volatility, risks, etc.

Identify any additional information you might, in practice, have looked at. Recognised any limitations of your ratio analysis (in a positive way in an exam).

Select and calculate an appropriate set of ratios, including any helpful non-standard or industry specific ratios.

Perform comparisons and suggest explanation. Remember the importance of keeping comments constructive.

Ensure your answer or report is relevant and helpful to the needs of the users.

8.2 Checklist for report writing

The following checklist for report writing is provided to help you identify factors that should be considered.

- (a)   **Purpose or terms of reference**

    - (i)   Who are the **users** of the report and what are their **interests**?

    - (ii)   What is the **purpose** of the report? What type of **focus** should it have?

    - (iii)   What is wanted, **definite recommendations or less specific advice**?

    - (iv)   What **outcomes** might the report have if its findings or **recommendations** are **implemented**?

    - (v)   What **previous reviews or reports** have there been on the subject, what did they find or recommend, and what action was taken on these findings, or recommendations?

- (b)   **Information in the report**

    - (i)   What is the **source** of each item of information in the report?

    - (ii)   What is the **age** of the information? Is it **up-to-date**?

    - (iii)   What **period** does the report **cover** – a month, a year?

    - (iv)   How can the **accuracy** of the information be checked and **verified**? To what extent might it be subject to error?

    - (v)   What **other information** might be useful.

(c) **Preparing the report**

 (i) Decide on **structure** of report; headings, sub headings, summary, appendices and other aspects.

 (ii) Decide on balance between **analysis** and **solution orientation**.

 (iii) Consider **style** and **tone**.

 (iv) For exam purposes, use an **easy** to follow **numbering system**.

 (v) Be aware of putting content over in bite-size (**mark oriented**) chunks!

 (vi) Beware of tact and diplomacy. Be **constructive**, not **critical**.

(d) **User-friendliness of the report**

 (i) What **use** will the report be in its present form? What **action** is it intended to **trigger**?

 (ii) Does the report meet the requirements of the **terms of reference**?

 (iii) Will the users who asked for the report be **delighted**?

8.3 Format of reports in the examination

Exam focus point

> In an examination your time is limited and you are under pressure. To make life a little easier, we suggest that you adopt the following format for any report you are requested to write.
>
> Remember that report writing involves skill – you need to practice it till you can write clearly, positively and quickly under exam conditions.

REPORT (OR MEMORANDUM)

To: Board of Directors (or Chief Accountant, etc)

From: Financial Controller   Date:

Subject: Report format

Body of report

Signed: Accountant

If you adopt this style in your practice questions, you should end up producing it automatically. This should ensure that you **do not lose any presentation marks**. Remember if the **question asks specifically for a report**, your **answer must look like a report**.

Now you have considered the knowledge and skills you will need to produce a report for the examiner. You might like to have a go at doing the following question.

The following information has been extracted from the recently published accounts of Seymour Marx plc.

SEYMOUR MARX PLC
EXTRACTS FROM THE PROFIT AND LOSS ACCOUNT

	20X9	20X8
	£'000	£'000
Sales	11,200	9,750
Cost of sales	8,460	6,825
Net profit before tax	465	320

This is after charging:

Depreciation	360	280
Debenture interest	80	60
Interest on bank overdraft	15	9
Audit fees	12	10

SEYMOUR MARX PLC
BALANCE SHEET AS AT 30 APRIL

	20X9	20X8
	£'000	£'000
Fixed assets	1,850	1,430
Current assets		
Stock	640	490
Debtors	1,230	1,080
Cash	80	120
	1,950	1,690
Current liabilities		
Bank overdraft	110	80
Creditors	750	690
Taxation	95	75
	955	845
Total assets less current liabilities	2,845	2,275
Long-term capital and reserves		
Ordinary share capital	800	800
Reserves	1,245	875
	2,045	1,675
10% debentures	800	600
	2,845	2,275

The following ratios are those calculated for Seymour Marx plc, based on its published accounts for the previous year, and also the latest industry average ratios:

	Seymour Marx plc *30 April 20X8*	*Industry* *average*
ROCE (capital employed = equity and debentures)	16.70%	18.50%
Profit/sales	3.90%	4.73%
Asset turnover	4.29	3.91
Current ratio	2.00	1.90
Quick ratio	1.42	1.27
Gross profit margin	30.00%	35.23%
Debtors control	40 days	52 days
Creditors control	37 days	49 days
Stock turnover	13.90	18.30

	Seymour Marx plc *30 April 20X8*	*Industry* *average*
Gearing	26.37%	32.71%

Required

(a) Calculate comparable ratios (to two decimal places where appropriate) for Seymour Marx plc for the year ended 30 April 20X9. All calculations must be clearly shown.

(b) Write a report to your board of directors analysing the performance of Seymour Marx plc, comparing the results against the previous year and against the industry average.

Answer

(a)

	20X8	*20X9*	*Industry average*
ROCE	$\frac{320+60}{2,275} = 16.70\%$	$\frac{465+80}{2,845} = 19.16\%$	18.50%
Profit/sales	$\frac{320+60}{9,750} = 3.90\%$	$\frac{465+80}{11,200} = 4.87\%$	4.73%
Asset turnover	$\frac{9,750}{2,275} = 4.29x$	$\frac{11,200}{2,845} = 3.94x$	3.91x
Current ratio	$\frac{1,690}{845} = 2.00$	$\frac{1,950}{955} = 2.04$	1.90
Quick ratio	$\frac{1,080+120}{845} = 1.42$	$\frac{1,230+80}{955} = 1.37$	1.27
Gross profit margin	$\frac{9,750-6,825}{9,750} = 30.00\%$	$\frac{11,200-8,460}{11,200} = 24.46\%$	35.23%
Debtors turnover	$\frac{1,080}{9,750} \times 365 = 40\text{ days}$	$\frac{1,230}{11,200} \times 365 = 40\text{ days}$	52 days
Creditors turnover	$\frac{690}{6,825} \times 365 = 37\text{days}$	$\frac{750}{8,460} \times 365 = 32\text{ days}$	49 days
Stock turnover	$\frac{6,825}{490} = 13.9x$	$\frac{8,460}{640} = 13.2x$	18.30x
Gearing	$\frac{600}{2,275} = 26.37\%$	$\frac{800}{2,845} = 28.12\%$	32.71%

(b) (i) REPORT

To: *Board of Directors*
From: *Management accountant*   Date: *xx/xx/xx*
Subject: *Analysis of performance of Seymour Marx plc*

This report should be read in conjunction with the appendix attached which shows the relevant ratios (from part (a)).

1 **Trading and profitability**

1.1 Return on capital employed has improved considerably between 20X8 and 20X9 and is now higher than the industry average.

1.2 Net income as a proportion of sales has also improved noticeably between the years and is also now marginally ahead of the industry average. Gross margin, however, is considerably lower than in the previous year and is only some 70% of the industry average.

1.3 The above suggests either that there has been a change in the cost structure of Seymour Marx plc or that there has been a change in the method of cost allocation between the periods. Either way, this is a marked change that requires further investigation.

1.4 The company appears to be in a period of transition as sales have increased by nearly 15% over the year and it would also appear that new fixed assets have been purchased.

1.5 Asset turnover has declined between the periods although the 20X9 figure is in line with the industry average. This reduction might indicate that the efficiency with which assets are used has deteriorated,

(a) The assets acquired in 20X9 have not yet fully contributed to the business.
(b) A longer term trend would clarify the picture.

2 **Liquidity and working capital management**

2.1 The current ratio has improved slightly over the year and is marginally higher than the industry average. It is also in line with what is generally regarded as satisfactory (2:1).

2.2 The quick ratio has declined marginally but is still better than the industry average. This suggests that Seymour Marx plc has no short term liquidity problems and should have no difficulty in paying its debts as they become due.

2.3 Debtors as a proportion of sales is unchanged from 20X8 and are considerably lower than the industry average. Consequently, there is probably little scope to reduce this further.

2.4 Consideration should be given to the likelihood that there may be pressure in the future from customers to increase the period of credit given.

2.5 The period of credit taken from suppliers has fallen from 37 days' purchases to 32 days' and is much lower than the industry average.

2.6 The above trends suggest that it may be possible to finance any additional debtors by negotiating better credit terms from suppliers.

2.7 Stock turnover has fallen slightly and is much slower than the industry average and this may partly reflect stocking up ahead of a significant increase in sales.

2.8 The above suggests that there may be some danger that the stock could contain certain obsolete items that may require writing off.

2.9 The relative increase in the level of stock has been financed by an increased overdraft which may reduce if the stock levels can be brought down.

2.10 The high levels of stock, overdraft and debtors compared to that of creditors suggests a labour intensive company or one where considerable value is added to bought-in products.

3 **Gearing**

3.1 The level of gearing has increased only slightly over the year and is below the industry average.

3.2 The return on capital employed is nearly twice the rate of interest on the debentures, hence profitability is likely to be increased by a modest increase in the level of gearing.

Signed: Accountant

Exam focus point

> The above is quite a brief and focused answer but clearly includes 17 points (5+10+2). Marks would also be allocated for the heading and the sign off.
>
> You may well find the above numbering system provides a marks-orientated approach for discursive questions generally.

8.4 Commercial awareness

Your interpretation should always demonstrate a **'real world' commercial awareness** sought by examiners. To develop this business acumen may involve a **variety of activities** on your part in addition to your formal academic studies.

(a) **Reading publications** such as the Financial Times, Economist etc.

(b) Watching the **business coverage** on **television** channels

(c) Taking on an **interest** in business of your **employer** or your **clients**, including discussing their **real concerns**

(d) Obtaining **published financial reports** for a range of companies in **different industry** sectors and developing an understanding of their financial structures and the **business factors** they face.

A useful address in this regard is the free FT annual reports service. Do have a look at the advert on the FT '*London share service*' page.

Exam focus point

> The June 2002 exam required candidates to describe the matters that might be relevant when entity financial statements are used to assess the performance of a wholly owned subsidiary.

Chapter Roundup

- There are five main categories of ratio:

  - Profitability and return
  - Long term solvency
  - Short term solvency
  - Efficiency
  - Shareholders' investment ratios

  You must select the most appropriate ratios to use.

- The ratios measuring profitability and return on capital are:

  - Gross margin on sales
  - Return on capital employed
  - Net profit %
  - Asset turnover ratio

- Long-term solvency and stability is assessed by means of the following ratios:

  - Debt ratio
  - Gearing ratio
  - Debt/equity ratio
  - Interest cover
  - Cash flow ratio

- Short-term solvency and liquidity is assessed by:

  - Current ratio
  - Quick ratio (acid test)
  - Creditors turnover

- The efficiency ratios are:

  - Stock turnover
  - Debtors turnover

- The shareholders' investment ratios are:

  - Earnings per share
  - Dividend cover
  - P/E ratio
  - Dividend yield
  - Earnings yield

  Earnings per share and dividend yield can be calculated from information in a company's published accounts. The other three ratios require the share price.

- Ratios provide information **through comparison**:

  - trends in a company's ratios **from one year to the next**
  - in some cases, against an industry norm or standard
  - comparison with the ratios of other companies in the same industry

  But note that the use of different accounting policies may distort comparisons between companies.

- Always bear in mind:

  (a) However many ratios you calculate, **numbers alone will not answer a question**. You must **interpret** all the available information and support your interpretation with ratio calculations.

  (b) Financial ratios must be viewed alongside **commercial and business issues** that may impact on a business. Your report must demonstrate **commercial awareness**.

Quick Quiz

1   Brainstorm a list of sources of information which would be useful in interpreting a company's accounts.

2   ROCE is $\dfrac{\text{Profit before interest and tax}}{\text{Capital employed}}$.

      True   ☐

      False   ☐

3   Company Q has a profit margin of 7%. Briefly comment on this.

4   The debt ratio is a company's long term debt over its net assets.

      True   ☐

      False   ☐

5   Cash flow ratio is the ratio of:

    A   Gross cash inflow to total debt
    B   Gross cash inflow to net debt
    C   Net cash inflow to total debt
    D   Net cash inflow to net debt

6   List six limitations to ratio analysis.

Answers to Quick Quiz

1   There are a number of sources (see Para 1 6 and Para 1.11). Information on competitors and the economic climate are obvious items of information.

2   True

3   You should be careful here. You have very little information. This is a low margin but you need to know what industry the company operates in. 7% may be good for a major retailer.

4   False. It is the ratio of total debt to total assets

5   C

6   Compare your list to that in Paragraph 7.7

Now try the questions below from the Exam Question Bank			
Number	**Level**	**Marks**	**Time**
Q24	Full examination	25	45 mins
Q25	Full examination	25	45 mins

Cash flow statements

Topic list	Syllabus reference
1 FRS 1 Cash flow statements	5 (c)
2 Preparing a cash flow statement	5 (c)
3 Interpretation of cash flow statements	5 (c)

Introduction

You have already covered basic cash flow accounting in your earlier studies. Here, the study of cash flow statement revolves around FRS 1, which governs the content and disclosure of cash flow statements in company accounts.

FRS 1 was the first standard produced by the Accounting Standards Board and it was revised in October 1996.

This chapter adopts a systematic approach to the preparation of cash flow statements in examinations; you should learn this method and you will then be equipped for any problems in the exam itself.

The third section in the chapter looks at the information which is provided by cash flow statements and how it should be analysed.

Study guide

- Prepare a cash flow statement, including relevant notes, for an individual company in accordance with relevant accounting standards

  Note: questions may specify the use of the direct or the indirect method.

- Appraise the usefulness of, and interpret the information in, a cash flow statement.

Exam guide

Preparation and analysis of cash flow statements is identified in the syllabus as a key area so make sure you master both techniques.

1 FRS 1 Cash flow statements

FAST FORWARD

Cash flow statements were made compulsory for companies because it was recognised that accounting profit is not the only indicator of a company's performance.

Cash flow statements concentrate on the **sources** and **uses of cash** and are a useful indicator of a company's **liquidity** and **solvency**.

Exam focus point

The June 2003, June 2004 and December 2004 papers asked candidates to prepare a cash flow statement. This is a fairly mechanical exercise where you can score a lot of marks: do practise the questions until you can do a cash flow statement accurately and quickly.

It has been argued that 'profit' does not always give a useful or meaningful picture of a company's operations. **Readers of a company's financial statements might even be misled by a reported profit figure**.

(a) Shareholders might believe that if a company makes a profit after tax of, say, £100,000 then this is the amount which it could afford to **pay as a dividend**. Unless the company has **sufficient cash** available to stay in business and also to pay a dividend, the shareholders' expectations would be wrong.

(b) Employees might believe that if a company makes profits, it can afford to **pay higher wages** next year. This opinion may not be correct: the ability to pay wages depends on the **availability of cash**.

(c) Survival of a business entity depends not so much on profits as on its **ability to pay its debts when they fall due**. Such payments might include 'profit and loss' items such as material purchases, wages, interest and taxation etc, but also capital payments for new fixed assets and the repayment of loan capital when this falls due (for example on the redemption of debentures).

From these examples, it may be apparent that a company's performance and prospects depend not so much on the 'profits' earned in a period, but more realistically on liquidity or **cash flows**.

The great advantage of a cash flow statement is that it is unambiguous and provides information which is additional to that provided in the rest of the accounts. It also describes to the cash flows of an organisation by activity and not by balance sheet classification.

1.1 FRS 1 Cash flow statements (revised)

FRS 1 sets out the structure of a cash flow statement and it also sets the minimum level of disclosure.
In October 1996 the ASB issued a revised version of FRS 1 *Cash flow statements*. The revision of FRS 1 was part of a normal process of revision, but it also responded to various criticisms of the original FRS 1. Although cash flow statements were found to be useful, some shortcomings were perceived, which we will discuss in Section 3.

Exam focus point

You only need to learn the revised version of the standard. Examination questions are likely to be computational, but some discussion and interpretation may be required.

1.2 Objective

The FRS begins with the following statement.

'The objective of this FRS is to ensure that reporting entities falling within its scope:

(a) Report their cash generation and cash absorption for a period by highlighting the significant components of cash flow in a way that facilitates comparison of the cash flow performance of different businesses

(b) Provide information that assists in the assessment of their liquidity, solvency and financial adaptability.'

1.3 Scope

The FRS applies to all financial statements intended to give a true and fair view of the financial position and profit or loss (or income and expenditure), except those of various exempt bodies in group accounts situations or where the content of the financial statement is governed by other statutes or regulatory regimes. In addition, **small entities are excluded** as defined by companies logislation.

1.4 Format of the cash flow statement

An example is given of the format of a cash flow statement for a single company and this is reproduced below.

A cash flow statement should list its cash flows for the period classified under the following **standard headings**.

Standard headings

(a) Operating activities (using either the direct or indirect method)
(b) Returns on investments and servicing of finance
(c) Taxation
(d) Capital expenditure and financial investment
(e) Acquisitions and disposals
(f) Equity dividends paid
(g) Management of liquid resources
(h) Financing

The last two headings can be shown in a single section provided a subtotal is given for each heading. Acquisitions and disposals are not on your syllabus; the heading is included here for completeness.

Individual categories of inflows and outflows under the standard headings should be disclosed separately either in the cash flow statements or in a note to it unless they are allowed to be shown net. Cash inflows and outflows may be shown net if they relate to the management of liquid resources or financing and the inflows and outflows either:

(a)   Relate in substance to a single financing transaction (unlikely to be a concern in Paper 2.5)

(b)   Are due to short maturities and high turnover occurring from rollover or reissue (for example, short-term deposits).

The requirement to show cash inflows and outflows separately does not apply to cash flows relating to operating activities.

Each cash flow should be classified according to the substance of the transaction giving rise to it.

1.5 Links to other primary statements

Because the information given by a cash flow statement is best appreciated in the context of the information given by the other primary statements, the FRS requires **two reconciliations**, between:

(a)   **Operating profit and the net cash flow from operating activities.**
(b)   The **movement in cash in the period and the movement in net debt.**

Neither reconciliation forms part of the cash flow statement but each may be given either adjoining the statement or in a separate note.

The **movement in net debt** should identify the following components and reconcile these to the opening and closing balance sheet amount:

(a)   The **cash flows** of the entity.
(b)   **Other non-cash changes**.
(c)   The recognition of **changes in market value** and **exchange rate movements**.

1.6 Definitions

The FRS includes the following **important definitions** (only those of direct concern to your syllabus are included here). Note particularly the definitions of cash and liquid resources.

(a)   An **active market** is a market of sufficient depth to absorb the investment held without a significant effect on the price. (This definition affects the definition of liquid resources below.)

(b)   **Cash** is cash in hand and deposits repayable on demand with any qualifying financial institution, less overdrafts from any qualifying financial institution repayable on demand. Deposits are repayable on demand if they can be withdrawn at any time without notice and without penalty or if a maturity or period of notice of not more than 24 hours or one working day has been agreed. Cash includes cash in hand and deposit denominated in foreign currencies.

(c)   **Cash flow** is an increase or decrease in an amount of cash.

(d)   **Liquid resources** are current asset investments held as readily disposable stores of value. A readily disposable investment is one that:

(i)   Is disposable by the reporting entity without curtailing or disrupting its business.
(ii)   Is either:

(1)   Readily convertible into known amounts of cash at or close to its carrying amount.

(2)   Traded in an active market.

(e) **Net debt** is the borrowings of the reporting entity less cash and liquid resources. Where cash and liquid resources exceed the borrowings of the entity reference should be to 'net funds' rather than to 'net debt'.

(f) **Overdraft** is a borrowing facility repayable on demand that is used by drawing on a current account with a qualifying financial institution.

1.7 Classification of cash flows by standard heading

The FRS looks at each of the cash flow categories in turn.

Exam focus point

If you are in a hurry or revising skim through these definitions, taking in the highlighted words and go straight to the example in Paragraph 1.12.

1.7.1 Operating activities

Cash flows from operating activities are in general the **cash effects of transactions** and other events **relating to operating or trading activities**, normally shown in the profit and loss account in arriving at operating profit. They include cash flows in respect of operating items relating to provisions, whether or not the provision was included in operating profit.

A **reconciliation** between the operating profit reported in the profit and loss account and the net cash flow from operating activities should be given **either adjoining the cash flow statement or as a note**. The reconciliation is not part of the cash flow statement: if adjoining the cash flow statement, it should be clearly labelled and kept separate. The reconciliation should disclose separately the movements in stocks, debtors and creditors related to operating activities and other differences between cash flows and profits.

1.7.2 Returns on investments and servicing of finance

These are **receipts resulting from the ownership of an investment and payments to providers of finance and non-equity shareholders** (eg the holders of preference shares).

Cash inflows from returns on investments and servicing of finance include:

(a) **Interest received**, including any related tax recovered.
(b) **Dividends received**, net of any tax credits.

Cash outflows from returns on investments and servicing of finance include:

(a) **Interest paid** (even if capitalised), including any tax deducted and paid to the relevant tax authority.

(b) Cash flows that are treated as **finance costs** (this will include issue costs on debt and non-equity share capital).

(c) The **interest element of finance lease rental** payments.

(d) **Dividends paid on non-equity shares** of the entity.

1.7.3 Taxation

These are cash flows to or from taxation authorities in respect of the reporting entity's revenue and capital profits. VAT and other sales taxes are discussed later.

(a) Taxation cash **inflows** include **cash receipts** from the relevant tax authority of tax rebates, claims or returns of overpayments.

(b) Taxation cash **outflows** include **cash payments** to the relevant tax authority of tax, including payments of advance corporation tax.

1.7.4 Capital expenditure and financial investment

These **cash flows** are those **related to the acquisition or disposal of any fixed asset** other than one required to be classified under 'acquisitions and disposals' (discussed below), **and any current asset investment** not included in liquid resources (also dealt with below). If no cash flows relating to financial investment fall to be included under this heading the caption may be reduced to 'capital expenditure'.

The **cash inflows** here include:

(a)   **Receipts from sales or disposals** of property, plant or equipment.

(b)   **Receipts from the repayment of** the reporting entity's **loans** to other entities.

Cash outflows in this category include:

(a)   **Payments to acquire property**, plant or equipment.

(b)   **Loans made** by the reporting entity.

1.7.5 Acquisitions and disposals

These cash flows are related to the acquisition or disposal of any trade or business, or of an investment in an entity that is either an associate, a joint venture, or a subsidiary undertaking (these group matters are beyond the scope of your syllabus).

(a)   Cash **inflows** here include **receipts from sales of trades or businesses**.

(b)   Cash **outflows** here include **payments to acquire trades or businesses**.

1.7.6 Equity dividends paid

The cash outflows are **dividends paid on** the reporting entity's **equity shares**, excluding any advance corporation tax.

1.7.7 Management of liquid resources

This section should include cash flows in respect of liquid resources as defined above. Each entity should explain what it includes as liquid resources and any changes in its policy. The cash flows in this section can be shown in a single section with those under 'financing' provided that separate subtotals for each are given.

Cash inflows include:

(a)   **Withdrawals from short-term deposits** not qualifying as cash.

(b)   Inflows from **disposal or redemption** of any other investments held as liquid resources.

Cash outflows include:

(a)   **Payments into short-term deposits** not qualifying as cash.

(b)   Outflows to **acquire any other investments** held as liquid resources.

1.7.8 Financing

Financing cash flows comprise receipts or repayments of principal from or to external providers of finance. The cash flows in this section can be shown in a single section with those under 'management of liquid resources' provided that separate subtotals for each are given.

Financing **cash inflows** include receipts **from issuing**:

(a)   **Shares** or other equity instruments.

(b)   **Debentures**, loans and from other long-term and short-term borrowings (other than overdrafts).

Financing cash **outflows** include:

(a)   **Repayments of amounts borrowed** (other than overdrafts).

(b)   The **capital element of finance lease rental** payments.

(c)   Payments to **reacquire or redeem the entity's shares**.

(d)   Payments of **expenses or commission on any issue of equity shares**.

1.8 Exceptional and extraordinary items and cash flows

Where cash flows relate to items that are classified as exceptional or extraordinary in the profit and loss account they **should be shown under the appropriate standard headings according to the nature of each item**. The cash flows relating to exceptional or extraordinary items should be identified in the cash flow statement or a note to it and the relationship between the cash flows and the originating exceptional or extraordinary item should be explained.

Where cash flows are exceptional because of their size or incidence but are not related to items that are treated as exceptional or extraordinary in the profit and loss account, **sufficient disclosure should be given to explain their cause and nature.**

1.9 Value added tax and other taxes

Cash flows should be shown net of any attributable value added tax or other sale tax unless the tax is irrecoverable by the reporting entity. The net movement on the amount payable to, or receivable from the taxing authority should be allocated to cash flows from operating activities unless a different treatment is more appropriate in the particular circumstances concerned. Where restrictions apply to the recoverability of such taxes, the irrecoverable amount should be allocated to those expenditures affected by the restrictions. If this is impracticable, the irrecoverable tax should be included under the most appropriate standard heading.

Taxation cash flows other than those in respect of the reporting entity's revenue and capital profits and value added tax, or other sales tax, **should be included within the cash flow statement** under the same standard heading as the cash flow that gave rise to the taxation cash flow, unless a different treatment is more appropriate in the particular circumstances concerned.

1.10 Material non-cash transactions

Material transactions not resulting in movements of cash of the reporting entity **should be disclosed in the notes** to the cash flow statement if disclosure is necessary for an understanding of the underlying transactions.

1.11 Comparative figures

Comparative figures **should be given for all items in the cash flow statement** and such notes thereto as are required by the FRS with the exception of the note to the statement that analyses changes in the balance sheet amount making up net debt.

1.12 Example: Single company

The following example is provided by the standard for a single company.

XYZ LIMITED
CASH FLOW STATEMENT FOR THE YEAR ENDED 31 DECEMBER 20X6

Reconciliation of operating profit to net cash inflow from operating activities

	£'000
Operating profit	6,022
Depreciation charges	899
Increase in stocks	(194)
Increase in debtors	(72)
Increase in creditors	234
Net cash inflow from operating activities	6,889

CASH FLOW STATEMENT

	£'000
Net cash inflow from operating activities	6,889
Returns on investments and servicing of finance (note 1)	2,999
Taxation	(2,922)
Capital expenditure (note 1)	(1,525)
	5,441
Equity dividends paid	(2,417)
	3,024
Management of liquid resources (note 1)	(450)
Financing (note 1)	57
Increase in cash	2,631

Reconciliation of net cash flow to movement in net debt (note 2)

	£'000	£'000
Increase in cash in the period	2,631	
Cash to repurchase debenture	149	
Cash used to increase liquid resources	450	
Change in net debt*		3,230
Net debt at 1.1.96		(2,903)
Net funds at 31.12.96		327

*In this example all change in net debt are cash flows.

The reconciliation of operating profit to net cash flows from operating activities can be shown in a note.

NOTES TO THE CASH FLOW STATEMENT

1   *Gross cash flows*

	£'000	£'000
Returns on investments and servicing of finance		
Interest received	3,011	
Interest paid	(12)	
		2,999
Capital expenditure		
Payments to acquire intangible fixed assets	(71)	
Payments to acquire tangible fixed assets	(1,496)	
Receipts from sales of tangible fixed assets	42	
		(1,525)
Management of liquid resources		
Purchase of treasury bills	(650)	
Sale of treasury bills	200	
		(450)

	£'000	£'000
Financing		
Issue of ordinary share capital	211	
Repurchase of debenture loan	(149)	
Expenses paid in connection with share issues	(5)	
		57

Note. These gross cash flows can be shown on the face of the cash flow statement, but it may sometimes be neater to show them as a note like this.

2   *Analysis of changes in net debt*

	As at 1 Jan 20X6 £'000	*Cash flows* £'000	*Other changes* £'000	*At 31 Dec 20X6* £'000
Cash in hand, at bank	42	847		889
Overdrafts	(1,784)	1,784		
		2,631		
Debt due within 1 year	(149)	149	(230)	(230)
Debt due after 1 year	(1,262)		230	(1,032)
Current asset investments	250	450		700
Total	(2,903)	3,230	-	327

Question	Cash flow statement format

Close the book for a moment and jot down the format of the cash flow statement.

2 Preparing a cash flow statement

FAST FORWARD

> You need to learn the **format** of the statement – this is the essential first stage in preparation. Always use the step-by-step procedure.

Exam focus point

> In essence, preparing a cash flow statement is very straightforward. You should therefore simply learn the format given above and apply the steps noted in the example below. Note that the following items are treated in a way that might seem confusing, but the treatment is logical if you think in terms of **cash**.

(a)   **Increase in stock** is treated as **negative** (in brackets). This is because it represents a cash **outflow**; cash is being spent on stock.

(b)   An **increase in debtors** would be treated as **negative** for the same reasons; more debtors means less cash.

(c)   By contrast an **increase in creditors** is **positive** because cash is being retained and not used to pay off creditors. There is therefore more of it.

2.1 Example: Preparation of a cash flow statement

Kitty Ltd's profit and loss account for the year ended 31 December 20X2 and balance sheets at 31 December 20X1 and 31 December 20X2 were as follows.

KITTY LIMITED
PROFIT AND LOSS ACCOUNT FOR THE YEAR ENDED 31 DECEMBER 20X2

	£'000	£'000
Sales		720
Raw materials consumed	70	
Staff costs	94	
Depreciation	118	
Loss on disposal	18	
		300
Operating profit		420
Interest payable		28
Profit before tax		392
Taxation		124
Profit after tax		268

KITTY LIMITED
BALANCE SHEETS AS AT 31 DECEMBER

	20X2		20X1	
	£'000	£'000	£'000	£'000
Fixed assets				
Cost		1,596		1,560
Depreciation		318		224
		1,278		1,336
Current assets				
Stock	24		20	
Trade debtors	76		58	
Bank	48		56	
	148		134	
Current liabilities				
Trade creditors	12		6	
Taxation	102		86	
	114		92	
Working capital		34		42
		1,312		1,378
Long-term liabilities				
Long-term loans		200		500
		1,112		878
Share capital		360		340
Share premium		36		24
Profit and loss		716		514
		1,112		878

During the year, the company paid £90,000 for a new piece of machinery.

Dividends paid amounted to £66,000.

Required

Prepare a cash flow statement for Kitty Ltd for the year ended 31 December 20X2 in accordance with the requirements of FRS 1 (revised).

Solution

STEP 1

Set out the proforma cash flow statement with all the headings required by FRS 1 (revised). You should leave plenty of space. Ideally, use three or more sheets of paper, one for the main statement, one for the notes (particularly if you have a separate note for the gross cash flows) and one for your workings. It is obviously essential to know the formats very well.

STEP 2

Complete the reconciliation of operating profit to net cash inflow as far as possible. When preparing the statement from balance sheets, you will usually have to calculate such items as depreciation, loss on sale of fixed assets and profit for the year (see Step 4).

STEP 3

Calculate the figures for tax paid, dividends paid, purchase or sale of fixed assets, issue of shares and repayment of loans if these are not already given to you (as they may be). Note that you may not be given the tax charge in the profit loss account. You will then have to assume that the tax paid in the year is last year's year-end provision and calculate the charge as the balancing figure.

STEP 4

If you are not given the profit figure, open up a working for the profit and loss account. Using the opening and closing balances, the taxation charge and dividends paid, you will be able to calculate profit for the year as the balancing figure to put in the statement.

STEP 5

Complete note 1, the gross cash flows. Alternatively this information may go straight into the statement.

STEP 6

You will now be able to complete the statement by slotting in the figures given or calculated.

STEP 7

Complete note 2 the analysis of changes in net debt.

KITTY LIMITED
CASH FLOW STATEMENT FOR THE YEAR ENDED 31 DECEMBER 20X2

Reconciliation of operating profit to net cash inflow

	£'000	£'000
Operating profit		420
Depreciation charges		118
Loss on sale of tangible fixed assets		18
Increase in stocks		(4)
Increase in debtors		(18)
Increase in creditors		6
Net cash inflow from operating activities		540

CASH FLOW STATEMENT

	£'000	£'000
Net cash flows from operating activities		540
Returns on investment and servicing of finance		
Interest paid		(28)
Taxation		
Corporation tax paid (W1)		(108)
Capital expenditure		
Payments to acquire tangible fixed assets (W2)	(90)	
Receipts from sales of tangible fixed assets (W2)	12	
Net cash outflow from capital expenditure		(78)
		326
Equity dividends paid		(66)
		260
Financing		
Issues of share capital (360 + 36 – 340 – 24)	32	
Long-term loans repaid (500 – 200)	(300)	
Net cash outflow from financing		(268)
Decrease in cash		(8)

NOTES TO THE CASH FLOW STATEMENT

Analysis of changes in net debt

	At 1 Jan 20X2	Cash flows	At 31 Dec 20X2
	£'000	£'000	£'000
Cash in hand, at bank	56	(8)	48
Debt due after 1 year	(500)	300	(200)
Total	(444)	292	(152)

Workings

1   *Corporation tax paid*

	£'000
Opening CT payable	86
Charge for year	124
Net CT payable at 31.12.X2	(102)
Paid	108

2   *Fixed asset disposals*

COST

	£'000		£'000
At 1.1.X2	1,560	At 31.12.X2	1,596
Purchases	90	Disposals	54
	1,650		1,650

ACCUMULATED DEPRECIATION

	£'000		£'000
At 31.1.X2	318	At 1.1.X2	224
Depreciation on disposals	24	Charge for year	118
	342		342

NBV of disposals	30
Net loss reported	(18)
Proceeds of disposals	12

2.2 Alternative methods

FRS 1 allows two possible layouts for cash flow statement in respect of operating activities:

(a) The **indirect method**, which is the one we have used so far

(b) The **direct method**.

Under the **direct method** the operating element of the cash flow statement should be shown as follows.

	£'000
Operating activities	
Cash received from customers	X
Cash payments to suppliers	(X)
Cash paid to and on behalf of employees	(X)
Other cash payments	(X)
Net cash flow from operating activities	X

Points to note are as follows.

(a) The **reconciliation** of operating profits and cash flows is **still required** (by note).

(b) **Cash received from customers** represents cash flows received during the accounting period in respect of sales.

(c) **Cash payments to suppliers** represents cash flows made during the accounting period in respect of goods and services.

(d) **Cash payments to and on behalf of employees** represents amounts paid to employees including the associated tax and national insurance. It will, therefore, comprise gross salaries, employer's National Insurance and any other benefits (eg pension contributions).

The direct method is, in effect, an analysis of the cash book. This information does not appear directly in the rest of the financial statements and so many companies might find it difficult to collect the information. Problems might include the need to reanalyse the cash book, to collate results from different cash sources and so on. The indirect method may be easier as it draws on figures which can be obtained from the financial statements fairly easily.

Question	Cash flow statement

The summarised accounts of Rene plc for the year ended 31 December 20X8 are as follows.

RENE PLC
BALANCE SHEET AS AT 31 DECEMBER 20X8

	20X8		20X7	
	£'000	£'000	£'000	£'000
Fixed assets				
Tangible assets		628		514
Current assets				
Stocks	214		210	
Debtors	168		147	
Cash	7		-	
	389		357	
Creditors: amounts falling due within one year				
Trade creditors	136		121	
Tax payable	39		28	
Overdraft	-		14	
	175		163	
Net current assets		214		194
Total assets less current liabilities		842		708
Creditors: amounts falling due after more than one year				
10% debentures		(80)		(50)
		762		658
Capital and reserves				
Share capital (£1 ords)		250		200
Share premium account		70		60
Revaluation reserve		110		100
Profit and loss account		332		298
		762		658

RENE PLC
PROFIT AND LOSS ACCOUNT
FOR THE YEAR ENDED 31 DECEMBER 20X8

	£'000
Sales	600
Cost of sales	(319)
Gross profit	281
Other expenses (including depreciation of £42,000)	(194)
Profit before tax	87
Tax	(31)
Profit after tax	56

You are additionally informed that there have been no disposals of fixed assets during the year. New debentures were issued on 1 January 20X8. Wages for the year amounted to £86,000. Dividends paid were £22,000.

Required

Produce a cash flow statement using the direct method suitable for inclusion in the financial statements, as per FRS 1 (revised 1996).

Answer

RENE PLC
CASH FLOW STATEMENT
FOR THE YEAR ENDED 31 DECEMBER 20X8

	£'000	£'000
Operating activities		
Cash received from customers (W1)	579	
Cash payments to suppliers (W2)	(366)	
Cash payments to and on behalf of employees	(86)	
		127
Returns on investments and servicing of finance		
Interest paid		(8)
Taxation		
UK corporation tax paid (W4)		(20)
Capital expenditure		
Purchase of tangible fixed assets (W5)	(146)	
Net cash outflow from capital expenditure		(146)
		(47)
Equity dividends paid		(22)
Financing		
Issue of share capital	60	
Issue of debentures	30	
Net cash inflow from financing		90
Increase in cash		21

NOTES TO THE CASHFLOW STATEMENT

1 *Reconciliation of operating profit to net cash inflow from operating activities*

	£'000
Operating profit (87 + 8)	95
Depreciation	42
Increase in stock	(4)
Increase in debtors	(21)
Increase in creditors	15
	127

2 *Reconciliation of net cash flow to movement in net debt*

	£'000
Net cash inflow for the period	21
Cash received from debenture issue	(30)
Change in net debt	(9)
Net debt at 1 January 20X8	(64)
Net debt at 31 December 20X8	(73)

3 *Analysis of changes in net debt*

	At 1 January 20X8 £'000	Cash flows £'000	At 31December 20X8 £'000
Cash at bank	–	7	7
Overdrafts	(14)	14	–
		21	
Debt due after 1 year	(50)	(30)	(80)
Total	(64)	(9)	(73)

Workings

1   *Cash received from customers*

DEBTORS CONTROL ACCOUNT

	£'000		£'000
B/f	147	Cash received (bal)	579
Sales	600	C/f	168
	747		747

2   *Cash paid to suppliers*

CREDITORS CONTROL ACCOUNT

	£'000		£'000
Cash paid (bal)	366	B/f	121
C/f	136	Purchases (W3)	381
	502		502

3   *Purchases*

	£'000
Cost of sales	319
Opening stock	(210)
Closing stock	214
Expenses (194 – 42 – 86 – 8 debenture interest)	58
	381

4   *Taxation*

TAXATION

	£'000		£'000
∴ Tax paid	20	Balance b/f	28
Balance c/f	39	Charge for year	31
	59		59

5   *Purchase of fixed assets*

	£'000
Opening fixed assets	514
Less depreciation	(42)
Add revaluation (110 – 100)	10
	482
Closing fixed assets	628
Difference = additions	146

BPP PROFESSIONAL EDUCATION

3 Interpretation of cash flow statements

FAST FORWARD

Cash flow statements provide **useful information** about a company which is not provided elsewhere in the accounts. Note that you may be expected to **analyse** or **interpret** a cash flow statement.

FRS 1 *Cash flow statements* was introduced on the basis that it would provide better, more comprehensive and more useful information than its predecessor standard. So what kind of information does the cash flow statement, along with its notes, provide?

Some of the **main areas where FRS 1 should provide information not found elsewhere in the accounts are as follows.**

(a) The **relationships between profit and cash** can be seen clearly and analysed accordingly.

(b) **Management of liquid resources** is highlighted, giving a better picture of the liquidity of the company.

(c) **Financing inflows and outflows must be shown, rather than simply passed through reserves**.

One of the most important things to realise at this point is that, as the ASB is always keen to emphasise, it is wrong to try to assess the health or predict the death of a reporting entity solely on the basis of a single indicator. When analysing cash flow data, the **comparison should not just be between cash flows and profit, but also between cash flows over a period of time** (say three to five years).

Cash is not synonymous with profit on an annual basis, but you should also remember that the 'behaviour' of profit and cash flows will be very different. **Profit is smoothed out** through accruals, prepayments, provisions and other accounting conventions. This does not apply to cash, so the **cash flow figures are likely to be 'lumpy' in comparison**. You must distinguish between this 'lumpiness' and the trends which will appear over time.

The **relationship between profit and cash flows will vary constantly**. Note that healthy companies do not always have reported profits exceeding operating cash flows. Similarly, unhealthy companies can have operating cash flows well in excess of reported profit. The value of comparing them is in determining the extent to which earned profits are being converted into the necessary cash flows.

Profit is not as important as the extent to which a company can convert its profits into cash on a continuing basis. This process should be judged over a period longer than one year. The cash flows should be compared with profits over the same periods to decide how successfully the reporting entity has converted earnings into cash.

Cash flow figures should also be considered in terms of their specific relationships with each other over time. A form of **'cash flow gearing' can** be determined by comparing operating cash flows and financing flows, particularly borrowing, to **establish the extent of dependence of the reporting entity on external funding.**

Other relationships can be examined.

(a) Operating cash flows and investment flows can be related to match cash recovery from investment to investment.

(b) Investment can be compared to distribution to indicate the proportion of total cash outflow designated specifically to investor return and reinstatement.

(c) A comparison of tax outflow to operating cash flow minus investment flow will establish a 'cash basis tax rate'.

The 'ratios' mentioned above can be monitored inter- and intra-firm and the analyses can be undertaken in monetary, general price-level adjusted, or percentage terms.

3.1 The advantages of cash flow accounting

The advantages of cash flow accounting are as follows.

(a)   Survival in business depends on the **ability to generate** cash. Cash flow accounting directs attention towards this critical issue.

(b)   Cash flow is **more comprehensive** than 'profit' which is dependent on accounting conventions and concepts.

(c)   **Creditors** (long and short-term) **are more interested in an entity's ability to repay them than in its profitability**. Whereas 'profits' might indicate that cash is likely to be available, cash flow accounting is more direct with its message.

(d)   Cash flow reporting provides a **better means of comparing the results** of different companies than traditional profit reporting.

(e)   Cash flow reporting satisfies the needs of all users better.

   (i)   For **management**, it provides the sort of information on which decisions should be taken: (in management accounting, 'relevant costs' to a decision are future cash flows); traditional profit accounting does not help with decision-making.

   (ii)   For **shareholders and auditors**, cash flow accounting can provide a satisfactory basis for stewardship accounting.

   (iii) As described previously, the information needs of **creditors and employees** will be better served by cash flow accounting.

(f)   Cash flow forecasts are **easier to prepare**, as well as more useful, than profit forecasts.

(g)   They can in some respects be **audited more easily** than accounts based on the accruals concept.

(h)   The accruals concept is confusing, and cash flows are **more easily understood**.

(i)   Cash flow accounting should be both retrospective, and also include a forecast for the future. This is of **great information value** to all users of accounting information.

(j)   **Forecasts** can subsequently be **monitored** by the publication of variance statements which compare actual cash flows against the forecast.

Question   Disadvantages

Can you think of some possible disadvantages of cash flow accounting?

Answer

The main disadvantages of cash accounting are essentially the advantages of accruals accounting (proper matching of related items). There is also the practical problem that few businesses keep historical cash flow information in the form needed to prepare a historical cash flow statement and so extra record keeping is likely to be necessary.

3.2 Why FRS 1 was revised

We mentioned at the beginning of this chapter that FRS 1 was revised, at least in part, because of certain criticisms. We will look at these briefly.

The original FRS 1 included 'cash equivalents' with cash. Cash equivalents were highly liquid investments with a maturity date of less than three months from the date of acquisitions (netted off against similar advances from banks). The inclusion of cash equivalents was criticised because it did not reflect the way in which businesses were managed: in particular, the requirement that to be a cash equivalent an investment had to be within three months of maturity was **considered unrealistic. In the revised FRS, only cash in hand and deposits repayable on demand, less overdrafts, are included in 'cash'.**

To distinguish the management of assets similar to cash (which previously might have been classed as 'cash equivalents') from other investment decisions, the revised FRS has a section dealing separately with the cash flows arising from the management of liquid resources.

The **new note** required by FRS 1 (revised) **reconciling movement in net debt** gives **additional information** on company performance, solvency and financial adaptability.

Chapter Roundup

- **Cash flow statements** were made compulsory for companies because it was recognised that accounting profit is not the only indicator of a company's performance.

- Cash flow statements concentrate on the **sources** and **uses of cash** and are a useful indicator of a company's **liquidity** and **solvency**.

- You need to learn the **format** of the statement – this is the essential first stage in preparation. Always use the step-by-step procedure.

- Cash flow statements provide **useful information** about a company which is not provided elsewhere in the accounts. Note that you may be expected to **analyse** or **interpret** a cash flow statement.

- **Cash flow forecasts** are of two main types

    - Cash budgets in **receipts and payments** form
    - Balance sheet and **financial statements based** forecasts.

Quick Quiz

1   List the aims of a cash flow statement.

2   The standard headings in the FRS1 cash flow statement are:

   * O.................................... a....................................

   * R.................................... on i.................................... and s.................................... of
     f....................................

   * T....................................

   * C.................................... e.................................... and f....................................
     i....................................

   * A.................................... and d....................................

   * E.................................... d.................................... p....................................

   * M.................................... of l.................................... r....................................

   * F....................................

3   Liquid resources are current asset investments which will mature or can be redeemed within three months
     of the year end.

     True   ☐

     False   ☐

4   Why are you more likely to encounter the indirect method as opposed to the direct method?

5   List five advantages of cash flow accounting.

Answers to Quick Quiz

1   Comparability and assessment of liquidity, solvency and financial adaptability.

2   See Paragraph 1.4.

3   False. See the definition in Paragraph 1.6 if you are not sure about this.

4   The indirect method utilises figures which appear in the financial statements. The figures required for the
     direct method may not be readily available.

5   See Paragraph 3.1 for ten advantages.

Now try the question below from the Exam Question Bank

Number	Level	Marks	Time
Q10	Full exam	25	45 mins

Related parties: segmental information

Topic list	Syllabus reference
1 FRS 8 *Related party disclosures*	5 (d)
2 SSAP 25 *Segmental reporting*	5 (e)

Introduction

FRS 8 is a fairly straightforward standard. Learn the definitions and the disclosures so that you can apply it or discuss it in the exam

SSAP 25 is also a straightforward standard - learn the definitions and formats.

Study guide

- Define and apply the definition of related parties in accordance with relevant accounting standards.

- Describe the potential to mislead users when related party transactions are included in a company's financial statements.

- Adjust financial statements (for comparative purposes) for the effects of non-commercial related party transactions.

- Describe the disclosure requirements for related party transactions.

- Discuss the usefulness and problems associated with the provision of segmental information.

- Define a reportable segment and the information that is to be reported.

- Prepare segmental reports in accordance with relevant accounting standards.

- Assess the performance of a company based on the information contained in its segmental report.

1 FRS 8 Related party disclosures

FAST FORWARD

> **FRS 8** is primarily a **disclosure statement**. It is concerned to increase transparency in information provided by published accounts and also to strengthen the stewardship role of management.

The ASB produced this FRS on related parties in 1995. FRS 8 *Related party disclosures* makes it clear why a standard was required on this subject.

'In the absence of information to the contrary, it is assumed that a reporting entity has independent discretionary power over its resources and transactions and pursues its activities independently of the interests of its individual owners, managers and others. Transactions are presumed to have been undertaken on an arm's length basis, ie on terms such as could have obtained in a transaction with an external party, in which each side bargained knowledgeably and freely, unaffected by any relationship between them.

These assumptions may not be justified when related party relationships exist, because the requisite conditions for competitive, free market dealings may not be present. Whilst the parties may endeavour to achieve arm's length bargaining the very nature of the relationship may preclude this occurring.'

FRS 8 can be summarised as follows.

(a)   FRS 8 *Related party disclosures* requires the **disclosure** of:

    (i)   **Information on related party transactions**.

    (ii)   The **name of the party controlling** the reporting entity and, if different, that of the ultimate controlling party whether or not any transactions between the reporting entity and those parties have taken place.

(b)   **No disclosure** is required in consolidated financial statements of **intragroup transactions** and balances eliminated on consolidation. A parent undertaking is not required to provide related party disclosures in its own financial statements when those statements are presented with consolidated financial statements of its group.

(c)   Disclosure is not required in the financial statements of **subsidiary undertakings**, 90% or more of whose voting rights are controlled within the group, of transactions with entities that are part of the group or investees of the group qualifying as related parties provided that the consolidated financial statements in which that subsidiary is included are publicly available.

Exam focus
point

Small and medium sized enterprises (SMEs) are becoming the bedrock of economic growth here in the UK and globally. This often entails related party scenarios. Be careful to spot any related party disclosures which the examiner might slip into a paper, albeit well camouflaged amongst a lot of other data, as would be the situation in real life.

1.1 Objective

The objective of FRS 8 is to ensure that financial statements contain the disclosures necessary to draw attention to the possibility that the reported financial position and results may have been affected by the existence of related parties and by material transactions with them. In other words, this is a standard which **is primarily concerned with disclosure**.

The definitions given in FRS 8 are fundamental to the effect of the standard.

Definitions

(a) **Close family** are those family members, or members of the same household, who may be expected to influence, or be influenced by, that person in their dealings with the reporting entity.

(b) **Control** means the ability of an undertaking to direct the financial and operating policies of another undertaking with a view to gaining economic benefits from its activities.

(c) **Key management** are those persons in senior positions having authority or responsibility for directing or controlling the major activities and resources of the reporting entity.

(d) **Persons acting in concert** comprise persons who, pursuant to an agreement or understanding (whether formal or informal), actively co-operative, whether through the ownership by any of them of shares in an undertaking or otherwise, to exercise control or influence over that undertaking.

The most important definitions are of *related parties* and *related party transactions*.

Related parties

(a) Two or more parties are related parties when at any time during the financial period:

    (i) One party has **direct or indirect control** of the other party

    (ii) The parties are **subject to common control** from the same source

    (iii) One party has **influence over the financial and operating policies** of the other party to an extent that that other party might be inhibited from pursuing at all times its own separate interests.

    (iv) The parties, in entering a transaction, are subject to **influence from the same source** to such an extent that one of the parties to the transaction has subordinated its own separate interests.

(b) For the avoidance of doubt, the following are **related parties** of the reporting entity:

    (i) Its ultimate and intermediate **parent undertakings**, subsidiary undertakings, and fellow subsidiary undertakings.

    (ii) Its **associates and joint ventures**.

    (iii) The **investor or venturer** in respect of which the reporting entity is an associate or a joint venture.

    (iv) **Directors*** of the reporting entity and the directors of its ultimate and intermediate parent undertakings.

    (v) **Pension funds** for the benefit of employees of the reporting entity or of any entity that is a related party of the reporting entity.

[* Directors include shadow directors, which are defined in companies legislation as persons in accordance with whose directions or instructions the directors of the company are accustomed to act.]

(c)   And the following are **presumed to be related parties** of the reporting entity unless it can be demonstrated that neither party has influenced the financial and operating policies of the other in such a way as to inhibit the pursuit of separate interests:

   (i)   The **key management** of the reporting entity and the key management of its parent undertakings or undertakings.

   (ii)   A person owning or able to exercise control over **20 per cent or more of the voting rights** of the reporting entity, whether directly or through nominees.

   (iii)   Each person **acting in concert** in such a way as to be able to exercise control or influence [in terms of part (a)(iii) of the definition of related party transitions, above] over the reporting entity.

   (iv)   An entity managing or managed by the reporting entity under a **management contract**.

(d)   Additionally, because of their relationship with certain parties that are, or are presumed to be, related parties of the reporting entity, the following are also presumed to be related parties of the reporting entity:

   (i)   **Members of the close family** of any individual falling under parties mentioned in (a) - (c) above.

   (ii)   Partnerships, companies, trusts or other **entities** in which any individual or member of the close family in (a) - (c) above has a **controlling interest**.

Sub-paragraphs (b), (c) and (d) are not intended to be an exhaustive list of related parties.

Related party transaction

The transfer of assets or liabilities or the performance of services by, or for a related party irrespective of whether a price is charged.'

The most important point is in paragraph (a) of the definition of related parties because it defines in **general terms** what related party transactions are; the succeeding paragraphs of definition only add **some specifics**.

1.2 Scope

The FRS does **not** require disclosure of the relationship and transactions between the reporting entity and the parties listed in (a) to (d) below simply as a result of their role as:

(a)   **Providers of finance** in the course of their business in that regard
(b)   **Utility companies**
(c)   **Government departments** and their sponsored bodies,
(d)   A customer, supplier, franchiser, distributor or general agent with whom an entity transacts a significant volume of business.

FRS 8 states the disclosures it requires, under two headings:

(a)   **Disclosure of control**
(b)   **Disclosure of transactions and balances**

1.3 Disclosure of control

When the reporting entity is controlled by another party, there should be disclosure of the related party relationship and the name of that party and, if different, that of the ultimate controlling party. If the controlling party or ultimate controlling party of the reporting entity is not known, that fact should be disclosed. This information should be disclosed **irrespective of whether any transactions have taken place** between the controlling parties and the reporting entity.

1.4 Disclosure of transactions and balances

Financial statements should **disclose material transactions** undertaken by the reporting entity with a related party. Disclosure should be made **irrespective of whether a price is charged**. The disclosure should include:

(a)   The **names** of the transacting parties.

(b)   A description of the **relationship** between the parties.

(c)   A description of the **transactions**.

(d)   The **amounts** involved.

(e)   **Any other elements** of the transactions necessary for an understanding of the financial statements.

(f)   The **amounts due** to or from related parties **at the balance sheet** date and provisions for doubtful debts due from such parties at that date.

(g)   **Amounts written off** in the period in respect of debts due to or from related parties.

1.5 Disclosable related party transactions

The explanatory notes also give examples of related party transactions which would require disclosure:

(a)   Purchases or sales of goods (finished or unfinished).
(b)   Purchases or sales of property and other assets.
(c)   Rendering or receiving of services.
(d)   Agency arrangements
(e)   Leasing arrangements.
(f)   Transfer of research and development.
(g)   Licence agreements.
(h)   Provision of finance (including loans and equity contributions in cash or in kind).
(i)   Guarantees and the provision of collateral security.
(j)   Management contracts.

The *materiality* of related party transactions is also an important question because **only material related party transactions must be disclosed**. You should be familiar with the general definition of materiality, that transactions are material when disclosure might reasonably be expected to influence decisions made by the users of general purpose financial statements. In the case of related party transactions, materiality:

'is to be judged, not only in terms of their significance to the reporting entity, but also **in relation to the other related party** when that party is:

(a)   A director, key manager or other individual in a position to influence, or accountable for stewardship of, the reporting entity.

(b)   A member of the close family of any individual mentioned in (a) above.

(c)   An entity controlled by any individual mentioned in (a) or (b) above.'

Question   Related parties

Which transactions are *excluded* by FRS 8?

Answer

The following transactions are excluded:

(a)   In consolidated accounts, transactions between group companies eliminated on consolidation

(b)   Transactions in parent company's accounts which also appear in consolidated accounts

(c)   Transactions with 90% subsidiaries in subsidiaries own accounts, where transactions are in publicly available consolidated accounts

(d)   Transactions with providers of finance, utility companies and government departments

(e)   Transactions with customers, suppliers, franchisers, distributors or general agents.

In the exam you are more likely to be tested on how related party relationships and transactions may affect the financial statements than on the detailed disclosure requirements.

Where group accounts are concerned, transfer pricing arrangements can be used to move profits from one group company to another, perhaps to benefit shareholders of the parent company at the expense of minority shareholders. Or transfer pricing can be manipulated to enhance the reported profits of a subsidiary which the group is planning to sell.

1.6 Current CA 1985 and Stock Exchange requirements

Some types of related party transactions are covered by existing statutory or Stock Exchange requirements, such as the provisions of the Companies Act 1985 covering transactions by directors and connected persons and 'Class IV' circulars which listed companies are required to send to shareholders when an acquisition or disposal of assets is made from or to a director, substantial shareholder or associate.

Exam focus point

The June 2002 exam tested the related party implications of a parent company and wholly owned subsidiary relationship.

2 SSAP 25 Segmental reporting

FAST FORWARD

SSAP 25 is primarily a **disclosure statements** concerned to improve the quality of information provided by published accounts. It gives shareholders and others details of **how** and **where** the entity generates turnover and profits.

SSAP 25 *Segmental reporting* was introduced in June 1990 and builds on the CA 1985 requirements to provide limited segmental analyses.

(a)   Where a company has two or more classes of business, it must show in a note the amount of turnover and operating profit attributable to each class of business; and

(b)   where a company operates in more than one geographical market, it must show in a note the amount of turnover attributable to each market.

Any or all of these analyses can be omitted on grounds of commercial sensitivity, but the directors must then state that these analyses would have been published but for these considerations.

2.1 Scope

SSAP 25 **applies only to** any entity which:

(a)   Is a **public company** or has a public limited company as a subsidiary undertaking, or

(b)   Is a **banking or insurance company or group,** or

(c)   **Exceeds the criteria, multiplied in each case by 10**, for defining a **medium-sized company** under s 248 of the Companies Act 1985, as amended from time to time by statutory instrument. (The criteria for defining a medium-sized company are given in Chapter 3.)

The standard adds:

'However, a subsidiary that is not a public limited company or a banking or insurance company need not comply with these provisions if its parent provides segmental information in compliance with this accounting standard.

All entities are encouraged to apply the provisions of this accounting standard in all financial statements intended to give a true and fair view of the financial position and profit or loss.

Where, in the opinion of the directors, the disclosure of any information required by this accounting standard would be seriously prejudicial to the interests of the reporting entity, that information need not be disclosed; but the fact that any such information has not been disclosed must be stated.'

2.2 Requirements

SSAP 25 extends the Companies Act requirements on analysis of turnover and profits as follows:

(a)   The **result** as well as turnover **must be disclosed for all segments**.

(b)   'Result' for these purposes is profit or loss before tax, minority interests and extraordinary items.

(c)   **Each segment's net assets should be disclosed** (so that return on capital employed can be calculated).

(d)   **Segmental turnover must be analysed between sales to customers outside the group and inter-segment sales/transfers** (where material).

Like the CA 1985, SSAP 25 requires analysis by two types of segment, class of business and geographical market.

Key term

> The SSAP defines a **class of business** as: 'a distinguishable component of an entity that provides a separate product or service or a separate group of related products or services.'

Factors to take into account in making this distinction are the nature of the products or services and production processes, markets distribution channels, organisation of activities and legislative framework relating to any part of the business.

SSAP 25 requires that turnover should be analysed by **geographical market** in two different ways, explained as follows.

Key terms

'A **geographical segment** is a geographical area comprising an individual country or a group of countries in which an entity operates, or to which it supplies products or services.

A **geographical analysis** should help the user of the financial statements to assess the extent to which an entity's operations are subject to factors such as the following:

(a)   Expansionist or restrictive economic climates
(b)   Stable or unstable political regimes
(c)   Exchange control regulations
(d)   Exchange rate fluctuations

The SSAP amplifies those statements as follows.

'The factors listed above apply both to the geographical locations of the entity's operations and to the geographical locations of its markets. The user of the financial statements gains a fuller understanding of the entity's exposure to these factors if turnover is disclosed according to both location of operations and location of markets. For the purposes of this accounting standard, origin of turnover is the geographical area from which products or services are supplied to a third party or another segment. Destination of turnover is the geographical area to which goods or services are supplied. Because disclosure relating to segment results and net assets will generally be based on location of operations, an analysis of turnover on the same basis will enable the user to match turnover, result and net assets on a consistent basis, and to relate all three to the perceived risks and opportunities of the segments. For these reasons this accounting standard requires the disclosure of sales by origin, but reporting entities should also disclose turnover by destination unless there is no material difference between the two. If there is no material difference, a statement to that effect is required.'

2.3 Identifying segments

FAST FORWARD

You must be able to prepare a **segmental analysis** and if necessary to use the results to help with interpretation of the accounts, as well as to discuss the **advantages and limitations** of segmental reporting.

Identifying segments could be difficult and the SSAP suggests as a **rule of thumb that a segment should normally be regarded as material if its third party turnover is ≥ 10% of the entity's total third party turnover or its profit is ≥ 10% of the combined results of all segments in profit (or its loss is ≥ 10% of the combined results of all loss making segments) or its net assets are ≥ 10% of total net assets of the entity.** The aim is to inform users of the accounts about activities earning a different rate of return from the rest of the business; or subject to different degrees of risk; or experiencing different growth rates; or with different potential for future development.

Reproduced below is the example given by SSAP 25 in its Appendix. Notice how the segmental results are reconciled to the entity's reported profit before taxation. This is a requirement of the SSAP. The example shows a segmental analysis based on a consolidated profit and loss account. However, SSAP 25 also applies to companies which do not need to prepare group accounts.

It is quite common for larger companies to operate through divisions or branches, and each of these could qualify as a segment, depending on the circumstances in each case. In both groups of companies and divisionalised single entity companies, there is frequently considerable trade between divisions.

Exam focus point

It is worth memorising this format. A question on SSAP 25 is likely to be quite straightforward.

The June 2004 paper had 50% of one question on segmental reporting.

CLASSES OF BUSINESS

	Industry A		Industry B		Other Industries		Group	
	20X2 £'000	20X1 £'000	20X2 £'000	20X1 £'000	20X2 £'000	20X1 £'000	20X2 £'000	20X1 £'000
Turnover								
Total sales	33,000	30,000	42,000	38,000	26,000	23,000	101,000	91,000
Inter-segment sales	(4,000)	-	-	-	(12,000)	(14,000)	(16,000)	(14,000)
Sales to third parties	29,000	30,000	42,000	38,000	14,000	9,000	85,000	77,000
Profit before taxation								
Segment profit	3,000	2,500	4,500	4,000	1,800	1,500	9,300	8,000
Common costs							(300)	(300)
Operating profit							9,000	7,700
Net interest							(400)	(500)
							8,600	7,200
Group share of the profit before taxation of associated undertakings	1,000	1,000	1,400	1,200	-	-	2,400	2,200
Group profit before taxation							11,000	9,400
Net assets								
Segment net assets	17,600	15,000	24,000	25,000	19,400	19,000	61,000	59,000
Unallocated assets*							3,000	3,000
							64,000	62,000
Group share of the net assets of associated undertakings	10,200	8,000	8,800	9,000	-	-	19,000	17,000
Total net assets							83,000	79,000

* Unallocated assets consist of assets at the group's head office in London amounting to £2.4 million (20X1: £2.5 million) and at the group's regional office in Hong Kong amounting to £0.6 million (20X1: £0.5 million).

GEOGRAPHICAL SEGMENTS

	United Kingdom		North America		Far East		Other		Group	
	20X2 £'000	20X1 £'000	20X2 £'000	20X1 £'000	20X2 £'000	20X1 £'000	20X2 £'000	20X1 £'000	20X2 £'000	20X1 £'000
Turnover										
Turnover by destination										
Sales to third parties	34,000	31,000	16,000	14,500	25,000	23,000	10,000	8,500	85,000	77,000
Turnover by origin										
Total sales	38,000	34,000	29,000	27,500	23,000	23,000	12,000	10,500	102,000	95,000
Inter-segment sales	-	-	(8,000)	(9,000)	(9,000)	(9,000)	-	-	(17,000)	(18,000)
Sales to third parties	38,000	34,000	21,000	18,500	14,000	14,000	12,000	10,500	85,000	77,000
Profit before taxation										
Segment profit	4,000	2,900	2,500	2,300	1,800	1,900	1,000	900	9,300	8,000
Common costs									(300)	(300)
Operating profit									9,000	7,700
Net interest									(400)	(500)
									8,600	7,200
Group share of the profit before taxation of associated undertakings	950	1,000	1,450	1,200	-	-	-	-	2,400	2,200
Group profit before taxation									11,000	9,400
Net assets										
Segment net assets	16,000	15,000	25,000	26,000	16,000	15,000	4,000	3,000	61,000	59,000
Unallocated assets*									3,000	3,000
									64,000	62,000
Group share of the net assets of associated undertakings	8,500	7,000	10,500	10,000	-	-	-	-	19,000	17,000
Total net assets									83,000	79,000

* Unallocated assets consist of assets at the group's head office in London amounting to £2.4 million (20X1: £2.5 million) and at the group's regional office in Hong Kong amounting to £0.6 million (20X1: £0.5 million).

2.3.1 Notes on the example

(a) **Common costs should be treated in the way that the directors deem most appropriate** in pursuance of the objectives of segmental reporting. For internal accounting purposes, some companies routinely apportion common costs between divisions, segments and so on and others do not; the same considerations prompting that decision should be applied to segmental reporting.

(b) **For companies in the financial sector it would normally be more sensible to include the net interest income or expense as part of the segment's operating results.** In the majority of cases non-interest bearing operating assets less non-interest bearing liabilities would be the most appropriate measure of capital employed; however, if interest is included in the segment results, then the relevant interest-bearing assets and liabilities should be included in calculating capital employed.

2.4 Arguments against reporting by segment

Those who argue against this form of disclosure generally emphasise the practical problems, which **include**:

(a) **Identifying segments** for reporting purposes.

(b) **Allocating common income** and costs among the different segments.

(c) **Reporting inter-segment transactions**.

(d) Providing information in such a way as to **eliminate misunderstanding** by investors.

(e) **Avoiding any potential damage** that may be done to the reporting entity by disclosing information about individual segments.

Question   Segmental report

The Multitrade Group has three divisions (all based in the UK), A. B and C. Details of their turnover, results and net assets are given below.

Division A	£'000
Sales to B	304,928
Other UK sales	57,223
Middle East export sales	406,082
Pacific fringe export sales	77,838
	846,071

Division B	
Sales to C	31,034
Export sales to Europe	195,915
	226,949

Division C	
Export sales to North America	127,003

	Division A	Division B	Division C
	£'000	£'000	£'000
Operational profit/(loss) before tax	162,367	18,754	(8,303)
Re-allocated costs from			
Head office	48,362	24,181	24,181
Interest costs	3,459	6,042	527

	Head office £'000	Division A £'000	Division B £'000	Division C £'000
Fixed assets	49,071	200,921	41,612	113,076
Net current assets	47,800	121,832	39,044	92,338
Long-term liabilities	28,636	16,959	6,295	120,841
Deferred taxation	1,024	24,671	9,013	4,028

Required

Prepare a segmental report in accordance with SSAP 25 for publication in Multitrade's group.

Answer

Ignoring comparative figures, Multitrade plc's segmental report would look like this.

CLASSES OF BUSINESS

	Group £'000	Division A £'000	Division B £'000	Division C £'000
Turnover				
Total sales	1,200,023	846,071	226,949	127,003
Inter-segment sales	335,962	304,928	31,034	–
Sales to third parties	864,061	541,143	195,915	127,003
Profit before taxation				
Segment profit/(loss)	172,818	162,367	18,754	(8,303)
Common costs **	96,724			
Operating profit	76,094			
Net interest	10,028			
Group profit before tax	66,066			
Net assets				
Segment net assets	427,016	281,123	65,348	80,545
Unallocated assets	67,211			
Total net assets	494,227			

GEOGRAPHICAL SEGMENTS

	Group	United Kingdom	Middle East	Pacific fringe	Europe	North America
Turnover						
Turnover by destination ***						
Sales to third parties	864,061	57,223	406,082	77,838	195,915	127,003

* Turnover, profit, net interest and net assets should be the same as those shown in the consolidated accounts.

** Common costs and unallocated assets are those items in the consolidated accounts which cannot reasonably be allocated to any one segment nor does the group wish to apportion them between segments. An example of a common cost is the cost of maintaining the holding company share register, and an example of an unallocated asset might be the head office building.

*** Turnover by destination must be disclosed in accordance with the Companies Act 1985. If Multitrade's divisions were not all in the UK, then another analysis would be required by SSAP 25 on the same lines as that shown for classes of business but analysed between the geographical origins of turnover.

Chapter Roundup

- **FRS 8** is primarily a **disclosure statement**. It is concerned to increase transparency in information provided by published accounts and also to strengthen the stewardship role of management.

- **SSAP 25** is primarily a **disclosure statement** concerned to improve the quality of information provided by published accounts. It gives shareholders and others details of **how** and **where** the entity generates turnover and profits.

- You must be able to prepare a **segmental analysis** and if necessary to use the results to help with interpretation of the accounts, as well as to discuss the **advantages and limitations** of segmental reporting.

Quick Quiz

1   Summarise the requirement of FRS 8.

2   Pension funds for the benefit of the employees of the reporting entity are deemed related parties by FRS 8.

    True   ☐

    False   ☐

3   How does FRS 8 define related parties?

4   What are the disclosure requirements of FRS 8?

5   What figure prefixes the following as the rule of thumb for identifying a segment under SSAP 25?

- .... of the entities total third party turnover

- .... ot the combined profit of all profit making segments

- .... of the net assets of the entity

6   How should common costs be allocated in segmental accounts?

Answers to Quick Quiz

1   FRS 8 requires (a) information on related party transactions and (b) the name of the party controlling the reporting entity. (See Para 1 for more details.)

2   True

3   Two or more parties are related parties when at any time during the financial period:

   (i)   one party has **direct or indirect control** of the other
   (ii)   they are subject to **common control** from the same source
   (iii)   one party has **influence over the financial and operating policies** of the other
   (iv)   they are subject to **influence** from the same source

   (See Para 1.1. for more detail.)

4   FRS 8 requires disclosure under two headings.

   (a)   disclosure of control (irrespective of whether any transactions have taken place)
   (b)   disclosure of transactions and balances involving related parties

   (See Para 1.4 for disclosure details.)

5   10   ≥ 10%. SSAP 25 suggests that 10% is the level at which turnover should be regarded as **material**.

6   In the way the directors deem most appropriate in pursuance of the objectives of segmental reporting.

Now try the questions below from the Exam Question Bank

Number	Level	Marks	Time
Q15	Introductory	n/a	15 mins
Q16	Introductory	n/a	10 mins

BPP
PROFESSIONAL EDUCATION

Appendix: Examination questions on published accounts

BPP
PROFESSIONAL EDUCATION

Introduction

(a) Before attempting these questions, you should be familiar with the requirements both of statute and of accounting standards (SSAPs and FRSs) in respect of the presentation and content of published accounts.

(b) Provided that you know the legal and accounting regulations, published accounts questions are not difficult to answer. They are, however, very time consuming and almost certainly you will not have time in the examination unless you adopt a clear and systematic approach. In this appendix we suggest an approach which should provide you with a useful guide. However, it is not the only approach, and you might develop your own method and means of answering such questions. Never be put off by the volume of detail given; it provides you with all the information necessary to produce a clear and detailed solution.

(c) Your aim in answering these questions should be to disclose the minimum information required by statute, SSAPs and FRSs. To disclose more than this might suggest to the examiner that you are unclear about what information is *required* to be disclosed and what information is sometimes *voluntarily* disclosed in practice.

(d) In the time available in the examination it is virtually impossible to provide the examiner with all the information normally given in an actual set of accounts, and indeed, the examiner does not expect you to do so. It is only necessary to comply with the statutory and quasi-statutory requirements so far as you are able from the information given. There is generally no need to embellish your solution with made-up information.

Suggested approach

(e) Read the question carefully to ensure you do not do more than the examiner wants. For example, questions often end with a statement that you may ignore the requirement to disclose accounting policies.

(f) It is likely that the examiner will ask you to prepare accounts for presentation to the members (ie the 'full' accounts rather than the modified versions for small and medium-sized companies) and it is suggested that you adopt the 'operational format' profit and loss account (unless otherwise requested) and the vertical balance sheet in your solutions. As far as possible, use the words given in the CA 1985 formats, but remember that certain alternative or additional headings are allowable and may be used in the examination.

(g) Head up a sheet of paper for the profit and loss account, a second sheet for the balance sheet and a third for the notes to the accounts. Keep a fourth sheet ready for your workings. Begin by writing a statement of accounting policies as note 1 to the accounts, unless the question has instructed you to ignore this requirement.

(h) Now, keeping in mind the 1985 Act pro-formas and the FRS 3 requirements, write out the profit and loss account, beginning with turnover and working line by line through the pro-forma. Search through the question for the information relevant to each line as you come to it and mark the question paper to indicate which bits of information have been used.

(i) While you are writing out the profit and loss account you should be building up the notes to the accounts, writing out each in conjunction with the profit and loss caption to which it refers and, of course, entering the cross reference on the face of the profit and loss account. The process of writing out the relevant note will often remove the need to prepare a working and thus save valuable time.

(j) Don't forget to disclose the EPS at the foot of the profit and loss account for a public company, if the figure is given. (You should assume that the company is listed unless told to the contrary.)

(k)   Once the profit and loss account and related notes are complete, follow the same procedure to construct the balance sheet, again working line by line through the pro-forma and writing out the relevant notes at the same time as entering the figures on the balance sheet.

(l)   Complete the notes to the accounts by considering whether any notes are necessary other than those arising directly from the profit and loss account and balance sheet. Common examples include:

      (i)   Events after the balance sheet date

      (ii)   Contingent liabilities

(m)   If you *are* asked to produce financial statements which comply with FRS 3, you may be asked to produce:

      (i)   A statement of total recognised gains and losses

      (ii)   A profit and loss account which shows the turnover and operating profit from continuing activities, acquisitions and discontinued activities

      (iii)   A note of historical cost profits and losses, reconciling P & L retained profit to historical cost profit

      (iv)   A reconciliation of movements in shareholders' funds

      (v)   A reserves note

We have ignored the requirements of FRS 3 in the two questions given here, partly because practice is given in those areas elsewhere in the text, but also to avoid distracting you from the main focus of the preparation of the standard CA 1985 pro-formas. Any FRS 3 requirements will be an 'extra' to your questions. Refer back to Chapter 3 to refresh your memory of these formats and notes.

(n)   Finally, do not forget that FRS 21 requires that the balance sheet should be dated. Indicate at the foot of the balance sheet where the date and director's signature are to appear.

(o)   You should now attempt to apply this approach to the illustrative questions which follow. Do not set yourself any time limit in answering these questions. Published accounts can only be mastered by absorbing the mass of detail required by statute and professional practice.

BPP
PROFESSIONAL EDUCATION

1 Kitchentech

The following list of balances was extracted from the books of Kitchentech Ltd on 31 December 20X8. The company is involved in the retailing of hardware through four shops which it owns in various parts of the country.

	£
Sales	1,875,893
Cost of sales	1,597,777
Administrative expenses	124,723
Directors' salaries	43,352
Debenture interest to 30.6.X8	3,000
Freehold premises at cost (land £100,000)	215,000
Motor vehicles, at cost	37,581
Accumulated depreciation on motor vehicles to 31.12.X7	16,581
Fixtures and fittings at cost	26,550
Accumulated depreciation on fixtures & fittings to 31.12.X7	8,200
Stock	88,452
Debtors	18,550
Creditors and accruals	47,609
Bank overdraft	11,433
Cash in hand	386
Debtors allowance (provision for doubtful debts) at 31.12.X7	1,200
Share capital	100,000
Profit and loss account at 31.12.X7	18,455
General reserve	16,000
10% debentures 20X8/Y6 (secured on the freehold buildings)	60,000

The following adjustments are to be made.

(a) Depreciation is to be provided in the accounts for the year as follows.

Buildings 2% on cost
Motor vehicles 25% on written down value
Fixtures and fittings 10% on cost

(b) Directors' remuneration is divided amongst the three directors as follows.

	£
Mr Adil - Chairman	4,000
Mr Beane – Marketing director	20,000
Mr Curruthers – Finance director	19,352
	43,352

Fees of £2,000 each are to be provided for the directors.

A pension of £1,900 paid to Mr Dingley-Jones, a former director, is included in the administration expenses.

The salary of Mr Frobisher, the company secretary, is £18,000 and is also included in the administrative expenses.

(c) Messrs Greene, Penn and partners, the company's auditors, rendered an account in early March 20X8 as follows.

	£
Assistance in preparation of taxation computation for the year ended 31.12.X7	500
Audit of accounts for the year ended 31.12.X7	1,000
	1,500

This bill was the subject of an accrual of £1,200 on 31 December 20X7. A similar bill for £1,500 is expected for the 20X8 accounts in due course.

(d)   The debtors include a balance of £400 owing from Catering Supplies Ltd. This is to be written off as it has proved irrecoverable. The debtors' allowance is to be adjusted to 10% of debtors.

(e)   Corporation tax based upon the profits for the year at the rate of 35% amounting to £40,000 is to be provided.

(f)   £30,000 is to be transferred to general reserve.

(g)   The basic rate of income tax should be taken as 25%.

(h)   The finance cost on the debentures is £6,000 per annum.

Required

Within the limits of the information given, prepare a profit and loss account and balance sheet for the year ended 31 December 20X8 for submission to the members of the company in accordance with statutory requirements and best professional practice.

2 Alpine

Alpine Athletic Training plc is a manufacturer of sports equipment. Set out below is a trial balance extracted from the books of the company as at 31 December 20X3.

	£	£
Sales		2,925,900
Cost of sales	1,785,897	
Selling expenses	120,000	
Administrative expenses	652,096	
Debtors/creditors	469,332	371,022
Debtors allowance		22,500
Directors' remuneration	181,500	
Audit fee	3,000	
Debenture interest	7,500	
Premises at cost	600,000	
Plant and machinery at cost	135,000	
Provision for depreciation on plant and machinery at 1.1.X3		60,000
Motor vehicles at cost (salesmen's cars)	54,000	
Provision for depreciation on motor vehicles at 1.1.X3		24,000
Stock in trade and work in progress	282,728	
Trade investment at cost	72,000	
Bank overdraft		354,528
Profit and loss account balance at 1.1.X3		65,103
General reserve		90,000
Ordinary share capital		300,000
10% debentures 20X9 secured on premises		150,000
	4,363,053	4,363,053

The following information is also related to the accounts for the year to 31 December 20X3.

(a)   The debtors' allowance is to be increased to an amount which is equal to 1% of the turnover for the year.

(b)   The directors' remuneration is divided amongst the four directors of the company as follows.

	£
Chairman	24,000
Managing director	60,000
Finance director	49,500
Sales director	48,000
	181,500

In addition provision must be made for directors' fees of £5,000 to each of the above directors.

(c) Depreciation is to be provided for the year as follows.

Buildings 2% on cost
Plant and machinery 10% on cost
Motor vehicles 25% on written down value

The only changes in fixed assets during the year were an addition to plant and machinery in early January 20X3 costing £30,000 and the purchase of premises for £600,000 comprising £150,000 for buildings and £450,000 for land.

(d) A provision of £60,000 is to be made for corporation tax at 35% based upon the profits for the year. This will be payable on 30 September 20X4.

(e) The sum of £15,000 is to be transferred to general reserve.

(f) The authorised ordinary share capital is £600,000 in 50p shares. All shares in issue are fully paid.

(g) Assume the basic rate of income tax to be 25%.

(h) Administrative expenses include £5,244 interest on the overdraft.

(i) The directors consider the value of the trade investment to be £75,000. It consists of 10,000 20p ordinary shares in Crampon Ltd, a company with an issued share capital of 200,000 ordinary shares.

(j) The finance charge on the debentures in £15,000 per annum.

Required

Within the limits of the above information, prepare the final accounts of Alpine Athletic Training plc for the year ended 31 December 20X3 in a form suitable for presentation to the members and which complies with the requirements of the Companies Act 1985.

The required information should be shown as part of the accounting statements or by way of note, whichever is considered most appropriate.

BPP
PROFESSIONAL EDUCATION

Appendix: Examination questions on published accounts (Solutions)

BPP
PROFESSIONAL EDUCATION

1 Kitchentech

PROFIT AND LOSS ACCOUNT FOR THE YEAR ENDED 31 DECEMBER 20X8

	Notes	£	£
Turnover	1		1,875,893
Cost of sales			(1,597,777)
Gross profit			278,116
Distribution costs (W1)		30,920	
Administrative expenses (W1)		156,175	
			(187,095)
Operating profit	2		91,021
Interest payable	3		(6,000)
Profit on ordinary activities before taxation			85,021
Tax on profit on ordinary activities	4		(40,000)
Profit on ordinary activities after taxation			45,021
Earnings per share	5		45.0p

STATEMENT OF MOVEMENT ON RESERVES

	£
Profit for the year	45,021
Transfer to general reserve	(30,000)
Retained profit for the year	15,021
Retained profits brought forward	18,455
Retained profits carried forward	33,476

BALANCE SHEET AS AT 31 DECEMBER 20X8

	Notes	£	£
Fixed assets			
Tangible assets	6		244,145
Current assets			
Stock		88,452	
Debtors £(18,550 – 400 – 1,815)		16,335	
Cash in hand		386	
		105,173	
Creditors: amounts falling due within one year			
Bank overdraft		11,433	
Creditors and accruals (W2)		58,409	
Taxation		40,000	
		109,842	
Net current liabilities			(4,669)
Total assets less current liabilities			239,476
Creditors: amounts falling due after more than one year			
10% debentures 20X8/Y6			(60,000)
			179,476
Capital and reserves			
Called up share capital			
£1 ordinary shares fully paid (authorised: £200,000)			100,000
Reserves			
General reserve		46,000	
Profit and loss account		33,476	
			79,476
			179,476

Approved by the Board of Directors on....................

..............................Director

NOTES TO THE ACCOUNTS

1   *Turnover*

Turnover is the value, net of VAT, of goods sold during the year in a single class of business in the UK.

2   *Operating profit*

Operating profit is stated after charging:

	£	£
Directors' remuneration		
Salaries	43,352	
Fees	6,000	
Pension to former director	1,900	
		51,252
Depreciation		10,205
Auditors' remuneration		1,000
Audit fees		1,300
Other services		500

(*Tutorial note*. No further details are required of directors' remuneration, since in total it is less than £200,000. Note that Mr Frobisher is *not* a director and so his salary is not included in the above total.)

3   *Interest payable*

Interest on 10% debentures 20X8/Y6	£6,000

4   *Tax on profit on ordinary activities*

UK corporation tax at 35% on the profit of the year	£40,000

5   *Earnings per share*

Earnings per share is based on earnings of £45,021 and 100,000 ordinary shares in issue during the year

6   *Fixed assets*

	Land and buildings £	Motor vehicles £	Fixtures & fittings £	Total £
Cost				
At 1 January and 31 December 20X8	215,000	37,581	26,550	279,131
Depreciation				
At 1 January 20X8	-	16,581	8,200	24,781
Charge for year	2,300	5,250	2,655	10,205
At 31 December 20X8	2,300	21,831	10,855	34,986
Net book value				
At 1 January 20X8	215,000	21,000	18,350	254,350
At 31 December 20X8	212,700	15,750	15,695	244,145

BPP
PROFESSIONAL EDUCATION

Workings

1 *Allocation of costs*

	Distribution costs £	Administrative expenses £
Per list of balances		124,723
Directors' salaries	20,000	23,352
Directors' fees	2,000	4,000
Depreciation:		
Buildings (2% × £115,000)		2,300
Motor vehicles 25% × £(37,581 − 16,581)	5,250	
Fixtures (10% × £26,550)	2,655	
Audit and tax advice; GPP		1,800
(includes £300 under-provided in previous year)		
Bad debt	400	
Debtors' allowance		
10% × £(18,550 − 400) − £1,200	615	
	30,920	156,175

(*Note.* The allocation above is somewhat arbitrary, especially as regards the depreciation costs. Other allocations would be acceptable.)

2 *Creditors and accruals*

	£
Per list of balances	47,609
Directors' fees	6,000
Half-year's debenture interest	3,000
20X8 audit and tax fee	1,500
Increase in accrual for 20X7 and audit tax fee	300
	58,409

2 Alpine

PROFIT AND LOSS ACCOUNT FOR THE YEAR ENDED 31 DECEMBER 20X3

	Note	£	£
Turnover (continuing operations)	1		2,925,900
Cost of sales (W1)			(1,799,397)
Gross profit			1,126,503
Distribution costs (W2)		187,259	
Administrative expenses (W3)		801,352	
			(988,611)
Operating profit	2		137,892
Interest payable	3		(20,244)
Profit before taxation			117,648
Taxation	4		(60,000)
Profit after taxation			57,648
Earnings per share	5		9.3p

STATEMENT OF MOVEMENT IN SHAREHOLDERS FUNDS

	£
Profit for the year	57,648
Transfer to general reserve	(15,000)
Retained profit for the financial year	42,648
Retained profits brought forward	65,103
Retained profits carried forward	107,751

BALANCE SHEET AS AT 31 DECEMBER 20X3

	Note	£	£
Fixed assets			
Tangible assets	6		681,000
Investments (directors' valuation: £75,000)			72,000
			753,000
Current assets			
Stocks and work in progress		282,728	
Debtors £(469,332 – 29,259)		440,073	
		722,801	
Creditors: amounts falling due within one year			
Bank overdraft		354,528	
Trade creditors		371,022	
Taxation		60,000	
Accruals (£7,500 deb int + £20,000 dir rem)		27,500	
		813,050	
Net current liabilities			(90,249)
Total assets less current liabilities			662,751
Creditors: amounts falling due after more than one year			
10% debentures 20X9			(150,000)
			512,751
Capital and reserves			
Called up share capital			
50p ordinary shares fully paid (authorised: £600,000)			300,000
Reserves			
General reserve (£90,000 + £15,000)		105,000	
Profit and loss account (£65,103 + £42,648)		107,751	
			212,751
			512,751

Approved by the Board of Directors on ....

...................Director

NOTES TO THE ACCOUNTS

1 *Turnover*

Turnover represents amounts invoiced, net of VAT, for goods and services supplied during the year in a single class of business in the UK.

2 *Operating profit*

Operating profit is stated after charging:

	£
Depreciation	24,000
Directors' emoluments	201,500
Auditors' remuneration	3,000

Directors' emoluments comprise fees of £20,000 and remuneration of £181,500.

The emoluments of the highest paid director were £63,000. (This information is required because the total of directors' emoluments is over £200,000.)

3   *Interest payable*

	£
On debentures repayable in more than five years	15,000
On bank overdraft	5,244
	20,244

4   *Taxation*

	£
UK corporation tax at 35% on the profits for the year	£60,000

5   *Earnings per share*

Earnings per share is based on earnings of £(59,748 - 4,200) = £55,548 and 600,000 ordinary shares in issue during the year.

6   *Fixed assets*

	Premises £	Plant and machinery £	Motor vehicles £	Total £
Cost				
At 1 January 20X3	-	105,000	54,000	159,000
Additions in year	600,000	30,000		630,000
At 31 December 20X3	600,000	135,000	54,000	789,000
Depreciation				
At 1 January 20X3	-	60,000	24,000	84,000
Charge for the year	3,000	13,500	7,500	24,000
At 31 December 20X3	3,000	73,500	31,500	108,000
Net book value				
At 1 January 20X3	–	45,000	30,000	75,000
At 31 December 20X3	597,000	61,500	22,500	681,000

Workings

1   *Cost of sales*

	£
Per TB	1,785,897
Add depreciation on plant (10% × £135,000)	13,500
	1,799,397

2   *Distribution costs*

	£	£
Selling expenses		120,000
Sales director's remuneration £(48,000 + 5,000)		53,000
Debtors' allowance:		
Allowance required (1% × £2,925,900)	29,259	
Less existing allowance	22,500	
Increase in allowance		6,759
Depreciation on motor vehicles (25% × £30,000)		7,500
		187,259

3   *Administrative expenses*

		£
Per TB		652,096
Directors' remuneration £(24,000 + 60,000 + 49,500 + 15,000)		148,500
Audit fee		3,000
Depreciation on buildings (2% × £150,000)		3,000
		806,596
Less overdraft interest		5,244
		801,352

BPP
PROFESSIONAL EDUCATION

Exam question bank

BPP
PROFESSIONAL EDUCATION

Examination standard questions are indicated by the mark and time allocations.

1 Conceptual framework (25 marks)   **45 mins**

(a) Outline the benefits of having a conceptual framework to help with the development of financial reporting standards.

(b) State the objectives of financial statements.

(c) Describe what you understand by the terms relevance and reliability in relation to financial reporting.

(d) Explain why materiality is an important concept in preparing true and fair financial statements.

(e) State the ASB definitions of assets and liabilities.

(f) Explain the ASB approach to the application of prudence and neutrality in the preparation of financial statements.

2 Setting and regulating standards (20 marks)   **36 mins**

(a) Describe how the ASB goes about developing and issuing new financial reporting standards.
(b) Briefly describe the ASB's approach to harmonisation of financial reporting standards.
(c) Explain the role of the Financial Reporting Review Panel.
(d) Briefly outline the role of the UITF.

3 Published accounts (25 marks)   **45 mins**

(a) Why is the disclosure of accounting policies required by the Companies Act 1985?

(b) The Companies Act 1985 regulates the concept of small and medium-sized companies and allows certain 'accounting exemptions' for such entities.

Required

(i) State the criteria which are taken into account to determine whether a company is 'small' or 'medium-sized'.

(ii) With regard to small companies only, list the exemptions which are allowed.

(c) List the contents of the directors' report.

4 Azrina (25 marks)   **45 mins**

The financial controller of Azrina plc is preparing forecast balance sheets as at 31 December 20X4, 20X5, 20X6 and 20X7.

The 20X4 forecast has been prepared and shows the following figure in respect of motor vehicles.

	£'000
Cost	540
Accumulated depreciation	130
Net book value	410

Depreciation on motor vehicles is charged at 25% on the reducing balance. A full year's depreciation is charged in the year of purchase and none in the year of sale.

The following information has been collated by the assistant accountant in order to help the financial controller prepare his forecast.

FORECAST PURCHASES OF MOTOR VEHICLES
FOR THE YEAR ENDED 31 DECEMBER

	20X5 £'000	20X6 £'000	20X7 £'000
List price			
Cash purchase	180	300	450
Hire purchase	–	400	–
Trade discount (20%)			
Cash purchase	36	60	90
Hire purchase	–	80	–
Cash discount (5% of net price)	7	12	18
Delivery costs (paid to supplier)	10	12	15
Costs of valeting old vehicles to prepare them for sale	2	3	4
Trade-in allowances on old vehicles to be set off against hire purchase deposit or finance lease first year rental		25	20
Hire-purchase deposit	–	85 (110 – 25)	
Finance lease first year rental			90 (110 – 20)
Total cash to be paid to the suppliers of the new vehicles in the year of purchase	147 (180 – 36 – 7 + 10)	97 (85 + 12)	105 (90 + 15)

FORECAST DISPOSALS OF MOTOR VEHICLES (AT COST)
IN THE YEARS ENDED 31 DECEMBER

	20X5 £'000	20X6 £'000	20X7 £'000
Vehicle			
Originally acquired in year ended 31 December			
20X0	30		
20X1	40		
20X2		45	
20X3		65	
20X4			75

The following methods of purchase will be used to acquire the vehicles.

Year ended 31 December 20X5: cash purchase.

Year ended 31 December 20X6: hire purchase. The agreement in question requires an initial deposit of £110,000, then in each of the three years following an instalment of £70,000.

Year ended 31 December 20X7: finance lease agreement. A rental of £110,000 will be payable in arrears for six years.

Required

For the asset motor vehicles in the forecast balance sheets of Azrina plc as at 31 December 20X5, 20X6, 20X7, produce a schedule showing cost, accumulated depreciation and net book value. You should show all your workings and make all calculations to the nearest £'000.

BPP
PROFESSIONAL EDUCATION

5 Bleco (30 marks)

54 mins

The following information relates to the R & D activities of Bleco plc. All projects are given designatory prefixes to indicate their nature.

PR = pure research
AR = applied research
D   = development

At 1 September 20X0, the balance brought forward as development costs consisted of:

		£
Project:	D363	198,300
	D367	242,700
	D368	nil

During the year ended 31 August 20X1 the following took place.

(a)   Project D368 satisfied the SSAP 13 deferment criteria. In previous years, a total of £47,830 expended on this project had been written off to the profit and loss account. The directors have resolved to defer, by capitalisation, the aggregate of the current year's expenditure together with the reinstated figure from previous years.

(b)   An applied research project, AR204, was converted into a development project and redesignated D369, but all expenditure up to this point is to be written off.

(c)   Two more development projects were instituted, D370 and D371. This latter project was commissioned by Lytax Ltd under a contract for full reimbursement of expenditure; to date, £24,000 has been received from Lytax Ltd.

(d)   It has become apparent that the technical feasibility and commercial viability of Project D370 are doubtful.

(e)   All other development projects satisfy the SSAP 13 deferment criteria.

(f)   (See below)

(g)   Project D363 entered full commercial production and is to be amortised on a straight line basis over six years.

Bleco plc depreciates fixed assets on a straight line basis, assuming no residual value, at the following rates.

	% per annum on cost
Laboratory buildings	10
Laboratory equipment	20

A full year's depreciation is charged in the year of acquisition.

Expenditure was incurred as follows.

	PR119	AR187	AR204	D367	D368	D369	D370	D371	Unallocated
	£	£	£	£	£	£	£	£	£
Wages, salaries and related charges	35,100	27,300	15,260	2,090	16,480	34,070	29,800	27,500	3,300
Materials	810	520	290	340	410	1,560	2,650	3,400	4,070
Direct expenses (other)	250	210	180	170	230	640	690	710	2,240
Production overheads	1,240	3,600	2,950	3,540	4,650	6,980	6,010	6,420	7,070
Fixed assets:									
Experimental laboratory buildings		200,000							
Testing laboratory buildings						310,000			
Laboratory equipment		170,000				472,000			
Related selling and administrative overheads									76,200
Market research									55,600

Required

Prepare extracts from the profit and loss account of Bleco plc for year ended 31 August 20X1 and from the company's balance sheet at that date, to incorporate the financial effects of the research and development expenditure.

Your answer should comply with the requirements of SSAP 13 Accounting for research and development.

Detailed workings for each item must be shown.

6 Winger (Pilot paper – 25 marks)   45 mins

The following trial balance relates to Winger plc at 31 March 20X1:

	£'000	£'000
Turnover (note i)		358,450
Cost of sales	185,050	
Distribution costs	28,700	
Administration expenses	15,000	
Lease rentals (note ii)	20,000	
Debenture interest paid	2,000	
Interim dividends (note vi)	12,000	
Land and buildings – cost (note iii)	200,000	
Plant and equipment – cost	154,800	
Depreciation 1 April 20X0 – plant and equipment		34,800
Development expenditure (note iv)	30,000	
Profit on disposal of fixed assets		45,000
Trade debtors	55,000	
Stocks – 31 March 20X1	28,240	
Cash and bank	10,660	
Trade creditors		29,400
Taxation – over provision in year to 31 March 20X0		2,200
Ordinary shares of 25p each		150,000
8% Debenture (issued in 20W8)		50,000
Profit and loss reserve 1 April 20X0		71,600
	741,450	741,450

BPP
PROFESSIONAL EDUCATION

The following notes are relevant:

(i)   Included in the turnover is £27 million, which relates to sales made to customers under sale or return agreements. The expiry date for the return of these goods is 30 April 20X1. Winger plc has charged a mark-up of 20% on cost for these sales.

(ii)   A lease rental of £20 million was paid on 1 April 20X0. It is the first of five annual payments in advance for the rental of an item of equipment that has a cash purchase price of £80 million. The auditors have advised that this is a finance lease and have calculated the implicit interest rate in the lease as 12% per annum. Leased assets should be depreciated on a straight-line basis over the life of the lease.

(iii)   On 1 April 20X0 Winger plc acquired new land and building at a cost of £200 million. For the purpose of calculating depreciation only, the asset has been separated into the following elements:

Separate asset	Cost	Life
	£'000	
Land	50,000	Freehold
Heating system	20,000	10 years
Lifts	30,000	15 years
Building	100,000	50 years

The depreciation of the elements of the building should be calculated on a straight-line basis. The new building replaced an existing building that was sold on the same date for £95 million. It had cost £50 million and had a carrying value of £80 million at the date of sale. The profit on this building has been calculated on the original cost. It had not been depreciated on the basis that the depreciation charge would not be material.

Plant and machinery is depreciated at 20% on the reducing balance basis.

(iv)   The figure for development expenditure in the trial balance represents the amounts capitalised in previous years in respect of the development of a new product. Unfortunately, during the current year, the Government has introduced legislation which effectively bans this type of product. As a consequence of this the project has been abandoned. The directors of Winger plc are of the opinion that writing off the development expenditure, as opposed to its previous capitalisation, represents a change of accounting policy and therefore wish to treat the write off as a prior adjustment.

(v)   A provision for corporation tax for the year to 31 March 20X1 of £15 million is required.

(vi)   The company has paid an interim ordinary dividend and half of the annual debenture interest. No final dividend is proposed.

(vii)   The finance cost on the debentures is £4,000 per annum.

Required

(a)   Prepare the profit and loss Account of Winger plc for the year to 31 March 20X1.   (9 marks)

(b)   Prepare a balance sheet as at 31 March 20X1 in accordance with the Companies Acts and current Accounting Standards so far as the information permits.   (11 marks)

Notes to the financial statements are not required.

(c)   Discuss the current acceptability of the company's previous policy in respect of non-depreciation of buildings.   (5 marks)

7 Bulwell (20 marks)   36 mins

Bulwell Aggregates Ltd wish to expand their transport fleet and purchased three heavy lorries with a list price of £18,000 each. Robert Bulwell has negotiated hire purchase finance to fund this expansion, and the company has entered into a hire purchase agreement with Granby Garages plc on 1 January 20X1. The agreement states that Bulwell Aggregates will pay a deposit of £9,000 on 1 January 20X1, and two annual instalments of £24,000 on 31 December 20X1, 20X2 and a final instalment of £20,391 on 31 December 20X3.

Interest is to be calculated at 25% on the balance outstanding on 1 January each year and paid on 31 December each year.

The depreciation policy of Bulwell Aggregates Ltd is to write off the vehicles over a four year period using the straight line method and assuming a scrap value of £1,333 for each vehicle at the end of its useful life.

The cost of the vehicles to Granby Garages is £14,400 each.

Required

(a)   Account for the above transactions in the books of Granby Garages plc, showing the entries in the hire purchase trading account for the years 20X1, 20X2 and 20X3. This is the only hire purchase transaction undertaken by this company.

(b)   Account for the above transactions in the books of Bulwell Aggregates Ltd showing the entries in the profit and loss account and balance sheet for the years 20X1, 20X2, 20X3. This is the only hire purchase transaction undertaken by this company.

Calculations to the nearest £.

8 Soap (15 marks)   27 mins

Soap plc is working on a number of short-term and long-term contracts. Its policy with regard to attributable profit on the long term contracts is to calculate it as follows.

Degree of completion (%) × total estimated profit (adjusted for known variations in costs accruing in the period)

The directors are sure that their cost calculations for the contracts are accurate, and the auditors concur with them in their belief that the degree of completion is sufficient to accrue profit. It is 31 December 20X7, the company's accounting year end. Further details of the contracts are as follows.

(a)   The short term contracts are 7 to 9 months in duration. Some of them will not be completed until 31 March 20X8. It is the directors' policy to accrue profit earned to date on these contracts in the accounts as at 31 December 20X7.

(b)   On 1 April 20X7 Soap plc commenced work on a contract with Emmerdale plc. The total contract price was £9 million and the total contract costs were expected to be £7.5 million. The contract is expected to run for two years.

During the year to 31 December 20X7, Soap plc incurred unforeseen additional costs of £500,000 on the contract in the light of which it revised its estimate of the total expected costs to £8 million. The following details are relevant to the position as at 31 December 20X7.

(i)   Costs incurred to date: £4m
(ii)   Payments on account: £3m
(iii)   Percentage complete per independent surveyor: 45%.

(c) On 1 July 20X7 Soap plc entered into a contract with Archers plc. The details of the contract were as follows.

(i) Duration of contract: 2 years

(ii) Total contract price: £150,000

(iii) Estimated total cost: £120,000

(iv) Percentage of completion (directors' estimate): 20% (The terms of the contract did not require an independent valuation by a surveyor.)

(v) Costs incurred up to 31 December 20X7: £47,500

(vi) Payments on account received: £40,000

A special machine had been purchased for the purposes of the contract and was being depreciated over the two year period on a straight line basis. The cost of the machine was £20,000, and the depreciation charge to date had been included in the costs incurred figure (v). On 31 December 20X7 it was decided that this machine should be written off. (Assume no residual value.)

(d) On 1 August 20X7, Soap plc entered into a contract with Neighbours Ltd. The details of the contract were as follows.

(i) Duration: 1½ years
(ii) Total contract price: £6.4 million
(iii) Estimated total costs: £5 million
(iv) Payments on account: £2.5 million
(v) Costs incurred up to 31 December 20X7: £1.8 million
(vi) Percentage of completion (independent surveyor's estimate): 25%

Neighbours Ltd was a new customer, so as a precaution, Soap plc had asked for a large deposit.

Required

(a) State whether you think it is good accounting practice to accrue profit on the short term contracts. Give reasons for your view. (4 marks)

(b) For the year ended 31 December 20X7, show the relevant extracts from the profit and loss account and balance sheet of Soap plc as regards the contracts with Emmerdale plc, Archers plc and Neighbours Ltd. You do not need to show the cash and bank balances. (11 marks)

9 Corax (20 marks)   36 mins

Corax plc has an allotted capital of £350,000 in fully paid 50p ordinary shares. At 31 December 20X6 the following balances were included in the company's balance sheet.

	£
Agreed corporation tax liability on 20X5 profits	16,300
Estimated corporation tax liability on 20X6 profits	5,000
Deferred taxation account	29,400
Profit and loss account (credit)	43,000

(No dividends had been paid or proposed in respect of 20X6)

The following information relates to the year ended 31 December 20X7.

(a) Corporation tax liability for 20X5 profits was settled (January).

(b) Interim dividend of 3p per share was paid (August).

(c) Corporation tax liability for 20X6 was agreed at £3,800 (December), paid January 20X8.

(d) Profit for 20X7 (before tax) on ordinary activities was calculated at £100,000.

(e)   Corporation tax based on the 20X7 profits was estimated at £36,000.

(f)   A transfer to the deferred taxation account of £7,000 for 20X7 is to be made in respect of capital allowances in excess of depreciation charges (the entire balance on the deferred tax account being of a similar nature).

Required

(a)   Make all relevant entries in the ledger accounts (except bank and share capital).

(b)   Complete the profit and loss account for 20X7 and show how the final balances would be included the balance sheet at 31 December 20X7. Show the details given in the notes to the accounts.

Assume income tax at 25%.

10 Emma

Set out below are the financial statements of Emma Ltd. You have been asked to prepare the cash flow statement of the company, implementing the *revised* version of FRS 1 *Cash flow statements.*

EMMA LIMITED
PROFIT AND LOSS ACCOUNT FOR THE YEAR ENDED 31 DECEMBER 20X2

	£'000
Turnover	2,553
Cost of sales	1,814
Gross profit	739
Distribution costs	125
Administrative expenses	264
Operating profit	350
Interest received	25
Interest paid	75
Profit on ordinary activities before taxation	300
Taxation	140
Profit after tax	160

BPP
PROFESSIONAL EDUCATION

EMMA LIMITED
BALANCE SHEETS AS AT 31 DECEMBER 20X2

	20X2	20X1
	£'000	£'000
Fixed assets		
Tangible assets	380	305
Intangible assets	250	200
Investments	–	25
	630	530
Current assets		
Stocks	150	102
Debtors	390	315
Short-term investments	50	–
Cash in hand	2	1
	592	418
Creditors: amounts falling due in less than one year		
Trade creditors	127	119
Bank overdraft	85	98
Taxation	120	110
	332	327
Net current assets	260	91
Total assets less current liabilities	890	621
Creditors amounts falling due after more than one year		
Long-term loan	100	
Provisions for liabilities and charges		
Deferred taxation	70	50
	720	571
Capital and reserves		
Share capital (£1 ordinary shares)	200	150
Share premium account	160	150
Revaluation reserve	100	91
Profit and loss account	260	180
	720	571

The following information is available.

(a)   The proceeds of the sale of fixed asset investments amounted to £30,000.

(b)   Fixtures and fittings, with an original cost of £85,000 and a net book value of £45,000, were sold for £32,000 during the year.

(c)   The current asset investments fall within the definition of liquid resources under FRS 1 (revised).

(d)   The following information relates to tangible fixed assets.

	31.12.20X2	31.12.20X1
	£'000	£'000
Cost	720	595
Accumulated depreciation	340	290
Net book value	380	305

(e)   50,000 £1 ordinary shares were issued during the year at a premium of 20p per share.

(f)   Dividends totalling £80,000 were paid during the year.

Required

Prepare a cash flow statement for the year to 31 December 20X2 using the format laid out in FRS 1 (revised), together with the relevant notes to the statement.

11 Justin Case

10 mins

One of Justin Case Ltd's employees suffered sever electric shock and nerve damage in trying to install a piece of equipment which was known to be faulty.

The company's solicitors suggest that the employee has a strong case. However, he has to undergo a series of medical tests before likely financial damages can be estimated.

Required

Explain how this matter should be treated in the year-end accounts of Justin Case Ltd in terms of FRS 12.

12 Multiplex (Pilot paper – 25 marks)

45 mins

The following transactions and events have arisen during the preparation of the draft financial statements of Multiplex for the year to 31 March 20X0.

(a)   On 1 April 20W9 Multiplex issued £80 million 8% convertible debentures at par. The debentures are convertible into equity shares, or redeemable at par, on 31 March 20X4, at the option of the debenture holders. The terms of conversion are that each £100 of debentures will be convertible into 50 equity shares of Multiplex. A finance consultant has advised that if the option to convert to equity had not been included in the terms of the issue, then a coupon (interest) rate of 12% would have been required to attract subscribers for the debenture issue.

The value of £1 receivable at the end of each year at a discount rate of 12% can be taken as:

Year	£
1	0.89
2	0.80
3	0.71
4	0.64
5	0.57

Required

Calculate the profit and loss account charge for the year to 31 March 20X0 and the balance sheet extracts at 31 March 20X0 in respect of the issue of the convertible debentures.   (5 marks)

(b)   On 1 January 20X1 Multiplex plc acquired Steamdays Ltd, a company that operates a scenic railway along the coast of a popular tourist area. The summarised balance sheet at fair values of Steamdays Ltd on 1 January 20X1, reflecting the terms of the acquisition was:

	£'000
Goodwill	200
Operating licence	1,000
Property – train stations and land	250
Rail track and coaches	250
Two steam engines	1,000
Other net assets	300
Purchase consideration	3,000

The operating licence is for ten years. It was renewed on 1 January 20X1 by the transport authority and is stated at the cost of its renewal. The carrying values of the property and rail track and coaches are based on their value in use. The engines, and other net assets are valued at their net selling prices.

On 1 February 20X1 the boiler of one of the steam engines exploded, completely destroying the whole engine. Fortunately no one was injured, but the engine was beyond repair. Due to its age a replacement could not be obtained. Because of the reduced passenger capacity the estimated value in use of the whole of the business after the accident was assessed at £2 million.

Passenger numbers after the accident were below expectations even after allowing for the reduced capacity. A market research report concluded that tourists were not using the railway because of their fear of a similar accident occurring to the remaining engine. In the light of this the value in use of the business was re-assessed on 31 March 20X1 at £1.8 million. On this date Multiplex plc received an offer of £600,000 in respect of the operating licence (it is transferable). The realisable value of the other net assets has not changed significantly.

Required

Calculate the carrying value of the assets of Steamdays Ltd (in Multiplex plc's consolidated balance sheet) at 1 February 20X1 and 31 March 20X1 after recognising the impairment losses.

(6 marks)

(c)   On 1 January 20X1 the Board of Multiplex plc approved a resolution to close the whole of its loss-making engineering operation. A binding agreement to dispose of the assets was signed shortly afterwards. The sale will be completed on 10 July 20X1 at an agreed value of £30 million. The costs of the closure are estimated at:

–   £2 million for redundancy
–   £3 million in penalty costs for non-completion of contracted orders
–   £1.5 million for associated professional costs
–   Losses on the sale of the net assets whose book value at 31 March 20X1 was £46 million
–   Operating losses for the period from 1 April 20X1 to the date of sale are estimated at £4.5 million.

Multiplex plc accounts for its various operations on a divisional basis.

Required

Advise the directors on the correct accounting treatment of the closure of the engineering division.

(5 marks)

(d)   Multiplex plc is in the intermediate stage of a long-term, construction contract for the building of a new privately owned road bridge over a river estuary. The original details of the contract are:

Approximate duration of contract: 3 years
Date of commencement: 1 October 20W9
Total contract price: £40 million
Estimated total cost: £28 million

An independent surveyor certified the value of the work in progress as follows:

– On 31 March 20X0   £12 million
– on 31 March 20X1   £30 million (including the £12 million in 20X0)

Costs incurred at:

– 31 March 20X0   £9 million
– 31 March 20X1   £28.5 million (including the £9 million in 20X0)

Payments received on account by 31 March 20X1 were £25 million

On 1 April 20X0 Multiplex plc agreed to a contract variation that would involve an additional fee of £5 million with associated additional estimated costs of £2 million.

The costs incurred during the year to 31 March 20X1 include £2.5 million relating to the replacement of some bolts which had been made from material that had been incorrectly specified by the firm of civil engineers who were contracted by Multiplex plc to design the bridge. These costs were not included in the original estimates, but Multiplex plc is hopeful that they can be recovered from the firm of civil engineers.

Multiplex plc calculates profit on long-term contracts using the percentage of completion method. The percentage of completion of the contract is based on the value of the work certified to date compared to the total contract price.

Required

Prepare the profit and loss account and balance sheet extracts in respect of the contract for the year to 31 March 20X1 only. (9 marks)

13 Dividend distribution (20 marks) 36 mins

(a) What do you understand by the statement that dividends must not be paid out of the capital of a company?

(b) What would be the effect on the maximum distributable profits of Donor plc, a public company, of the following transactions:

(i) An upward revaluation of a fixed asset by £20,000 on 1 January, and a consequential increase in the depreciation charge of £4,000 in the year to 31 December.

(ii) The sale of some land for £500,000, which had a historical cost of £150,000 but which was valued in the balance sheet at £440,000.

14 Revenue recognition (Pilot paper – 25 marks) 45 mins

The timing of revenue (income) recognition has long been an area of debate and inconsistency in accounting. Industry practice in relation to revenue recognition varies widely, the following are examples of different points in the operating cycle of businesses that revenue and profit can be recognised.

– On the acquisition of goods
– During the manufacture or production of goods
– On delivery/acceptance of goods
– When certain conditions have been satisfied after the goods have been delivered
– Receipt of payment for credit sales
– On the expiry of a guarantee or warranty

In the past the 'critical event' approach has been used to determine the timing of revenue recognition. The Accounting Standards Board (ASB) in its 'Statement of Principles for Financial Reporting' has defined the 'elements' of financial statements, and it uses these to determine when a gain or loss occurs.

Required

(a) Explain what is meant by the critical event in relation to revenue recognition and discuss the criteria used in the Statement of Principles for determining when a gain or loss arises. (5 marks)

(b) For each of the stages of the operating cycle identified above, explain why it may be an appropriate point to recognise revenue and, where possible, give a practical example of an industry where it occurs. (12 marks)

(c) Jenson plc has entered into the following transactions/agreements in the year to 31 March 20X1:

(i) Goods, which had cost £20,000 were sold to Wholesaler plc for £35,000 on 1 June 20X0. Jenson plc has an option to repurchase the goods from Wholesaler plc at any time within the next two years. The repurchase price will be £35,000 plus interest charged at 12% per annum from the date of sale to the date of repurchase. It is expected that Jenson plc will repurchase the goods.

(ii) Jenson plc owns the rights to a fast food franchise. On 1 April 20X0 it sold the right to open a new outlet to Mr Cody. The franchise is for five years. Jenson plc received an initial fee of £50,000 for the first year and will receive £5,000 per annum thereafter. Jenson plc has continuing service obligations on its franchise for advertising and product development that amount to approximately £8,000 per annum per franchised outlet. A reasonable profit margin on the provision of the continuing services is deemed to be 20% of revenues received.

(iii) On 1 September 20X0 Jenson plc received total subscriptions in advance of £240,000. The subscriptions are for 24 monthly publications of a magazine produced by Jenson plc. At the year end Jenson plc had produced and despatched six of the 24 publications. The total cost of producing the magazine is estimated at £192,000 with each publication costing a broadly similar amount.

Required

Describe how Jenson plc should treat each of the above examples in its financial statements in the year to 31 March 20X1. (8 marks)

15 Related party transactions 15 mins

(a) Give ten examples of related party transactions which would require disclosure in terms of FRS 8.
(b) List what has to be disclosed in the financial statements of a company in respect of related parties.

16 Segmental reporting 10 mins

Explain how SSAP 25, Segmental Reporting, helps users of financial information to make sensible decisions about the performance and position of a company.

17 Group accounts (20 marks) 36 mins

For many years, under UK law, companies with subsidiaries have been required to publish group accounts, usually in the form of consolidated accounts. You are required to state why you feel the preparation of group accounts is necessary and to outline their limitations, if any.

18 Arlene and Sandra 36 mins

Arlene plc acquired 135,000 shares in Sandra Ltd in 20X3. The reserves of Sandra Ltd at the date of acquisition comprised: revenue reserve £20,000; capital reserve £10,000. The draft balance sheets of both companies are given below as at 31 December 20X5.

	Arlene plc		Sandra Ltd	
	£	£	£	£
Fixed assets				
Tangible assets		350,000		210,000
Investments				
Shares in Sandra Ltd at cost		190,000		
		540,000		
Current assets				
Stocks	83,000		42,000	
Debtors	102,000		48,000	
Current account with Sandra Ltd	5,000			
Bank and cash	40,000		12,000	
	230,000		102,000	
Current liabilities				
Trade creditors	120,000		47,000	
Current account with Arlene Ltd	–		1,000	
	120,000		48,000	
Net current assets		110,000		54,000
Total assets less current liabilities		650,000		264,000
Share capital and reserves				
Ordinary shares of £1 each		400,000		150,000
Revenue reserve		190,000		99,000
Capital reserve		60,000		15,000
		650,000		264,000

On 29 December 20X5 Sandra Ltd sent a cheque for £4,000 to Arlene Ltd, which was not received until 3 January 20X6.

You are required to prepare the consolidated balance sheet of Arlene plc as at 31 December 20X5. (Goodwill arising on consolidation is deemed to have an indefinite useful life and is therefore to remain in the balance sheet.)

19 Plate (25 marks)   45 mins

(a)   When an acquisition takes place, the purchase consideration may be in the form of share capital. Where no suitable market price exists (for example, shares in an unquoted company) how may the fair value of the purchase consideration be estimated?   (4 marks)

(b)   On 1 May 20X7, Plate plc acquired 70% of the ordinary share capital of Spoon Ltd by issuing 500,000 ordinary £1 shares at a premium of 60p per share. The costs associated with the share issue were £50,000.

As at 30 June 20X7, the following financial statements for Plate plc and Spoon Ltd were available.

PROFIT AND LOSS ACCOUNTS
FOR THE YEAR ENDED 30 JUNE 20X7

	Plate plc	Spoon Ltd
	£'000	£'000
Turnover	3,150	1,770
Cost of sales	(1,610)	(1,065)
Gross profit	1,540	705
Distribution costs	(620)	(105)
Administrative expenses	(325)*	(210)
Operating profit	595	390
Interest payable	(70)	(30)
Dividends from Spoon plc	42	–
Profit on ordinary activities before taxation	567	360
Tax on profit	(283)	(135)
Profit after tax	284	225

*Note. The issue costs of £50,000 on the issue of ordinary share capital are included in this figure.

Dividends paid during the year were: Plate plc £38,000; Spoon Ltd £60,000.

BALANCE SHEETS AS AT 30 JUNE 20X7

	Plate plc	Spoon Ltd
	£'000	£'000
Fixed assets		
Tangible fixed assets	1,750	350
Investment in Spoon Ltd	800	–
	2,550	350
Current assets		
Stock	150	450
Debtors	238	213
Cash	187	112
	575	775
Creditors: amounts falling due within one year	(400)	(250)
Net current assets	175	525
Total assets less current liabilities	2,725	875
Creditors: amounts falling due after one year	(1,050)	(175)
	1,675	700
Capital and reserves		
Ordinary shares of £1 each	750	100
Share premium	300	150
Profit and loss account	625	450
	1,675	700

You have been asked to prepare the consolidated financial statements, taking account of the following further information.

(i) Any goodwill arising on acquisition is to be amortised over 5 years on a straight line basis, with a full year's amortisation charged in the year of acquisition. The charge is to be included in administrative expenses.

(ii) Plate plc accounts for pre-acquisition dividends by treating them as a deduction from the cost of the investment. Spoon Ltd paid an ordinary dividend of 60p per share on 1 June 20X7. No dividends were proposed as at 30 June 20X7.

(iii) The profit of Spoon Ltd may be assumed to accrue evenly over the year.

(iv) The tangible fixed assets of Spoon Ltd had a net realisable value of £400,000 at the date of acquisition. Their open market value was £500,000. It has been decided that, as Spoon Ltd was acquired so close to the year end, no depreciation adjustment will be made in the group accounts; the year end value will be taken as the carrying value of the tangible fixed assets in the accounts of Spoon Ltd. The remaining assets and liabilities of Spoon Ltd were all stated at their fair value as at 1 May 20X7.

(v)   Spoon Ltd did not issue any shares between the date of acquisition and the year end.

(vi)   There were no intercompany transactions during the year.

Required

Prepare the consolidated balance sheet and the consolidated profit and loss account of the Plate Group plc for the year ended 30 June 20X7. You should work to the nearest £'000. You do not need to prepare notes to the accounts.   (21 marks)

(25 marks)

20 Enterprise and Vulcan (20 marks)

Enterprise plc purchased 30% of Vulcan Ltd on 1 July 20X4. At all times, Enterprise participates fully in Vulcan's financial and operating policy decisions. Goodwill is to be capitalised and amortised over five years.

EXTRACT FROM VULCAN LTD'S BALANCE SHEET AT ACQUISITION

	£'000
Share capital	2,000
Revaluation reserve	200
Profit and loss reserve	900
	3,100

BALANCE SHEETS AS AT 30 JUNE 20X8

	Enterprise plc group £'000	Enterprise plc group £'000	Vulcan Ltd £'000	Vulcan Ltd £'000
Fixed assets				
Tangible fixed assets		8,000		7,000
Investment in associate		2,000		–
		10,000		7,000
Current assets				
Stock	1,340		860	
Debtors	1,000		790	
Cash	260		430	
	2,600		2,080	
Creditors (due within one year)	(1,500)		(1,140)	
		1,100		940
		11,100		7,940
		£'000		£'000
Capital and reserves				
Equity share capital		4,000		2,000
Revaluation reserve		2,000		1,000
Profit and loss reserve		5,100		4,940
		11,100		7,940

PROFIT AND LOSS ACCOUNTS FOR THE YEAR ENDING 30 JUNE 20X8

	Enterprise plc group £'000	Vulcan Ltd £'000
Turnover	10,000	6,0000
Cost of sales	(6,000)	(3,000)
Gross profit	4,000	3,000
Expenses	(1,500)	(880)
Operating profit	2,500	2,120
Interest	(100)	(20)
Profit before tax	2,400	2,100
Taxation	(800)	(700)
Profit after tax	1,600	1,400

Note: Dividends paid are: Enterprise plc £600,000; Vulcan Ltd £100,000.

Required

Prepare the consolidated balance sheet and P&L account for the year ended 30 June 20X8. Ignore any additional disclosure requirements of FRS 9.

21 Hepburn and Salter (Pilot paper – 25 marks) 45 mins

(a) On 1 October 20X0 Hepburn plc acquired 80% of the ordinary share capital of Salter Ltd by way of a share exchange. Hepburn plc issued five of its own shares for every two shares it acquired in Salter Ltd. The market value of Hepburn plc's shares on 1 October 20X0 was £3 each. The share issue has not yet been recorded in Hepburn plc's books. The summarised financial statements of both companies are:

PROFIT AND LOSS ACCOUNTS FOR THE YEAR TO 31 MARCH 20X1

	Hopburn plc £'000	Salter Ltd £'000
Turnover	1,200	1,000
Cost of sales	(650)	(660)
Gross profit	550	340
Operating expenses	(120)	(88)
Finance charge on debentures	nil	(12)
Profit before tax	430	240
Taxation	(100)	(40)
Profit after tax	330	200

Note: Hepburn paid dividends totalling £80,000 during the year. Salter has paid no dividends.

BALANCE SHEETS AS AT 31 MARCH 20X1

	Hepburn plc		Salter Ltd	
	£'000	£'000	£'000	£'000
Fixed assets		400		150
Land and Buildings		220		510
Plant and Machinery		20		10
Investments		640		670
Current Assets				
Stock	240		280	
Debtors	170		210	
Bank	20		40	
	430		530	
Creditors: amounts falling due within one year				
Trade creditors	210		155	
Taxation	50		45	
	(260)		(200)	
Net current assets		170		330
Creditors: amounts falling after more than one year				
8% Debentures		nil		(150)
Net assets		810		1,000
		810		850
Capital and reserves				
Ordinary shares of £1 each		400		150
Profit and loss account		410		700
		810		850

The following information is relevant.

(i)   The fair value of Salter Ltd's assets were equal to their book values with the exception of its land, which had fair value of £125,000 in excess of its book value at the date of acquisition.

(ii)   In the post acquisition period Hepburn plc sold goods to Salter Ltd at a price of £100,000, this was calculated to give a mark-up on cost of 25% to Hepburn plc. Salter Ltd had half of these goods in stock at the year end.

(iii)   Consolidated goodwill is to be written off as an operating expense over a five-year life. Time apportionment should be used in the year of acquisition.

(iv)   The current accounts of the two companies disagreed due to a cash remittance of £20,000 to Hepburn plc on 26 March 20X1 not being received until after the year end. Before adjusting for this, Salter Ltd's debtor balance in Hepburn plc's books was £56,000.

Required

Prepare a consolidated profit and loss account and balance sheet for Hepburn plc for the year to 31 March 20X1.   (20 marks)

(b)   At the same date as Hepburn plc made the share exchange for Salter Ltd's shares, it also acquired 6,000 'A' shares in Woodbridge Ltd for a cash payment of £20,000. The share capital of Woodbridge Ltd is made up of:

Ordinary voting A shares	10,000
Ordinary non-voting B shares	14,000

All of Woodbridge Ltd's equity shares are entitled to the same dividend rights; however during the year to 31 March 20X1 Woodbridge Ltd made substantial losses and did not pay any dividends.

Hepburn plc has treated its investment in Woodbridge Ltd as an ordinary fixed asset investment on the basis that:

PROFESSIONAL EDUCATION

(i)   It is only entitled to 25% of any dividends that Woodbridge Ltd may pay

(ii)   It does not have any directors on the Board of Woodbridge Ltd

(iii)   It does not exert any influence over the operating policies or management of Woodbridge Ltd.

Required

Comment on the accounting treatment of Woodbridge Ltd by Hepburn plc's directors and state how you believe the investment should be accounted for.   (5 marks)

Note. You are not required to amend your answer to part (a) in respect of the information in part (b).   **(25 marks)**

Approaching the answer

(a)   On 1 October Hepburn acquired 80% of the equity share capital of Salter by way of a share

exchange. Hepburn issued five of its own shares for every two shares in Salter. The market value of

Hepburn's shares on 1 October 20X0 was £3 each. The share issue has not yet been recorded in

You can work out the cost of the investment or the goodwill calculation

Hepburn's books. The summarised financial statements of both companies are:

PROFIT AND LOSS ACCOUNTS
YEAR TO 31 MARCH 20X1

		Hepburn		Salter
	£'000	£'000	£'000	£'000
Turnover		1,200		1,000
Cost of sales		(650)		(660)
Gross profit		550		340
Operating expenses		(120)		(88)
Debenture interest		Nil		(12)
Profit before tax		430		240
Taxation		(100)		(40)
Profit after tax		330		200

Note: Hepburn paid dividends totalling £80,000 during the year. Salter has paid no dividends.

BALANCE SHEETS AS AT 31 MARCH 20X1

	Hepburn plc		Salter Ltd	
	£'000	£'000	£'000	£'000
Fixed assets		400		150
Land and Buildings		220		510
Plant and Machinery		20		10
Investments		640		670
Current Assets				
Stock	240		280	
Debtors	170		210	
Bank	20		40	
	430		530	
Creditors: amounts falling due within one year				
Trade creditors	210		155	
Taxation	50		45	
	(260)		(200)	
Net current assets		170		330
Creditors: amounts falling after more than one year				
8% Debentures		nil		(150)
Net assets		810		1,000
		810		850
Capital and reserves				
Ordinary shares of £1 each		400		150
Profit and loss account		410		700
		810		850

The following information is relevant:

You will use this to calculate goodwill

(i)   The fair values of Salter's assets were equal to their book values with the exception of its

land, which had fair value of £125,000 in excess of its book value at the date of acquisition.

(ii)   In the post acquisition period Hepburn sold goods to Salter at a price of £100,000, this was

There will be an unrealised profit

calculated to give a mark-up on cost of 25% to Hepburn. Salter had half of these goods in

stock at the year end.

(iii)   Consolidated goodwill is to be written off as an operating expense over a five-year life. Time

Unusual - don't overlook

apportionment should be used in the year of acquisition.

(iv)   The current accounts of the two companies disagreed due to a cash remittance of £20,000

Agree current accounts before eliminating inter-company items

to Hepburn on 26 March 20X1 not being received until after the year end. Before adjusting

for this, Salter's debit balance in Hepburn's books was £56,000.

Required

Prepare a consolidated profit and loss and balance sheet for Hepburn for the year to 31 March
20X1.   (20 marks)

(b) At the same date as Hepburn made the share exchange for Salter's shares, it also acquired 6,000 'A' shares in Woodbridge for a cash payment of £20,000. The share capital of Woodbridge is made up of:

The % age of shares with voting rights is important

Equity voting A shares   10,000

Equity non-voting B shares   14,000

All of Woodbridge's equity shares are entitled to the same dividend rights; however during the year to 31 March 20X1. Woodbridge made substantial losses and did not pay any dividends.

Hepburn has treated its investment in Woodbridge as an ordinary long-term investment on the basis that:

(i)   It is only entitled to 25% of any dividends that Woodbridge may pay

(ii)   It does not any have directors on the board of Woodbridge

(iii) It does not exert any influence over the operating policies or management of Woodbridge

Required

This is a big hint that the treatment may be wrong

Comment on the accounting treatment of Woodbridge by Hepburn's directors and state how you believe the investment should be accounted for.   (5 marks)

Note. You are not required to amend your answer to part (a) in respect of the information in part (b).   (25 marks)

22 CPP and CCA (25 marks)   45 mins

(a)   'It is important that managements and other users of financial accounts should be in a position to appreciate the effects of inflation on the business with which they are concerned.'   (PSSAP 7)

Required

Explain how inflation obscures the meaning of accounts prepared by the traditional historical cost convention, and discuss the contribution which CPP accounting could make to providing a more satisfactory system of accounting for inflation.

(b)   Compare the general principles underlying CPP and CCA accounting.

(c)   Define the term 'realised holding gain'.

(d)   Explain briefly the use in CCA accounting of:

(i)   The cost of sales adjustment
(ii)   The monetary working capital adjustment
(iii)   The depreciation adjustment
(iv)   The gearing adjustment

23 Statement of Principles (20 marks)

36 mins

'A major achievement of the ASB was the development of its Statement of Principles. However, it is too theoretical to be applied to accounting standards.'

What are the merits of the Statement of Principles and do you agree with the criticism that it is too theoretical?

24 XYZ Group (25 marks)

45 mins

A new managing director will soon be taking over the management of the XYZ Group which consists of three companies carrying on similar businesses in the same trade. The group accountant has produced a summary and comparison of the balance sheets, sales and profits for the most recent years to help the new managing director to familiarise himself with the main figures. These are reproduced below.

As the new managing director is essentially a production and marketing expert rather than being from a financial background, he has not had too much experience in reading accounting and financial statements for a group of companies and would find some additional information helpful for use in preliminary discussion with the managers of each of the group companies. However, he has specifically asked that the extra information should not be another extensive statement showing long lists of ratios and percentages which would need yet another statement to interpret the figures. Further, he has managed to obtain a checklist which suggests some 'Criteria for a healthy company' against which the group companies could be compared.

He thinks this checklist could be helpful to the person preparing the report giving the extra information. It suggest the following criteria.

(a)   There should be a strong asset base.

(b)   There should be adequate control of working capital such as stocks and debtors.

(c)   There should be adequate liquidity to ensure that debts can be paid as they arise.

(d)   If new funds are likely to be required for any reasons, there should be sufficient borrowing capacity available, or a potential shareholder should be able to invest with confidence.

(e)   The operating performance of any individual group company should generally be as good as any other group company, unless there are special reasons otherwise.

(f)   A fair commercial return should be earned for the shareholders which covers the risk taken in running the business.

(g)   The figures in the accounts should represent accurate valuations of assets and liabilities. Any item of concern should be the subject of further investigations in the context of good account practices.

One immediate problem that the new managing director has to face, when he visits company Y for the first time, is to advise the directors about this year's ordinary dividend. The directors are anxious to keep up good relations with one of the minority shareholders who happens to be a director of their main materials supplier. They therefore wish to pay a dividend of £60,000 as usual, even though a loss was made this particular year. They wish to use the capital redemption reserve to make up any balance not available in general reserve.

BPP
PROFESSIONAL EDUCATION

SUMMARY AND COMPARISON OF THE BALANCE SHEETS, SALES AND PROFIT OF THE XYZ GROUP FOR THE YEAR 20X5/X6

	Company X		Company Y		Company Z		Group	
	£'000	£'000	£'000	£'000	£'000	£'000	£'000	£'000
Fixed assets								
Intangible assets								
Goodwill					200			866
Research/development		180						180
Licences/trade marks		140	–		–			140
		320				200		1,186
Tangible assets								
Freehold at cost or revaluation		300				800		1,100
Leasehold at cost					600		600	
Less amortisation	–		–		580		580	
						20		20
Plant at cost	1,200		900		1,000		3,100	
Less depreciation	600		400		200		1,200	
		600		500		800		1,900
		1,220		500		1,820		4,206
Investments								
in group companies		2,000						
Current assets								
Stock and work in progress	516		250		198		964	
Debtors	468		418		312		1,198	
Bank	100		–		36		136	
	1,084		668		546		2,298	
Liabilities due within one year								
Bank overdraft			172				172	
Trade creditors	442		330		86		858	
Customers prepayments	–		106		–		106	
		642		60		460		1,162
		3,862		560		2,280		5,368
Liabilities due after one year								
Debentures (19Y7)		1,000						1,000
Loan capital		724						724
Minority interest		–		–		–		620
		2,138		560		2,280		3,024

	Company X		Company Y		Company Z		Group	
	£'000	£'000	£'000	£'000	£'000	£'000	£'000	£'000
Capital and reserves								
Share capital		1,300		340		1,500		1,300
Reserves								
Revaluation					300		300	
Capital redemption			200				200	
General	838		20		480		1,224	
		838		220		780		1,724
		2,138		560		2,280		3,024
Sales		1,752		1,136		2,316		5,204
Cost of sales		1,488		1,182		1,890		4,560
Net profit (before interest)		264		(46)		426		644
Finance charges on loans								
and debentures	108						108	
Taxation	50		–		98		148	
		158		–		98		256
		106		(46)		328		388
Less minority interest		–		–		–		45
Earnings (loss) after tax		106		(46)		328		343
Extraordinary item		–		–		73		73
Net earnings (loss)								
available for shareholders		106		(46)		255		270

Required

(a)   Prepare a report for the use of the new managing director which highlights any major weaknesses, or other special features, of each of the group companies in the light of the suggested criteria for a healthy company as mentioned above. Use may be made of any appropriate accounting ratios to illustrate specific points.

(b)   Identify any items in the summary which you think may require some 'further investigation in the context of good accounting practices' giving reasons for specifying each of these items for special examination and quoting the particular accounting assumption, precept, rule or standard under which it should be examined.

(c)   Advise the new managing director as to whether any dividend can be paid by Company Y this year.

BPP
PROFESSIONAL EDUCATION

25 Webster (Pilot paper – 25 marks)   45 mins

Webster plc is a diversified holding company that is looking to acquire a suitable engineering company. Two private limited engineering companies, Cole Ltd and Darwin Ltd, are available for sale. The summarised financial statements for the year to 31 March 20X1 of both companies are as follows:

PROFIT AND LOSS ACCOUNTS

	Cole Limited		Darwin Limited	
	£'000	£'000	£'000	£'000
Sales (note (i))		3,000		4,400
Opening stock	450		720	
Purchases (note (ii))	2,030		3,080	
	2,480		3,800	
Closing stock	(540)		(850)	
		(1,940)		(2,950)
Gross profit		1,060		1,450
Operating expenses	480		964	
Debenture interest	80		nil	
Overdraft interest (note (v))	nil		10	
		(560)		(974)
Net profit		500		476

BALANCE SHEETS

	Cole Limited		Darwin Limited	
	£'000	£'000	£'000	£'000
Fixed assets				
Premises (note iii)		1,140		1,900
Plant (note iv)		1,200		1,200
		2,340		3,100
Current assets				
Stock	540		850	
Debtors	522		750	
Bank	20		nil	
	1,082		1,600	
Current liabilities				
Creditors	438		562	
Overdraft	nil		550	
	(438)		(1,112)	
		644		488
Net current assets		2,984		3,588
10% Debenture		(800)		nil
Net assets		2,184		3,588
Share capital and reserves				
Ordinary shares of £1 each		1,000		500
Reserves				
Revaluation reserve		nil		700
Profit and loss – 1 April 20X0	684		1,912	
Profit for year to 31 March 20X1	500		476	
		1,184		2,388
		2,184		3,588

Webster plc bases its preliminary assessment of target companies on certain key ratios. These are listed below together with the relevant figures for Cole Ltd and Darwin Ltd calculated from the above financial statements:

	Cole Limited		Darwin Limited
Return on capital employed (500 + 80)/(2,184 + 800) × 100	19.4%	(476/3,588) × 100	13.3%
Asset turnover (3,000/2,984)	1.01 times	(4,400/3,588)	1.23 times
Gross profit margin	35.3%		33.0%
Net profit margin	16.7%		10.8%
Debtors collection period	64 days		62 days
Creditors payment period	79 days		67 days

Note. Capital employed is defined as shareholders' funds plus long-term, debt at the year end; asset turnover is sales revenues divided by gross assets less current liabilities.

The following additional information has been obtained.

(i)   Cole Ltd is part of the Velox Group. On 1 March 20X1 it was permitted by its holding company to sell goods at a price of £500,000 to Brander Ltd, a fellow subsidiary. Cole Ltd's normal selling price for these goods would have been £375,000. In addition Brander Ltd was instructed to pay for the goods immediately. Cole Ltd normally allows three months credit.

(ii)   On 1 January 20X1 Cole Ltd purchased £275,000 (cost price to Cole Ltd) of its materials from Advent Ltd, another member of the Velox Group. Advent Ltd was also instructed to depart from its normal trading terms that would have resulted in a charge of £300,000 to Cole Ltd for these goods. The Group's finance director also authorised a four-month credit period on this sale. Normal credit terms for this industry are two months credit from suppliers. Cole Ltd had sold all of these goods at the year-end.

(iii)   Fixed assets:

Details relating to the two companies' fixed assets at 31 March 20X1 are:

	Cost/revaluation £'000	Depreciation £'000	Book value £'000
Cole Ltd – property	3,000	1,860	1,140
– plant	6,000	4,800	1,200
			2,340
Darwin Ltd – property	2,000	100	1,900
– plant	3,000	1,800	1,200
			3,100

Both companies own very similar properties. Darwin Ltd's property was revalued to £2,000,000 at the beginning of the current year (ie. 1 April 20X0). On this date Cole Ltd's property, which is carried at cost less depreciation, had a book value of £1,200,000. Its current value (on the same basis as Darwin Ltd's property) was also £2,000,000. On this date (1 April 20X0) both properties had the same remaining life of 20 years.

(iv)   Darwin Ltd purchased new plant costing £600,000 in February 20X1. In line with company policy a full year's depreciation at 20% per annum has been charged on all plant owned at the year-end. The plant is still being tested and will not come on-stream until next year. The purchase of the plant was largely financed by an overdraft facility that resulted in the interest cost shown in the profit and loss account. Both companies depreciate plant over a five-year life.

(v)   The bank overdraft that would have been required but for the favourable treatment towards Cole Ltd in respect of the items in (i) and (ii) above, would have attracted interest of £15,000 in the year to 31 March 20X1.

Required

(a)   Restate the financial statements of Cole Ltd and Darwin Ltd for the year to 31 March 20X1 in order that they may be considered comparable for decision making purposes. State any assumptions you make.   (10 marks)

(b)   Recalculate the key ratios used by Webster plc and, together with any other relevant points, comment on how the revised ratios may affect the relative assessment of the two companies.
                                                                                                                          (10 marks)

(c)   Discuss whether the information in notes (i) to (v) above would be publicly available, and if so, describe its source(s).   (5 marks)

Exam answer bank

BPP
PROFESSIONAL EDUCATION

1 Conceptual framework

(a) **Benefits of a conceptual framework**

A conceptual framework to underpin the development of financial reporting standards affords several benefits.

(i) It enables standards to be developed on a **consistent basis** from standard to standard

(ii) General **principles** are **clearly laid out** so that an *ad hoc* or piecemeal basis that responds to issues as they arise is avoided

(iii) Standards are likely to be **up-to-date** with **modern developments** and business practices

(iv) There is a **reduction** in the **need to debate fundamental issues** each time a standard is addressed

(v) It **assists auditors** in **arriving at their opinion** on whether a set of financial statements conforms with accounting standards

(vi) **Users** of financial statements can **better understand** the **information contained** therein

(vii) It provides a **framework** for the **future development of financial reporting standards**

(b) **Objectives of financial statements**

(i) The objective of financial statements is to provide information about the reporting entity's financial performance and financial position that is useful to a wide range of users for **assessing the stewardship** of the entity's management and for making **economic decisions**

(ii) That objective can usually be met by **focusing exclusively** on the information needs of **present and potential investors**, the defining class of user

(iii) Present and potential investors need information about the reporting entity's **financial performance** and **financial position** that is useful to them in evaluating the entity's **ability to generate cash** (including the timing and certainty of its generation) and in **assessing the entity's financial adaptability**

(c) **Relevance and reliability**

Relevance

(i) Information is **relevant** if it possess **certain qualities**

- Ability to influence economic decisions of users
- Is sufficiently timely to influence the decision
- Has predictive or confirmatory value, or both

Eg the FRS 3 requirement for separate analyses of the results of discontinued operations can be said to improve the predictive value of a set of financial statements

Reliability

(ii) Financial information is reliable if:

- It can be depended upon by users to **represent faithfully** what it either purports to represent or could reasonably be expected to represent, and therefore reflects the **substance of the transactions** and other events that have taken place
- It is **free** from deliberate or systematic **bias** (ie it is **neutral**)
- It is **free** from **material error**
- It is **complete** within the bounds of **materiality**
- Under conditions of **uncertainty**, it has been **prudently prepared**

(d) **Materiality**

   (i)   Materiality exerts a **quality threshold** on financial statements. It provides a basis for deciding whether the views of a user of the financial statements might be adversely influenced when making **economic decisions** or trying to assess the **stewardship of management**

   (ii)   It also ensures that **trivial information** does **not clutter** the financial statements and thereby **cloud** the **true and fair view** that should be shown. However, care must be taken to ensure that several items that are individually immaterial do not, when taken together, exert a material effect on the view shown by the financial statements

   (iii)   We are concerned not only about the accuracy of the numbers included, but also the **manner in which the information** is **presented** and how wording is used

(e) **Definitions**

   (i)   **Assets** are **rights** or other access to **future economic benefits** controlled by an entity as a result of **past transactions** or **events**

   (ii)   **Liabilities** are **obligations** of an entity to **transfer economic benefits** as a result of **past transactions** or **events**

(f) **Prudence and neutrality**

   (i)   **Prudence** relates to the **uncertainty** that may be associated with the **recognition** and **measurement** of **assets** and **liabilities**

   (ii)   Different levels of confirmatory evidence may be required regarding the recognition of assets and liabilities, where uncertainty exists. In such circumstances, the existence of an **asset or gain** requires **stronger confirmatory evidence** than that required to acknowledge the existence of a liability or loss

   (iii)   Prudence may only be called upon to justify setting up a provision if uncertainty exists. **Prudence** should **not** be **invoked** to **justify setting up hidden reserves, excessive provisions** or **understating assets**. Prudence should not be seen as a tool for smoothing profits in financial statements.

   (iv)   However, where there is **uncertainty** either about the **existence** of a **liability** or about the **amount** at which it should be **measured**, prudence requires that the accounting treatment used takes into consideration such uncertainty

   (v)   Financial statements should be **free from deliberate or systematic bias**

   (vi)   **If financial statements are not neutral they cannot be reliable**. Tension often exists between neutrality and prudence. This should be reconciled by finding a balance that ensures that the deliberate and systematic understatement of assets and gains, and overstatement of liabilities and losses, does not occur.

Note. This is a fairly full response, provided for overall learning purposes.

2   Setting and regulating standards

(a) **ASB standards setting process**

The following is a summary drawn from the ASB website.

   (i)   **Identify topic** based on ASB research or input from outside.

   (ii)   Set up **project management structure** and identify project resources and expertise.

(iii)   Publish a *Discussion Paper.* The objective here is to canvass the **views** of the **interested public** on possible approaches.

(iv)   Analyse and publish **feedback** received.

(v)   Publish **Financial reporting exposure draft** (FRED); sometimes comments on alternative approaches might be invited.

(vi)   Analyse and consider **further feedback** received from interested parties.

(vii)   Issue **final pronouncement** in the form of a *Financial Reporting Standard* (FRS) or other publication, which specifies the date on which it becomes effective.

(b)   **ASB convergence approach**

(i)   The ASB liases with the IASB to secure convergence between UK and international financial reporting standards

(ii)   The ASB is implementing a phased replacement of existing UK standards with new UK standards that have been aligned with the international version

(c)   **Financial Reporting Review Panel**

(i)   The role of the Review panel is to examine departures from the accounting requirements of the Companies Act 1985, including applicable accounting standards, and if necessary to seek an order from the court to remedy them

(ii)   By agreement with the Department of Trade and Industry the normal ambit of the Panel is public and large private companies, the Department dealing with all other cases.

(iii)   The Panel is concerned with an examination of **material departures** from accounting standards with a view to considering whether the accounts in question nevertheless meet the statutory requirement to give a **true and fair view**. While such a departure does not necessarily mean that a company's accounts fail the true and fair test it will raise that question. Remember that the Companies Act 1985 requires large companies to disclose in their accounts any such departures together with the reasons for them, thus enabling them to be readily identified and considered.

(iv)   The Panel does not scrutinise on a routine basis all companies accounts falling within its ambit. Instead it acts on matters drawn to its attention, either directly or indirectly.

(v)   The Panel normally aims to discharge its tasks by **seeking voluntary agreement** with the directors of a company on any **necessary revisions** to the accounts in question. But if that **approach fails** and the Panel believes that revisions to the accounts are necessary, it will seek a **declaration from the court** that the annual accounts of the company concerned do not comply with the requirements of the Companies Act 1985, **and** for **an order** requiring the directors of the company to **prepare revised accounts**.

(vi)   Where accounts are revised at the instance of the Panel, either voluntarily or by order of the court, but the company's **auditor** had **not qualified his audit report** on the **defective accounts** the Panel will draw this fact to the **attention** of the **auditor's professional body**.

(d)   **Role of UITF**

(i)   The main role of the UITF is to **assist the ASB** in areas where an accounting standard or Companies Act provision exists, but where **unsatisfactory** or **conflicting interpretations** have developed or seem likely to develop.

(ii)   Its **consensus pronouncements** are issued as UITF Abstracts, which the ASB expects to be regarded as **accepted practice** in the area in question, and part of the body of practices forming the basis for what determines a true and fair view.

(iii)   A UITF Abstract may be taken into **consideration** by the **FRRP** in deciding whether a company's financial statements **call for review**.

3   Published accounts

(a)   Before the development of accounting standards it was argued that a 'credibility gap' had developed in financial reporting. Some companies were producing accounts based on the principle of prudence; others were selecting from the range of accounting bases available to achieve the most favourable profit figure. Users of accounts could not tell which were which.

The range of profit figures which a single enterprise can present by choosing different accounting policies in respect of, say, depreciation, research and development expenditure and deferred taxation is very wide. Investors are unable to take rational decisions if the information presented to them may be interpreted with such latitude. Loan creditors and potential loan creditors cannot decide on the security of their investment unless they are aware of the basis adopted in valuing the assets of the enterprise.

These problems are more serious in the case of quoted companies because of the far greater number of people who have an interest in the activities of such companies. People who may in some degree rely on the accounts of quoted companies, apart from investors and loan creditors, include the companies' employees and business contacts, all kinds of investment analysts and advisers, and the government. Many (particularly investors and employees) will be interested primarily in the future prospects of the company, but others (particularly loan creditors and the government) will be more concerned about the degree of reliance they can place on reported figures.

There are several ways in which disclosure of accounting policies can help to achieve these aims.

(i)   It enables a comparison to be made between companies with different policies. This is useful not only for investment and lending decisions, but also for the purpose of collecting statistics, for example, by government agencies.

(ii)   It prevents possible abuse of the range of accounting bases available so as to distort a company's results and financial position.

(iii)   It enables a proper computation to be made of certain figures important for legal reasons (for example, the amount of corporation tax due; the amount which may be distributed by way of dividend).

(b)   (i)   A company which qualifies to be treated as a *small or medium-sized company* is exempted from delivering its full accounts to the registrar of companies. Full accounts must still be presented to and approved by the members of the company, but the exemptions allow for a reduction in the information which must be published and available (through the registrar) to the general public.

A company cannot benefit from the relevant exemptions for individual accounts in respect of any accounting reference period if it is (or was at any time within the financial year to which the accounts relate):

(1)   A public company.

(2)   A banking company or insurance company.

(3)   An authorised person under the Financial Services Act 1986.

(4)   A member of an ineligible group (which is one in which any of its members is a public company, banking company, insurance company or authorised under the Financial Services Act 1986).

An eligible company or group will qualify for treatment as a small or medium sized company (or group) if it satisfies any two or more of the qualifying conditions for both the current and the previous year. (*Note*. Once qualified, a company will not cease to be so, unless the conditions are not satisfied for two successive years.)

The conditions (which relate to company size) in respect of each company category may be summarised in tabular form.

Category	*Turnover*	*Gross assets*	*Average employees per week*
Small company	Up to £5.6m	Up to £2.8m	Up to 50
Medium company	Up to £22.8m	Up to £11.4m	Up to 250

(ii)   The directors of a company which is entitled to the benefit of a small company exemption (for individual accounts in respect of any accounting reference period) may file, with the registrar of companies, 'abbreviated accounts' (formerly 'modified accounts') as follows:

(1)   A summarised balance sheet.

(2)   Notes only on accounting policies, fixed assets (aggregate movements for tangible and intangible fixed assets and fixed asset investments), share capital, allotments, debts, foreign currency translation and corresponding amounts.

(3)   No profit and loss account.

(4)   No information on directors' emoluments or auditors' remuneration.

(5)   No directors' report.

(c)   The directors' report is expected to contain the following information.

(i)   A fair review of the development of the business of the company and its subsidiary undertakings during that year and of their position at the end of it. No guidance is given on the form of the review, nor the amount of detail it should go into.

(ii)   The amount, if any, recommended for dividend.

(iii)   The principal activities of the company and its subsidiaries in the course of the financial year, and any significant changes in those activities during the year.

(iv)   Where significant, an estimate should be provided of the difference between the book value of land held as fixed assets and its realistic market value.

(v)   Information about the company's policy for the employment for disabled persons.

(vi)   The names of persons who were directors at any time during the financial year.

(vii)   For those persons who were directors at the year end, the interests of each (or of their spouse or infant children) in shares or debentures of the company or subsidiaries:

(1)   At the beginning of the year, or at the date of appointment as director, if this occurred during the year.

(2)   At the end of the year.

If a director has no such interests at either date, this fact must be disclosed. (The information in (e) may be shown as a note to the accounts instead of in the directors' report.)

(viii)   Political and charitable contributions made, if these together exceeded more than £200 in the year, giving:

(1)   Separate totals for political contributions and charitable contributions.

(2)   The amount of each separate political contribution exceeding £200, and the name of the recipient.

Wholly owned British subsidiaries are exempt from requirement (g) because the information will be disclosed in the directors' report of the holding company.

(ix)   Particulars of any important events affecting the company or any of its subsidiaries which have occurred since the end of the financial year (significant 'post-balance sheet events').

(x)   An indication of likely future developments in the business of the company and of its subsidiaries.

(xi)   An indication of the activities (if any) of the company and its subsidiaries in the field of research and development.

(xii)   Particulars of purchases (if any) of its own shares by the company during the year, including reasons for the purchase.

(xiii)   Particulars of other acquisitions of its own shares during the year (perhaps because shares were forfeited or surrendered, or because its shares were acquired by the company's nominee or with its financial assistance).

(xiv)   Details of any measures taken by the company directed at increasing employee participation and information.

(xv)   Details of the company's creditor payment policy.

4   Azrina

SCHEDULE OF MOTOR VEHICLES
FOR THE YEARS ENDED 31 DECEMBER 20X5, 20X6, 20X7

	£'000
20X5	
Cost: At 1 January 20X5	540
Additions	147
Disposals	70
At 31 December 20X5	617
Accumulated depreciation: At 1 January 20X5	130
Disposals (W1)	50
Charge for year $25\% \times (617 - (130 - 50))$	134
At 31 December 20X5	214
Net book value at 31 December 20X5	403
20X6	
Cost: At 1 January 20X6	617
Additions*	252
Disposals	110
At 31 December 20X6	759
Accumulated depreciation: At 1 January 20X6	214
Disposals (W2)	68
Charge for year $25\% \, (759 - (214 - 68))$	153
At 31 December 20X6	299
Net book value at 31 December 20X6	460

* *Note*. The acquisitions in 20X6 are capitalised at cash price less trade discount (for cash purchases), plus delivery costs £(300 − 60 + 12) = £252,000.

20X7	£'000
Cost: At 1 January 20X7	759
Additions**	375
Disposals	75
At 31 December 20X7	1,059

20X7		£'000
Accumulated depreciation:	At 1 January 20X7	299
	Disposals (W3) (1,059 − (299 − 43)) × 25%	43
	Charge for year 25%	201
	At 31 December 20X7	457
Net book value at 31 December 20X5		602

** *Note.* The acquisitions in 20X7 are capitalised at cash price less trade discount (for cash purchase) plus delivery cost: £(450 − 90 + 15) = £375.

Workings

1 Accumulated depreciation on 20X5 disposals

Vehicles acquired in 20X0:

		£
20X0	25% × £30,000	7,500
20X1	25% × £(30,000 − 7,500)	5,625
20X2	25% × £(30,000 − (7,500 + 5,625))	4,219
20X3	25% × £(30,000 − (7,500 + 5,625 + 4,219))	3,164
20X4	25% × £(30,000 − (7,500 + 5,625 + 4,219 + 3,164))	2,373
Total		22,881

Vehicles acquired in 20X1:

		£
20X1	25% × £40,000	10,000
20X2	25% × £(40,000 − 10,000)	7,500
20X3	25% × £(40,000 − (10,000 + 7,500))	5,625
20X4	25% × £(40,000 − (10,000 + 8,500 + 5,625))	4,219
Total		27,344

Total accumulated depreciation on disposals: £(22,881 + 27,344) = £50,225.

2 *Accumulated depreciation on 20X6 disposals*

Vehicles acquired in 20X2:

		£
20X2	25% × £45,000	11,250
20X3	25% × £(45,000 − 11,250)	8,438
20X4	25% × £(45,000 − (11,250 + 8,438))	6,328
20X5	25% × £(45,000 − (11,250 + 8,438 + 6,328))	4,746
Total		30,762

Vehicles acquired in 20X3:

		£
20X3	25% × £65,000	16,250
20X4	25% × £(65,000 − 16,250)	12,188
20X5	25% × £(65,000 − (16,250 + 12,188))	9,141
Total		37,579

Total accumulated depreciation on 20X6 disposals £(30,762 + 37,579) = £68,341

3 *Accumulated depreciation on 20X7 disposals*

Vehicles acquired in 20X2:

		£
20X4	25% × £75,000	18,750
20X5	25% × £(75,000 − 18,750)	14,063
20X6	25% × £(75,000 − (18,750 + 14,063))	10,547
Total		43,360

Note. The hire purchase was treated as though it was an operating lease as the finance leases were already separately identified in the question. If in doubt, always explain your assumptions in your answer.

5   Bleco

Notes

(a) Under the original SSAP 13, development expenditure written off could not be reinstated if it subsequently met the SSAP's criteria for capitalisation. The revised SSAP permits such expenditure to be reinstated.

(b) Project D371 is contract WIP, not a development project, because costs are being reimbursed in full and so Bleco is taking no risk itself.

(c) SSAP 13 requires that depreciation on assets used in R & D should be included in the expenditure on R & D to be disclosed and it should also be disclosed separately in accordance with FRS 15.

(d) It is possible (but not obligatory) to capitalise depreciation, just like the other expenses deferred.

(e) Common errors in this question include capitalisation of pure and applied research projects, omission of opening balances, treating the contract WIP as an intangible asset and taking individual expenses to P & L rather than a global figure for R & D written off.

BLECO PLC
PROFIT AND LOSS ACCOUNT
FOR THE YEAR ENDED 31 AUGUST 20X1 (EXTRACT)

	£
Included in cost of sales (or other appropriate category):	
Research and development costs written off (W2)	329,340
Amortisation of development costs (W1)	33,050
	362,390

BLECO PLC
BALANCE SHEET AS AT 31 AUGUST 20X1 (EXTRACTS)

	£
Fixed assets	
Intangible assets	
Deferred development expenditure	652,340
Current assets	
Stocks	
Contract work in progress	14,030
Profit and loss account	
At 1 September 20X0:	
As previously reported	X
Development expenditure previously written off,	
now reinstated	47,830
As restated	X + 47,830

Workings

1   *Deferred development expenditure/long-term contract*

	D369 £	D368 £	D363 £	D367 £	Total £	D371 £
Brought forward	–		198,300	242,700	488,830	–
Reinstated		47,830				
Current year expenditure						
Staff costs	34,070	16,480	–	2,090	52,640	27,500
Materials	1,560	410	–	340	2,310	3,400
Other direct expenses	640	230	–	170	1,040	710
Production overheads	6,980	4,650	–	3,540	15,170	6,420
Depreciation (W3):						
buildings	31,000	–	–	–	31,000	
equipment	94,400	–	–	–	94,400	–
	168,650	21,770	–	6,140	196,560	
Reimbursed						(24,000)
Contract WIP						14,030
Amortisation ($1/6$)		–	33,050	–	33,050	
Carried forward	168,650	69,600	165,250	248,840	652,340	

2   *Expenditure to be written off*

	Total £	PR119 £	AR187 £	AR204 £	D370 £	Unallocated £
Staff costs	110,760	35,100	27,300	15,260	29,800	3,300
Materials	8,340	810	520	290	2,650	4,070
Direct expenses	3,570	250	210	180	690	2,240
Production overheads	20,870	1,240	3,600	2,950	6,010	7,070
	143,540	37,400	31,630	18,680	39,150	16,680
Sales/admin o'hds	76,200					76,200
Market research	55,600					55,600
Depreciation:						
buildings (W3)	20,000		20,000		–	
equipment (W3)	34,000		34,000		–	
	329,340	37,400	85,630	18,680	39,150	148,480

3   *Depreciation*

	AR187 £	D369 £
Buildings		
£200,000 × 10%	20,000	
£310,000 × 10%		31,000
Equipment		
£170,000 × 20%	34,000	
£472,000 × 20%		94,400

6 Winger

(a) WINGER PLC
PROFIT AND LOSS ACCOUNT FOR THE
YEAR ENDED 31 MARCH 20X1

	£'000	£'000
Turnover (358,450 – 27,000)		331,450
Cost of sales (W1)		(208,550)
Gross profit		122,900
Distribution expenses		(28,700)
Administration expenses		(15,000)
Operating profit		79,200
Exceptional items		
Profit on disposal of land and buildings		
(95,000 - 80,000)		15,000
Loss on abandonment of research project		(30,000)
Profit on ordinary activities before interest		64,200
Interest expense (W3)		(11,200)
Profit before tax		53,000
Taxation (15,000 - 2,200)		(12,800)
Profit after tax		40,200

(b) BALANCE SHEET AS AT 31 MARCH 20X1

	£'000	£'000
Fixed assets: tangible		
Land and buildings (200,000 - 6,000 (W2))		194,000
Plant and machinery (W5)		160,000
		354,000
Current assets		
Stock (28,240 + 22,500 (W1))	50,740	
Debtors (55,000 – 27,000 (W1))	28,000	
Cash	10,660	
	89,400	
Creditors due within one year		
Trade and other creditors (W6)	51,400	
Taxation	15,000	
	66,400	
Net current assets		23,000
Total assets less current liabilities		377,000
Creditors due after one year		
Lease creditor (W7)		(47,200)
8% debentures		(50,000)
Net assets		279,800
Capital and reserves		
Ordinary shares 25p each		150,000
Profit and loss account (W4)		129,800
Shareholders' funds		279,800

Workings

1	*Cost of sales*	£'000
	Per question	185,050
	Less sale/return goods (27,000 × 100/120)	(22,500)
	Add depreciation (W2)	46,000
		208,550

2	*Depreciation*	£'000
	Building (100,000 ÷ 50)	2,000
	Heating system (20,000 ÷ 10)	2,000
	Lifts (30,000 ÷ 15)	2,000
		6,000
	Leased plant (80,000 × 20%)	16,000
	Owned plant (154,800 - 34,800) × 20%	24,000
		46,000

3	*Interest expense*	£'000
	Debenture interest (50,000 × 8%)	4,000
	Finance lease (80,000 - 20,000) × 12%	7,200
		11,200

4	*Profit and loss reserve*	£'000
	B/f 1 April 20X0	71,600
	Transfer to profit and loss on revaluation surplus on building sold 1 April 20X0	30,000
	Profit for the year	40,200
	Dividend paid	(12,000)
		129,800

5	*Plant and machinery*	£'000
	Cost: owned plant	154,800
	leased plant	80,000
		234,800
	Depreciation: owned plant (34,800 + 24,000 (W2))	(58,800)
	leased plant (80,000 × 20%)	(16,000)
		160,000

6	*Trade and other creditors*	£'000
	Trial balance	29,400
	Lease creditor (W7)	20,000
	Accrued debenture interest	2,000
		51,400

7	*Lease creditor*	£'000
	Total payments due	80,000
	Less amount paid	(20,000)
		60,000
	Add accrued interest (60,000 × 12%)	7,200
	Total creditor	67,200
	Due within one year	20,000
	Due after one year	47,200

(c) Prior to the issue of FRS 15 *Tangible fixed assets*, companies often used to justify the non-depreciation of buildings on several grounds, including:

(i) That the current value of the buildings was **higher than cost**.

(ii) That the level of **maintenance** meant that no deterioration or consumption had taken place.

(iii) That the depreciation charge would **not be material**.

FRS 15 dismisses the first two of them as being **insufficient grounds** for a policy of non-depreciation. Depreciation is **not** a valuation model; rather it is a means of **allocating the depreciable amount** of the asset to accounting periods.

However, it is still permissible not to charge depreciation on the grounds of non-materiality, but only when **both** the depreciation charge for the period **and** the accumulated depreciation that would have been charged against the value of the asset at that point in time, are immaterial. Thus assets with very long lives and/or high residual values may fall not to be depreciated. FRS 15 also requires that, for depreciation to be classed as immaterial:

(i)   There must be a policy of **regular maintenance**.

(ii)   The asset is unlikely to **suffer obsolescence**.

(iii) There is a policy **and** practice of disposing of similar assets long **before** the **end of their useful lives** at proceeds not materially less than their carrying amounts.

An annual **test for impairment** is also required (except for land).

On the facts given, Winger's policy may have complied with FRS 15.

7 Bulwell

(a)   BOOKS OF BULWELL AGGREGATES LIMITED

LORRIES ACCOUNT

20X1		£			£
1 Jan	Granby Garages	54,000			

PROVISION FOR DEPRECIATION ON LORRIES

20X1		£	20X1		£
			31 Dec	P & L account: ¼ ×	
31 Dec	Balance c/d	12,500		£(54,000 − (3 × 1,333))	12,500
20X2			20X2		
31 Dec	Balance c/d	25,000	1 Jan	Balance b/d	12,500
			31 Dec	P & L account	12,500
		25,000			25,000
20X3			20X3		
31 Dec	Balance c/d	37,500	1 Jan	Balance b/d	25,000
			31 Dec	P & L account	12,500
		37,500			37,500
20X4			20X4		
31 Dec	Balance c/d	50,000	1 Jan	Balance b/d	37,500
			31 Dec	P & L account	12,500
		50,000			50,000
			20X5		
			1 Jan	Balance b/d	50,000

HP INTEREST PAYABLE

20X1		£	20X1		£
31 Dec	Bank (W)	11,250	31 Dec	P & L account	11,250
20X2			20X2		
31 Dec	Bank (W)	8,063	31 Dec	P & L account	8,063
20X3			20X3		
31 Dec	Bank (W)	4,078	31 Dec	P & L account	4,078

GRANBY GARAGES PLC

20X1		£	20X1			£
1 Jan	Bank – deposit	9,000	1 Jan	Lorries a/c		54,000
31 Dec	Bank (W)	12,750				
	Balance c/d	32,250				
		54,000				54,000
20X2			20X2			
31 Dec	Bank (W)	15,937	1 Jan	Balance b/d		32,250
	Balance c/d	16,313				
		32,250				32,250
20X3			20X3			
31 Dec	Bank (W)	16,313	1 Jan	Balance b/d		16,313

PROFIT AND LOSS ACCOUNTS (EXTRACTS)

	20X1 £	20X2 £	20X3 £	20X4 £
HP interest	11,250	8,063	4,078	
Depreciation on lorries	12,500	12,500	12,500	12,500

BALANCE SHEETS AT 31 DECEMBER (EXTRACTS)

		20X1 £	20X2 £	20X3 £	20X4 £
Fixed assets					
Lorries:	at cost	54,000	54,000	54,000	54,000
	depreciation	12,500	25,000	37,500	50,000
		41,500	29,000	16,500	4,000
Current liabilities					
HP obligations		15,937	16,313	–	–
Long-term liabilities					
HP obligations		16,313	–	–	–

(b)   BOOKS OF GRANBY GARAGES PLC

BULWELL AGGREGATES LIMITED

20X1		£	20X1		£
1 Jan	Sales	54,000	1 Jan	Bank	9,000
			31 Dec	Bank	12,750
				Balance c/d	32,250
		54,000			54,000
20X2			20X2		
1 Jan	Balance b/d	32,250	31 Dec	Bank	15,937
				Balance c/d	16,313
		32,250			32,250
20X3			20X3		
1 Jan	Balance b/d	16,313	31 Dec	Bank	16,313

HP INTEREST RECEIVABLE

20X1		£	20X1		£
31 Dec	P & L account	11,250	31 Dec	Bank	11,250
20X2			20X2		
31 Dec	P & L account	8,063	31 Dec	Bank	8,063
20X3			20X3		
31 Dec	P & L account	4,078	31 Dec	Bank	4,078

TRADING AND PROFIT AND LOSS ACCOUNTS (EXTRACTS)

	£	20X1 £	20X2 £	20X3 £
Sales	54,000		–	–
Cost of sales on HP	43,200		–	–
Gross profit on HP sales		10,800	–	–
HP interest receivable		11,250	8,063	4,078

Working

Apportionment of HP instalments between interest and capital repayment.

	20X1 £	20X2 £	20X3 £
Opening liability (after deposit)	45,000	32,250	16,313
Interest at 25%	11,250	8,063	4,078
	56,250	40,313	20,391
Instalment	(24,000)	(24,000)	(20,391)
Closing liability	32,250	16,313	Nil
Interest element as above	11,250	8,063	4,078
∴ Capital repayment	12,750	15,937	16,313
Total instalment	24,000	24,000	20,391

8 Soap

Tutorial note. The key to avoiding getting muddled in part (b) of this question is to set out the proformas (including those for workings) and present your workings logically. Remember, only 11 out of a total of 30 marks are available for the computational aspects of this question.

(a) The definition of a long term contract in SSAP 9 *Stocks and long term contracts* generally applies to contracts which last for more than one year, but does not exclude contracts of less than one year which fall into different accounting periods. The relevant wording of the definition is as follows.

'(A long term contract is) one where the time taken substantially to complete the contract is such that the contract activity falls into different accounting periods. A contract that is required to be accounted for as long term ... will usually extend for a period exceeding one year ... Some contracts with a shorter duration than one year should be accounted for as long term contracts if they are sufficiently material ... that not to record turnover and attributable profit would lead to distortion'.

The accounting treatment adopted by Soap plc for the shorter contracts would appear to be consistent with this SSAP 9 definition. It is also consistent with the treatment of the other contracts. It is important, however, that the same accounting treatment is used every year, even if the results are not as favourable, unless there are good reasons for changing it.

(b) SOAP PLC
PROFIT AND LOSS ACCOUNT
FOR THE YEAR ENDED 31 DECEMBER 20X7 (EXTRACT)

	£'000
Turnover	5,680
Cost of sales	(5,165)
Gross profit on long term contracts	515

SOAP PLC
BALANCE SHEET AS AT 31 DECEMBER 20X7

	£'000
Current assets	
Stock	
Long term contract balances	137.5
Debtors	
Amounts recoverable on contracts	1,050
Current liabilities	
Payments on account	(350)

Workings

1   *Archers plc*

	£
Costs incurred to date	47,500
Machine write-off $(20,000 - (^6/_{12} \times 10,000))$	15,000
	62,500
Cost of sales (W4)	(40,000)
Long term contract balance	22,500
Excess of payments on account over turnover (40 – 30)	(10,000)
	12,500

2   *Neighbours Ltd*

	£'000
Costs incurred to date	1,800
Cost of sales (W4)	(1,250)
Long term contract balance	550
Excess of payments on account over turnover (2,500 – 1,600)	(900)
Current liability	(350)

3   *Emmerdale plc*

	£'000
Costs incurred to date	4,000
Cost of sales (W4)	(3,875)
Long term contract balance	125
Turnover (W4)	4,050
Payments on account	3,000
Amounts recoverable on contracts	1,050

4   *Profit and loss account*

	Emmerdale £'000		Archers £'000		Neighbours £'000	Total £'000
Turnover (45% × 9)	4,050	(20% × 150)	30	(25% × 6.4)	1,600	5,680
Cost of sales (45% × 7.5)	3,375	(20% × 120 – 20*)	20	(25% × 5)	1,250	4,645
Additional costs (8 – 7.5)	500		20			520
	(3,875)		(40)		(1,250)	(5,165)
Profit (loss) on long term contracts	175		(10)		350	515

* *Note.* Because the machine is being written off in one year, its total cost, rather than a percentage, is allocated to that year.

5   *Balance sheet*

	Emmerdale £'000	Archers £'000	Neighbours £'000	Total £'000
Current assets				
Stocks				
Long term contract balances	125 (W3)	12.5 (W1)		137.5
Debtors				
Amounts recoverable on contracts	1,050 (W3)			1,050
Current liabilities				
Payments on account			(350) (W2)	(350)

9   Corax

(a)

CORPORATION TAX (20X5) ACCOUNT

	£		£
Bank	16,300	Balance b/f	16,300

CORPORATION TAX (20X6) ACCOUNT

	£		£
Profit and loss a/c over provision	1,200	Balance b/f	5,000
Balance c/d	3,800		
	5,000		5,000

CORPORATION TAX (20X7) ACCOUNT

	£		£
		Profit and loss a/c	36,000
Balance c/d	36,000		
	36,000		36,000

DEFERRED TAXATION ACCOUNT

	£		£
		Balance b/f	29,400
		Profit and loss a/c	
Balance c/d	36,400	(increase in provision)	7,000
	36,400		36,400

(b)   PROFIT AND LOSS ACCOUNT
FOR THE YEAR ENDED 31 DECEMBER 20X7 (EXTRACT)

	Note	£
Profit for the year on ordinary activities		100,000
Tax on profit for the year	1	(41,800)
Profit for the financial year		58,200

PROFIT AND LOSS RESERVE

	£
Retained profit brought forward	43,000
Profit for the financial year	58,200
Dividend paid	(21,000)
Retained profit carried forward	80,200

BALANCE SHEET AS AT 31 DECEMBER 20X7 (EXTRACT)

	Note	£
Note		
Creditors: amounts falling due within one year		
Other creditors including taxation		
(£3,800 + £36,000)		39,800
Provisions for liabilities		
Taxation, including deferred taxation	3	36,400
Capital and reserves		
Called up share capital – 700,000 ordinary shares of 50p each, allotted and fully paid		350,000
Profit and loss account		80,200

NOTES ON THE ACCOUNTS (EXTRACTS)

		£
1	The tax on profit for the year comprises:	
	UK corporation tax (provided at X% on taxable profits for the year)	36,000
	Less over provision on profits of previous year	1,200
		34,800
	Transfer to deferred taxation account	7,000
		41,800
2	Dividends for the year on the allotted ordinary share capital are:	£
	Paid: 3p on 700,000 shares	21,000
3	Deferred tax balance at 31 December 20X6	£ 29,400
	Charge for the year	7,000
	Balance at 31 December 20X7	36,400

10 Emma

EMMA LIMITED
CASH FLOW STATEMENT
FOR THE YEAR ENDED 31 DECEMBER 20X2
Reconciliation of operating profit to net cash inflow from operating activities

	£'000
Operating profit	350
Depreciation charge (W1)	90
Loss on sale of tangible fixed assets (45 – 32)	13
Profit on sale of fixed asset investments	(5)
Increase/decrease in stocks	(48)
Increase/decrease in debtors	(75)
Increase/decrease in creditors	8
Net cash inflow from operating activities	333

CASH FLOW STATEMENT

	£'000
Net cash inflow from operating activities	333
Returns on investments and servicing of finance (note 1)	(50)
Taxation (W2)	(110)
Capital expenditure	(189)
	(16)
Equity dividends paid	(80)
	(96)
Management of liquid resources (note 1)	(50)
Financing (note 1)	160
Increase in cash	14

Reconciliation of net cash flow to movement in net debt (note 2)

	£'000	£'000
Increase in cash in the period	14	
Cash received from long-term loan	(100)	
Cash used to increase liquid resources	50	
Change in net debt		(36)
Net debt at 1.1.X2		(97)
Net debt at 31.12.X2		(133)

NOTES TO THE CASH FLOW STATEMENT

1   *Gross cash flows*

	£'000	£'000
Returns on investments and servicing of finance		
Interest received	25	
Interest paid	(75)	
		50
Capital expenditure		
Payments to acquire intangible fixed assets	(50)	
Payments to acquire tangible fixed assets (W3)	(201)	
Receipts from sale of tangible fixed assets	32	
Receipts from sale of fixed asset investments	30	
		(189)
Management of liquid resources		
Purchase of short-term investments		(50)
Financing		
Issue of ordinary share capital	60	
Issue of long-term loan	100	
		160

2   *Analysis of changes in net debt*

	At 1 Jan 20X2 £'000	Cash flows £'000	At 31 Dec 20X2 £'000
Cash in hand, at bank	1	1	2
Overdraft	(98)	13	(85)
		14	
Debt due within 1 year	–	–	–
Debt due after 1 year	–	(100)	(100)
Current asset investments	–	50	50
Total	(97)	(36)	(133)

PROFESSIONAL EDUCATION

Workings

1   *Depreciation charge*

	£'000	£'000
Depreciation at 31 December 20X2		340
Depreciation 31 December 20X1	290	
Depreciation on assets sold (85 − 45)	40	
		250
Charge for the year		90

2   *Tax paid*

CORPORATION TAX

	£'000		£'000
Tax paid	110	1.1.X2 balance b/d	110
		Profit and loss	
		140 − (70 − 50)*	120
31.12.X2 balance c/d	120		
	230		230

* Note. The taxation charge in the profit and loss account includes the increase in deferred taxation provision. This must be excluded when calculating the amount of corporation tax paid.

3   *Purchase of tangible fixed assets*

TANGIBLE FIXED ASSETS

	£'000		£'000
1.1.X2 Balance b/d	595	Disposals	85
Revaluation (100 − 91)	9		
Purchases (bal fig)	201	31.12.X2 Balance c/d	720
	805		805

11 Justin Case

FRS 12 states that an entity should **never recognise** a **contingent liability** in the financial statements. The FRS requires a contingent liability to be **disclosed unless** the possibility of any **outflow of economic benefits to settle it is remote**.

In **this case** the contingent liability would merely be **disclosed** in the **notes** to the accounts as follows.

(i)   The **nature** of the contingency
(ii)   The **uncertainties** which are expected to **affect** the **ultimate outcome**
(iii)   A **statement** that it is **not practicable** to make an **estimate** of the **financial effect**

The employee's claim should be included in contingent liabilities, since it is likely that a payment will have to be made.

12 Multiplex

Tutorial note. Compound or hybrid instruments such as convertible debentures (part (a)) are required by FRSs 25 and 26 to be treated according to the substance of the contractual agreement. Here, the equity element and liability (debt) element must be separately identified on the balance sheet. Although in theory this split can be calculated in many ways, with the information available in the question, the only available methodology is the 'residual value of equity' approach. This involves calculating the present value of the cash flows attributable to the 'pure' debt element and treating the difference from the proceeds received as the equity component.

(a)   PROFIT AND LOSS ACCOUNT (EXTRACTS)

	£'000	£'000
Debenture interest paid (£80m × 8%)	6,400	
Required accrual of finance cost	1,844	
Total finance cost (£68.704m (W) × 12%)		8,244

BALANCE SHEET (EXTRACTS)

	£'000	£'000
Equity		
Share options (W)		11,296
Long-term liabilities		
8% debenture 20X4 (W)	68,704	
Accrual of finance costs	1,844	
		70,548

Working

Year		Cash flow £'000	Factor	PV cash flow $'000
1	Interest	6,400	0.89	5,696
2	Interest	6,400	0.80	5,120
3	Interest	6,400	0.71	4,544
4	Interest	6,400	0.64	4,096
5	Interest + capital	86,400	0.57	49,248
PV of debt cash flows				68,704
Residual equity element (= share options)				11,296
				80,000

(b)   The impairment losses are allocated as required by FRS 11 *Impairment of fixed assets and goodwill.*

	Asset at 1.1.20X1 £'000	1st provision (W1) £'000	Assets at 1.2.20X1 £'000	2nd provision (W2) £'000	Revised asset £'000
Goodwill	200	(200)	–	–	–
Operating licence	1,000	(300)	700	(100)	600
Property: stations/land	250	–	250	(50)	200
Rail track/coaches	250	–	250	(50)	200
Steam engines	1,000	(500)	500	–	500
Other net assets	300	–	300	–	300
	3,000	(1,000)	2,000	(200)	1,800

Workings

1   *First provision*

£500,000 relates directly to an engine and its recoverable amount can be assessed directly (ie zero).

FRS 11 then requires goodwill to be written off. Any further impairment must be written off intangible assets.

2   *Second provision*

The first £100,000 of the impairment loss is applied to the operating licence to write it down to NRV.

The remainder is applied pro rata to assets carried at other than their net selling prices.

(c)   At the year end of 31 March 20X1, the company has committed itself to a **binding decision** to close the engineering operation. The expected losses on closure **must** therefore **be provided** for and, as they are **material**, they will be classed as **exceptional**. FRS 3 *Reporting financial performance* requires **separate disclosure** of losses on the closure of an operation on the face of the profit and loss account.

However, again under FRS 3, the closure of the division appears to meet **only three** of the four criteria for it to be treated as a discontinued operation, ie:

(i)   The activities have **ceased permanently**.
(ii)   The closure has a **material effect** on the nature and focus of Multiplex's operations.
(iii)   The results are **separately distinguishable**.
(iv)   But the closure will *not* be completed **within three months** of the year end.

The provision must therefore be shown as part of **continuing operations**, although it can be disclosed separately in the notes as discontinuing.

	£m
The amount will be:	
Loss on sale of net assets (46 – 30)	16.0
Other costs: redundancies	2.0
Professional costs	1.5
Penalty costs	3.0
	22.5

FRS 12 *Provisions, Contingent Liabilities and Contingent Assets* does not permit future operating losses to be recognised as a provision unless they relate to 'onerous contracts' (which is not indicated in this question).

(d)
Profit and loss account	£m
Turnover (W2)	18.0
Cost of sales (balancing figure)	(14.1)
Profit (W3)	3.9

Balance sheet:£m

Current assets	
Long-term contract balances (W5)	6.0
Debtors: amounts recoverable on long-term	
Contracts (W6)	5.0

Workings

1   *Percentage completion*

$$\text{Percentage completion} = \frac{\text{Work certified}}{\text{Contract price}}$$

20X0   *20X1 (including variation)*

$\dfrac{£12m}{£40m} = 30\%$ $\dfrac{£30m}{£45m} = 66.7\%$ (ie $^2/_3$)

2   *Turnover*

Accumulated turnover to 31 March 20X1 = £45m × $^2/_3$ = £30m
In 20X1 turnover = £30m – £12m (20X0) = £18m

3   *Profit*

Revised estimated total profit = £45m – £30m = £15m
Accumulated to 31 March 20X1 = £15m × $^2/_3$ = £10m
Total profit for year ended 31 March 20X1:

	£m
Accumulated to date	10.0
Less 20X0 profit taken (W4)	(3.6)
Less rectification costs	(2.5)
	3.9

4   *Profit for 20X0*

	£m
Turnover	12.0
Cost of sales (bal fig)	(8.4)
Profit = (£40m – £28m) × 30%	3.6

5   *Long-term contract balance*

		£m
Costs incurred to 31 March 20X1		28.5
Cost of sales charged:	20X0 (W4)	(8.4)
	20X1	(14.1)
		6.0

6   *Debtors: amounts recoverable*

	£m
Value of work certified 31 March 20X1	30.0
Payments on account	(25.0)
Amounts due	5.0

13 Dividend Distribution

(a)   (i)   This statement of principle is now expressed in a statutory rule (s 263 CA 1985) that a distribution (a dividend) may only by made out of profits available for that purpose, namely, accumulated realised profits less accumulated realised losses (so far as the losses have not already been written off). However, 'realised' profits have been defined by the Act only in rather obscure terms, and this leaves a query over such items as profits on long-term contract work in progress.

(ii)   A public company is subject to the additional requirement that it may only distribute a surplus of its net assets over the aggregate of its called-up share capital and undistributable reserves (s 264 CA 1985). The statement that profits shall be 'accumulated' requires a company to make good losses of past years out of profits. In effect, this means that any surplus of unrealised losses over unrealised profits must be deducted from realised profits less realised losses in determining the maximum amount available for distribution.

(iii) The requirement that profits shall be realised prevents a company from distributing a revaluation surplus on retained assets.

(iv)   Provisions made in the accounts, for example for depreciation, are generally treated as realised losses which must be deducted in computing profits available for dividend: s 275(2), but this rule does not apply to an increased provision for depreciation made necessary by revaluation of fixed assets.

(v)   There is no objection to payment of dividends out of capital profits (that is, surplus over book value of fixed assets) but such profits must have been realised by sale. An unrealised capital profit arising from revaluation of retained fixed assets may only be distributed by a bonus issue of shares, not as a dividend: s 263 (2) CA 1985.

(vi)   The amount of profit available for distribution is determined by the 'relevant accounts' which are in a typical case the latest audited accounts (provided that the auditor has not qualified his report).

(b)   (i)   The revaluation represents an unrealised holding gain of £20,000. The net difference between unrealised profits and unrealised losses would thus improve, thereby providing a greater 'safety margin' for a public company under s 264 CA 1985. Depreciation is usually regarded as a realised loss, but this does not apply to additional depreciation arising as a consequence of an asset revaluation, therefore the extra depreciation charge would not be treated as a realised loss in computing the maximum amount available for distribution.

(ii) The company had an unrealised gain of £(440,000 – 150,000) = £290,000 prior to the sale. This would have been included in the 'safety margin' under s 264, as described in (a) above, but it disappears when the sale occurs, because a realised profit of £350,000 is now made, and this is a distributable capital profit.

14 Revenue recognition

(a) In revenue recognition, the 'critical event' is the point in the earnings process or operating cycle at which the transaction is deemed to have been **sufficiently completed** to allow the **profit** arising from the transaction, or a distinct component part of it, to be **recognised** in income in a particular period. This has to be addressed in order to allocate transactions and their effects to different accounting periods and is a direct result of the episodic nature of financial reporting. For most companies the **normal earnings cycle** is the purchase of raw materials which are transformed through a manufacturing process into saleable goods, for which orders are subsequently received, delivery is made and then payment received.

In the past the approach has been to **match costs with revenues** and record both once the critical event has passed; in most systems this critical event has been full or near **full performance of the transaction**, so that no material uncertainties surround either the transaction being completed or the amounts arising from the transaction. This is encompassed in the notion of prudence, so that revenue is recognised only in cash or near cash form. However, any point in the cycle could be deemed to be the critical event. This approach leaves the balance sheet as a statement of uncompleted transaction balances, comprising unexpired costs and undischarged liabilities.

UITF abstract 40 has been published as an amendment to FRS 5 and changes how revenue is recognised by professional firms. Work that was unbilled at the year end would previously have been classified as WIP. Now, when work is unbilled at the year end for which a fee note could be raised, it is treated as revenue and valued at its estimated sales value.

In contrast, the *Statement of Principles* defines gains and losses (or income and expenses) in terms of **changes** in assets and liabilities other than those arising from transactions with owners as owners, not in terms of an earnings or matching process. The balance sheet thus assumes primary importance in the recognition of earnings and profits. A gain **can only be recognised** if there is an **increase** in the **ownership interest** (ie net assets) of an entity not resulting from contributions from owners. Similarly, a loss is recognised if there is a **decrease** in the ownership interest of an entity not resulting from distributions to owners. Thus gains arise from recognition of assets and derecognition of liabilities, and losses arise from derecognition of assets and recognition of liabilities. The Statement explains that it is not possible to reverse this definitional process, ie by defining assets and liabilities in terms of gains and losses, because it has not been possible to formulate robust enough base definitions of gains and losses (partly because the choice of critical event can be subjective). Nevertheless the two approaches are linked by the Statement, which says that '**sufficient evidence**' for recognition or derecognition will be met at the critical event in the operating cycle.

(b) *On the acquisition of goods*

This would be **unlikely** to be a critical event for most businesses. However, for some the acquisition of the raw materials is the most important part of the process, eg extraction of gold from a mine, or the harvesting of coffee beans. Only where the goods in question could be **sold immediately in a liquid market** would it be appropriate to recognise revenue, ie they would have to have a **commodity value**.

During the manufacture or production of goods

This is also **unlikely** to be the critical event for most businesses because **too many uncertainties** remain, eg of damaged goods or overproduction leading to obsolete stock. An **exception** would be **long-term contracts** for the construction of specific assets, which tend to earn the constructing company revenues over the length of the contract, usually in stages, ie there is a **series of critical events** in the operating cycle (according to the *Statement of Principles*). It would **not** be appropriate to recognise all the revenue at the end of the contract, because this would reflect profit earned in past periods as well as the present period. Profit is therefore recognised during manufacture or production, usually through certification of a qualified valuer. Some would argue that this is not really a critical event approach, but rather an 'accretion approach'.

On delivery/acceptance of goods

Goods are frequently sold on **credit**, whereby the vendor hands over the inventory asset and receives in its place a **financial asset of a debt** due for the price of the goods. At that point legal title passes and **full performance** has taken place. In general, the bulk of the risks of the transaction have gone and the only ones remaining relate to the creditworthiness of the purchaser and any outstanding warranty over the goods. Many trade sales take place in this way, with periods of credit allowed for goods delivered, eg 30 days. This therefore tends to be the critical event for many types of business operating cycles.

Where certain conditions have been satisfied after the goods have been delivered

In these situations the customer had a right of return of the goods without reason or penalty, but usually within a time and non-use condition. A good example is clothes retailers who allow **non-faulty goods to be returned**. Another example is that the goods need only be paid for once they are sold on to a third party. Traditionally, recognition of revenue is delayed until, eg the **deadline to allowed return passes**. However, in circumstances where goods are never returned, it might be argued that the substance of the transaction is a sale on delivery.

Receipt or payment for credit sales

Once payment is received, only warranty risk remains. A company may wait until this point to recognise income if receipt is considered uncertain, eg when goods have been sold to a company resident in a country that has **exchange controls**. It would otherwise be **rare** to delay recognition until payment.

On the expiry of a guarantee or warranty

Many businesses may feel unable to recognise revenue in full because of **outstanding warranties**, eg a construction company which is subject to fee retention until some time after completion of the contract. Other businesses, such as car manufacturers, may make a **general provision** for goods returned under warranty as it will not be possible to judge likely warranty costs under individual contracts.

(c)   (i)   This agreement is worded as a **sale**, but it is fairly obvious from the terms and assessed substance that it is in fact a **secured loan**. Jensen should therefore continue to recognise the stock on balance sheet and should treat the receipt from Wholesaler as a loan, not revenue. Finance costs will be charged to the profit and loss account, of £35,000 × 12% × 9/12 = £3,150.

       (ii)   Years 2 to 5 of the franchise contract would be **loss making** for Jensen and hence part of the initial fee of £50,000 should be **deferred over the life of the contract**. Since Jensen should be making a profit margin of 20% on this type of arrangement, revenues of £10,000 will be required to match against the costs of £8,000. The company will receive £5,000 pa and so a further £5,000 × 4 = £20,000 of the initial fee should be deferred, leaving £50,000 – £20,000 = £30,000 to be recognised in the first year. However, this may not represent a liability under FRS 12 *Provisions, contingent liabilities and contingent assets*, where a liability is defined as an obligation to transfer economic benefits as a result of past transactions or events. It will be necessary to consider the terms of the initial fee and whether it is returnable.

(iii)   The cost of the first 6 months' publications is £192,000 ÷ 24 × 6 = £48,000. On an accruals basis, income of £240,000 ÷ 24 × 6 = 60,000 should be recognised. This would leave deferred income of £240,000 − £60,000 = £180,000 in Jensen's balance sheet (ie as a liability). As in (ii), however, this may not represent a liability. In fact, the liability of the company may only extend to the cost of the future publications, ie £192,000 − £48,000 = £144,000. This would allow Jensen to **recognise all the profit** on the publications **immediately**. In want of an accounting standard on revenue recognition, it will be necessary to consider the extent of Jensen's commitments under this arrangement.

15 Related party transactions

(a)   Disclosure is required for all material related party transactions. Related party transactions are required to be disclosed whether or not a price is charged. The following are examples of related party transactions that require disclosure by a reporting entity in the period in which they occur:

(i)   Purchases or sales of goods (finished or unfinished)
(ii)   Purchases or sales of property and other assets
(iii)   Rendering or receiving of services
(iv)   Agency arrangements
(v)   Leasing arrangements
(vi)   Transfer of research and development
(vii)   Licence agreements
(viii) Provision of finance
(ix)   Guarantees and the provision of collateral security
(x)   Management contracts

(b)   Financial statements should disclose material transactions undertaken by the reporting entity with a related party. Disclosure should be made irrespective of whether a price is charged. The disclosure should include:

(i)   The names of the transacting related parties

(ii)   A description of the relationship between the parties

(iii)   A description of the transactions

(iv)   The amounts involved

(v)   Any other elements of the transactions necessary for an understanding of the financial statements

(vi)   The amounts due to or from related parties at the balance sheet date and provisions for doubtful debts due to such parties at this date

(vii)   Amounts written off in the period in respect of debts due to or from related parties

Transactions with related parties may be disclosed on an aggregated basis (aggregation of similar transactions by type of related party) unless disclosure of an individual transaction, or connected transactions, is necessary for an understanding of the impact of the transactions on the financial statements of the reporting entity or is required by law.

16 Segmental reporting

SSAP 25 requires larger companies (ie plcs, banking and insurance companies or those meeting ten times the medium sized company criteria) to provide, where applicable, an analysis of turnover and operating profit attributable to different classes of business and an analysis of turnover attributable to each geographical market.

Segmental net assets are also required to be disclosed.

The purpose of **SSAP 25 disclosures** is **to provide users with information as to which classes of business**:

(1) **Earn the best rate of return**
(2) **Have a lower degree of risk**
(3) **Show the best growth rates**
(4) **Demonstrate the best potential for future development.**

17 Group accounts

The object of annual accounts is to help shareholders exercise control over their company by providing information about how its affairs have been conducted. The shareholders of a holding company would not be given sufficient information from the accounts of the holding company on its own, because not enough would be known about the nature of the assets, income and profits of all the subsidiary companies in which the holding company has invested. The primary purpose of group accounts is to provide a true and fair view of the position and earnings of the holding company group as a whole, from the standpoint of the shareholders in the holding company.

A number of arguments have been put forward, however, which argue that group accounts have certain limitations.

(a) Group accounts may be misleading.

  (i) The solvency (liquidity) of one company may hide the insolvency of another.

  (ii) The profit of one company may conceal the losses of another.

  (iii) They imply that group companies will meet each others' debts (this is certainly not true: a parent company may watch creditors of an insolvent subsidiary go unpaid without having to step in).

(b) There may be some difficulties in defining the group or 'entity' of companies, although the Companies Act 1989 has removed many of the grey areas here.

(c) Where a group consists of widely diverse companies in different lines of business, a set of group accounts may obscure much important detail unless supplementary information about each part of the group's business is provided.

18 Arlene and Sandra

Workings:

Minority interests

	£
Ordinary share capital (10% × 150,000)	15,000
Revenue reserves (10% × 99,000)	9,900
Capital reserves (10% × 15,000)	1,500
	26,400

Goodwill

	£	£
Cost of investment		190,000
Share of net assets acquired as represented by:		
Ordinary share capital	150,000	
Revenue reserves on acquisition	20,000	
Capital reserves on acquisition	10,000	
	180,000	
Group share 90%		162,000
Goodwill		28,000

Consolidated revenue reserve

	£
Arlene plc	190,000
Share of Sandra Ltd's post acquisition reserves	
(99,000 − 20,000) × 90%	71,100
	261,100

Consolidated capital reserve

	£
Arlene plc	60,000
Share of Sandra's post-acquisition reserve	
(15,000 − 10,000) × 90%	4,500
	64,500

ARLENE PLC
CONSOLIDATED BALANCE SHEET AS AT 31 DECEMBER 20X5

	£	£
Intangible fixed assets: goodwill		28,000
Tangible fixed assets		560,000
Current assets		
Stocks	125,000	
Debtors	150,000	
Bank and cash	56,000	
	331,000	
Current liabilities		
Trade creditors	167,000	
Net current assets		164,000
Total assets less current liabilities		752,000

	£	£
Capital and reserves		
Ordinary shares of £1 each		400,000
Reserves		
Revenue reserves	261,100	
Capital reserves	64,500	
		325,600
		725,600
Minority interest		26,400
		752,000

19 Plate

Tutorial note. This question may look intimidating because it involves an acquisition part of the way through the year, some FRS 7 issues and both the consolidated profit and loss account and balance sheet. It is, however, fairly straightforward. You should not have overlooked FRS 3 aspects in the consolidated profit and loss account.

(a) FRS 7 *Fair values in acquisition accounting* states that quoted shares should be valued at market price on the date of acquisition. However, the standard acknowledges that the market price may be difficult to determine if it is unreliable because of an inactive market. In particular, where the shares are not quoted, there may be no suitable market. In such cases the value must be estimated using:

(i) The value of similar quoted securities
(ii) The present value of the cash flows of the shares
(iii) Any cash alternative which was offered
(iv) The value of any underlying security into which there is an option to convert

It may be necessary to undertake a valuation of the company in question should none of the above methods prove feasible.

(b) PLATE GROUP PLC
CONSOLIDATED BALANCE SHEET AS AT 30 JUNE 20X7

	£'000	£'000
Fixed assets		
Tangible assets (1,750 + 500)		2,250
Goodwill (W3)		151
		2,401
Current assets		
Stocks	600	
Debtors	451	
Cash at bank and in hand	299	
	1,350	
Creditors: amounts falling due within one year	(650)	
Net current assets		700
Total assets less current liabilities		3,101
Creditors: amounts falling due after one year		(1,225)
		1,876
Capital and reserves		
Ordinary share capital		750
Share premium (W6)		250
Profit and loss account (W5)		621
		1,621
Minority interests (W4)		255
		1,876

PLATE GROUP PLC
CONSOLIDATED PROFIT AND LOSS ACCOUNT
FOR THE YEAR ENDED 30 JUNE 20X7

	£'000	£'000
Turnover		
Continuing operations	3,150	
Acquisitions $(^2/_{12}) \times 1,770$	295	
		3,445
Cost of sales		(1,788)
Gross profit		1,657
Distribution costs	638	
Administrative expenses (W7)	348	
		(986)
Operating profit		
Continuing operations	606	
Acquisitions	65	
		671
Interest payable		(75)
Profit on ordinary activities before taxation		596
Tax on profit on ordinary activities		(306)
Profit after tax		290
Minority interests (equity) (W8)		(11)
Profit for the financial year		279

Workings

1   *Revaluation surplus*

	£'000
Spoon Ltd: tangible fixed assets at market value	500
Carrying value	350
Revaluation surplus	150

FRS 7 *Fair values in acquisition accounting* states that open market values should be used to value tangible fixed assets, and it is this figure which is compared with the carrying value here, rather than the net realisable value. The latter is lower because the costs of realisation are deducted. However, as the group does not intend to dispose of the asset, the market value is more appropriate.

2   *Pre-acquisition dividend*

Dividend paid by Spoon to Plate: £42,000
Pre-acquisition element $^{10}/_{12} \times$ £42,000 = £35,000

3   *Goodwill*

	£'000	£'000
Cost of investment		800
Pre-acquisition dividend (W2)		(35)
		765
Share capital	100	
Share premium	150	
Revaluation surplus	150	
Profit and loss account		
Prior year: 450 – 165	285	
Current year: $^{10}/_{12} \times$ 165	138	
	823	
Group share: 70%		576
Goodwill		189
Amortisation for period (189 × 1/5)		(38)
Unamortised goodwill		151

4   *Minority interests (balance sheet)*

	£'000
Share capital	100
Share premium	150
Revaluation surplus	150
Profit and loss account	450
	850

MI = £850,000 × 30% = £255,000.

5   *Profit and loss account*

	Plate Ltd £	Spoon Ltd £
As per accounts	625	450
Adj pre-acquisition dividend (W2)	(35)	
Adj issue costs (W7)	50	
Pre-acquisition profit Prior year (W3)		(285)
Current year (W3)		(138)
Group share in Spoon Ltd (27 × 70%)	19	27
Goodwill amortised (W3)	(38)	
	621	

6   *Share premium account*

	£'000
Plate plc	300
Less issue costs	(50)
	250

7   *Administrative expenses*

		£'000
	Plate plc	325
	Spoon Ltd $(^2/_{12} \times 210)$	35
	Goodwill written off	38
		398
	Issue costs	(50)
		348

8   Minority interests (p & l)

$225 \times {}^2/_{12} \times 30\% = £11,250$

20 Enterprise and Vulcan

Step 1

Calculate the goodwill in the investment in Vulcan Ltd. This will be needed in order to calculate the 'Investment in associated undertakings' line on the balance sheet since goodwill is being amortised, and is not yet fully amortised.

Goodwill

	£'000	£'000
Cost of investment		2,000
Share capital	2,000	
Revaluation reserve	200	
Profit and loss reserve	900	
	3,100	
	$\times 30\%$	(930)
		1,070

£1,070,000 ÷ 5 = 214,000 amortised per year
3 years amortised already × £214,000 = 642,000

Add this year's amortisation of £214,000 = 856,000

£	
856,000	amortised to date
214,000	unamortised
1,070,000	total goodwill

Step 2

Complete the top half of the balance sheet including the 'Investments in associates' line as below, and insert the share capital of Enterprise plc.

	£'000
Investment in associate's net assets	
(30% × 7,940,000)	2,382
Unamortised goodwill (see Step 1))	214
	2,596

Step 3

Calculate the balance sheet reserves.

1   *Revaluation reserve*

	Enterprise £'000	Vulcan £'000
Per question	2,000	1,000
Pre-acquisition		(200)
		800
Share in Vulcan (800 × 30%)	240	
	2,240	

2   *Profit and loss reserve*

	Enterprise £'000	Vulcan £'000
Per question	5,100	4,940
Pre-acquisition		(900)
		4,040
Share in Vulcan (4,040 × 30%)	1,212	
Goodwill amortisation (Step 1)	(856)	
	5,456	

Step 4

Complete the consolidated P&L account up to the group operating profit line, and calculate the share of operating profit in the associate. Any adjustments to the P&L account for the amortisation of goodwill should be charged now to reduce this figure.

Share of operating profit in associate

	£'000
Operating profit × 30% (£2,120,000 × 30%)	636
Amortisation for the year (see task one)	(214)
	422

Step 5

Complete the balance sheet and profit and loss account.

ENTERPRISE PLC
CONSOLIDATED BALANCE SHEET AS AT 30 JUNE 20X8

	£'000	£'000
Fixed assets		
Tangible assets		8,000
Investments:		
Investments in associates		2,596
		10,596
Current assets		
Stock	1,340	
Debtors	1,000	
Cash	260	
	2,600	
Creditors (due within one year)	(1,500)	
Net current assets		1,100
		11,696
Capital and reserves		
Equity share capital		4,000
Revaluation reserve		2,240
Profit and loss reserve		5,456
		11,696

BPP
PROFESSIONAL EDUCATION

ENTERPRISE PLC GROUP
CONSOLIDATED PROFIT AND LOSS ACCOUNT
FOR THE YEAR ENDING 30 JUNE 20X8

	£'000	£'000
Group turnover		10,000
Cost of sales		(6,000)
Gross profit		4,000
Expenses		(1,500)
Group operating profit		2,500
Share of operating profit in associates	636	
Amortisation in associate	(214)	
		422
		2,922
Interest payable:		
Group		(100)
Associates (30% × 20,000)		(6)
Profit before tax		2,816
Taxation		(1,010)
Profit after tax		1,806

* Tax relates to the following:

Parent and subsidiaries	£800,000
Associates (30% × £700,000)	£210,000

Note: As the share in the associates is equal to more than 25% of the group figure (before associates) for operating profit, additional disclosures required under FRS 9 would need to be given, if not specifically excluded from the question requirements.

21 Hepburn and Salter

(a)   HEPBURN PLC
CONSOLIDATED PROFIT AND LOSS ACCOUNT
FOR THE YEAR ENDED 31 MARCH 20X1

	£'000
Turnover (W1)	1,600
Cost of sales (W2)	(890)
Gross profit	710
Operating expenses (W3)	(184)
Debenture interest (12 × 6/12)	(6)
Operating profit	520
Taxation (100 + (40 × 6/12)	(120)
Profit after tax	400
Minority interest (200 × 20% × 6/12)	(20)
Profit after tax and minority interest	380

HEPBURN PLC
CONSOLIDATED BALANCE SHEET
AS AT 31 MARCH 20X1

	£'000	£'000
Fixed assets		
Intangible: goodwill (W4)		180
Tangible fixed assets		
Land and buildings (400 + 150 + 125)		675
Plant and machinery (220 + 510)		730
Investments (20 + 10)		30
		1,615
Current assets		
Stock (240 + 280 – 10 (W2))	510	
Debtors (170 + 210 – 56)	324	
Bank (20 + 40 + 20)	80	
	914	
Creditors: amounts due < 1 year		
Trade creditors (210 + 155 - 36)	329	
Taxation (50 + 45)	95	
	424	
Net current assets		490
		2,105
Creditors: amounts due > 1 year		
8% Debentures		150
Net assets		1,955
Capital and reserves		
Ordinary shares £1 each (400 + 300 (W4))		700
Share premium account (900 – 300 (W4))		600
Profit and loss account (W5)		460
		1,760
Minority interests (W6)		195
Shareholders' funds		1,955

Workings

1	*Turnover*	£'000
	Hepburn	1,200
	Salter (1,000 × 6/12)	500
	Intercompany sale	(100)
		1,600

2	*Cost of sales*	£'000
	Hepburn	650
	Salter (660 × 6/12)	330
	Intercompany sales	(100)
	Unrealised profit in stock (100 × 50% × 25/125)	10
		890

3	*Operating expenses*	£'000
	Hepburn	120
	Salter (88 × 6/12)	44
	Goodwill amortisation (W4)	20
		184

4	Goodwill	£'000	£'000
	Cost of investment in Salter 150 × 80% × 5/2 (= 300) × £3		900
	Fair value of net assets acquired		
	Share capital	150	
	Profit and loss account		
	At 1 April 20X0 (700 - 200)	500	
	Profit to 1 Oct 20X0 (200 × 6/12)	100	
	Fair value adjustment	125	
		875	
	Group share (80%)		700
	Goodwill		200
	Amortisation (200 ÷ 5 × 6/12)		20
	Unamortised		180

5	Profit and loss account		Hepburn Ltd £	Salter Ltd £
	As per accounts 31.3.X1		410	700
	Unrealised profit in stock (W2)		(10)	
	Pre-acquisition profit	At 1 April 20X0 (W4)		(500)
		Profit to 1 Oct 20X0		(100)
				100
	Group share of Salter Ltd (100 ×80%)		80	
	Goodwill amortisation (W4)		(20)	
			460	

6	Minority interest	£'000
	Share capital: 20% × 150	30
	Profit and loss account: 20% × 700	140
	Fair value adjustment of land: 20% × 125	25
		195

(b) In **voting rights**, Hepburn's interest in Woodbridge Ltd is **60%**; however it is correct that it is only entitled to 6,000/24,000 = 25% of any dividends paid.

The approach taken by Hepburn to its investment in Woodbridge seems to be based on the view that, with a **25% equity holding**, the investment would normally be treated as an associate and equity accounting applied. However, Hepburn does not exert any significant influence over Woodbridge and hence under FRS 9 *Associates and joint ventures* it can rebut the presumption of associate status.

Key point ▷ This overlooks the fact that FRS 2 *Accounting for subsidiary undertakings* bases the treatment of an investment in another entity on the notion of control rather than **ownership**. Hepburn can control Woodbridge by virtue of its holding the **majority of the voting rights** in the company.

Woodbridge is thus a **subsidiary** and should be **consolidated in full** in Hepburn's group accounts, **from the date of acquisition**.

Hepburn's directors may wish to avoid consolidation because of Woodbridge's **losses**. But these **losses** may indicate that the **value of the investment** in Woodbridge in Hepburn's own individual accounts may be **overstated**. A test for **impairment**, as required by FRS 11 *Impairment of fixed assets and goodwill* may reveal that the **recoverable amount** of the investment has fallen below £20,000, thus requiring a write down in Hepburn's own accounts and a write down of Woodbridge's assets in the consolidated accounts.

22 CPP and CCA

(a) In accounting, the value of income and capital is measured in terms of money. In simple terms, profit is the difference between the closing and opening balance sheet values (after adjustment for new sources of funds and applications such as dividend distribution). If, because of inflation, the value of assets in the closing balance sheet is shown at a higher monetary amount than assets in the opening balance sheet, a profit has been made. In traditional accounting, it is assumed that a monetary unit of £1 is a stable measurement; inflation removes this stability.

CPP accounting attempts to provide a more satisfactory methods of valuing profit and capital by establishing a stable unit of monetary measurement, £1 of current purchasing power, as at the end of the accounting period under review.

A distinction is made between monetary items, and non-monetary items. In a period of inflation, keeping a monetary asset (eg debtors) results in a loss of purchasing power as the value of money erodes over time. Non-monetary assets, however, are assumed to maintain 'real' value over time, and these are converted into monetary units of current purchasing power as at the year end, by means of a suitable price index. The equity interest in the balance sheet can be determined as a balancing item.

The profit or deficit for the year in CPP terms is found by converting sales, opening and closing stock, purchases and other expenses into year-end units of £CPP. In addition, a profit on holding net monetary liabilities (or a loss on holding net monetary assets) is computed in arriving at the profit or deficit figure.

CPP arguably provides a more satisfactory system of accounting since transactions are expressed in terms of 'today's money' and similarly, the balance sheet values are adjusted for inflation, so as to give users of financial information a set of figures with which they can:

(i) Decide whether operating profits are satisfactory (profits due to inflation are eliminated)

(ii) Obtain a better appreciation of the size and 'value' of the entity's assets

(b) CPP and CCA accounting are different concepts, in that CCP accounting makes adjustments for general inflationary price changes, whereas CCA makes adjustments to allow for specific price movements (changes in the deprival value of assets). Specific price changes (in CCA) enable a company to determine whether the operating capability of a company has been maintained; it is not a restatement of price levels in terms of a common unit of money measurement. The two conventions use different concepts of capital maintenance (namely operating capability with CCA, and general purchasing power with CPP).

In addition CPP is based on the use of a general price index. In contrast, CCA only makes use of a specific price index where it is not possible to obtain the current value of an asset by other means (eg direct valuation).

(c) In CCA, holding gains represent the difference between the historical cost of an asset and its current cost. If the asset is unsold, and appears in the balance sheet of a company at current cost, there will be an 'unrealised' holding gain, which must be included in a current cost reserve. When the asset is eventually sold, the profit (equal to the sale price minus the historical cost) may be divided into:

(i) An operating profit which would have been made if the cost of the asset were its current value

(ii) A *realised* holding gain which has arisen because of the appreciation in value of the asset between the date of its acquisition and the date of its sale

The handbook's method of CCA excludes realised holding gains from the calculation of current cost operating profit, and the implication is that realised holding gains should not be made available for distribution as a dividend, because to do so would result in a loss of 'business substance' or 'operating capability' by the business.

(d)   (i)   The cost of sales adjustment is the difference between the historical cost of goods sold and their current cost. In a CCA statement, the COSA is therefore used to adjust 'historical cost profit' towards 'current cost profit' by, in effect, changing the cost of sales from an historical cost to a current cost basis.

     (ii)   The COSA does not allow for the fact that purchased goods are acquired on credit and finished goods are likewise sold on credit. In a period of inflation, a company benefits from creditors (because payments are made at 'yesterday's prices') but loses with debtors, because a delay in the receipt of cash means that more money is required to purchase replacement assets (at 'tomorrow's prices') in order to maintain the operating capability of the business. The MWCA is therefore a charge, if the company has positive, rather than negative, monetary working capital (MWC defined roughly as debtors minus creditors) which takes account of the effect of deferred payments on business substance in arriving at the current cost operating profit.

     (iii)   The depreciation adjustment is the difference between the depreciation share based on the historical cost of fixed assets and the charge based on their current cost. In a CCA statement, the depreciation adjustment is therefore used to adjust 'historical cost profit' towards 'current cost operating profit' in order to reflect the current value of fixed assets 'consumed'.

     (iv)   The gearing adjustment is applied to the total of the other adjustments to allow for the fact that some of the loss in value is being borne by outside creditors. During a period of inflation the debts owed to outside parties are also declining in value.

23 Statement of principles

The merits of the ASB's *Statement of Principles* should, ideally, be summarised in its objective, which is given in the *Foreword to Accounting Standards*:

> 'to provide a framework for the consistent and logical formulation of individual accounting standards (and to provide) a basis on which others can exercise judgement in resolving accounting issues.'

The following points may be made in favour of the *Statement of Principles*.

(a)   The principles have in fact been used in the formulation of standards, for example its definitions of assets and liabilities have been used in FRS 5 *Reporting the substance of transactions*.

(b)   The *Statement* helps reduce scope for individual judgement and the potential subjectivity that this implies.

(c)   Financial statements should be more comparable because, although alternative treatments will still be available, there will be a consistent and coherent framework on which to base one's choice of a particular alternative.

(d)   The *Statement* puts forward a consistent terminology and consistent objectives, for example in the definitions and the qualitative characteristics.

It could be argued that the *Statement of Principles* is too theoretical. It is certainly general rather than particular. However, as has been seen with FRS 5, the general principles can be applied to very specific issues in accounting standards. Moreover, in areas not at present covered by accounting standards, the statement can give general guidance. Nevertheless, in the short term, the principles in the *Statement* may conflict with some accounting standards which had already been issued before it was written.

24 XYZ Group

(a) To: Managing director
From: Company Secretary
Date: 3 June 20X6

Subject: XYZ *Group performance 20X5/X6*

In accordance with your instructions, I have prepared a report on the XYZ Group. The report is presented under the 'criteria for a healthy company' suggested by you. Appropriate ratios are listed in the appendix.

Asset base

The fixed assets are in each case covered by the shareholders' funds. The asset base of company X appears adequate, although substantial investments in intangible assets appear in the balance sheet. The freehold property is reported at cost and is therefore likely to be undervalued. Plant is on average half-way through its useful life. Company Y does not own its own property and rental agreements should be examined to check on security of tenure. Again plant is approximately half-way through its useful life. Company Z has a substantial asset base and its plant has been purchased fairly recently. However, the term of the lease appears to have almost expired and details of arrangement for renewal or replacement need to be investigated.

Control of working capital

There are unexpectedly large variations in the stock holding period, in view of the fact that all three companies are engaged in the same trade. The reason why Y and X, respectively, carry stocks for twice and three times the period of Z needs to be examined. Similarly the debt collection periods of X (14 weeks) and Y (19 weeks) appear excessive. Systems of stock and debtor control in companies X and Y require investigation.

Liquidity

All three companies are engaged in manufacturing. The current and liquid ratios of X appear adequate for this type of operation. The liquidity position of Y is weak, which may be the reason why it takes 14½ weeks to pay suppliers. Also the company has a large bank overdraft in relation to its scale of operations. The solvency ratios of Z appear excessive and, with suppliers representing 2½ weeks purchases, it does not seem as if maximum credit is being taken. The possibility of transferring resources from Z to Y should be explored.

Borrowing capacity

The gearing of both X and Y is high. At X, the amounts due to suppliers and providers of loan finance (£2,166,000) exceed the equity interest; at Y, there is a substantial balance of liabilities due within one year. In neither of these cases is a great deal of borrowing capacity apparent. Z has no borrowings, low creditors and cash at the bank; its borrowing capacity is therefore more promising.

Operating performance

Again there are substantial unexplained variations in performance. The net profit ratio of Z (18.4%) is well above the average for the group (10.3%). The negative net margin of Y requires careful investigation.

Commercial return for shareholders

The return on shareholders' funds earned by Z appears adequate, that of X is low while Y produces a negative return on the shareholders' investment.

Appendix: accounting ratios

Ratio	Calculation	X	Y	Z	Group
Stock turnover *	$\dfrac{\text{Closing stock}}{\text{Cost of goods sold}} \times 52$ (weeks)	18	11	5½	11
Debt collection *	$\dfrac{\text{Closing debtors}}{\text{Sales}} \times 52$ (weeks)	14	19	7	12
Payment of creditors	$\dfrac{\text{Creditors}}{\text{Cost of sales**}} \times 52$ (weeks)	15½	14½	2½	9¾
Current ratio	$\dfrac{\text{Current assets}}{\text{Current liabilities}}$:1	2.5:1	1.1:1	6.4:1	2:1
Liquid ratio	$\dfrac{\text{Debtors + bank}}{\text{Current liabilities}}$:1	1.3:1	0.7:1	4:1	1.2:1
Gearing ratio	$\dfrac{\text{External finance}}{\text{Total finance}} \times 100$	50%	52%	4%	44%
Net profit ratio	$\dfrac{\text{Net profit***}}{\text{Sales}} \times 100$	8.9%	(4%)	18.4%	10.3%
Return on capital employed	$\dfrac{\text{Net profit**}}{\text{Shareholders equity}} \times 100$	7.3%	(8.2%)	18.7%	14.7%

*   Closing balances used as insufficient data provided to calculate averages.

**   Cost of goods sold used as an approximation of purchases.

***   Net profit after interest and before tax.

(b)   *Items requiring further investigation*

Company X. Research and development of £180,000 needs to be investigated to check that the requirements of SSAP 13 are satisfied. According to this standard, and the Companies Act, research expenditure should be written off immediately it is incurred. Development expenditure may only be capitalised where stringent conditions are met, including the requirement for a clearly defined project where commercial viability is reasonably certain.

Freehold property, £300,000. FRS 15 and the Companies Act require fixed assets to be written off either immediately or over its useful economic life. There is no evidence that this is being done.

Company Y. Customer prepayments of £106,000. The nature of this item should be investigated. Is the company able to supply the goods at the agreed price?

Company Z. Goodwill £200,000. FRS 10 and the Companies Act require purchased goodwill to be written off over its useful economic life. Non-purchased goodwill should not appear in the accounts. The accounting policy followed should be investigated to ensure compliance with these regulation.

Freehold property at valuation £800,000. Again a check needs to be made to ensure that the asset is being depreciated over its estimated useful life.

Extraordinary item £73,000. FRS 3 contains regulations regarding the treatment of rare, unusual items. Only extraordinary items may be reported 'below the line' and evidence must be produced to prove that this item has been properly classified.

(c)   A company may, legally, pay a dividend out of accumulated realised profits less accumulated realised losses. The available balance is £20,000 and so the company is clearly unable to make the proposed payment of £60,000. The capital redemption reserve is, for all purposes, to be treated as share capital, and is therefore not available to back the proposed payment. Apart from legal regulations, cash availability is the crucial practical constraint on proposals to pay a dividend. The company's bank overdraft of £172,000 suggest that even a dividend payment of £20,000 would be ill-advised at this stage.

25 Webster

(a)   PROFIT AND LOSS ACCOUNTS (Restated)

	Cole Ltd £'000	Cole Ltd £'000	Darwin Ltd £'000	Darwin Ltd £'000
Sales (W1)		2,875		4,400
Opening stock	450		720	
Purchases (W2)	2,055		3,080	
	2,505		3,800	
Closing stock	(540)		(850)	
		(1,965)		(2,950)
Gross profit		910		1,450
Operating expenses (W3)	520		844	
Debenture interest	80		–	
Overdraft interest	15		–	
		(615)		(844)
Net profit		295		606

BALANCE SHEETS (restated)

	Cole Ltd £'000	Cole Ltd £'000	Darwin Ltd £'000	Darwin Ltd £'000
Fixed assets (W4)				
Premises		1,900		1,900
Plant		1,200		720
		3,100		2,620
Current assets				
Sales	540		850	
Debtors (522 + 375)	897		750	
Bank (W5)	-		60	
	1,437		1,660	
Current liabilities				
Creditors (438 – 275)	163		562	
Overdraft (W5)	795		–	
	958		562	
Net current assets		479		1,098
		3,579		3,718
10% debenture		(800)		–
Net assets		2,779		3,718
Share capital and reserves				
Ordinary shares £1 each		1,000		500
Revaluation reserve (800 – 40)		760		700
Profit and loss account		1,019		2,518
(684 + 295 + 40)/(1,912 + 606)		2,779		3,718

Workings

		£'000
1	*Cole's sales*	
	Per P&L account	3,000
	Over-priced intra group sales (500 – 375)	(125)
		2,875
2	*Cole's purchases*	
	Per P&L account	2,030
	Under-priced intra group sales (300 – 275)	25
		2,055

BPP
PROFESSIONAL EDUCATION

3   *Operating expenses*   £'000
     Cole: as if property is revalued
     Per P&L account   480
     Additional depreciation (2,000 − 1,200) ÷ 20   40
     520

     Darwin's as if plant not yet acquired   £'000
     Per P&L account   964
     Depreciation on plant (600 × 20%)   (120)
     844

4   *Fixed asset balance*

	Cole	Darwin
	£'000	£'000
Property	2,000	2,000
Depreciation	(100)	(100)
	1,900	1,900
Plant	1,200	1,200
Plant not on stream (600 − (600 × 20%))	–	(480)
	1,200	720

5   *Bank balances*   £'000
     Cole
     Per balance sheet   20
     Intra group sale   (500)
     Intra group purchase   (300)
     Overdraft interest   (15)
     (795)

     Darwin
     Per balance sheet   (550)
     Plant purchase reversed   600
     Overdraft interest reversed   10
     60

6   *Ratios*

	Cole Limited		Darwin Limited	
	Original	Restated	Original	Restated
ROCE (W1)	19.4%	10.5%	13.3%	16.3%
Asset turnover (W2)	1.01 times	0.80 times	1.23 times	1.18 times
Gross profit margin (W30	35.3%	31.7%	33.0%	33.0%
Net profit margin (W4)	16.7%	10.3%	10.8%	13.8%
Debtors collection period (W5)	64 days	114 days	62 days	62 days
Creditors payment period (W6)	79 days	29 days	67 days	67 days

Workings

1   ROCE

Cole   = $\dfrac{295 + 80}{2,779 + 800}$ =   10.5%

Darwin   = $\dfrac{606}{3,718}$ =   16.3%

2   Asset turnover

Cole   = $\dfrac{2,875}{3,579}$ =   0.80 times

Darwin   = $\dfrac{4,400}{3,718}$ =   1.18 times

3   *Gross profit margin*

Cole   = $\dfrac{910}{2{,}875}$ =   31.7%

4   *Net profit margin*

Cole   = $\dfrac{295}{2{,}875}$ =   10.3%

Darwin = $\dfrac{606}{4{,}400}$ =   13.8%

5   *Debtors collection period*

Cole   = $\dfrac{897}{2{,}875} \times 365$ = 114 days

6   *Creditors payments period*

Cole   = $\dfrac{163}{2{,}055} \times 365$ = 29 days

The general effect of the restatement is to **improve Darwin's results** in comparison to Cole's. Once the impact of the **beneficial intra-group purchases** and sales are removed, Cole is shown to have a **poorer gross profit margin** than Darwin. This has fed through to the net margin, which is also affected in Cole's case by the impact of a **higher depreciation charge**. The **cash flow** situation for Cole is significantly **worse**, thus increasing interest payable which also impacts on net profit margin.

Darwin's **return on capital** has been **improved** by removing the asset that had yet to make a contribution to the company's profitability. It is significant that the revaluation of Cole's property along the same lines as Darwin has **failed to compensate** for the increase in depreciation and the decrease in gross margin caused by the adjustments to the intra-group transactions.

These adjustments have also had a marked effect on **Cole's collection periods**; whereas these are evenly matched between debtors and creditors by Darwin; Cole's figures indicate an **imbalance**, with far longer taken to pay by debtors than Cole can take to pay its own debts to creditors.

In summary, **Darwin** looks much the **better investment opportunity**. However, Webster will also have to consider:

(i)   The relative **asking prices** of the companies.

(ii)   The likelihood that the **historical results** are a **true reflection** of future profitability (eg what is the likely effect of Darwin's new machinery coming on stream?).

(c)   **Some** but **not all** of the **information** is likely to be available, although each company may disclose voluntarily beyond that required by legislation or standards.

Items (i) and (ii)

FRS 8 Related party transactions requires the disclosure of transactions and balances, between **related parties**. These would be included, but may be aggregated with other similar transactions, as permitted by the standard. Further, if Cole is 90% + owned by Velox, then an exemption from disclosure is permitted.

Item (iii)

Companies that do not follow a policy of revaluation are **not required** to state **market values**, other than in the Directors' Report, where considered significant. However, those that **do revalue** are required to give **historical cost information**; in any case, the additional depreciation would appear in the note of historical cost profits and losses.

Item (iv)

The company's **depreciation policy** would be disclosed, but not necessarily that a certain asset is yet to come on-line, nor how the purchase had been financed.

Item (v)

Without the information in (i) and (ii), it would **not** be possible to work out how much overdraft interest Cole would have to pay.

Index

BPP
PROFESSIONAL EDUCATION

> Note: **Key Terms** and their page references are given in **bold**.

Review Form & Free Prize Draw – Paper 2.5 Financial Reporting (6/06)

All original review forms from the entire BPP range, completed with genuine comments, will be entered into one of two draws on 31 January 2007 and 31 July 2007. The names on the first four forms picked out on each occasion will be sent a cheque for £50.

Name: _____   Address: _____

_____

_____

How have you used this Interactive Text?
(Tick one box only)

☐ Home study (book only)

☐ On a course: college _____

☐ With 'correspondence' package

☐ Other _____

Why did you decide to purchase this Interactive Text? *(Tick one box only)*

☐ Have used BPP Texts in the past

☐ Recommendation by friend/colleague

☐ Recommendation by a lecturer at college

☐ Saw advertising

☐ Saw information on BPP website

☐ Other _____

During the past six months do you recall seeing/receiving any of the following?
(Tick as many boxes as are relevant)

☐ Our advertisement in *ACCA Student Accountant*

☐ Our advertisement in *Pass*

☐ Our advertisement in *PQ*

☐ Our brochure with a letter through the post

☐ Our website www.bpp.com

Which (if any) aspects of our advertising do you find useful?
(Tick as many boxes as are relevant)

☐ Prices and publication dates of new editions

☐ Information on Text content

☐ Facility to order books off-the-page

☐ None of the above

Which BPP products have you used?

Text	☑	Success CD	☐	Learn Online	☐
Kit	☐	i-Learn	☐	Home Study Package	☐
Passcard	☐	i-Pass	☐	Home Study PLUS	☐

Your ratings, comments and suggestions would be appreciated on the following areas.

	Very useful	Useful	Not useful
Introductory section (Key study steps, personal study)	☐	☐	☐
Chapter introductions	☐	☐	☐
Key terms	☐	☐	☐
Quality of explanations	☐	☐	☐
Case studies and other examples	☐	☐	☐
Exam focus points	☐	☐	☐
Questions and answers in each chapter	☐	☐	☐
Fast forwards and chapter roundups	☐	☐	☐
Quick quizzes	☐	☐	☐
Question Bank	☐	☐	☐
Answer Bank	☐	☐	☐
Index	☐	☐	☐

Overall opinion of this Study Text	Excellent ☐	Good ☐	Adequate ☐	Poor ☐

Do you intend to continue using BPP products?   Yes ☐   No ☐

On the reverse of this page are noted particular areas of the text about which we would welcome your feedback. The BPP author of this edition can be e-mailed at: marymaclean@bpp.com

Please return this form to: Nick Weller, ACCA Publishing Manager, BPP Professional Education, FREEPOST, London, W12 8BR

Review Form & Free Prize Draw (continued)

TELL US WHAT YOU THINK

Please note any further comments and suggestions/errors below

Free Prize Draw Rules

1   Closing date for 31 January 2007 draw is 31 December 2006. Closing date for 31 July 2007 draw is 30 June 2007.

2   Restricted to entries with UK and Eire addresses only. BPP employees, their families and business associates are excluded.

3   No purchase necessary. Entry forms are available upon request from BPP Professional Education. No more than one entry per title, per person. Draw restricted to persons aged 16 and over.

4   Winners will be notified by post and receive their cheques not later than 6 weeks after the relevant draw date.

5   The decision of the promoter in all matters is final and binding. No correspondence will be entered into.